THE CHRISTIAN FAITH

THE
CHRISTIAN FAITH

BY

FRIEDRICH SCHLEIERMACHER

*English Translation of the
Second German Edition*

EDITED BY

H. R. MACKINTOSH, D.Phil., D.D.
PROFESSOR OF THEOLOGY, NEW COLLEGE, EDINBURGH

AND

J. S. STEWART, M.A., B.D.
MINISTER OF BEECHGROVE UNITED FREE CHURCH, ABERDEEN

T&T CLARK
EDINBURGH

T&T CLARK LTD
59 GEORGE STREET
EDINBURGH EH2 2LQ
SCOTLAND

First published 1989
Reprinted 1994

ISBN 0 567 02239 0

British Library Cataloguing-in-Publication Data
A catalogue record for this book is available from the British Library

Printed and bound in Great Britain by Bookcraft, Avon

EDITORS' PREFACE

THIS translation of Schleiermacher's chief dogmatic work was projected some years ago by a group of persons interested in the study of nineteenth-century theology, and anxious that one exceptionally influential source should be made accessible to English readers. Since the war, as everyone knows, the costs of publication have been high. It therefore was resolved in 1924 to send out an appeal for financial aid to Theological Colleges and Seminaries throughout the English-speaking world. To this appeal a response came so prompt and generous that the way for action opened up, and incidentally the urgency of the demand for a translation was made clearer than ever. A special debt of gratitude for timely assistance is due to the Hibbert Trustees and to a number of friends associated with Hartford Seminary, Connecticut.

In the opinion of competent thinkers the *Christian Faith* of Schleiermacher is, with the exception of Calvin's *Institutes*, the most important work covering the whole field of doctrine to which Protestant theology can point. To say this is not necessarily to adopt either his fundamental principles or the detailed conclusions to which these principles have guided him. On all such matters a nearly unbroken controversy has long prevailed. Indeed, at the moment a formidable attack is being delivered upon his main positions by a new and active school of thought in Germany. But, whether for acceptance or rejection, it is necessary for serious students to know what Schleiermacher has to say. Books devoted to the interpretation and criticism of his views have been not merely numerous but of unusually good quality. Surprise may not unnaturally be felt that during the century which has elapsed since the German original was issued, no attempt has been made to render it in English. For this delay, doubtless, good reasons could be assigned. But it was all the more desirable, in view of the growing sense of united

v

purpose among Christian thinkers everywhere, that no more time should be lost before making Schleiermacher's great treatise available for a wider circle.

The translation has been executed by various hands. Paragraphs 1–31 were translated by the Rev. D. M. Baillie, M.A., of Cupar ; 32–61 by the Rev. Professor W. R. Matthews, D.D., of King's College, London, and Miss Edith Sandbach-Marshall, M.A., B.D. ; 62–85 by the Rev. Professor A. B. Macaulay, D.D., of the United Free Church College, Glasgow, and the late Rev. Alexander Grieve, Ph.D., of that city ; 86–105 by the Rev. Professor J. Y. Campbell, M.A., of the Divinity School, Yale University ; 106–125 by the Rev. R. W. Stewart, B.D., of Cambuslang ; and 126–172 by the Rev. Professor H. R. Mackintosh, D.D., of New College, Edinburgh, who also has exercised a general supervision over the work as a whole. Dr. Grieve had promised to act as joint-editor, and the book would have gained much from his scholarly and unselfish care ; but his too early death in 1927 broke off the plan. His place was taken by the Rev. J. S. Stewart, B.D., of Aberdeen, who assumed a full share in preparing the MS. for press and has collaborated in reading the whole proof.

The Editors wish to express their cordial thanks to the Publishers for the courteous and unfailing help they have given in the production of the book.

AUTHOR'S PREFACE TO THE SECOND EDITION

THERE lies before me, at this moment, the Preface with which I accompanied this work on its first appearance nine years ago. And just because I do not intend to reprint it, I dwell with pleasure on the wish expressed at its conclusion—namely, that, if possible by its own contents, but if not, then by the antagonism which its imperfections must excite, the book might contribute to an ever clearer understanding as to the meaning of our Evangelical Faith. That wish, thank God, has not remained unfulfilled ; though I cannot quite make out how much of the excitement it has aroused among the theological public, or of the antagonism it has encountered, is to be set down to the truth it contains, and how much to its imperfections.   This point facts will decide, as the controversy, now so vigorous, goes on its way.   May this controversy keep its proper limits ;   and may no one suppose that acts of violence, even if perpetrated within the Church itself, are the fire which will most surely declare who has built with stubble, and who with precious stones.   The issue of conflicts so alien in character can never guarantee the goodness of a cause.

My procedure in this new edition, in essentials, I have already explained elsewhere.[1] None the less, many readers may possibly find the difference between the two editions, even apart from the Introduction, greater than they had expected. Yet however great it may be, no leading proposition has been omitted, and none has had its specific content modified.   With all my efforts, I have not on the whole succeeded in attaining greater brevity.   Success, indeed, was hardly possible, for experience has shown that explanations themselves stood much in need of explanation.   Still I did the best I could, and my hope is that many points have been put, if not with greater brevity, at least with greater clearness, and that misapprehensions have been eased or avoided.   This chiefly has strengthened my confidence that the time is not far off when

[1] Cf. *Dr. Schleiermacher's Sendschreiben über seine Glaubenslehre an Dr. Lücke.*

it will no longer be necessary to write with fulness on topics many of which either are by now finally antiquated or even yet are misunderstood. When that time comes, some later thinker occupying the same standpoint will be able to write a much shorter Dogmatic. That in the future such a Dogmatic will be written, I have no doubt at all ; though at the same time I must protest most emphatically against the honour recently done me in some quarters of bringing me forward as the head of a new theological school. I protest against this, because I am without either of the two requisite qualifications. In the first place, I have invented nothing, so far as I remember, except my order of topics and here or there a descriptive phrase ; and similarly in my thinking I have never had any other aim than that of communicating my thoughts by way of stimulus, for each to use in his own fashion. Further, it is only in this sense—not as a mine of formulæ by the repetition of which members of a school might recognize each other—that I issue this book for the second and certainly the last time. Even if I am permitted longer life, I should prefer to attempt what would be at least brief outlines treating of other theological disciplines.

In my first edition I assumed too much when I said that my book was the first Dogmatic which had been composed with special reference to the Union of the two Protestant communions—the Lutheran and the Reformed. This honour I now gladly yield to my dear friend, Herr G. K. R. Schwarz, of Heidelberg ; merely remarking that it ought to be regarded as a fundamental characteristic of the Union accomplished in these lands that there exists no necessity for any dogmatic adjustment between the two sides, still less for a new Confession ; and that accordingly it was specially incumbent upon me, not only to proceed on this assumption, but also to the best of my power to give effect to it as a fixed principle, by a free and conciliatory treatment of the relevant documents.

Finally, I may observe that as the two volumes of the first edition proved so very unequal in size, I have included one part of the former second volume in the first volume of this edition ; but this external change has no bearing on the inner structure of the whole work.

BERLIN, *April* 22, 1830.

CONTENTS

INTRODUCTION

FIRST PART OF THE SYSTEM OF DOCTRINE

CONTENTS

THE CHRISTIAN FAITH

INTRODUCTION

§ 1. *The purpose of this Introduction is, first, to set forth the conception of Dogmatics which underlies the work itself; and secondly, to prepare the reader for the method and arrangement followed in it.*

1. It can never be superfluous to begin the treatment of any branch of study with a definition of that branch, except when complete agreement on the matter can be confidently taken for granted. And this can only be done when there has never been any controversy as to how the study is to be practised, or when it belongs to a larger scientific whole which is always delimited and articulated in the same way.

As regards the first of these conditions : we can, of course, start from the fact that most Christian churches have made use of Dogmatics in their internal tradition and in their external intercourse with other churches ; but what it really is, and what gives propositions of religious and Christian import a dogmatic status— on these questions agreement would be hard to find. As regards the second condition : Dogmatics would indeed by general consent be placed in that province which we designate by the term ' theological sciences.' But one need only compare the most reputed of the encyclopædic surveys of this department to see how variously it is articulated, how differently different writers understand the individual disciplines, relate them to each other, and estimate their value ; and this is true in an especial degree of Dogmatics. It would doubtless be a natural thing for me to take as my basis the definition of Dogmatics given in my own *Outline* ; [1] but that book is so short and aphoristic that it is not superfluous to come to its aid with some elucidations. The very title of the present work, in which the name ' Dogmatics ' is avoided, contains the

[1] *Kurze Darstellung*, § 3. [Eng. trans., *Brief Outline of the Study of Theology*, p. 92.]

elements of a definition, but not with completeness ; and, moreover, the component parts of the title are themselves not beyond all need of definition. Therefore this part of the Introduction will go its own way independently, and only as the argument gradually unfolds itself will the reader be referred to the relevant passages of the *Brief Outline*. And since the preliminary process of defining a science cannot belong to the science itself, it follows that none of the propositions which will appear in this part can themselves have a dogmatic character.

2. The method and arrangement of a work, when the nature of the subject permits of diversities (and this is the case in a marked degree with Dogmatics, as the facts themselves show), will of course best justify themselves by the result. But the most favourable results can only be obtained if the reader is made acquainted with both method and arrangement at the outset. For that will make it possible for him to view each proposition at once in all its manifold relations. Moreover, the comparison of particular sections with the corresponding sections of similar works which have a different structure may under these conditions become instructive, while they would otherwise be merely confusing.

The greatest diversities in order and method will, of course, be those which follow from the particular way in which Dogmatics is conceived, and which thus disappear when a different conception of Dogmatics is taken as basis. But there are also lesser diversities among which choice may be exercised even by those who start from the same definition of the subject.

CHAPTER I

THE DEFINITION OF DOGMATICS

§ 2. *Since Dogmatics is a theological discipline, and thus pertains solely to the Christian Church, we can only explain what it is when we have become clear as to the conception of the Christian Church.*

NOTE.—Cf. the *Brief Outline*, Introduction, §§ 1, 2, 5, 22, 23; and in the First Part, Introd., §§ 1, 2, 3, 6, 7; First Section, §§ 1, 2. Also Sack's *Apologetik*, Introd., §§ 1–5.

1. The expression ' theological discipline ' is here taken in the sense which is explicated in the first of the above-mentioned passages. From this it follows that the present work entirely disclaims the task of establishing on a foundation of general principles a Doctrine of God, or an Anthropology or Eschatology either, which should be used in the Christian Church though it did not really originate there, or which should prove the propositions of the Christian Faith to be consonant with reason. For what can be said on these subjects by the human reason in itself cannot have any closer relation to the Christian Church than it has to every other society of faith or of life.

2. Granted, then, that we must begin with a conception of the Christian Church, in order to define in accordance therewith what Dogmatics should be and should do within that Church : this conception itself can properly be reached only through the conception of ' Church ' in general, together with a proper comprehension of the peculiarity of the Christian Church. Now the general concept of ' Church,' if there really is to be such a concept, must be derived principally from Ethics; since in every case the ' Church ' is a society which originates only through free human action and which can only through such continue to exist. The peculiarity of the Christian Church can neither be comprehended and deduced by purely scientific methods nor be grasped by mere empirical methods.[1] For no science can by means of mere ideas reach and elicit what is individual, but must always stop short with what is

[1] Cf. *Brief Outline*, Introd., § 22 ; *Phil. Theol.*, § 1.

3

general. Just as all so-called *a priori* constructions in the realm
of history come to grief over the task of showing that what has
been in such-and-such wise deduced from above is actually identical
with the historically given—so is it undeniably here also.   And the
purely empirical method, on the other hand, has neither standard
nor formula for distinguishing the essential and permanent from
the changeable and contingent.   But if Ethics establishes the
concept of the ' Church,' it can, of course, also separate, in that
which forms the basis of these societies, the permanently identical
from the changeable elements, and thus by dividing up the whole
realm it can determine the places at which the individual forms
could be placed as soon as they put in an appearance historically.
And the task of thus exhibiting in a conceptually exhaustive way,
according to their affinities and gradations, the totality of all those
' Churches ' which are distinguished from each other by peculiar
differences of basis—this task would be the business of a special
branch of historical science, which should be exclusively designated
Philosophy of Religion ; just as, perhaps, the name Philosophy of
Right would best be reserved for an analogous critical study which,
as bearing on the general conception of the State as developed in
Ethics, would have to do the same thing for the different individual
forms of civic organization.   The performance of this task of the
Philosophy of Religion has, of course, been attempted in a variety
of ways ; but these attempts do not rest upon a sufficiently universal
scientific method, nor do they sufficiently maintain the balance
between the historical and the speculative, for us to be able to
appeal to them in our theological studies as admittedly satisfactory.
To begin with, these results of the Philosophy of Religion would
have to be accepted by Apologetics, which, starting from that
point, would lay down as foundation a description of the peculiar
essence of Christianity and its relation to other ' Churches.'   If,
however, it were duly recognized that Apologetics is a theological
discipline which needs to be refashioned for these present times, it
would not be advisable to defer its appearance until the arrival of
a satisfactory exposition of the Philosophy of Religion.   Rather
would Apologetics have to strike out in the interval upon an
abbreviated course of its own.   It would then begin at the same
point as the Philosophy of Religion, and take the same road, but
would leave aside, without working it out, all that does not directly
contribute to the purpose of ascertaining the nature of Christianity.
But now, since this discipline of Apologetics is only just beginning

to come to life again, the following exposition has to perform this task for itself.

3. Thus this first part of our Introduction has only to collate and apply borrowed propositions, *i.e.* propositions which belong to other scientific studies, in this case to Ethics, Philosophy of Religion, and Apologetics. Of course, the results of an investigation which is put together out of such component parts cannot lay claim to any general recognition, except when that form of Ethics and of the Philosophy of Religion which underlies the investigation is likewise recognized.   From this it is clear that even here at the very beginning there is plenty of opportunity for very diverse definitions and conceptions of Dogmatics, each of which can only regard itself as preparatory for a future one when the scientific studies of which it has to take account will be more firmly established, while, nevertheless, Christianity itself remains entirely the same.

Postscript 1.—In this connexion it is by no means intended to assert that these propositions must, in the independent treatment of the sciences to which they belong, occur in the same form in which they are here set forth.   That is in itself improbable, since in this work we have before us none of the matter which would in those sciences lead up to the propositions.

Postscript 2.—By Ethics is here understood that speculative presentation of Reason, in the whole range of its activity, which runs parallel to natural science. By Philosophy of Religion is understood a critical presentation of the different existing forms of religious communion, as constituting, when taken collectively, the complete phenomenon of piety in human nature.   The expression Apologetics is explained in the *Brief Outline*, § 39.

I. THE CONCEPTION OF THE CHURCH : PROPOSITIONS BORROWED FROM ETHICS.

§ 3. *The piety which forms the basis of all ecclesiastical communions is, considered purely in itself, neither a Knowing nor a Doing, but a modification of Feeling, or of immediate self-consciousness.*

NOTE.—Cf. the *Speeches on Religion* (Eng. trans.), pp. 28 ff.

1. That a Church is nothing but a communion or association relating to religion or piety, is beyond all doubt for us Evangelical (Protestant) Christians, since we regard it as equivalent to degeneration in a Church when it begins to occupy itself with other matters as well, whether the affairs of science or of outward organization ;

just as we also always oppose any attempt on the part of the leaders of State or of science, as such, to order the affairs of religion. But, at the same time, we have no desire to keep the leaders of science from scrutinizing and passing judgment from their own point of view upon both piety itself and the communion relating to it, and determining their proper place in the total field of human life ; since piety and Church, like other things, are material for scientific knowledge.   Indeed, we ourselves are here entering upon such a scrutiny.   And, similarly, we would not keep the leaders of State from fixing the outward relations of the religious communions according to the principles of civil organization—which, however, by no means implies that the religious communion is a product of the State or a component part of it.

However, not only we, but even those Churches which are not so clear about keeping apart Church and State, or ecclesiastical and scientific association, must assent to what we have laid down.   For they cannot assign to the Church more than an indirect influence upon these other associations ; and it is only the maintenance, regulation, and advancement of piety which they can regard as the essential business of the Church.

2. When Feeling and Self-consciousness are here put side by side as equivalent, it is by no means intended to introduce generally a manner of speech in which the two expressions would be simply synonymous.   The term ' feeling ' has in the language of common life been long current in this religious connexion ; but for scientific usage it needs to be more precisely defined ; and it is to do this that the other word is added.   So that if anyone takes the word ' feeling ' in a sense so wide as to include unconscious states, he will by the other word be reminded that such is not the usage we are here maintaining.   Again, to the term ' self-consciousness ' is added the determining epithet ' immediate,' lest anyone should think of a kind of self-consciousness which is not feeling at all ; as, e.g., when the name of self-consciousness is given to that consciousness of self which is more like an objective consciousness, being a representation of oneself, and thus mediated by self-contemplation.   Even when such a representation of ourselves, as we exist in a given portion of time, in thinking, e.g., or in willing, moves quite close to, or even interpenetrates, the individual moments of the mental state, this kind of self-consciousness does appear simply as an accompaniment of the state itself.   But the real immediate self-consciousness, which is not representation but in the proper sense

feeling, is by no means always simply an accompaniment. It may
rather be presumed that in this respect everyone has a twofold
experience. In the first place, it is everybody's experience that
there are moments in which all thinking and willing retreat behind
a self-consciousness of one form or another ; but, in the second place,
that at times this same form of self-consciousness persists unaltered
during a series of diverse acts of thinking and willing, taking up no
relation to these, and thus not being in the proper sense even an
accompaniment of them. Thus joy and sorrow—those mental
phases which are always so important in the realm of religion—are
genuine states of feeling, in the proper sense explained above ;
whereas self-approval and self-reproach, apart from their subsequently passing into joy and sorrow, belong in themselves rather
to the objective consciousness of self, as results of an analytic contemplation. Nowhere, perhaps, do the two forms stand nearer to
each other than here, but just for that reason this comparison puts
the difference in the clearest light.

NOTE.—Steffen's account of feeling is closely akin to mine, and the passage
from it to mine is easy (*Falsche Theologie*, pp. 99, 100). ' The immediate
presence of whole undivided Being, etc.' On the other hand, the account
given by Baumgarten-Crusius (*Einleitung in das Studium der Dogmatik*, p. 56),
apart from its antithesis between feeling and self-consciousness, (*a*) does not
comprehend the whole, but only the higher regions, of feeling, and (*b*) seems
to transfer feeling into the realm of the objective consciousness by using the
word ' perception ' (*Wahrnehmung*).

3. Our proposition seems to assume that in addition to Knowing, Doing, and Feeling, there is no fourth. This is not done,
however, in the sense which would be required for an apagogic
proof ; but those other two are placed alongside of Feeling simply
in order that, with the exposition of our own view, we may at the
same time take up and discuss those divergent views which are
actually in existence. So that we might leave the question entirely
aside whether there is a fourth such element in the soul, but for two
reasons : namely, in the first place, that it is our duty to convince
ourselves as to whether there is still another region to which piety
might be assigned ; and, in the second place, that we must set
ourselves to grasp clearly the relation which subsists between
Christian piety in itself, on the one hand, and both Christian belief
(so far as it can be brought into the form of knowledge) and Christian
action, on the other. Now, if the relation of the three elements
above-mentioned were anywhere set forth in a universally recognized
way, we could simply appeal to that. But, as things are, we must

in this place say what is necessary on the subject ; though this is to be regarded as simply borrowed from Psychology, and it should be well noted that the truth of the matter (namely, that piety is feeling) remains entirely independent of the correctness of the following discussion. Life, then, is to be conceived as an alternation between an abiding-in-self (*Insichbleiben*) and a passing-beyond-self (*Aussichheraustreten*) on the part of the subject. The two forms of consciousness (Knowing and Feeling) constitute the abiding-in-self, while Doing proper is the passing-beyond-self. Thus far, then, Knowing and Feeling stand together in antithesis to Doing. But while Knowing, in the sense of possessing knowledge, is an abiding-in-self on the part of the subject, nevertheless as the act of knowing, it only becomes real by a passing-beyond-self of the subject, and in this sense it is a Doing. As regards Feeling, on the other hand, it is not only in its duration as a result of stimulation that it is an abiding-in-self : even as the process of being stimulated, it is not effected by the subject, but simply takes place in the subject, and thus, since it belongs altogether to the realm of receptivity, it is entirely an abiding-in-self ; and in this sense it stands alone in antithesis to the other two—Knowing and Doing.

As regards the question whether there is a fourth to these three, Feeling, Knowing, and Doing ; or a third to these two, abiding-in-self and passing-beyond-self : the unity of these is indeed not one of the two or the three themselves ; but no one can place this unity alongside of these others as a co-ordinate third or fourth entity. The unity rather is the essence of the subject itself, which manifests itself in those severally distinct forms, and is thus, to give it a name which in this particular connexion is permissible, their common foundation. Similarly, on the other hand, every actual moment of life is, in its total content, a complex of these two or these three, though two of them may be present only in vestige or in germ. But a third to those two (one of which is again divided into two) will scarcely be found.

4. But now (these three, Feeling, Knowing, and Doing being granted) while we here set forth once more the oft-asserted view that, of the three, Feeling is the one to which piety belongs, it is not in any wise meant, as indeed the above discussion shows, that piety is excluded from all connexion with Knowing and Doing. For, indeed, it is the case in general that the immediate self-consciousuess is always the mediating link in the transition between moments in which Knowing predominates and those in which Doing pre-

dominates, so that a different Doing may proceed from the same Knowing in different people according as a different determination of self-consciousness enters in. And thus it will fall to piety to stimulate Knowing and Doing, and every moment in which piety has a predominant place will contain within itself one or both of these in germ. But just this is the very truth represented by our proposition, and is in no wise an objection to it ; for were it otherwise the religious moments could not combine with the others to form a single life, but piety would be something isolated and without any influence upon the other mental functions of our lives. However, in representing this truth, and thus securing to piety its own peculiar province in its connexion with all other provinces, our proposition is opposing the assertions from other quarters that piety is a Knowing, or a Doing, or both, or a state made up of Feeling, Knowing, and Doing ; and in this polemical connexion our proposition must now be still more closely considered.

If, then, piety did consist in Knowing, it would have to be, above all, that knowledge, in its entirety or in its essence, which is here set up as the content of Dogmatics (*Glaubenslehre*) : otherwise it must be a complete mistake for us here to investigate the nature of piety in the interests of our study of Dogmatics. But if piety *is* that knowledge, then the amount of such knowledge in a man must be the measure of his piety. For anything which, in its rise and fall, is not the measure of the perfection of a given object cannot constitute the essence of that object. Accordingly, on the hypothesis in question, the most perfect master of Christian Dogmatics would always be likewise the most pious Christian. And no one will admit this to be the case, even if we premise that the most perfect master is only he who keeps most to what is essential and does not forget it in accessories and side-issues ; but all will agree rather that the same degree of perfection in that knowledge may be accompanied by very different degrees of piety, and the same degree of piety by very different degrees of knowledge. It may, however, be objected that the assertion that piety is a matter of Knowing refers not so much to the content of that knowledge as to the certainty which characterizes its representations ; so that the knowledge of doctrines is piety only in virtue of the certainty attached to them, and thus only in virtue of the strength of the conviction, while a possession of the doctrines without conviction is not piety at all. Then the strength of the conviction would be the measure of the piety ; and this is undoubtedly what those people have chiefly in mind who so love to paraphrase the word *Faith* as ' fidelity to one's convictions.'   But in all other more typical fields of knowledge the only measure of conviction is the clearness and completeness of the thinking itself.   Now if it is to be the same with *this* conviction, then we should simply be back at our old point, that he who thinks the religious propositions most clearly and completely, individually and in their connexions, must likewise be the most pious man,   If, then, this conclusion is still to be rejected, but the hypothesis is to be retained (namely, that conviction is the measure of piety), the conviction in this case must be of a different kind and must have a different measure.   However closely, then, piety may be connected with this conviction, it does not follow that it is connected in the same way with that knowledge. And if, nevertheless, the knowledge which forms Dogmatics has to relate itself to piety, the explanation of this is that while piety is, of course, the object of this knowledge, the knowledge can only be explicated in virtue of a certainty which inheres in the determinations of self-consciousness.

If, on the other hand, piety consists in Doing, it is manifest that the Doing which constitutes it cannot be defined by its content ; for experience teaches that not only the most admirable but also the most abominable, not only the most useful but also the most inane and meaningless things, are done as pious and out of piety. Thus we are thrown back simply upon the form, upon the method and manner in which the thing comes to be done.   But this can only be understood from the two *termini*, the underlying motive as the starting-point, and the intended result as the goal.   Now no one will pronounce an action more or less pious because of the greater or less degree of completeness with which the intended result is achieved.   Suppose we then are thrown back upon the motive.   It is manifest that underlying every motive there is a certain determination of self-consciousness, be it pleasure or pain, and that it is by these that one motive can most clearly be distinguished from another.   Accordingly an action (a Doing) will be pious in so far as the determination of self-consciousness, the feeling which had become affective and had passed into a motive impulse, is a pious one.

Thus both hypotheses lead to the same point : that there are both a Knowing and a Doing which pertain to piety, but neither of these constitutes the essence of piety : they only pertain to it inasmuch as the stirred-up Feeling sometimes comes to rest in a thinking which fixes it, sometimes discharges itself in an action which expresses it.

Finally, no one will deny that there are states of Feeling, such as penitence, contrition, confidence, and joy in God, which we pronounce pious in themselves, without regard to any Knowing or Doing that proceeds from them, though, of course, we expect both that they will work themselves out in actions which are otherwise obligatory, and that the reflective impulse will turn its attention to them.

5. From what we have now said it is already clear how we must judge the assertion that piety is a state in which Knowing, Feeling, and Doing are combined. Of course we reject it if it means that the Feeling is derived from the Knowing and the Doing from the Feeling. But if no subordination is intended, then the assertion might just as well be the description of any other quite clear and living moment as of a religious one. For though the idea of the goal of an action precedes the action itself, at the same time it continues to accompany the action, and the relation between the two expresses itself simultaneously in the self-consciousness through a greater or less degree of satisfaction and assurance ; so that even here all three elements are combined in the total content of the state. A similar situation exists in the case of Knowing. For the thinking activity, as a successfully accomplished operation, expresses itself in the self-consciousness as a confident certainty. But simultaneously it becomes also an endeavour to connect the apprehended truth with other truths or to seek out cases for its application, and thus there is always present simultaneously the commencement of a Doing, which develops fully when the opportunity offers ; and so here also we find Knowing, Feeling, and Doing all together in the total state. But now, just as the first-described state remains, notwithstanding, essentially a Doing, and the second a Knowing, so piety in its diverse expressions remains essentially a state of Feeling. This state is subsequently caught up into the region of thinking, but only in so far as each religious man is at the same time inclined towards thinking and exercised therein ; and only in the same way and according to the same measure does this inner piety emerge in living movement and representative action. It also follows from this account of the matter that Feeling is not to be thought of as something either confused or inactive ; since, on the one hand, it is strongest in our most vivid moments, and either directly or indirectly lies at the

root of every expression of our wills, and, on the other hand, it can be grasped by thought and conceived of in its own nature.

But suppose there are other people who would exclude Feeling altogether from our field, and therefore describe piety simply as a Knowledge which begets actions or as a Doing which proceeds from a Knowing : these people not only would have to settle first among themselves whether piety is a Knowing or a Doing, but would also have to show us how a Doing can arise from a Knowing except as mediated by a determination of self-consciousness. And if they have eventually to admit this point, then they will also be convinced by the above discussion that if such a complex does bear the character of piety, nevertheless the element of Knowing in it has not in itself got the length of being piety, and the element of Doing is in itself no longer piety, but the piety is just the determination of self-consciousness which comes in between the two.   But that relationship can always hold in the reverse order also : the Doing has not got the length of being piety in those cases in which a determinate self-consciousness only results from an accomplished action ; and the Knowing is in itself no longer piety when it has no other content than that determination of self-consciousness caught up into thought.

§ 4. *The common element in all howsoever diverse expressions of piety, by which these are conjointly distinguished from all other feelings, or, in other words, the self-identical essence of piety, is this : the consciousness of being absolutely dependent, or, which is the same thing, of being in relation with God.*

NOTE.—For the word *schlechthinig* [translated ' absolute '], which occurs frequently in the following exposition, I am indebted to Professor Delbrück. I was unwilling to venture upon its use, and I am not aware that it has occurred anywhere else.   But now that he has given it me, I find it very convenient to follow his lead in using it.

1. In any actual state of consciousness, no matter whether it merely accompanies a thought or action or occupies a moment for itself, we are never simply conscious of our Selves in their unchanging identity, but are always at the same time conscious of a changing determination of them.   The Ego in itself can be represented objectively ; but every consciousness of self is at the same time the consciousness of a variable state of being.   But in this distinction of the latter from the former, it is implied that the variable does not proceed purely from the self-identical, for in

that case it could not be distinguished from it.   Thus in every self-consciousness there are two elements, which we might call respectively a self-caused element (*ein Sichselbstsetzen*) and a non-self-caused element (*ein Sichselbstnichtsogesetzthaben*) ; or a Being and a Having-by-some-means-come-to-be (*ein Sein und ein Irgendwiegewordensein*).   The latter of these presupposes for every self-consciousness another factor besides the Ego, a factor which is the source of the particular determination, and without which the self-consciousness would not be precisely what it is. But this Other is not objectively presented in the immediate self-consciousness with which alone we are here concerned.   For though, of course, the double constitution of self-consciousness causes us always to look objectively for an Other to which we can trace the origin of our particular state, yet this search is a separate act with which we are not at present concerned.   In self-consciousness there are only two elements : the one expresses the existence of the subject for itself, the other its co-existence with an Other.

Now to these two elements, as they exist together in the temporal self-consciousness, correspond in the subject its *Receptivity* and its (spontaneous) *Activity*.   If we could think away the co-existence with an Other, but otherwise think ourselves as we are, then a self-consciousness which predominantly expressed an affective condition of receptivity would be impossible, and any self-consciousness could then express only activity—an activity, however, which, not being directed to any object, would be merely an urge outwards, an indefinite ' agility ' without form or colour.   But as we never do exist except along with an Other, so even in every outward-tending self-consciousness the element of receptivity, in some way or other affected, is the primary one ; and even the self-consciousness which accompanies an action (acts of knowing included), while it predominantly expresses spontaneous movement and activity, is always related (though the relation is often a quite indefinite one) to a prior moment of affective receptivity, through which the original ' agility ' received its direction.   To these propositions assent can be unconditionally demanded ; and no one will deny them who is capable of a little introspection and can find interest in the real subject of our present inquiries.

2. The common element in all those determinations of self-consciousness which predominantly express a receptivity affected from some outside quarter is the *feeling of Dependence*.   On the other hand, the common element in all those determinations which

predominantly express spontaneous movement and activity is the *feeling of Freedom*. The former is the case not only because it is by an influence from some other quarter that we have come to such a state, but particularly because we *could* not so become except by means of an Other. The latter is the case because in these instances an Other is determined by us, and without our spontaneous activity could not be so determined. These two definitions may, indeed, seem to be still incomplete, inasmuch as there is also a mobility of the subject which is not connected with an Other at all, but which seems to be subject to the same antithesis as that just explained. But when we become such-and-such from within outwards, for ourselves, without any Other being involved, that is the simple situation of the temporal development of a being which remains essentially self-identical, and it is only very improperly that this can be referred to the concept ' Freedom.' And when we cannot ourselves, from within outwards, become such-and-such, this only indicates the limits which belong to the nature of the subject itself as regards spontaneous activity, and this could only very improperly be called ' Dependence.'

Further, this antithesis must on no account be confused with the antithesis between gloomy or depressing and elevating or joyful feelings, of which we shall speak later. For a feeling of dependence may be elevating, if the ' having-become-such-and-such ' which it expresses is complete ; and similarly a feeling of freedom may be dejecting, if the moment of predominating receptivity to which the action can be traced was of a dejecting nature, or again if the manner and method of the activity prove to be a disadvantageous combination.

Let us now think of the feeling of dependence and the feeling of freedom as *one*, in the sense that not only the subject but the corresponding Other is the same for both. Then the total self-consciousness made up of both together is one of *Reciprocity* between the subject and the corresponding Other. Now let us suppose the totality of all moments of feeling, of both kinds, as one whole : then the corresponding Other is also to be supposed as a totality or as one, and then that term ' reciprocity ' is the right one for our self-consciousness in general, inasmuch as it expresses our connexion with everything which either appeals to our receptivity or is subjected to our activity. And this is true not only when we particularize this Other and ascribe to each of its elements a different degree of relation to the twofold consciousness within us,

but also when we think of the total ' outside ' as one, and moreover (since it contains other receptivities and activities to which
we have a relation) as one together with ourselves, that is, as a
World. Accordingly our self-consciousness, as a consciousness of
our existence in the world or of our co-existence with the world,
is a series in which the feeling of freedom and the feeling of dependence are divided. But neither an absolute feeling of dependence,
i.e. without any feeling of freedom in relation to the co-determinant, nor an absolute feeling of freedom, *i.e.* without any feeling
of dependence in relation to the co-determinant, is to be found in
this whole realm. If we consider our relations to Nature, or those
which exist in human society, there we shall find a large number of
objects in regard to which freedom and dependence maintain very
much of an equipoise : these constitute the field of equal reciprocity.
There are other objects which exercise a far greater influence upon
our receptivity than our activity exercises upon them, and also
vice versa, so that one of the two may diminish until it is imperceptible. But neither of the two members will ever completely
disappear. The feeling of dependence predominates in the relation
of children to their parents, or of citizens to their fatherland ; and
yet individuals can, without losing their relationship, exercise upon
their fatherland not only a directive influence, but even a counter-
influence. And the dependence of children on their parents,
which very soon comes to be felt as a gradually diminishing and
fading quantity, is never from the start free from the admixture
of an element of spontaneous activity towards the parents : just
as even in the most absolute autocracy the ruler is not without
some slight feeling of dependence. It is the same in the case of
Nature : towards all the forces of Nature—even, we may say,
towards the heavenly bodies—we ourselves do, in the same sense
in which they influence us, exercise a counter-influence, however
minute. So that our whole self-consciousness in relation to the
World or its individual parts remains enclosed within these limits.

3. There can, accordingly, be for us no such thing as a feeling
of absolute freedom. He who asserts that he has such a feeling
is either deceiving himself or separating things which essentially
belong together. For if the feeling of freedom expresses a forth-
going activity, this activity must have an object which has
been somehow given to us, and this could not have taken place
without an influence of the object upon our receptivity. Therefore in every such case there is involved a feeling of dependence

which goes along with the feeling of freedom, and thus limits it. The contrary could only be possible if the object altogether came into existence through our activity, which is never the case absolutely, but only relatively. But if, on the other hand, the feeling of freedom expresses only an inward movement of activity, not only is every such individual movement bound up with the state of our stimulated receptivity at the moment, but, further, the totality of our free inward movements, considered as a unity, cannot be represented as a feeling of absolute freedom, because our whole existence does not present itself to our consciousness as having proceeded from our own spontaneous activity. Therefore in any temporal existence a feeling of absolute freedom can have no place. As regards the feeling of absolute dependence which, on the other hand, our proposition does postulate : for just the same reason, this feeling cannot in any wise arise from the influence of an object which has in some way to be *given* to us ; for upon such an object there would always be a counter-influence, and even a voluntary renunciation of this would always involve a feeling of freedom. Hence a feeling of absolute dependence, strictly speaking, cannot exist in a single moment as such, because such a moment is always determined, as regards its total content, by what is *given*, and thus by objects towards which we have a feeling of freedom. But the self-consciousness which accompanies all our activity, and therefore, since that is never zero, accompanies our whole existence, and negatives absolute freedom, is itself precisely a consciousness of absolute dependence ; for it is the consciousness that the whole of our spontaneous activity comes from a source outside of us in just the same sense in which anything towards which we should have a feeling of absolute freedom must have proceeded entirely from ourselves. But without any feeling of freedom a feeling of absolute dependence would not be possible.

4. As regards the identification of absolute dependence with ' relation to God ' in our proposition : this is to be understood in the sense that the *Whence* of our receptive and active existence, as implied in this self-consciousness, is to be designated by the word ' God,' and that this is for us the really original signification of that word. In this connexion we have first of all to remind ourselves that, as we have seen in the foregoing discussion, this ' Whence ' is not the world, in the sense of the totality of temporal existence, and still less is it any single part of the world. For we have a feeling of freedom (though, indeed, a limited one) in relation

to the world, since we are complementary parts of it, and also since
we are continually exercising an influence on its individual parts ;
and, moreover, there is the possibility of our exercising influence
on all its parts ; and while this does permit a limited feeling of
dependence, it excludes the absolute feeling. In the next place,
we have to note that our proposition is intended to oppose the
view that this feeling of dependence is itself conditioned by some
previous knowledge about God. And this may indeed be the more
necessary since many people claim to be in the sure possession of
a concept of God, altogether a matter of conception and original,
i.e. independent of any feeling ; and in the strength of this higher
self-consciousness, which indeed may come pretty near to being
a feeling of absolute freedom, they put far from them, as something
almost infra-human, that very feeling which for us is the basic
type of all piety. Now our proposition is in no wise intended to
dispute the existence of such an original knowledge, but simply
to set it aside as something with which, in a system of Christian
doctrine, we could never have any concern, because plainly enough
it has itself nothing to do directly with piety. If, however, word
and idea are always originally one, and the term ' God ' therefore
presupposes an idea, then we shall simply say that this idea, which
is nothing more than the expression of the feeling of absolute
dependence, is the most direct reflection upon it and the most
original idea with which we are here concerned, and is quite independent of that original knowledge (properly so called), and
conditioned only by our feeling of absolute dependence. So that
in the first instance God signifies for us simply that which is the
co-determinant in this feeling and to which we trace our being in
such a state ; and any further content of the idea must be evolved
out of this fundamental import assigned to it. Now this is just
what is principally meant by the formula which says that to feel
oneself absolutely dependent and to be conscious of being in relation with God are one and the same thing ; and the reason is that
absolute dependence is the fundamental relation which must include
all others in itself. This last expression includes the God-consciousness in the self-consciousness in such a way that, quite in accordance
with the above analysis, the two cannot be separated from each
other. The feeling of absolute dependence becomes a clear self-
consciousness only as this idea comes simultaneously into being.
In this sense it can indeed be said that God is given to us in feeling
in an original way ; and if we speak of an original revelation of

God to man or in man, the meaning will always be just this, that, along with the absolute dependence which characterizes not only man but all temporal existence, there is given to man also the immediate self-consciousness of it, which becomes a consciousness of God.   In whatever measure this actually takes place during the course of a personality through time, in just that measure do we ascribe piety to the individual.   On the other hand, any possibility of God being in any way *given* is entirely excluded, because anything that is outwardly given must be given as an object exposed to our counter-influence, however slight this may be.   The transference of the idea of God to any perceptible object, unless one is all the time conscious that it is a piece of purely arbitrary symbolism, is always a corruption, whether it be a temporary transference, *i.e.* a theophany, or a constitutive transference, in which God is represented as permanently a particular perceptible existence.

§ 5. *What we have thus described constitutes the highest grade of human self-consciousness ; but in its actual occurrence it is never separated from the lower, and through its combination therewith in a single moment it participates in the antithesis of the pleasant and the unpleasant.*

1. The relation between these two forms of self-consciousness, namely, the feeling of absolute dependence and the self-consciousness which, as expressing the connexion with perceptible finite existence, splits up into a partial feeling of dependence and a partial feeling of freedom, will best be seen if we bring in yet a third form. If we go back to the first obscure period of the life of man, we find there, all over, the animal life almost solely predominating, and the spiritual life as yet entirely in the background ; and so we must regard the state of his consciousness as closely akin to that of the lower animals.   It is true, indeed, that the animal state is to us really entirely strange and unknown.   But there is general agreement that, on the one hand, the lower animals have no knowledge, properly so called, nor any full self-consciousness which combines the different moments into a stable unity, and that, on the other hand, they are nevertheless not entirely devoid of consciousness.   Now we can hardly do justice to this state of affairs except by postulating a consciousness of such a sort that in it the objective and the introversive, or feeling and perception, are not really distinct from each other, but remain in a state of unresolved

confusion. The consciousness of children obviously approximates to this form, especially before they learn to speak. From that time on, this condition tends more and more to disappear, confining itself to those dreamy moments which form the transition between sleep and waking ; while in our wide-awake hours feeling and perception are clearly distinct from each other, and thus make up the whole wealth of man's sensible life, in the widest sense of the term. In that term we include (speaking simply of the consciousness, and leaving out action proper), on the one hand, the gradual accumulation of perceptions which constitute the whole field of experience in the widest sense of the word, and, on the other hand, all determinations of self-consciousness which develop from our relations to nature and to man, including those which we described above (§ 4, 2) as coming nearest to the feeling of absolute dependence ; so that by the word ' sensible ' we understand the social and moral feelings no less than the self-regarding, since they all together have their place in that realm of the particular which is subject to the above-mentioned antithesis. The former division [*i.e.* the accumulation of perceptions] which belongs to the objective consciousness, we pass over, as it does not concern us here. But in the whole of the latter class, consisting of feelings which we have designated sensible, the corresponding co-determinant to which we trace the constitution of the present state belongs to the realm of reciprocal action ; so that, whether we are at the moment more conscious of dependence or of freedom, we take up towards it, in a sense, an attitude of equal co-ordination, and indeed set ourselves as individuals (or as comprised within a larger individual, as, *e.g.*, in our patriotic feelings) over against it as another individual. Now it is in this respect that these feelings are most definitely distinguished from the feeling of absolute dependence. For while the latter from its very nature negatives absolute freedom (§ 4, 3), though it does it under the form of self-consciousness, this is not the consciousness of ourselves as individuals of a particular description, but simply of ourselves as individual finite existence in general ; so that we do not set ourselves over against any other individual being, but, on the contrary, all antithesis between one individual and another is in this case done away. Hence there seems to be no objection to our distinguishing three grades of self-consciousness : the confused animal grade, in which the antithesis cannot arise, as the lowest ; the sensible self-consciousness, which rests entirely upon the antithesis, as the middle ; and the feeling of absolute dependence, in which the antithesis again disappears and the subject unites and identifies itself with everything which, in the middle grade, was set over against it, as the highest.

2. If there did exist a feeling of absolute freedom, in it also the above antithesis would be done away. Only, such a subject could never stand in any relation with other similarly constituted subjects, but whatever is given to it must be given as purely susceptible or passive material. And since, for this reason alone, such a feeling is never found in man, the only immediate self-consciousness in man on that grade is the feeling of absolute dependence which we have described. For every moment which is made up of a partial feeling of freedom and a partial feeling of dependence places us in a position of co-ordinate antithesis to a similar Other. But now there remains the question, whether there exists any other self-consciousness, not immediate but accompanying some kind of knowledge or action as such, which can be ranked along with that which we have described. Let us then conceive, as the act or state of an individual, a highest kind of knowledge in which all subordinate knowledge is comprised. This, indeed, in its province is likewise elevated above all antithesis. But its province is that of the objective consciousness. However, it will of course be accompanied by an immediate self-consciousness expressive of certainty or conviction. But since this concerns the relation of the subject as knower to the known as object, even this self-consciousness which accompanies the highest knowledge remains in the realm of the antithesis. In the same way, let us conceive a highest kind of action, in the form of a resolve which covers the whole field of our spontaneous activity, so that all subsequent resolves are developed out of it, as individual parts,[1] which were already contained in it. This also in its province stands above all antithesis, and it is likewise accompanied by a self-consciousness. But this also concerns the relation of the subject as agent to that which may be the object of its action, and thus has its place within the antithesis. And since obviously this must be equally true of every self-consciousness which accompanies any particular knowledge or action, it follows that there is no other self-consciousness which is elevated above the antithesis, and that this character belongs exclusively to the feeling of absolute dependence.

3. While the lowest or animal grade of consciousness gradually disappears as the middle grade develops, the highest cannot develop

[1] See *Ueber die Behandlung des Pflichtbegriffs*, 1824, pp. 4–6.

at all so long as the lowest is present ; but, on the other hand, the middle grade must persist undiminished even when the highest has reached its perfect development. The highest self-consciousness is in no wise dependent on outwardly given objects which may affect us at one moment and not at another. As a consciousness of absolute dependence it is quite simple, and remains self-identical while all other states are changing. Therefore, in itself it cannot possibly be at one moment thus and at another moment otherwise, nor can it by intermission be present at one moment and absent at another. Either it is not there at all, or, so long as it is there, it is continuously there and always self-identical. Now if it were impossible for it to co-exist with the consciousness of the second grade (as it cannot with that of the third), then either it could never make an appearance in time, but would always remain in the concealment in which it lay during the predominance of the lowest grade, or it must drive out the second and exist alone, and, indeed, in ever-unchanging identity. Now this latter supposition is controverted by all experience, and indeed is manifestly impossible unless our ideation and action are to be entirely stripped of self-consciousness, which would irrevocably destroy the coherence of our existence for our own minds. It is impossible to claim a constancy for the highest self-consciousness, except on the supposition that the sensible self-consciousness is always conjoined with it. Of course, this conjunction cannot be regarded as a fusion of the two : that would be entirely opposed to the conception of both of them which we have established. It means rather a co-existence of the two in the same moment, which, of course, unless the Ego is to be split up, involves a reciprocal relation of the two. It is impossible for anyone to be in some moments exclusively conscious of his relations within the realm of the antithesis, and in other moments of his absolute dependence in itself and in a general way ; for it is as a person determined for this moment in a particular manner within the realm of the antithesis that he is conscious of his absolute dependence. This relatedness of the sensibly determined to the higher self-consciousness in the unity of the moment is the consummating point of the self-consciousness. For to the man who once recognizes what piety is, and appropriates it as a requirement of his being, every moment of a merely sensible self-consciousness is a defective and imperfect state. But even if the feeling of absolute dependence in general were the entire content of a moment of self-consciousness, this also would be an imperfect state ; for it would lack the definiteness and clearness which spring from its being related to the deter-mination of the sensible self-consciousness. This consummation, however, since it consists in the two elements being related to each other, may be described in two different ways. Described from below it is as follows: when the sensible self-consciousness has quite expelled the animal confusion, then there is disclosed a higher tendency over against the antithesis, and the expression of this tendency in the self-consciousness is the feeling of absolute depend-ence. And the more the subject, in each moment of sensible self-consciousness, with his partial freedom and partial dependence, takes at the same time the attitude of absolute dependence, the more religious is he. Described from above it is as follows: the ten-dency which we have described, as an original and innate tendency of the human soul, strives from the very beginning to break through into consciousness. But it is unable to do so as long as the anti-thesis remains dissolved in the animal confusion. Subsequently, however, it asserts itself. And the more it contributes to every moment of sensibly determined self-consciousness without the omission of any, so that the man, while he always feels himself partially free and partially dependent in relation to other finite existence, feels himself at the same time to be also (along with everything towards which he had that former feeling) absolutely dependent—the more religious is he.

4. The sensibly determined self-consciousness splits up of itself, in accordance with its nature, into a series of moments that differ in their content, because our activity exercised upon other beings is a temporal one, and their influence upon us is likewise temporal. The feeling of absolute dependence, on the other hand, being in itself always self-identical, would not evoke a series of thus distinguishable moments ; and if it did not enter into relation with such a series in the manner described above, either it could never become an actual consciousness in time at all, or else it must accompany the sensible self-consciousness monotonously without any relation to the manifold rising and falling variations of the latter. But, as a matter of fact, our religious consciousness does not take either of these forms, but conforms to the description we have given above. That is to say : being related as a constituent factor to a given moment of consciousness which consists of a partial feeling of freedom and a partial feeling of dependence, it thereby becomes a particular religious emotion, and being in another moment related to a different datum, it becomes a different religious emotion ;

yet so that the essential element, namely, the feeling of absolute
dependence, is the same in both, and thus throughout the whole
series, and the difference arises simply from the fact that it becomes
a different moment when it goes along with a different determination of the sensible self-consciousness. It remains always, however, a moment of the higher power ; whereas, where there is no
piety at all, the sensible self-consciousness breaks up (as was likewise described) into a series of moments of the lower power, while
in the period of animal confusion there does not even take place a
definite separation and antithesis of the moments for the subject.

It is the same with the second part of our proposition. That
is to say : the sensible self-consciousness splits up also, of itself and
from its very nature, into the antithesis of the pleasant and the
unpleasant, or of pleasure and pain. This does not mean that the
partial feeling of freedom is always pleasure, and the partial feeling
of dependence always pain, as seems to be assumed by those who
wrongly think that the feeling of absolute dependence has, of its
very nature, a depressing effect. For the child can have a feeling
of perfect well-being in the consciousness of dependence on its
parents, and so also (thank God) can the subject in his relation to
the government ; and other people, even parents and governments,
can feel miserable in the consciousness of their freedom. So that
each may equally well be either pleasure or pain, according to
whether life is furthered or hindered by it. The higher self-consciousness, on the other hand, bears within it no such antithesis.
Its first appearance means, of course, an enhancement of life, if a
comparison arises with the isolated sensible self-consciousness. But
if, without any such reference, we think of it in its own self-identity,
its effect is simply an unchanging identity of life, which excludes
any such antithesis. This state we speak of under the name of the
Blessedness of the finite being as the highest summit of his perfection. But our religious consciousness, as we actually find it,
is not of that character, but is subject to variation, some pious
emotions approximating more to joy, and others to sorrow. Thus
this antithesis refers simply to the manner in which the two grades
of self-consciousness are related to each other in the unity of the
moment. And thus it is by no means the case that the pleasant
and the unpleasant, which exist in the sensible feeling, impart the
same character to the feeling of absolute dependence. On the
contrary, we often find, united in one and the same moment (as
a clear sign that the two grades are not fused into each other or

neutralized by each other so as to become a third) a sorrow of the lower and a joy of the higher self-consciousness ; as, *e.g.*, whenever with a feeling of suffering there is combined a trust in God. But the antithesis attaches to the higher self-consciousness, because it is the nature of the latter to become temporal, to manifest itself in time, by entering into relation with the sensible self-consciousness so as to constitute a moment. That is to say : as the emergence of this higher self-consciousness at all means an enhancement of life, so whenever it emerges *with ease*, to enter into relation with a sensible determination, whether pleasant or unpleasant, this means an easy progress of that higher life, and bears, by comparison, the stamp of joy. And as the disappearance of the higher conscious-ness, if it could be perceived, would mean a diminution of life, so whenever it emerges *with difficulty*, this approximates to an absence of it, and can only be felt as an inhibition of the higher life.

Now this alternation undeniably forms the feeling-content of every religious life, so that it seemed superfluous to illustrate these formulæ by examples. But we may now go on to ask how this usual course of the religious life is related to that which we have at an earlier point described, if only problematically, as the highest development of it. Suppose that the opposite characters are both continuously being strongly imprinted upon the individual religious emotions, so that both alternately rise to a passionate level : this gives to the religious life an instability which we cannot regard as of the highest worth. But suppose that the difficulties gradually disappear, so that facility of religious emotions becomes a permanent state ; and that gradually the higher grade of feeling comes to pre-ponderate over the lower, so that in the immediate self-conscious-ness the sensible determination asserts itself rather as an oppor-tunity for the appearance of the feeling of absolute dependence than as containing the antithesis, which is therefore transferred into the realm of mere perception : then this fact, that the antithesis has almost disappeared again from the higher grade of life, indisputably means that the latter has attained its richest content of feeling.

5. From the above it follows directly that (and in what sense) an uninterrupted sequence of religious emotions can be required of us, as indeed Scripture actually requires it ; and it is confirmed every time a religious soul laments over a moment of his life which is quite empty of the consciousness of God (since no one laments the absence of anything which is recognized to be impossible). Of course, it goes without saying in this connexion that the feeling of

absolute dependence, when it unites with a sensibly determined self-consciousness, and thus becomes an emotion, must vary as regards strength.   Indeed, there will naturally be moments in which a man is not directly and definitely conscious of such a feeling at all. And yet, indirectly, it can be shown that in these moments the feeling was not dead ; as, *e.g.*, when such a moment is followed by another in which the feeling strongly asserts itself, while the second is not felt to be of a different character from the first or a definite departure from it, but to be linked up with it tranquilly as a continuation of its essentially unchanged identity (which is not the case when the preceding moment was one from which the feeling was definitely excluded).   Also, of course, the different formations assumed by the sensible self-consciousness in virtue of the highly manifold minglings of the feeling of freedom and the feeling of dependence, differ in the degree in which they evoke or encourage the appearance of the higher self-consciousness ; and in the case of those which do it in a lesser degree, a weaker appearance of the higher need not be felt as an inhibition of the higher life.   But there is no determination of the immediate sensible self-consciousness which is incompatible with the higher ; so that there is no kind of necessity for either of the two ever to be interrupted, except when the confused state of consciousness gains ground, and both retire behind it.

Postscript.—If thus the direct inward expression of the feeling of absolute dependence is the consciousness of God, and that feeling, whenever it attains to a certain clearness, is accompanied by such an expression, but is also combined with, and related to, a sensible self-consciousness : then the God-consciousness which has in this way arisen will, in all its particular formations, carry with it such determinations as belong to the realm of the antithesis in which the sensible self-consciousness moves.   And this is the source of all those anthropomorphic elements which are inevitable in this realm in utterances about God, and which form such a cardinal point in the ever-recurring controversy between those who accept that fundamental assumption and those who deny it.   For those who rejoice in the possession of an original idea of the Supreme Being derived from some other quarter, but who have no experience of piety, will not tolerate the statement that the expression of that feeling posits the action of the very same thing which is expressed in their original idea.   They assert that the God of feeling is a mere fiction, an idol, and they may perhaps even hint that such a fancy is more tenable in the form of Polytheism. And those who will not admit either a conception of God or a feeling which represents Him, base their position on the contention that the representation of God which is put together out of such utterances, in which God appears as human, destroys itself. Meanwhile, religious men know that it is only in speech that they cannot avoid the anthropomorphic : in their immediate consciousness they keep the object separate from its mode of representation, and they endeavour to show their opponents that without this integration of feeling no certainty is possible even for the strongest forms of objective consciousness or of transitive action, and that, to be consistent, they must limit themselves entirely to the lower grade of life.

§ 6. *The religious self-consciousness, like every essential element in human nature, leads necessarily in its development to fellowship or communion ; a communion which, on the one hand, is variable and fluid, and, on the other hand, has definite limits, i.e. is a Church.*

1. If the feeling of absolute dependence, expressing itself as consciousness of God, is the highest grade of immediate self-consciousness, it is also an essential element of human nature. This cannot be controverted on the ground that there is for every individual man a time when that consciousness does not yet exist. For this is the period when life is incomplete, as may be seen both from the fact that the animal confusion of consciousness has not yet been overcome, and from the fact that other vital functions too are only developing themselves gradually. Nor can it be objected that there are always communities of men in which this feeling has not yet been awakened ; for these likewise only exhibit on a large scale that undeveloped state of human nature which betrays itself also in other functions of their lives. Similarly it cannot be argued that the feeling is accidental (non-essential), because even in a highly developed religious environment individuals may be found who do not share it. For these people cannot but testify that the whole matter is not so alien to them but that they have at particular moments been gripped by such a feeling, though they may call it by some name that is not very honouring to themselves. But if anyone can show, either that this feeling has not a higher value than the sensible, or that there is besides it another of equal value—only then can anyone be entitled to regard it as a merely accidental form, which, while it

may perhaps exist for some people in every age, is nevertheless not to be reckoned as part of a complete human nature for everybody.

2. The truth that every essential element of human nature becomes the basis of a fellowship or communion, can only be fully explicated in the context of a scientific theory of morals. Here we can only allude to the essential points of this process, and then ask everybody to accept it as a fact. Fellowship, then, is demanded by the *consciousness of kind* which dwells in every man, and which finds its satisfaction only when he steps forth beyond the limits of his own personality and takes up the facts of other personalities into his own. It is accomplished through the fact that everything inward becomes, at a certain point of its strength or maturity, an outward too, and, as such, perceptible to others. Thus feeling, as a self-contained determination of the mind (which on the other side passes into thought and action, but with that we are not here concerned), will, even *qua* feeling, and purely in virtue of the consciousness of kind, not exist exclusively for itself, but becomes an outward, originally and without any definite aim or pertinence, by means of facial expression, gesture, tones, and (indirectly) words ; and so becomes to other people a revelation of the inward. This bare expression of feeling, which is entirely caused by the inward agitation, and which can be very definitely distinguished from any further and more separate action into which it passes, does indeed at first arouse in other people only an idea of the person's state of mind. But, by reason of the consciousness of kind, this passes into living imitation ; and the more able the percipient is (either for general reasons, or because of the greater liveliness of the expression, or because of closer affinity) to pass into the same state, the more easily will that state be produced by imitation. Everybody must in his own experience be conscious of this process from both its sides, the expressing and the perceiving, and must thus confess that he always finds himself, with the concurrence of his conscience, involved in a multifarious communion of feeling, as a condition quite in conformity with his nature, and therefore that he would have co-operated in the founding of such a communion if it had not been there already.

As regards the feeling of absolute dependence in particular, everyone will know that it was first awakened in him in the same way, by the communicative and stimulative power of expression or utterance.

3. Our assertion that this communion is at first variable and fluid follows from what we have just been saying. For as individuals in general resemble each other in variable degrees, both as regards the strength of their religious emotions and as regards the particular region of sensible self-consciousness with which their God-consciousness most easily unites, each person's religious emotions have more affinity with those of one of his fellows than with those of another, and thus communion of religious feeling comes to him more easily with the former than with the latter. If the difference is great, he feels himself attracted by the one and repelled by the others ; yet not repelled directly or absolutely, so that he could not enter into any communion of feeling with them at all ; but only in the sense that he is more powerfully attracted to others ; and thus he could have communion even with these, in default of the others, or in circumstances which specially drew them together. For there can hardly exist a man in whom another would recognize no religious affection whatever as being in any degree similar to his own, or whom another would know to be quite incapable of either moving or being moved by him. It remains true, however, that the more uninterrupted the communion is to be, *i.e.* the more closely the kindred emotions are to follow each other, and the more easily the emotions are to communicate themselves, so much the smaller must be the number of people who can participate. We may conceive as great an interval as we like between the two extremes, that of the closest and that of the feeblest communion ; so that the man who experiences the fewest and feeblest religious emotions can have the closest kind of communion only with those who are equally little susceptible to these emotions, and is not in a position to imitate the utterances of those who derive religious emotion from moments where he himself never finds it. A similar relation holds between the man whose piety is purer, in the sense that in every moment of it he clearly distinguishes the religious content of his self-consciousness from the sensible to which it is related, and the man whose piety is less pure, *i.e.* more confused with the sensible. However, we may conceive the interval between these extremes as being, for each person, filled up with as many intermediate stages as we like ; and this is just what constitutes the fluidity of the communion.

4. This is how the interchange of religious consciousness appears when we think of the relation of individual men to each other   But if we look at the actual condition of men, we also find

well-established relationships in this fluid, and therefore (strictly speaking) undefined communion or fellowship. In the first place, as soon as human development has advanced to the point of a domestic life, even if not a completely regulated one, every family will establish within itself such a communion of the religious self-consciousness—a communion which, however, has quite definite limits as regards the outside world. For the members of the family are bound together in a peculiar manner by definite congruity and kinship, and, moreover, their religious emotions are associated with the same occasions, so that strangers can only have an accidental and transitory, and therefore a very unequal, share in them.

But we also find families not isolated but standing collectively in distinctly defined combinations, with common language and customs, and with some knowledge or inkling of a closer common origin. And then religious communion becomes marked off among them, partly in the form of predominating similarity in the individual families, and partly by one family, which is particularly open to religious emotions, coming to predominate as the paramountly active one, while the others, being as it were scarcely out of their nonage, display only receptivity (a state of affairs which exists wherever there is a hereditary priesthood). Every such relatively closed religious communion, which forms an ever self-renewing circulation of the religious self-consciousness within certain definite limits, and a propagation of the religious emotions arranged and organized within the same limits, so that there can be some kind of definite understanding as to which individuals belong to it and which do not—this we designate a *Church*.

Postscript.—This will be the best place to come to an understanding, from our own point of view, as to the different senses in which the word *Religion* is customarily used—though indeed, as far as possible, we here confine ourselves to an occasional and cursory employment of the word for the sake of variety.[1] In the first place, then, when people speak of *a particular religion*, this is always with reference to one definite ' Church,' and it means the totality of the religious affections which form the foundation of such a communion and are recognized to be identical in the various members, in its peculiar content as set forth by

---

[1] [That is to say, Schleiermacher normally uses the word *Frömmigkeit*, which we *usually* translate ' piety,' while we translate the adjective *fromm* sometimes by ' pious ' and sometimes by ' religious.'—TRANSL.]

contemplation and reflection upon the religious emotions. Correspondingly, the individual's susceptibility (which admits of different degrees) to the influence of the fellowship or communion, as also his influence upon the latter, and thus his participation in the circulation and propagation of the religious emotions—this is designated *Religiosity* (*Religiosität*). Now if a man, on the analogy of ' Christian Religion ' and ' Mohammedan Religion,' begins to speak also of ' *Natural Religion*,' he is again abandoning the rule and confusing the use of words, because there is no natural ' Church ' and no definite compass within which the elements of natural religion can be sought. If the expression ' *Religion in general* ' be employed, it again cannot signify such a whole. Nothing can fitly be understood by it but the tendency of the human mind in general to give rise to religious emotions, always considered, however, along with their expression, and thus with the striving for fellowship, *i.e.* the possibility of particular religions (but without regard to the distinction between fluid and defined fellowships). It is only that tendency, the general susceptibility of individual souls to religious emotion, that could be called ' religion in general.' These expressions, however, are seldom clearly distinguished in actual use.

Now, in so far as the constitution of the religious affections of the individual contains more than can be recognized as uniform in the communion, this purely personal element is usually, in regard to its content, called *Subjective Religion*, while the common element is called *Objective Religion*. But this usage becomes in the highest degree inconvenient whenever (as is now the case among ourselves) a large Church splits up into several smaller communions without entirely giving up its unity. For the peculiarities of the smaller Churches would then also be ' subjective religion ' in comparison with what was recognized as common to the larger Church, while they would be ' objective ' in comparison with the peculiarities of their particular members. Finally, in the religious emotions themselves, a distinction can be made between the inner determination of self-consciousness and the manner of its outward expression, though these are closely connected ; and thus the organization of the communicative expressions of piety in a community is usually called *Outward Religion*, while the total content of the religious emotions, as they actually occur in individuals, is called *Inward Religion*.

Now, while these definitions may well be the best, as comprehending the various and very arbitrary usages, we have only to compare the expressions with the explanations given, in order to realize how indeterminate it all is. Therefore it is really better to avoid these designations in scientific usage, especially as the term 'religion,' as applied to Christianity, is quite new in our language.

II. THE DIVERSITIES OF RELIGIOUS COMMUNIONS IN GENERAL: PROPOSITIONS BORROWED FROM THE PHILOSOPHY OF RELIGION.

§ 7. *The various religious communions which have appeared in history with clearly defined limits are related to each other in two ways : as different stages of development, and as different kinds.*

1. The religious communion which takes the form of household worship within a single family cannot fitly be regarded as an appearance in the realm of history, because it remains in the obscurity of an inner circle. Moreover, the transition from this to a really historical appearance is often very gradual. The beginning of it is seen in the large style of the patriarchal household, and the persisting association between families of sons and grandsons that live near each other ; and it is out of these alone that the two fundamental forms previously mentioned (§ 6, 4) can be developed. In these transitions, if several of them are placed beside each other, both kinds of difference can be found at least in germ.

Now in the first place, as regards the different stages of development : the historical appearance is in itself a higher stage, and stands above the mere isolated household worship, just as the civic condition, even in its most incomplete forms, stands above the formless association of the pre-civic condition. But this difference by no means relates only to the form or the compass of the fellowship itself, but also to the constitution of the underlying religious affections, according as they attain to clearness in conscious antithesis to the movements of the sensible self-consciousness. Now this development depends partly on the whole development of the mental powers, so that for that reason alone many a communion cannot continue longer in its own peculiar mode of existence ; as, *e.g.*, many forms of idol-worship, even though they might claim a high degree of mechanical skill, are incompatible with even a moderate scientific and artistic education, and perish when confronted by it. Yet it is also partly true that the development takes its own course ; and there is no contradiction in saying that, in one and the same whole, the piety may develop to its highest consummation, while other mental functions remain far behind.

But all differences are not to be thus regarded as distinct stages or levels. There are communal religions (Greek and Indian poly-theism are good cases in point), of which one might well seem to be at the same point in the scale as the other, but which are yet very definitely different from each other. If, then, several such exist which belong to the same stage or level, the most natural course will be to call them different kinds or species. And indisputably it can be shown, even at the lowest stage, that most religious communions which are geographically separated from each other are also divided by inner differences.

2. But of course these two distinctions, into stages of develop-ment and into kinds (genera) or species, cannot in this realm, or indeed generally in the realm of history or of so-called moral ' persons,' be maintained so definitely or carried through so surely as in the realm of Nature. For we are not here dealing with invariable forms which always reproduce themselves in the same way. Each individual communion is capable of a greater or lesser development within the character of its kind or genus. Let us, now, consider that in this way, just as the individual may pass from a more imperfect religious communion to a higher one, so a parti-cular communion might, without prejudice to its generic character, develop beyond its original level, and that this may happen equally to all. Then the idea of stages would naturally disappear, for the last phase of the lower and the first of the higher might be con-tinuously connected, and it would then be more correct to say that each genus works itself up by a series of developments from the imperfect to the more perfect. But, on the other hand, we may take the fact that, just as we say an individual becomes in a certain sense a new man by passing to a higher form of religion, so the generic character of a communion must be lost when it rises to a higher level. Then even on any one level, if the inner development is to go on, the generic character would become uncertain and altogether unstable, while the levels or stages would be all the more sharply and definitely distinguished.

This variability, however, does not discredit the reality of our twofold distinction. For every religious communion which appears in history will be related to the others in this twofold way. It will be co-ordinate with some, and subordinate or superior to others ; and thus it is distinguished from the former in the one manner and from the latter in the other.   And if those who busy themselves most with the history and criticism of religions have given less attention to the task of fitting the different forms into this framework, this may be partly because they confine themselves almost exclusively to the individual, and partly also because it may be difficult in particular cases to lay bare these relationships and properly to distinguish and separate co-ordinates and subordinates.   It may here suffice us to have established the twofold distinction in a general way, since our sole concern is to investigate how Christianity is related, in both respects, to other religious communions and forms of faith.

3. Our proposition does not assert, but it does tacitly presuppose the possibility, that there are other forms of piety which are related to Christianity as different forms on the same level of development, and thus so far similar.   But this does not contradict the conviction, which we assume every Christian to possess, of the exclusive superiority of Christianity.   In the realm of Nature also we distinguish perfect and imperfect animals as different stages of the development of animal life, and again on each of these stages different genera, which thus resemble each other as expressions of the same stage ; but this does not mean that one genus of the lower stage may not be nearer to the higher, and thus more perfect, than the others.   Similarly, though several kinds of piety belong to the same stage as Christianity, it may yet be more perfect than any of them.

Our proposition excludes only the idea, which indeed is often met with, that the Christian religion (piety) should adopt towards at least most other forms of piety the attitude of the true towards the false.   For if the religions belonging to the same stage as Christianity were entirely false, how could they have so much similarity to Christianity as to make that classification requisite ? And if the religions which belong to the lower stages contained nothing but error, how would it be possible for a man to pass from them to Christianity ?   Only the true, and not the false, can be a basis of receptivity for the higher truth of Christianity.   The whole delineation which we are here introducing is based rather on the maxim that error never exists in and for itself, but always along with some truth, and that we have never fully understood it until we have discovered its connexion with truth, and the true thing to which it is attached.   With this agrees what the apostle says when he represents even Polytheism as a perversion of the original consciousness of God which underlies it, and when, in this evidence of the longing which all these fancies have failed to satisfy, he finds an obscure presentiment of the true God.[1]

§ 8. *Those forms of piety in which all religious affections express the dependence of everything finite upon one Supreme and Infinite Being, i.e. the monotheistic forms, occupy the highest level ; and all others are related to them as subordinate forms, from which men are destined to pass to those higher ones.*

1. As such subordinate stages we set down, generally speaking, Idol-worship proper (also called Fetichism) and Polytheism ; of which, again, the first stands far lower than the second. The idol-worshipper may quite well have only one idol, but this does not give such Monolatry any resemblance to Monotheism, for it ascribes to the idol an influence only over a limited field of objects or processes, beyond which its own interest and sympathy do not extend. The addition of several idols is merely an accident, usually caused by the experience of some incapacity in the original one, but not aiming at any kind of completeness. Indeed, the main reason why people remain on this level is that the sense of totality has not yet developed. The old ξόανα of the original Greek tribes were probably idols in the proper sense, each being something in itself alone. The unification of these different worships, by which one Being was substituted for several such idols, and the rise of several cycles of myths by which these creations were brought into connexion with each other—this was the development through which the transition from Idol-worship to Polytheism proper took place. But the more the idea of a multiplicity of local habitations clung to the Beings thus constituted, the more did Polytheism continue to savour of Idol-worship. Polytheism proper is present only when the local references quite disappear, and the gods, spiritually defined, form an organized and coherent plurality, which, if not exhibited as a totality, is nevertheless presupposed and striven after as such. The more, then, any single one of these Beings is related to the whole system of them, and this system, in turn, to the whole of existence as it appears in consciousness, the more definitely is the dependence of everything finite, not indeed on a Highest One, but on this highest totality, expressed in the religious self-consciousness. But in this state of religious faith there

[1] Rom. 1²¹ᶠ·, Acts 17²⁷⁻³⁰.

cannot fail to be here and there at least a presentiment of One Supreme Being behind the plurality of higher Beings ; and then Polytheism is already beginning to disappear, and the way to Monotheism is open.

2. As for this difference, of believing in one God on whom the religious man regards himself as being (along with the world of which he is a part) absolutely dependent, or in a group of gods to whom he stands in different relations according as they divide the government of the world among them, or finally in particular idols which belong to the family or the locality or the particular occupation in which he lives : it seems at first, indeed, to be only a difference in the mode of representation, and therefore, from our point of view, only a derivative difference. And only a difference in the immediate self-consciousness can for us be a fit measure of the development of religion. But it is also very easy to show that these different representations depend on different states of self-consciousness. Idol-worship proper is based upon a confused state of the self-consciousness which marks the lowest condition of man, since in it the higher and the lower are so little distinguished that even the feeling of absolute dependence is reflected as arising from a particular object to be apprehended by the senses. So, too, with Polytheism : in its combination of the religious susceptibility with diverse affections of the sensible self-consciousness, it exhibits this diversity in such a very preponderant degree that the feeling of absolute dependence cannot appear in its complete unity and indifference to all that the sensible self-consciousness may contain ; but, instead, a plurality is posited as its source. But when the higher self-consciousness, in distinction from the sensible, has been fully developed, then, in so far as we are open in general to sensible stimulation, *i.e.* in so far as we are constituent parts of the world, and therefore in so far as we take up the world into our self-consciousness and expand the latter into a general consciousness of finitude, we are conscious of ourselves as absolutely dependent. Now this self-consciousness can only be described in terms of Monotheism, and indeed only as we have expressed it in our proposition. For if we are conscious of ourselves, as such and in our finitude, as absolutely dependent, the same holds true of all finite existence, and in this connexion we take up the whole world along with ourselves into the unity of our self-consciousness. Thus the different ways of representing that existence outside of us to which the consciousness of absolute dependence refers, depend

partly on the different degrees of extensiveness of the self-consciousness (for as long as a man identifies himself only with a small part
of finite existence, his god will remain a fetich) ; and partly on the
degree of clearness with which the higher self-consciousness is
distinguished from the lower. Polytheism naturally represents in
both respects an indeterminate middle stage, which sometimes is
very little different from Idol-worship, but sometimes, when in the
handling of the plurality there appears a secret striving after unity,
may border very closely on Monotheism ; whether it be that the
gods rather represent the forces of Nature, or that they symbolize
the human qualities which are operative in social relationships, or
that both these tendencies are united in the same cult. Otherwise
it could not in itself be explained how the correlative term in the
feeling of absolute dependence could be reflected as a plurality of
beings. But if the higher consciousness has not become quite
distinct from the lower, then the correlative can only be conceived
in a sensible way, and then for that very reason it contains the
germs of plurality. Thus it is only when the religious consciousness
expresses itself as capable of being combined with all the states of
the sensible self-consciousness without discrimination, but also as
clearly distinct from the latter, in such a way that in the religious
emotions themselves no sharper distinction appears than that
between the joyful and the depressing tone—it is only then that
man has successfully passed beyond those two stages, and can
refer his feeling of absolute dependence solely to one Supreme Being.

3. It can therefore justly be said that as soon as piety has anywhere developed to the point of belief in one God over all, it may be
predicted that man will not in any region of the earth remain
stationary on one of the lower planes. For this belief is always
and everywhere very particularly engaged, if not always in the best
way, in the endeavour to propagate itself and disclose itself to the
receptive faculties of mankind ; and this succeeds eventually, as
we can see, even among the rudest human races, and by a direct
transition from Fetichism without any intermediate passage through
a stage of Polytheism. On the other hand, there is nowhere any
trace, so far as history reaches, of a relapse from Monotheism, in
the strict sense. In the case of most of those Christians who under
persecution went back to heathenism, it was only an apparent
return. Where it was a matter of real earnest, these people must,
previously, at their conversion to Christianity, have been simply
carried on by a general movement, without having appropriated

the essence of this belief into their own personal consciousness.
However, we must not, from all this, draw the conclusion that the
existence of Fetichism requires for its explanation the assumption
of a still lower stage, in which religious emotion would be altogether
lacking. ·Many have, indeed, described the original state of mankind as such a brute-existence ; but, even if we cannot deny all
trace of such a state, it can be neither proved historically nor
imagined in a general way how of itself this state should have given
rise to the development of something higher. No more can it be
shown that Polytheism has anywhere transformed itself, by a sheer
process from within, into genuine Monotheism ; although this can
at least be conceived as possible, as has been indicated above. In
any case, we must secure ourselves against the demand that, since
we have definitely exhibited such a gradation, we are bound also
to give a definite account of such an original state of religion ; for
in other connexions also it is the case that we never get back to
origins. If, then, we keep simply to our presuppositions, without
resorting to any historical statements about a period which is
altogether prehistoric, we are left with a choice between two ways
of conceiving it. Either that quite obscure and confused form of
religion was everywhere the original form, and advanced to Polytheism through the concentration of several small tribes into one
larger community ; or a childish Monotheism (which for that very
reason was subject to a confused mingling of the higher and the
lower) was the original stage, and among some people darkened
completely into idol-worship, while among others it clarified into a
pure belief in God.

4. On this highest plane, of Monotheism, history exhibits only
three great communions—the Jewish, the Christian, and the Mohammedan ; the first being almost in process of extinction, the other
two still contending for the mastery of the human race. Judaism,
by its limitation of the love of Jehovah to the race of Abraham,
betrays a lingering affinity with Fetichism ; and the numerous
vacillations towards idol-worship prove that during the political
heyday of the nation the monotheistic faith had not yet taken fast
root, and was not fully and purely developed until after the Babylonian Exile. Islam, on the other hand, with its passionate character, and the strongly sensuous content of its ideas, betrays, in
spite of its strict Monotheism, a large measure of that influence of
the sensible upon the character of the religious emotions which elsewhere keeps men on the level of Polytheism. Thus Christianity,

because it remains free from both these weaknesses, stands higher than either of those other two forms, and takes its place as the purest form of Monotheism which has appeared in history.   Hence there is strictly no such thing as a wholesale relapse from Christianity to either Judaism or Mohammedanism, any more than there is from any monotheistic religion to Polytheism or idol-worship.   Individual exceptions will always be connected with pathological states of mind ; or, instead of religion, it will prove to be simply one form of irreligion that is exchanged for another, which indeed is what always happens in the case of renegades.   And so this comparison of Christianity with other similar religions is in itself a sufficient warrant for saying that Christianity is, in fact,[1] the most perfect of the most highly developed forms of religion.

Postscript 1.—The above account is at variance with the view which sees no real piety at all, but only superstition, in the religions of the lower levels, mainly because they are supposed to have had their source simply in fear.   But the honour of Christianity does not at all demand such an assertion.   For since Christianity itself affirms [2] that only perfect love casts out all fear, it must admit that imperfect love is never entirely free from fear.   And likewise it is always the case, even in idol-worship, if the idol is worshipped as a protector at all, and not as an evil being, that the fear is by no means quite without any impulses of love, but is rather an adaptation. corresponding to the imperfect love, of the feeling of absolute dependence.   Moreover (quite apart from the fact that many of these religions are too cheerful to be explicable by fear), if we should set out to discover for them a quite different origin from that of true religion, it would be difficult to show what sort of tendency this is in the human soul, and what its inner aim is, which engenders idol-worship, and which must again be lost when the latter gives place to Religion.   The truth is, rather, that we must never deny the homogeneity of all these products of the human spirit, but must acknowledge the same root even for the lower powers.

Postscript 2.—But for the assonance of the names there would scarcely be any occasion for us expressly to remark that it is not at all our present business to say anything about that way of thinking which is called Pantheism.   For it has never been the confession of a religious communion which actually appeared in history, and it is only with these that we are concerned.   Moreover, this name was not originally used even by individuals to designate their own

---

[1] Cf. § 7, 3.   [2] 1 John 4[18].

views, but crept in as a taunt and nickname ; and in such cases it
always remains difficult to hold consistently to any one meaning.
The one thing concerning the subject which can be discussed in this
place (and indeed *only* in such a place as this) is the question of the
relation of this way of thinking to piety.　It is admitted that it
does not, like the three above-described theories, spring from the
religious emotions, by direct reflection upon them.　But it may be
asked whether, having once arisen in some other way—by the way
of speculation or simply of reasoning—it is yet compatible with
piety.　To this question an affirmative answer may be given without
hesitation, provided that Pantheism is taken as expressing some
variety or form of Theism, and that the word is not simply and
solely a disguise for a materialistic negation of Theism.　If we look
at idol-worship, and consider how it is always conjoined with a
very limited knowledge of the world, and is also full of magic and
sorcery of every sort, it is very easy to see that in very few cases
can one speak of a clear distinction on this level between what is
assigned to God and what is assigned to the world.　And why
could not a Hellenic polytheist, embarrassed by the entirely human
shapes of the gods, have identified his great gods with the evolved
gods of Plato, leaving out the God whom Plato represents as
addressing them, and positing only the enthroned Necessity ?
This would not imply any change in his piety, yet his representation
of it would have become pantheistic.　But let us think of the
highest stage of religion, and let us accordingly hold Pantheism
fast to the usual formula of One and All : then God and world will
remain distinct at least as regards function, and thus such a man,
since he reckons himself as belonging to the world, can feel himself,
along with this All, to be dependent on that which is the corresponding One.　Such states of mind can scarcely be distinguished
from the religious emotions of many a Monotheist.　At any rate,
the distinction (always rather a curious one, and, if I may say so,
roughly drawn) between a God who is outside of and above the
world, and a God who is in the world, does not particularly meet
the point, for nothing can strictly be said about God in terms of the
antithesis between internal and external without imperilling in
some way the divine omnipotence and omnipresence.

§ 9. *The widest diversity between forms of piety is that which exists,*
　　　with respect to the religious affections, between those forms
　　　which subordinate the natural in human conditions to the

moral and those which, on the contrary, subordinate the moral to the natural.

1. It is primarily in the interests of Christianity, and therefore only for the highest level, that we shall here attempt a conceptual division of religions which appear as co-ordinate (a cross-division, *i.e.*, in relation to our division of the whole field). Whether this division holds for the subordinate stages too, is a question that does not here concern us. But for the highest stage the attempt is necessary. For even if this stage is, as a matter of history, exhausted in the three above-mentioned communions, yet we need a more exactly defined position in which to fix Christianity; for otherwise we could only distinguish it empirically from the other two, and could never be certain whether the more essential differences were being brought to light or whether we were only getting hold of accidental characteristics. Hence our attempt cannot be held to have succeeded until we find a basis of division by which Christianity is either clearly distinguished, in itself, from the two others, or along with one of the others distinguished from the third.

Now, since the feeling of absolute dependence is in itself perfectly simple, and the conception of it provides no basis of differentiation, such a basis can be derived only from the fact that that feeling, in order to realize itself in an actual moment, must first unite with a sensible stimulation of self-consciousness, and that these sensible stimuli must be regarded as infinitely various. Now it is true that the feeling of absolute dependence in itself is equally related to all these stimulations, and is highly susceptible to them all alike. But nevertheless it may, by analogy, be assumed that this relationship in actual reality differentiates itself variously not only in individual men but also in larger masses. And thus with some people a certain class of sensible feelings develops easily and surely into religious emotion, and another opposite class with difficulty or not at all, while with other people the case is precisely reversed. Or it may be that the same sensible states of self-consciousness develop into religious moments with some people in one set of conditions, and with other people in the opposite set of conditions. As regards the former alternative, we might first of all divide these states into the more physical and the more spiritual, into those which arise through the influence of men and their actions and those which arise through the influence of external Nature. But this could only hold of individual men, that some are more susceptible to religious emotion through the impressions of external Nature, and others through social relationships and the temper which they produce. The difference between one religious communion and another cannot be thus explained, since every such communion includes all these diversities, and none excludes from its pale either the one or the other kind of emotion, or even makes the one less prominent than the other to any significant extent. Again, we might point to the fact that, our whole life being an inter-penetration and succession of activity and passivity, a man is sometimes more conscious of himself as active and sometimes more as passive. And this might be held better to provide a common constitution for larger masses of people—the fact that in certain quarters the active form of self-consciousness more easily rises into religious emotion, and the passive remains on the sensible level, while in other quarters this is reversed. Only, of course, this so simply conceived distinction remains a merely fluid one between a more and a less, so that the same moment may be conceived as either more active or more passive according as it is compared with one or with another. If a grand division of universal application is to be made between the different forms of piety, the above fluid distinction must be transformed into such a subordination as is indicated in our proposition. This subordination is on the one side most strongly marked when the passive states (whether pleasant or unpleasant, whether occasioned by external Nature or by social relationships) only arouse the feeling of absolute dependence in so far as they are referred to the spontaneous activity, *i.e.* in so far as we know that some particular thing (just because we stand in that relation to the totality of existence which is expressed in our passive state) has to be done by us, so that the action which depends on and proceeds from that state has thus precisely this God-conscious-ness as its impulse. Thus where piety has taken this form, the passive states, having risen into religious emotion, become simply an occasion for the development of a definite activity which can only be explained as the result of a God-consciousness of that particular description. And in the realm of such religious emotions all passive relations of man to the world appear as simply means for evoking the totality of his active states, whereby the antithesis between the sensibly pleasant and the unpleasant therein is over-come and retires into the background ; while, on the contrary, it of course remains predominant in the cases in which the sensible feeling does not rise into religious emotion. This subordination we designate *teleological* Religion ; an expression which indeed is else-where somewhat differently used, but which is here meant to signify simply that a predominating reference to the moral task constitutes the fundamental type of the religious affections. Now if the action which is prefigured in the religious emotion is a practical contribution to the advancement of the Kingdom of God, the mental state is an elevating one, whether the feeling which occasioned it be pleasant or unpleasant. But if the action is a retreat into oneself, or a seeking for help to relieve a perceptible obstruction of the higher life, the mental state is a subduing one, whether the feeling which occasioned it was pleasant or unpleasant. The reverse form of this subordination appears in its completeness when the self-consciousness of a state of activity is taken up into the feeling of absolute dependence only in proportion as the state itself appears as a result of those relations which exist between the subject and all the rest of existence, and is thus referred to the passive side of the subject. But every individual state of activity is simply a particular expression of the disposition of common human faculties which exists in the subject and constitutes his personal peculiarity. Con-sequently, in every religious emotion of this sort, that disposition itself is posited as the result of the influences, ordered by the Supreme Being, of all things upon the subject ; and thus in the elevating emotions, as harmony, *i.e.* as beauty of the individual life, and in the unpleasant or subduing emotions, as discord or ugliness. Now this form of piety, in which each moment of spontaneous activity, simply as a determination of the individual by the whole of finite existence, and thus as referred to the passive side, is taken up into the feeling of absolute dependence, we will call *æsthetic* Religion. These two fundamental forms are definitely opposed to each other, in virtue of the opposite subordination of the elements which are common to both ; and every kind of religious fellow-feeling or sympathy is naturally found in both forms, just as is the personal feeling, since the former is simply an expanded, the latter a con-tracted, self-consciousness.

2. A general demonstration as to whether the actual historical faiths can best be classified according to this antithesis would be the business only of a general critical History of Religions. Here we are simply concerned as to whether the division so far justifies itself, as to provide a means of distinguishing Christianity from religions co-ordinate with it, and by more narrowly determining its position to facilitate the task of isolating its peculiar essence.

As a matter of fact, the religion which is chiefly present to our minds, as being sharply opposed in this respect to Christianity, is not co-ordinate with it, but belongs to a lower level, namely, Greek Polytheism. In this religion the teleological trend falls entirely into the background. Neither in their religious symbols nor even in their Mysteries is there any considerable trace of the idea of a totality of moral ends to which a man's mental states are in general to be related. On the contrary, what we have called the æsthetic outlook very definitely predominates, inasmuch as even the gods are principally intended to exhibit different dispositions of the activities of the human soul, and thus a peculiar form of inward beauty. Now no one can well deny that Christianity, even apart from the fact that it belongs to a higher level, is sharply opposed to this type. In the realm of Christianity the consciousness of God is always related to the totality of active states in the idea of a Kingdom of God. As for the idea of a beauty of the soul, regarded as the result of all the influences of Nature and the world, this has always remained so foreign to Christianity (in spite of Christianity's early absorption of Hellenism *en masse*) that it has never been adopted into the cycle of current expressions in the realm of Christian piety, and has never been maintained in any treatise of Christian morals. But that figure of a Kingdom of God, which is so important and indeed all-inclusive for Christianity, is simply the general expression of the fact that in Christianity all pain and all joy are religious only in so far as they are related to activity in the Kingdom of God, and that every religious emotion which proceeds from a passive state ends in the consciousness of a transition to activity.

But now we have to determine whether the above-mentioned antithesis between the teleological and the æsthetic trend is not, after all, necessarily bound up with the distinction between the two levels, so that all Polytheism would necessarily belong to the æsthetic side and all Monotheism to the teleological. To this end we must simply take our stand upon the highest level, and ask whether the two other monotheistic faiths are like Christianity in this respect or not. As for Judaism, then, though it relates the passive states to the active rather in the form of divine punishments and rewards than in the form of moral challenge and influence, nevertheless the predominating form of God-consciousness is that of the commanding Will ; and thus, even when it proceeds from passive states, it necessarily turns to the active. Islam, on the other hand, in no way shows this subordination of the passive

to the active. Rather does this form of piety come to complete
rest in the consciousness of immutable divine appointments, and
even the consciousness of spontaneous activity is only united with
the feeling of absolute dependence in the sense that its determination is supposed to rest upon those appointments. And this
fatalistic character reveals in the clearest manner a subordination
of the moral to the natural. Thus the monotheistic stage appears
divided, the teleological type being most expressed in Christianity,
and less perfectly in Judaism, while Mohammedanism, which is
quite as monotheistic, unmistakably expresses the æsthetic type.
All this points us for our present task to a definitely limited field,
and what we are going to establish as the peculiar essence of Christianity must no more deviate from the teleological line than it may
descend from the monotheistic level.

§ 10. *Each particular form of communal piety has both an outward
unity, as a fixed fact of history with a definite commencement, and an inward unity, as a peculiar modification of
that general character which is common to all developed faiths
of the same kind and level ; and it is from both of these taken
together that the peculiar essence of any particular form is
to be discerned.*

NOTE.—Cf. *Speeches on Religion* (Eng. trans.), pp. 210 ff.

1. The first part of this proposition would be false if it could
be shown, or even conceived as possible, that Christian piety could
anywhere arise, as it were of itself, quite apart from any historical
connexion with the impulse which proceeded from Christ. The
same thing would in that case be true of Mohammedan and Jewish
piety too, with reference to Moses and Mohammed. But the
possibility of it will be admitted by nobody. Of course this outward
unity is not so rigid on the subordinate levels of religion ; partly
because in these cases the starting-point often falls in the prehistoric period (as it does in the case of the pre-Mosaic monotheistic worship of Jehovah) ; partly because many of these
historical forms, such as the Greek, and still more the Roman,
Polytheism, present to us a composite whole which, from many
very diverse starting-points, has gradually been woven together or
even grown together of itself. The same might indeed be said of
the Norse and Indian systems. But these apparent exceptions
rather confirm the rule laid down in our proposition. For the less
the outward unity can be definitely exhibited, the more precarious

becomes the inward unity too. It appears that, just as in the realm of Nature the species are less definite on the lower levels of life, so in this realm of religion also the uniform consummation of the outward and the inward unity is reserved for the higher development ; and thus in the most perfect form (which we may say in advance is Christianity) the inward peculiarity must be most intimately bound up with that which forms the historical basis of the outward unity.

The second part of our proposition would be false if it could be asserted that the different religious communions were really separated only by space and time without having any genuinely inward difference. But this would imply that whenever two such communions came into contact spatially they would necessarily recognize their identity with each other, and so become one, and that nothing could hinder this except (to a certain extent) a foolish self-will which was anxious to cling to the name of the founder. It would also imply that each individual could, without undergoing any inward change, pass from his own religious communion to a quite different one, simply by dissolving the one historical con-nexion and entering into another. But this would be contrary to all experience. Indeed it would, on this hypothesis, be im-possible that one religious communion should spring up within another and break away from it ; for if nothing new came in, there could be no new beginning where the same elements had been already present.

2. With respect to the actual beginning of each religious com-munion there need be no further discussion. Whether a new variety of the feeling of absolute dependence takes shape first simply in one individual or in several simultaneously, is a matter of indifference, though everyone will see that the latter is, generally speaking, less probable than the former. It would also be futile to try to distinguish the different ways in which such a new form can arise in the soul, since the communion can only arise through its communication and transmission. But what our proposition says about the inward difference requires some further discussion. Our proposition makes the statement (which, however, in accord-ance with our present purpose, we are going to apply only to the religious communions of the highest level) that the same thing is present in all, but present in a quite different way in each. The pre-vailing view, on the contrary, is that the greater part is the same in all communions of the highest level, and that to this common matter

there is simply added in each some special element of its own ; so that perhaps, to give a rough illustration, the belief in one God, with all that it involves, is the element common to all these communions, but in the one there is added obedience to commandment, in another the belief in Christ, and in a third the belief in the prophets. But if the belief in Christ had no influence upon the separately pre-existing consciousness of God and on its mode of uniting with the sensible emotions, either that belief would stand quite outside the realm of religion, and would consequently (since no other realm can be assigned to it) be a mere nothing, or Christ would at any rate be only one particular object producing impressions which could be united with the consciousness of God, in which case also one could not properly speak of a belief in Christ. Suppose however the meaning is that the belief in Christ has an influence only on *some* of the religious emotions, while the majority of them take exactly the same form in Christianity as in other monotheistic faiths. This would involve the assertion that this belief has not so much an influence on the consciousness of God (which, after all, must be the same in all religious emotions of the same man at the same time, *i.e.* so long as he belongs to the same religious communion), but rather has an influence merely upon the sensibly stimulated consciousness ; and such an influence could not be the basis of a distinctive way of faith. Hence there remains for us only the view adopted in our proposition, which implies that in each really distinctive religious communion the self-consciousness itself must have a different determination, since only on this condition can the religious emotions be all differently determined. Now just as each individual instance necessarily makes it clear that the presence of an absolutely identical element in two different ways of faith can be only in appearance, if the God-consciousness itself is differently determined in the two : so also it is only in appearance that each faith has some element which is entirely absent in others. Otherwise, if in other faiths also we find God becoming Man, and a communication of the Divine Spirit, what would be the absolutely new thing in Christianity ? But the same thing may be seen in a general way. For if, on the supposition of a quite similarly determined consciousness of God, some element is found in one faith which is not found in another, this could only be caused by a different field of experience, and so the whole difference would necessarily disappear if the experiences were brought into line with each other.

3. Though it was only in a somewhat indefinite way that we were able to establish the conception of *kind* in our present province, the conception of the *Individual* has here a firmer basis, and the formula set up in our proposition is the same which holds for all individual differences within the same kind. For every man has in him all that another man has, but it is all differently determined ; and the greatest similarity is only a diminishing or (relatively) vanishing difference. So also every species has the same characteristics as every other species of its genus, and everything which is really additional is merely accidental. But the discovery of this differentiating matter in any individual existence is a task which can never be perfectly, but only approximately, discharged in words and sentences. And hence naturalists and historians are wont to bring forward only certain marks as distinguishing signs, without meaning to assert that these express everything distinctive and characteristic ; and the man who describes religion must in most cases be content with the same procedure. But if we must make an attempt at some kind of general statement, in order that the apologist of any particular faith may be the less likely to fall into error, we should be content with saying this : in every individual religion the God-consciousness, which in itself remains the same everywhere on the same level, is attached to some relation of the self-consciousness in such an especial way that only thereby can it unite with other determinations of the self-consciousness ; so that all other relations are subordinate to this one, and it communicates to all others its colour and its tone. If it should seem that by this we are expressing merely a different rule for the *connecting* of religious moments, rather than a difference of form or of content, we have only to note that every moment is itself a connexion, as being the transition from the preceding to the following moment, and thus must become a different moment when the religious self-consciousness is placed in a different connexion.

Postscript.—It is only by means of the two points set up in our proposition (namely, the distinctive beginning to which each religious communion goes back, and the peculiar form which the religious emotions and their utterances take in each communion) that it is possible to regulate the usage of the familiar terms ' *positive* ' and ' *revealed*.' It is well known that these terms are used somewhat confusedly, being often applied in exactly the same manner at one moment to the individual doctrines, at another to the faith in general, and being at one time opposed to the natural, at another to the rational. Hence it would be a difficult task so to fix their meaning as to secure for them a uniformly consistent usage in the realm of scientific theology. For the former of the two terms we are given a good lead by the use made of it in the theory of Law, where positive rights are contrasted with natural rights. If we compare the two, one finds that natural right never appears in the same sense as positive, namely, as the basis of a civic community. Even the simplest and most original relationships, such as paternal authority or the marriage union, are in each society defined in a distinctive manner—in the developed State by express legislation, and in earlier stages by prevailing custom. Natural right, however, is simply what can be abstracted in a similar manner from the legislation of all societies. And even if, as pure knowledge, it were to come into existence in another way, yet everyone would admit that when you come to the application of it, it must first be more precisely defined, and therefore, as applicable to practice, can only be traced back to this act of more precise definition. Now it is the same with Natural Religion. It never appears as the basis of a religious communion,[1] but is simply what can be abstracted uniformly from the doctrines of all religious communions of the highest grade, as being present in all but differently determined in each. Such a natural religion would mark out the common elements in all religious affections which are found in the ecclesiastical communions, and if we conceive of all religious communions as already given, and also of all the different philosophical systems as having adjusted their differences as regards the terminology of such a doctrine, this natural religion would be everywhere the same, and would remain ever self-identical. But it would never anywhere be more than a mere private possession, which would belong, in addition to their definite type and manner of piety and its expression in doctrine, to those individuals in the various religious communions who, acknowledging from their own standpoint the other communions in their inter-relation, were able to view together in a higher unity things which are separated in actuality. Moreover, it would not be difficult to show that what is called natural religion did actually arise in this way, and, further, that any attempt to make this secondary product the basis of an ecclesiastical communion has always failed, and must always fail. But that is hardly our business here. Agreed, then, that in any case, even if it should have arisen in a different way, such a natural

---

[1] Cf. § 6, *Postscript.*

religion, or rather, properly speaking, natural theology, being a mere collocation of doctrines, would be simply the common element in all monotheistic faiths : then the positive element in each would be seen to be the individualized element, which, as shown above, is found in each of them not simply here and there but, strictly considered, all over them, though it may be more prominent at one point than at another. It simply betrays a misapprehension when people attempt to distinguish the actually existing religious communions from each other by the principle that the positive element is found in one at one point and in another at another point, as, e.g., that in Christianity it is the doctrines, in Judaism the commandments.[1] For if in one communion the commands are more elaborated and the doctrines less, and in another vice versa, it is simply that in the one case the doctrine is concealed in the command as in a symbol, and in the other the doctrine itself appears as a command that it be expressed and confessed. Moreover, it would be equally false to deny that the precepts of Christian morals are positive and to deny that the doctrine of Jehovah in Judaism is positive. In any case, neither the command, as the expression of a common mode of action, nor the doctrine, as the expression of a common mode of representation, is an original element : both are based on a common distinctive quality of the religious emotions. Now since without this the particular communion itself could not have come into existence, and since it has maintained an existence dating from, and in relation to, the fact which marked its beginning, it must be dependent on that fact for the peculiar stamp of its religious emotions. This, then, is what is to be signified by the term ' positive ' : the individual content of all the moments of the religious life within one religious communion, in so far as this content depends on the original fact from which the communion itself, as a coherent historical phenomenon, originated.

The words ' reveal,' ' revealed,' ' revelation,' present still further difficulties, since even originally they sometimes signify the illumination of what was obscure, confused, unobserved, and sometimes rather the disclosing and unveiling of what was hitherto concealed and kept secret, and still further confusion has been introduced by the distinction between mediate and immediate (direct and indirect) revelation. To begin with, all will at once agree that the word ' revealed ' is never applied either to what is discovered in the realm of experience by one man and handed on to others, or to

[1] See M. Mendelssohn's *Jerusalem*.

what is excogitated in thought by one man and so learned by others ; and further, that the word presupposes a divine communication and declaration. And in this sense we find the word very generally applied to the origin of religious communions. For of what religious mysteries and varieties of worship, either among the Greeks or among the Egyptians and Indians, would it not be asserted that they originally came from heaven or were proclaimed by Deity in some way which fell outside the human and natural order ? Not seldom, indeed, we find even the beginning of civic communities (just as from the beginning we often find the moral and the religious unseparated) traced to a divine sending of the man who first gathered the tribe together into a civic union, and so the new organization of life is based on a revelation. Accordingly we might say that the idea of revelation signifies the *originality* of the fact which lies at the foundation of a religious communion, in the sense that this fact, as conditioning the individual content of the religious emotions which are found in the communion, cannot itself in turn be explained by the historical chain which precedes it.

Now the fact that in this original element there is a divine causality requires no further discussion ; nor does the fact that it is an activity which aims at and furthers the salvation of man. But I am unwilling to accept the further definition that it operates upon man as a cognitive being. For that would make the revelation to be originally and essentially *doctrine* ; and I do not believe that we can adopt that position, whether we consider the whole field covered by the idea, or seek to define it in advance with special reference to Christianity. If a system of propositions can be understood from their connexion with others, then nothing supernatural was required for their production. But if they cannot, then they can, in the first instance, only be apprehended (we need only appeal for confirmation to the first principles of Hermeneutics) as parts of another whole, as a moment of the life of a thinking being who works upon us directly as a distinctive existence by means of his total impression on us ; and this working is always a working upon the self-consciousness. Thus the original fact will always be the appearing of such a being, and the original working will always be upon the self-consciousness of those into whose circle he enters. That this does not exclude doctrine, but implies it, is obvious. For the rest, it always remains very difficult, indeed almost impossible, to give definite limits to this idea, and, if it is thus definitely grasped, to explain its rise wherever it appears. For everywhere in the realm of mythology, Greek as well as Oriental and Norse, these divine communications and declarations border so closely on the higher states of heroic and poetic inspiration that it is difficult to distinguish them from each other. And thus it becomes difficult to avoid a widened application of the idea, to the effect that every original ideal which arises in the soul, whether for an action or for a work of art, and which can neither be understood as an imitation nor be satisfactorily explained by means of external stimuli and preceding mental states, may be regarded as revelation. For the fact that the one is greater and the other less cannot here make a dividing line. And, indeed, the inward generation of a new and peculiar idea of God in a moment of inspiration has often been one and the same thing with the rise of a distinctive worship. Indeed, it would be difficult to draw any clear dividing line at all between what is revealed and what comes to light through inspiration in a natural way, unless we are prepared to fall back on the position that revelation is only to be assumed when not a single moment but a whole existence is determined by such a divine communication, and that what is then proclaimed by such an existence is to be regarded as revealed. This, in the polytheistic religions, would include not only the divine declarations and oracles attached to certain holy places which the divinity has made known to be his specially chosen habitations, but also those persons who, because they are descended from the divinity, make known the divine archetype in a human life in an original way which cannot be explained by the historical context. In this same sense Paul calls even the world the original revelation of God.[1] But this may again lead us to the conclusion that no particular thing, since it always belongs to the world, can in itself be regarded as divine revelation. For just as the dawning of an archetypal idea in an individual soul, even if it cannot be explained by the previous states of that very soul, can certainly be explained by the total state of the society to which the individual belongs : so even the men who are credited with divine descent always appear as determined by the character of their people, and thus it is from the total energy of the people that their existence is to be explained or comprehended. Hence even if we do venture to establish, in the way we have done above, the relation of the idea of ' revelation ' and ' revealed ' to the idea of the ' positive ' for the whole realm of historically actual religious communions, we shall nevertheless naturally and inevitably find

[1] Rom. 1[20].

that the application of the idea to the fact which forms the basis of any particular religious communion will be contested by all other communions, while each will claim it for its own basal fact.

Finally, this must be added : that if one faith wishes to establish the validity of its own application of the idea as against the others, it cannot at all accomplish this by the assertion that its own divine communication is pure and entire truth, while the others contain falsehood. For complete truth would mean that God made Himself known as He is in and for Himself. But such a truth could not proceed outwardly from any fact, and even if it did in some incomprehensible way come to a human soul, it could not be apprehended by that soul, and retained as a thought ; and if it could not be in any way perceived and retained, it could not become operative. Any proclamation of God which is to be operative upon and within us can only express God in His relation to us ; and this is not an infra-human ignorance concerning God, but the essence of human limitedness in relation to Him. On the other hand, there is the connected fact that a consciousness of God which arose in a realm of complete barbarity and degradation might be really a revelation, and might nevertheless, through the fault of the mind in which it arose, become, in the form in which it was apprehended and retained, an imperfect one. And therefore it may truly be said even of the imperfect forms of religion, so far as they can be traced, in whole or in part, to a particular starting-point and their content cannot be explained by anything previous to that point, that they rest upon revelation, however much error may be mingled in them with the truth.

III. Presentation of Christianity in its Peculiar Essence : Propositions borrowed from Apologetics.

§ 11. *Christianity is a monotheistic faith, belonging to the teleological type of religion, and is essentially distinguished from other such faiths by the fact that in it everything is related to the redemption accomplished by Jesus of Nazareth.*

1. The only pertinent way of discovering the peculiar essence of any particular faith and reducing it as far as possible to a formula is by showing the element which remains constant throughout the most diverse religious affections within this same communion, while it is absent from analogous affections within other communions. Now since we have little reason to expect that this peculiarity is equally strongly marked in all the different varieties of

emotions, there is all the greater possibility of our missing the mark
in this attempt, and so coming in the end to the opinion that there
is no hard-and-fast inward difference at all, but only the outward
difference as determined by time and place. However, we may
with some certainty conclude from what has been said above,[1]
that we shall be least likely to miss the peculiarity if we keep
principally to what is most closely connected with the basal fact,
and this is the procedure which underlies the formula of our proposition. But Christianity presents special difficulties, even in
this fact alone, that it takes a greater variety of forms than other
faiths and is split up into a multiplicity of smaller communions
or churches ; and thus there arises a twofold task, first, to find the
peculiar essence, common to all these communions, of Christianity
as such, and secondly, to find the peculiar essence of the particular
communion whose right is to be authenticated or whose system of
doctrine is to be established. But still further difficulty lies in the
fact that even in each particular ecclesiastical communion almost
every doctrine appears with the most multifarious variations at
different times and places ; and this implies as its basis, not indeed,
perhaps, an equally great diversity in the religious affections themselves, but always at least a great diversity in the manner of understanding and appraising them. Indeed, the worst of all is that,
owing to this variation, the bounds of the Christian realm become
a matter of dispute even among Christians themselves, one asserting
of this form of teaching, and another of that form, that though it
was indeed engendered within Christianity it is nevertheless really
un-Christian in content. Now, if he who wishes to solve our problem
belongs himself to one of these parties, and assumes at the outset that
only what is found within the realm of that one view ought to be
taken into account in ascertaining what is distinctive of Christianity,
he is at the outset taking controversies as settled, for the settle-
ment of which he professes to be only discovering the conditions.
For only when the peculiar essence of Christianity has been ascertained can it be decided how far this or that is compatible or incompatible with it. But if the investigator succeeds in freeing himself
from all partiality, and therefore takes into account everything,
however opposed, so long as it professes to be Christian, then on the
other hand he is in danger of reaching a result far scantier and more
colourless in its content, and consequently less suitable to the aims
of our present task. That is the present state of affairs, and it

[1] § 10, *Postscript.*

cannot be concealed. Now since each man, the more religious he
is, usually brings his individual religion the more into this investigation, there is a large majority of the people who form their idea of
the peculiar essence of Christianity according to the interests of
their party. But for the interests of Apologetics as well as of
Dogmatics it seems advisable rather to be content with a scanty
result at the beginning and to hope for its completion in the course
of further procedure, than to begin with a narrow and exclusive
formula, which is of necessity confronted by one or more opposing
formulæ, with which there must be a conflict sooner or later. And
it is in this sense that the formula of our proposition is set up.

2. It is indisputable that all Christians trace back to Christ the
communion to which they belong. But here we are also presupposing that the term *Redemption* is one to which they all confess : not only that they all *use* the word, with perhaps different
meanings, but that there is some common element of meaning which
they all have in mind, even if they differ when they come to a more
exact description of it. The term itself is in this realm merely
figurative, and signifies in general a passage from an evil condition,
which is represented as a state of captivity or constraint,[1] into a
better condition—this is the passive side of it. But it also signifies
the help given in that process by some other person, and this is the
active side of it. Further, the usage of the word does not essentially
imply that the worse condition must have been preceded by a better
condition, so that the better one which followed would really
be only a restoration : that point may at the outset be left quite
open. But now apply the word to the realm of religion, and suppose
we are dealing with the teleological type of religion. Then the evil
condition can only consist in an obstruction or arrest of the vitality
of the higher self-consciousness, so that there comes to be little
or no union of it with the various determinations of the sensible
self-consciousness, and thus little or no religious life. We may
give to this condition, in its most extreme form, the name of *Godlessness*, or, better, *God-forgetfulness*. But we must not think this
means a state in which it is quite impossible for the God-consciousness to be kindled. For if that were so, then, in the first place, the
lack of a thing which lay outside of one's nature could not be felt
to be an evil condition ; and in the second place, a re-creating in

[1] [This does not apply as precisely to the English word *redemption* as to
the German word *Erlösung*, which primarily means release or deliverance.—
TRANSL.]

the strict sense would then be needed in order to make good this lack, and that is not included in the idea of redemption. The possibility, then, of kindling the God-consciousness remains in reserve even where the evil condition of that consciousness is painted in the darkest colours.[1] Hence we can only designate it as an absence of facility for introducing the God-consciousness into the course of our actual lives and retaining it there. This certainly makes it seem as if these two conditions, that which exists before redemption and that which is to be brought about by redemption, could only be distinguished in an indefinite way, as a more and a less ; and so, if the idea of redemption is to be clearly established, there arises the problem of reducing this indefinite distinction to a relative opposition. Such an opposition lies in the following formulæ. Given an activity of the sensible self-consciousness, to occupy a moment of time and to connect it with another : its ' exponent ' or ' index ' will be greater than that of the higher self-consciousness for uniting itself therewith ; and given an activity of the higher self-consciousness, to occupy a moment of time through union with a determination of the sensible, its ' exponent ' or ' index ' will be less than that of the activity of the sensible for completing the moment for itself alone. Under these conditions no satisfaction of the impulse towards the God-consciousness will be possible ; and so, if such a satisfaction is to be attained, a redemption is necessary, since this condition is nothing but a kind of imprisonment or constraint of the feeling of absolute dependence. These formulæ, however, do not imply that in all moments which are so determined the God-consciousness or the feeling of absolute dependence is at zero, but only that in some respect it does not dominate the moment ; and in proportion as that is the case the above designations of Godlessness and God-forgetfulness may fitly be applied to it.

3. The recognition of such a condition undeniably finds a place in all religious communions. For the aim of all penances and purifications is to put an end to the consciousness of this condition or to the condition itself. But our proposition establishes two points which in this connexion distinguish Christianity from all other religious communions. In the first place, in Christianity the incapacity and the redemption, and their connexion with each other, do not constitute simply one particular religious element among others, but all other religious emotions are related to this, and this

<hr>

[1] Rom. 1[18ff].

accompanies all others, as the principal thing which makes them distinctively Christian. And secondly, redemption is posited as a thing which has been universally and completely accomplished by Jesus of Nazareth. And these two points, again, must not be separated from each other, but are essentially interconnected. Thus it could not by any means be said that Christian piety is attributable to every man who in all his religious moments is conscious of being in process of redemption,even if he stood in no relation to the person of Jesus or even knew nothing of Him—a case which, of course, will never arise. And no more could it be said that a man's religion is Christian if he traces it to Jesus, even supposing that therein he is not at all conscious of being in process of redemption—a case which also, of course, will never arise. The reference to redemption is in every Christian consciousness simply because the originator of the Christian communion is the Redeemer ; and Jesus is Founder of a religious communion simply in the sense that its members become conscious of redemption through Him. Our previous exposition ensures that this will not be understood to mean that the whole religious consciousness of a Christian can have no other content than simply Jesus and redemption, but only that all religious moments, so far as they are free expressions of the feeling of absolute dependence, are set down as having come into existence through that redemption, and, so far as the feeling appears still unliberated, are set down as being in need of that redemption. It likewise goes without saying that, while this element is always present, different religious moments may and will possess it in varying degrees of strength or weakness, without thereby losing their Christian character. But it *would*, of course, follow from what has been said, that if we conceive of religious moments in which all reference to redemption is absent, and the image of the Redeemer is not introduced at all, these moments must be judged to belong no more intimately to Christianity than to any other monotheistic faith.

4. The more detailed elaboration of our proposition, as to how the redemption is effected by Christ and comes to consciousness within the Christian communion, falls to the share of the dogmatic system itself. Here, however, we have still to discuss, with reference to the general remarks we made above,[1] the relation of Christianity to the other principal monotheistic communions. These also are traced back each to an individual founder. Now if the difference of founder were the only difference, this would be a

---

[1] § 10.

merely external difference, and the same thing would be true if
these others likewise set up their founder as a redeemer and thus
related everything to redemption. For that would mean that in
all these religions the religious moments were of like content, only
that the personality of the founder was different. But such is not
the case : rather must we say that only through Jesus, and thus
only in Christianity, has redemption become the central point of
religion. For inasmuch as these other religions have instituted
particular penances and purifications for particular things, and
these are only particular parts of their doctrine and organization,
the effecting of redemption does not appear as their main business.
It appears rather as a derivative element. Their main business is
the founding of the communion upon definite doctrine and in
definite form. If, however, there are within the communion considerable differences in the free development of the God-consciousness, then some people, in whom it is most cramped, are more in
need of redemption, and others, in whom it works more freely, are
more capable of redemption ; and thus through the influence of the
latter there arises in the former an approximation to redemption ;
but only up to the point at which the difference between the two
is more or less balanced, simply owing to the fact that there exists
a communion or fellowship. In Christianity, on the other hand,
the redeeming influence of the Founder is the primary element, and
the communion exists only on this presupposition, and as a communication and propagation of that redeeming activity. Hence
within Christianity these two tendencies always rise and fall
together : the tendency to give pre-eminence to the redeeming
work of Christ, and the tendency to ascribe great value to the
distinctive and peculiar element in Christian piety. And the same is
true of the two opposite tendencies : the tendency to regard Christianity simply as a means of advancing and propagating religion
in general (its own distinctive nature being merely accidental and
secondary), and the tendency to regard Christ principally as a
teacher and the organizer of a communion, while putting the redeeming activity in the background.

Accordingly, in Christianity the relation of the Founder to
the members of the communion is quite different from what it is
in the other religions. For those other founders are represented as
having been, as it were, arbitrarily elevated from the mass of similar
or not very different men, and as receiving just as much for themselves as for other people whatever they do receive in the way of

divine doctrine and precept. Thus even an adherent of those faiths will hardly deny that God could just as well have given the law through another as through Moses, and the revelation could just as well have been given through another as through Mohammed. But Christ is distinguished from all others as Redeemer alone and for all, and is in no wise regarded as having been at any time in need of redemption Himself ; and is therefore separated from the beginning from all other men, and endowed with redeeming power from His birth.

Not that we mean here to exclude at the outset from the Christian communion all those who differ from this presentation of the matter (which is itself capable of manifold shades of variation) in holding that Christ was only later endowed with redeeming power, provided only that this power is recognized as something different from the mere communication of doctrine and rule of life. But if Christ is regarded entirely on the analogy of the founders of other religions, then the distinctive peculiarity of Christianity can only be asserted for the content of the doctrine and rule of life, and the three monotheistic faiths remain separate only in so far as each holds unflinchingly to what it has received. But now suppose them all together capable of advancing still to perfection, and suppose they were able to find for themselves, sooner or later, the better doctrines and precepts of Christianity : then the inward difference would entirely disappear. Suppose that finally the Christian Church is likewise to move on beyond what has been received from Christ : then nothing else remains for Christ but to be regarded as an outstanding point in the development, and this in such a sense that there is a redemption *from* Him as well as a redemption through Him. And since the perfecting principle can only be Reason, and this is everywhere the same, all distinction between the progress of Christianity and that of other monotheistic faiths would gradually disappear, and all alike would only have a validity limited to a definite period, so far as their distinctive character was concerned.

In this way the difference becomes clear between two widely divergent conceptions of Christianity. But at the same time the lines leading from the one to the other become visible. If the latter of the two conceptions were ever to present itself as a complete doctrine, such a communion would perhaps of its own accord sever its connexion with the other Christian communions. But otherwise it could still be recognized as a Christian communion, unless

it actually declared itself to be now freed from the necessity of
adherence to Christ.   Still less should participation in the Christian
communion be denied to *individuals* who approximate to that
view, so long as they desire to maintain in themselves a living consciousness of God along with, and by means of, that communion.

5. This development of the argument will, it is hoped, serve to
confirm what we have established for the purpose of determining
the distinctive element of Christianity.   For we have tried, as it
were by way of experiment, to single out from among the common
elements of Christian piety that element by which Christianity is
most definitely distinguished externally ; and in this attempt we
were guided by the necessity of regarding the inner peculiarity and
the outward delimitation in their interconnexion.   Perhaps in a
universal Philosophy of Religion, to which, if it were properly
recognized, Apologetics could then appeal, the inner character of
Christianity in itself could be exhibited in such a way that its
particular place in the religious world would thereby be definitely
fixed.   This would also mean that all the principal moments of
the religious consciousness would be systematized, and from their
interconnexion it would be seen which of them were fitted to have
all the others related to them and to be themselves a constant concomitant of all the others.   If, then, it should be seen that the
element which we call ' redemption ' becomes such a moment as
soon as a liberating fact enters a region where the God-consciousness
was in a state of constraint, Christianity would in that case
be vindicated as a distinct form of faith and its nature in a sense
construed.   But even this could not properly be called a proof of
Christianity, since even the Philosophy of Religion could not
establish any necessity, either to recognize a particular Fact as
redemptive, or to give the central place actually in one's own consciousness to any particular moment, even though that moment
should be capable of occupying such a place.   Still less can this
present account claim to be such a proof ; for here, in accordance
with the line we have taken, and since we can only start from a
historical consideration, we cannot even pretend to do as much as
might be done in a complete Philosophy of Religion.   Moreover, it
is obvious that an adherent of some other faith might perhaps be
completely convinced by the above account that what we have set
forth is really the peculiar essence of Christianity, without being
thereby so convinced that Christianity is actually the truth, as to
feel compelled to accept it.   Everything we say in this place is

relative to Dogmatics, and Dogmatics is only for Christians ; and so this account is only for those who live within the pale of Christianity, and is intended only to give guidance, in the interests of Dogmatics, for determining whether the expressions of any religious consciousness are Christian or not, and whether the Christian quality is strongly and clearly expressed in them, or rather doubtfully. We entirely renounce all attempt to prove the truth or necessity of Christianity ; and we presuppose, on the contrary, that every Christian, before he enters at all upon inquiries of this kind, has already the inward certainty that his religion cannot take any other form than this.

§ 12. *Christianity does indeed stand in a special historical connexion with Judaism ; but as far as concerns its historical existence and its aim, its relations to Judaism and Heathenism are the same.*

1. We here take Judaism to mean primarily the Mosaic institutions, but also, as preparing the way for these, every earlier usage which helped to separate the people from other peoples. With this Judaism, then, Christianity has an historical connexion through the fact that Jesus was born among the Jewish people, as indeed a universal Redeemer could scarcely spring from any other than a monotheistic people, once such a people was in existence. But we must not represent the historical connexion in a too exclusive manner. At the time of the appearance of Christ the religious thought of the people was no longer based exclusively on Moses and the prophets, but had been in many ways remoulded through the influence of non-Jewish elements which it had absorbed during and after the Babylonian Dispersion. And, on the other hand, Greek and Roman Heathendom had been in many ways prepared for Monotheism, and in these quarters the expectation of a new phase was most intense ; while contrariwise among the Jews the Messianic promises had been partly given up and partly misunderstood. So that when one puts together all the historical circumstances, the difference becomes much smaller than it appears at the first glance. And Christ's descent from Judaism is largely counterbalanced by the facts that so many more heathen than Jews went over to Christianity, and that Christianity would not have been received by the Jews even as much as it was, had they not been permeated by those foreign elements.

2. The truth rather is that the relations of Christianity to

Judaism and Heathenism are the same, inasmuch as the transition from either of these to Christianity is a transition to another religion. The leap certainly seems greater in the case of Heathenism, since it had first to become monotheistic in order to become Christian. At the same time, the two processes were not separated, but Monotheism was given to the heathen directly in the form of Christianity, as it had been previously in the form of Judaism. And the demand made upon the Jews, to give up their reliance upon the law, and to put a different interpretation upon the Abrahamitic promises, was just as large a demand. Accordingly we must assume that Christian piety, in its original form, cannot be explained by means of the Jewish piety of that or of an earlier time, and so Christianity cannot in any wise be regarded as a remodelling or a renewal and continuation of Judaism. Paul does indeed regard the faith of Abraham as the prototype of Christian faith, and represents the Mosaic Law simply as something slipped in between ; [1] and from this it might, of course, be inferred that he meant to represent Christianity as a renewal of that original and pure Abrahamitic Judaism. But his meaning was only that Abraham's faith was related to the promise as ours is to the fulfilment, and not by any means that the promise was the same to Abraham as the fulfilment is to us. Where he expressly speaks of the relation of the Jews and the Heathen to Christ, he represents it as being exactly the same : [2] he represents Christ as being the same for both, and both as being alike very far from God and so in need of Christ. Now if Christianity has the same relation to Judaism as to Heathenism, it can no more be regarded as a continuation of the former than of the latter : if a man comes from either of them to Christianity, he becomes, as regards his religion, a new man. But the promise to Abraham, so far as it has been fulfilled in Christ, is represented as having had its reference to Christ only in the divine decree, not in the religious consciousness of Abraham and his people. And since we can only recognize the self-identity of a religious communion when there is a uniformity of the religious consciousness, we can no more recognize an identity between Christianity and Abrahamitic Judaism than between it and the later Judaism or Heathenism. And neither can it be said that that purer original Judaism carried within itself the germ of Christianity, so that it would have developed of itself by natural progress from Judaism without the intervention of any new factor ; nor

[1] Gal. 3[9. 14. 23-25].   [2] Rom. 2[11. 12] 3[21-24], 2 Cor. 5[16. 17], Eph. 2[13-18].

that Christ Himself lay in the line of this progress in such a way that a new communal life and existence could not begin with Him.

3. The widely prevalent notion of one single Church of God, existing from the beginning of the human race to the end of it, is opposed to our proposition more in appearance than in reality. If the Mosaic Law belongs to the one chain of this divine economy of salvation, then we must, according to approved Christian teachers, include also the Greek philosophy,[1] especially that which tended towards Monotheism ; and yet we cannot, without quite destroying the peculiarity of Christianity, assert that its teaching forms a single whole with the heathen philosophy. If, on the other hand, this doctrine of the one Church is chiefly intended to express the fact that Christ's active relation to all that is human knows no limits, even with regard to the time that was past, this is an intention upon which we cannot yet pass judgment, but which is quite compatible with our proposition. And even in Old Testament prophecy there is ascribed to the New Covenant a different character from the Old,[2] and this direct antithesis expresses the inward separation in the most definite way. Hence the rule may be set up that almost everything else in the Old Testament is, for our Christian usage, but the husk or wrapping of its prophecy, and that whatever is most definitely Jewish has least value. So that we can find rendered with some exactness in Old Testament passages only those of our religious emotions which are of a somewhat general nature without anything very distinctively Christian. For those which are distinctively Christian, Old Testament sayings will not provide a suitable expression, unless we think certain elements away from them and read other things into them. And that being the case, we shall certainly find quite as near and accordant echoes in the utterances of the nobler and purer Heathenism ; as indeed the older Apologists were no less glad to appeal to what they held to be heathen Messianic prophecies, and thus recognized there a striving of human nature towards Christianity.

§ 13. *The appearance of the Redeemer in history is, as divine revelation, neither an absolutely supernatural nor an absolutely supra-rational thing.*

1. As regards revelation, it has already[3] been granted that the starting-point of any entity which has a distinctive constitu-

---

[1] Εἰκότως οὖν Ἰουδαίοις μὲν νόμος Ἕλλησι δὲ φιλοσοφία μέχρι τῆς παρουσίας· ἐντεῦθεν δὲ ἡ κλῆσις ἡ καθολικὴ εἰς περιούσιον δικαιοσύνης λαόν. Clemens Alex., *Strom.* vi.
[2] Jer. 31[31-34].   [3] § 10, *Postscript.*

tion of its own, still more of any communion and especially a religious communion, can never be explained by the condition of the circle in which it appears and operates ; for if it could, it would not be a starting-point, but would itself be the product of a spiritual process.   But though its existence transcends the nature of the circle in which it appeared, there is no reason why we should not believe that the appearing of such a life is the result of the power of development which resides in our human nature—a power which expresses itself in particular men at particular points according to laws which, if hidden from us, are nevertheless of divine arrangement, in order through these men to help the others forward. And indeed, apart from such a supposition, any progress of the human race as a whole or any part of it would be inconceivable. Every outstanding endowment of an individual, through whose influence any spiritual institution within a particular circle takes shape anew, is such a starting-point ; only, the more such expressions are temporally and spatially limited in their influence, the more do they appear, if not explicable by what went before, yet conditioned by it.   Therefore when we designate all these men as heroes, each in his own sphere, and ascribe to them a higher inspiration, this is what is meant : that for the good of the definite circle in which they appear they have been quickened and inspired from the universal fountain of life.   And the fact that such men appear from time to time must be regarded as due to the working of a law, if we are to maintain the higher significance of human nature at all.   The case of all such individuals is therefore analogous to that of the idea of revelation, which it is better to apply only to the region of the higher self-consciousness.   No one will object to the supposition that in all founders of religions, even on the subordinate levels, there is such an endowment, if only the doctrine and communion which proceed from them have a distinctive and original character.   But if this is to be applied in the same sense to Christ, it must first of all be said that, in comparison with Him, everything which could otherwise be regarded as revelation again loses this character.   For everything else is limited to particular times and places, and all that proceeds from such points is from the very outset destined to be submerged again in Him, and is thus, in relation to Him, no existence, but a non-existence ; and He alone is destined gradually to quicken the whole human race into higher life.   Anyone who does not take Christ in this universal way as divine revelation cannot desire that Christianity should be an

enduring phenomenon. But notwithstanding, it must be asserted
that even the most rigorous view of the difference between Him
and all other men does not hinder us from saying that His appearing, even regarded as the incarnation of the Son of God, is a natural
fact. For in the first place : as certainly as Christ was a man, there
must reside in human nature the possibility of taking up the divine
into itself, just as did happen in Christ. So that the idea that the
divine revelation in Christ must in this respect be something
absolutely supernatural will simply not stand the test. Even the
Protevangelium,[1] by linking the prediction of Christ directly to the
Fall, declares entirely against the idea that human nature is somehow incapable of taking up into itself the restorative divine element
and that the power to do so must first be introduced into it. But
secondly : even if only the *possibility* of this resides in human nature,
so that the actual implanting therein of the divine element must be
purely a divine and therefore an eternal act, nevertheless the
temporal appearance of this act in one particular Person must at
the same time be regarded as an action of human nature, grounded
in its original constitution and prepared for by all its past history,
and accordingly as the highest development of its spiritual power
(even if we grant that we could never penetrate so deep into those
innermost secrets of the universal spiritual life as to be able to
develop this general conviction into a definite perception). Otherwise it could only be explained as an arbitrary divine act that the
restorative divine element made its appearance precisely in Jesus,
and not in some other person. But the supposition of divine
arbitrariness in particular matters belongs to an anthropopathic
view of God, and Scripture does not declare itself in favour of such
a view, but rather seems itself to point to our view that the act
is conditioned.[2]

2. We now come to the supra-rational. Christ could not in
any way be distinguished as Redeemer from the totality of mankind if those phases of His life by which He accomplishes redemption were explicable by means of the reason which dwells equally
in all other men. For then those conditions would also be found
in the others, and they also could work redemption. We may
further take for granted that in redeemed people there are states
of mind which are conditioned solely by Christ's communication
or influence, and apart from this, one could not say that redemption has taken place in them. Consequently, these states cannot

---

[1] [*i.e.* Gen. 3[15].]   [2] Gal. 4[4].

be explained solely by the reason which has dwelt in them from
their birth—though, indeed, this does play an indispensably
necessary part, since such states can never exist in a soul devoid
of reason.   Accordingly, the supra-rational certainly has a place
in the Redeemer and the redeemed, and consequently in the whole
compass of Christianity ; and anybody who refused to recognize
this in any form would be incapable of understanding redemption
in the proper sense, and could only acknowledge Christianity as an
institution, to continue until a better appeared, for the transmission
of the influence of a human reason which, especially in the form of
its self-consciousness, was affected in a remarkable and superior
manner.   This supra-rational quality is also recognized almost
without exception in the utterances of those who confess Christ,
and is expressed in various forms as an indwelling (either from the
beginning, or coming in later and continuing, or confined to one
moment) of God or of the λόγος in Christ, and as a moving of the
redeemed by the Holy Spirit.   But however great a difference
we make between this supra-rational and the common human
reason, it can never, without falling into self-contradiction, be set
up as an *absolutely* supra-rational element.   For the highest goal
that is set for these workings of redemption is always a human
state which not only would obtain the fullest recognition from the
common human reason, but in which also it is impossible always to
distinguish, even in the same individual, between what is effected
by the divine Spirit and what is effected by the human reason.
Inasmuch, then, as the reason is completely one with the divine
Spirit, the divine Spirit can itself be conceived as the highest
enhancement of the human reason, so that the difference between
the two is made to disappear.   But further : even at the very
outset, whatever opposes the movements of the divine Spirit is
the same as what conflicts with human reason ; for otherwise
there could not exist in man (as there does), before the entry of
those divine influences, a consciousness of the need of redemption,
which these very influences set at rest.   If, then, the human reason
itself in a sense contains that which is produced by the divine
Spirit, the latter does not in this connexion, at least, go beyond
the former.   Now what is true of the redeemed may also be said
of the Redeemer.   For even the people who do not assume any
kind of divine indwelling in Him do nevertheless, for their part,
extol the very same activities, ideas, and practical precepts of His
(which others explain by divine indwelling) as being the highest

pitch of the rational, and thus with their human reason apprehend them with approval ; which apprehension, again, those others do not reproach or reject, but likewise recognize with approval.

Postscript.—According to the view of religion which we have taken as our basis, the peculiar being of the Redeemer and of the redeemed in their connexion with Him is the original point at which this question of the supernatural and the supra-rational in Christianity emerges ; so that there is no ground whatever for admitting anything supernatural or supra-rational which is not connected with the appearing of the Redeemer but would in itself form another original element. The question is usually handled, partly with reference to the individual facts for which a supernatural quality is especially claimed (we cannot yet speak of them here), and partly with reference to the Christian doctrines, which are for us nothing but the expressions given to the Christian self-consciousness and its connexions. But if the supernatural in the Christian self-consciousness consists in the fact that it cannot, in the form in which it actually exists, be produced by the activity of reason, it by no means follows from this that the expressions given to this self-consciousness must also be supra-rational. For in the same sense in which the Christian self-consciousness is supra-rational, the whole of Nature is supra-rational too, and yet we do not apply that epithet to the things we say *about* Nature, but call them purely rational. But the whole process of formulating our expressions concerning the religious self-consciousness is just as much a rational process as in the case of Nature ; and the difference is merely that this objective consciousness is given at first hand only to him who is affected by Nature, while that (Christian) self-consciousness is given only to him who is affected by the Redeemer in the manner which is peculiar to His followers. Now this itself makes plain what we are to think of the prevalent view that Christian doctrine consists partly of rational and partly of supra-rational dogmas. It is, indeed, of itself obvious that this can be no more than a juxtaposition, and that these two kinds of dogmas cannot form one whole. Between the rational and the supra-rational there can be no connexion. This further becomes pretty clearly evident in all treatises upon Christian doctrine which divide themselves into a natural theology, purely rational and thus valid not only within, but also outside of Christianity, and a positive supra-rational theology, valid only within the compass of Christianity. For then the two are and remain separate from each other. The

apparent practicability of a union of the two arises from the fact
that there are, of course, Christian dogmas in which the peculiarly
Christian element retreats considerably into the background, so
that they may be taken to be purely rational in those respects in
which the others are recognized as supra-rational. But if that
peculiarly Christian element were not in them at all, they would,
of course, not be Christian dogmas. Hence the truth of the matter
is as follows. In one respect all Christian dogmas are supra-
rational, in another they are all rational. They are supra-rational
in the respect in which everything experiential is supra-rational.
For there is an inner experience to which they may all be traced :
they rest upon a *given* ; and apart from this they could not have
arisen, by deduction or synthesis, from universally recognized and
communicable propositions. If the reverse were true, it would
mean that you could instruct and demonstrate any man into being
a Christian, without his happening to have had any experience.
Therefore this supra-rationality implies that a true appropriation
of Christian dogmas cannot be brought about by scientific means,
and thus lies outside the realm of reason : it can only be brought
about through each man willing to have the experience for himself,
as indeed it is true of everything individual and characteristic, that
it can only be apprehended by the love which wills to perceive.
In this sense the whole of Christian doctrine is supra-rational. It
may, however, be further asked whether the dogmas which give
expression to the religious affections of the Christian and their
connexions are not subject to the same laws of conception and
synthesis as regulate all speech, so that the more perfectly these
laws are satisfied in such a presentation, the more will each individual be constrained to apprehend correctly what is thought
and intended, even if he cannot, for lack of the fundamental inward experience, convince himself of the truth of the matter. It
must be answered that in this sense everything in Christian doctrine
is entirely according to reason. Accordingly, the supra-rationality
of all particular Christian dogmas is the measure by which it can be
judged whether they succeed in expressing the peculiarly Christian
element ; and again, their rationality is the test of how far the
attempt to translate the inward emotions into thoughts has
succeeded. But to assert that it cannot be demanded that what
goes beyond reason should be rationally presented, appears to be
only a subterfuge designed to cover up some imperfection in the
procedure ; just as the opposite view that in Christian doctrine

everything must be, in every sense, based on reason, is simply meant to cover up the lack of a fundamental experience of one's own.

The usual formula, that the supra-rational in Christianity must not be contrary to reason, seems intended to say the same thing as our proposition. For it implies, on the one hand, the recognition of the supra-rational, and, on the other hand, the task of showing that it is not contrary to reason, and this can only be achieved by means of a rational presentation.

§ 14. *There is no other way of obtaining participation in the Christian communion than through faith in Jesus as the Redeemer.*

1. To participate in the Christian communion means to seek in Christ's institution an approximation to the above-described [1] state of absolute facility and constancy of religious emotions. No one can wish to belong to the Christian Church on any other ground. But since each can only enter through a free resolve of his own, this must be preceded by the certainty that the influence of Christ puts an end to the state of being in need of redemption, and produces that other state ; and this certainty is just faith in Christ. That is to say, this term always signifies, in our present province, the certainty which accompanies a state of the higher self-consciousness, and which is therefore different from, but not for that reason less than, the certainty which accompanies the objective consciousness. In the same sense we spoke above [2] of faith in God, which was nothing but the certainty concerning the feeling of absolute dependence, as such, *i.e.* as conditioned by a Being placed outside of us, and as expressing our relation to that Being. The faith of which we are now speaking, however, is a purely factual certainty, but a certainty of a fact which is entirely inward. That is to say, it cannot exist in an individual until, through an impression which he has received from Christ, there is found in him a beginning— perhaps quite infinitesimal, but yet a real premonition—of the process which will put an end to the state of needing redemption. But the term ' faith in Christ ' here (as the term ' faith in God ' formerly) relates the state of redemption, as effect, to Christ as cause. That is how John describes it. And so from the beginning only those people have attached themselves to Christ in His new community whose religious self-consciousness had taken the form of a need of redemption, and who now became assured in themselves

[1] § 5, 4.   [2] § 4, 4.

of Christ's redeeming power.[1] So that the more strongly those two
phases appeared in any individual, the more able was he, by representation of the fact (which includes description of Christ and
His work) to elicit this inward experience in others. Those in
whom this took place became believers, and the rest did not.[2]
This, moreover, is what has ever since constituted the essence of all
direct Christian preaching. Such preaching must always take the
form of testimony ; testimony as to one's own experience, which
shall arouse in others the desire to have the same experience. But
the impression which all later believers received in this way from
the influence of Christ, *i.e.* from the common Spirit communicated
by Him and from the whole communion of Christians, supported
by the historical representation of His life and character, was just
the same impression which His contemporaries received from Him
directly. Hence those who remained unbelieving were not blamed
because they had not let themselves be persuaded by reasons, but
simply because of their lack of self-knowledge, which must always
be the explanation when the Redeemer is truly and correctly
presented and people show themselves unable to recognize Him as
such. But even Christ Himself represented this lack of self-
knowledge, *i.e.* of the consciousness of needing redemption, as the
limit to His activity. And so the ground of unbelief is the same
in all ages, as is also the ground of belief or faith.

2. The attempt has often been made to demonstrate the
necessity of redemption, but always in vain. We need not, however, appeal to these cases, for it is clear in itself that the thing
is impossible. Any man who is capable of being satisfied with
himself as he is will always manage to find a way out of the argument. And no more can it be demonstrated, once the consciousness of this need has been awakened, that Christ is the only One
who can work redemption. In His own time there were many who
did believe that redemption was near, and yet did not accept Him.
And even when we have a more correct idea of the end to be sought,
it is not easy to see how it could be proved that any particular
individual is in a position to achieve the desired effect. For in this
matter we are concerned with amount of spiritual power, which we
have no means of calculating ; and even if we had, we should also
require some fixed datum against which the calculation could be
set. It cannot even be proved in a general way that such a redemption is bound to come, even if we presuppose a general know-

---

[1] John 1[45. 46] 6[68. 69], Matt. 16[15-18].   [2] Acts 2[37. 41].

ledge not only of what men are like but also of what God is like. There would still be plenty of room for different sophistical arguments to draw opposite conclusions from the same data, according as God's purpose for man was conceived in one way or in another.

Agreed. then, that we must adhere to the kind of certainty which we have just described, and that faith is nothing other than the incipient experience of the satisfaction of that spiritual need by Christ : there can still be very diverse ways of experiencing the need and the succour, and yet they will all be faith.   Moreover, the consciousness of need may be present for a long time in advance, or it may, as is often the case, be fully awakened only by the contrast which the perfection of Christ forms with our own condition, so that the two things come into existence simultaneously, the supreme consciousness of need and the beginning of its satisfaction.

3. It is true that in the Scriptures themselves proofs are often mentioned, which the witnesses of the Gospel employed.[1]   Yet it is never asserted that faith sprang from the proof, but from the preaching.   Those proofs were only applied among the Jews, with reference to their current ideas of the coming Messiah, in order to repulse the opposition presented by these ideas to the witness of the Gospel, or to anticipate any such opposition.   This was an indispensable line of defence for witnesses of Christ who were Jews and who were dealing with Jews.   If they wished to assert that they themselves had never expected any other kind of redemption than this, or that their expectations had been transformed by the appearing and the influence of Christ, they must either break with the whole Jewish religion, which they had no warrant for doing, or show that the prophetic representations were applicable to this Jesus as Redeemer.   If we took the other view of the matter, it would mean that the faith of the Gentile Christians was not the same as that of the Jewish Christians ; and then it would not have been possible for these two to become really one, but the Gentiles would have had to become Jews first, in order then to be brought to Christ by the authority of the prophets.

Postscript.—Our proposition says nothing of any intermediate link between faith and participation in the Christian communion, and is accordingly to be taken as directly combining the two, so that faith of itself carries with it that participation ; and not only as depending on the spontaneous activity of the man who has become a believer, but also as depending on the spontaneous

---

[1] Acts 6$^{9. 10}$ 9$^{20-22}$, also 18$^{27. 28}$.

activity of the communion (Church), as the source from which the testimony proceeded for the awakening of faith. At the same time, in shutting up the whole process between these two points, the witness or testimony and its effect, our proposition is intended to make an end of everything which, in the form of demonstration, is usually brought to the aid of the proper witness or even substituted for it. This refers principally to the attempts to bring about a recognition of Christ by means of the miracles which He performs, or the prophecies which predicted Him, or the special character of the testimonies originally borne to Him, regarded as the work of divine inspiration. In all this there seems to be more or less illusion on the following point : that the efficacy of these things somehow always presupposes faith, and therefore cannot produce it.

First consider *Miracle*, taking the word in its narrower sense, so that prophecy and inspiration are not included, but simply phenomena in the realm of physical nature which are supposed not to have been caused in a natural manner. Whether we confine ourselves to those performed by Jesus Himself, or include those which took place in connexion with Him, these miracles cannot bring about a recognition of Him at all. In the first place, we know of these miracles only from those same Holy Scriptures (for the miracles related in less pure sources are never adduced along with them) which relate similar miracles of people who did not adhere to Christianity at all, but are rather to be reckoned among its enemies ; and Scripture gives us no marks for distinguishing evidential miracles from non-evidential. But further, Scripture itself bears witness that faith has been produced without miracles, and also that miracles have failed to produce it ; from which it may be concluded that even when it has existed along with miracles it was not produced by miracles but in its own original way. Hence if the purpose of miracles had been to produce faith, we should have to conclude that God's breaking into the order of Nature proved ineffectual. Accordingly, many find the purpose of miracles simply in the fact that they turn the attention to Christ. But this, again, is at least so far contradicted by Christ's oft-repeated command not to make the miracles more widely known, that we should have to limit their efficacy to the immediate eye-witnesses, and thus this efficacy would no longer exist to-day. But, finally, the following question cannot be avoided. In any other context than that of such faith and its realm, we may encounter any number of facts which we cannot explain naturally, and yet we never think

of miracle, but simply regard the explanation as deferred until we
have a more exact knowledge both of the fact in question and of
the laws of Nature. But when such a fact occurs in connexion
with some faith-realm which has to be established, we think at
once of miracle ; only, each man claims miracle as real for the
realm of his own faith alone, and sets down the others as false.
On what is this distinction based ? The question can hardly be
answered except as follows. In general we do, perhaps, assume so
exclusive a connexion between miracles and the formation of a
new faith-realm, that we only admit miracle for this kind of case ;
but the state of each individual's faith determines his judgment of
the alleged miracle, and so the miracle does not produce the faith.
As regards that universal connexion, however, the state of the
case seems to be as follows. Where a new point in the development of the spiritual life, and indeed primarily of the self-consciousness, is assumed to exist, new phenomena in physical Nature,
mediated by the spiritual power which is manifested, are also expected, because both the contemplative and the outwardly active
spiritual states all proceed from the self-consciousness, and are
determined by its movements. Thus, once Christ is recognized as
Redeemer, and consequently as the beginning of the supreme development of human nature in the realm of the self-consciousness,
it is a natural assumption that, just because at the point where
such an existence communicates itself most strongly, spiritual
states appear which cannot be explained from what went before,
He who exercises such a peculiar influence upon human nature
around Him will be able, in virtue of the universal connexion of
things, to manifest also a peculiar power of working upon the physical
side of human nature and upon external Nature. That is to say,
it is natural to expect miracles from Him who is the supreme
divine revelation ; and yet they can be called miracles only in a
relative sense, since our ideas of the susceptibility of physical
Nature to the influence of the spirit and of the causality of the
will acting upon physical Nature are as far from being finally settled
and as capable of being perpetually widened by new experiences as
are our ideas of the forces of physical Nature themselves. Now,
since, in connexion with the divine revelation in Christ, phenomena
presented themselves which could be brought under this concept of
miracle, it was natural that they should actually come to be regarded
from this point of view, and adduced as confirmation of the fact
that this was a new point of development. But this confirmation

will be effectual only where there is already present a beginning of faith ; failing that, the miracle would either be declared false or be reserved, as regards the understanding of it, for some natural explanation which the future would reveal. Still less could it be proved from the miracles which accompanied it that Christianity is the supreme revelation, since similar phenomena are on the same grounds to be expected in the lower faiths too, and miracles themselves cannot, as such, be divided into higher and lower. Indeed, the possibility cannot be excluded that similar phenomena might occur even apart from all connexion with the realm of religion, whether as accompanying other kinds of development or as signalizing deeper movements in physical Nature itself. Similarly, on the other hand, it seems to be a matter of course that such supernatural phenomena, which accompany revelation, disappear again in proportion as the new development, freed from its point of origin in the external realm, is organized, and so becomes Nature.

The same thing may be said with regard to *Prophecies*, in case anyone should wish to assign to them a more powerful rôle than that which we have granted above. Let us confine ourselves to the prophecies of the Jewish prophets regarding Christ, for in more recent times the heathen prophecies have been universally set aside, and we are not here immediately concerned with the prophecies of Christ and His apostles. Suppose, then, that we wished to make more use of those prophetic utterances among Jews. It is quite conceivable that a Jew should become a Christian because he came to see that those prophecies were to be referred to Jesus, and that nevertheless he should possess neither the real faith nor the true participation in the Christian communion, understanding it all, perhaps, in a quite different way, because he did not feel any need of redemption. But suppose these prophecies were to be universally set before unbelievers, in order to produce in them the will to enter into communion with Christ. It might be made out at the start that these prophecies are all to be regarded as belonging together, that they all have in view an individual, and indeed one and the same individual (for otherwise the fulfilment of them all in one and the same person would really be a non-fulfilment), and further that they have all come to fulfilment in Christ, each in the sense in which it was meant, not those figuratively meant being fulfilled in a literal sense and those literally meant in a figurative sense (for that also would not be a real fulfilment). But, after all, it always comes to this in the end : that Jesus must be taken to be the

Redeemer, because the Redeemer was predicted with descriptive details which are found in Him. But this argument presupposes that people already have faith in the prophets who predicted, as such ; and it is impossible to imagine how an unbeliever outside of Judaism should come to have such a faith, except on the supposition that the inspiration of the prophets is proved to him, and with this we shall deal below. Without such a faith the collocation of prophecies and their fulfilments would be a mere signpost, giving an impulse to seek fellowship with Christ only to those people who were already feeling the need of redemption ; and this only in so far as the need expressed in the prophecies is analogous to their own, and at the same time the thing prophesied has a manifest connexion with that need ;[1] that is to say, in so far as each man could himself have prophesied the same thing out of his own need. The impulse, however, could only issue in his seeking to have the experience for himself,[2] and only when this attempt succeeded would there be faith. And certainly this impulse can now, when facts speak so loud, be given much more powerfully and surely in other ways than by means of the prophecies. This becomes especially clear when we reflect how the case really stands with regard to the above-mentioned presuppositions ; namely, that it can never be proved that those prophets foresaw Christ as He really was, and still less the Messianic kingdom as it really developed in Christianity. Thus it must be admitted that a proof from prophecy of Christ as the Redeemer is impossible ; and in particular, the zealous attempt to seek out for this purpose prophecies or prototypes which relate to accidental circumstances in the story of Christ must appear simply as a mistake. A clear distinction must, therefore, be made between the apologetical use which the apostles made of the prophecies in their intercourse with the Jews, and a general use which might be made of them as evidences. When, however, faith in the Redeemer is already present, then we can dwell with great pleasure on all expressions of the longing for redemption awakened by earlier and inadequate revelations. And this is the real significance (and it has, of course, a confirmative and corroborative value) of Messianic prophecies, wherever they appear and in however obscure presentiments they are shrouded : they disclose to us a striving of human nature towards Christianity, and at the same

[1] In this sense perhaps the prophecy quoted in Matt. 12[19. 20] is the most pregnant prophecy.

[2] John 1[41. 46]

time give it as the confession of the best and most inspired of earlier religious communions, that they are to be regarded only as preparatory and transitory institutions. As for the prophecies made by Christianity itself, it is, of course, natural that at the beginning of the development of a new thing the outlook is directed very much towards the future, *i.e.* towards its completion, and so one can understand the questions of the disciples, to which answers —on the basis of which they afterwards made further prophecies— could not altogether be denied. But Christ's prophecies cannot serve as a proof of His unique office and His exclusive vocation as Redeemer, for the simple reason that others also have admittedly prophesied. Again, it was equally natural that the more the new dispensation became established as an historical phenomenon, the more the interest in the future decreased and prophecy disappeared.

Now from all this it follows that, if faith in the revelation of God in Christ and in redemption through Him has not already arisen in the direct way through experience as the demonstration of the Spirit and of power, neither miracles nor prophecies can produce it, and indeed that this faith would be just as immovable even if Christianity had neither prophecies nor miracles to show. For the lack of these could never refute that demonstration, or prove a mere delusion ,the experience of need satisfied in the fellowship of Christ. From the lack of these, indeed, nothing could be concluded except that those natural assumptions do not always prove true, and that the beginning of the most perfect form of religious self-consciousness appeared more suddenly, and confined its working more closely to its own immediate realm.

We come finally to *Inspiration*. In Christianity this conception has a wholly subordinate significance. It cannot be related at all to Christ, since the divine revelation through Him, however it is conceived, is always conceived as identical with His whole being, and not as appearing fragmentarily in sporadic moments. And as for what the apostles received from the Spirit, Christ traces that entirely to His own instruction, and those who through their testimony became believers did not believe because the testimony sprang from inspiration, for of that they knew nothing. The conception therefore relates only in the first place to the prophets of the Old Covenant, and in the second place to the composition of the New Testament Scriptures ; and so we have to deal with it here only in so far as concerns the attempt to compel faith demonstratively by means of Holy Scripture, when this is first assumed to be inspired. But as regards the Old Testament, Prophecy cannot be understood alone without Law and History ; and this whole, taken all together, is so consistently theocratic that (while we can indeed distinguish in it two ' poles,' one of which exercises attraction, the other repulsion, towards the New Testament), if, apart from the New Testament, we succeeded in making anyone believe in the prophetic inspiration (which, however, could hardly be accomplished except upon their own testimony that the word of God came to them), yet from this there could not be developed a faith in Christ as the end of the Law. We shall rather express the whole truth if we say that we believe in the prophetic inspiration simply because of the use which Christ and His apostles make of the utterances of the prophets. As regards the New Testament, the faith had been disseminated for two hundred years before that Testament was unanimously established as having peculiar validity. And, moreover, it was not a matter of Christian faith being in the meantime always mediated by faith in the Old Testament, for among the great mass of the heathen, who went over to Christianity without having been previously Judaized, this was by no means the case. But even now, and even supposing that the inspiration of the New Testament Scriptures can be proved from these Scriptures themselves, this would nevertheless presuppose a very perfect understanding of these Scriptures. And thus, since this is possible only for a few, we should still require some other way in which faith might arise, so that there would be two kinds of faith. And further, it is still impossible to see how an objective conviction of this kind could exercise such an influence on the self-consciousness, that, from the mere knowledge that those people were inspired who asserted that men need redemption and that Christ is their Redeemer, this assertion would immediately come to contain for all an inward truth. All that this conviction in itself can do is merely to give an impulse towards the awakening of a fuller self-consciousness and towards the winning of a total impression of Christ ; and only from this will faith then proceed.

IV. THE RELATION OF DOGMATICS TO CHRISTIAN PIETY.

§ 15. *Christian doctrines are accounts of the Christian religious affections set forth in speech.*

NOTE.—Cf. § 3, 5.

1. All religious emotions, to whatever type and level of religion they belong, have this in common with all other modifications of

the affective self-consciousness, that as soon as they have reached a certain stage and a certain definiteness they manifest themselves outwardly by mimicry in the most direct and spontaneous way, by means of facial features and movements of voice and gesture, which we regard as their expression. Thus we definitely distinguish the expression of devoutness from that of a sensuous gladness or sadness, by the analogy of each man's knowledge of himself. Indeed, we can even conceive that, for the purpose of maintaining the religious affections and securing their repetition and propagation (especially if they were common to a number of people), the elements of that natural expression of them might be put together into sacred signs and symbolical acts, without the thought having perceptibly come in between at all. But we can scarcely conceive such a low development of the human spirit, such a defective culture, and such a meagre use of speech, that each person would not, according to the level of reflection on which he stands, become in his various mental states likewise an object to himself, in order to comprehend them in idea and retain them in the form of thought. Now this endeavour has always directed itself particularly to the religious emotions ; and this, considered in its own inward meaning, is what our proposition means by an account of the religious affections. But while thought cannot proceed even inwardly without the use of speech, nevertheless there are, so long as it remains merely inward, fugitive elements in this procedure, which do indeed in some measure indicate the object, but not in such a way that either the formation or the synthesis of concepts (in however wide a sense we take the word ' concept ') is sufficiently definite for communication. It is only when this procedure has reached such a point of cultivation as to be able to represent itself outwardly in definite speech, that it produces a real doctrine (*Glaubenssatz*), by means of which the utterances of the religious consciousness come into circulation more surely and with a wider range than is possible through the direct expression. But no matter whether the expression is natural or figurative, whether it indicates its object directly or only by comparison and delimitation, it is still a doctrine.

2. Now Christianity everywhere presupposes that consciousness has reached this stage of development. The whole work of the Redeemer Himself was conditioned by the communicability of His self-consciousness by means of speech, and similarly Christianity has always and everywhere spread itself solely by preaching. Every proposition which can be an element of the Christian preaching

(κήρυγμα) is also a doctrine, because it bears witness to the determination of the religious self-consciousness as inward certainty. And every Christian doctrine is also a part of the Christian preaching, because every such doctrine expresses as a certainty the approximation to the state of blessedness [1] which is to be effected through the means ordained by Christ. But this preaching very soon split up into three different types of speech, which provide as many different forms of doctrine : the poetic, the rhetorical (which is directed partly outwards, as combative and commendatory, and partly inwards, as rather disciplinary and challenging), and finally the descriptively didactic. But the relation of communication through speech to communication through symbolic action varies very much according to time and place, the former having always retreated into the background in the Eastern Church (for when the letter of doctrine has become fixed and unalterable, it is in its effect much nearer to symbolic action than to free speech), and having become ever more prominent in the Western Church. And in the realm of speech it is just the same with these three modes of communication. The relation in which they stand to each other, the general degree of richness, and the amount of living intercourse in which they unfold themselves, as they nourish themselves on one another and pass over into one another—these things testify not so much to the degree or level of piety as rather to the character of the communion or fellowship and its ripeness for reflection and contemplation. Thus this communication is, on the one hand, something different from the piety itself, though the latter cannot, any more than anything else which is human, be conceived entirely separated from all communication. But, on the other hand, the doctrines in all their forms have their ultimate ground so exclusively in the emotions of the religious self-consciousness, that where these do not exist the doctrines cannot arise.

§ 16. *Dogmatic propositions are doctrines of the descriptively didactic type, in which the highest possible degree of definiteness is aimed at.*

NOTE.—Cf. § 3, 4 and 5 ; and § 13, 1 and 2.

1. The poetic expression is always based originally upon a moment of exaltation which has come purely from within, a moment of enthusiasm or inspiration ; the rhetorical upon a moment whose exaltation has come from without, a moment of stimulated interest

[1] See § 5, 4.

which issues in a particular definite result. The former is purely descriptive (*darstellend*), and sets up in general outlines images and forms which each hearer completes for himself in his own peculiar way. The rhetorical is purely stimulative, and has, in its nature, to do for the most part with such elements of speech as, admitting of degrees of signification, can be taken in a wider or narrower sense, content if at the decisive moment they can accomplish the highest, even though they should exhaust themselves thereby and subsequently appear to lose somewhat of their force. Thus both of these forms possess a different perfection from the logical or dialectical perfection described in our proposition. But, nevertheless, we can think of both as being primary and original in every religious communion, and thus in the Christian Church, in so far as we ascribe to everyone in it a share in the vocation of preaching. For when anyone finds himself in a state of unusually exalted religious self-consciousness, he will feel himself called to poetic description, as that which proceeds from this state most directly. And, on the other hand, when anyone finds himself particularly challenged by insistent or favourable outward circumstances to attempt an act of preaching, the rhetorical form of expression will be the most natural to him for obtaining from the given circumstances the greatest possible advantage. But let us conceive of the comprehension and appropriation of what is given in a direct way in these two forms, as being now also wedded to language and thereby made communicable : then this cannot again take the poetic form, nor yet the rhetorical ; but, being independent of that which was the important element in those two forms, and expressing as it does a consciousness which remains self-identical, it becomes, less as preaching than as confession (ὁμολογία), precisely that third form —the didactic—which, with its descriptive instruction, remains distinct from the two others, and is made up of the two put together, as a derivative and secondary form.

2. But let us confine ourselves to Christianity, and think of its distinctive beginning, namely, the self-proclamation of Christ, Who, as subject of the divine revelation, could not contain in Himself any distinction of stronger and weaker emotion, but could only partake in such a diversity through His common life with others. Then we shall not be able to take either the poetic or the rhetorical form of expression as the predominating, or even as the really primary and original, form of His self-proclamation. These have only a subordinate place in parabolic and prophetic discourses. The essential

thing in His self-proclamation was that He had to bear witness regarding His ever unvarying self-consciousness out of the depths of its repose, and consequently not in poetic but in strictly reflective form ; and thus had to set Himself forth, while at the same time communicating His alone true objective consciousness of the condition and constitution of men in general, thus instructing by description or representation, the instruction being sometimes subordinate to the description, and sometimes *vice versa*. But this descriptively didactic mode of expression used by Christ is not included in our proposition, and such utterances of the Redeemer will hardly be set up anywhere as dogmatic propositions ; they will only, as it were, provide the text for them. For in such essential parts of the self-proclamation of Christ the definiteness was absolute, and it is only the perfection of the apprehension and appropriation which reproduces these, that can be characterized by the endeavour after the greatest possible definiteness. Subordinate to these, however, there do appear genuinely dogmatic propositions in the discourses of Christ, namely, at those points at which He had to start from the partly erroneous and partly confused ideas current among His contemporaries.

3. As regards the poetic and rhetorical forms of expression, it follows directly from what we have said, that they may fall into apparent contradiction both with themselves and with each other, even when the self-consciousness which is indicated by different forms of expression is in itself one and the same. And a solution will only be possible, in the first place, when it is possible in interpreting propositions that are apparently contradictory to take one's bearings from the original utterances of Christ (a thing which can in very few cases be done directly), and, in the second place, when the descriptively didactic expression, which has grown out of those three original forms put together, is entirely or largely free from those apparent contradictions. This, however, will not be possible of achievement so long as the descriptively didactic expression itself keeps vacillating between the emotional and the didactic, in its presentation to the catechumens or the community, and approaches sometimes more to the rhetorical and sometimes more to the figurative. It will only be possible in proportion as the aim indicated in our proposition underlies the further develop-ment of the expression and its more definite separation from the rhetorical and the poetic, both of which processes are essentially bound up with the need of settling the conflict. Now, of course,

this demand, that the figurative expression be either exchanged for a literal one or transformed into such by being explained, and that definite limits be imposed on the corresponding element in the rhetorical expressions, is unmistakably the interest which science has in the formation of language ; and it is mainly with the formation of religious language that we are here concerned. Hence dogmatic propositions develop to any considerable extent and gain recognition only in such religious communions as have reached a degree of culture in which science is organized as something distinct both from art and from business, and only in proportion as friends of science are found and have influence within the communion itself, so that the dialectical function is brought to bear on the utterances of the religious self-consciousness, and guides the expression of them. Such a union with organized knowledge has had a place in Christianity ever since the earliest ages of the Church, and therefore in no other religious communion has the form of the dogmatic proposition evolved in such strict separation from the other forms, or developed in such fulness.

Postscript.—This account of the origin of dogmatic propositions, as having arisen solely out of logically ordered reflection upon the immediate utterances of the religious self-consciousness, finds its confirmation in the whole of history. The earliest specimens of preaching preserved for us in the New Testament Scriptures already contain such propositions ; and on closer consideration we can see in all of them, in the first place, their derivation from the original self-proclamation of Christ, and, in the second place, their affinity to figurative and rhetorical elements which, for permanent circulation, had to approximate more to the strictness of a formula. Similarly in later periods it is clear that the figurative language, which is always poetic in its nature, had the most decided influence upon the dogmatic language, and always preceded its development, and also that the majority of the dogmatic definitions were called forth by contradictions to which the rhetorical expressions had led.

But when the transformation of the original expressions into dogmatic propositions is ascribed to the logical or dialectical interest, this is to be understood as applying only to the form. A proposition which had originally proceeded from the speculative activity, however akin it might be to our propositions in content, would not be a dogmatic proposition. The purely scientific activity, whose task is the contemplation of existence, must, if it is to come to anything, either begin or end with the Supreme Being ; and so there may be forms of philosophy containing propositions of speculative import about the Supreme Being which, in spite of the fact that they arose out of the purely scientific interest, are, when taken individually, difficult to distinguish from the corresponding propositions which arose purely out of reflection upon the religious emotions, but have been worked out dialectically. But when they are considered in their connexions, these two indubitably show differences of the most definite kind. For dogmatic propositions never make their original appearance except in trains of thought which have received their impulse from religious moods of mind ; whereas, not only do speculative propositions about the Supreme Being appear for the most part in purely logical or natural-scientific trains of thought, but even when they come in as ethical pre-suppositions or corollaries, they show an unmistakable leaning towards one or other of those two directions. Moreover, in the dogmatic developments of the earliest centuries, if we discount the quite unecclesiastical Gnostic schools, the influence of speculation upon the content of dogmatic propositions may be placed at zero. At a later time, certainly, when the classical organization of know-ledge had fallen into ruins, and the conglomerate-philosophy of the Middle Ages took shape within the Christian Church, and at the same time came to exercise its influence upon the formation of dogmatic language, a confusion of the speculative with the dog-matic, and consequently a mingling of the two, was almost in-evitable. But this was for both an imperfect condition, from which philosophy freed itself by means of the avowal, growing ever gradually louder, that at that time it had stood under the tutelage of ecclesiastical faith, and therefore under an alien law. Having, however, since then made so many fresh starts in its own proper development, it was able to escape from the wearisome task of inquiring exactly as to what kind of speculative propositions were at that time taken to be dogmatic, and *vice versa*. For the Christian Church, however, which is not in a position ever and anon to begin the development of its doctrine over again from the start, this separa-tion is of the greatest importance, in order to secure that speculative matter (by which neither the poetic and rhetorical nor the popular expression can consent to be guided) may not continue to be offered to it as dogmatic. The Evangelical (Protestant) Church in parti-cular is unanimous in feeling that the distinctive form of its dogmatic propositions does not depend on any form or school of philosophy, and has not proceeded at all from a speculative interest, but simply from the interest of satisfying the immediate self-consciousness solely through the means ordained by Christ, in their genuine and uncorrupted form. Thus it can consistently adopt as dogmatic propositions of its own no propositions except such as can show this derivation. Our dogmatic theology will not, however, stand on its proper ground and soil with the same assurance with which philosophy has so long stood upon its own, until the separation of the two types of proposition is so complete that, *e.g.*, so extraordinary a question as whether the same proposition can be true in philosophy and false in Christian theology, and *vice versa*, will no longer be asked, for the simple reason that a proposition cannot appear in the one context precisely as it appears in the other : however similar it sounds, a difference must always be assumed. But we are still very far from this goal, so long as people take pains to base or deduce dogmatic propositions in the speculative manner, or even set themselves to work up the products of speculative activity and the results of the study of religious affections into a single whole.

§ 17. *Dogmatic propositions have a twofold value—an ecclesiastical and a scientific ; and their degree of perfection is determined by both of these and their relation to each other.*

1. The ecclesiastical value of a dogmatic proposition consists in its reference to the religious emotions themselves. Every such emotion, regarded singly, is indeed for description an infinite, and all dogmatic concepts, as well as all concepts of psychology, would have to be used to describe one moment of life. But just as in such a moment the religious strain may be the dominant one, so again in every such strain some one relation of the higher self-consciousness stands out as determinative ; and it is to this strain, uniformly for all analogous moments of religious emotion, that the dogmatic propositions refer. Thus, in all completely expressed dogmatic propositions, the reference to Christ as Redeemer must appear with the same measure of prominence which it has in the religious consciousness itself. Naturally, however, this is not equally strongly the case in all religious moments, any more than in the life of any civic state the distinctive character of its constitution can appear equally strongly in all moments. Accordingly, the less strongly the reference to Christ is expressed in a dogmatic proposition, as, *e.g.*, in the religious emotions mediated by our relation to the external world, the more easily may it resemble a

doctrinal proposition of another religious communion, in cases where the distinctive character of that communion too remains for the most part in the background. Now this occurs even within the Christian Church itself, in respect of the various modifications of the Christian consciousness which separate into larger or smaller groups. Now, if a dogmatic proposition is so formed that it satisfies the Christian consciousness for all alike, then it actually holds good in a larger circle, but it is not calculated to show up differences, which are thus indirectly marked as unimportant or in process of disappearing. If, on the other hand, it has respect only to one of these different modifications, then it holds good only within this smaller compass. Sometimes the former kind of dogma may seem colourless, and the latter be the right kind ; at other times the latter may be factious or sectarian, and the former be the right kind. But such differences in dogmatic propositions dealing with the same subject, which do not represent any differences at all in the immediate religious self-consciousness, are of no significance for their ecclesiastical value.

2. The scientific value of a dogmatic proposition depends in the first place upon the definiteness of the concepts which appear in it, and of their connexion with each other. For the more definite these become, the more does the proposition pass out of the indefinite realm of the poetic and rhetorical, and the more certain will it be that the proposition cannot enter into apparent contradiction with other dogmatic propositions belonging to the same form of religious consciousness. But in forming its concepts Dogmatics has not succeeded—indeed, one might say that from the nature of the subject it cannot succeed—in everywhere substituting the exact expression for the figurative ; and thus the scientific value of dogmatic propositions depends, from this side, for the most part simply upon the highest possible degree of precision and definiteness in explaining the figurative expressions which occur. And we can the more readily leave it at that, since, even if the exact expression could throughout be substituted for the figurative, the latter is the original, and therefore the identity of the two would have to be shown, which would come to the same thing in the end. In the second place, the scientific value of a dogmatic proposition consists in its fruitfulness, that is to say, its many-sidedness in pointing us towards other kindred ones ; and not so much in a heuristic way (since no dogmatic proposition is based on another, and each one can only be discovered from contemplation of the Christian self-

consciousness) as in a critical way, because then it can be the more easily tested how well one dogmatic expression harmonizes with others. For it is undeniable that, of a number of dogmatic expressions which are supposed to refer to the same fact of the Christian consciousness, that one will deserve the preference which opens up and enters into combination with the largest range of other expressions referring to kindred facts. And when we find a realm or system of dogmatic language which is closely bound together and forms a self-contained whole, that is an account of the facts which we may presume to be correct.

A proposition which lacks the first of these two properties, and which thus belongs entirely to the poetic or the rhetorical realm of language, has not got the length of being a dogmatic proposition. A proposition which, as regards the second of the two properties, goes beyond the principle we have set up, and seeks to establish anything objectively without going back to the higher self-consciousness, would not be a religious doctrine (*Glaubenssatz*) at all, and would simply not belong to our field.

3. Now since every doctrine of the faith has, as such, an ecclesiastical value, and since these doctrines become dogmatic when they acquire a scientific value, dogmatic propositions are the more perfect the more their scientific character gives them an outstanding ecclesiastical value, and also the more their scientific content bears traces of having proceeded from the ecclesiastical interest.

§ 18. *The collocation of dogmatic propositions, for the purpose of connecting them and relating them to each other, proceeds from the very same need which led to the formation of them, and is simply a natural sequel to it.*

1. We distinguish Christ's own preaching (which was the starting-point of everything) from dogmatic material, chiefly because when He went didactically into particular details, He verged upon the poetic and the rhetorical, and when He proclaimed Himself in precise and unfigurative language, He never went beyond a quite summary presentation of His being and His work.[1] But every religious emotion which was the direct effect of that preaching became, in the given life-context of the moment, a particular emotion, and therefore the apprehension of it in thought, as an appropriation of that original self-proclamation, was only

[1] Cf. John 3[17] 8[12] 10[30] 12[46].

partial and imperfect ; so that the total mass of the doctrines which thus arose and were worked out with the greatest possible definiteness as dogmatic propositions, is simply, taken all together, the unfolding, ever more and more complete, of that original preaching. Therefore each individual proposition which has so arisen implies a striving after the remaining ones, and thus an endeavour to connect each with others ; and each, just in so far as it is definitely one individual proposition, obtains its place only on the presupposition that it has other more or less kindred propositions beside it and around it.

2. Let us begin with the rhetorical and poetic preaching both of Christ Himself and of His witnesses, which did go into particular details. From this point the didactic form of expression certainly arises mainly out of the problem of settling the apparent conflict between individual metaphors and figures, but partly too out of the need for freeing the expression from the ambiguity and uncertainty which attach to it outside of the given context, and of setting it forth more independently as the same for all. But every apparent contradiction of that sort makes one apprehensive of a number of others, because each casts suspicion upon the whole realm of language in which it occurs, as possibly concealing contradictions. Thus if in a given case an exact and didactic form of expression is set up, by which one may orientate oneself in relation to the apparent opposition, our assurance depends entirely upon the condition that the reconciling expression does not in turn stand in apparent contradiction with itself, but that this whole realm of language is immune from any such danger. But certainty on this point can only be gained by the relating of several such expressions to each other, and by ever repeated attempts to connect them together. Now, although the didactic expression is both more definite and in itself more comprehensible, yet it is always a combination of general ideas which become perfectly definite only when considered along with the higher ones above them and the lower ones under them ; just as every such idea, as subject, can only be fully contemplated in the totality of its predicates, and as predicate, only in the whole range of its applicability. So that every such proposition points towards others, in which occur both kindred ideas and the same ideas in other connexions.

3. Thus it is unthinkable that the religious self-consciousness should be sufficiently alive to utter and communicate itself, without at the same time fashioning for itself the didactic form of expression,

whether in the looser form of popular usage or in the stricter form of the schools. And it is equally unthinkable that the particular elements of this expression should exist in any religious communion without forming themselves into a wealth of thought-series, which would partly aim at the original object of describing the religious emotions themselves in a real succession or in their natural connexion, and partly at working out the didactic expression itself into the greatest possible lucidity.

When we speak of Christian *Preaching*, we mean chiefly the utterance and presentation which have a directly rousing effect. But when we speak of Christian *Teaching* or *Doctrine* (*Lehre*), we mean rather that communication which employs the didactic form of expression, whether in order to rouse by bringing the idea in its clarity home to the consciousness, as happens in homiletic practice, or in order to isolate more definitely, through the clarity of the idea, the immediate religious self-consciousness, and reliably to establish its independence, which is the business of the dogmatic schools. But manifestly this can only reach a satisfactory conclusion when the system of doctrine has become a complete system, in which every essential moment of the religious and Christian consciousness is given its developed dogmatic expression, and all the dogmatic propositions are brought into relation with each other. Hence it is far from praiseworthy when respected theologians, perhaps confounding the thing itself with a perversion of it, reckon the scholarly study of doctrine as a degeneracy of the Christian communion or as a result of such degeneracy. Rather is it, on the one hand, the more necessary for the preaching office itself, as modes of presentation multiply with the variety of languages, that there should be a system of doctrine elaborated with dialectical precision. And on the other hand, it is natural that the more the Christian communion recruits and renews itself out of its own resources, the more does preaching itself take the form of popular *teaching* or *doctrine*, and the more does this doctrine (which itself in turn, however, requires the scholarly teaching as norm and limit) become the most important means to promote the living circulation of the religious consciousness.

Postscript.—If from this position we survey the whole procedure proper for dogmatic propositions, which indeed is just the subject of Dogmatic Theology, we arrive at the conclusion that it may begin at any point, wheresoever the requirements most demand it. The syntheses are, then, in part, of the kind which by preference are occasional, immediately serving the purpose of directly communicating the religious consciousness, and claiming only ecclesiastical value for the propositions in question, as doctrine which belongs to the realm of preaching and edification. But they are also, in part, of the kind where more depends upon their scientific value, and which keep strictly to the realm of Dogmatic Theology itself. These may take the form of *Monographs*, *i.e.* explications of some single proposition in its various relations as these may be surveyed from the standpoint of the proposition itself. Or they may take the form of *loci theologici* (*i.e.* collections of such monographs), which, of course, may be complete, so as to include the whole range of propositions which can be connected with each other, though this will be seen to be merely accidental, since such completeness has nothing to do with the form. Or, finally, they may take the form of a complete *System of Doctrine*, such as has been already described. Such a system, again, may be purely positive, and in that case either merely aphoristic or provided with an apparatus of explanations. Or it may include the polemical element, by taking account of other modifications of the religious and Christian consciousness, or other expressions of the same modification. Or, finally, it may also include the historical, by taking account of the development of dogmatic propositions and the changes which have occurred in the realm of dogmatic terminology.

§ 19. *Dogmatic Theology is the science which systematizes the doctrine prevalent in a Christian Church at a given time.*

NOTE.—See *Brief Outline*, §§ 3, 15, 18, 19, 26, 27.

1. This definition does not seem to exclude the possibility that a person could be a master of Dogmatic Theology and could even communicate it to others without himself believing in what he expounded, just as a man may have knowledge of the interconnexion of propositions in philosophical systems which he does not himself accept. But since the dogmatic procedure has reference entirely to preaching, and only exists in the interests of preaching, all who busy themselves therewith must be assumed to possess the relevant faith, if they are to offer anything profitable, because otherwise it would be a case of a professed reference and relation without any real congruity. The thing, however, is inconceivable except on the supposition that the exponent was not conscious of any religious emotions, even of a different variety. For otherwise no one could, without doing violence to himself, conceal the

contradiction between the position which he expounds as internally coherent and derived from the Christian consciousness, and the position which he himself accepts. And so a dogmatic presentation which takes no sides but is purely historical will always be sufficiently distinct from a presentation which is also apologetic— the only kind now in view. Moreover, it can hardly be denied that those dogmatic presentations (perhaps not uncommon even in our own Church) which, without any firm personal conviction, keep strictly to what is ecclesiastically received, either lack rigorous coherence and inward harmony, or involuntarily betray a weakening of the conviction.

2. Limitation to the doctrine of one particular Church is not a characteristic universally valid, for Christendom has not always been divided into a number of communions definitely separated by diversity of doctrine. But for the present this characteristic is indispensable ; for, to speak only of the Western Church, a presentation suitable for Protestantism cannot possibly be suitable for Catholics, there being no systematic connexion between the doctrines of the one and those of the other. A dogmatic presentation which aimed at avoiding contradiction from either of these two parties would lack ecclesiastical value for both in almost every proposition.

That each presentation confines itself to the doctrine existing at a certain time, is indeed seldom expressly avowed, but it nevertheless seems to be a matter of course ; and this seems, for the most part, to be the only possible explanation of the large number of dogmatic presentations which follow upon each other. It is obvious that the text-books of the seventeenth century can no longer serve the same purpose as they did then, but now in large measure belong merely to the realm of historical presentation ; and that in the present day it is only a different set of dogmatic presentations that can have the ecclesiastical value which these had then ; and the same fate will one day befall the present ones too. But of course it is only from the more universal crises of development that large alterations in doctrine arise, while the alterations which are continually going on amount to so little that it takes a long time to render them perceptible.

3. Now ' the prevalent doctrine ' is not by any means to be taken as signifying merely what is expressed in (confessional) Symbols, but rather all doctrines which are dogmatic expressions of that which, in the public proceedings of the Church (even if only

in certain regions of it), can be put forward as a presentation of its common piety without provoking dissension and schism. Hence this characterization admits of considerable variety in the dogmatic presentations. None the less it might be held that this makes the definition too narrow, partly because it seems as if no alterations could ever come into the dogmatic presentations unless at some time or other something not yet prevalent were adopted, and partly because in this way everything individually distinctive is excluded. But, in the first place, everyone will admit that a system, however coherent, of purely and entirely individual opinions and views, which, even if really Christian, did not link themselves at all to the expressions used in the Church for the communication of religion, would always be regarded as simply a private confession and not as a dogmatic presentation, until there came to be attached to it a like-minded society, and there thus arose a public preaching and communication of religion which found its norm in that doctrine. Consequently it may in a general way be said that the less there is of publicly accepted matter in any such presentation, the less does it answer to the conception of a Dogmatic. Yet this does not mean that the individuality of the author may not have an influence upon the form and manner of treatment, and even assert itself at particular points by intentional correction of the usual position. And this of itself makes it clear that our definition by no means excludes improvements and new developments of Christian doctrine. But this becomes still clearer when we add the fact that such improvements and developments hardly ever proceed directly from the dogmatic discussions themselves, but are for the most part occasioned, in one way or another, by the proceedings of public worship or by popular literature for the dissemination of religion.

4. The correctness of our definition is also made clear by the following considerations : that when a presentation of Christian doctrine lacks one of the above characteristics, it no longer falls within the real field of Dogmatics ; and that the most fundamental aberrations in the dogmatic field are caused by some one of these requirements being torn out of its natural connexions and taken by itself as the only rule for the treatment of the subject.

As for the popular presentation of doctrine, in catechisms and similar works, for the general instruction of the Church, this does indeed require completeness and coherence, but it makes no claim to erudition and systematic arrangement and connexion ; and therefore we separate this from the properly dogmatic field. Further, many religious books which aim either at mystical depth or at rational clarity are more of the descriptively didactic type than of the directly rousing, and these too handle doctrine with a certain completeness ; but they lack the historical attitude, and the reference to the public ecclesiastical understanding of the faith, so that they inform us only ·about the individual, or one isolated fragmeni of the whole ; and therefore we do not give them the title of dogmatic, however coherently systematic they may be in themselves. Finally let us take the canonical and symbolical definitions of doctrine which have from time to time entered into the traffic of dogmatics. These, of course, should always pre-suppose the science of the complete systematization of doctrine, and in that sense they of course belong to dogmatic theology. Only they do not themselves go so far as to give a complete presentation of this systematic coherence, but are concerned only with particular points of doctrine.

Similarly, the most fundamental aberrations in the dogmatic field are accounted for by the one-sided attention paid to one or other of the characteristics which we established. If from time to time dogmatic presentations of doctrine come to appear as pretty much a mere tradition which has become static, this happens be-cause people aim at no more than establishing the doctrine which is already publicly accepted, and thus look upon it as an absolutely given quantity. If, on the other hand, there are to be found dogmatic presentations which in their time enjoyed a widespread acceptance, but which, viewed from some distance and compared with earlier and later ones, appear entirely arbitrary, these are the ones which, having sprung from some transient and confused move-ment in the ecclesiastical realm, comprehended that movement alone, and thus were one-sided, never getting any further than the one particular phase ; in which circumstances it is easy for arbitrary caprice and sophistry to take the place of scientific rigour. Finally, if there are presentations which, while they of course handle Christian doctrine and profess to be dogmatic, do not go back at all to the religious affections, these are the ones which aim only at satisfying the demand for scientific system and coherence, as if that could at the same time produce what a genuinely dogmatic presentation must presuppose, namely, faith. Thus they attempt either directly to deduce and prove what is distinctively Christian from the universal reason, or to make it disappear, as an imperfect thing, in a purely rational and universally valid doctrine of religion.

Postscript.—Many theologians are in complete agreement with the definition of dogmatic theology which we have here established, but assign this actual Dogmatic to a pretty low level, as being only concerned with the presentation of ecclesiastical opinions, and assert that there must stand above it another and higher theology which, even with disregard of these ecclesiastical opinions, would bring out and make evident the essential truths of religion.[1] But the Christian science of God and Salvation cannot possibly recognize such a distinction between ecclesiastical doctrines and essential truths of religion (which are yet supposed to be Christian, for otherwise there can be no talk of them in this connexion at all), either in the sense that these truths of religion have another source, or in the sense that their content is of a different type. For there is only one source from which all Christian doctrine is derived, namely, the self-proclamation of Christ ; and there is only one type of doctrine, for, whether more perfect or less perfect, it all arises out of the religious consciousness itself and its direct expression. Therefore, if anybody is disposed to say that the ecclesiastical doctrine of any given time and place is mere opinion, because it does not remain ever self-identical and is not unmixed with error, it must be replied that nevertheless there is nothing else superior to it in the realm of Christian knowledge, except the purer and more perfect ecclesiastical doctrine which may be found in some other period and in other presentations. But this purifying and perfecting is just the work and the task of Dogmatic Theology.

But let us suppose this task to have been fully discharged, and Dogmatic Theology thus to have reached its completion. Even then we could not agree with those other theologians who make Dogmatics the whole of Christian theology, and who thus regard all the other branches of theological study, Scriptural Exegesis and Church History, both in their widest range and with all their accessories, as merely auxiliary sciences to Dogmatics. For even though both of these are necessary to Dogmatics, nevertheless their whole value does not consist in the service they render to it : each of them has also its own peculiar value directly for the advancement and guidance of the Church, which is the ultimate purpose of all

---

[1] See, among other works, Bretschneider's *Entwicklung*, § 25, and *Handbuch der Dogmatik*, § 5, where in the end one is in doubt whether Dogmatics belongs to Christian theology at all.

Christian theology, Dogmatics included. Rather would we say that, though Scriptural Exegesis and Church History are, each in its own peculiar office, dependent on the study of Dogmatics, and suffer when Dogmatics is neglected, so that all these different branches can only approach completion by reciprocally influencing each other, yet it would be a very suspicious thing if it were just Dogmatics that principally set the tone in this progress, because it depends more than the other branches (if only in form) upon Philosophy (*Weltweisheit*). For philosophy makes frequent new beginnings, and most of these revolutions engender new combinations and new expressions for the field from which Dogmatics draws its vocabulary; hence it is in this branch of theology that those variations most easily arise which provoke irrelevant controversy, and also those restatements which do not exactly represent progress but rather hinder than advance the theoretic development.

CHAPTER II

THE METHOD OF DOGMATICS

§ 20. *Since every system of doctrine, as a presentation of Dogmatic Theology, is a self-contained and closely-connected whole of dogmatic propositions, we must, with regard to the existing mass of such propositions, establish in the first place a rule according to which some will be adopted and others excluded; and in the second place, a principle for their arrangement and interconnexion.*

1. It is here presupposed that the individual propositions are the original, and are in existence earlier than the systematizing tendency itself; and this is entirely in line with the foregoing discussion. Thus it is by no means the case that first of all a principle is either somehow given externally or invented specially by each investigator, and that the individual propositions only proceed from the explication of this principle. That is indeed conceivable in the speculative realm, but not here. For the Christian self-consciousness must be already developed in the community before really dogmatic elements come to be formed, and it is only through the fragmentary, and perhaps chaotic, presence of these, that the task of making an orderly connexion arises. This last, however, only fulfils its purpose when it makes the collocation so complete that we can be certain we have in the doctrine a record of all the common elements of the Christian consciousness. Such completeness is, therefore, the aim of every system of doctrine. For without it we could not even have the assurance that our dogmatic expression of the distinctive essence of Christianity was correct, since the very region which was omitted might furnish proof of the contrary. This conviction of being correct can only proceed from having an outline of the whole, which clearly exhibits a comprehensive and exhaustive division.

2. It is undeniable that there has been great diversity in systems of doctrine even at the same times and in the same Churches. And since this is at least partly due to the differences of procedure in

adopting and connecting doctrines, it is only in very indefinite form that rules can be established for these two processes. But each individual system of doctrine characterizes itself best when, within these forms, it shows its own distinctive point of view with the greatest possible definiteness.

A double method naturally presents itself here. We could, starting from our general conception of the Christian consciousness, sketch an outline of the different ways in which it can express itself according to the nature of the human soul and of human life, and seek to fill in this outline with the existing doctrinal material ; and with this method the only concern would be to make sure that we were not adopting any mutually incompatible elements. But we could also take the line of bringing together all expressions of religious emotion which had developed in one particular region of Christianity and belonged to one and the same type ; and then it would only remain to arrange this material in the most convenient and synoptical way. To place the methods thus side by side is enough to show that we must combine the two, because each finds only in the other a security for what it lacks itself.

I. THE SELECTION OF THE DOGMATIC MATERIAL.

§ 21. *In order to build up a system of doctrine, it is necessary first to eliminate from the total mass of dogmatic material everything that is heretical, and to retain only what is ecclesiastical.*

1. If we think of the Christian Church as being what we call a moral Person, *i.e.* as being, though of course made up of many personalities, nevertheless a genuine individual life, then it must at once be admitted that in every such life, just as in individual lives in the narrower sense, there is a distinction between healthy and diseased conditions. The latter are always conditions which do not arise from the inward foundation of the life and in its clear course, but are to be explained only by foreign influences. So when among any race of people individuals arise who exhibit a quite alien physiological type, so that they do not take very kindly to the majority and their mode of life, or when in a republican state citizens arise with monarchist sentiments, or *vice versa*, we regard this as a disease of the whole, and also assume that it can only be explained by foreign influences. Now, even if this last point might not be admitted by everybody, yet everybody will reserve the name of ' heretical ' in the realm of Christian doctrine for that which he cannot explain from his idea of the distinctive essence of

Christianity, and cannot conceive as accordant therewith, but which nevertheless gives itself out as Christian and seeks to be regarded as such by others. Now, it is a matter of fact that during the period of the actual development of Christian doctrine a multitude of such elements appeared which the majority persistently rejected as of alien type, while they recognized the remainder, as self-consistent and as forming a coherent continuum, under the name of Catholic, *i.e.* common to the whole Church. In this connexion it may, of course, sometimes be the case that the religious emotions set forth in the doctrine are themselves at variance with the true essence of Christian piety ; but sometimes it is only in the working out of the doctrine that this variance arises, so that the religious affections themselves are not diseased, and only misunderstanding or false method produces an appearance of heresy. Now these two cases are of course seldom properly distinguished, and therefore many things have been too hastily declared heretical. But, nevertheless, real heresy has not been lacking ; and in its case foreign influences will readily be admitted, when one reflects that the Christian Church originally sprang solely from people who belonged before to other faiths, so that alien matter could easily creep in unawares.

2. It is undeniable that this makes the determination of what is heretical, and must therefore be excluded from the system of doctrine, appear a very uncertain thing, and people will all fix it differently who start from different formulæ of the distinctive essence of Christianity. But that cannot be otherwise, as the whole course of events in the Christian Church proves. For new heresies no longer arise, now that the Church recruits itself out of its own resources ; and the influence of alien faiths on the frontier and in the mission-field of the Church must be reckoned at zero so far as regards the formation of doctrine, though there may long remain in the piety of the new converts a great deal which has crept in from their religious affections of former times, and which, if it came to clear consciousness and were expressed as doctrine, would be recognized as heretical. But concerning the earlier heresies, on the other hand, there are the most diverse judgments, just as there are different ways and modes of conceiving the essence of Christianity. Hence anyone who aims at setting up a system of doctrine can only follow the rule of our proposition in the sense that he will not adopt anything which, according to the fundamental type of Christian doctrine which he has established, can only be traced to a foreign

source. If, however, we are not to proceed by haphazard but with due certainty, we cannot hold by the antithesis of Catholic and heretical as it presented itself in history down to a certain point, especially as subsequent revindications of this or that heresy have not been unheard-of. We must rather start from the essence of Christianity, and seek to construe the heretical in its manifold forms by asking in how many different ways the essence of Christianity can be contradicted and the appearance of Christianity yet remain. Conducted in this way, the inquiry into the heretical serves to supplement the inquiry into the essence of Christianity, and the two confirm each other. The more it turns out that what is thus set up problematically as heretical is also actually given in history, the more ground have we to regard the formula upon which the construction is based as a correct expression of the essence of Christianity. And the more naturally there develops out of this same formula the form of doctrine which Christianity has constantly professed, the more ground have we to regard as really diseased and worthy of rejection whatever conflicts on any side with that formula.

§ 22. *The natural heresies in Christianity are the Docetic and the Nazarean, the Manichean and the Pelagian.*

1. If in using these expressions we think only of the historical phenomena which have been so called, the choice of them as designating the whole range of heresy may seem very arbitrary and very disproportionate. For while the last two have been very widespread and have frequently recurred, the first two were very transitory and confined to narrow circles, and there are other names which are far more important and far more in everybody's mouth. But these names are here intended only to denote universal forms which we are here going to unfold, and the definitions of which they are intended to remind us proceed from the general nature of the situation, even if, *e.g.*, Pelagius himself should not be a Pelagian in our sense. But the nature of the situation means primarily the number of different ways in which the distinctive fundamental type of Christian doctrine can be contradicted while the appearance of Christianity yet remains. The question, from what foreign influences these can have sprung, is a matter of purely historical investigation, which does not properly concern us here : though, of course, the conviction that all alien material, if it is to lay claim at all to the name of Christian, must fit into one of these

forms, would be the only complete security for the truth of our presentation of the matter.

2. Now, if the distinctive essence of Christianity consists in the fact that in it all religious emotions are related to the redemption wrought by Jesus of Nazareth, there will be two ways in which heresy can arise. That is to say : this fundameñtal formula will be retained in general (for otherwise the contradiction would be manifest and complete, so that participation in Christian communion could not even be desired), but *either* human nature will be so defined that a redemption in the strict sense cannot be accomplished, *or* the Redeemer will be defined in such a way that He cannot accomplish redemption. But each of these two cases, again, can appear in two different ways. As regards the former : if men are to be redeemed, they must both be in need of redemption and be capable of receiving it. Now, if one of these conditions is openly posited, but the other covertly denied, the contradiction at the same time touches the fundamental formula itself, only this is not directly apparent. If, then, in the first place, the need of redemption in human nature, *i.e.* its inability to bring the feeling of absolute dependence into all human states of consciousness, is posited in such an absolute way that the ability to receive redeeming influences is made actually to disappear, so that human nature is not simultaneously in need of redemption and capable of receiving it, but only becomes capable of receiving it after a complete transformation, this is equivalent to an annulling of our fundamental formula. Now this is the unfailing consequence, if we suppose an Evil-in-itself as being original and opposed to God, and think of human nature as suffering from that inability by reason of a dominion which this original Evil exercises over it ; and therefore we call this deviation the Manichean. But, on the other hand, suppose the ability to receive redemption is assumed so absolutely, and consequently any hindrance to the entry of the God-consciousness becomes so utterly infinitesimal, that at each particular moment in each individual it can be satisfactorily counterbalanced by an infinitesimal overweight. Then the need of redemption is reduced to zero, at least in the sense that it is no longer the need of one single Redeemer, but merely, for each person in one of his weak moments, the need of some other individual who, if only for the moment, is stronger as regards the eliciting of the God-consciousness. Thus redemption would not need to be the work of one particular Person, but would be a common work of all for all, in which, at most, some would only

have a greater share than others ; and this aberration we may with good reason call, as above, the Pelagian.

Turn now to the other kind of heresy. If Christ is to be the Redeemer, *i.e.* the real origin of constant living unhindered evocation of the God-consciousness, so that the participation of all others in it is mediated through Him alone, it is, on the one hand, necessary that He should enjoy an exclusive and peculiar superiority over all others, and, on the other hand, there must also be an essential likeness between Him and all men, because otherwise what He has to impart could not be the same as what they need. Therefore on this side also the general formula can be contradicted in two different ways, because each of these two requisites may be conceived so unlimitedly that the other no longer remains co-posited, but disappears. If the difference between Christ and those who are in need of redemption is made so unlimited that an essential likeness is incompatible with it, then His participation in human nature vanishes into a mere appearance ; and consequently our God-consciousness, being something essentially different, cannot be derived from His, and redemption also is only an appearance. Now though the Docetics, properly so called, directly denied only the reality of the body of Christ, yet this likewise excludes the reality of human nature in His Person generally, since we never find body and soul given in separation from each other ; and therefore we may fitly call this aberration the Docetic. Finally, if on the other hand the likeness of the Redeemer to those who are to be redeemed is made so unlimited that no room is left for a distinctive superiority as a constituent of His being, which must then be conceived under the same form as that of all other men, then there must ultimately be posited in Him also a need of redemption, however absolutely small, and the fundamental relationship is likewise essentially annulled. This aberration we call by the name given to those who are supposed first to have regarded Jesus entirely as an ordinary man, the Nazarean or Ebionitic.

Other kinds of heresy than can be comprehended under one or other of these four forms cannot be conceived, if the conception of the Christian religion (piety) is to remain unchanged. For there are no more points at which the conception can be indirectly attacked. And if the conception of redemption is roundly denied, or another redeemer is set up, and thus it is roundly asserted either that men are not in need of redemption or that there is no redeeming power in Jesus, then the assertion is no longer heretical but anti-Christian.

3. These concepts of the natural heresies likewise serve, from our point of view, in the construction of any system of Christian doctrine, as limiting points which one must avoid if the agreement of particular details with the remainder is not to be destroyed. But then this also implies that no formula, in whatever division of the system it may occur, which avoids the two opposite aberrations, is to be regarded as heretical : however disproportionate the one side may appear as compared with the other, so long as neither completely disappears, the formula is still ecclesiastical or catholic. On the other hand, every formula must be suspect which can be identified with any one of these aberrations. Only, let everybody guard in this matter against the illusions so easily produced by the ' foreshortening ' natural to distance. For the nearer a man stands to the Pelagian line himself, the more easily will he believe that he sees actually on the Manichean side the man who really is still standing almost in the middle ; and so, too, with other cases. And therefore, unless the confusion is to grow ever greater, it is highly important that people should go to work with the greatest caution when it comes to declaring anything heretical.

But further, these heresies are specially bound up in pairs. That is to say, in their relation to the essence of Christianity the Manichean and the Docetic belong together, and so again do the Pelagian and the Ebionitic. For if human nature is essentially infected with positively original Evil, then the Redeemer cannot have any real participation in human nature ; and if the higher self-consciousness is hindered by the lower in Christ in the same way as in all other men, then His contribution to redemption can only be related to any other man's contribution as the more to the less. But if, on the other hand, we have regard to the fact that what cannot be understood from the essence of Christianity must have arisen through foreign influences, and that in the period of the original development of doctrine Christianity came into contact almost exclusively with Judaism and Greek Heathenism, then the Manichean and the Nazarean seem rather to belong together, as being of Judaizing tendency, the one in a purer form, and the other rather imbued with Orientalism ; while the Docetic and the Pelagian seem to be of Hellenizing tendency, since mythology led to the former, and the ethical trend of the Mysteries to the latter.

Postscript.—We are far from wishing to drag in here the antithesis, at present so intense, between Supernaturalism and Rationalism. But nevertheless let us note that since in accordance with the above discussion we have to admit, even within the range of the ecclesiastical, manifold approximations to these heretical extremes, they also are divided between those two modes of treatment ; and that in supernaturalistic presentations—not only in the properly dogmatic ones, but in the popular ones too—echoes may be found of the Docetic and Manichean, just as rationalistic presentations may with some justice be reproached with approximating to the Ebionitic and Pelagian. And the fact that any treatment of doctrine which does not escape one-sidedness altogether, necessarily inclines to one or other of these two sides, seems to testify to the correctness of this account of the heretical.

§ 23. *A system of doctrine drawn up at the present time within the Western Church cannot be indifferent to the antithesis between Roman Catholic and Protestant, but must adhere to one or the other.*

1. Some justification seems to be required for our here making the antithesis between the Eastern and the Western Church greater than the antithesis which we have expressed (between Roman Catholic and Protestant), and then, nevertheless, passing over the former. The first of these two steps seems to have against it the fact that the Eastern Church, as anti-Papal, appears to stand on the side of Protestantism. But suppose it were admitted that that antithesis *is* greater : then to pass over it seems inconsistent ; and the common character of the Western Church would first have to be specified, in order that we might discover within it the principle for the subordinate antithesis between Romanism and Protestantism. As against this, however, it is to be noted that this cannot at all be the place to construe these antitheses in a completely graduated scale, but only in their relation to the study of doctrine. And how little the anti-Papal character of the Eastern Church signifies in this respect, may be seen from the facility with which individual fragments of that Church acknowledge the Roman Primacy without giving up their Eastern type, and especially without making any considerable alteration in their doctrine. The antithesis *is* indeed a greater one in the precise connexion with which we are here concerned, in the sense that a lively activity in the realm of doctrine has remained common to the two Western Churches even since their separation, whereas the Eastern Church since its break-away has in this realm become more and more torpid, and in it the combination of knowledge about religion

with a really scientific organization is almost entirely destroyed. But just because of this purely negative character there was the less to be said here about that Church, since it cannot be determined whether it will again step back more into connexion with the world's intellectual intercourse, and so have the strength to elicit and develop within itself an antithesis analogous to the Western one.

2. This antithesis has not affected the whole range of doctrine, for alongside of the doctrines over which the two Churches are avowedly in conflict there are others for which they set up the same formulæ, and yet others about which analogous differences are found within both Churches. And the antithesis itself, like every similar one within the Christian communion, must be regarded as destined some day and somehow to disappear. So one can certainly conceive of very different modes of procedure in the construction of the system of doctrine, according as one believes that the antithesis has not yet reached its culminating-point, or that it has already passed it. In the latter case, it would be a true progress if we were to seek for, or prepare in advance, mediating formulæ in the controversial doctrines, in order to facilitate and help to bring about, from every standpoint, the approaching abrogation of the antithesis. Then it would likewise be the correct thing to establish as firmly as possible the common matter in the non-controversial doctrines, in order to make it as difficult as possible for well-meaning zealots who misconceived the whole condition of the Church, to delay unnecessarily the union of its two parts by stirring up new and unprofitable controversies. But, in the other case, we should have to assume the probability that, if the tension between the two parts is destined still to increase generally, it will also increase in the realm of doctrine. And in that case we should, in the same spirit (namely, with a view to accelerating the whole process in a steady course as much as possible), have to adopt the opposite line of procedure. A Protestant system of doctrine has in that case to aim at exhibiting the antithesis in those portions of doctrine where it has not hitherto appeared ; for only when it had been developed in all portions could we be quite sure that it had reached its culminating-point in doctrine. Now since the course of such an antithesis is seldom quite direct, the main trend being from time to time interrupted by reactions towards the opposite side, there may easily arise in the first half of the course an appearance of one's being in the second, and *vice versa*. Therefore, both modes of treatment are usually found simultaneously

alongside of each other ; but in both there is also found sometimes
more consciousness, sometimes less, of the particular point at which
they stand.

3. The proposition which we have set up therefore excludes
neither of these two modes of treatment. For even he who regards
the tension as now decreasing, and prepares means of accommodation, cannot (if he remains within the realm of Dogmatics) help
putting forward the distinction as still valid, and professing the side
which corresponds to the rest of his presentation of Christian
doctrine. A system of doctrine could only remain neutral on controversial points if it went back to older formulæ, and that means,
of course, to less definite ones, out of which the more definite ones
have only developed in the course of controversy. But it is impossible in a scientific exposition to confine oneself to the indefinite
when the definite is already given.

We, however, cannot regard the tension as already on the decrease. For when there arises in the Evangelical (Protestant)
Church a variety of views regarding any portion of doctrine, the
result of it is never a greater approximation to Roman formulæ ;
and similarly in the Roman Church those movements which take
an anti-Protestant direction seem to be the most successful. It is
therefore rather to be presumed that, even when the doctrines
sound the same, there are still hidden differences, than that, when
the formulæ diverge considerably, the difference in the religious
affections themselves is inconsiderable.

§ 24. *In so far as the Reformation was not simply a purification and
reaction from abuses which had crept in, but was the origination of a distinctive form of the Christian communion, the
antithesis between Protestantism and Catholicism may provisionally be conceived thus : the former makes the individual's relation to the Church dependent on his relation to
Christ, while the latter contrariwise makes the individual's
relation to Christ dependent on his relation to the Church.*

1. If we confine our attention to the rise of Protestantism, it is
certainly undeniable that the Reformers and their first adherents
were conscious only of the wish to purify. They had no intention
whatsoever of forming a Church of their own, but were simply
driven to it. If, on the other hand, we confine our attention to
the present time, and reflect that the Evangelical (Protestant)
Church never exercises an organized missionary activity upon the

Catholic Church, and indeed never expresses, as part of its essential nature, the desire to bring over the whole Catholic Church into the Evangelical ; and if we reflect that we could not help doing these things if we regarded all elements which are alien to us and peculiar to Roman Catholicism, whether doctrines or institutions and usages, as simply corruptions of Christianity ; then it follows that, while we do not cease to combat by word and deed what we really reckon as corruptions, we at the same time assume that other matter, which is indigenous there but equally alien to us, is yet of such a kind that we feel we may leave it standing alongside of our own religion, as being of a different formation but equally Christian. It will also be evident that even supposing the Catholic Church leant towards our definitions in all doctrines that have become controversial, this would not cause a reunion of the two Churches ; and this can only be explained by the existence of a spirit alien to ours, which repels us. But it is plain that the two conclusions go together : we ascribe such a peculiarity of character to our own Church, just as we do to the Catholic. And in case we should be disposed to keep solely to the idea of purification, this also must be added : in the first place, that, as a universal rule, what has previously existed never recurs at a later time in quite the same form ; and, in the second place, that no one particular point of time could be given, all over, to which the Church should have been brought back by the Reformation. For the Apostolic Age cannot be brought back, partly because we cannot sacrifice the dogmatic precision of our ideas, partly because we can as little re-establish the then relations to Judaism and Heathenism as we can the political passivity. Some things in the Evangelical Church may point to earlier periods, and some to later ; but its self-reproducing unity is of a kind which did not formerly exist, though there may have been individuals whose religion was analogous to it.

2. Now this naturally creates for the Evangelical theologian the task of bringing to clear consciousness the distinctive character of Protestantism in antithesis to Catholicism, and thus fixing the antithesis itself, if possible, in a formula. Otherwise he will no more be able to perform his work with some degree of security and completeness than will the Christian theologian in general who has similarly failed to fix the distinctive essence of Christianity. Now it is of course very natural that such a formula should not arise out of the controversy between the two parties themselves ; but unfortunately even we Protestants among ourselves have by no

means come to agree upon such a formula.   Usually we reduce the
antithesis to some one salient point which does not explain everything, and we do it in such a way that one of the two parties appears
only negatively defined ; or we treat the antithesis as a more or
less accidental aggregate of individual differences.   Some people,
perhaps, have thought that for Evangelical Dogmatics it is already,
unfortunately, too late for such a formula, because the doctrine
of our Church is completely settled in our Symbols, so that no new
element can be gained for it.   And others, perhaps, have thought
it is not yet time for such a formula, because the spirit of Protestantism has not yet in doctrine fully developed itself on all sides.   But,
as a matter of fact, the relation of the two Churches is at present
such that it is now possible, and also now necessary, to come to a
complete orientation on the point ; and, for another thing, we have
to provide against un-Protestant matter creeping in unawares even
into our own further development.   Since, however, so little has
yet been done upon this task, the attempt here made can claim to
be no more than a provisional one.

3. Just as the distinctive essence of Christianity could never be
discovered from the mere concept of religion and of the religious
communion, so the distinctive essence of Protestantism cannot be
discovered from the general expression which we have given to
Christianity.   And just as the essence of Christianity could not be
discovered by a merely empirical method, so it would be difficult
to arrive in that way at the principle of the inner unity of the
Evangelical Church.   Here, indeed, the difficulty would be still
greater.   For, on the one hand, at the rise of Protestantism the
purificatory aim alone appeared definitely, and the distinctive spirit
which began to develop lay unconscious and concealed behind that
aim.   And, on the other hand, even the outward unity of the new
Church is much more difficult to define, because there was no unity
of starting-point, and yet there did not arise as many new communions as there were starting-points.   Hence amid the great mass
of very diverse and independently developed personal peculiarities,
it must be almost impossible to determine what there was to unite
them apart from that purificatory aim, and how far they belonged
together.   Now since the antithesis can be most clearly seen from
the present consolidated existence of the two Churches alongside of
each other, it seemed best to attempt the solution of the problem
by considering what kind of qualities of the one communion most
strongly arouse in the common mind of the other the consciousness

of the antithesis. Now it is the charge most generally made by the Roman Church against Protestantism, that it has so much destroyed the old Church, and yet, by reason of its own fundamental principles, is not in a position to build up again a stable and durable communion, but leaves everything uncertain and in solution, and each individual standing by himself. The main reproach which we, contrariwise, bring against Catholicism is that, in ascribing everything to the Church and tracing everything to the Church, it deprives Christ of the honour due to Him, and puts Him in the background, and even in a measure subordinates Him to the Church. To this add the fact, that ecclesiastical Protestantism is as little chargeable in the latter respect as Catholicism in the former; and consider how nevertheless each party is disposed to point out in the other chiefly what could most easily lead it astray from the common ground of Christianity. Plainly the opinion of the Catholics is that, even though we were to hold fast the reference to Christ, we should nevertheless be in danger of giving up the Christian principle by dissolving the communion; and our opinion of the Roman Church is that, however fast it may hold this communion, it is nevertheless in danger of becoming un-Christian by neglecting the reference to Christ. Now add to this the further fact that the spirit of Christianity which rules in both Churches does not allow either of them ever to reach that extreme. Then there follows from this the formula which we have set up. In the controversial doctrines themselves this formula can only justify itself gradually in the course of the further discussion (unless we want to anticipate in a fragmentary way a large part of our system of doctrine). Here we can only make some preliminary remarks in support of the formula, and draw some conclusions from it regarding the treatment of Evangelical Dogmatics.

4. In support of our formula it may be said (though we could not take this as our starting-point) that it ascribes to the two parties antithetical characters which modify the essence of Christianity in antithetical ways. For since Christian piety never arises independently and of itself in an individual, but only out of the communion and in the communion, there is no such thing as adherence to Christ except in combination with adherence to the communion. That the two should be subordinated to each other in opposite ways is only possible because the same fact which *we* regard as the institution of the Church, to serve the work or influence of Christ, is regarded by *them* as a transference to the Church of the

work of Christ. So this, too, speaks well for our formula, that here, where we are primarily seeking to define the antithesis for the *theoretic* side of the doctrine, the formula fastens mainly upon the concept of the Church. This makes it probable that what is opposed in the *practice* of the two Churches and in the principles of their constitution can also be evolved out of this formula.

But as regards the treatment of Evangelical Dogmatics, what follows is that in those portions of doctrine to which the formula can be most directly applied, the greatest care must be taken not to carry the antithesis too far, lest we should fall into un-Christian positions. And, on the other hand, that in those doctrines in which the antithesis is least prominent, especial care must be taken not to set up formulæ which have never got rid of the antithetical character, or which have perhaps even taken on something of it once again. In this way it can best be ascertained how far the distinctive Evangelical spirit has everywhere become developed in doctrine. At the same time it seems natural that that Church which places the communion above the relation to Christ also most easily takes over matter from the earlier religious communions, and consequently that whatever has a certain flavour of the Jewish or the Heathen is more in keeping with the Roman Church, just as every opposition to these elements, even in earlier times, contained something akin to Protestantism.

Postscript.—What has been said about the indefiniteness of the outward unity of the Evangelical (Protestant) Church refers especially to the different branches of it, and in particular to the separation between the Reformed and the Lutheran Church. For the original relation was such that, notwithstanding their different starting-points, they might just as well have grown together into an outward unity as have come to separate from each other. Now this presentation of doctrine, even in its very title, professes adherence only to the Protestant Church in general, without naming either of those two in particular. Thus it starts from the assumption that the separation of the two has lacked sufficient grounds, inasmuch as the differences in doctrine are in no sense traceable to a difference in the religious affections themselves, and the two do not diverge from each other, either in morals and moral theory or in constitution, in any way which at all corresponds to those differences of doctrine. Therefore we can only treat of such differences in the same way as writers in other subjects take notice of divergent presentations by different teachers—in short, simply as an academic matter.

§ 25. *Every Evangelical (Protestant) Dogmatic ought to contain a peculiar and distinctive element; only, this will be more prominent in some systems than in others, and sometimes more in some points of doctrine, sometimes in others.*

NOTE.—Cf. *Brief Outline*, p. 118.

1. We could not at all grant the name of Dogmatics to a presentation composed purely of original doctrines peculiar to itself. Even the earliest coherent presentations of the Evangelical Faith could only bear that name, in so far as they linked themselves to what went before, and had most of their system in common with what was ecclesiastically given. And so an epitome of doctrine which claimed no connexion with that which at the time of the Reformation either took shape or was for the Evangelical Church recognized anew, could not by any means pass as an Evangelical system of doctrine, however opposed all its contents might be to Romanism. And if we had nothing to show but such an epitome, then indeed the unity and identity of our Church would not appear at all in its doctrine, and there would, from this side, be no guarantee whatever of the mutual kinship of those who call themselves Protestants. If, on the other hand, our system of doctrine were so perfectly and precisely definite that there could be no divergence unless one were willing to exclude oneself from the communion of the Church, then new presentations of the system of doctrine within our Church would be entirely superfluous and useless. If repetitions of a hard-and-fast letter are to mean anything, there must at least be change in the turns of expression or in the arrangement of the propositions. But both of these really always indicate characteristic alterations, since there never are two expressions meaning exactly the same thing, and since every proposition acquires a somewhat different meaning when it is placed in a different context. And so even where there was only a slight tinge of difference in a number of different presentations, there would always likewise be divergent and distinctive doctrines. As a matter of fact, however, our system of doctrine is very far from having such a thoroughgoing definiteness, for even in the different confessional documents the same thing is not always comprehended in the same letters, and these solely official and perhaps universally recognized presentations have, after all, only individual parts of the system

of doctrine as their subject.   And just as in the Reformation age
this common matter sprang simply out of the free agreement of
individuals, it is still true, since the Protestant Church has become
firmly established, that there is no other way in which anything
can become generally accepted than by the free concurrence of the
results obtained by individuals who are engaged upon the same
subject.   The fact that, notwithstanding, common doctrine is not
lacking, sufficiently proves that the individuals are united by something distinctive which they have in common ; and anything more
than this, as regards unity of doctrine, is not to be expected in the
Evangelical Church, nor is it required.

2. Let us then start from the facts that the system of doctrine
in our Church all over is not a thing absolutely settled, and that it
may indeed be asserted that its distinctive character has not yet
become fully manifest in doctrine.   Then we can only proceed on
the supposition that in the further development also of the system
of doctrine in the future these two elements will appear together,
and will penetrate each other—matter which is common to all, and
which makes good its claim as a pure and universally recognizable
expression of the distinctive Protestant spirit ; and peculiar
matter which expresses the personal views of its exponents.   And
every particular presentation of the substance of the doctrine,
which lays claim to an ecclesiastical character, will be the more
perfect the more inwardly it unites in itself and relates together
the common and the peculiar.   The common matter naturally
starts from, and becomes most prominent in, those portions of
doctrine which are most akin to the original efforts to purify the
faith.   Now if this effort at the time of the Reformation itself did
not transform the whole tenor of doctrine, but allowed much to be
simply taken over unaltered from earlier definitions, this realm will
naturally become a controversial one, and much of what has
hitherto passed as common matter will gradually become obsolete.
The element of peculiarity lies originally in the arrangement of
the individual doctrines, in which there is, and can be, practically
nothing which would be recognized as necessarily of general acceptance.   But further, all points of doctrine, even while keeping
within the universally recognized mode of expression, permit of
more exact definition in many ways ; and everyone achieves
something who makes people recognize this capacity for modification, and in his own way makes use of his rights in the matter.
Finally, the element of peculiarity in the presentation touches also

the area of what is gradually becoming antiquated, with a view to remodelling individual doctrines in a way more true to the Protestant spirit. But even the most lively originality cannot aim at anything higher than to set the common doctrine in the clearest light ; just as, again, for the common element there is no higher aim than to encourage the peculiar and original development of doctrine without disturbing the communion, by establishing as definitely as possible the Protestant character of the system. The more the two elements thus interpenetrate each other, the more ecclesiastical, and at the same time the more favourable to progress, is the presentation. The more they are detached from each other, and merely stand side by side as unconnected, the more does the element which clings to the historical, and is set up as of common acceptance, appear to be of merely antiquarian interest, and the original element to be simply ultra-modern.

Postscript.—The terms *orthodox* and *heterodox*, which even etymologically do not form a proper antithesis, are too uncertain for me to have any great desire to employ them. Consider, however, how much there is which was originally decried as heterodox in our Church, and which afterwards came to pass muster as orthodox, but always through an earlier orthodoxy becoming obsolete. Then it becomes plain how this antithesis refers solely to what professes to be common matter. The name of orthodox is then given to what is in unmistakable conformity with the matter fixed in the confessional documents ; and what is not thus in conformity is heterodox. But now, if heterodox matter succeeds in vindicating itself as being more accordant with the spirit of the Evangelical Church than is the letter of the confessional documents, then the latter becomes antiquated and the former becomes orthodox. Now, since such changes in our Church can never by a special act be declared universally valid, the employment of these two terms, for things which are still subject to discussion, is always doubtful policy. The situations which occasion it will probably never cease to arise, because what is fixed in the confessional documents contains exegeses of Scripture, and thus the progress of the art of exegesis may render doubtful that part of the Symbols. And similarly, on the other hand, even if the heterodox cannot be definitely distinguished in content and expression from the heretical of older times, yet it must not be regarded as heretical, if only it seeks to make good its claim in connexion with the commonly accepted elements of our Church's system of doctrine.

For, in the case of those people who do not desire to separate themselves from our Church's system of doctrine, we must not, even when there are such divergences, put them down to anything more than misunderstandings, which are sure to disappear again through scientific interchange of views within the Church itself. And especially we must not think there has been any hidden influence of principles which belong to other religious communions.

§ 26. *In the Evangelical (Protestant) Church the Science of Christian Doctrine and that of Christian Morals have long been separated : and so here too, for the purposes of our presentation, we eliminate from the totality of the dogmatic material such propositions as are elements of the Science of Christian Morals.*

NOTE.—Cf. *Brief Outline*, §§ 31 ff.

1. Even the propositions of the Science of Christian Morals are in the above sense propositions or doctrines of the faith. For the modes of action which they describe under the form of theorems or precepts (for the two come to the same thing) are likewise expressions of the religious affections of the Christian. That is to say, every religious emotion is essentially a modification of human existence, and if it is understood as a quiescent state, there arises a proposition which belongs to the Science of Christian Doctrine. But every such emotion, unless it either gets interrupted in its natural course or is too weak from the beginning (and we cannot here take account of either of these cases), issues just as essentially in activity ; and if the different modifications of the Christian's religious consciousness are understood as activities which arise in different ways in accordance with the circumstances which at the time occasion and determine them, there arise propositions which belong to the Science of Christian Morals. But rules of life and formulæ for modes of action which were not of that type would not belong to the Science of Christian Morals, but either to the purely rational Science of Morals or to some special technical or practical study.

2. Now it is clear that only the two taken together represent the whole reality of the Christian life. For it is inconceivable that a man should everywhere and always have in his self-consciousness the emotions which are expressed in the doctrines of the Christian faith, without also acting, everywhere and always, in the way set forth by Christian morals. And it is equally easy to

understand how the two could have been for a long time unified in presentation, so that they formed a single discipline. For the issues of the religious emotions in activity can always, when taken together at suitable points, be described in a supplemental way even in the Science of Doctrine, as natural consequences of the described states themselves ; as, *e.g.*, what are called duties to God may come after the treatment of the Divine Attributes. Similarly there are doctrines which in themselves belong equally to both studies, and which thus provide in the Science of Doctrine a place where particular parts of the Science of Morals, or even the whole of it, could easily be introduced. Such are the portions of doctrine which treat of Sanctification and of the Church. But in the nature of the case the Science of Doctrine could equally well be introduced into the Science of Morals, and in the same twofold manner ; *i.e.* the religious affections could be described, each as something which preceded the developing activities in general, but which also accompanied and was, as it were, echoed in these ; but they could also be described at particular points. For since the expression of the self-consciousness is a moral activity, it would be possible in a treatment of this latter to introduce the whole Science of Doctrine as an explication of the thing which is to be expressed. But (when the two were united) the relation was always a purely one-sided one, the treatment of the Science of Morals being included in the Science of Doctrine. The Science of Doctrine in this way became shapeless in consequence of unevenly distributed appendices, and the need for viewing as a connected whole the modes of action accepted in the Christian Church was not satisfied. Hence it was inevitable that the ethical interest should sooner or later lead to the two studies being separated from each other.

II. THE FORMATION OF THE DOGMATIC SYSTEM.

§ 27. *All propositions which claim a place in an epitome of Evangelical (Protestant) doctrine must approve themselves both by appeal to Evangelical confessional documents, or in default of these, to the New Testament Scriptures, and by exhibition of their homogeneity with other propositions already recognized.*

1. It may seem strange that here the confessional documents of the Evangelical Church, collectively, are, as it were, given a prior place to the New Testament Scriptures themselves. But this

must not by any means be taken as establishing a precedence for
these documents. That, indeed, would contradict the documents
themselves, since they always appeal to Scripture. Thus the
appeal to them in fact always implies indirectly an appeal to
Scripture. But the appeal to Scripture can directly prove only
that a proposition which has been set up is Christian, while its
distinctively Protestant content is not decided upon, except in the
few cases where it can be shown that the Catholic Church has
sanctioned an opposite use of the same passages of Scripture. Thus
for the Protestant content there remain only the other two kinds
of proof ; and, of these, the first place is assured to the proof from
the confessional documents, in virtue of the general demand made
upon Dogmatics to set forth doctrine prevalent in the Church. For
these documents are plainly the first common possession of Protestantism ; and just as all Protestant communities grew together
into the Church primarily through attachment to these, so every
system of doctrine which desires to pass as Protestant must strive
to attach itself to this history. Indeed, this holds of its original and
distinctive elements as much as of its common elements, only that
for the former, it is naturally enough to have an indirect demonstration that its propositions are compatible with the Symbols.
Thus the direct appeal to Scripture is only necessary either when
the use which the confessional documents make of the New Testament books cannot be approved of (and we must at least admit the
possibility that in individual cases all the testimonies adduced,
even if not falsely applied, may nevertheless be unsatisfying, since
other passages of Scripture must be applied as means of proof), or
when propositions of the confessional documents do not themselves
seem sufficiently scriptural or Protestant, and these must accordingly be superannuated and other expressions substituted, which
will then certainly the more easily find acceptance, the more it is
shown that Scripture on the whole favours them or even perhaps
demands them. Therefore this method of always going back in
the first instance to the confessional documents affords at the same
time the advantage, that the ecclesiastical status of any proposition
thereby at once becomes clear, and consequently the significance of
the whole presentation for the further development of the system
of doctrine is much more easily perceived.

From this it follows that, if we look at individual cases, the
proving of a proposition by exhibiting its relation to other propositions already proved in another way is a merely subordinate

matter, and only suitable to propositions of second rank, which neither appear directly in the Symbols nor are represented in any definite way in Scripture. But, on the other hand, when this reference is added at each point to that original method of proof, it does properly illuminate for the first time the suitability both of the arrangement of the system of doctrine and of the terminology which prevails in it.

2. Now, as we here class together all confessional documents of the Evangelical Church, in both its main branches, as of equal right, there is for us no single one which could have proceeded from the whole Church or even have been recognized by it. And so the distinction between the greater and more universal authority of some, and the more doubtful and scantier authority of others, vanishes as of no significance at all. Indeed, since in the confessional documents, at least of the second stage, Reformed modes of presentation are directed against Lutheran, and *vice versa*, it must be admitted at the outset that only that part of the confessional documents in which they all agree can be really essential to Protestantism ; and indeed that, through this conflict between the different particular confessional documents, the right of holding different views on all non-essential points has itself, as it were, received symbolic recognition for the whole Evangelical Church. Further, it is unquestionable that in a certain sense all our Symbols, though some more than others, are merely occasional documents, in which therefore the precise mode of statement of many points depends upon time and place ; and we have no reason to suppose that the authors themselves would offer the selected expression as the only perfectly right one. And here is another related point : the authors themselves (certainly quite in accordance with their then convictions, but nevertheless too precipitately for the character of a confessional document, since they were still engaged in inquiry) repudiated views then held to be heretical, and, in all points which had not yet become definitely controversial, testified to their agreement with the then prevalent doctrine. That sentence of condemnation may have fallen on many a divergence which had proceeded from the same spirit as the Reformation itself, because this spirit had not learnt to recognize itself promptly. And similarly many an older doctrinal view might be taken over, simply because people failed to see at once how it conflicted with the essence of Protestantism. From this it follows that, in going back to the Symbols, if we are to avoid making that procedure a

hindrance to the further development of doctrine, we must, in the first place, rather have regard to the spirit than cling to the letter, and, in the second place, we must apply the exegetical art to the letter itself, in order to make a right use of it.

3. Our proposition mentions only the New Testament Scriptures, not the Bible in general. We have already to some extent prepared the reader for this in what we said above about the relation of Christianity to Judaism.[1] But, further, everyone must admit that if a doctrine had neither direct nor indirect attestation in the New Testament, but only in the Old, no one could have much confidence in regarding it as a genuinely Christian doctrine ; whereas if a doctrine is attested by the New Testament, no one will object to it, because there is nothing about it in the Old. Hence the Old Testament appears simply a superfluous authority for Dogmatics. Now it is indeed true that even New Testament passages can demonstrate no more than that a proposition or doctrine is Christian. But, nevertheless, this is a thoroughly Protestant mode of procedure, in the case of every dogmatic proposition to go back to Scripture itself, and to human claims only in so far as they are attested by Scripture, but in this use of Scripture to allow everyone the free application of the exegetical art, as based on linguistic science. Naturally, however, the use made of Scripture varies itself a great deal, according to the differing character of the propositions. When the original trend towards purification of the Church is uppermost, the agreement must be so exact that Scripture can be used polemically against the assertions of the Roman Church. When it is rather the distinctive character of Protestantism that is concerned, it is enough to show that this more particularized form of doctrine is embraced within what Scripture says, without having to show that this particular form is the only scriptural one. And, similarly, all that the original and peculiar element in the presentation can with certainty venture to assert is, that it contains nothing demonstrably contrary to Scripture ; the common element, on the other hand, must definitely attach itself to Scripture.

But this must not by any means be understood to mean that the Biblical vocabulary should itself be adopted in the system of doctrine. For since the New Testament is but partially didactic in form, and is nowhere properly systematic, a mode of expression which there is perfectly suitable would in most cases only very

[1] See § 12, 2 and 3.

imperfectly answer the demands which are made of a system of doctrine. And, further, the didactic parts of Scripture are for the most part occasional discourses and writings, and therefore full of special references which in a dogmatic presentation must simply cause confusion. Hence our task cannot be anything like perfectly discharged by the adducing of some passages of Scripture under each proposition. This procedure has actually become hurtful in many ways, to Dogmatics on the one hand, and to Scriptural exegesis on the other. The relating of particular passages of Scripture to particular dogmatic propositions can therefore only be done in-directly, by showing that the former are based on the same religious emotions which are set forth in the latter, and that the differences of expression are only such as are occasioned by the different con-nexions in which they appear. But since this can only be done by explaining these connexions, there ought to be developed more and more in this branch of study a large-viewed use of Scripture, not stressing individual passages torn out of their context, but only taking account of larger sections, and these particularly fruitful ones, so as to exhibit in the trains of thought of the sacred writers those same combinations on which the dogmatic results also are based. Such an application of Scripture can, however, only be made allusively in the system of doctrine itself, and its success depends entirely upon agreement in hermeneutic principles and methods. Therefore, on this side, Dogmatics can only reach its con-summation simultaneously with the theory of Scriptural exegesis.

4. Thus there is room for great variety on this side too, so that Protestant systems of doctrine may be of very different stamp without losing their ecclesiastical character. When in a Dogmatic the appeal to the confessional documents and to analogy falls very much into the background, while the reference to Scripture pre-dominates throughout, we have what I should call, for the most part, a *Scriptural Dogmatic*. In such a Dogmatic, the arrangement will be the thing of least importance ; but it will be a perfectly ecclesi-astical arrangement, except where (say) the recognizedly common Protestant element is sacrificed to what is merely local and tem-porary in Scripture, or even to an eccentric interpretation of Scripture, or where it gives up the dialectical development of the ideas and goes back to the often indefinite and ambiguous language of the Bible. On the other hand, I should give the name of *Scientific Dogmatic* preferably to a Dogmatic which, starting from some recognized principal points, would make everything clear by its

orderly sequence, the parallelism of its members, and the coherence of its individual propositions, in which case citation from Scripture and application of the Symbols, of course, falls automatically into the background. Only, of course, those principal points must be none other than the fundamental facts of the religious self-consciousness conceived in a Protestant spirit. For if they were speculations, the system of doctrine might indeed be very scientific, but it would not be Christian doctrine. Finally, if a Dogmatic attaches itself principally to the confessional documents alone, and contents itself with proving everything from these and making everything dependent on these, without either going back to Scripture in details or linking up everything more closely by strict arrangement, this would be a *Symbolical Dogmatic* ; and in such we cannot fail to see a certain approximation to the Roman Catholic Church, since it lays the whole stress on every detail being recognized by the Church. But so long as it does not, on the one hand, set up the principle that Scriptural exegesis is subject to authority, and does not, on the other hand, ascribe to its own propositions a value independent of their expressing the inner experience of each individual, its Protestant character is not endangered. Since, however, each of these forms exposes itself the more to its own peculiar danger, the more it steers clear of the others, it would certainly seem that the common aim of all must be to diverge from each other as little as possible.

Postscript.—Our proposition is completely silent as to the very general custom of appealing in dogmatic systems to the dicta of other teachers, from the Church Fathers down to the most recent ; and this certainly means declaring such a procedure to be non-essential. Nevertheless, these citations may have a value, though not always the same value. In so far as what is established in our confessional documents passes over into a system of doctrine, citation of later theologians cannot increase the conviction of the ecclesiastical character of the propositions ; and it has a value only in compendiums, for the purpose of referring the reader to the most outstanding of later developments. Even ancient Patristic citations can in this case be of use only in an apologetical or polemical connexion as against the Roman Church. But it is different in cases of divergence, whether only in terminology or in content as well, from the symbolical documents. For the more a proposition has made itself heard from different quarters, the more claim has it to present itself as current in the Church. In particular, when a system of doctrine belongs definitely to one of the three above-mentioned forms, it becomes the more complete the more closely it connects itself with systems which bear equally strongly the stamp of one of the other forms.

§ 28. *The dialectical character of the language and the systematic arrangement give Dogmatics the scientific form which is essential to it.*

NOTE.—Cf. § 13, *Postscript*; § 16, § 18.

1. The term ' dialectical ' is here taken in exactly the ancient sense. The dialectical character of the language therefore consists simply in its being formed in a technically correct manner, that it may be used in all intercourse for the communication and correction of the knowledge in question. Now this cannot be said of either the poetic or the rhetorical form of expression, nor even of the descriptively didactic, which, having sprung from the other two, has not become quite separate from them. Thus the expressions amid which the system of doctrine moves, form (inasmuch as they go back to the religious feeling) a special realm of language within the didactically religious, *i.e.* the strictest region of it. The questions of how religious feeling becomes diversified, and what object it refers to, encroach upon the ground of Psychology, Ethics, and Metaphysics ; and the proper language of Dogmatics is distinguished more definitely from the didactically religious in general by its affinity to the scientific terminology of those realms : a terminology which is as sedulously avoided in the homiletical and poetical communication of the religious consciousness as it is eagerly sought after in the dogmatic. Hence the great diversity of views and of their expressions in all these philosophical realms makes the suitable management of language in dogmatic presentation a most difficult problem. However, the only views which are primarily unfit for use in dogmatic language are those which make no separation between the conceptions of God and the World, admit no contrast between good and evil, and thus make no definite distinction in man between the spiritual and the sensible. For these distinctions are the original presuppositions of the religious self-consciousness, because without these the self-consciousness, when widened into a world-consciousness, could not be set in antithesis to the God-consciousness,[1] nor could one speak of a distinction between a free and an inhibited higher self-consciousness, nor, consequently, of redemption and the need for it.[2] Now the more frequently philo-

[1] § 8, 2.   [2] § 11, 2.

sophical systems change within those limits, the more frequent also are the revolutions in dogmatic language. These revolutions are indeed inevitable only when a system has become antiquated, *i.e.* when thinking really no longer conforms to its type. But they often take place earlier through the more intense zeal of theologians who have been caught away by a rising system, and who hope that the new system will be better fitted than any previous one to make an end of all divisions and misunderstandings in the realm of Dogmatics. Others again, by the spectacle of that very zeal, are made apprehensive lest one particular philosophical system should set itself up as lord and judge in theological matters. But the apprehension is, as a rule, as unfounded as the hope. The hope is illusory, because the important misunderstandings are always there before the expressions used upon the controversial points take on a strictly dogmatic complexion, and consequently the change resulting from the influence of another system does not in itself touch the origin of the misconceptions, unless the language should thereby gain a higher degree of clearness and definiteness. And it is the same with the apprehension referred to. For, in the first place, a system never, at least in our day, continues to have sole supremacy for a sufficiently long time. And secondly, as a general consideration, so long as it is really an interest in Christian piety that evokes the dogmatic presentation, this latter can never turn against that interest : such a danger can only arise when the whole procedure has not sprung from that interest, but is alien in type. Apart from this, there are two other opposite complaints which one sometimes hears made concerning the language used by theologians, as regards its connexion with philosophy. The more frequent complaint is that the language is too abstract and too far removed from the immediate language of religion, for the sake of which alone Dogmatics exists. The other one is less frequent—that one cannot tell from the language used which philosophical system the theologian assumes as his starting-point. Both complaints appear to be unfounded. For in our Church it is only the scientifically educated who can be expected to take their bearings from Dogmatics for the realm of popular religious teaching, and the key for this they are bound to have. And as regards the other complaint, for this purpose it is neither necessary nor profitable to know which philosophical system a theologian adheres to, so long as his language is correct and self-consistently formed. In all sciences the Schools always more or less discard their own language for the universal language of educated people, and yet the language of the Schools does always tend to keep itself distinct. Now the more a theologian keeps to the strictest language of the Schools, the more readily will he give occasion for the first complaint ; and for the second, the more use he makes of the elements which have been adopted into the universal language of humanity. In this latter, indeed, there remain for long enough elements collected from different periods and systems. But even out of these, by means of skilful selection and due explanation, there can be formed a whole which is perfectly well adapted for dogmatic usage. And thus the danger of an influence hurtful to the interests of Christian piety completely disappears, and a balance is maintained amid the influences of various contemporary systems.

2. If, however, Dogmatics is to fulfil its proper vocation, *i.e.* both to clear up the misconceptions which ever and again tend to arise in the whole business of making communications from the immediate religious life of the Christian, and also, so far as in it lies, to prevent such misconceptions by the norm it has established, not only is a dialectically formed vocabulary indispensable in the establishing of the system of doctrine, but also as strict and systematic an arrangement of the subject-matter as possible. For the more indefinite and more imperfectly formed material offered by every fragmentary opinion can only be rightly appraised by comparison with the perfectly definite and ordered material of the self-contained system, and only so can it be rectified. For even the most definite idea and the clearest proposition do not lose every trace of instability until they have been placed in an absolute context, for the simple reason that the sense of any proposition is not fully given except in some definite context. But this is the very essence of systematic arrangement, that by comprehensive co-ordination and exhaustive subordination each proposition should be brought into a perfectly definite relation with all others. Now a dogmatic system of doctrine is capable of this in so far as the subject treated of forms a self-contained whole, *i.e.*, on the one hand, in so far as all Christian religious emotions of the Protestant type, wherever they appear, can be represented in a complex of coherent formulæ, and, on the other hand, in so far as it is true that facts of consciousness which can be subsumed under these formulæ are not to be found anywhere outside of this communion. Now in this sense the Evangelical (Protestant) Church, it is true, is not so perfectly self-contained that there might not be doctrines which

the Roman Church expresses in exactly the same way, or that, on the other hand, its doctrines might not for the most part be also found in other anti-Roman communions which do not form a single whole with the Evangelical Church.   But this latter contingency is due simply to the fact that outward unity does not depend solely on doctrine.   As far as doctrine is concerned, those small communions do for us really form a single whole with the Evangelical Church.   And the former case disappears when we come to regard the propositions, not by themselves alone, but in their context ; and thus at suitable points an Evangelical Dogmatic may legitimately set itself to dispel that impression.   In Dogmatics, however, the arrangement of material can have no resemblance to that employed in those sciences which are built upon some fundamental principle or can be developed from within themselves, or in those either which comprise a definite field of external perception and in this sense are historical.   Instead of a fundamental law, Dogmatics has simply the fundamental inner fact of Christian piety which it postulates ; and what it has to arrange consists simply in the different modifications of this fact which emerge, according to its differing relations with the other facts of consciousness.[1]   Thus the task of arrangement consists simply in so comparing and so distinguishing those different relations that the different modifications themselves appear as a complete whole, and that consequently, by means of the formulæ all taken together, the infinite multiplicity of the particular can be synoptically viewed in a definite plurality. But the dialectical language and the systematic arrangement require one another, and also they promote one another.   The dialectical language is too sharply defined for any other kind of religious communication, and outside of the complete doctrinal system itself it is permissible only in passages which are extensions of or outflows from the latter.   But a systematic arrangement would never stand out so clearly, and still less could it win recognition, if it did not make use of language which admits of a strict calculus-like procedure for the trying and testing of all connexions of ideas.   But it is self-evident how very much the task of systematic arrangement is facilitated when the particulars are given in dialectical language of uniform consistency, and also how the most precise expression for the particular is more easily found when a schematism of sharp distinctions and close connexions has already been fashioned for that purpose.

[1] § 10, 3.

3. After all we have already said on this point, it seems superfluous now expressly to remark or to demonstrate that there is no other connexion than that which we have exhibited between Christian Dogmatics and speculative philosophy ; especially since, in a treatment of the subject developed on the lines we have described above, there scarcely remains any point at which speculation could force its way into the system of doctrine. Our method indeed would seem to be the one that will most easily get rid of all traces of the Scholastic mode of treatment, by which philosophy (transformed as it was by the spread of Christianity) and real Christian Dogmatics were frequently mingled in one and the same work. There is only one point remaining for discussion here. Those members of the Christian communion through whose agency alone the scientific form of Dogmatics arises and subsists are also those in whom the speculative consciousness has awakened. Now as this is the highest objective function of the human spirit, while the religious self-consciousness is the highest subjective function, a conflict between the two would touch essential human nature, and so such a conflict can never be anything but a misunderstanding. Now it is certainly not sufficient merely that such a conflict should not arise : the man of knowledge is bound to reach the positive consciousness that the two are in agreement ; only, this is not the work of Dogmatics, since even for the same religious standpoint the procedure would necessarily vary with every different type of philosophy. If, on the other hand, such a conflict does arise, and some one rightly or wrongly finds the occasion of misunderstanding to be on the religious side, that circumstance may of course lead to his giving up religion altogether, or at least the Christian religion. But to guard against this, otherwise than by taking care not to occasion misunderstandings by unconsidered formulæ—that again is not the business of Dogmatics, which has nothing whatever to do with those who do not admit the fundamental fact. It is rather the business of Apologetics.

Postscript.—Those expositions of Christian doctrine which have long flourished under the name of Practical Dogmatics or Popular Dogmatics do indeed dispense both with dialectical language and with systematic arrangement. But these lie outside of the realm to which we here appropriate the name of Dogmatics. They are sometimes compromises between a system of doctrine and a catechism, and sometimes adaptations of Dogmatics to homiletical ends. The former have for the most part the aim of communicating the results of dogmatic developments with a certain coherence to those who would not find it easy to follow a scientific argument. But as that aim is itself somewhat arbitrary, the undertaking seems to lead to too much confusion and to foster too great superficiality for anything really useful to be achieved. As for the latter kind, its place will be completely filled if in Practical Theology the needful general directions are added concerning the matter of religious communications as well as concerning the form.

§ 29. *We shall exhaust the whole compass of Christian doctrine if we consider the facts of the religious self-consciousness, first, as they are presupposed by the antithesis expressed in the concept of redemption, and secondly, as they are determined by that antithesis.*

NOTE.—Cf. §§ 8, 9, and 11.

1. It is clear, to begin with, that the antithesis between the inability to inform all moments of life with the feeling of absolute dependence and the corresponding ability communicated to us by the Redeemer, presupposes that feeling itself and a knowledge of it. For since it is never presented to us except in man, we cannot know about it except in so far as it exists in ourselves ; and without knowing about it we could not know about an incapacity for it, nor even about the difference between the Redeemer and ourselves. Thus the state which precedes the communication of the capacity cannot be either absolute forgetfulness of God or a mere empty striving after the God-consciousness, but must somehow contain this last as a datum in the self-consciousness. It might, however, be said that such facts of the religious self-consciousness, which precede fellowship with the Redeemer, cannot belong to the system of *Christian* doctrine, but only to some general system of doctrine, or to the system of some religious communion from which one could pass to Christianity. To this we must reply that these states of the religious mind do not disappear when the mind has been laid hold of by Christianity, but are facilitated and encouraged in proportion as the communicated capacity is less or more. Thus they belong to the religious consciousness of the Christian too, and they might have been described as states not determined by that antithesis but remaining unchanged on all its different levels ; while the facts which are determined by the antithesis itself must differ in their content according as the incapacity or the communicated capacity has the preponderance. Only, the former kind of facts,

remaining as they do ever self-identical, will never by themselves
alone occupy completely any moment of the religious life in the
realm of Christian piety, but only partially ; and it is for that
reason, and because none the less we have to consider these facts
in themselves, on account of their different nature, that the mode
of expression used in our proposition has been preferred.

2. If, then, this first element in our proposition does thus belong
to Christian piety, because it necessarily appears in combination
with the second, we further venture to assert that the two taken
together enclose the whole realm of Christian piety.   For even if
we assume that by degrees the incapacity disappears completely,
this will not give rise to any new modifications of the religious self-
consciousness, but will simply bring the reality nearer to the formulæ
which express the condition in its purity.   And so our only concern
is to measure out the provinces of the two elements precisely and
completely, that we may be sure of the completeness of the whole.
The two will, then, of course, be so related to each other that the
first part will contain those doctrines (the possibility in general of
which has already been admitted) in which the distinctively
Christian element is less prominent, and which may therefore most
easily be coincident in expression with those of other faiths.   These
doctrines, however, are by no means constituent parts of a universal
or so-called natural theology.   Not only are they in every case
expressions of the religious self-consciousness, and thus genuinely
dogmatic propositions, but they are also definitely Christian, in
virtue of the distinctively Christian reference which is inherent in
the arrangement of the whole, and which we might repeat in every
proposition.   But apart from this, it certainly could be said—
especially as all that belongs to the realm of the Science of Christian
Morals remains excluded—that there are dogmatic propositions
which only express monotheism in general, without making it clear
whether they belong to the teleological or the æsthetic point of
view.   Therefore it is necessary that, if general allusions to the
Science of Christian Morals are not given in Dogmatics, we should
nevertheless always keep in mind the fact that to a system of
Christian doctrine, of whatever form, there essentially belongs also
a system of Christian morals developing in harmony with it.

3. These two, then, may be identified with each other : facts
which are presupposed by the antithesis, and facts which remain
unchanged throughout the whole development of the antithesis ;
and we have further asserted that these, together with the facts

which are determined by the antithesis, comprise the whole of Christian doctrine. Now from this it follows that, strictly considered, nothing which belongs exclusively to a period preceding the Christian development of that antithesis, and also nothing which belongs to a period which will only begin when the incapacity has been completely overcome and has disappeared, can be brought within the compass of Christian doctrine in the proper sense. No matter can be thus introduced except in so far as it has a demonstrable and definite connexion with the religious affections which are found within the antithesis. Now since all Christian piety rests upon the appearing of the Redeemer, the same thing is true of Him too, namely, that nothing concerning Him can be set up as real doctrine unless it is connected with His redeeming causality and can be traced to the original impression made by His existence. Whatever falls outside these limits either must have its proper place elsewhere or can make good its position only in virtue of some more distant relationship to be demonstrated in a special way.

§ 30. *All propositions which the system of Christian doctrine has to establish can be regarded either as descriptions of human states, or as conceptions of divine attributes and modes of action, or as utterances regarding the constitution of the world; and all three forms have always subsisted alongside of each other.*

1. Since the feeling of absolute dependence, even in the realm of redemption, only puts in an appearance, *i.e.* becomes a real self-consciousness in time, in so far as it is aroused by another determination of the self-consciousness and unites itself therewith,[1] every formula for that feeling is a formula for a definite state of mind; and consequently all propositions of Dogmatics must be capable of being set up as such formulæ. But any such sensible determination of the self-consciousness points back to a determinant outside of the self-consciousness. Now since, in virtue of the general coherence always postulated in every human consciousness, this determinant always appears as a part thereof, any modification which has so arisen of the feeling of absolute dependence may be known if we can get a description of that element of existence on which the state in question is based. Thus conceived, the dogmatic propositions become utterances regarding the constitution of the world, but only for the feeling of absolute dependence and with

[1] Cf. § 5.

reference to it. Finally, not only is the feeling of absolute dependence in itself a co-existence of God in the self-consciousness, but the
totality of being from which, according to the position of the subject,
all determinations of the self-consciousness proceed, is comprehended under that feeling of dependence ; and therefore all modifications of the higher self-consciousness may also be represented
by our describing God as the basis of this togetherness of being in
its various distributions.

2. If we compare these three possible forms with each other,
it is clear that descriptions of human states of mind with this
content can only be taken from the realm of inner experience,
and that therefore in this form nothing alien can creep into the
system of Christian doctrine ; whereas, of course, utterances regarding
the constitution of the world may belong to natural science, and
conceptions of divine modes of action may be purely metaphysical ;
in which case both are engendered on the soil of science, and so
belong to the objective consciousness and its conditions, and are
independent of the inner experience and the facts of the higher
self-consciousness. Thus these two forms (the first of which includes, of course, all propositions of a generally anthropological
content) do not in themselves afford any guarantee that all propositions so conceived are genuinely dogmatic. Hence we must
declare the description of human states of mind to be the fundamental dogmatic form ; while propositions of the second and third
forms are permissible only in so far as they can be developed out
of propositions of the first form ; for only on this condition can
they be really authenticated as expressions of religious emotions.

3. If, then, all propositions which belong to the system of
Christian doctrine can indisputably be expressed in the fundamental form, and propositions which assert attributes of God and
qualities of the world must be reduced to propositions of that
first form before we can be safe from the creeping in of alien and
purely scientific propositions, then it would seem that Christian
Dogmatics has only to carry through consistently that fundamental
form in order to complete the analysis of Christian piety, while the
other two forms might be entirely set aside as superfluous. But if
anyone were to attempt at the present time to treat Christian
Dogmatics in this way, his work would be left isolated without
any historical support ; and not only would it lack a really ecclesiastical character, but, however perfectly it rendered the content
of Christian doctrine, it could not fulfil the real purpose of all

Dogmatics. For since dogmatic language only came to be formed gradually out of the language which was current in the public communication of religion, the rhetorical and hymnic elements in this latter must have been especially favourable to the formation of conceptions of divine attributes, and indeed these became necessary in order that those expressions should be kept within due proportions. Similarly there arose, partly out of these, and partly out of the need for fixing the relation between the Kingdom of God and the world, utterances regarding the constitution of the world. Then, as the habit increased of treating Metaphysics in combination with Dogmatics, these two kinds of proposition became more numerous through the addition of similar ones of alien content, whereas the fundamental form naturally came to be left behind, and scarcely found any place except in presentations of a less scientific character. Hence a work which at the present time tried to confine itself entirely to the proper fundamental form would have no link with the past, and just for that reason would be of little practical use, either for purging the doctrinal system of alien elements, or for maintaining the clarity and verity of the rhetorical and poetic communications.

§ 31. *Thus the division outlined above will have to be fully worked out according to all these three forms of reflection upon the religious affections ; but always and everywhere on this same basis, namely, the direct description of the religious affections themselves.*

1. As the elements of Dogmatics have taken shape in a fragmentary manner, and the science itself has therefore been fitted together externally out of these elements rather than generated organically, it is easy to understand how, generally speaking, propositions of all three kinds have been placed together without distinction, while none of the forms has been worked out with completeness and perspicuity. But such a state of affairs by no means satisfies the demands which may justly be made of dogmatic science ; and in place of that we must of necessity (since, as we have seen, we cannot confine ourselves to the fundamental form alone) introduce that completeness of treatment which our proposition indicates. Nothing else can satisfy the present need. Now the general description of the Christian religion given above [1] underlies this whole presentation so fundamentally that even our

[1] See § 11.

division of the subject-matter rests upon it. And so each individual section will have to be prefaced by a similar general description, to which in turn the further articulation of that section will have reference ; and with this the ecclesiastical doctrines belonging to the same province will be brought into connexion : first, those which come nearest to the direct exposition of the religious affections, and then those which express the same thing in the form of divine attributes and qualities of the world.

2. From this it follows that the doctrine of God, as set forth in the totality of the divine attributes, can only be completed simultaneously with the whole system : whereas it is usually treated continuously and without a break, and before any other points of doctrine. But this divergence from the usual order can hardly be viewed as a disadvantage. For, not to mention the fact that divine attributes and modes of action which bear exclusively on the development of human soul-states (and this can be said of all the so-called moral attributes of God) cannot be understood without previous knowledge of these states, it is in general undeniable that the usual arrangement is peculiarly apt to conceal the relation of those doctrines both to the feeling of absolute dependence in general and to the fundamental facts of the Christian religion, and to give the impression of a quite independent speculative theory. Whereas our method not only makes that connexion most luminous, but also places in closer juxtaposition things which can only be understood alongside of and by means of each other.

Postscript.—Further comparison of the schematism here set forth with those more common in our older and newer textbooks and systems would exceed the limits of an Introduction which is not obliged to be polemical. The method here adopted can only be justified by the finished argument itself.

FIRST PART OF
THE SYSTEM OF DOCTRINE

FIRST PART

The Development of that Religious Self-Consciousness which is always both presupposed by and contained in every Christian Religious Affection.

INTRODUCTION

§ 32. *The immediate feeling of absolute dependence is presupposed and actually contained in every religious and Christian self-consciousness as the only way in which, in general, our own being and the infinite Being of God can be one in self-consciousness.*

1. The fact that the whole Christian religious consciousness is here presupposed is entirely legitimate, for here we abstract entirely from the specific content of the particular Christian experiences, and what we have stated is in no way affected by these differences. Hence nothing can be deduced from the above proposition either for or against any dogmatic formulation of such specific content. But if anyone should maintain that there might be Christian religious experiences in which the Being of God was not involved in such a manner, *i.e.* experiences which contained absolutely no consciousness of God, our proposition would certainly exclude him from the domain of that Christian belief which we are going to describe. Our proposition appeals, therefore, against such a person to the religious self-consciousness as it appears and is recognized everywhere in the Evangelical (Protestant) Church: that is, we assert that in every religious affection, however much its special contents may predominate, the God-consciousness must be present and cannot be neutralized by anything else, so that there can be no relation to Christ which does not contain also a relation to God. At the same time, we also assert that this God-consciousness, as it is here described, does not constitute by itself alone an actual moment in religious experience, but always in connexion with other particular determinations; so that this God-consciousness maintains its identity through its particular moments in all mani-

festations of Christian piety, just as in life generally the self-consciousness of an individual does in the different moments of his existence.   Hence the view that in every Christian affection there must be a relation to Christ does not in the least contradict our proposition.   Much more is this the case when the pious feeling comes to expression as an actual moment in the form of pleasure or pain.   For the Christian faith, however, the incapacity implied in religious pain must be ascribed to lack of fellowship with the Redeemer, while, on the other hand, the ease in evoking pious feeling which goes along with religious pleasure is regarded as a possession which comes to us from this fellowship.   Thus it is evident that, within the Christian communion, there can be no religious experience which does not involve a relation to Christ.

2. It is possible to give a non-religious explanation of this sense of absolute dependence ; it might be said that it only means the dependence of finite particulars on the whole and on the system of all finite things, and that what is implied and made the centre of reference is not God but the world.   But we can only regard this explanation as a misunderstanding.   For we recognize in our self-consciousness an awareness of the world, but it is different from the awareness of God in the same self-consciousness.   For the world, if we assume it to be a unity, is nevertheless in itself a divided and disjointed unity which is at the same time the totality of all contrasts and differences and of all the resulting manifold determinations, of which every man is one, partaking in all the contrasts. To be one with the world in self-consciousness is nothing else than being conscious that we are a living part of this whole ; and this cannot possibly be a consciousness of absolute dependence ; the more so that all living parts stand in reciprocal interaction with each other.   This oneness with the whole in each several part is essentially twofold : a feeling of dependence, indeed, so far as the other parts act spontaneously upon it, but also a feeling of freedom in so far as it likewise reacts spontaneously on the other parts. The one is not to be separated from the other.

The feeling of absolute dependence, accordingly, is not to be explained as an awareness of the world's existence, but only as an awareness of the existence of God, as the absolute undivided unity. For neither is there in relation to God an immediate feeling of freedom, nor can the feeling of dependence in relation to Him be such that a feeling of freedom can be its counterpart.   On the contrary, at the highest point of Christian devotion and with the clearest

consciousness of the most unimpeded self-activity, the absolute-
ness of the feeling of dependence remains undiminished. This
is what is indicated by the statement that the realization of oneself
as absolutely dependent is the only way in which God and the ego
can co-exist in self-consciousness. If we abolish this distinction
and mistake the self-consciousness which refers to God as referring
only to the world, then we must dispute in the latter the reality of
this feeling of freedom and, indeed, consequently entirely reject
it, since there is no moment in self-consciousness in which we do
not think of ourselves as one with the world. This non-religious
explanation, which casts aside what we hold to be the characteristic
of the religious consciousness as a deception, comes sometimes from
those who explain all feeling of freedom as illusion and sometimes
even from those who, maintaining that there is nothing upon which
we could feel ourselves absolutely dependent, reject all distinction
between the ideas of God and the world.

3. It is obvious that, as we are no longer moving outside the
province of Christian piety, we do not here concern ourselves with
the only partially developed and differentiated religious feeling
which constitutes polytheistic types of belief ; the Christian feeling
can only exist side by side with monotheism. On the other hand,
it may be objected that the foregoing statement is not pertinent
to our subject, because it is not so much peculiarly Christian as
characteristic of monotheism in general. The answer is that there
is no purely monotheistic piety in which the God-consciousness
alone and by itself forms the content of religious experiences.
Just as there is always present in Christian piety a relation to
Christ in conjunction with the God-consciousness,[1] so in Judaism
there is always a relation to the Lawgiver, and in Mohammedanism
to the revelation given through the Prophet. In our Holy Scriptures for this reason God is constantly referred to by the name of
the Father of our Lord Jesus Christ. The saying of Christ also
(John 14[7-9]) implies that every relation to Christ includes also the
God-consciousness.

§ 33. *This feeling of absolute dependence, in which our self-conscious-*
　　　ness in general represents the finitude of our being (cf. § 8, 2),
　　　is therefore not an accidental element, or a thing which varies
　　　from person to person, but is a universal element of life ; and
　　　the recognition of this fact entirely takes the place, for the

[1] Quare in omni cogitatione de Deo et omni invocatione mentes intueantur
Christum, etc. Melanchthon, *Loc. de Deo.*

system of doctrine, of all the so-called proofs of the existence of God.

Melanchth., *loc. de Deo* : Esse Deum et praecipere obedientiam juxta discrimen honestorum et turpium impressum humanis mentibus.—Zwingl., *d. ver. et fals. rel.*, p. 9. Fucus ergo est et falsa religio, quicquid a Theologis ex philosophia, quid sit Deus, allatum est.—Clem., *Strom.* vii. p. 864, πίστις μὲν οὖν ἐνδιάθετόν τί ἐστιν ἀγαθὸν, καὶ ἄνευ τοῦ ζητεῖν τὸν θεὸν ὁμολογοῦσα τοῦτον εἶναι καὶ δοξάζουσα ὡς ὄντα· ὅθεν χρὴ ἀπὸ ταύτης ἀναγόμενον τῆς πίστεως, καὶ αὐξηθέντα ἐν αὐτῇ χάριτι θεοῦ τὴν περὶ αὐτοῦ κομίσασθαι ὡς οἷόν τέ ἐστι γνῶσιν.

1. One cannot concede the postulated self-consciousness with the content we have already described, and yet maintain that it is something unessential, *i.e.* that it may or may not be present in a man's life according to whether, in the course of his life, he meets with this or that experience. For its emergence does not depend at all upon the fact that something definite and objective is given in the experience of a partially developed subject, but only on the fact that in some way or other the sensory consciousness has been stimulated from without. But what is presupposed on the subjective side is only that which is common to all—the intelligence in its subjective function, in which the disposition towards God-consciousness is a constituent element.

That the feeling of absolute dependence as such is the same in all, and not different in different persons, follows from the fact that it does not rest upon any particular modification of human nature but upon the absolutely general nature of man, which contains in itself the potentiality of all those differences by which the particular content of the individual personality is determined.

Further, if a difference is admitted between perfection and imperfection as measured by greater or less development, this arises from the fact that the emergence of this feeling depends upon a contrast having been apprehended in consciousness ; the lack of development is simply the lack of differentiation of functions. For when the objective consciousness and self-consciousness are not yet clearly differentiated in such a way as nevertheless to be distinctly connected together, in that case the consciousness as a whole has not yet become genuinely human. And if sensuous self-consciousness and the higher self-consciousness are not thus differentiated from one another and related to one another, development is incomplete.

2. We may conclude then that godlessness within the Christian community has its cause simply in defective or arrested development. Should it occur however in spite of a complete development,

we can only regard this as illusion and appearance. It is nevertheless possible to distinguish in the main three types of godlessness.

The first is the childish complete lack of God-consciousness,
which as a rule disappears in the course of the natural development
of the individual, and only in exceptional cases degenerates into
brutal godlessness in such as bitterly resist their own wider
development. Both things are to be met with outside the Christian
community for the most part among peoples that innocently or
voluntarily remain on the lowest grade of development. The
existence of this type, however, is hardly to be proved historically.

The second type of godlessness is the sensual. This occurs
when a feeling of absolute dependence actually appears, but intimately associated with awareness of that on which there can be
no absolute dependence ; since what is conceived as capable of
passion can give no absolute dependence, for it implies the possibility of self-initiated activity upon it. Face to face with this
contradiction, it may be doubted whether the disposition towards
God-consciousness has really been operative, the appearance merely
being obscured by perverted reflexion, or whether the inner reflexion
corresponds to the original, inner fact, so that the latter does not
really belong to the province of piety. But a comparison of the
way in which in childhood the God-consciousness at first manifests
itself shows that here certainly the disposition to God-consciousness
is already effective ; it is only on account of the imperfect development of self-consciousness that the process cannot fully be carried
to its conclusion. This condition is obviously akin to Polytheism,[1]
for the same germ of multiplicity is there also, only it is restrained
by opposing influences ; further, this anthropomorphic conception
is sometimes of a more pure and spiritual kind and sometimes verges
on Fetichism.

Finally, the third type of godlessness is the so-called definite
denial of God—Atheism, which is propounded as a speculative
theory in the midst of a Christian society, in a condition of full
development and even in the highest stage of culture. This again
is twofold. In part it is a wicked fear of the sternness of the
God-consciousness, and hence, though moments of enlightenment
intervene, clearly a product of licentiousness and thus a sickness of
the soul usually accompanied by contempt of everything intellectual ; and of this (godlessness) it can be said that it is naught,
because it entirely lacks inner truth. And in part it is simply a

[1] § 8, 2.

reasoned opposition to the current and more or less inadequate representations of the religious consciousness. Moreover, the atheism of the eighteenth century was, for the most part, a struggle against the petrified, anthropomorphic presentations of doctrine, a struggle provoked by the tyranny of the Church. But when, over and above the defects of representation, the inner facts of self-consciousness themselves are thus wholly misconstrued, this serious misunderstanding is none the less merely a disease of the understanding which may revive sporadically and from time to time, but never produces anything that is historically permanent. This fact cannot therefore be pled against our assertion that the feeling of absolute dependence, as here expounded, and the God-consciousness contained in it are a fundamental moment of human life.

3. But even supposing its universality could be disputed, still no obligation would arise for the system of doctrine to prove the existence of God ; that would be an entirely superfluous task. For since in the Christian Church the God-consciousness should be developed in youth, proofs, even if youth were capable of understanding them, could only produce an objective consciousness, which is not the aim here, nor would it in any way generate piety. We are not concerned here with the question whether there are such proofs, and whether, if we have no immediate certitude of God, then that of which we do have immediate certitude, and by which God could be proved, must not itself be God. Our point simply is that these proofs can never be a component part of the system of doctrine ; for that is only for those who have the inner certainty of God, as we have already described it, and of that they can be directly conscious at every moment. On our interpretation of Christian doctrine it would be quite unnecessary to enlarge on this point did it not seem essential to protest against the general custom of furnishing Dogmatics at this point with such proofs, or at least of referring to them as already familiar from other sciences. It is obvious that for the purpose of Dogmatics this reference is quite useless : for neither in catechetical nor in homiletical nor in missionary work can such proofs be of any value. Experience, too, shows how little can be accomplished by such a polemic against theoretical atheism as above described. Dogmatics must therefore presuppose intuitive certainty or faith ; and thus, as far as the God-consciousness in general is concerned, what it has to do is not to effect its recognition but to explicate its content. That such proofs are not the concern of Dogmatics is obvious also from

the fact that it is impossible to give them dogmatic form ; for we cannot go back to Scripture and symbolical books, since they themselves do not prove, but simply assert. Moreover, he for whom such assertion is authoritative needs no further proof.

The prevalent method of inflating Christian doctrine with rational proofs and criticism had its origin in the confusion of Dogmatics and philosophy in old Patristic times.[1] Closely related to this, and therefore to be named here, is the equally erroneous view that Christian theology, to which Dogmatics also belongs, is differentiated from Christian religion by its sources of knowledge. Religion, for instance, it is argued, draws from Scripture only, but theology draws also from the Fathers, reason and philosophy. But as theology itself draws from Scripture, and the Scriptures themselves have arisen out of the Christian religion, what originates in reason and philosophy cannot be Christian theology. It is certainly a great gain here, and elsewhere, to banish all material of this kind from the Christian system of doctrine, for only thus is a uniformity of method to be established. Such a difficult choice as that between moral proofs, geometrical proofs, and probable proofs [2] is not a task for any dogmatic theologian to take up, even if it be only for his own personal satisfaction.

Postscript.—Though it lies outside our present scheme we may remark here that there can be a precisely similar awareness of God in the objective consciousness, an awareness which in itself does not take the form of a temporal consciousness, but which in a like manner can be aroused and brought into existence through sense-perception ; and in fact all scientific construction, whether in the sphere of nature or of history, is based upon it. But just as it could only injure science to employ expressions belonging to the religious consciousness or to mingle with science anything belonging to that sphere, so it can only be harmful to faith and the system of doctrine to intersperse them with scientific propositions or to make them dependent on scientific foundations. For the system of doctrine has as little to do immediately with the objective consciousness as pure science with the subjective.

§ 34. *The feeling of absolute dependence is contained in every Christian religious affection, in proportion as in the latter,*

---

[1] Augustin., *d. ver. rel.* 8: Sic enim creditur et docetur, quod est humanae salutis caput, non aliam esse philosophiam, id est sapientiae studium, et aliam religionem.

[2] Reinhard's *Dogmatik*, § 7 and § 30.

through its co-determining stimuli, we become conscious that
we are placed in a universal nature-system, i.e. in propor-
tion as we are conscious of ourselves as part of the world.

1. To be conscious of oneself as part of the world is the same thing as to find oneself placed in a universal nature-system. In every actual self-consciousness there is either an awareness of a relation of our being to some object opposed to it or the comprehension at one and the same time of a being and a having. That which is set in opposition to us must naturally decrease as our self-consciousness .widens. Whether we widen it to the self-consciousness of the human race or are simply aware of ourselves as finite spirit, in either case there is nothing set over against us except what the spirit does not possess. The expansion takes place only in virtue of a partial identity (between subject and object), and hence in virtue of a system of nature ; thus in every such process we discover ourselves to be in a nature-system of spiritual being.

But though in our self-consciousness we constantly distinguish the system of relations from the spirit in ourselves, nevertheless the system is seated in the spirit as its original possession, original just because there is a system of nature. It exists in our self-consciousness always as influenced by being other than itself and thus as co-existent with such being in the system of nature. This system, however, is not posited as having limits ; hence it contains within itself all finite being, only in undeveloped form. If we extend our self-consciousness to that of the human species, then the whole earth co-posited with its external relations is equally undeveloped, partly as that which is possessed by us and partly as that which stands over against us. But that which stands over against us is only in self-consciousness so far as it affects us, and consequently exists along with us in a nature-system ; and thus also the whole system of nature or the world exists in our self-consciousness in so far as we recognize ourselves to be a part of the world. But this must be the case in every Christian and religious emotion because it is (at each moment) accompanied by the sensuous self-consciousness. Even if we were known to ourselves only as presentational activity (*vorstellende Thätigkeit*)—that is to say, as being centres for ideas—even so the self-consciousness is a centre for truth ; and that implies a relation of being in the self-consciousness, corresponding to the relation of ideas in the objective consciousness.

It is true, one frequently encounters the view that the more prominent the system of nature is in self-consciousness, the more the feeling of absolute dependence recedes; and that, on the other hand, the latter is most in evidence when something is posited which abrogates the systematic connexion of nature, *i.e.* something miraculous. This we can only regard as an error. The real fact is that we most abrogate the systematic connexion of nature when we posit either a dead mechanism or chance and arbitrariness; and in both cases the God-consciousness recedes—a clear proof that it does not exist in inverse proportion to our consciousness of the relatedness of nature. But the miraculous obviously presupposes the system of nature : for universal chance excludes everything miraculous. If, then, the miraculous really aroused the God-consciousness in a special degree, we should have to find the cause in the fact that many people only become aware of the rule through the exception. But this view in itself would justify the conclusion that this universal God-consciousness emerges more strongly and frequently in the religious experience of the Roman Church than in ours : because its adherents, properly speaking, are all immersed in the miraculous and may expect it at any moment. The proportion in which the God-consciousness appears is in fact the reverse of this.

Our proposition can be verified also in detail. The daily revolution of the atmospheric changes frequently appears to us as a mechanism; on the other hand, it is pre-eminently the abode of the seemingly contingent; whereas the periodical renewing of life's functions gives us the most vivid feeling of nature, but obviously the God-consciousness is more clearly posited in the latter than in the former.

3. Moreover, no Christian religious emotion can be imagined in experiencing which we do not find ourselves placed in a nature-system. Whatever the emotion may express, and whether it issue in action or in speculation, we must always be conscious of ourselves in this manner, and this consciousness must also be united to the God-consciousness; because otherwise the moment would be at one and the same time religious and non-religious. The only thing to which we ought still to call attention is that this element of our pious moments, so far as their content is concerned, is the same at each stage of Christian development. It will certainly occur more frequently when a soul in fellowship with Christ has already attained a very marked facility in the development of the

God-consciousness ; and will occur very little in one whom the sensuous impulse sways so quickly from moment to moment that such a development can rarely follow. The content, however, is always the same, for it does not at all depend on any definite relation or condition, but the individual regards his absolute dependence as exactly the same as that of every other finite being.

All we have to do in the first part of our exposition is, to the best of our ability, to describe this religious feeling of nature in general, apart from the specifically Christian content which is always attached to it.

§ 35. *According to the criterion of the three forms established in § 30 we shall have to treat, first, the relation present in the religious self-consciousness between the finite being of the world and the infinite Being of God ; then, in the second section, the attributes of God in relation to the world as they appear in that self-consciousness ; and lastly, in the third section, the constitution of the world as therein conceived in virtue of its absolute dependence on God.*

1. Considered as finite being and hence as representing all finite being, this consciousness of the absolute dependence of the self as an inward permanent datum which can be made apparent at any moment, is a state of our heart or soul (*Gemüthszustand*) : so that the first part of our proposition entirely corresponds with what we expect of the dogmatic basal form. In it must be expressed the relation of the world (regarded as absolutely dependent on God) and God (regarded as the Being on Whom the world absolutely depends), and if the propositions still to be established keep within these limits it cannot be said that they go outside the real province of Dogmatics.

2. But that danger certainly does exist in the other two forms. For these do not immediately reflect the religious self-consciousness, in which are given only the antithesis and the relation of the antithetic entities to each other ; but since the one makes God the subject of its thesis, and the other the world, great discrimination must be used lest either of them should express concerning their subject anything in excess of the immediate content of that self-consciousness.

The second dogmatic form, which treats of the divine attributes, is based proximately on the poetical and theoretical expressions which occur in hymns and sermons. Since it does not sufficiently conform these expressions to dialectical usage, it may easily be led into saying something about the Infinite Being which would contradict the antithesis contained in self-consciousness and represent the Infinite Being as dependent on the finite, while in fact the latter was posited as absolutely dependent on the Infinite. Those expressions would then not correspond to the religious self-consciousness which they ought to set forth.

From another point of view the third form needs careful thought. For here the world is made the subject of dogmatic propositions ; and for various reasons—partly on account of the customary confusion between speculative thought and dogmatic, and partly because those who are ignorant of science like to borrow from it those general conceptions which they think desirable and which make clearer their own higher self-consciousness—for such reasons it can easily occur that, through weak compliance with these mistaken demands, objective statements should find their way into catechetical and homiletic utterances, and that these again should pass, in a slightly different form, into Dogmatics.

3. If, then, the statements of these two latter forms have gone beyond the sphere of Dogmatics, and if in practice they have come to predominate, it is only too natural that statements of the first form should be more and more assimilated to them, and in this manner should partake of errors which by themselves they would have escaped. How far this has occurred up to the present time in the development of Dogmatics the following argument will show.

FIRST SECTION

A Description of our Religious Self-Consciousness in so far as the Relation between the World and God is expressed in it.

INTRODUCTION

§ 36. *The original expression of this relation, i.e. that the world exists only in absolute dependence upon God, is divided in Church doctrine into the two propositions—that the world was created by God, and that God sustains the world.*

NOTE.—πιστεύω εἰς θεὸν παντοκράτορα is also the original simple expression of the Roman Symbol.—Docent . . . Deum . . . semper adorandum ut omnium Dominum ac regem summum in aevum regnantem ; ab eoque solo pendere omnia. *Conf. Bohem.*, Art. iii.—Omnia ipsum habere sub potestate et manu. *Catech. Genev.*

1. The proposition that the totality of finite being exists only in dependence upon the Infinite is the complete description of that basis of every religious feeling which is here to be set forth. We find ourselves always and only in a continuous existence ; our life is always moving along a course ; consequently just so far as we regard ourselves as finite being, apart from all other things, our self-consciousness can represent this being only in its continuity. And this in so complete a sense that (the feeling of absolute dependence being so universal an element in our self-consciousness) we may say that in whatever part of the whole or at whatever point of time we may be placed, in every full act of reflection we should recognize ourselves as thus involved in continuity, and should extend the same thought to the whole of finite being. The proposition that God sustains the world, considered in itself, is precisely similar. At least it only seems to have acquired another and lesser content because we have grown accustomed to think of preservation and creation together, and thus a beginning is excluded from the range of the idea of preservation. On the other hand, the proposition, ' God has created,' considered in itself, lays down absolute dependence, but only for the beginning, with the exclusion of development ;

142

and whether the creation is conceived as taking place once for all or in the manner of one part after another, it lays down something which is not immediately given in our self-consciousness. Thus this proposition appears to belong to Dogmatics only so far as creation is complementary to the idea of preservation, with a view of reaching again the idea of unconditional all-inclusive dependence.

2. Thus there is no sufficient reason for retaining this division instead of the original expression which is so natural. And there can have been no reason for bringing this distinction into Dogmatics originally except that it was already to be found in traditional religious teaching, and that both the suitability of such expressions and the right measure of their use could be better guarded and established if the distinction were also adopted in the system of doctrine. Thus it did not originally arise on purely dogmatic grounds ; and not only so, but it is not the outcome of any purely religious interest (which would find complete satisfaction in the simple expression) ; and thus, left to itself, the distinction between creation and preservation would fall into oblivion.

But for a human imagination only partially awakened, the beginning of all spatial and temporal existence is a subject which it cannot leave alone ; consequently the treatment of the question is older than the abstract scientific phase of speculation, and belongs to the period of mythology. The question is linked up for us with the Mosaic account of creation, but that by itself does not give it a religious or Christian character any more than other things in the Pentateuch which have been brought over in the same way from primitive and prehistoric times. Yet for a long time this representation had to submit to being used for purposes of speculation and of science as well, and, indeed, for the purpose of supporting opposing theories or even as their source.

§ 37. *As the Evangelical (Protestant) Church has adopted both doctrines, but has not in her confessional documents given to either of them any distinctive character, it behoves us so to treat them that, taken together, they will exhaust the meaning of the original expression.*

NOTE.—*Augsburg Conf.* i. : ' A Creator and Sustainer of all things— visible and invisible.'—*Ibid.* xix. : ' Almighty God has created the whole of Nature and sustains it, etc.'—*Conf. et expos. simpl.* iii. : Deum credimus . . . creatorem rerum omnium cum visibilium tum invisibilium . . . et omnia vivificantem et conservantem.'—*Conf. Gall.* vii.: Credimus Deum cooperantibus tribus personis—condidisse universa, non tantum coelum et terram omniaque

iis contenta, sed etiam invisibiles spiritus.—*Conf. Angl.* i. : Unus est Deus
. . . creator et conservator omnium tum visibilium tum invisibilium.—
Conf. Scot. i. : . . . unum Deum . . . per quem confitemur omnia in coelo
et in terra tam visibilia quam invisibilia creata in suo esse retineri, etc.—
Conf. Hung. : Confitemur Deum verum esse et unum auctorem et conser-
vatorem omnium.

1. These juxtapositions of creation and preservation are all
derived from the later additions made in the Roman creed to the
simple statement cited above,[1] and still further enlarged in the
Creed of Constantinople.[2] As nothing definite is here said about
the manner of creation, there is nothing on which to remark in this
distinction except the intention that nothing, no point of space and
no point of time, should be exempted from the Divine All-Sove-
reignty.   Further, the expressions relating to the Trinity are neither
peculiar to the Gallican Confession nor do they first appear in this
period ; the same expressions occur in the Augsburg Confession,
where the Trinity is said to be Creator and Preserver ; and they
originate in the creed *Quicunque vult*, where *omnipotens* and *dominus*
are predicated of the three Persons, which clearly means the same
thing.   Since the doctrine of the Trinity is neither presupposed
in every Christian religious experience nor contained in it, these
definitions do not belong to our present discussion.

But there is unmistakably a gradation in these expressions, so
that the original expression in the Roman symbol and the Gallican
Confession form the extremes.   While in the former there is no
separation, in the latter it is so complete that the doctrine of preservation is not treated at all in connexion with the creation, but is
merged later in the government of the world.   The Bohemian and
Scots Confessions are therefore nearest to the former, the Augsburg
and Swiss Confessions to the latter.   Moreover, all belong under our
formulation, though they do not all go back to the stimulated
religious self-consciousness as definitely as the expression in the
Bohemian Confession ; for they describe attributes of God as little as
attributes of the world, and concerning God state only ideas of relation
and operation.   For it is only by describing God as the sole original
activity that the relation of absolute dependence can be expressed.

2. From this situation it follows [3] that we of the Evangelical
Church not only have a very wide field for a more diversified exposition of this article of doctrine, but are also called upon to make use
of it.   For, by returning to the first source, we are free not only to

---

[1] εἰς θεὸν πατέρα παντοκράτορα ποιητὴν οὐρανοῦ καὶ γῆς.
[2] ὁρατῶν τε πάντων καὶ ἀοράτων.   [3] Cf. § 27, 2.

adhere more closely to the oldest and simplest expression, and develop it without any such distinction as far as the purpose of Dogmatics requires it, but also in the formulation of the distinction between the two topics in the Evangelical Church everything must rank as an opinion men are free to hold which, equally with the rather broad and vague statements of the different Confessions, can be traced back to the simple expression of primitive feeling. If we consider that the attention of the Reformers was not directed to this doctrine because of its remoteness from what at first was matter of dispute in the early days of our Church, then (especially as these doctrines are exposed to so many foreign influences, which ought to be resisted) it is our duty to inquire whether traces of such influences are not to be found in the credal formulas themselves. Even if that is not the case, it is our duty to discover whether they satisfy our present need and whether, perhaps, the further development of the evangelical spirit, and the many revolutions in the province of philosophy as well as of the natural sciences, do not necessitate other definitions ; in which case we need have no scruples in completely abandoning the credal expression.

3. Now in this respect the standard adopted for our treatment appears to be not only appropriate but adequate. For although the aim of Dogmatics does undoubtedly compel us to develop the simple expression to such a point that the language of popular religious teaching on this fundamental relation of the world to God can be regulated and guarded, it is clearly appropriate at the present time to consider the separation of Creation from Preservation. But the danger threatens us of losing ourselves on alien ground, and passing from the more peculiarly religious province into the speculative, and such a danger will be best averted if every individual proposition, no matter how we may have arrived at it, is constantly traced back to that simple expression which most truly interprets the immediate religious self-consciousness. But, if each of these doctrines completely coincided with that original expression, so that both ideas were contained in each later doctrine just as much as in the original one—the doctrine of Preservation in that of Creation and *vice versa*—then one or other doctrine would be superfluous. We should then have either to present the whole content of the fundamental feeling twice over, or else so to arrange the two that only when taken together did they make explicit the undeveloped content of the original expression. This latter method is evidently to be preferred.

§ 38. *The content of the original expression can be evolved out of either of the two doctrines, provided that in both of them, as in the original expression, God is regarded as the sole Determinant.*

Calvin, *Inst.* i. 16. 1 : In hoc praecipue nos a profanis hominibus differre convenit, ut non minus in perpetuo mundi statu quam in prima ejus origine praesentia divinae virtutis nobis eluceat.—Nemesius, *d. nat. hom.*, p. 164, Ed. Ant. : 'Ει γὰρ λέγοι τὶς, ὅτι κατὰ τὴν ἐξ ἀρχῆς γένεσιν εἱρμῷ προβαίνει τὸ πρᾶγμα, τοῦτο ἂν εἴη λέγων, ὅτι τῇ κτίσει συνυπάρχει πάντως ἡ πρόνοια. τὸ γὰρ εἱρμῷ προβαίνειν τὸ κτισθέν, δηλοῖ τῇ κτίσει συγκαταβεβλῆσθαι τὴν πρόνοιαν· καὶ οὕτως οὐδὲν ἂν ἄλλο λέγοι, ἢ τὸν αὐτὸν εἶναι ποιητὴν ἅμα καὶ προνοητὴν τῶν ὄντων.

1. If, with the statements of the Confessions, which uniformly speak of all things, not of an All, we refer the idea of creation primarily to particular things, what from this point of view we conceive of as their origin will really be simply the preservation of species, which is conditioned by the renewal or re-emergence of individual things.[1] Since the underlying self-consciousness here represents the whole of finite being, the concept of species suggests itself as naturally as that of the individual life, for in our self-consciousness we always posit ourselves as men ; and thus the statement that the re-emergent things exist through God, will correspond to the content of this self-consciousness just as adequately as the statement that individual things arise through God.

Now, with our increased knowledge of the world, we may indeed conceive the heavenly bodies and all the life developing upon them as particular things which have not all necessarily come into existence simultaneously ; yet their successive origination must obviously be also conceived as the active continuance of formative forces which must be resident in finite existence. And thus, however far our consciousness extends, we find nothing the origin of which cannot be brought under the concept of Preservation, so that the doctrine of Creation is completely absorbed in the doctrine of Preservation. In the same way, if we regard individual things as created, and follow this a step further, we find that the preservation of these same things is equivalent to that alternation of changes and movements in which their being perdures. But as these always form more or less coherent series, there is always something new implied either in the beginning of each series of activities or in the effects produced by a subject—something which was not formerly contained in that particular thing. This is, therefore, a new beginning and can be regarded as a creation, and the more properly

[1] So also Nemesius, p. 163 : πῶς οὖν ἕκαστον ἐκ τοῦ οἰκείου σπέρματος φύεται καὶ οὐκ ἐξ ἄλλου προνοίας ἀπούσης ;

so regarded the more such a beginning appears to be an important link in development : nevertheless ' more ' and ' less ' here do not give us ground for a definite distinction. But as every individual activity forms in itself a fresh series, and its beginning is a new origin, so, as far as our consciousness extends, all that we are accustomed to regard as object of the divine preservation falls under the conception of creation. Thus the concept of creation if taken in its whole range makes the concept of preservation superfluous, just as we have already seen happens inversely ; for what does not wholly fall under one of the two is not given for the other.

Popular religious teaching cannot be blamed for clinging to this freedom and regarding the same event alternatively as either new creation or preservation in accordance with natural law. And devotion will scarcely consent to recognize the precedence of either, as if the one more perfectly, or in a loftier style than the other, corresponded to the absolute feeling of dependence.

2. This equivalence, however, is certainly dependent on our conceiving of the divine origination on the one side, and the dependence of the finite being on the other as equally complete, whether we imagine a thing to be created by God or sustained by Him. If we think of the creation of the world as a single divine act and including the whole system of nature, then this conception may be a complete expression of the feeling of absolute dependence, so long as we do not conceive of that act as having ceased, and consequently imagine on the one side, in God, an alternation of activity and rest relatively to the world, and on the other side, in the world, an alternation between a determination of the whole through God and a determination of all single individuals through each other. In the same way if we regard Preservation as a continuous divine activity exerted on the whole course of the world, covering the first beginning no less than each subsequent state, then this is a complete expression of the self-consciousness in question, provided we do not think the origin of the world is conditioned by something else before and after that activity. For, otherwise, in every situation only some elements would be dependent on the divine activity, while the rest, though ever so small a part, would be conditioned by what had previously existed. And thus the divine activity, whose object should be the whole world, would be always mingled with passiveness.

The same results follow in another way if we conceive of the divine creative activity, not indeed as momentary, yet as recurring

only at particular points and certain times. For even though the
sustaining activity extended between these points so that divine
activity never alternated at any point with inactivity, yet creative
activity would then come in distinguishably from sustaining
activity, and each in limiting the other would exclude it ; and thus
the world would certainly remain entirely dependent on God but
irregularly, and on divine activities which mutually restrict each
other.   And the position is not altered if we think of the sustaining
activity as unmixed with passivity but suppose either that, following on a pure creative act, it has to overcome an opposition which
develops therefrom, or suppose that the creative activity enters
at individual points as another activity.   The tendency, however,
to such perverted formulas, which in no way express the pure feeling
of dependence but misrepresent it in every way, is nearly always
unmistakably present.   This naturally has its roots, not in Christian piety, but in a confused world-view which in ordinary life
is only too common—a view which only uses dependence on God
as an explanation of the course of the world where the causal nexus
is concealed, and thus makes use of it mostly where something
severed from what went before as well as separated from its context, appears either as a beginning or in isolation.

§ 39. *The doctrine of Creation is to be elucidated pre-eminently with
a view to the exclusion of every alien element, lest from the
way in which the question of Origin is answered elsewhere
anything steal into our province which stands in contradiction to the pure expression of the feeling of absolute dependence. But the doctrine of Preservation is pre-eminently
to be elucidated so as to bring out this fundamental feeling
itself in the fullest way.*

1. Our self-consciousness, in its universality, as both these
doctrines relate to it, can only represent finite being in general
so far as it is a continuous being ; for we only know ourselves in
this manner but have no consciousness of a beginning of being.
Hence as we have seen, though not impossible, it would be
extremely difficult to develop the same material principally or
exclusively under the form of the doctrine of Creation.   Such an
attempt would be just as arbitrary as it would be inappropriate
for the purpose of Dogmatics, in view of the fact that in popular
religious teaching the doctrine of Preservation has a far greater
importance.   In general the question of the origin of all finite

being is raised not in the interest of piety but in that of curiosity, hence it can only be answered by such means as curiosity offers. Piety can never show more than an indirect interest in it ; *i.e.* it recognizes no answer to it which brings the religious man into contradiction with his fundamental feeling. And this is the position given the doctrine, both when it occurs in the New Testament and in all regular Confessions of Faith. Whereas the Old Testament basis of it lies in the beginnings of a history-book which as such chiefly satisfies the desire for knowledge.

2. In the doctrine of Creation, then, we have pre-eminently to prevent anything alien from slipping in from the field of knowledge. But the opposite danger is also certainly to be kept in view, namely, the development of our self-consciousness must not be so conceived as to set the man who desires knowledge in contradiction with the principles of research he follows in the sphere of nature or of history. But as the self-consciousness we have here to consider itself implies that we are placed in a nature-system, any doctrine of Preservation which could immediately follow from this would find no motive in the working out of this self-consciousness for wishing to overthrow that assumption. And this mistake will be the less likely to occur if the treatment of the doctrine of Creation already specified has gone before.

3. If the immediate higher self-consciousness which is to be represented in both doctrines be one and the same, then the aim of Christian Dogmatics is twofold. On the one hand, to bring together the various presentations current within our Church in the different spheres of religious teaching, to show their true content, and to make them clear and coherent ; on the other hand, to set up safeguards in order to ensure that nothing should insinuate itself which—though in any given context the fact might not be noticed—might contradict what really belongs here. Both doctrines taken together will then exhaust the dogmatic presentation of the fundamental feeling of absolute dependence, if in the one we seek more particularly to secure the necessary precautions, and if in the other we have predominantly in view its positive development.

First Doctrine : Creation

§ 40. *The religious consciousness which is here our basis contradicts every representation of the origin of the world which excludes anything whatever from origination by God, or which places*

God under those conditions and antitheses which have arisen in and through the world.

Acts 17²⁴, Rom. 1¹⁹·²⁰, Heb. 11³.

1. The New Testament passages quoted above lead us to reject any more definite conception of the Creation. The expression ῥήματι is merely the negative of any closer definition, so as to exclude all idea of instrument or means. It is quite consistent with it and equally correct to say that the world itself, since it came into existence through the spoken word, is the word of God.[1] Thus we may be satisfied to put forward this negative character as a standard of criticism for that which has, as it seems to us, wrongly intruded itself as a more exact definition of this conception in Dogmatics. For as our immediate self-consciousness represents finite being only in the identity of origination and continuance, we find in that self-consciousness neither motive nor guidance for a treatment of origination taken by itself, and therefore we can take no particular interest in it.

The further elaboration of the doctrine of Creation in Dogmatics comes down to us from times when material even for natural science was taken from the Scriptures and when the elements of all higher knowledge lay hidden in Theology. Hence the complete separation of these two involves our handing over this subject to natural science, which, carrying its researches backward into time, may lead us back to the forces and masses that formed the world, or even further still. On this assumption we may patiently await the result, since every scientific endeavour which works with the ideas 'God' and 'world' must, without being dependent on Christian doctrine or becoming so, be limited by the very same determinations, if these two ideas are not to cease to be two.

2. As the New Testament passages give no material for a further development of the doctrine of Creation, and dogmaticians have always referred back to the Scriptures even when confusing their problem with that of philosophy, we must, in the first place, pass in review the Mosaic narrative and the Old Testament passages, which really in a sense are wholly dependent on it.

The Mosaic account was undeniably received by the Reformers as a genuinely historical narrative.[2] Luther's statements, how-

---

[1] 'What is the whole creation else than a word of God, said and spoken by God? . . . thus it is for God no harder to create than for us to speak.'—Luther in *Genesis*, i. § 51.

[2] Luther in *Genesis*, i. 3, § 43: 'Moses is writing a history and narrates things that happened.'—Calvin, *Instit.* i. 14. 3: Moses vulgi ruditati se accom-

ever, are chiefly directed against the allegorical interpretation, and
Calvin's view really excludes any use of the narrative for the
development of a genuine theory. It is an advantage in every
way that nothing on the subject has become a part of Confessions
of Faith, especially as (if we do not force ourselves to look upon
the second account in Genesis as a recapitulating continuation of
the first) the difference between the two is of such importance that
we can hardly attribute to them a genuine historical character.
If we further take into consideration that in the Old Testament
passages referring to the Creation sometimes the same simplicity
prevails as in the New Testament,[1] and that sometimes the Mosaic
statements, although made fundamental, are very freely handled : [2]
also that nowhere is a purely didactic use made of this account, and
that Philo, who absolutely rejects the ' six days ' in the literal
sense, must certainly have had predecessors who did the same—
in view of all this we may conclude pretty certainly that in that
age the literal interpretation was never universally prevalent, but
that there always survived a somewhat obscure but healthy feeling
that the old record must not be treated as historical in our sense of
the word. We have therefore no reason to maintain a stricter
historical interpretation than the Hebrews themselves did in their
best days.

Supposing, however, we were right in assuming that the Mosaic
description was an historical account communicated in an extraordinary way, it would only follow that in this way we had attained
to a scientific insight we could not otherwise have acquired. But
the particular pieces of information would never be articles of faith
in our sense of the phrase, for our feeling of absolute dependence
does not gain thereby either a new content, a new form, or clearer
definition. That is why it cannot be the task of Dogmatics to give
an explanatory commentary or a criticism of such comments.

3. As regards the stated definitions themselves, it is quite clear
that our feeling of absolute dependence could not refer to the
universal condition of all finite being if anything in it (*i.e.* that
being) were independent of God or ever had been. It is just as
certain that if there could be anything in the whole of finite existence
as such which entered into it at its origin independently of God,
then because it must exist in us too, the feeling of absolute depend-

modans non alia Dei opera commemorat in historia creationis, nisi quae oculis
nostris occurrunt.
[1] Isa. 45[18], Jer. 10[12].   [2] Ps. 33[6-9], Ps. 104, Job 33[4f.]

ence could have no truth even in relation to ourselves. But if, on the other hand, we think of God the Creator in any way as limited, and thus in His activity resembling that which should be absolutely dependent on Him, then the feeling expressing this dependence likewise could not be true (since equality and dependence neutralize each other), and thus the finite in that it resembled God could not be absolutely dependent upon Him. But except in one of these two forms, a contradiction between any theory of creation and the universal basis of our religious self-consciousness is not conceivable. With the Christian form of religious self-consciousness, which presupposes an experience, the doctrine of mere creation cannot be in contradiction, because it disregards continuity. Christian piety can, then, have no other interest in these researches than to avoid both these dangers. Whether this is easy, or if in avoiding one we only too easily fall into the other, must be seen from a closer consideration of the corollaries accepted by Dogmatics.

§ 41. *If the conception of Creation is to be further developed, the origin of the world must, indeed, be traced entirely to the divine activity, but not in such a way that this activity is thought of as resembling human activity ; and the origin of the world must be represented as the event in time which conditions all change, but not so as to make the divine activity itself a temporal activity.*

Conf. Belg. xii. : Credimus Patrem per verbum hoc est filium suum coelum et terram ceterasque creaturas omnes quandoque ipsi visum fuit, ex nihilo creasse.—Joh. Dam., *d. orth. f.* ii. 5: . . . ἐκ τοῦ μὴ ὄντος εἰς τὸ εἶναι παραγαγὼν τὰ σύμπαντα.—Luther on *Genesis*, ii. 2, § 7 : ' And God is in short outside all means and circumstances of time.'—*Ibid.* : ' Everything which God has willed to create He created at that moment when He spake, though certainly everything does not at once appear before our eyes. . . . I am indeed something new . . . but . . . for God I have been born and preserved even from the beginning of the world, and this word when He said, " Let us make man," created me as well.'—Hilar., *d. f. Tr.* xii. 40 : Nam etsi habeat dispensationem sui firmamenti solidatio—sed coeli terrae ceterorumque elementorum creatio ne levi saltem momento operationis discernitur.— Anselm, *Monol.* 9: Nullo namque pacto fieri potest aliquid rationabiliter ab aliquo, nisi in facientis ratione praecedat aliquod rei faciendae quasi exemplum, sive ut aptius dicitur forma . . . quare cum ea quae facta sunt, clarum sit nihil fuisse antequam fierent, quantum ad hoc quia non erant quod nunc sunt, nec erat ex quo fierent, non tamen nihil erant quantum ad rationem facientis. —Phot., *Bibl.*, p. 302, Bekk. : ὅτι ὁ Ὠριγένης ἔλεγε συναΐδιον εἶναι τῷ . . . θεῷ τὸ πᾶν. Ἐι γὰρ, ἔφασκε, οὐκ ἔστι δημιουργὸς ἄνευ δημιουργημάτων . . . οὐδὲ παντοκράτωρ ἄνευ τῶν κρατουμένων . . . ἀνάγκη ἐξ ἀρχῆς αὐτὰ ὑπὸ τοῦ θεοῦ γεγενῆσθαι.

καὶ μὴ εἶναι χρόνον, ὅτε οὐκ ἦν ταῦτα. εἰ γὰρ ἦν χρόνος, ὅτε οὐκ ἦν τὰ ποιήματα . . .
καὶ ἀλλοιοῦσθαι καὶ μεταβάλλειν τὸν ἄτρεπτον καὶ ἀναλλοίωτον συμβήσεται θεόν· εἰ γὰρ
ὕστερον πεποίηκε τὸ πᾶν, δῆλον ὅτι ἀπὸ τοῦ μὴ ποιεῖν εἰς τὸ ποιεῖν μετέβαλε.—Hilar.,
d. f. Tr. xii. 39: Cum enim praepararetur coelum aderat Deo. Numquid
coeli praeparatio Deo est temporalis ? ut repens cogitationis motus subito
in mentem tamquam antea torpidam . . . subrepserit, humanoque modo
fabricandi coeli impensam et instrumenta quaesierit ? . . . Quae enim
futura sunt, licet in eo quod creanda sunt adhuc fient, Deo tamen, cui in
creandis rebus nihil novum ac repens est, iam facta sunt : dum et temporum
dispensatio est ut creentur, et iam in divinae virtutis praesciente efficientia
sint creata.—Augustin., d. civ. D. xi. 4. 2 : Qui autem a Deo factum fatentur,
non tamen eum volunt temporis habere sed suae creationis initium, ut modo
quodam via intelligibili semper sit factus : dicunt quidem aliquid, etc.—
Ibid. xii. 15: Sed cum cogito cuius rei dominus semper fuerit, si semper
creatura non fuit, affirmare aliquid pertimesco.—Ibid. 17 : Una eademque
sempiterna et immutabili voluntate res, quas condidit, et ut prius non
essent egit, et ut posterius essent, quando esse coeperunt.—Ibid. xi. 6 :
Procul dubio non est mundus factus in tempore sed cum tempore.—Idem, de
Genes. c. Man. i. 2 : Non ergo possumus dicere fuisse aliquod tempus quando
Deus nondum aliquid fecerat.

1. The expression 'out of nothing' excludes the idea that
before the origin of the world anything existed outside God, which
as 'matter' could enter into the formation of the world. And
undoubtedly the admission of 'matter' as existing independently
of the divine activity would destroy the feeling of absolute dependence, and the actual world would be represented as a mixture
of that which existed through God and that which existed independently of God. But since this phrase undeniably recalls
Aristotle's category ἐξ οὗ and is formed on it, it reminds us on
the one hand of human methods in construction which give form
to an already existing matter, and on the other hand of the processes of nature in the composition of bodies out of many elements.
The expression is harmless if everything that is a part of the processes of nature is strictly separated from the first beginning of
things, and creation is thus raised above mere formation.

Yet from Hilary and Anselm we can see how easily, behind the
denial of matter, may lie the idea of the pre-existence of form
before things, though of course in God and not outside God. This
position, too, appears to be quite harmless in itself, but as the two
terms of the antithesis, matter and form, are not in the same
relation to God, He is drawn away from an attitude of neutrality
to the antithesis and placed in some degree under it. Hence the
existence of forms in God prior to the existence of things but already
related to it may naturally be called a 'preparation.' But in this
way the other rule is violated, and we must regard as valid Luther's

contention that if there are two divine activities which, like preparation and creation, can be conceived of only in a definite time-
sequence, then God is no longer outside all contact with time.
Anselm in his own way has expressed this time-relationship most
bluntly and frankly. Hilary would have done away with it, but
he only succeeded in eliminating it with regard to things now
happening separately in time and not in respect of the original
creation. For it cannot be said of the original creation that it was
created by the activity of foreknowledge prior to its actual existence.

Here it can only be remarked.in passing that the phrase ' out of
nothing ' is also used frequently to differentiate the creation of the
world from the generation of the Son.[1] If it were generally understood that the latter is eternal and the former temporal, or if we
could come to a general agreement as to the difference between
generation and creation, there would be no necessity to draw any
further distinction. But even so the expression is not essential for
this purpose, for even if we do not at all identify the ' Word ' and
the ' Son,' the phrase ' to be created through the " Word " ' [2]
sufficiently obviates any confusion of this kind ; even if the difference between creation and generation is not emphasized.

2. If, as suggested above, we strictly isolate the first creation,
so that all things not absolutely primitive are regarded as part of
the developing processes of nature and thus brought under the
conception of preservation, then the question whether the creation
occupied time, is answered in the negative. The distinction between
a first and second creation, or an indirect and direct creation,
always comes back in general to the evolving of the complex from
the simple [3] and of the organic from the elementary.[4] But to
acknowledge another creation here is either again entirely to
abolish the difference between creation and preservation or to
assume different kinds of matter devoid of inherent forces, which
is surely meaningless. But even if in the case of creation we think

[1] Fecisti enim coelum et terram non de te, nam esset aequale unigenito
tuo—et aliud praeter te non erat unde faceres ea, et ideo de nihilo fecisti
coelum et terram.—Augustin., *Conf.* xii. 7.

[2] ' All things are so made through God's word that they may more rightly
be said to be born than made or renewed, for no instrument or means comes in.'
—Luth., Th. v. p. 1102.

[3] Τῇ μὲν πρώτῃ ἡμέρᾳ ἐποίησεν ὁ θεὸς ὅσα ἐποίησεν ἐκ μὴ ὄντων. ταῖς δὲ ἄλλαις
οὐκ ἐκ μὴ ὄντων, ἀλλ' ἐξ ὧν ἐποίησε τῇ πρώτῃ ἡμέρᾳ μετέβαλεν ὡς ἠθέλησε.—Hippolyt.
in *Genesis*.

[4] Τὰ μὲν οὐκ ἐκ προϋποκειμένης ὕλης, οἷον οὐρανὸν (where οὐρανός is the Aristo-
telian fifth substance) γῆν ἀέρα πῦρ ὕδωρ· τὰ δὲ ἐκ τούτων, οἷον ζῷα φυτά, etc.—
Joh. Damasc. ii. 25.

first of matter (though we might equally well think of forces), then, from that point, living mobile being must have existed and undergone a continuous development. Otherwise the creation of bare matter would only have been a preparation, that is an external material corresponding to the previously mentioned inner formal one. We must refer these definitions back to a time when men delighted in such abstractions because there was then no question of a dynamic aspect of nature.

Another point with respect to the relation of the creation to time which does not lie in our purview is the question whether there was time before the world existed or whether time began with the world. If we take the world in its widest sense, we cannot admit the first, since a time before the world could only have referred to God, and He would then be placed in time. The *Confessio Belgica* with its ' quando ipsi visum fuit ' clearly falls into this error, and in opposition to it we must return to Augustine's formula.

Finally, the controversy over the temporal or eternal creation of the world (which can be resolved into the question whether it is possible or necessary to conceive of God as existing apart from created things) has no bearing on the content of the feeling of absolute dependence, and it is therefore a matter of indifference how it is decided. But in so far as the idea of a creation in time must be related to that of a beginning of divine activity *ad extra* or a beginning of divine sovereignty as Origen suggested, God would be brought within the region of change and subjected to time. Thus the antithesis between Him and finite beings would be lessened, and the purity of the feeling of absolute dependence endangered.

Augustine is hardly more satisfactory when, in order to avoid this position, he declares that a single act of the Divine Will is sufficient to account for the earlier non-existence and the later existence of the world. For if a similar action of the Divine Will is required to explain the prior non-existence of the world, then we must suppose that, apart from this Divine Will, the world would have come into existence earlier, and consequently that there was a possibility of its coming into existence independently of the Divine Will. But if we regard the one Divine Will as ineffectual prior to the existence of the world, neither preventing nor producing anything, then the transition from non-activity to activity remains, even though it be differently expressed as a transition from willing to doing ;[1] while, on the other hand, it is impossible to see how

[1] Addamus eum ab aeterno id voluisse. Quicquid enim vult, id voluit

the idea that God does not exist without something absolutely dependent on Him could weaken or confuse the religious self-consciousness. Just so the tracing of the Word through which God created the world (a subject not to be considered here) back to the Word which was with God from eternity, can never be made clearly intelligible [1] if there is not an eternal creation through the eternal Word.

Postscript.—We can also attach to this the definition that God created the world through a *free* decree. Now it is self-evident that He on Whom everything is absolutely dependent is absolutely free. But if we suppose that the free decision implies a prior deliberation followed by choice, or interpret freedom as meaning that God might equally well have not created the world (because we think that there must have been this possibility, otherwise God was compelled to create), we have then assumed an antithesis between freedom and necessity, and, by attributing this kind of freedom to God, have placed Him within the realm of contradictions.

FIRST APPENDIX. THE ANGELS

§ 42. *This conception is indigenous to the Old Testament and has passed over into the New. It contains in itself nothing impossible and does not conflict with the basis of the religious consciousness in general. But at the same time it never enters into the sphere of Christian doctrine proper. It can, therefore, continue to have its place in Christian language without laying on us the duty of arriving at any conclusion with regard to its truth.*

1. The narratives of Abraham, Lot, Jacob, of the call of Moses and Gideon and the prophecy of Samson, bear the stamp very clearly of what we are accustomed to call ' myth.' Indeed, in many of them God Himself and the Angels of the Lord are so interchanged that the whole can be thought of as a Theophany in which the appearance perceived by the senses need not be that of a being independent and different from God. In this indefinite form the idea is older than these narratives, perhaps even older than the narrated events. That they are not exclusively Hebraic in the narrower sense seems clear from many other traces, such as the history of Balaam. Poetical representations of many kinds in the Psalms

ab aeterno. Jam quod voluerat ab aeterno id aliquando tandem factum est. ' Thus He now worked and was active that the world should come into being.' —Morus, *Comment.*, t. i. § 292.
    [1] Cf. Luther, *W. A.*, i. pp. 23–28, and iii. pp. 36–40.

and the Prophets lead to the same conclusion ; anything can be called an angel that is a bearer of a divine message. So that sometimes definite individual beings are to be conceived under this term and sometimes not. Of the former we have scarcely any other explanation to give than that in general different peoples have imagined many kinds of spiritual beings in different forms because of a consciousness of the power of spirit over matter ; and the less this problem is solved the more that consciousness gives rise to a tendency to suppose there is more spirit than that manifested in the human race and different from that in the living animal, whose powers and mechanical instincts with their own power over matter, must themselves as matter be brought within our power.

Now we, to whom the majority of the heavenly bodies are known, satisfy this longing by the familiar supposition that most or all of these are filled with animated beings of varying grades. Previously there was no alternative but to people either the earth or the heavens with hidden and spiritual beings. The Jewish people seem to have decidedly adhered to the latter method, especially after the highest Being came to be thought of also as the King of the people, who therefore must have servants around Him to send as He chose to every part of His kingdom and to allow them to share in every branch of administration. This is certainly the most developed conception of the angels. Consequently we must distinguish them clearly from our conception of spiritual life developed on other planets according to their nature and in association with an organism, since the Biblical idea cannot be connected with this, but is something quite different.[1] We ought rather to think of them as spiritual beings, not belonging to any definite heavenly body, who could embody themselves temporarily, according to their tasks, in the manner in which they have appeared from time to time in our world. And obviously we know far too little of the interstellar spaces, as also of the possible relations between spirit and body, to deny outright the truth of such a notion. Indeed, if we regard the appearance of such beings as something miraculous, this is not so much because we must necessarily hold that such a temporary incursion of alien beings into the order of our lives would interrupt the course of nature, but much more because (in Christianity generally and also to a great extent in the Old Testament) their appearance is associated with special points of development and revelation. In the New Testament angels appear at the

[1] Cf. Reinh., *Dogm.*, § 50.

Annunciation of Christ and of His forerunner and at Christ's Birth in narratives of a more or less poetical character which lie outside the proper field of the Gospel tradition. This is true also in some measure of the strengthening angel in Gethsemane, with respect to whom at any rate no witness is quoted. In the case of the Resurrection and the Ascension, as well as the conversion of Cornelius and the liberation of Peter, it is possible to doubt whether angels or men are meant. In the account of Philip, the expressions ' angel of the Lord ' and ' spirit ' alternate as they do in the Old Testament. But after this angels disappear altogether even from the Apostolic history.

2. Everywhere, however, in our Holy Scriptures the angels are assumed ; but nowhere is anything taught respecting them. Apart from the usual prophetic and poetical language in descriptions of the Last Day,[1] Christ Himself refers to them only in His warning against despising little ones [2] and in connexion with Peter's useless defence of Him.[3] If we want to take this as definite teaching we must also put forward the doctrine that children (and perhaps every individual) have special angels, that the angels behold the face of God, and that they can be employed in legions.[4] The same applies to the Apostolic passages if we refer to angels all the obscure and ambiguous expressions about thrones and principalities.[5] Even in the Epistle to the Hebrews [6] the angels are not so much subjects of dogmatic teaching as mediums for such teaching. The writer maintains that Christ is more exalted than all the angels, as they are mentioned in the Old Testament, in the Prophets, and the Psalms ; to the angelic appearances in the New Testament there is no reference. Christ and the Apostles might have said all these things without having had any real conviction of the existence of such beings or any desire to communicate it, just as everyone adopts popular ideas and makes use of them in discussing other things, as, for example, we might talk of ghosts or fairies, although these ideas had no definite sort of relation to our actual convictions. We do not mean to suggest what is usually understood by ' accommodation,' which is often taken to mean adapting oneself to prevailing ideas whilst holding opposite convictions.

The Confessions of the Protestant Church have accepted these conceptions only incidentally, and the statements show clearly enough ·that they place no value on any teaching about angels.[7]

---

[1] Matt. 16²⁷ and 25³¹.   [2] Matt. 18¹⁰.   [3] Matt. 26⁵³.
[4] John 1⁵¹ is plainly figurative.   [5] Col. 1¹⁶.   [6] Heb. 1⁴ff..
[7] Apol. Conf. Art. ix.: Praeterea et hoc largimur quod angeli orent pro nobis.   Art. Smalc.: Etsi angeli in coelo pro nobis orent, etc.

This does not in the least mean that the Reformers were unfamiliar with the subject or doubted the literal truth of the angelic appearances in the Biblical narratives : their Church hymns prove the contrary, but in the sphere of piety they attached no great value to the matter.

§ 43. *The only tenet which can be established as a doctrine concerning angels is this : that the question whether the angels exist or not ought to have no influence upon our conduct, and that revelations of their existence are now no longer to be expected.*

1. It is not without considerable hesitation that the confidence of Christians in the protection of angels can be encouraged. For in the first place, that they avert the power of evil spirits [1] could hardly be told to any but children without detriment, because against all that is usually ascribed to the devil, we should use the spiritual armour recommended by the Bible, and not rely on angelic protection.[2] It is not less serious to teach an external protection through angels.[3] For we must teach that God has no need of angels for our protection, unless we assume a continual activity on the part of angels, and thus do away with the entire interdependence of nature. But it is said that it affords more consolation if God makes use of angels than if our preservation is effected by natural means, so that God, in view of our weakness, employs angels and then reveals the fact to us. On the one hand, this theory could not be carried through without very limited and almost childish conceptions of God, and on the other hand, it can only feed our vanity if we accept the idea that a whole species of higher beings exists only for our service. Wisely, therefore, in our Confessions— although strictly in opposition to the saints of the Roman Church— the intercessions of the angels have taken the place of their active influence. We cannot, however, take the Biblical passage on which this is founded as a convincing proof.[4]

That this conception is losing its influence among Christians follows naturally from the fact that it belongs to a time when our knowledge of the forces of nature was very limited, and our power over them at its lowest stage. In every such situation our reflections now instinctively take another direction, so that in active life we do not easily turn to angels. The argument of Luther [5]

---

[1] Luth., *Catech. Min.* : Tuus sanctus angelus sit mecum ne diabolus quidquam in me possit.
[2] Eph. 6[11ff.], 1 Pet. 5[8, 9].   [3] Cf. Calvin, *Instit.* i. xiv. 6–11.   [4] Zech. 1[12].
[5] In *Genesis*, ii. § 19 : ' The angels must be our protectors and guard us,

has, moreover, as regards the angels, tended to repress the levity so easily elicited by the supernatural. But the confidence he wishes to strengthen will be the same even if we do not think of the angels, but expect the divine protection in the usual way. Since the Church has itself declared against the veneration of angels, we can rightly say it would be the worst form of veneration if, in deference to their unknown service to us, we believed we might omit any of the care recommended us for ourselves and others.

2. But more closely considered, nothing can be concluded from all the angelic appearances of which we have knowledge, either for present or future times, partly because these appearances occurred in that primitive period when the interdependence of man with nature was not yet settled and he himself was undeveloped ; and, as even to many a philosopher at that time the notion of an education through higher beings was not unfamiliar, these warning and prophetic appearances might be an echo of that connexion of ideas. At a later time we find angels almost exclusively at great points of development when other wonderful events are wont to happen. Moreover, when the earlier teachers of the Church [1] assert that the intercourse between men and angels, which for so long a period had been interrupted, was only restored through Christ, this, too, must be understood in the same way, for this restoration did not extend beyond the Apostolic times.

Since they are so entirely outside our province, there is no reason for more accurate inquiry into the creation of angels either in itself or in relation to the Mosaic creation story, nor again into their general nature, manner of life, and activities.[2] On the contrary, for the actual province of Dogmatics the subject remains wholly problematic, and none but a private and liturgical use of this conception is to be recognized. The private use of the conception will always confine itself to visualizing the higher protection so far as that does not make use of conscious human activities. In the liturgical use the thought which has been specially in view is that God must be represented as surrounded by pure and innocent spirits.[3]

but only so far as we remain in our path. Christ points to this explanation when He confronts the devil with the command from Deut. 6[16]. For thereby He shows that man's appointed path is not to fly in the air. Hence, when we are in our calling or office and have a command from God or from the men who have the right to direct our calling, then we must believe that the protection of the dear angels cannot fail us.'

[1] Cf. Chrysost. on Col. 1[20].
[2] Cf. Reinhard, *Dogm.*, §§ 53, 54.   [3] Cf. Heb. 12[22].

SECOND APPENDIX : THE DEVIL

§ 44. *The idea of the Devil, as developed among us, is so unstable that we cannot expect anyone to be convinced of its truth ; but, besides, our Church has never made doctrinal use of the idea.*

1. The chief points in this idea are as follows : spiritual beings of a high degree of perfection, who lived in close relation with God, voluntarily changed from this state to a state of antagonism and rebellion against God.

Now we cannot ask anyone to accept this unless we are able to help him over a great number of difficulties. First, as to the so-called fall of the good angels : the more perfect these good angels are supposed to have been, the less possible it is to find any motive but those presupposing a fall already, *e.g.* arrogance and envy ; [1] furthermore, if after the Fall the natural powers of the devil remained undiminished,[2] it is impossible to conceive how persistent evil could exist side by side with superlative insight. For such insight must, in the first place, have shown every conflict with God to be an entirely useless undertaking. It can only be thought to afford a momentary satisfaction even to one lacking true understanding, whereas an intelligent being, to undertake such a conflict and persevere in it, must of necessity will to be and remain unblessed. Now in speaking of such a man we say he is ' possessed,' because no explanation of his attitude can be derived from the subject himself. Is it not, then, still more impossible to find an explanation in the more perfect condition of the angels— by whom would *they* be possessed ? Again, if the devil at the time of his fall lost the finest and the purest intelligence (and it is indeed the worst possible derangement to become the bitterest and most obdurate enemy of God after being His friend), then it is inconceivable, on the one hand, how through one error of the will the intelligence could be for ever lost, unless the error was already due to a lack of intelligence ; and on the other hand, how could the devil, after such a loss of intelligence, be so dangerous an enemy ? For nothing is easier than to contend with senseless wickedness. It is just as difficult to explain the relation of the fallen angels to other

---

[1] So rightly Luther (Hall. ed.), Th. i. p. 36. In Bernard, too, the idea is to be found that Lucifer perceived in God that man was to be raised above the angelic nature ; hence that *arrogant* spirit had *envied* man such blessedness, and thus had fallen. Such ideas have their own value. But I should not care to compel anyone to yield to them.

[2] Cf. Luther, *ibid.* pp. 261, 262.

angels. For if they were all alike, and in that case no special personal motive could be felt by one group, how is it to be explained that the one group sinned and the other did not ? It is certainly no less difficult if we assume that,[1] prior to the fall of one group, all the angels may have been in a partially unstable state of innocence, but that one group because of one deed have been for ever judged and condemned while the other group, because of their resistance, have been for ever confirmed and established, so that henceforth they cannot fall. Lastly, with regard to the condition of the fallen angels after the Fall, it is difficult to see how the two following ideas can be held consistently : The fallen angels, already oppressed by great ills and expecting still greater, at the same time out of hatred to God and to relieve their feeling of distress, engage in active opposition to God, while yet they are unable to effect anything except by God's will and permission,[2] and thus would find far greater alleviation for their distress as well as satisfaction for their hatred of God in absolute inactivity.

Finally, can the devil and his angels be thought of as a kingdom, and thus working unanimously although only outwardly and mostly in human affairs ? Now, with the limitations already outlined and generally acknowledged, such a kingdom is inconceivable unless the overlord is omniscient and therefore knows in advance what God will permit ; and besides not only does the evil in one man mostly hinder the same evil in another, but in each man one evil hinders another.

2. There are two ways, in particular, in which a doctrinal use might be made of this conception. The evil in man may be traced back to the prior evil in Satan and explained by it ; and the devil may be represented as active in the punishment of sin. Our Confessions, however, are too cautious to base anything concerning this doctrine on so hazardous an idea. As regards the former, they only group the devil with the wicked by making him their leader,[3] in which case the existence of evil in man is in no way explained by its existence in Satan, and the latter requires just as much elucidation as the former. In other passages, moreover, if evil is traced back to the temptation of Satan,[4] the purpose in some

---

[1] Cf. Luther, *ibid.* p. 202.

[2] Mosh., *Th. dogm.*, t. i. p. 417 sq. ; Calv., *Instit.* i. 14, 16.

[3] Aug., *Conf.* 19: Causa peccati est voluntas diaboli et malorum quae . . . avertit se a Deo.

[4] *Conf. Belg.* xiv.: verbis diaboli aurem praebens.—*Conf. Helv.* viii.: instinctu serpentis et sua culpa.—*Sol. decl.* i.: seductione Satanae iustitia concreata amissa est.

of them is less to provide an explanation than a modification of the opinion that the devil was instrumental in putting quite another creature in the place of the original man.   But, indeed, the fact that man allowed himself to be tempted presupposes aberration and evil, so that the explanation is seen to be no explanation at all. If, again, here and there the power and might of the devil is included under the punishment of sin, on the one hand we find that this does not have any special bearing on the deliverance of man from sin and its punishment, and we might as well speak simply of the influence of evil apart from a personal overlord of evil ; on the other hand, if the power of the devil (and his greatest power lies in tempting to sin) were the result of sin, then when he accomplished his greatest act of temptation he must have been powerless —which is plainly inconsistent.   Elsewhere, however, punishment too is represented as something that the devil and sinful men have in common.[1]   And again, the fairly frequent idea that the devil is the instrument of God in the punishment of the wicked, is inconsistent with his antagonism to the divine purpose.

§ 45. *In the New Testament Scriptures the Devil is, indeed, frequently mentioned, but neither Christ nor the Apostles set up a new doctrine concerning him, and still less do they associate the idea in any way with the plan of salvation ; hence the only thing we can establish on the subject for the system of Christian doctrine is this : whatever is said about the Devil is subject to the condition that belief in him must by no means be put forward as a condition of faith in God or in Christ. Furthermore, there can be no question of the Devil having any influence within the Kingdom of God.*

1. There is not a single passage in the New Testament where Christ or His Apostles definitely and indisputably refer to the devil with the intention either of teaching anything new or peculiarly their own, or of correcting and supplementing current beliefs.   They make use of the conception in its current popular form.   If, nevertheless, we wished to formulate a Christian doctrine of the devil we should be obliged to assume that this conception as known to Christ and His disciples corresponded perfectly with the truth and could not be improved.   This position must certainly be taken up by anyone who is unwilling to admit that Christ made use of what

---

[1] *Conf. Aug.* xvii. : impios autem homines et diabolos condemnabit ut sine fine crucientur.

we usually call accommodation. Such a complete development of the idea is the more improbable because its chief characteristics have no basis even in the Old Testament, their origin being wholly apocryphal. It is apparent from the incidental way in which the subject occurs that neither Christ nor His disciples desired either to give support to the idea or vouch for its truth. For Christ seems to introduce it for no particular reason into parables, maxims, and short instructions dealing with quite other subjects. In the parable of the Sower, the expressions [1] are of doubtful meaning, and the hostility of man to the divine message would be just as relevant as the hostility of the devil. If it were only a question of his relation to the human soul and his influence on it, then the uncertainty would be removed and we could draw up a doctrine about him. But, at best, he is represented as a quite unknown cause of rapid transitions from one state of feeling to another of an opposite kind. It is equally impossible to base a doctrine on the parable of the Tares in the Field. The Sower is like the Son of Man Who sows openly by teaching : and the Sower of Tares does the same, but by night, *i.e.* not openly. Thus here, too, we are brought to see the real meaning of the name ' the Slanderer.' The Apostles, at least, did not understand the parable to teach doctrinally that it was the devil who sowed tares in the field tilled by Christ ; for when speaking of false brethren and unworthy members of the community, they never quote the devil as the cause of the evil, but at most they deliver such men over to the devil. If we remember that ' his seed ' is explained as ' children of the evil one,' [2] we are reminded of an important passage [3] where Christ tells the hostile Jews that ' they are of their father the devil.' Obviously, according to the Hebrew idiom, these expressions are used only of the relations of likeness and affinity. Nobody can propose to take the expression literally, as if they could be descended from the devil in the same sense as they gloried in descending from Abraham, or in the sense in which Christ, Whose words they were mocking, had originally asserted that God was His Father. Thus we cannot take this passage literally and assume the real existence of the devil without either placing the devil on an equality with God, as the Manichæans did, or else applying the phrase ' Son of God ' to Christ merely in the wider sense in which the Jews could really be termed ' sons of the devil.' There is certainly here a reference to a story

---

[1] πονηρός in Matt. 13[19], διάβολος in Luke.
[2] υἱοὶ τοῦ πονηροῦ Matt. 13[38].   [3] John 8[44].

about the devil, but only as to something well known, and this description, like the other, only stands here as related to the central statement that ' they were not of God.' [1]

The expression that ' Satan had desired to have the disciples that he might sift them ' [2] bears the stamp of a proverb, and does not imply that the devil is to be regarded as the overlord of the wicked. The phrase, as a whole, is derived from Job, and in both passages Satan is pictured as bargaining with God. So that here what is being uttered is only a warning borrowed from a truly Biblical idea, and there is no intention either to teach anything with regard to Satan or to confirm that older belief.

The phrase ' to be overreached by Satan ' [3] is a similar proverbial expression. Here certainly it is used in connexion with the fact that one had been delivered over to Satan; but apart from this instance, it is applicable to any case in which something done from a good motive proves to be detrimental to the good. Only, we must not think here of Satan as simply bringing evil to light, but as the one who fights against good. The ' roaring lion ' of Peter [4] obviously hovers between these two meanings, for ' devouring,' points to the deadly enemy, but ' adversary ' to the accuser. So that these three passages should be taken together, supplementing each other perfectly and forming a useful adaptation of a varying Biblical tradition. If we compare the relevant passages, we shall find that the expression ' Prince of this world,' [5] used frequently by Christ, admits equally well of a different interpretation. At any rate, if Christ's disciples did refer this saying to the devil, he is passed over without any specifically Christian doctrine being opposed to the popular tradition. For some New Testament writings refer the ' binding of Satan ' to an earlier time, [6] and others, though admittedly of doubtful interpretation, assume a still continuing conflict with him. [7] Thus if Christ had intended to formulate a doctrine in the above-quoted passages He certainly would have failed in His intention.

The story of the Temptation is equally unsuited for the purpose. Even if we must accept it as literal fact (and there is much to be said against this), it does not give us material to construct a complete idea of the devil or to apply it in any further way. In the two

---

[1] John 8⁴⁷.   [2] Luke 22³¹.   [3] 2 Cor. 2¹¹.   [4] 1 Pet. 5⁸.

[5] John 12³¹ : ὁ ἄρχων τοῦ κόσμου τούτου ἐκβληθήσεται.—John 14³⁰ : ἔρχεται ὁ τοῦ κόσμου ἄρχων, καὶ οὐκ ἔχει ἐν ἐμοὶ οὐδέν.—John 16¹¹ : ὁ ἄρχων τοῦ κόσμου τούτου κέκριται.

[6] 2 Pet. 2⁴, Jude 6.   [7] 2 Cor. 12⁷, Eph. 6¹¹,¹².

passages where Christ is specially led to mention the devil,[1] the question is of so-called ' possession,' and therefore concerns the natural explanation of this phenomenon, which has nothing to do with faith. Though the first passage may be obscure, still it is closely connected with the casting out of demons. The same is true of the saying concerning the ' divided kingdom of Satan,' and the highly figurative representation of the return of an evicted spirit, which is a continuation of the same story, is not intended in any way to throw doubt on the certainty of salvation ; it bears on the same realm of phenomena as ' possession ' and indicates primarily the difference between the real and permanent healings of Christ and the merely apparent and transitory healings of the Jewish exorcists. In these cases and in others which may have happened without being recorded there was no occasion to examine critically the current ideas, nor is there any ground for regarding their use as indicating an intention to sanction them as divine teaching. If we consider that John in his Epistle [2] sees the relation between the devil and the sinner (doer of evil) exactly as Christ saw it in the above-quoted discussions with the Jews, we must give a similar explanation of the fact that John attributes the betrayal of Judas to the devil, as Christ never does. The few remaining Apostolic passages [3] cannot be used doctrinally any more than those already cited. For if Christ and the Apostles had ever desired to combine Christian piety with the fear of the devil, and, at the same time, had wished to establish a particular doctrine drawn from and corresponding to this element of the religious consciousness, they would have had to allow proper space for the idea when treating didactically of the origin and propagation of evil in mankind generally, when dealing with the manner in which sin remains in believers, and when discussing the necessity of redemption. It is just at this latter point that the question arises whether the Son of God was not necessary in some way because of the power the devil had over man. But of this there is not the slightest trace,[4] nor do we find any mention of the devil,[5] even when sin is being discussed, and we should most expect it. Such a complete silence in every essentially didactic passage ought to have been seriously considered.

[1] Luke 10[18], Matt. 12[43], Luke 11[24]   [2] 1 John 3[8]
[3] 2 Cor. 4[4] 11[14], 2 Thess. 2[9].
[4] The passage Heb. 2[14, 15] has little relevance here, for it is not said of the devil that he has power over men, but only over death, so that we must think here chiefly of the angel of death ; and men are not said to be in slavish fear of the devil but of death.
[5] Cf. Matt. 15[19], Rom. 5[12-19] 7[7ff.], Jas. 1[12]

2. But even if we could regard some or, indeed, all of the above-quoted passages of Scripture as referring to the devil, there is still no reason for our accepting this notion as a permanent element in Christian doctrine and defining it accordingly so accurately that everything attributed to the devil could be conceived as a consistent whole. For Christ and His disciples did not hold this idea as one derived from the sacred writings of the Old Testament, or in any way acquired through Divine revelation ; it was drawn from the common life of the period just as it is still present more or less in all our minds in spite of our utter ignorance as to the existence of such a being. Since that from which we are to be redeemed remains the same (as does also the manner of our redemption) whether there be a devil or no, the question as to his existence is not one for Christian Theology but for Cosmology, in the widest sense of that word. It is exactly similar to questions as to the nature of the firmament and the heavenly bodies. In Christian Dogmatics we have nothing either to affirm or deny on such subjects ; and similarly we are just as little concerned to dispute the conception of the devil as to establish it. The Biblical usage merely shows that among the Jewish people the idea was really a fusion of two or three quite different elements. The first element is that of the servant of God who, while searching out the evil, has his rank and function among the other angels and cannot be regarded as expelled from the presence of God. Another element is that of the original source of evil in Oriental dualism, the conception being modified in such a way that the Jews alone were able to assimilate it. Now this function to some extent suggests joy in evil, and thus easily enough through some such fictitious story as the apostasy, the former could become the latter, or rather the name of the former pass over to the latter. It was obviously from these two elements that the acute mind of Calvin composed his formulas,[1] though they will not harmonize in one consistent view.

The third element, the angel of death, though not quite so certain, is also a combination of native and foreign ideas ; this angel, too, can be represented as having his kingdom in the underworld. On the other hand, the spirits active in the possessed are always represented differently, and are only indirectly brought into connexion with the devil. The conception was probably developed

---

[1] *Instit.* i. 14, 17 : Quamvis voluntate et conatu semper Deo aversetur tamen nisi annuente et volente Deo nihil facere potest.—Legimus illum se sistere coram Deo nec pergere audere ad facinus, nisi impetrata facultate . . . 18, Deus illi fideles cruciandos tradit, impios gubernandos.

through the assimilation of these various elements ; but apart from this it has obtained a strong hold by reason of the manifold enigmas presented to introspection by sudden changes of feeling—so strong, indeed, that we might almost say that it suggests itself to nearly everyone who has not the gift for self-analysis of the more accurate kind. For all too frequently we find that evil emotions arise in us in a strange and abrupt manner, having no connexion with our ruling tendencies, but up to a certain point gaining strength irresistibly, so that we feel obliged to look upon them as not belonging to us but alien, while at the same time we are unable to indicate any external cause. And as good, for the most part unexpected, its origin not being easily perceived, was attributed to the ministry of angels, in the same way the origin of wickedness and evil, not being discoverable, has been explained as due to the craft and influence of the devil and of evil spirits. Thus the idea is always recurring, especially when we reach the limits of our observations in regard to evil. But since in this matter the Scriptures always refer us to our own inner life, we ought to carry our observations further ; and then more and more it would cease to be possible to consider things as the work of the devil, and the conception would thus gradually become obsolete. The same holds good of the interlocking and co-operation of evil,[1] which, at important junctures, when it is a question of antagonism to some sudden development of good, seems to reveal it as a kingdom and a power. But the more the good establishes itself as a whole in history, the less often will such antagonisms appear, and the more disintegrated will they be, so that here too the devil will no more be thought of.

On the other hand, anyone seeking to put forward, as a part of Christian doctrine, belief in a permanent influence of the devil either in the Kingdom of God itself or in a permanent kingdom of Satan opposed to the Kingdom of God, will not only be in direct contradiction to many of the above-quoted passages of Scripture, but will also be making very dangerous assertions. For in the first case at every difficult point he makes harder the endeavour, which cannot be sufficiently encouraged for the sake of inward blessedness, to explain all the phenomena (even the strangest) of the individual soul by its own peculiar qualities and by the influences of common life. And at the same time he gravely strengthens the already strong inclination of men to deny their own guilt. It would be bad enough if anyone neglected due care for himself and others because of his

[1] Cf. § 43, 1.

trust in the protection of angels ; but it would certainly be more dangerous if at will, in place of severe self-examination, he attributed his growing wickedness to the influence of Satan—a purely arbitrary proceeding, since no definite marks and limits can be given and the merest caprice has free scope. If, then, the influence of Satan in the strictest sense can only be directly inward, and must therefore be magical, a firm belief in any such doctrine must destroy the joyful consciousness of a sure inheritance in the Kingdom of God ; for everything wrought by the Spirit of God must then be at the mercy of the antagonistic influences of the devil, and all confidence in the guidance of one's own mind be abolished. Even if we only believed in such influences as existing outside the Christian Church, it would hinder the true Christian treatment of the individuals to whom the Gospel is to be preached. Moreover, belief in a lasting kingdom of Satan, which still implies that individual men are regarded as his instruments, is bound not only to impair joy of heart and to endanger steadfastness in conduct, but also to destroy Christian love. But those who actually go so far as to maintain that living faith in Christ is in some way conditioned by belief in the devil ought to be on their guard lest, by so doing, they depreciate Christ and unduly exalt themselves. For the ultimate meaning is that salvation by Christ would be less necessary if there were no devil ; and so, on the one hand, salvation appears to be only a help against an external enemy, while, on the other hand, man would be well able to help himself if there were no devil and evil had its seat solely in human nature.

Postscript.—So long as it is not a question of connected doctrine but of particular applications of this or that feature of a vague notion, we cannot deprive any Christian of the right, not only (within the limits defined above) to set forth elements of his own religious self-consciousness in terms of this kind, but also to make use of this idea in religious teaching—as indeed everything mentioned in the New Testament Scriptures proper may legitimately be given a place in our religious teaching as well. The idea may be so used if we find it suitable, or perhaps apparently indispensable, in order to make clear the positive godlessness of evil in itself, or to emphasize the fact that it is only in a higher protection that we can find help against an evil the source of whose power our will and intelligence seem unable to reach. So long as in this way the idea finds support in the living tradition of religious language, there will occasionally be a liturgical use of it which must, however, conform in every respect to the scriptural type, since deviation from that would only introduce more confusion, and this confusion would be increased the more, on the one hand, the susceptibility of people to the idea diminishes in course of time and, on the other hand, the liturgical expressions tend to assume a scientific character or to acquire confessional authority. The poetic use is therefore the freest and the least harmful. For in poetry personification is quite in place, and no disadvantage is to be feared from an emphatic use of this idea in pious moods. It would therefore be inexpedient and in many ways unjustifiable to wish to banish the coneeption of the devil from our treasury of song.

SECOND DOCTRINE : PRESERVATION (CONSERVATION)

§ 46. *The religious self-consciousness, by means of which we place all that affects or influences us in absolute dependence on God, coincides entirely with the view that all such things are conditioned and determined by the interdependence of Nature.*

1. It is not in the least meant that the pious self-consciousness is realized with every stimulation of the sensuous consciousness, any more than every perception causes us actually to visualize the interrelatedness of nature. But whenever objective consciousness reaches this degree of clarity we assume afresh the interdependence of nature as universal and as determining everything which has not led to our consciousness of it ; and in the same way we recognize in the moments when the pious self-consciousness is present that those in which it is lacking are really imperfect states, and we postulate the feeling of absolute dependence as valid for everything without exception, because we apply it to our own existence in so far as we are a part of the world.

But neither is our proposition meant to fall short of the conception of preservation, although in accordance with the nature of self-consciousness it is limited to what affects us ; and, indeed, only the movements and changes of things stimulate us directly, not the things themselves or their inner being. For every impulse directed towards perception and knowledge which yet has the qualities, essence, and being of things as its object, begins with a stimulation of self-consciousness which thus accompanies the process of apprehending ; and, consequently, the being and nature of things belongs to that which affects us. Within this range our proposition admits no distinction ; in each and every situation we ought to be conscious of, and sympathetically experience, absolute dependence on God just as we conceive each and every thing as completely conditioned by the interdependence of nature.

But we find the opposite idea to this very widely spread. Namely, the idea that these two views do not coincide, but that each excludes the other as its contradictory. It is said that the more clearly we conceive anything to be entirely conditioned by the interdependence of nature, the less can we arrive at the feeling of its absolute dependence upon God; and, conversely, the more vivid this latter feeling is the more indefinitely must we leave its interrelatedness with nature an open question. But it is obvious that, from our standpoint and in consistency with what we have already said, we cannot admit such a contradiction between the two ideas. For otherwise (since everything would present itself to us as always in the system of nature), as our knowledge of the world grew perfect, the development of the pious self-consciousness in ordinary life would cease; which is quite contrary to our presupposition that piety is of the essence of human nature. And on the other hand, conversely, the love of religion would be opposed to all love of research and all widening of our knowledge of nature; which would entirely contradict the principle that the observation of creation leads to the consciousness of God. And besides, prior to the completion of both tendencies the most competent naturalist would have to be the least religious of men, and *vice versa*. Now, as the human soul is just as necessarily predisposed towards a knowledge of the world as towards a consciousness of God, it can only be a false wisdom which would put religion aside, and a misconceived religion for love of which the progress of knowledge is to be arrested.

The only apparent ground for this assertion is the fact that, as a rule, the more strongly the objective consciousness predominates at any given moment, the more at that identical moment the consciousness of self is repressed and *vice versa*, because in the one case, through absorption in ourselves, we lose consciousness of the object affecting us, just as in the other case we are entirely merged in the object. But this in no way prevents the one activity, after having satisfied itself, from stimulating and passing over into the other. We are clearly quite wrong if we allege, as a general experience, that the incomprehensible as such is more conducive to the awakening of the religious feeling than that which is understood. The favourite example is the great natural phenomena, produced by elementary forces ; but in point of fact the religious feeling is not destroyed even by the completest confidence with which we accept this or that hypothetical explanation of these phenomena. The reason why these manifestations so readily arouse religious feeling lies rather in the immensity of their operations both in the promotion and destruction of human life and works of skill, and thus in the awakening of the consciousness of the limitation of our activity by universal forces. But this precisely is the most complete re-cognition of the universal interrelatedness of nature, and thus it turns out in fact to be the other way round, a support for our thesis. It is certainly, however, an expedient often adopted by human indolence to attribute what is not understood to the super-natural immediately ; but this does not at all belong to the tendency to piety. Since the Supreme Being here takes the place of the system of nature, we find ourselves tending rather to know-ledge ; besides, in that case not everything but only the incompre-hensible would be placed in absolute dependence upon God. Start-ing from this men have imagined evil and destructive supernatural powers in the same way as they have gone back to a highest good Power ; which makes it immediately evident that this kind of linking up (with the supernatural) has not arisen in the interests of religion, for such a setting of one over against the other would inevitably destroy the unity and completeness of the relation of dependence.

As furthermore we regard everything stimulating us as an object of the pious consciousness, it follows that not even the least and most unimportant thing should be excluded from the relation of absolute dependence. But here it should be remarked that frequently, on the one hand, an undue value is placed on expressly tracing back the least detail to this relation ; while on the other hand, with no greater justice, we often oppose such a relation. The first mistake appears in the view that, because the greatest events often arise from small, the smallest detail must be expressly ordained by God. For it appears to be only an empty, and by no means trustworthy, play of the fantasy, when we so often hear people describing great events as arising from small causes, and thereby drawing away our attention from the universal relatedness in which the true causes really lie hidden. A clear judgment can only be formed on the principle of the similarity of cause and effect in the domain of history or of nature, and it is only under definite conditions that individual changes with their causes can be severed from the universal interrelatedness and taken separately. But as soon as the pious feeling combines with such a view, thought has no choice but to recur to the universal interdependence of nature ; otherwise an isolated and separate activity would be ascribed in too human fashion to God. The second point, *i.e.* that the application of absolute dependence to the smallest matters is felt to be objectionable, has its origin in the fear that religion might be drawn into blasphemy, if, say, our free choices in little things were to be traced back to divine appointment : for instance, the point which foot shall be put forward first, or chance in matters of no serious importance such as winning or losing in sports and contests. Still, the incongruity here does not lie in the object, but in our way of thinking about it : that is, in the isolation of single events, because in cases of the first kind the apparent free choice is sometimes only an individual instance of a general situation, from which many similar events follow, and sometimes it is the expression of a more general law by which many similar events are controlled ; while in cases of the second kind, the issue can always be regarded as submission to a universal will. Neither of these can be regarded as insignificant, and thus no reason can be found against treating both as subsumed under absolute dependence on God.

2. If now we examine our proposition purely in itself, it must be directly evident in its wider scope to everyone who accepts it as a general principle of experience that the feeling of absolute dependence can be aroused through stimulations of our sensuous self-consciousness. For that feeling is most complete when we identify ourselves in our self-consciousness with the whole world and feel ourselves in the same way as not less dependent. This identification can only succeed in so far as in thought we unite everything that in appearance is scattered and isolated, and by means of this unifying association conceive of everything as one. For the most complete and universal interdependence of nature is posited in this ' All-One ' of finite being, and if we also feel ourselves to be absolutely dependent, then there will be a complete coincidence of the two ideas—namely, the unqualified conviction that everything is grounded and established in the universality of the nature-system, and the inner certainty of the absolute dependence of all finite being on God. From this follows, on the one hand, the possibility of pious self-consciousness in every moment of the objective consciousness, and on the other the possibility of com-

plete world-consciousness in every moment of pious self-consciousness. For with regard to the latter, where a pious feeling is actually existent, there the interdependence of nature is always posited ; and therefore the effort to extend the idea of the latter and perfect it in a world-representation will not be detrimental to the former, but can be effected just in so far as the tendency towards knowledge is predominant. And as regards the former, wherever there is an objective idea, there is always a stimulated self-consciousness ; and from this the pious self-consciousness can develop without prejudice to the objective idea (with its world-conception, which is more or less clearly co-posited), in proportion as the tendency in each towards feeling is dominant. Now if we conceive both tendencies as fully developed in a given man, then each would with perfect ease call forth the other, so that every thought, as part of the whole world-conception, would become in him the purest religious feeling, and every pious feeling, as evoked by a part of the world, would become a complete world-conception. On the contrary, if the one did not call forth the other, but in some way limited it, then the more completely the one developed, the more would it destroy the other. It has been always acknowledged by the strictest dogmaticians [1] that divine preservation, as the absolute dependence of all events and changes on God, and natural causation, as the complete determination of all events by the universal nexus, are one and the same thing simply from different points of view, the one being neither separated from the other nor limited by it. If anyone should detect in this an appearance of Pantheism, he ought to bear in mind that so long as philosophy does not put forward a generally accepted formula to express the relation of God and the world, even in the province of Dogmatics, directly we begin to speak not of the origin of the world but of its co-existence with God and its relatedness to God, we cannot avoid an oscillation between formulas, on the one hand, which approach to the identification of the two, and formulas, on the other, which go near to putting them in opposition to one another. Moreover, in order not to confuse ourselves in this way, we ought to observe

---

[1] Quenstedt, *Syst. theol.*, p. 761 : . . . ita ut idem effectus non a solo Deo nec a sola creatura, sed unâ eâdemque efficientiâ totali simul a Deo et creatura producatur . . . actum dico (*sc.* concursum Dei) non praevium actioni causae secundae nec subsequentem . . . sed talis est actus, qui intime in ipsa actione creaturae includitur, imo eadem actio creaturae est.—*Ibid.* p. 782 : Non est re ipsa alia actio influxus Dei, alia operatio creaturae, sed una et indivisibilis actio utrùmque respiciens et ab utràque pendens, a Deo ut causa universali, a creatura ut particulari.

more carefully the difference between a universal and an individual cause. For in the totality of finite being only a particular and partial causality is given to each individual, since each is dependent not on one other but on all the others; the universal causality attaches only to that on which the totality of this partial causality is itself dependent.

Postscript.—In Dogmatics the analytical method originating with the Scholastics has led to a division of our simple proposition in a number of different ways into many elements and sections, and it will not make much difference which of these divisions we select in order to show its relation to our statement. Some have divided the conception of preservation, which is expressed in our proposition as referring both to the whole and the parts, into the following: the *general*, which is related to the whole world as a unity; the *special*, which is concerned with species; and the *most special*, which is concerned with individuals (*generalis, specialis et specialissima*). This classification does not appear to be made in the interest of religion (from which here everything should start), for the simple reason that it leads to a question which is purely one for natural science, *i.e.* whether there is anything in the world which cannot be brought under the idea of a species. But supposing this question must be answered in the affirmative and the division be made complete, nevertheless universal preservation must include everything, and the division thus becomes quite superfluous to us, since our fundamental feeling rests solely on the finiteness of being as such. But a further purpose of this division may be surmised, if we take into account the addition usually made to the third member of it—namely, that God sustains individual things in their existence and their powers as long as He wills. For in that case the species, as reproductions of individual things, are in a sense immortal, but the individual is mortal; and the wish arose to establish a difference between the preservation of what endures and of what is mortal.

For those, however, who accept a beginning and an end of the world there is absolutely no reason to differentiate between the world and individual things. But in any case the proposition must cover equally the beginning and the end; and we know fairly certainly of our earth that there have been species on it which are no longer extant and that the present species have not always existed; so that our proposition must be stretched to embrace these also. It really affirms nothing except that the temporality or the duration of the finite is to be conceived solely in absolute dependence upon God. But since the duration of individual as well as of universal things is simply an expression for the degree of their power as each coexists with all the rest, it follows that the addition taken in itself contains nothing which our statement had not expressed already. But the way in which the addition is framed might easily give rise to the idea that the sustaining will of God began or ended at some particular time, and in anticipation of this it must be said that God, in sustaining as in creating, must remain apart from all means and occasions of time.

Another similar division is to discriminate between the work of God as *preserving* and as *co-operating*; but the distinction is not made in the same way by all teachers of doctrine, for some connect the expression ' preservation ' only with matter and form, and ' co-operation ' with powers and actions ; others again connect preservation with the existence and powers of things, and co-operation only with activity. The fact, however, that the expression ' co-operation' contains a hidden meaning should not be overlooked, as if there were in the finite an activity in and for itself and thus independent of the sustaining divine activity. This tendency must be entirely avoided and not merely covered over by indefiniteness.[1] If, however, such a distinction ought not to be drawn, and if the powers of things are something as little separated from the divine sustaining activity as their being itself (the latter we only divide into matter and form by an abstraction which has no place here), then the difference between preservation and co-operation rests also on a similar abstraction. For being posited for itself can only exist where there is also power, just as power always exists only in activity ; thus a preservation which did not include the placing of all the activities of any finite being in absolute dependence on God would be just as empty as creation without preservation. And in the same way, if we conceived co-operation without conceiving that the existence of a thing in its whole duration was dependent on God, then this thing might be independent of God even at its first moment of existence, and this would be equivalent to conceiving preservation in such a way that it did not include creation and positing it without creation. It should be added here that even theologians who have treated the subject quite correctly on

---

[1] *E.g.* Morus, i. p. 306 : limites non definiuntur quousque operatur sol, agricola, et ubi incipiat Deus . . . adjuvando et limitando efficit Deus, ut fiat consilium suum.

the whole have allowed themselves to be led into describing co-operation as something more immediate than preservation,[1] so that deeds, as distinct from the preservation of powers, proceed from a divine activity. The result of this would be, if we took it seriously, to reduce the preservation of power to nothing, for in the system of nature power is always dependent on the activity of the rest of things. Thus we can only say that, in the region of absolute dependence on God, everything is equally direct and equally indirect, some in one relation and some in another.

Some combine the idea of divine *government* immediately with these two ideas. But if by that is meant the fulfilment of divine decrees [2] or the guidance of all things to divine ends, and if it be taken as signifying anything else than that everything can happen and has happened only as God originally willed and always wills, by means of the powers distributed and preserved in the world—this is already included in our proposition, and we cannot consider it here. For here we are concerned in general with the description of the feeling of absolute dependence, and must set completely aside a view which is based upon the distinction between means and end without reference to the question whether this distinction can exist for God. On the one hand, for our Christian conscious-ness it could only be the Kingdom of God, established by means of redemption (*i.e.* something quite foreign to our present purpose), to which everything else is related as its goal : and on the other, if our self-consciousness is to represent finite existence in general, and end and means are related to one another as that which is posited for its own sake and that not posited for its own sake, or more exactly as what is willed by God and what is not willed by God, then we must take up into our religious self-conscious-ness an antithesis of which our present discussion knows nothing. The only thing then that this conception [divine government] could suggest to us at this point would be that so far as the divine preservation relates, as co-operation, to powers and activities taken separately, we require a counterpart to it to cover the passive state of finite things ; but since these are just as essential parts for the attainment of the divine purpose, their absolute dependence is included in the conception of government. Even this is, however,

---

[1] Quenst., *l.c.* : Observandum quod Deus non solum vim agendi dat causis secundis et etiam conservat, sed quod immediate influit in actionem et effectum creaturae.

[2] Morus, i. p. 319 : Gubernatio est opus Dei efficientis ut in mundo ipse suum semper adsequatur consilium.

superfluous so far as we are concerned. For since preservation has as its object the being of things, and in this, so far as they are centres of power, the antithesis of self-activity and susceptibility is included, the passive states are already subsumed under absolute dependence ; and particularly when they also belong to that which affects our self-consciousness, whether in the form of perception or of sympathy, they are included in our general proposition. But, in addition, the passive states of one thing are only the result of the active states of others ; while, on the other hand, the way in which the active states emerge successively and the strength which they display depends not only on each thing's peculiar mode of existence. but also on its concurrence with other things, hence on the influence of others and on its own passive states. From this we may think that perhaps we should differentiate better if we said that what proceeds from the intrinsic characteristics of each individual thing and what proceeds from its co-existence with all other things are both alike to be placed in absolute dependence upon God. But even this would be an abstraction without importance for our religious self-consciousness, for which the two are not distinguished from one another as stimulating objects ; and thus we should do better to include everything which stimulates our consciousness together in the idea of finite being which is only relatively individual and is conditioned in its individuality by the universal co-existence. And this is wholly identical with what our proposition denotes by the term interdependence of nature.

§ 47. *It can never be necessary in the interest of religion so to interpret a fact that its dependence on God absolutely excludes its being conditioned by the system of Nature.*

1. This proposition is so much a direct consequence of what went before that there would be no reason to make an express statement of it, but that ideas which have still a circulation in the Christian Church must be considered in their appropriate place in any Dogmatic. Now there is a general idea that the miracles which are interwoven with the beginnings of Christianity or at least in some form are reported in the Scriptures, should be regarded as events of the kind described : and yet if the idea itself is inadmissible, it cannot be applied to this or that particular fact. It is in this way that theologians from of old have generally treated the question. We have not to pass judgment here on its inherent possibility, but only on the relation of the theory to the feeling of

absolute dependence. If, then, this relation is what our proposition declares it to be, we must in our field try, as far as possible, to interpret every event with reference to the interdependence of nature and without detriment to that principle.

Now some have represented miracle in this sense as essential to the perfect manifestation of the divine omnipotence. But it is difficult to conceive, on the one side, how omnipotence is shown to be greater in the suspension of the interdependence of nature than in its original immutable course which was no less divinely ordered. For, indeed, the capacity to make a change in what has been ordained is only a merit in the ordainer, if a change is necessary, which again can only be the result of some imperfection in him or in his work. If such an interference be postulated as one of the privileges of the Supreme Being, it would first have to be assumed that there is something not ordained by Him which could offer Him resistance and thus invade Him and His work ; and such an idea would entirely destroy our fundamental feeling. We must remember, on the other hand, that where such a conception of miracles is commonly found, namely, in conditions where there is least knowledge of nature, there, too, the fundamental feeling appears to be weakest and most ineffectual. But where a knowledge of nature is most widely spread, and therefore this conception seldom occurs, more is found of that reverence for God which is the expression of our fundamental feeling. It follows from this that the most perfect representation of omnipotence would be a view of the world which made no use of such an idea.

Other teachers [1] defend the conception in a more acute but scarcely more tenable way, by saying that God was partly in need of miracles that He might compensate for the effects of free causes in the course of nature, and partly that He might generally have reasons for remaining in direct contact with the world. The latter argument presupposes, for one thing, a wholly lifeless view of the divine preservation, and for another, an opposition in general between the mediate and immediate activities of God which cannot be conceived without bringing the Supreme Being within the sphere of limitation. The former sounds almost as if free causes were not themselves objects of divine preservation, and (since preservation includes in itself the idea of creation) had not come into being and been maintained in absolute dependence upon God. But if, on the contrary, they are in this condition there can be just

[1] Cf. Storr, *Dogm.*, § 25.

as little necessity for God to counteract their influences as to counteract the influences which a blind natural force exercises in the domain of another natural force. But none of us understands by 'the world' which is the object of the divine preservation a nature-mechanism alone, but rather the interaction of the nature-mechanism and of free agents, so that in the former the latter are taken into account just as in the latter the former is reckoned.

Moreover, the Biblical miracles, on account of which the whole theory has been devised, are much too isolated and too restricted in content for any theory to be based on them which should assign them the function of restoring in the nature-mechanism what free agents had altered. That one great miracle, the mission of Christ, has, of course, the aim of restoration, but it is the restoration of what free causes have altered in their own province, not in that of the nature-mechanism or in the course of things originally ordained by God. Nor does the interest of religion require that the free cause which performs the function of restoration in the sphere of phenomena should have a different relation to the order of nature from that of other free causes.

Two other reasons may be put forward why an absolute suspension of the interrelatedness of nature by miracles may be held to be in the interests of religion. And it cannot be denied that it is mostly for these reasons, even though they may never have been formulated as actual Church doctrine, that this conception of miracle has maintained its practical hold over many Christians. The first is that of answer to prayer ; for prayer seems really to be heard only when because of it an event happens which would not otherwise have happened : thus there seems to be the suspension of an effect which, according to the interrelatedness of nature, should have followed. The other is that of regeneration, which, represented as a new creation, in part requires some such suspension and in part introduces a principle not comprised in the system of nature. Neither subject can be discussed in this place ; but it may suffice to remark in relation to the first, which more concerns piety in general, that our statement places prayer, too, under divine preservation, so that prayer and its fulfilment or refusal are only part of the original divine plan, and consequently the idea that otherwise something else might have happened is wholly meaningless. With regard to the second we need only refer here to what was said above. If the revelation of God in Christ is not necessarily something absolutely supernatural, Christian piety cannot be held bound in advance to regard as absolutely supernatural anything that goes along with this revelation or flows from it.

2. The more accurate definitions by which the acceptance of such miracles is brought into connexion with the propositions and concepts which indicate the complete dependence of the system of nature on God show very clearly how little that idea is demanded by our religious emotions. For the more they try definitely to fix an absolute miracle, the further off they are from making it the expression of a religious emotion, and, instead of genuine dogmatic material, something of quite a different character [1] comes in. Speaking generally, the question can most easily be considered if we start from the point that the event in which a miracle occurs is connected with all finite causes, and therefore every absolute miracle would destroy the whole system of nature. There are, therefore, two ways of looking at such a miracle—a positive way when we consider the whole future, and a negative way when we consider it as affecting in some sense the whole of the past. Since, that is, that which would have happened by reason of the totality of finite causes in accordance with the natural order does not happen, an effect has been hindered from happening, and certainly not through the influence of other normally counteracting finite causes given in the natural order, but in spite of the fact that all active causes are combining to produce that very effect. Everything, therefore, which had ever contributed to this will, to a certain degree, be annihilated, and instead of introducing a single supernatural power into the system of nature as we intended, we must completely abrogate the conception of nature.

From the positive point of view we must consider that some

---

[1] Mosheim, *op. cit.*, p. 462, calls the divine activity which works miracles ' gubernatio immediata ' or ' inordinata,' and, by so doing, introduces an antithesis between miracle and the sustaining activity of God, to the advantage of the last-named in the latter formula, but to its disadvantage in the former. But religious feeling would equally refuse to interpose anything between that which is and the divine activity through which it is, and to impute something to the divine activity which is at the same time regarded as unordained. At the same time, the expression conflicts with the general explanation which he gives of ' gubernatio '—namely, that it stands for a ' directio virium alienarum,' if, that is to say, the miracle is not to be explained by means of the relevant natural forces.—Reinhard calls (*Dogm.*, p. 236) the same divine activity ' providentia miraculosa,' and explains it by ' cura divina, qua Deus aliquid effici mutationibus a consuetudine naturae plane abhorrentibus.' If, as here, we look to find the antithesis in the divine care, then preservation would be an absence of care ; if in the custom of nature, then the custom of nature is apparently something independent of the divine providence. Religious feeling would, necessarily, declare equally against both views.

event follows which is not to be explained by the totality of finite causes. But as this event now enters into the interrelatedness of nature as an active member, throughout the whole future everything will be different from what it would have been had this single miracle not occurred. Thus every miracle not only suspends the entire continuity of the original order for all future time, but every later miracle annuls all earlier ones, in so far as they have become part of the continuity of active causes. But now, in order to describe the origin of the effect, we have to allow for the entrance of a divine activity apart from natural causes.[1] Yet at whatever point we admit the entrance of this particular divine activity, which must always seem like magic, in each case there will always appear a number of possibilities according to which the same result could have been attained by natural causes if they had been opportunely directed towards this end. In this way we shall be driven to hold either that miracles have a purely epideictic tendency in view of which God purposely did not so order the system of nature that His whole will should be accomplished in it (a view against which we directed our earlier discussion of the relation between omnipotence and this conception of miracle), or if the totality of finite causes could not have been so directed, then what can be explained by the order of nature can never rightly evoke in us the feeling of the absolute dependence of all finite being.

Now, if others think it would be easier to establish this conception of miracles by first dividing the divine co-operation into ordinary and extraordinary (which, however, is only ostensibly different from the unordered), and then attributing the former to the natural and the latter to the supernatural, so that the negative aspect of a miracle would be the withdrawal of the ordinary co-operation,[2] but the positive aspect the entrance of the extraordinary, this means, on the one hand, that the ordinary co-operation is no longer ordinary if it can be withdrawn, and is not to be definitely

---

[1] The formula that in such a case God acts without intermediary causes is in contradiction to our fundamental feeling, if for no other reason than that it represents God as under constraint within the ordinary course of nature. At bottom, however, this use of terms which describes natural causes as intermediary causes, is itself infected by the radical error of conceiving the dependence on God of what happens as dependence on particular finite causes—a dependence of the same kind, only lying further back. And, in fact, Storr (*Dogm.*, p. 336), when seeking to show how God can act directly on the world, and change the course of nature without abrogating natural laws, seems to conceive Him in the manner of a finite free cause.

[2] Quenstedt, *l.c.* : Deo concursum suum subtrahente cessat creaturae actio.

distinguished from the extraordinary ; only that we call that which occurs more frequently the ordinary, and what seldom occurs, the extraordinary, a relation which might equally well be reversed. On the other hand, the miracle is effected in the first instance by finite causes, even if by means of extraordinary divine co-operation ; but since thereby something comes into existence which according to its natural character would not have come into existence, it follows that in this case either they are not causes, and the expression 'co-operation' is inaccurate, or they have become something different from what they were formerly.   In that case, every such extra-ordinary co-operation is really a creation, on which afterwards the re-establishment of actual things in their original state must follow as a further creation cancelling the former one.   Moreover, it should be recognized with regard to these explanations that the one corre-sponds more closely to the one class of Biblical miracle [1] and the other to the other class, and therefore the different characteristics of these events have had an important influence on the development of these different formulæ.   If, however, anyone finds it difficult to accept this view, yet it must be admitted that although the older theologians on the whole [2] still maintain this conception of miracle, the younger ones [3] do not maintain its exclusive validity, but also admit the legitimacy of another hypothesis—namely, that God has prepared miracles in nature itself in some way incomprehensible to us ; and this, in the interests of religion itself, we must admit to be pure gain.

3. On the whole, therefore, as regards the miraculous, the general interests of science, more particularly of natural science, and the interests of religion seem to meet at the same point, *i.e.* that we should abandon the idea of the absolutely supernatural because no single instance of it can be known by us, and we are nowhere required to recognize it.   Moreover, we should admit, in general, that since our knowledge of created nature is continually growing, we have not the least right to maintain that anything is impossible and also we should allow, in particular (by far the greater number

[1] Morus (*op. cit.*) describes it thus : aut enim mentio quidem fit adminiculi naturalis ; aut ne fit quidem mentio talis, sed praegresso verbo res facta est.
[2] Buddeus, *Thes. de atheism.*, p. 291 : Operatio, qua revera naturae leges, quibus totius huius universi ordo et conservatio innititur, suspenduntur. According to Thomas, p. 1, cap. cx. : ex hoc aliquid dicitur miraculum, quod sit praeter ordinem totius naturae creatae.
[3] Cf. Reinhard, *Dogmat.*, p. 238 : the above-quoted expression 'consuetudo naturae ' is in this respect carefully chosen.—Morus treats the matter in the same sense but superficially in his *Commentary*, part i. p. 97 sq.

of New Testament miracles being of this kind), that we can neither define the limits of the reciprocal relations of the body and mind nor assert that they are, always and everywhere, entirely the same without the possibility of extension or deviation. In this way, everything—even the most wonderful thing that happens or has happened—is a problem for scientific research; but, at the same time, when it in any way stimulates the pious feeling, whether through its purpose or in some other way, that is not in the least prejudiced by the conceivable possibility of its being understood in the future. Moreover, we free ourselves entirely from a difficult and highly precarious task with which Dogmatics has so long laboured in vain,[1] i.e. the discovery of definite signs which shall enable us to distinguish between the false and diabolical miracle and the divine and true.

§ 48. *Excitations of self-consciousness expressing a repression of life are just as much to be placed in absolute dependence on God as those expressing an advancement of life.*

1. This statement deals more particularly with the contrast between the serene and the sad moments of life, but it follows so directly from our principal proposition,[2] or rather is so completely involved in it, that we should have had no reason for putting it specially forward if long experience had not taught us that imperfect piety has always found it difficult to harmonize the existence of sad and unhappy experiences with the God-consciousness, whether because it is overwhelmed by life's repressions or led astray by sceptical and unbelieving arguments. On this account almost every religious doctrine, and particularly the Christian doctrine of faith, must make it a special duty to show their compatibility. This has generally involved, however, a false complacency towards these imperfect emotions, partly by way of vindicating the Supreme Being with respect to the existence of such experiences and partly by admitting a variation in the absolute feeling of dependence in relation to them. It is sufficient here to enter a protest against both, as much against the counterfeit emotion itself as against the weak and obscure treatment of it, in order that the simple and complete apprehension of the fundamental feeling may not be endangered. Now if sad experiences only occurred separately, although frequently, and were such that we could trace no connexion between them, then they would hardly have been able to

[1] Cf. Gerhard, *loc. th. loc.* xxiii. § 271.   [2] § 46.

produce such an effect ; but it is dependent on the fact that there
are conditions which bring a persistent and regularly renewed consciousness of life's obstacles. These, then, are what we usually
characterize by the term *evil*: and it is to be maintained that all
evil, in the full meaning of that word, is just as much wholly dependent upon God as that which is in opposition to it, *i.e.* good.
But clearly we must reckon moral evil under the term ' evil,' since
where it exists it always shows itself to be an inexhaustible source
of life's difficulties ; only here we have not to consider it as a human
activity but as a state. Therefore, just as later we shall have to
treat more fully the connexion of evil with moral evil and from a
different standpoint, here, in the reverse order, moral evil is to be
included under the term ' evil.' Thus it is to be considered now
apart from ethics, and only as it appears and is given as a state
affecting the self-consciousness as one of life's obstacles ; and after
the present discussion it will not later be treated separately. There
is, however, a further division of evil which we need only consider
in order to make clear that, just as (we maintain) evil and good are
alike rooted in universal dependence on God, from this point of view
there is no difference between these two types or classes of evil.
To the one belong those conditions which we call natural evil, in
which human existence is partially negated. To the other, which
we name social evil, belong those conditions in which human
activity is in conflict with another activity and is partially overcome and depressed ; and here the influence of moral evil specially
comes in. But clearly these two kinds of evil not only give rise to
each other (since where there is diminution of being activity will
more easily be depressed, and a depressed activity which is always
decreasing reacts again on the whole being), but they also overlap
in thought, for the being of man consists only in the totality of his
activities, and *vice versa.* The difference consists then principally
in this, that the one is much more determined by the total forces
of nature, and the other by the collective conditions of human
activity.

2. In order to solve our problem within the prescribed limits we
do not at all require to enter deeply into teleological speculations
or, in addition to evil itself, to consider what has resulted from it ;
for it can never be proved that the results might not have been
caused in some other way. It is just as unnecessary for us to work
back from the idea of Preservation to that of Creation or beyond it,
to show that evil was unavoidable. But remaining strictly within

our province, we have only to show that apparent oppositions come together under the universal dependence. And here two points arise with regard to both kinds of evil. First, the relation of the fluctuating and transitory to the permanent in all finite being. Individual beings belong to the transitory in the form primarily of a vital activity that takes a progressive development up to a certain climax, from thence gradually decreasing until death. Since, regarded as a whole, every relation which determines development arouses the consciousness of life as stimulated, and conversely what tends to bring death nearer is interpreted as an arrest of life, there is throughout the whole course a casual fluctuation between these two. Clearly then, on the one hand, it is the same entire relatedness of men with nature which determines both progress and arrest, so that the one cannot be apart from the other. It is just the same, again, in the sphere of social life, where, for example, a later formation of community life cannot grow and expand without the earlier formation being repressed and brought to decay ; and thus there are here again two modes of life, progress and limitation, each conditioning the other. The second point is the relation of what is only relatively self-existent and the corresponding and mutual limitations of the finite. That is to say, there is no absolute isolation in the finite : each is only self-existent as it conditions another, and is in turn only conditioned in so far as it is self-existent. But another thing is only conditioned by me if I can in some way cause it to progress ; but then this equally implies that I can be a hindrance. The whole relation can only be presented to consciousness in so far as both terms (in both forms, that of self-existence and that of conditionedness) are presented ; and consequently both obstacles and progress are equally ordained by God. This is equally valid of personal feeling and of sympathetic and social feeling. So that without a very far-reaching misunderstanding, no one can find difficulty in the fact that even what appears to him an evil (be it his own, someone else's, or one common to many) exists as a consequence of absolute dependence, and therefore is to be regarded as ordained by God. Otherwise we should in general be neither willing nor able to think of the transitory and finite as existing through God—that is, we could not think any world at all as dependent on God ; and in this way our fundamental proposition would be denied.

Now this misunderstanding is due, on one side, to the fact that we look at states themselves apart from their natural conditions ;

and it is increased by the fact that we wrongly represent these influences which produce permanent life-repressions as if they were a separate self-contained province and thus could be isolated and eliminated—in short, that the world could exist apart from evil. The fact is rather that the very same activity or condition of a thing by which it enters on the one hand into human life as an evil, on the other hand is a cause of good, so that if we could remove the source of life's difficulties the conditions of life's progress too would disappear. This is true even of moral evil which only functions as evil in so far as it appears in external action : and it holds good not only accidentally because sin produces good effects sometimes in individuals and sometimes as a great historical lever, but as a general truth since sin only comes to be done by reason of that capacity of man to express his inner nature outwardly which is the source of all good. On the other hand, since in the same way it can be held as a general truth that in the universal system that which is the source of most of life's advancement, from some point of view has an aspect of evil, and that in virtue of the very character-istic which makes it helpful (as indeed all forces of nature and all social relations which originate in intelligence, with the single ex-ception perhaps of intelligence itself, may be said to have this two-fold aspect of good and evil), it is absolutely correct to say in another sense that evil as such is not ordained by God, because evil in isolation is never found, and the same is true of good, but each thing or event is ordained by God that it should be both.

There is an important point for us here—that it is an imperfec-tion of self-consciousness when a limitation, as such, completely and exclusively engrosses a moment of experience, whether this imperfection be that of immediate self-consciousness or of that which accompanies the activities of the objective consciousness ; and in the same way it is an erroneous view when its being the source of difficulties is regarded as the essence of any object that exists in absolute dependence on God. And even this imperfection is one which disappears with the increasing development of the good, like every evil vanishing into the good itself—that is, in the susceptibility of the sensuous consciousness in general for union with the God-consciousness.

3. The usual dogmatic definitions which try under the headings of preservation and co-operation to throw light on this subject, certainly appear to have the same solution in view but to reach it very inadequately. Thus, for this purpose they sometimes differ-

entiate a divine co-operation that is helpful from one that is not, and sometimes a merely material co-operation from one that is also formal. These terms seem to have been originally thought out with special reference to the antithesis between good and evil, and to the latter was assigned the co-operation which is not helpful or only material. But apart from the fact that co-operation and help are inseparable ideas, and no definite conception can be formed of a co-operation which is not helpful, we must observe that if co-operation with activity is in question there is no activity without form, so that there can be no co-operation with an activity which is not also a co-operation with the form of that activity, and a merely material co-operation would be nothing more than preservation without co-operation. The consequence of this would be that all activity so described would be placed outside the relation of absolute dependence. Hence, according to both these formulas, evil seems to be stronger and more powerful than good, since the latter can only be accomplished with the helpful or (in addition) formal co-operation, while the former needs neither of them. But, apart from this, I say that there can be no question in this place of treating evil as a purely inward disposition prior to all activity, because it could not then stimulate the self-consciousness of the individual, much less could it stimulate the self-consciousness of someone else. But, if we consider evil as active, then all sinful actions are performed not only by means of the material powers of men, but just like good actions, in a way appropriate to them ; so that there is no ground for making such a distinction.

Suppose now that all social evil was in some way bound up with moral evil, this distinction would no longer be applicable. But how about natural evil ? Since destructive events are precisely the strongest expressions of natural forces, they are thus less able to take place without helpful co-operation than other events, and just as little without formal co-operation, since no specific form can be ascribed to them. Thus if the intention is to maintain that in so far as co-operation is admitted, evil, too, comes within the absolute dependence on God, but that in so far as the co-operation is not helpful or only material, God cannot be the originator, this intention has, strictly speaking, not been fulfilled. Consequently, it appears to be a better expedient if we say that everything real without exception is the result of divine co-operation, so that this can suffer no diminution : but all evil, including moral evil as such, has its ground in a mere defect ; and, a mere defect being a partial *non-ens*, divine co-operation cannot be concerned with it. If then each finite thing is ordained simultaneously by God as an entity with its own dimensions, this does not mean that it exerts activities outside this limit ; on the contrary, the divine co-operation would be lacking to these, and consequently it could not resist external influences beyond this limit. But difficulties or obstacles do not arise from the circumstance that no opposition can be offered because divine assistance is lacking, but because an attack is made in a manner which is beyond the finite thing's power of resistance, whereas divine co-operation is available for the attack. Nothing remains but on the one hand to attribute the divine co-operation equally to everything that happens, and on the other to maintain that evil as such is not ordained by God, but only as related to the good and as one condition of it.

§ 49. *Whether or not that which arouses our self-consciousness and consequently influences us, is to be traced back to any part of the so-called nature-mechanism or to the activity of free causes—the one is as completely ordained by God as the other.*

1. The proposition is in itself only the expression of the undoubtedly generally admitted fact that we do not feel ourselves less absolutely dependent on God when anything happens to us through the actions of other men than in other cases. Also it is completely contained in the principal proposition of this Second Doctrine, and is only put forward in explanation in order to prevent a not infrequent misunderstanding, namely, that the consciousness of our free-will is in opposition to the feeling of absolute dependence. The question first of all is as to the effect of free actions, primarily on the lives of others but also on our own. But however much freedom resides in determination of will and resolution, action, emerging as it does under influences beyond itself, is always so conditioned that it only becomes what it is because it belongs to the very same universal system which is the essential indivisible subject of the feeling of absolute dependence ; and this would lose its significance in the whole province of history if we should think of free causes as excluded from this system. Indeed, what was put incidentally above must here be brought out in its full significance.[1] Just because free causes form a part of the general system, we must be able to assert the same of the moment of activity itself and of the accompanying self-consciousness. It

[1] See § 47, 1.

was in this sense that in our first elucidations of the fundamental feeling we explained how the relative feeling of freedom and the absolute feeling of dependence each involves and pervades the other, so that the latter cannot exist apart from the former.[1]

Let us consider now the moment of action, starting from the point that every other free agent in the same position would have acted differently, just as the same free agent would have acted differently in another position, and that this position, whatever it may be, is within the universal system. Then no one can doubt that the results of free activity take place in virtue of absolute dependence. What is certain, moreover, about the accompanying self-consciousness is that we are only capable of the feeling of absolute dependence as freely acting agents—that is to say, that we are conscious of our freedom as something which is received and is gradually developed in a universal system. Therefore in every religious experience of free self-activity the self-consciousness must contain both the feeling of absolute dependence and the relative feeling of freedom.

In our proposition, the expression ' free causes ' clearly makes a difference between freedom and causality in general, and implies causes which are not free. And yet they are still causes. But in the customary conception of the universal nature-mechanism there is, strictly speaking, no causality apart from free causes. For by it we imagine a coherence and interaction of things which only react as such in so far as they have been acted upon ; and in that case we can only think of each in its activity as a point of inter-section : so that causality is only applicable to the first mover existing outside this sphere. That is to say that, according to this conception, free causes having been excluded, there is no causality in finite things, while outside there is only the free infinite cause, the divine causality which is presupposed as originally setting the whole sphere in motion by a first push. If we include in this mechanism all inferior life, animal and vegetable (since there can, in this conception, be no question of a universal life of the heavenly bodies), then free causes, by which we mean men, are the sole finite causality, and it only needs one step to leave the divine causality as the only one, *i.e.* to hold what we have already shown to be destructive of the feeling of absolute dependence, and with it all piety—that men should regard themselves too as simply part of this mechanism, and should treat consciousness of self-activity

[1] See § 4, 3.

as only an unavoidable illusion. Fortunately, few have ever been capable of this self-annihilating renunciation by which, after robbing the whole world of life, they sacrifice their own selves also to the completeness of their theory. By this method all causality of the finite is transformed into appearance, and consequently there is no ground for regarding individual finite being as existing for itself, and therefore no reason why a finite being should come to rest at one point rather than another in this universal flux of moving and being moved ; but all things are either an indivisible unity or else an innumerable multitude of points of transition, *i.e.* atoms.

Let us now attribute to ourselves free causality along with absolute dependence, and causality also to every living being as assuredly as we hold it to have being for itself ; and let us see complete absence of freedom only where a thing does not move itself and moves other things only in so far as it is moved ; in that case we should be able to regard the causality of living beings as simply a diminished freedom, and we should have to say that true causality only exists where there is life, and the complete absence of freedom is also a complete absence of causality, since the impulse which sets the lifeless thing in motion so that it moves other things always comes itself from what is living. In our proposition, then, the expression ' nature-mechanism ' is not used as our own, for we should be wrong to reduce anything which stimulates our self-consciousness and thus influences us to mere mechanism, to active points of transition. It lies, however, outside our province to inquire how far the sphere of true causality and therefore of life extends, and how in each particular case the true cause is to be discovered. But our self-consciousness, in so far as it is the consciousness of a finite being and we distinguish in it a partial consciousness of freedom and a partial feeling of dependence as belonging together, from the feeling of absolute dependence as including both, requires for every stimulation a finite causality in the sphere of the universal system of nature which, as a consequence of this, must be taken up into absolute dependence. For this feeling would not retain its uniform character if there were a sphere, *i.e.* that of natural causes, in which finite and divine causation met, and alongside it two others, that of mechanical or rather apparent causation where only divine causality reigned and finite causality was absent, and that of free causality where only finite cause reigned and divine causality was absent. At the same time we must observe, with reference to absolute dependence, that we assume no sharp antithesis between freedom and natural necessity in finite being, since anything which actually has a being for itself moves itself in some sense or other, even if it has no part in spiritual life ; but even in the most free cause its range is ordained by God.

2. In the dogmatic terminology which now prevails, this truth is expressed sometimes by the idea of preservation and sometimes by the idea of co-operation. The most usual form of the first kind is that God upholds each thing in its being, and therefore also free causes as such. In this statement we can find everything which we have ascertained, namely, that the activities of free beings are determined from within, without prejudice to the absolute dependence which is indicated by the expression preservation. Considered in itself, however, this formula may be open to the censure that it appears to obscure the essential difficulties in a superficial way rather than actually solve them.

In a similar way a distinction is drawn in the concept of co-operation between a co-operation after the manner of free cause and a co-operation after the manner of natural cause.[1] But this expression requires at least to be treated very cautiously if the differences of finite being are not to be placed within the Supreme Being and thus God Himself appear as the totality, a view which can scarcely be differentiated from that of Pantheism. The meaning can only be that God co-operates in every case with activities which are appropriate to the nature of the active thing, but only and always according to His own causality, which is entirely different from that which belongs to the sphere of reciprocal action.

Postscript to this Doctrine.—It seemed advisable to state these separate propositions, though it must be admitted that they were already implied in essence in the principal proposition of the doctrine, for two reasons. First, because it is easy here to put forward definitions which obscure the right relationship between creation and preservation. This is done when the miraculous is regarded as entirely supernatural, since in this way a secondary creative act comes in which partially suspends preservation and thus stands in opposition to it. The same result follows if we believe that evil was less ordained by God than other things, because, in that case, of the things equally created by Him, He would leave some in the lurch rather than others. And it occurs, finally, if

---

[1] Concursus ad modum causae liberae, *and* ad modum causae naturalis.

we oppose free causes to natural ones so strongly that the former in their activity appear to be less dependent on God ; for then they must derive their effectiveness partly from elsewhere while their existence itself they derive from God, and thus an inequality is introduced between creation and preservation.

Secondly, it was supremely important here to show the harmony between the interests of piety and science on the one hand and morality on the other. Indeed, morality must always be endangered or must endanger religion if the absolute dependence be so conceived that free self-determination cannot co-exist with it, or *vice versa*. Scientific knowledge, however, is twofold—that of natural science and that of history. Natural science is so hampered by the assumption of the absolutely supernatural within the course of nature that it would thereby be made entirely nugatory. History deals more particularly with the opposition between good and evil, and on account of the way in which they are clearly interwoven one with another, necessarily becomes fatalistic (that is to say, it must give up its relation to the idea of the good) if evil is either not ordained by God or less ordained by Him than its opposite. Our propositions, however, retain their purely dogmatic content and do not trench upon the ground of speculation, in spite of these connexions with it, because they are all implied in the principal proposition. Their common relation to it is not everywhere equally clear. It consists in this, that each in its own province puts forward a greatest and a least and, showing that the feeling of dependence holds good in an equivalent way for both limiting cases, establishes this equivalence as the rule for all religious expression. The antithesis between the ordinary and the miraculous goes back to the greatest and least in the sphere of nature from which both are to be explained ; the antithesis between good and evil goes back to the greatest and least in the harmony of universal reciprocal activity with the independent being of the individual ; the antithesis between freedom and mechanism goes back to the greatest and least in individualized life. It had, therefore, to be shown that if at any of these points the similarity of treatment failed, then the main proposition of the doctrine itself would fall to the ground, and neither the conditioned feeling of dependence nor the conditioned feeling of freedom could be combined with the absolute feeling of dependence. Beyond these there are no difficult cases to consider.

SECOND SECTION

The Divine Attributes which are related to tne Religious Self-consciousness so far as it expresses the General Relationship between God and the World.

§ 50. *All attributes which we ascribe to God are to be taken as denoting not something special in God, but only something special in the manner in which the feeling of absolute dependence is to be related to Him.*

1. If an adequate expression of the absolute feeling of dependence here indicated has been given in the expositions of the preceding section, we cannot believe that the theory of the divine attributes originally issued from a dogmatic interest. But history teaches us concerning speculation that, ever since it took the divine essence as an object of thought,[1] it has always entered the same protest against all detailed description, and confined itself to representing God as the Original Being and the Absolute Good. And, indeed, it has frequently been recognized that even in these concepts (of which the first only is relevant here) there remains a certain inadequacy, in so far as they still contain an element of opposition or other analogy with finite being. This method of treatment, therefore, owes its origin first of all to religious poetry, particularly to hymns and other lyrics, and also to the more uncultured experience of common life which harmonizes with poetry and tries to vivify and establish the simple idea of the Supreme Being by the employment of expressions which we use about finite beings. Both methods proceed from religious interests, and have far more the

---

[1] As we can only deal here with Christian speculation it may be sufficient to refer to Dionys. Areop., *de myst. theol.* cc. iv. and v.: Λέγομεν οὖν ὡς ἡ πάντων αἰτία καὶ ὑπὲρ πάντα οὖσα οὔτε ἀνούσιός ἐστιν οὔτε ἄζωος . . . οὔτε ποιότητα, ἢ ποσότητα ἢ ὄγκον ἔχει . . . οὔτε ψυχή ἐστιν οὔτε νοῦς . . . οὔτε λόγος ἐστιν, οὔτε νόησις . . . οὔτε ζῇ οὔτε ζωή ἐστιν . . . οὐδέ τι τῶν οὐκ ὄντων, οὐδέ τι τῶν ὄντων ἐστιν, and to Augustin., *de Trin.* v. 1 : ut sic intelligamus Deum, si possumus, quantum possumus sine qualitate bonum sine quantitate magnum, sine indigentia creatorem sine situ praesidentem sine habitu omnia continentem sine loco ubique totum sine tempore sempiternum, sine ulla sui mutatione mutabilia facientem. And Hilary, *de Trin.* ii. 7 : Perfecta scientia est sic Deum scire, ut licet non ignorabilem tamen inenarrabilem scias. Cf. Anselm, *Proslog.* cc. xviii. and xxii.

aim of representing the immediate impression in its different forms than of establishing scientific knowledge. Therefore, just because both have been taken over from Judaism, it has been from the beginning the business of Christian Dogmatics to regulate these representations, so that the anthropomorphic element, to be found more or less in all of them, and the sensuous which is mixed in with many, may be rendered as harmless as possible, and that no retrogression towards polytheism should result. And in this direction the age of Scholasticism contributed much that was profound and excellent. But as afterwards Metaphysics came to be treated separately and apart from Christian Doctrine, in conformity with the nature of the subject, it was for long overlooked (as only too easily happens in such divisions of territory) that these representations of divine attributes are not of philosophical but of religious origin ; and they were taken over into that philosophical discipline which went by the name of Natural Theology. There, however, the more science developed a purely speculative character, the more these representations, which had not arisen on the soil of speculation were bound to be treated in a merely critical or sceptical way. Dogmatic Theology, on the other hand, tried more and more to systematize them, not, if it understood itself rightly, in order to arrive at the consciousness that they contained a complete knowledge of God, but only to assure itself that the God-consciousness which dwells in us in all its differentiations and as it realizes itself at the prompting of different elements of life, was included in them. As, however, the separation was not complete, and intercourse was always lively and manifold between the two disciplines, much has remained permanently under philosophical treatment which belonged only to the dogmatic, and *vice versa*. It is still therefore always necessary to premise that, without making any speculative demands but at the same time without bringing in any speculative aids, we keep ourselves altogether within the limits of purely dogmatic procedure, both with regard to the content of individual definitions and also as to method.

2. It is precisely in this connexion that our proposition denies in general the speculative character of the content of all the divine attributes to be affirmed in Christian doctrine, just for that reason and in so far as they are manifold. For if as such they present a knowledge of the Divine Being, each one of them must express something in God not expressed by the others ; and if the knowledge is appropriate to the object, then, as the knowledge is com-

posite, the object too must be composite.[1] Indeed, even if these attributes only asserted relations of the Divine to the world, God Himself, like the finite life, could only be understood in a multiplicity of functions ; and as these are distinct one from another, and relatively opposed one to another, and at least partly exclusive one of another, God likewise would be placed in the sphere of contradiction. This does not fulfil the requirements of the speculative reason, and definitions of this kind could not pass for speculative propositions ; and just as little could the interests of religion be satisfied if dogmatic definitions were interpreted in this way. For if differentiations were assumed in God, even the feeling of absolute dependence could not be treated as such and as always and everywhere the same. For, in that case, there must be differences having their source in something beyond the difference of the life-moments through which the feeling (of dependence) makes its appearance in the mind. So that while we attribute to these definitions only the meaning stated in our proposition, at the same time everyone retains the liberty, without prejudice to his assent to Christian Doctrine, to attach himself to any form of speculation so long as it allows an object to which the feeling of absolute dependence can relate itself.

3. But as concerns method, in the treatment of Dogmatics up to the present a double procedure is found to predominate. First, rules are put forward as to how one can arrive at right ideas of the divine attributes, and then further, certain rubrics are given under which the various conceptions of divine attributes are to be divided. Now since both aim at systematizing these ideas, the same general assumption has to be made. If the list of these attributes be regarded as a complete summary of definitions to be related to God Himself, then a complete knowledge of God must be derivable from conceptions, and an explanation in due theoretic form would take the place of that ineffability of the Divine Being which the Scriptures—so far as they mention divine attributes—recognize so clearly on every page that we need not quote passages. We have therefore to strive after that completeness alone which guards against letting any of the different moments of the religious self-

---

[1] Mosheim, *Theol. dogm.* i. p. 232 : Si essentia Dei vere differet ab attributis, et si attributa realiter inter se differrent, Deus esset natura composita. Nevertheless many theologians come very near to admitting such differences in God ; *e.g.* Endemann, *Instit.*, p. 51, who distinguishes ea attributa sine quibus Deus nequit esse Deus and determinationes internas Dei, quae salva eius essentia et actualitate abesse possunt, which he therefore calls analoga accidentium.

consciousness pass without asking what are the divine attributes corresponding to them. And with this procedure the classification emerges of its own accord, because in each division only the attributes belonging there can be subjects of exposition. All the more necessary is it to make clear at this point how little is lost for the real matter in hand when we set aside, as we do, the apparatus which has hitherto been employed.

Now we may remark concerning these methods that there are three accepted ways of arriving at the divine attributes—the way of removal of limits (*via eminentiæ*), the way of negation or denial (*via negationis*), and the way of causality (*via causalitatis*). Now it is self-evident that these are by no means homogeneous or co-ordinate. For in the first two a something apart from God must be posited as an attribute; and this, after it has been freed from all limitations, is ascribed to Him, or else its negation is ascribed to Him; while on the other hand causality stands in the closest connexion with the feeling of absolute dependence itself. And if the first two be viewed in their relation to each other, it is clear that negation by itself is no way to posit any attribute, unless something positive remains behind the negation. In that case the negation will consist simply in the fact that the limits of the positive are denied. But in the same manner the way of the removal of limits is a negation, for something is posited of God, but the limits which elsewhere would be co-posited are not posited of God. The identity of these two methods becomes quite obvious in the idea of Infinity, which is at the same time the general form of absence of limits, for what is posited as infinite is also freed from limitation; but at the same time it shows quite generally (by the fact that it is a negation in which nothing is immediately posited but in which everything may be posited which can be thought of as either limited or unlimited), that by negation we can only posit an attribute in so far as something positive remains behind the negation. Both these methods then can only be applied either haphazard with reference to the question whether something, which as such could only be absolutely denied of God, can be conceived as unlimited and posited as a divine attribute; or if this is to be avoided, the application of these methods must be preceded by a definition as to what kind of attribute-conceptions are rightly to be ascribed to God in an unlimited fashion, and what kind simply must be denied of Him. The third method, on the contrary, is certainly an independent one. And even if we do not wish to maintain that all divine attributes corresponding to any modification of our feeling of dependence can equally be derived immediately from the idea of causality, but rather here at the start must premise for one thing that to this conception the other methods must first be applied, *i.e.* that the finitude of causality must be denied and its productivity posited as unlimited ; and again, that in so far as a plurality of attributes is developed out of the idea of the divine causality, this differentiation can correspond to nothing real in God ; indeed, that neither in isolation nor taken together do the attributes express the Being of God in itself (for the essence of that which has been active can never be known simply from its activity alone)—yet this at least is certain, that all the divine attributes to be dealt with in Christian Dogmatics must somehow go back to the divine causality, since they are only meant to explain the feeling of absolute dependence.

Finally, with regard to the divisions of the divine attributes, their great diversity shows how little certainty attaches to the whole procedure and how little any division has been able to count on general agreement ; but of some of them we can here give only brief indications.   Some [1] put forward as chief division that into natural (also called metaphysical, which of course in the case of God must be the same thing) and the moral (which of course has a very objectionable sound, since it leads to the inference that the moral attributes do not belong to God in the same way).[2]   Others first of all divide all divine attributes into active and inactive ; but this is difficult to understand if God cannot be represented otherwise than as living, for in the living as such all is activity.   The one class may indeed be described as inhering in God as determinations of the most perfect Substance, which include no activity *ad extra* ; yet even the inactive attributes can be thought as possessing a purely inward activity ; and in that case this division coincides with another, into absolute and relative attributes.   Apart, however, from the fact that the presupposition of a creation in time implies either that the active attributes first came into being along with time or must previously have been inactive (and on this assumption the division is meaningless), the result is always a duality in God—a purely inner life in virtue of the inactive attributes, and a life related to the world in virtue of the active attri-

---

[1] Particular passages are not quoted, but the reader is referred to the doctrine of the divine attributes in Mosheim, Reinhard, and Schott.

[2] It would belong to the *locus* which some designate as *analogon accidentium.*

butes—and as in this way the two classes seem quite separated, still a third class of attributes might seem to be needed to combine them.   Only if it be asked which are those inactive attributes, we find that there is really no inner life described by them ; in part they are simply formal, as unity, simplicity, eternity ; partly, like independence and unchangeability, they are merely negative ; and partly, as infinity and immeasurability, they are only the measure and quality of the active attributes.   In addition, these divisions turn out not to be exhaustive, since often outside the division isolated attributes are added as inferences, *e.g.* blessedness, glory, majesty, or even that God is the Highest Good.   Hence to avoid this kind of thing it at first sight seems commendable that some should from the outset divide the divine attributes into original and derived ;   and although it is not easy to see how such a division could be made unless the attributes were themselves already given, it might be all the more genuinely dogmatic on that account.   Yet, if it be generally conceded that the difference of the attributes is nothing real in God, each attribute is then only another expression for the whole Being of God, which remains always the same ;   and consequently all are original, and the derived are not attributes at all in the same sense.   But if the attributes so divided be developed from the religious self-consciousness, and the division in this sense be dogmatic, then again there would be no original attribute, but all would equally be very much derived.   In fact, however, the division has not arisen from any such view, but from the view which holds that in another respect the Divine Essence alone may be regarded as original, and all the attributes derived.   Such a derivation of the divine attributes from the Divine Essence would presuppose the latter as known, and would be a purely speculative proceeding.   True, even the purely dogmatic presentation of the attributes can take no other form, except that here nothing can be taken as fundamental save that in the Divine Essence which explains the feeling of absolute dependence.   But if the simple expression that ' everything depends upon God,' is further supplemented by the negative ' but He Himself upon nothing,' at once a fresh opening is given for a division into positive and negative attributes.   And since here in the basis of division the relationship between the highest Essence and all other being is presupposed, it is evident that here absolute or inactive or natural or metaphysical attributes can only be considered as negative, and therefore, strictly taken, without definite content.

4. From this discussion it follows : (a) that the presupposition on which the idea is based that those attributes which express God's relation to the world have the appearance of mere additions and accidents, *i.e.* the presupposition of a separation between what God is, in and for Himself, and what He is in relation to the world, is also the source of the idea that the purely internal (*innerlichen*) attributes can only be conceived negatively ; (b) that the rules laid down to secure the collection of all the divine attributes in one *locus* evoke conceptions which are quite foreign to the interests of religion, and result in a confusion of what it was intended to distinguish. We may hope, therefore, to solve our problem equally well without this apparatus and apart from any such collection if only we treat each individual part of our scheme as adequately as possible. Still, we too shall be able to make use of many of these formulas in our own way. For instance, since we have not to do as yet with the actual manifestation of religious self-consciousness in the form of pleasure and pain, but only with what lies uniformly at the root of these phenomena, *i.e.* with the inner creative disposition towards God-consciousness apart from the consideration whether it is hindered or encouraged, we may call those attributes which come up here ' original ' in so far as the tendency itself is original, and we may call ' derived ' those which will come to our notice in the Second Part. And in considering the manifestations of the religious self-consciousness, if we find that everything which would destroy His presence in us must specially be denied of God, and everything which favours His presence in us specially be affirmed of Him, we can say in our own way that thus divine attributes are formulated by the methods of removal of limits and negation ; but those which arise from present observation, and there will be such, are reached by the method of causality. Still, this diverges fairly widely from the general usage of those formulæ, which rather betrays an analogy with speculation.

§ 51. *The Absolute Causality to which the feeling of absolute dependence points back can only be described in such a way that, on the one hand, it is distinguished from the content of the natural order and thus contrasted with it, and, on the other hand, equated with it in comprehension.*

1. We experience the feeling of absolute dependence as something which can fill a moment both in association with a feeling of partial and conditional dependence and also in association with a

partial and conditioned feeling of freedom ; for self-consciousness always represents finite being as consisting in this mingling of conditioned dependence and conditioned freedom or of partial spontaneity and partial passivity. But whenever dependence or passivity is posited in a part of finite existence, then spontaneity and causality is posited in another part to which the former is related, and this condition of mutual relation of differently distributed causality and passivity constitutes the natural order. It necessarily follows that the ground of our feeling of absolute dependence, *i.e.* the divine causality, extends as widely as the order of nature and the finite causality contained in it ; consequently the divine causality is posited as equal in compass to finite causality. And further, the feeling of absolute dependence stands in exactly the same relationship with the partial dependence-feeling as with the partial freedom-feeling, and so in that relationship the antithesis between these two last disappears ; but finite causality is what it is only by means of its contrast with finite passivity, so it is to be inferred that the divine causality is contrasted with the finite. The divine causality as equivalent in compass to the sum-total of the natural order is expressed in the term, the divine *omnipotence* ; this puts the whole of finite being under the divine causality. The divine causality as opposed to the finite and natural is expressed in the term, the divine *eternity*. That is, the interrelationship of partial causality and passivity makes the natural order a sphere of reciprocal action, and thus of change as such, in that all change and all alteration can be traced back to this antithesis. It is therefore just in the relationship in which the natural causality is set over against the divine, that the essence of the former is to be temporal ; and consequently, so far as eternal is the opposite of temporal, the eternity of God will also be the expression of that antithesis.

In regard to what both terms according to general usage appear to imply as to something more than, and transcending, divine causality or the range of finite being—of this we shall speak in our further elucidation of both concepts. Here it is to be noted generally, that since these two ideas—omnipotence and eternity—are here related only to the divine causality, it may at once be proved in their case also that the individual attributes in their differences correspond to nothing real in God. It is always an inexactitude, which as such must be pointed out when we present these as two different attributes. For the divine causality is only equal in compass to the finite in so far as it is opposite to it in kind, since if it were like it in kind, as it is often represented as being in anthropomorphic ideas of God, it too would belong to the sphere of interaction and thus be a part of the totality of the natural order. In the same way, if the divine causality were not equal in compass to the finite, it could not be set over against it without at the same time disrupting the unity of the natural order ; because otherwise for some finite causality there would be a divine causality, but not for some other. Instead, therefore, of saying God is eternal and almighty, we should rather say He is almighty-eternal and eternal-almighty, or God is eternal omnipotence or almighty eternity. Still, in view of unavoidable comparisons with the more exact definitions of both attributes hitherto current, we must treat of each by itself.

2. It is however natural that, as people always started with a comparison of the divine causality with the finite, these two ideas should, in religious poetry as well as in religious speech, have been associated with two further ideas—the idea of eternity with that of omnipresence, and the idea of omnipotence with that of omniscience. If the two terms just dealt with completely corresponded with the two members of the relationship set forth in our proposition, we should not have to deal in the same manner with the two ideas just mentioned ; it would only be necessary to set forth precautionary rules to ensure that nothing should be included in the thought of them contrary to the two principal ideas and to our proposition. The situation, however, is not quite like that. The idea of eternity does, of course, express a contrast to the causality contained in the natural order, but primarily only as far as this is conditioned by time ; and actually it is conditioned just as much by space, and this no less in the case of the spiritual than of the corporeal. True, if we think of their equality in compass or comprehension, this itself implies that the finite causality everywhere in space is dependent upon the divine ; but the conception which expresses contrast is obscured by this relationship, and the complete expression of it is found only in eternity and omnipresence taken together.

Further, with regard to the conception of omniscience, it perhaps arose in the first place in the sphere of popular, poetical, and religious teaching, to indicate the relationship between God and that which goes on in man's inner life. In Dogmatics, however, it is always dealt with at this point, and taken in its widest application it belongs here ; for we are accustomed to make an antithesis in the sphere of finite causality between living and ' dead ' forces, and notwithstanding that in the doctrine of preservation even conscious finite causality is brought under the divine, the possibility is still not excluded (if once, rightly or wrongly, ' dead ' forces are assumed) of conceiving the idea of omnipotence itself after the analogy of ' dead ' forces. Since consciousness is the highest form of life known to us, this danger is averted by the idea of omniscience. Naturally, however, these additional attributes can just as little each for itself denote anything special and distinct in God as those set forth at the beginning ; and as with reference to that pair it appeared that the most correct expression was to say that God, in His causality, was eternal omnipotence or the almighty-eternal, so this other pair of ideas also would best be included in a similar compound expression. But each of these two ideas also must in itself be an expression for the Divine Essence, because neither can betoken anything different in God ; and thus omnipresence too, when ascribed to the divine causality, is itself eternity, and omniscience is itself omnipotence. But to express the identity of all these attributes in the briefest manner, still another usage may be chosen. If, that is, time and space everywhere represent externality, and we here always presuppose a something which, by extending itself in time and space, becomes an external object, in the same way the antithesis to time and space may be described as the absolutely inward. In the same way, if the term ' omniscience ' well emphasizes the fact that omnipotence is not to be thought of as a ' dead ' force, the same result would be reached by the expression ' Absolute Vitality.' And this pair, inwardness and vitality, would be just as exhaustive a mode of presentation, and one perhaps even more secure against all admixture of alien elements.

FIRST DOCTRINE : GOD IS ETERNAL

§ 52. *By the Eternity of God we understand the absolutely timeless causality of God, which conditions not only all that is temporal, but time itself as well.*

1. If the eternity of God be separated from His omnipotence, which is here confined to its special relation to eternity, it becomes only a so-called ' inactive ' attribute ; and thus is often described as infinity or immeasurability applied to time. To represent it

thus, however, would only encourage the representation of God apart from the manifestations of His power, an idea quite out of harmony with the religious consciousness and so quite empty for us. Such an idea would in any case include the antithesis of rest or idleness and activity, always suspect in relation to God, but in the sphere of Christian religion quite inapplicable. The religious consciousness, however (since we relate the world as such to God), becomes actual only as consciousness of His *eternal power*.[1] On the other hand, poetical representations express the eternity of God as an existence before all time;[2] but this cannot be taken up into didactic language without harm, for in this sphere a comparison of more or less can only be made between similars; but the divine causality, since time itself is conditioned by it,[3] must so much the more be thought of as utterly timeless.[4] This is achieved through expressions denoting the temporal, and therefore as it were pictorially, since the temporal oppositions of before and after, older and younger disappear in coincidence when applied to God.[5]

While, however, we relate the eternity of God to His omnipotence, and make it equal and identical therewith, it still does not by any means follow that the temporal existence of the world must reach back into infinity, so that no beginning of the world can be thought of.[6] For as what now arises in time is yet grounded in the omnipotence of God, and therefore willed and enacted by Him in an eternal, *i.e.* timeless, manner, the world also could be timelessly willed to emerge in the beginning of time. On the other hand, we need not be anxious lest, if the world is given no beginning or end, the difference between divine causality and causality within the natural order should be cancelled, and the world be as eternal as God. On the contrary, the eternity of God remains none the less unique, since the antithesis between the temporal and the

---

[1] Rom. 1[20]. [2] Ps. 90[2].

[3] Augustin., *de Gen. c. Man.* i. 3: Deus enim fecit et tempora . . . Quomodo enim erat tempus, quod Deus non fecerat, cum omnium temporum ipse sit fabricator.—The same meaning seems to be indicated by the phrase ἄφθαρτος βασιλεὺς τῶν αἰώνων, 1 Tim. 1[17].

[4] Aug., *Conf.* xi. 16: Nec tu tempore tempora praecedis, alioquin non omnia tempora praecederes; sed praecedis omnia celsitudine semper praesentis aeternitatis.—Boeth., p. 137: Interminabilis vitae tota simul et perfecta possessio. Aeternum necesse est et sui compos praesens sibi semper assistere, et infinitatem mobilis temporis habere praesentem.

[5] Augustin., *de Gen. ad litt.* viii. 48: Nullo temporum vel intervallo vel spatio incommutabili aeternitate et antiquior est omnibus, quia ipse est ante omnia, et novior omnibus, quia idem ipse post omnia. The same as 2 Pet. 3[8], in another form.

[6] Cf. Joh. Damasc., *c. Man.* vi.: οὐ γὰρ πρότερον μὴ θέλων ὕστερον ἠθέλησεν, ἀλλ᾽ ἀεὶ ἤθελεν ἐν τῷ ὑπ᾽ αὐτοῦ ὡρισμένῳ καιρῷ γίνεσθαι τὴν κτίσιν.

eternal is not in the least diminished by the infinite duration of time.[1]

2. But, of course, this relationship is much obscured by all explanations of the eternity of God which either equate it with apparent eternity,[2] *i.e.* endless time, or even merely compare it therewith.[3] Even the common formula to the effect that the eternity of God is the attribute in virtue of which He has neither begun nor will cease to exist, is of this kind. For since here only the terminal points of temporal duration are negated, while between them the existence of God is made equivalent to a temporal one, the intrinsically temporal character and the measurability of the Divine Being, and therefore also His activity through time, are not denied but rather indirectly affirmed. We must therefore reject as inadequate all those explanations which abrogate for God only the limits of time and not time itself, and would form eternity from time by the removal of limits, while in fact these are opposites. Even if poetical passages cannot describe eternity except by pictures of unending time,[4] the New Testament itself teaches us how for didactic purposes these must be supplemented.[5] While therefore it must be admitted of some theologians that, with Socinus, only for other dogmatic reasons, they have here rejected the perfectly scriptural statements of Augustine and Boethius, in the case of others that rejection can only be explained as due to the fear that if eternity be taken as timelessness nothing really is affirmed at all. But this can only happen if eternity is placed among the inactive attributes, while yet it is also thought that each such attribute by itself alone expresses the Essence of the Divine Being. On the other hand, it disappears if, as we demand, this conception is combined with that of omnipotence. For, in that a divine activity is posited, something may be posited, unknown indeed and perhaps not clearly conceivable, but by no means simply nothing. Indeed, finite being offers us some real help in

---

[1] Augustin., *de mus.* vi. 29: tempora fabricantur et ordinantur aeternitatem imitantia.—Idem, *de Gen. c. Man.* i. 4: Non enim coaevum Deo mundum istum dicimus, quia non ejus aeternitatis est hic mundus, cuius aeternitatis est Deus.

[2] Socin., *Praelectt.* cap. viii. : Nec vero in mundi creatione tempus primum extitit . . . quamobrem ipsius quoque Dei respectu aliquid praeteritum aliquid vero praesens, aliquid etiam futurum est. Mosheim, *Theol. dogm.* i. p. 254 : Aeternitas est duratio infinita. Cf. Cudw., *Syst. intell.*, p. 780.—Reinh., p. 104 : Aeternitas est existentiae divinae infinita continuatio, which assumes an inadmissible distinction between substance and existence in God.

[3] Eckermann, *Dogm.* i. p. 123, calls it a necessity, because he compares it with the immortality of the soul and the indestructibility of force.

[4] Job 36[26], Ps. 102[28].   [5] Cf. 2 Pet. 3[8] with Ps. 90[2].

conceiving the idea of eternity, since to a great degree time is merely an adjunct to finite being in so far as it is caused, and to a less degree in so far as it is cause. But in so far as finite being produces time-series with their content, thus remaining the same and identical with itself (as, *e.g.*, the Ego, as the enduring ground of all changing spiritual states, especially of resolves, each of which again as a moment of the Ego produces a concrete time-series), then, as the enduring causal ground relatively to the changing caused, it is posited as timeless. And with some such kind of analogy we must rest content.

Postscript : The Unchangeability of God

If the idea of eternity is thus conceived, there is no reason to introduce unchangeability as a separate attribute : it is already contained in the idea of eternity. For if God, in His relation to the world, conditioning its absolute dependence, is completely time-less, there is in His being no manifold of parts following one upon another. It appears to be different if, setting out from a distinction between substance and existence in God, eternity is presented merely as one aspect of unchangeability.[1] But for us it comes to the same thing, since the other aspect is an inactive attribute which expresses nothing actually present in the religious consciousness. We may do better, therefore, to take the principle, that God is unchangeable, merely as a cautionary rule to ensure that no religious emotion shall be so interpreted, and no statement [2] about God so understood, as to make it necessary to assume an alteration in God of any kind.

Second Doctrine : God is Omnipresent

§ 53. *By the Omnipresence of God we understand the absolutely space-less causality of God, which conditions not only all that is spatial, but space itself as well.*

1. This proposition is quite similar in verbal form to the fore-going ; and the idea of omnipresence, indeed, is only taken up here because the contrast between the divine causality and the finite in the term eternity has been predominantly referred to time. It

---

[1] Cf. Reinhard, *Dogm.*, p. 105. If we regard unchangeableness in relation to the essence of God, it is simplicity; if in relation to His existence, it is eternity. But previously he had treated simplicity as a separate attribute, and eternity was unendingness contemplated as belonging to God's existence.

[2] Ex. 32^{14}, Jer. 26^{13} 42^{10}.

seems unnecessary then to do more than to carry over in the same form everything belonging to the former proposition, changing time into space.   In religious poetry from of old, indeed, this conception has been more splendidly and more widely honoured than that of eternity.[1]   Indeed, it must be said in general that far more religious moments evoke the idea of omnipresence, and therefore it is a more living idea and has a more general currency.   The relation of God and time expressed in the conception of eternity, on the other hand, pervades the religious life to a lesser degree, and is marked by a colder tone in consequence.   This is probably due to the fact that the majority of religious people are bound up in their consciousness with the present.   The equivalence of divine causality with the whole content of the finite enables every act to excite the religious consciousness, every act, that is, in which we take up into ourselves a part of the natural order or identify ourselves with such a part, every moment of our self-consciousness as it extends over the whole world.   And thus, whenever a person either moves or is moved, he is also drawn to a conscious apprehension of the power of the Highest directly near to him in all finite causality.   It is natural, then, that we are far more prone to transfer ourselves in thought to the farthest point of space, which after all comes immediately to our apprehension, than to go back to the remotest time.   And yet from our standpoint this difference appears unjustifiable, however natural it may be ; and it is incumbent on Dogmatics as a scientific discipline to see whether it can remove the discrepancy arising from the immediate juxtaposition in this way of the two ideas.   At the same time it must take care lest the greater vividness of the conception now to be dealt with should be associated with a large admixture of the sensuous, and should be affected by it.

Now, just as the divine causality as eternity may easily appear to have lost its invariableness if the non-existence of the finite causality be asserted prior to its existence, in the same way a like result easily appears to hold in connexion with space.   For we have to admit that finite causality is greater and less at different points in space ; least, *i.e.* where the space is occupied with so-called ' dead ' forces, and greater where there is a greater development of life, and greatest where clear human consciousness is active, and so upwards.   Now as against this it must be said, first of all, that, of course, no distinction in the almighty presence of God is hereby

[1] Ps. 139, and elsewhere in the Psalter.

posited, but only in the receptivity of the finite being to the causal activity of which the divine presence is related.[1] For thus the receptivity of man is greater for it than that of any other earthly being, but amongst men it is greatest in the religious. Yet even this only becomes plain when it is remembered that, according to the statement given in our proposition, the divine omnipresence ought to be thought of as completely spaceless,[2] and consequently not as greater or smaller at different places.

2. It is, however, difficult successfully to avoid all such definitions as put something spatial into the divine omnipresence, if we try to carry over the poetical and popular descriptions (which almost always set forth the space-conditioning causality of God by the figure of unlimited space itself), into the dogmatic sphere. It is no less difficult if we begin by looking on the divine omnipresence, without relation to the divine causality as an inactive attribute. In relation to the first, we may not without advantage employ the description of the divine causality, as current in Greek theology, by the expressions ἀδιαστασία and συνουσία—both, of course, related to God's almighty presence. For the negation of all remoteness expresses the contrast with finite causality, which—as well in the case of the spiritual as in that of the corporeal—becomes weakened by distance from its place of origin or central point, so that each force, as it is no longer present where it no longer works, is also less as such where it effects less. This difference it is which is denied, and thus an everywhere uniform self-identity of the divine causality is affirmed. The relation to space, however, which lurks in the expression ' not *outside* one another,' and thus also in ' *everywhere* uniform self-identity,' applies only to the finite as that which is effected, but not to God. The same is to be noted of the term συνουσία, which can only lay down that finite causality is nowhere without the divine, but not also that the divine with the finite is in space. For not only is the συνουσία ἐνεργετικὴ related to finite causality, but also the ὑποστατικὴ in so far as it lays down the divine omnipresence as the maintenance of things in their being

---

[1] Joh. Damasc., *de fid. orth.* i. 13 : αὐτὸς μὲν γὰρ διὰ πάντων ἀμιγῶς διήκει, καὶ πᾶσι μεταδίδωσι τῆς ἑαυτοῦ ἐνεργείας κατὰ τὴν ἑκάστου ἐπιτηδειότητα καὶ δεκτικὴν δύναμιν.

[2] Augustin., *de div. quaest.* xx. : Deus non alicubi est, quod enim alicubi est, continetur loco ; et tamen quia est, et in loco non est, in illo sunt potius omnia quam ipse alicubi. Nec tamen ita in illo, ut ipse sit locus.—Idem, *Ep.* 187, 11 : Et in eo ipso quod dicitur Deus ubique diffusus carnali resistendum est cogitationi . . . ne quasi spatiosa magnitudine opinemur Deum per cuncta diffundi, sicut aër aut lux.

and in their powers. Any other explanation would find it difficult
to avoid the suspicion of a mixture of the divine being with the
finite, and therefore a semblance of pantheism. This semblance
belongs also very strongly to the definition that God is everywhere
not *circumscriptivè* but *repletivè*. For when there is space-filling,
we cannot get away from the analogy with expansive forces, and
then the notion of an infinite extension to be predicated of God lies
too near ; and even the improvement which is introduced when we
say that this is not to be understood corporeally (as though the
existence of a finite in space were hindered by the divine space-
filling), but in a divine way, is seldom interpreted with proper
caution.[1] And if the expression used be that God includes all places
in Himself,[2] this easily suggests the opposite, namely, that God is
that which universally includes all things even spatially ; and if
this omnipresence be thought of as inactive instead of active, nothing
almost remains except that God is that which is in itself empty.
So, too, the kindred expression, that God Himself is the place of all
things, ought on this very account to be used only with the greatest
caution.[3] Hence in this matter there remains a fundamental
improvement, one which removes the spatial element altogether,
namely, the formula that God is in Himself ; [4] but, of course, along
with this it must be asserted that the effects of His causal being-in-
Himself are everywhere. The same result is reached indirectly
and, as it were, pictorially by the abrogation of spatial contrasts.[5]
As far as other matters are concerned, the distinction between the
divine omnipresence as an inactive and as an active attribute
almost inevitably destroys the essential self-identity of the divine
causality, and thus only produces confusion. If, for example, one
distinguishes between the omnipresence of God so far as related to
Himself and omnipresence in relation to the creatures,[6] and in

---

[1] This is to be commended in Joh. Damas., *l.c.*: Ἔστι δὲ καὶ νοητὸς τόπος,
ἔνθα νοεῖται καὶ ἔστιν ἡ νοητὴ καὶ ἀσώματος φύσις, ἔνθαπερ πάρεστι καὶ ἐνεργεῖ . . .
ὁ μὲν οὖν θεὸς . . . λέγεται καὶ ἐν τόπῳ εἶναι, καὶ λέγεται τόπος θεοῦ, ἔνθα ἔκδηλος ἡ
ἐνέργεια αὐτοῦ γίνεται.
[2] Hilar., *d. f. Trin.* i. 6 : Nullus sine Deo, neque ullus non in Deo locus
est.
[3] Theoph., *ad Aut.* ii. : Θεὸς γὰρ οὐ χωρεῖται, ἀλλ᾽ αὐτός ἐστι τόπος τῶν ὅλων.
[4] Augustin., *Ep.* 187, 14: Nullo contentus loco, sed in se ipse ubique totus.
[5] Augustin., *de Gen. ad litt.* viii. 48: incommutabili excellentique potentia
et interior omni re quia in ipso sunt omnia, et exterior omni re, quia ipse est
super omnia.—Hilar., *l.c.*: ut in his cunctis originibus creaturarum Deus intra
extraque et supereminens et internus, id est circumfusus et infusus in omnia
nosceretur, cum . . . exteriora sua insidens ipse, rursum exterior interna
concluderet atque ita totus ipse intra extraque se continens neque infinitus
abesset a cunctis, neque cuncta ei, qui infinitus est, non inessent.
[6] radicaliter et relative. Cf. Gerh., *loc. th.* t. iii. p. 136.

addition accepts a creation in time, then before creation there would only be the first kind of omnipresence and the other would be then added. Or if one makes the world finite in space, and thus, of course, at the limit supposes an always empty space outside, then again the first kind of omnipresence stretches further than the other, and it very easily comes to be said that in and for Himself God is outside the world, but, in relation to the creatures He is present only *in* the world—which introduces a similar inequality. Here, too, the Socinians have gone furthest,[1] but principally in order to avoid the appearance of pantheism,[2] which they thought could only be achieved in this way; for they could not quite free themselves from spatiality in thinking of the being and activity of God. And this becomes most clearly apparent when in defence of this view it is alleged that it is a perfection in finite things if their power extends further than their essence. As opposed to this, the everywhere-ness of God must, of course, be related equally to His essence and His power.

Postscript : The Immensity of God

It follows clearly that we shall not need to treat further of this term as the designation of a special divine attribute. Its use is bound up with the greatest difficulties.[3] Partly it is equated with the infinity of God, and in part it is derived therefrom ; since of course infinity regarded as substance yields immensity, but regarded as existence eternity. But just as when taken so time is not done away in eternity, but only its limits ; so too with immensity, it is not space but its limits that are abrogated ;[4] and we should then in this way have only an omnipresence separated from omnipotence, and consequently conceived as inactive but always spatial. But if immensity is thought of as infinity itself, this again is frequently presented as the attribute of all God's attributes. In that case we should have no reason whatever to speak of it here, nor indeed would it ever come up for discussion ; for in virtue of its negative content it could be no true attribute, not even of the attributes, but only a reservation with regard to

[1] Smalcius, *refut. Franc.*, p. 4 : Essentia et praesentia Dei in locis omnibus nulla datur, nec enim frustra in coelis Deus esse dicitur.

[2] Thom. Pisecius, *respon. ad rat. Camp.* : Virtutem Dei infinitam permeare omnia scripturae testantur, non essentiam, cujus infinitate concessa universa orbis machina, quam cernimus, corpus quoddam divinum esset.

[3] Cf. Gerh., *loc. T.* iii. p. 122, and Reinhard, *Dogm.*, pp. 101–104.

[4] See Mosheim, *Theol. dogm.* i. p. 247 : Quando infinitas cum respectu loci seu spatii consideratur dicitur *immensitas*.

them.   It would then have to repudiate for all the attributes every analogy with the finite, and would be the general anti-anthropo-morphic and anti-somatomorphic formula.   As such it has guided us even here and will do so also in the future, without our finding it right on that account to erect it into an attribute.   For since here we have to do only with the causality of God, the con-ception of the infinity of God is useful only as warding off analogy with finite causality.   But all finite causality is measurable in time and space ;   consequently we have made the Divine infinite in the most proper sense, since we made it absolutely timeless and non-spatial.   And the term immensity is easily brought round to equivalence with this proper meaning of infinity, if one only says *immeasurability* ;   because all measure may be resolved into time and space determinations.   Immensity is usually defined by laying down, on the one hand, a being everywhere, and, on the other, a warning that this is not to be taken to imply extension. But once the activity of God has been separated from the being of God, and only the latter regarded, there of course remains for this immensity only a negation with no positive substratum which could have emerged from religious emotion.   Whereas, on the contrary, it is self-evident that the contrast between the feeling of absolute dependence and the feeling of either partial dependence or partial freedom (both being equally spatial and temporal) includes in itself the implication that the causality which evokes the former feeling cannot be temporal and spatial.

THIRD DOCTRINE : GOD IS OMNIPOTENT

§ 54. *In the conception of the divine Omnipotence two ideas are con-tained : first, that the entire system of Nature, comprehending all times and spaces, is founded upon divine causality, which as eternal and omnipresent is in contrast to all finite causality ; and second, that the divine causality, as affirmed in our feeling of absolute dependence, is completely presented in the totality of finite being, and consequently everything for which there is a causality in God happens and becomes real.*

1. Since the natural order is naught but the twofold mutually determined sum of the finite causing and the finite caused, the first part of our proposition first of all implies that each finite given as such, in virtue of its foundation in the divine omnipotence, effects everything which the causality implanted in it makes it capable of

effecting in the sphere of universal causality. It is, however, equally
implied that every effect within the natural order is also, in virtue
of its being ordained by the divine causality, the pure result of
all the causes within the natural order, according to the measure
in which it stands in relation with each of them. As now everything that we can regard as a separate thing for itself within the
totality of finite being must be ' cause ' as well as effect, there is
never anything of any kind which can begin to be an object of the
divine causality, though previously—hence somehow independent
of God and opposed to Him—in existence. Rather on such a view
(whether it be that the activity of the divine omnipotence as
such begins in this way, or that by such opposition its activity
is interrupted, whether seldom or often matters not), the
foundation feeling of religion would thereby be destroyed.
If this is not the immediate result, it at once appears when
we extend our self-consciousness to cover the whole of finite
being and so represent that object also ; for then there
would no longer be absolute dependence but only partial
dependence.

Further, since divine omnipotence can only be conceived as
eternal and omnipresent, it is inadmissible to suppose that at any
time anything should begin to be through omnipotence ; on the
contrary, through omnipotence everything is already posited
which comes into existence through finite causes, in time and space.
Similarly, because a thing can be recognized as having happened
through finite causation, it is not on this account the less posited
through the divine omnipotence, nor is that which cannot be traced
to finite causation the more on that account to be referred to
divine omnipotence. Thus the divine omnipotence can never in
any way enter as a supplement (so to speak) to the natural causes in
their sphere ; for then it must like them work temporally and
spatially ; and at one time working so, and then again not so,
it would not be self-identical and so would be neither eternal nor
omnipresent. Rather everything is and becomes altogether by
means of the natural order, so that each takes place through all
and all wholly through the divine omnipotence, so that all in-
divisibly exists through One.

2. The second part of our proposition rests upon the fact that
in our sphere we only come to the idea of the divine omnipotence
through the conception of the feeling of absolute dependence, and
we lack any point of connexion for making demands upon the

divine causality which extend beyond the natural order embraced
by this feeling. As against this it seems as though it might be said
that what we call ' all ' consists of the actual and the potential,
and omnipotence must therefore embrace both of these ; but that
if it presents itself completely and exhaustively in the totality of
finite being, then it includes only the actual but not also the potential.
But how little the difference between actual and potential can exist
for God will appear very clearly, if we only notice in what cases we
ourselves chiefly apply it. We conceive, in the first place, much to
be possible in a thing by virtue of the general conception of the
species to which it belongs, which is not actual, however, because
excluded by its special character ; whilst in the case of other individuals of the same species other determinations, possible in virtue
of the idea of the species, remain excluded for the same reason.
Here, however, something appears to us as possible only because
we find that the particularity of the individual is a problem we are
never fully in a position to solve. But with regard to God such a
distinction between the general and the individual is not applicable ; in Him the species exists originally as the sum-total of its
individual existences, and these in turn are given and established
together with their place in the species, so that what does not
hereby become actual, is also, so far as He is concerned, not potential.
In the same way, we say that much is possible by virtue of the
nature of a thing (when we take together its determinations by its
species and as an individual being), which yet does not become
actual because it is hindered by the position of the thing in the
sphere of general interaction. We rightly make this distinction
and attribute truth, as in the former case, to that which is thought
of in this way as being possible, because it is only by this indirect
method that we pass from the unfruitful sphere of abstractions and
put together a view of the conditioned development of individual
existence. On the other hand, if we could have taken into account
for each point the influence of the whole system of interaction, we
should then have had to say that what was not actual was also not
possible within the system of nature. In God, however, the one is
not separated from the other, that which exists for itself having
one ground and the system of interaction another, but both these
are grounded with and through each other, so that in relation to
Him only that is possible which has its foundation in both equally.
But every case which has any validity for us, may be reduced under
one of these heads. The idea of a potentiality outside the sum of

the actual [1] has no validity even for our minds ; for not only does the religious self-consciousness not lead us to such a point, but, in addition, however we arrived at it, we should then have to accept a self-limitation of the divine omnipotence which can never be given in experience. Nor can we conceive any ground for such a self-limitation, unless that which is thought of as potential could enter into existence, not as an increase, but only in some way or other as a diminution of the actual, whereby the whole assumption is destroyed.[2]

3. Since in relation to God no distinction between the potential and the actual can be allowed, it is easy to pass judgment on the popular explanation of God's omnipotence, which has often been adopted even in scientific discussions, namely, that it is the attribute in virtue of which God is able to effect all that is possible, or all which contains no contradiction in itself. If, of course, contradiction is taken *realiter* and that is called contradictory which can find no place in the whole of existence, this is perfectly correct ; for all the compossible is certainly produced by the divine omnipotence. Objection might still be made to the one point of saying that, in virtue of omnipotence, God *can* effect, not *does* effect, everything ; for thereby a distinction is made between ' can ' and ' will,' and the explanation comes near to another, namely, that omnipotence is the attribute by which God can do what He will. There is, however, as little distinction between ' can ' and ' will ' in God, as between the actual and the possible.[3] For whichever is greater than the other, the will or the ability, there is always a limitation, which can only be done away with if both be made equal in range. Moreover the very separation of each in itself, as though, that is, ability were a different condition from will, is an imperfection. For should I think of an ability without will, the will must proceed from an individual impulse, and so also always from a caused impulse ; and should I think of a will without

---

[1] Statements such as that of Basil, *hom. I. in hexaëm.* : τὸν τοῦ παντὸς τούτου δημιουργὸν οὐχ ἑνὶ κόσμῳ σύμμετρον ἔχειν τὴν ποιητικὴν δύναμιν, ἀλλ᾽ εἰς τὸ ἀπειροπλάσιον ὑπερβαίνουσαν, we must explain by the limits of contemporary knowledge of the universe, in contrast to which we have already arrived at the ἀπειροπλάσιον.

[2] Abelard rightly says, *Introd.* iii. 5 : Potest, quod convenit, non convenit quod praetermittit, ergo id tantum facere potest, quod quandoque facit. Cf. August., *Enchirid.* 24 : Neque enim ob aliud veraciter vocatur omnipotens, nisi quoniam quicquid vult potest.

[3] Joh. Damasc., *d. fid. orth.* i. 8, calls God indeed δύναμιν οὐδενὶ μέτρῳ γνωριζομένην, μόνῳ τῷ οἰκείῳ βουλήματι μετρουμένην. But this is only meant to bring out one side, for he says, i. 13 : πάντα μὲν ὅσα θέλει δύναται, οὐχ ὅσα δὲ δύναται θέλει.

ability, the ability cannot be grounded in the inner power, but must be given from without. And if, since in God there is no willing through individual impulses, and no ability given from without, waxing and waning, the two in God cannot be separated even in thought, so also, since ' can ' and ' will ' together are necessarily doing, neither willing and doing are to be separated, nor ' can ' and ' do,' but the entire omnipotence is, undivided and unabbreviated, the omnipotence that does and effects all. But it is useless to say anything further on this view on account of its inevitable separation between ' can ' and ' will.' [1]

4. With the misunderstanding just exposed there are connected many distinctions within the divine omnipotence, as well as divisions of it, given currency especially by the scholastics, which can be ruled out without loss. To these belongs, in the first place, the contrast between a mediate and immediate, or absolute and ordered, exercise of the divine omnipotence, *i.e.* between cases when it acts without or with intermediary causes. Now when individual effects are referred some only to the former and some only to the latter, the distinction is false. For everything which happens in time and space has its determinations in the totality of that which is outside it in space and before it in time, however much they may be hidden, and so far come under the ordered power ; and if some, to the exclusion of others, be referred back to the immediate power, the whole order of nature would be abrogated. If, however, we think not of the individual but of the world itself as the effect of the divine omnipotence, we have no choice but to recur to its immediate exercise. Hence in so far as we can apply the idea of creation in detail, we apply at the same time and equally the idea of the absolute exercise of omnipotence ; but in so far as we use the idea (rightly understood) of concurrence or preservation, [2] in this aspect of it, everything is referred to the ordered exercise of power which establishes the dependence of each individual on the totality of existence eternally, and for the maintenance of the general interaction makes use of the forces of individual things. There is no point, however, which we can relate only to the absolute (which by way of stricter contrast we ought to call not ' unordered ' but ' ordering ') exercise of omnipotence and not to the ordered exercise and conversely.

---

[1] This is true of all such formulæ as Deus absolutâ suâ potentiâ multa potest, quae non vult nec forte unquam volet ; or Nunquam tot et tanta efficit Deus, quia semper plura et majora efficere possit (cf. Gerh., *loc. theol.* i. pp. 132 f.).

[2] Cf. § 38. 1 and § 45, *Postscript.*

The case is similar with the distinction almost everywhere drawn between the divine will as absolute and as conditioned. It is clear that on this view ability is still made greater than will, because in the former no such distinction is drawn ; and there arises a gradation, so that of what God can do some things He wills absolutely, some under conditions, and still others not at all. But it is by no means the case that God wills some things absolutely and others conditionally ; just as with regard to every event there is something of which one can say, if this were not then that event would not be ; so with regard to every individual thing—the fact that it exists and that it exists in this way—we can say that God wills it conditionally, because everything is conditioned by something else. But that whereby something else is conditioned is itself conditioned by the divine will ; indeed in such a way that the divine will upon which the conditioning rests, and the divine will upon which the conditioned rests is not different in each case, but one only and the same ; it is the divine will embracing the whole framework of mutually conditioning finite being : and this naturally is the absolute will, because nothing conditions it. In this way everything individual would be willed by God conditionally, but the whole willed absolutely as a unity. On the other hand, if for once we take an individual out of the order, and relate it *so* to the divine will, we shall have to say that each individual existing for itself, so far as we regard it not as conditioned by, but as co-conditioning the whole, is so fully willed by God as what it is, that everything else must be so, and cannot be otherwise than as follows from its action ; which is as much as to say that it is absolutely willed by God. In this respect, therefore, it can be said that every individual, so far as it must be affected by the rest, is also only conditionally willed by God ; but, of course, not as though on that account it were any the less willed, or any the less came to reality. Everything, however, so far as it is itself effective, and in various ways conditions other things, is absolutely willed by God.

But the whole idea of the divine omnipotence appears most endangered, when an active and an inactive, and a free and a necessary, divine will are set one over against the other. The *necessary* will would be related to what God wills in virtue of His essence, the *free* to that which, so far as His essence is concerned, He could just as well not will ; [1] where it is assumed that it does

---

[1] Gerh., *loc. th.* iii. p. 203 : *Ex necessitate naturae* vult quae de se ipso vult,

not belong to His essence to reveal Himself. Thus by means of
the necessary will God wills Himself, and by means of the free will
He wills what is other than Himself. But a ' self-willing ' of God
is always a most awkward formula, and almost inevitably raises
the hair-splitting question whether, just as the world exists by
reason of His free will, so also God exists because, by reason of His
necessary will, He wills Himself, or whether He wills Himself because
He is. Or, to express it rather differently, whether this self-willing
is more in the way of self-preservation, or more in the way of self-
approval, or (if both are taken together) after the manner of self-
love.[1] Now since self-preservation can scarcely be thought of as
a real will unless there is something to be striven for or averted,[2]
and self-approval almost necessarily implies a divided consciousness, it is easily seen that this self-willing can mean nothing but the
very existence of God posited under the form of will. But this,
which is in God purely inward and related solely to Himself, can
never come into our religious self-consciousness. In any case,
therefore, this necessary will of God, as in no way belonging here,
would fall under speculative theology. Moreover, it seems that this
contrast cannot be applied to God at all, and what has been brought
under the contrasted heads respectively is not really separable.
For where such a contrast exists the necessary must be unfree, and
the free be grounded in no necessity, and so arbitrary. Each, however, is an imperfection ; and consequently this contrast has its
place solely in that existence in which each being is co-determined
by the rest. We must therefore think of nothing in God as
necessary without at the same time positing it as free, nor as free
unless at the same time it is necessary. Just as little, however,
can we think of God's willing Himself, and God's willing the world,
as separated the one from the other. For if He wills Himself, He
wills Himself as Creator and Sustainer, so that in willing Himself,
willing the world is already included ; and if He wills the world,
in it He wills His eternal and ever-present omnipotence, wherein
willing Himself is included ; that is to say, the necessary will is
included in the free, and the free in the necessary. Obviously, too,

nulla re sive extra se sive intra se permotus. *Libere* vult, quae de creaturis
vult, quae *poterat* et velle et nolle.
  [1] Wegscheider, *Institt.*, § 67 : Voluntas necessaria, *i.e.* actus voluntatis quae
e scientia necessaria promanare dicitur, amor nimirum quo Deus . . . se ipsum
complectatur necesse est.
  [2] Many, of course, still describe the divine will in this way, *e.g.* Mosheim,
Th. dogm., p. 277 : actus appetendi quae bona sunt et aversandi quae mala
sunt.

there is nothing in the way in which God comes into our religious self-consciousness which corresponds to this contrast, and it lacks dogmatic content.

And finally as to the contrast between the *active* and *inactive* divine will : it first of all contradicts the generally recognized proposition that the divine will extends no further than divine ability.[1] For how should a true and real will be inactive unless it lacked the ability ? But it is to be noted that the one all-embracing divine will is identical with the eternal omnipotence ; and if then, as eternal, it is timeless, the content of no definite time can quite correspond with it, and so from this point of view the divine will is always inactive. But it is also always active, because there is no fraction of time which does not pass in fulfilment of it, and what seems to resist or repress the divine will is always simply co-operating in its temporal fulfilment.[2] If, then, we hold this fast and distinguish between will and command, it is quite unnecessary to deal with the idea of a precedent and a consequent will, expressions which again suggest the appearance of a change in the will of God.

POSTSCRIPT : THE INDEPENDENCE OF GOD

If the feeling of absolute dependence comprises a reference to divine omnipotence, it is no longer necessary to bring out the independence of God as a special attribute. For if one remains at all true to the derivation of the word, it is, as the opposite of that dependence in which we find ourselves, simply a negative attribute and, as it were, a shadow-picture of omnipotence, and only states that God has no foundation or cause of His being outside Himself, which coincides with the scholastic ' *aseitas*,' virtually ' existence-from-self.' If, now, this be changed into a formula of quite similar content, namely, that in relation to God there can be no question of a ground, one sees at once how this is already completely contained in our two main conceptions, eternity and omnipotence. But, of course, the term independence is dealt with in very different ways. Some include in the idea that God is Lord over all.[3] But

---

[1] Cf. Gerh., *loc. th.* i. p. 154 : Praeter voluntatem non indiget aliqua potentia.

[2] On this are also based the formulæ of Augustine, to which we must always come back, *Enchirid.* 26 : Omnipotentis voluntas semper invicta est—nec nisi volens quicquam facit, et omnia quaecunque vult facit. 27 : dum tamen credere non cogamur aliquid omnipotentem Deum voluisse fieri, factumque non esse.

[3] Reinhard's *Dogm.*, p. 106 : Independentia est illud attributum, quo nemini quicquam debet, et ipse solus est omnium rerum dominus.—Joh. Damasc., *de orth. fid.* i. 19, can scarcely have regarded αὐτεξούσιος (which, for

Lordship is connected with independence only on the presupposition that the independent is at the same time in need of something, for otherwise one can be completely independent without having even the slightest Lordship.   Thus if the divine attributes are to be separated at all, this combination is not practicable.   Then if ' indebted to no one ' has only a moral sense, and denies the applicability of the conception of obligation in relation to God, the conception is thereby divided, and there is, according to the usual procedure, a physical and a moral independence.   About the latter we have nothing to say here ; and since ' to be Lord over all ' can be only an expression of omnipotence (if, that is, we leave out in advance the moral consideration which here too enters, that God as Lord cannot be obligated, *i.e.* can stand under no law), we have nothing left but the above-mentioned ' existence-from-self ' of God—a speculative formula which, in the dogmatic sphere, we can only convert into the rule that there is nothing in God for which a determining cause is to be posited outside God.   But this is so clearly defined in our first explanation,[1] that it is unnecessary to bring it up specially here.

FOURTH DOCTRINE : GOD IS OMNISCIENT

§ 55. *By the divine Omniscience is to be understood the absolute spirituality of the divine Omnipotence.*

1. This explanation is quite in keeping with the manner in which we arrived at this conception above.[2]   And yet even here it is to be premised that everywhere it is chiefly intended much more to bring out the truth that the divine causality should be thought of as absolutely living than that a similarity should be definitely established between God and that which we designate as spirit in the existence presented to us.   The former is essential if the feeling of absolute dependence, or piety, is to be true and real ; for a lifeless and blind necessity would not really be something with which we could stand in relation ; and such a necessity, conceived as equal to the whole of finite causality yet contrasted with it, would really mean positing the latter alone, and thus declaring an absolute dependence unreal, because as self-caused beings we are not absolutely dependent on finite causality.   But to define the similarity

the most part, corresponds to *independent*) as forming one predicate together with αὐτοκρατής and ἀνενδεής.

[1] Cf. § 4, 4.   [2] § 51, 2.

between God and the spiritual in a finite sense is certainly a problem only to be solved by endless approximation ; for owing to the intermixture of receptivity and passivity in some degree to be found (even if unrecognized) in every available term, we inevitably co-posit something which must then be got rid of again by the use of some other term. If then here (where we are considering the feeling of absolute dependence only in its essence, and so have to do with the divine causality also only in its essence), Spirituality be denoted by the function of knowing, our first rule must be to exclude from the spirituality of the Divine Essence everything which necessarily contains in itself receptivity or passivity. Therefore just as the divine will must not be thought of as a faculty of desire, so the divine omniscience must not be considered as a perceiving or experiencing, a thinking together or a viewing together. Now since we are acquainted with no other kind of knowledge than that in which spontaneity and receptivity pervade each other, only in different degrees, we distinguish, according as one of the two predominates, between the knowledge which is chiefly constructed from within and that which is chiefly derived from without ; and still more, since the greater part of our thinking presupposes existence as its object, and is related only slightly to our productive activity, we distinguish between the purposive activity of thought upon which production follows, and the observing activity which relates to something already present. But this last distinction is completely inapplicable to God, for there are no objects of observation for Him other than those which exist through His will, but the divine knowledge is exclusively a knowledge of the willed and produced, not a knowledge for which an object could be given from any other source.[1] Indeed, since there is for Him no succession, it can never be said that in Him the purposive thought-activity precedes the will-activity.[2] In consequence of the above, there can be in God no distinction between resolving and the execution of the resolve (where in our case purposive ideas remain wholly or in part ideal), since otherwise the divine omnipotence would not perfectly express itself in the finite.[3] Just as little can any activities more analogous with the corporeal or any kind of matter [4] be added to the divine

[1] This is Calvin's meaning, *Instit.* iii. 23. 6 : Quum nec alia ratione quae futura sunt praevideat, nisi quia ut fierent decrevit ; where only the idea of seeing *beforehand* is awkward. Erigena puts it better, *de praedest.*, p. 121 : Ea ergo videt quae facere voluit, neque alia videt, nisi ea quae fecit.

[2] Idem, *ibid.* p. 125 : Non in eo praecedit visio operationem, quoniam coaeterna est visioni operatio.

[3] Cf. § 53. 2.   [4] Cf. Anselm, *Monol.* cap. xi.

thinking, so as to make its object real. Hence the divine thinking is the same as the divine will, and omnipotence and omniscience are one and the same. And since in God there is no duality between thought and word (nay, even the term ' word ' can only mean the activity of the thought outwards), this precisely is the point expressed in all formulæ which exhibit the divine Word as creating and preserving ; and it is quite correct to say, as has been said in multifarious ways, that everything exists by reason of God's speaking or thinking it.[1]

Since then this divine knowledge is recognized as the very productivity of God, the creative as well as the preservative, it follows at once that it is entirely the same divine knowledge which constitutes the divine omniscience and the divine wisdom.[2] If the two are separated, something out of our existence is transferred to God, which even if we make it infinite can still be for Him only an imperfection. Since it is the least part in the existence which surrounds us that proceeds from our own activity, a knowledge of things independent of our influence upon them certainly is for us a good and a perfection. But if in thought we shut off the sphere of our formative production by itself, for all that it is so limited, then it will always indicate an imperfection if the later cognition by the artist of the whole of his works contains something besides what was in his purposive idea, whether it be that the original image or the formative activity was imperfect, or that the sphere was not so completely shut off but that some foreign influence could have told upon his works. But now the world as the whole content of the divine formation and production is so self-enclosed that there is nothing external which could gain an influence upon it. Thus every distinction in content between wisdom and omniscience must presuppose an imperfection in God. But even as to form, a distinction between the two can hardly be granted ; for neither can the one have a more inner and the other a more outward origin, nor can the one be more and the other less bound up with the divine will. If omniscience is simply the absolute livingness of the divine will, this must be just as true of the divine

---

[1] Hilar. in *Ps. cxviii. sgm 4 :* Ergo omne ex quo vel in quo mundi totius corpus creatum est, originem sumit ex dicto, et subsistere in id, quod est ex verbo Dei, coepit.—Anselm, *Monol.* cap. xii. : Quicquid fecit, per suam intimam locutionem fecit, sive singula singulis verbis, sive potius uno verbo simul omnia dicendo.

[2] Augustin., *de div. qu. ad Simpl.* ii. 2. 3 : Quamquam et in ipsis hominibus solet discerni a sapientiâ scientia . . . in Deo autem nimirum non sunt haec duo sed unum.

wisdom, if wisdom be a comprehensive name for the divine purposes.

Hence it can only be from a special point of view that wisdom is regarded as a special attribute, and in this respect there will be something to say about it elsewhere. But it also follows, that finite existence must merge as completely in the divine knowledge as in the divine omnipotence, and that in finite existence the divine knowledge is exhibited as completely as the divine omnipotence ; so that when both are held one against another, there is nothing left in the divine knowledge to which there is no correlative in existence, or which stands in a different relationship to existence, so that the latter would always have to be presupposed in order that the former might be posited. Or, to put it briefly, God knows all that is ; and all that God knows is, and these two are not two-fold but single ; for His knowledge and His almighty will are one and the same.

2. It is in the light of what has already been said that the further, and for the most part later, definitions concerning divine omniscience must be judged. Of these it may, of course, be said in general that they transfer to God human activities, so conceived as still to include imperfection, and in such a way that by illimitation the imperfection is by no means done away. The first case where this holds good is when, in God's knowledge of existence, perception, memory, and prescience are distinguished, and then the divine omniscience, as the absolutely perfect cognition of things, is made up compositely of these three.[1] For as the same thing which now is present directly after is past, as it was previously future, in God all these three kinds of knowledge must either be simultaneous even for the same object, in which case the distinctions would be quite blurred by their simultaneity ; or, if they remain distinct and outside one another, they must follow one upon another even in God, according as the thing known passes out of the future into the past. And then this means that in the case of the divine knowledge the rule that in God there is no change is broken.[2] If

---

[1] So Reinhard, *Dogm.*, § 25 : Omniscientia divina est attributum, quo omnium rerum cognitionem habet longe perfectissimam. But this very superlative contains in it an analogy, and thus ascribes to the divine knowledge a similarity with that of finite beings, thus making it temporal. From this we get praescientia, visio, and reminiscentia.

[2] Augustin., *l.c.* : Quid est enim praescientia, nisi scientia futurorum ? Quid autem futurum est Deo, qui omnia supergreditur tempora ? Si enim scientia Dei res ipsas habet, non sunt ei futurae sed praesentes, ac per hoc non jam praescientia sed tantum scientia dici potest. Si autem sicut in ordine temporalium creaturarum, ita et apud eum nondum sunt, quae futura sunt,

then we say (as indeed already by combining opposites we have often sought to present the divine as raised above all opposition) that the perfect knowledge of a thing's existence for itself is the same as the knowledge of the inner law of its development, and the perfect knowledge of a thing's place in the sphere of universal interaction is one with the knowledge of the influence of all other things on it, but that both these perfect kinds of knowledge form in God one and the same timeless knowledge, determining the existence of the object, while with us both are incomplete and so temporally distinct, because our knowledge does not determine the existence of a thing, but is determined by it—then we have at least an indication as to how to avoid as far as possible too great a humanizing of the divine knowledge.[1]

Nor is a better scheme achieved by the division into *free* or intuitive knowledge and *necessary* knowledge or pure thought ; [2] for as the first member comprehends in itself those three modes of thought already noticed, the other would comprehend that divine knowledge which would have God Himself and all that is possible for its object.[3]   It must strike everyone as peculiar as well as most unfortunate that under one name there should be comprised God's knowledge of Himself, and His knowledge of that which is merely possible.   For whether one thinks of the merely possible as including only that which never becomes real, or whether one also includes that which comes to reality, in abstraction from its reality, God always remains that which is truest and most original, but the simply possible that which is most shadow-like and ineffectual ; so that such a combination almost assumes that God knows even Himself only through an abstract shadow-like presentation.[4]

sed ea praevenit sciendo, bis ergo ea sentit, uno quidem modo secundum futurorum praescientiam, altero vero secundum praesentium scientiam. Aliquid ergo temporaliter accedit scientiae Dei quod absurdissimum et falsissimum est.

[1] Augustin., *l.c.* : Cum enim demsero de humana scientia mutabilitatem et transitus quosdam a cogitatione in cogitationem, cum . . . de parte in partem crebris recordationibus transilimus . . . et reliquero solam vivacitatem certae atque inconcussae veritatis una atque aeterna contemplatione cuncta lustrantis, immo non reliquero, non enim habet hoc humana scientia, sed pro viribus cogitavero : insinuatur mihi utcumque scientia Dei ; quod tamen nomen, ex eo quod sciendo aliquid non latet hominem potuit esse rei utrique commune.

[2] Scientia libera or visionis and scientia necessaria or simplicis intelligentiae.

[3] Gerhard, *loc. th.* i. p. 148 note.

[4] This is only very slightly modified by such a remark as that of Thomas (in Gerh., *l.c.*) : Deus se ipsum videt in se ipso, quia se ipsum videt per essentiam suam : alia a se videt non in ipsis sed in se ipso, in quantum essentia sua continet similitudinem aliorum ab ipso.   Here the question is rather of the actual, and the meaning really is that God knows about finite

Thus we should have to admit besides a divine self-consciousness partaking of the nature of intuitive knowledge and resembling it ; the latter would be the living consciousness of God in His reality, but the former an inactive and, as it were, passive element of the Divine Essence.   Only, since all are at one in asserting that God's essence and God's attributes (and so also the active attributes) are one and the same, this distinction comes to nothing, as also does this aspect of pure thought in God.   Next, the one description appears to be formed very much on the analogy of the fact that with us the indefinite idea of what is simply possible must have an immediate sense-impression added to it, if it is to pass over into the consciousness of an object as real.   If now in all cases perceptual knowledge is richer in content than pure thought (since the former has a real existence corresponding to it and the latter has not), and if none the less finite existence is dependent on divine thought, the question inevitably arises why God, who must will to have the absolute maximum of cognition in Himself, knows with intuitive knowledge only *some* of what is possible, *i.e.* that which at any time becomes real, and not *all*.   And if we do not wish to fall back upon simple arbitrariness, which in thought is always an imperfection, and so a self-diminution of God, there can hardly be any other answer to this question than that some of what is possible lacks the possibility of existing along with the rest.   But that, the existence of which conflicts with the existence of all else, is also contradictory to itself.   Thus there is no divine knowledge of it even on the traditional explanation of the divine omniscience, for the self-contradictory is neither a thing nor cognizable.   But if we look at the matter from the point of view of the other description, that intuitive knowledge is free, while the other is necessary, then (since the free is something other than the necessary), God thereby is brought under this antithesis, and the necessity whereby anything not free exists in Him is not anything in Him (otherwise it would be His freedom itself), but something outside and above Him—which conflicts with the conception of the Supreme Being.

From the foregoing it is now very easy to conclude what is to be held regarding the so-called *mediate knowledge* of God,[1] by means of which He would know just what would have resulted had something happened which did not happen.   It rests altogether upon

being in the same way that He knows about Himself without reference to the possible.

[1] Scientia media also futuribilium, or de futuro conditionato.

the assumption of a possible outside the real, which we have already put aside. As soon, then, as we express it so, namely, that God knows what would have resulted if at any point the impossible had become real, this knowledge, as a whole, dissolves into nothing, because what rests solely upon the becoming real of the impossible is itself impossible. However, even apart from this it would follow that if anywhere even for God anything is possible outside the real, then infinitely much is possible at every point, and as each point is co-determinant for all the rest, a different world arises for each case from each point. The infinitely many times infinitely many worlds which thus, infinitely often, are formed (amid which the real world is lost as something infinitely small), are thus the object of this mediate knowledge—an object which still multiplies itself to infinity, if one considers that the necessary knowledge of God already of itself contains an infinite number of worlds originally different from the real world, for each of which again there obtains a mediate knowledge just as full as that which relates to the real world. So, measured thus, even the works of the divine omnipotence appear in the divine omniscience as something infinitely small in comparison with what omnipotence does not bring to reality, and consequently there is in God eternally and imperishably a mass of rejected thoughts ; and, if we accept this mediate knowledge, the imperfection of a human artist, who, because his formative capacity is fluctuating and uncertain, thinks out the individual parts of his work in various ways other than as he afterwards fashions them, will, freed from all limitations and made infinite, be transferred to God. Looked at by itself, this whole apparatus of rejected thoughts is simply a knowledge of nothing ; and it can only have a meaning if we could suppose that God also decides and produces by choice and deliberation, a view which from of old every form of teaching in any degree consistent has repudiated.[1] Hence it would have been far safer, if one does start from what is human, to transfer to God, illimited and perfect, the certainty of the perfect artist, who in a state of inspired discovery thinks of nothing else, to whom nothing else offers itelf, save what he actually produces. This also agrees very well with the story of the Creation, which knows nothing of any intervening deliberation and deciding choice, but keeps contemplation entirely to the end,

---

[1] Joh. Damasc., *d. f. orth.* ii. 22 : χρὴ δὲ γινώσκειν, ὅτι ἐπὶ θεοῦ βούλησιν μὲν λέγομεν, προαίρεσιν δὲ κυρίως οὐ λέγομεν· οὐ γὰρ βουλεύεται θεός· ἀγνοίας γάρ ἐστι τὸ βουλεύεσθαι· περὶ γὰρ τοῦ γινωσκομένου οὐδεὶς βουλεύεται.

where it appears simply as absolute approval, without ascribing to God any contemplation of what He did not make or any comparison of the real world with those possible worlds. If, however, the edifying and tranquillizing effect of the conception of such a mediate knowledge of God be alleged,[1] what that really amounts to is this, that, if we lift ourselves up to the religious consciousness in our pain over disappointed expectations, we should think that our wishes were also among God's thoughts, but amongst the rejected. But (we may take it) true religious submission makes no such demand as that God should have had our foolish thoughts as His own, but is content with seeing from the result that our plans were not contained in that original or rather eternal sanction.

The name ' mediate knowledge ' does, however, call for special consideration, since its reference can only be to the naming of the other two kinds of knowledge. Should it be a mediate between the necessary and the free, then God would be (as it were) more tied up in thinking that which from a given point is possible than in thinking the real, in spite of the fact that the last presents the greatest degree of ' tied-up-ness,' namely, the whole of the natural order. Or if the free knowledge of God is at the same time the productive, the mediate would present a transition from productivity to the idle, ineffective activity of pure thought. Thus the mediate, as a diminishing production, would be, as it were, the divine preservation and co-operation restraining itself in all directions, as in us the ever-stimulating idea of the real shades off into that of the probable, still lively-coloured and affecting us through hope and fear, and then loses itself in indifferent shadow-pictures of the merely possible. But we may reasonably hesitate to transfer such things from ourselves to God. If, however, this knowledge is the mean between perceptual and pure thought, it affords a passage from the former to the latter, which is inconceivable without a diminution of living power. And so, even from this point of view, we reach the final result, that the possible as distinct from the real cannot be an object of the divine knowledge.

3. If one adds to this the fact that unquestionably there exists at least a strong appearance as though, on the one side, a dual self-consciousness—an original and a reflected—were attributed to God, and as though, on the other, the piece-by-piece character of His knowledge were being assumed, it follows that till now the theory of these divine attributes has transferred to the Supreme

[1] Reinhard, *Dogm.*, p. 112.

Being all the imperfections of our consciousness. The appearance of a dual consciousness issues from the fact that the whole of God's knowledge about Himself (which is similar to His knowledge of all that is possible, as it remains wholly separate from the Divine activity) can only be thought of as objective and indeed on the lines of our most abstract knowledge ; yet as such it cannot be the only knowledge He possesses, but has necessarily beside it an original knowledge. This, indeed, does not come out immediately in the language of the Schools, but mediately, and as presupposed wherever emotional excitations attributed to God in popular preaching and religious poetry are treated dogmatically—which means that there is all too easily suggested such a sensibility on the part of the Supreme Being as destroys the basal relationship of absolute dependence. But such excitation of itself always implies the second imperfection we have to prove—the piece-by-piece quality of knowledge in God. For it is only the influence of a definite moment (which we feel is making such a demand upon us that in relation to it something must happen) that evokes an emotion in us. And so for a right theory on this point there is nothing left but the formula that God is related to the object in an eternal and omnipresent way, as in us the evocation of the emotion is related to the momentary impression. Then there will no longer be any cause either to introduce in the divine self-consciousness the above-mentioned contrast between original and reflected, or even to make a contrast between the latter and the objective, to avoid which the above formula [1] was chosen. The second point, namely, the piece-by-piece character of the divine knowledge, still lurks curiously in the treatment of the question whether even the trivial is an object of the divine knowledge. For this question could simply not have been raised if a start had been made from the formula that God knows each in the whole, as also the whole in each—a formula which utterly abolishes the contrast between great and small, and which alone is correct because already given in the idea of a settled natural order. This, however, follows of itself on the customary method of illimitation, for in fact we consider even a human consciousness more perfect the more there is present to it in each individual moment.

And this leads us to consider still further, in the light of this divine attribute, a subject which might really be regarded as already done with,[2] namely, whether the divine knowledge about

---

[1] Page 217, l. 29.   [2] § 49.

the free actions of men can co-exist with their freedom. Most thinkers, indeed, perhaps even the Socinians, would have felt ashamed to answer the question in the negative, or even to raise it, if they had reflected that in that case not only could there have been no further question of an eternal decree of God regarding salvation, but that history in general would become something which God only gradually experienced, and consequently the idea of providence must be wholly given up.[1] If, then, the temptation to answer the question in the negative, and the need to raise it is grounded in the interests of human freedom, it must be considered that one's own foreknowledge of free actions and the foreknowledge of others must destroy freedom still more than divine foreknowledge does. And yet we deem those people least free who cannot in general know their actions beforehand, *i.e.* those who are not conscious of any definite course of action. But in such cases this special foreknowledge is lacking only because foreknowledge is lacking of the special relevant outer conditions and inner conditions produced from without. In the same way we estimate the intimacy of relationship between two persons by the foreknowledge one has of the actions of the other, without supposing that in either case the one or the other's freedom has thereby been endangered. So even divine foreknowledge cannot endanger freedom.

APPENDIX TO THE SECOND SECTION : SOME OTHER DIVINE ATTRIBUTES

§ 56. *Among the divine attributes usually mentioned, the Unity, Infinity, and Simplicity of God especially might conveniently come in here, as having no relation to the antithesis in the excitations of the religious consciousness ; only they could not be regarded as divine attributes in the same sense as those already dealt with.*

1. The attributes mentioned here are not related (as are those to be dealt with in the Second Part of this Dogmatic) to the ease or difficulty with which the consciousness of God develops in us at different moments ; and so far they would belong here, if they

---

[1] The Socinian principle when fully applied really seems to imply this. We may find directly contrasted formulæ in Augustine, *de civ. Dei* v. 9 : Non est consequens ut si Deo *certus* est causarum omnium ordo, ideo nihil sit in nostrae voluntatis arbitrio ; and in Socin., *Praelect.* cap. viii. : Namque non entium nullae sunt qualitates. Atqui ea quae nec fuerunt nec sunt, nec *certo* futura sunt, nullo modo sunt, itaque ea Deo praesentia esse nequeunt. Eiusmodi autem sunt voluntariae hominum actiones, quae nondum revera extiterunt.

had any dogmatic content. But this they lack because, unlike the other four, they do not issue from the relationship between the feeling of absolute dependence and the sensibly stimulated self-consciousness, nor are they statements about it. But even the three attributes here appended stand in close relationship with the four former ones, in so far at least as they negate, if only in a pictorial way, the similarity of divine and finite causality ; but not even such a place can be given them in Dogmatics. There arises then only the question whether to turn these expressions out of our province, and send them back to the speculative doctrine of God, or whether there is really some meaning to be gained from them for Dogmatics. This, however, must be examined in each instance by itself, since we cannot maintain in advance that in this respect they are in the same case.

And first as to the *Unity* of God—strictly taken it can never be an attribute of a thing that it only exists in a definite number. It is not an attribute of the hand to be dual ; but it is the attribute of a man to have two hands, and of a monkey to have four. In the same way it could be an attribute of the world to be ruled by One God only, but not of God to be One only. And so if a divine attribute is here in question, we must turn away from mere number ; and in that case what we have first to insist upon is the general expression that God has no equal,[1] which, of course, our language can more distinctly express by ' uniqueness.' And inasmuch as many similars are always of the same kind or species, the individual beings representing the existence of the species and the species the essence of the individuals, it might be said that the unity or uniqueness of God is that attribute in virtue of which there is no distinction of essence and existence. Now this as such could belong only to speculative theology. But if, on the other hand, we abstract from what in strictness must be understood by an attribute, and if we consider that the excitations of the religious consciousness are individual moments, while that upon which in those excitations we feel ourselves absolutely dependent is not objectively given, then this term ' unity ' expresses the fact that all those excitations are meant and comprehended as indications of One, and not of many. And, indeed, if we go back to the earlier explanation of the original meaning of the expression, ' God,' [2] what is stated in the expression

---

[1] Mosheim, *Th. dogm.* i. p. 241 : Quando ergo dicimus Deum esse unum, negamus Deum habere socium.

[2] Cf. § 4, 4.

'unity of God' is that this homogeneity (*Zusammengehörigkeit*) of the religious excitations is given with the same certainty as these excitations themselves. Since now it is only on the assumption of this homogeneity that concepts of divine attributes can be developed from observation of the content of religious moments, this expression, the 'unity of God,' is not so much a single attribute as the principle of monotheism,[1] lying from the first at the foundation of all inquiry into the divine attributes, and can no more be proved than the existence of God itself. In fact an attempt to discuss this unity further or to prove it will scarcely be able altogether to escape making a distinction between the idea of God and the idea of the Supreme Being. Moreover, these attempts always occur in controversy with Polytheism[2] and, indeed, proceed from the assumption that the same idea underlies both. This assumption, however, we have already discarded.

The term *Infinity* is likewise too negative to be a proper attribute-conception; and indeed it has been dealt with in very different ways. The customary explanation,[3] 'negation of limits,' is most indefinite. For if one had already a description of the Supreme Being, there could be no question at all of any possibility of conceiving this as limited. But if this description is first formed by means of the term 'infinite' itself, we can see that all we have is a precautionary rule for the formation of ideas of divine attributes, the rule, *i.e.*, that attributes which cannot be conceived as without limits ought not to be ascribed to God; and thus indirectly infinity becomes an attribute of all the divine attributes. Hence every discussion leads over to other attributes which partake of infinity.[4] Only it is a sign that even this rule is not being properly applied to the formation of the divine attributes, if instead of taking omnipotence as the infinity of the divine productivity and omniscience as the infinity of the divine thought, one distinguishes rather between an infinity of substance and an infinity of existence; and so a distinction which has to do with the finite only is made fundamental in the description of the Divine Being. For infinite does not really mean that which has no end, but that which is in con-

---

[1] It is rightly taken so in Rufinus, *Expos. symb.* : Deum non numero unum dicimus sed universitate.

[2] Lactant., i. 3 : Virtutis perfecta natura non potest esse nisi in eo, in quo totum est . . . Deus vero si perfectus est . . . non potest esse nisi unus ut in eo sint omnia.

[3] Mosheim, *l.c.*, p. 299 : Infinitas itaque sic absoluta nihil aliud est, quam absentia finium in Deo.

[4] Cf. Mosheim, *ibid.*, and Reinhard, *Dogm.*, § 33, 3.

trast to the finite, *i.e.* to that which is co-determined by other things. Interpreted thus the term stands in the closest connexion with the monotheistic basic rule stated above, and, under the form of a cautionary predicate, expresses the difference of the divine causality from all finitude.	For already we have often seen how this formula only produces confusion if it is treated as a means of transferring to God by illimitation attributes which essentially are only attached to the finite.

The idea of *Simplicity* too is constantly treated as a negative— although regarded literally it is not so—either as simply negating matter of God or as excluding all idea of parts or of composition.[1] As regards the former, it is pretty clear that, if God and the world are to be kept distinct, in whatever way, all matter must belong to the world.	But simplicity strictly taken excludes not only materiality but also participation in everything by which we characterize the finite spirit as such ; and the finite spirit can in no way be called simple in the strictest sense of the word,[2] but must belong solely to the world, just as much as matter does.	For the relative separation of function itself conflicts with simplicity,[3] and each temporal moment of spiritual manifestation [4] is just as really a result of the mutual inherence of the relatively opposed as in the case of matter, which we declare to be composite in this sense only in so far as we can develop oppositions within it.	As therefore infinity on the one hand is an attribute of all the divine attributes, so simplicity, as here expounded in general and in each particular case, is the unseparated and inseparable mutual inherence of all divine attributes and activities.	And as on the other hand infinity ensures that nothing shall be ascribed to God which can be thought of only as limited, so simplicity ensures that nothing shall be adopted which belongs essentially to the sphere of contrast and opposition.

Postscript to this Section.—The whole circle of divine attributes here dealt with thoroughly illustrates the characteristic feature of this First Part of Dogmatic, namely, that of being derived from the

---

[1] The former in Reinhard, *Dogm.*, § 33, 2.	The latter in Mosheim, *Th. Dogm.* i. p. 243.

[2] What the older writers called μονοειδές and ἀμερές.

[3] The Socinians consequently were not wrong when they maintained that there is always a synthesis where there is either a connexion or union of the diverse (see Vorst., *Parasceve*, p. 50).	But they were wrong to separate the being of God from the will of God.

[4] Augustin., *Tract.* xix. 9 *in Joan.* : Non est Deus mutabilis spiritus . . . Nam ubi invenis aliter et aliter, ibi facta est quaedam mors.

religious self-consciousness as it is presupposed in every Christian religious life-moment. This is clear for the following reasons among others. In view of the teleological character of Christianity we can conceive no completely developed moment of religious experience which does not either itself pass over into some activity or in a definite way influence activities already going on and combine with them. Every such moment must be capable of description just as well under the form of this section as under that of the first or third. So if one individual attribute of these, or all of them together, were to condition a definite religious moment, out of it it would have to be possible to derive either a sentiment or a so-called duty towards God, or at least a course of action in general or in relation to others demanded by this God-consciousness. This, however, is not the case ; and no proposition in the Christian Doctrine of Morals can be based solely on the attributes dealt with here, either individually or taken together, but there are always others that go along with them. Hence even these attributes, however completely viewed together and related to each other, can in no way suffice as a description of the Divine Being. But it must be clearly understood here in advance, that whatever additional divine attributes may emerge later, those described here will always have to be thought of as inhering in the others ; so that an activity which does not admit of being conceived under the form of eternal omnipotence ought not to be posited as divine.

THIRD SECTION

The Constitution of the World which is indicated in the Religious Self-Consciousness, so far as it expresses the General Relationship between God and the World.

§ 57. *The universality of the feeling of absolute dependence includes in itself the belief in an original perfection of the World.*

1. By the *perfection* of the world nothing is to be understood here except what we must name so in the interests of the religious self-consciousness, namely, that the totality of finite existence, as it influences us (including also those human influences upon the rest of existence resulting from our place in the same), works together in such a way as to make possible the continuity of the religious self-consciousness. For since the religious self-consciousness can only fill a moment when combined with an excitation of the sensuous self-consciousness, and every such excitation is an impression of the world, the demand that the God-consciousness should be able to unite itself [1] with every sensuous determination of the self-consciousness would be in vain unless all the world-impressions (and this is only another way of saying the relation of all other finite being to the being of men) concurred in making the direction of the spirit to God-consciousness compossible with them. The same also holds good from the other side of the relationship, namely, from the determinability of the given through our spontaneity, because this also is always accompanied by a self-consciousness capable of such excitation. Inasmuch, however, as we have laid down that the feeling of absolute dependence does not diminish, still less cease, if we extend our self-consciousness to a consciousness of the whole world [2] (that is, so far as we represent in it finite existence in general), this implies that all different gradations of existence are comprehended in this feeling, and consequently no closer definition of it could destroy that co-existence of the God-consciousness with the consciousness of the world, nor the fact

<hr>

[1] See § 5, 5, pp. 24 f.   [2] Cf. § 8, 2, pp. 35 f.

of the former being excited by the latter. It must be premised, however, that the term *original* does not refer to any definite condition of the world or of men nor of the God-consciousness in men, all of which are a developed perfection admitting of a more and less ; the question is rather of self-identical perfection prior to all temporal development and based on the inner relations of the relevant finite existence. Such perfection is affirmed in the above sense, *i.e.* it is laid down that all finite being, so far as it co-determines our self-consciousness, is traceable back to the eternal omnipotent causality, and all the impressions of the world we receive, as well as the particular way (consequent on human nature) in which the predisposition towards God-consciousness becomes realized, include the possibility that the God-consciousness should combine with each impression of the world in the unity of a moment. This is implied in the certainty which is directly bound up with the God-consciousness. For were the God-consciousness not grounded thus inwardly, it would be something accidental, and so uncertain and arbitrary. From this it also follows that this belief naturally and necessarily belongs together with belief in the eternal omnipresent and living omnipotence, since both are related in exactly the same way to our basic assumption. For, as the former belief expresses the fact that in all excitations of the religious consciousness, the consciousness of God, as united with consciousness of the world, is related to One, so the latter belief asserts that in every such excitation the world-consciousness as united with the God-consciousness is related to All. And just as in belief in the eternal omnipotence it is implied that the world is the complete revelation of it, so in belief in the original perfection of the world it is implied that through the feeling of absolute dependence the divine omnipotence in all its livingness reveals itself everywhere in the world, as eternal omnipresent and omniscient, without any distinction of more or less, without even a contrast in respect of dependence between one part and another.

2. Inasmuch as the selected terms are to be taken in this sense, it at once follows that here any content of an actual life-moment mediated through a definite world-impression must be disregarded, since we have to do only with the original, ever-identical and enduring, inner demands of the lower and higher self-consciousness, and with the constitution of all given existence, as the perpetually effective cause of the world-impressions co-determining the predisposition to God-consciousness. And so we shall not directly

deal at all here with any temporal condition of the world and of mankind in particular, whether past, present, or yet to come ; but only with those relationships which uniformly underlie the whole temporal development and throughout it remain the same. As to what in the sphere of experience we call perfection or imperfection, the former is simply that which by means of the original perfection has already come to pass, the latter that which has not yet come to pass by the same means ; both taken together, however, are the perfection which is coming to pass. Hence we can say that for each given moment the original perfection is in that which underlies it as pure finite causality ; but the definitive perfection is in the totality of all the effects thereof, the development being thought of as included in the moment. But now what underlies each moment as finite causality is nothing but the totality of all enduring forms of existence and all contrasted functions of the same ; and consequently the original perfection is the coherence of all these in virtue of which they are equal in compass to the divine causality, and on account of the contrast evoke the consciousness of it.

The original expression of this belief, though in another form, is the divine approval of the world [1] which, in relation to the act of creation as such, has for its object no temporal condition arising out of an earlier one, but only the origin of finite existence, but this, of course, as the source of the whole temporal development. Hence, just as this divine approval cannot be abrogated by anything temporal, so no more can the truth of our proposition be prejudiced by the differing content of the temporal moments, though they appear now as accomplished perfection, and now as lessening imperfection. On the other hand, what is usually dealt with in Dogmatics under this phrase is historical moments—for instance, a paradisical condition of the world and a condition of moral perfection of man, both of which lasted for a period of time ; but it is clear that such a doctrine could not be given the same place as that advanced here. For an actual condition, one therefore in any case subject to change, cannot be related in the same way to the divine omnipotence, as that in finite existence which lies at the base of all succeeding conditions, and least of all one which has altogether disappeared ; for then the divine omnipotence itself could not have remained the same. Whereas if we on our part were to take up into the idea of original perfection something which, on closer scrutiny, revealed itself as changeable, it would be

[1] Gen. I[31].

only an oversight resting on an incorrect subsumption which could be corrected as soon as discovered without making any change in the doctrine. But even if the course of our presentation had not led us to it, this idea of a historically given real perfection, posited as original, is at all events to be found in Dogmatics ; and we must therefore inquire whether, in fact, there is any place at all for such a doctrine, or whether it always rests simply on a misunderstanding.

§ 58. *The belief described is to be set forth in two doctrines, of which one deals with the perfection of the rest of the world in relation to man, the other with the perfection of man himself.*

1. The belief described is nothing but a statement of the common factor in the religious excitations, only related to the finite co-determining them (although this too is taken in its generality), *i.e.* to the world-impressions which we receive ; hence this division follows naturally. For the God-consciousness could not be excited by these world-impressions if they were of a nature discordant with it, or if man were not so constituted that these impressions reached, as it were, the region of his higher self-consciousness, or again, unless there existed in him that relation of the lower and the higher self-consciousness to each other which occasions the whole process of the excitation of the God-consciousness. Accordingly, these two conditions come to be considered each in itself. It could of course be said that man himself, with his constitution, is an integral part of the world, and that it is only in virtue of this constitution that he is precisely the part he is ; and hence that the original perfection of man is already included in the original perfection of the world. This is quite correct ; and in a purely scientific inquiry, where what was in question was a view of finite existence in itself, such a division would only be permissible in so far as other divisions were made, and the idea of the perfection of the world analysed into the perfection of all its different parts, and their relations to one another. It is different in the dogmatic sphere, where the original object is not the objective consciousness at all but self-consciousness, especially in so far as in self-consciousness man contrasts himself with the world, and stands in the relationship of interaction to the rest of existence.

2. For the same reason there can even here be no question of the original perfection of the world in itself and in relation to the idea of finite existence, but only in relation to man. But if in

addition it were maintained that there is no other perfection of the world—this being regarded purely teleologically, in the usual sense of that word—such a position would call for a more precise explanation, in order to avoid the appearance of representing man as the central-point of all finite existence, in relation to which alone everything had a perfection. This explanation would not be hard to give, for, assuming an organic construction of the whole, all is just as much for each as each for all ; hence it is true even of the most remote thing (since, after all, its condition corresponds to the totality of its mediate and immediate relationships) not only that it stands in relationship with man, but also, on a complete view, that precisely this relationship might be an expression of the peculiarity of its nature. But we need not go into such explanations, for we have not to advance any exhaustive doctrine of the perfection of the world (which would be a task for cosmology) ; the belief to be set forth here will not go beyond the sphere of religious excitations, which is only touched by the relationships of the world to man. But, in going back to the common ground of these relationships, we at the same time lay it down that no still future development of them can ever involve what would abrogate this belief. As regards the perfection of man, it would not be in keeping to add that it also is only to be interpreted in relation to the world. Man's original perfection is primarily meant rather in relation to God, *i.e.* to the presence in him of the God-consciousness, and his endowments relatively to the world belong here only in so far as they awaken the God-consciousness. The whole tone of the proposition, however, certainly does imply that all those endowments, in virtue of which man is this specific part of the world, belong here—a proposition which, in the sphere of Christian morals, has regulative importance averting a crowd of misunderstandings.

3. This of itself makes clear how natural it is that the doctrine of the peculiar original perfection of man should have been much more fully elaborated in Dogmatic than that of the perfection of the world in relation to man. If, however, the latter be entirely lacking, this certainly is no advantage to the former ; and not only so, but the treatment of developed perfection, whether under the heading of Divine Providence or otherwise, often takes a wrong line, because a right idea of original perfection has not been taken as basis. But the less urgent and therefore also the less elaborate inquiry ought reasonably to precede the more important and more complex as an introduction.

FIRST DOCTRINE : THE ORIGINAL PERFECTION OF THE WORLD

§ 59. *Every moment in which we confront externally given existence*
involves the implication that the world offers to the human
spirit an abundance of stimuli to develop those conditions
in which the God-consciousness can realize itself, and at the
same time that in manifold degrees the world lends itself to
being used by the human spirit as an instrument and means of
expression.

1. It has been taken for granted above (§ 5, 3) that the God-consciousness may develop in every state of consciousness which has risen above animal confusion, so that in it there is expressed the contrast between the self and the 'given,' and the contrast between self-consciousness and objective consciousness, inasmuch as the two elements in the antithesis confront each other simultaneously. The same holds good also of the contrast between passive and active. But while in the sphere we are dealing with the God-consciousness, owing to the teleological character of Christian piety,[1] can unite with the passive only as it is related to self-activity, the interposition of the passive none the less is necessary to mark out clearly the moments of self-activity, because clarity of consciousness only arises through a successive contrast of distinct moments. Passive states, however, can only arise through operative influences, and hence the original perfection of the world in relation to men consists primarily in this, that in it is temporally grounded the excitation of passive states which are to pass into active states (these we name *incentives*), or, in other words, that they sufficiently determine the receptivity of man to the awakening and shaping of his self-activity. If now we take man first of all purely on his inner side, as a self-active being in whom God-consciousness is possible—that is, as spirit ; then, from this point of view, his bodily side, which is not the man himself, belongs originally to this material world into which the spirit enters. Only gradually does it become for the spirit instrument and means of expression—as later, mediately through it, all other things likewise become instrument and means of expression—but first of all and primarily it mediates the stimulating influences of the world upon the spirit. Thus the whole of this aspect of the original perfection of the world can be summarily expressed by saying that in it there is given for the spirit

---

[1] See § 9, 1 and § 11.

such an organism as the human body in living connexion with all else—an organism which brings the spirit into contact with the rest of existence.

Clarity of consciousness, however, is also conditioned by the contrasted distinction of self-consciousness and objective consciousness, and this is closely connected with the fact that different kinds of influences can be related to the same self-consciousness, so that the self-consciousness can be regarded as an entity existing independently of every particular influence (upon this all experience and eventually all science depend, though here we are only interested in the latter for the sake of the former). Hence we may summarily express this aspect of the original perfection of the world by the concept of its knowability. The two aspects are essentially bound up together, for without an organism such as ours there would be no interrelation between finite spirit and corporeal existence, however suitably adapted to such interrelation the latter might be. And without such an ordered distinction of existence the human organism would be a meaningless phenomenon. So, then, the two together are one : the knowability of existence is the ideal side of the original perfection of the world, and the natural subsistence of the human organism is the real side of the same perfection as directly related to human receptivity.

2. We must now put the same series in the reverse order. For if all self-activity in men were determined by the influences of the (external) world it would be merely reaction, and every feeling of freedom, even partial freedom, would be illusory. But if the receptivity is at least living and individual, so that the same influence is not the same thing for all, still more, if irrespective of influence, we can attribute to the spirit an original self-activity that is not simply immanent in the individual spiritual personality (which indeed might be the root of that consciousness of species which is so distinctively human), then to the perfection of the world there belongs also such a receptivity for the influences of the spiritual self-activity of man as is, considered in itself, unlimited. This receptivity must naturally begin at the human organism regarded as a constitutive part of the world ; but from this it broadens out more and more until it reaches those constitutive elements of the world which are of such a nature that they are subject to no other influences except that of being known— which brings us to the borders of the preceding section. Though we sum up this receptivity of the world under the two terms,

instrument and means of expression, we do not in the least mean to indicate a division, as if one thing could only be one and another the other. Rather the organism is itself both, the most immediate instrument and the most immediate means of expression ; and so every thing, if it is the one, is always the other also. Nevertheless, these are the two relations through which the self-consciousness accompanying states of self-activity becomes a means of awakening the God-consciousness. For it is only in connexion with his organs that man realizes sovereignty over the world,[1] of which he can only be conscious as something based upon the divine omnipotence ; and it is only inasmuch as the simple activity of spirit is expressed through the medium of space and time that it awakens, as a copy thereof, the consciousness of the divine causality.[2]

3. That these two chief moments of the original perfection of the world essentially go together is self-evident. For the first moment would be simply an imperfection—that is, an arrangement leading to nothing—apart from the second ; the knowability of the world would be empty if it did not include in itself the expression of its being known ; and the human organism would be lost among the more imperfect kinds of existence as similar to them, even though it were supposed to include the inner life of the spirit, if there did not proceed from it a new power of organization into which everything else could be taken up. On the other hand, the receptivity of the rest of existence to the influence of the spirit would be empty and meaningless unless the spirit could be filled by it. But now both these together embrace completely the relations of the world to the spirit as the seat of God-consciousness, since in the existence presented to it the human spirit can find no means other than this for developing this consciousness. And indeed in this relation to the passive states which arise through the influence of the world, taken in itself, the human spirit has precisely the same means of development whether these states as life-moments are pleasant or unpleasant, elevating or depressing ; and the same holds good of its acquired instruments and gathered means of expression in so far as, being external, they are capable of reacting upon men in various ways and of exciting passive states. For the relation of either to man's self-activity is not thereby altered, nor is the God-consciousness as such more tardily aroused by the unpleasant than by the pleasant.

Postscript.—Two doctrines must be distinguished from the

---

[1] Gen. 1[28].   [2] Gen. 1[26].

proposition here laid down : on the one hand, that known as the doctrine of the Best World ; and on the other, the assertion that there was a perfection of the world which can be called original, though not in the sense used above, but in the sense that prior to its present condition it endured for a period of time and afterwards became changed into its present imperfect condition.

The doctrine of the Best World originally belongs, especially since Leibniz, to the so-called natural or rational theology, and thus did not arise as a statement about the religious consciousness but as a product of speculation.   Hence there would have been no mention of it here if various theologians [1] had not taken it over in the same form into Christian Dogmatics.   The doctrine is concerned not only with what lies at the basis of temporal existence but with temporal existence itself, in which it is impossible to separate between the historical (*i.e.* the activity of the human spirit) and the natural (*i.e.* the activity of physical forces) ; and it maintains that, notwithstanding all the mists and imperfections of the world, no greater amount of being and of well-being could have been attained. It is true, our two doctrines also imply the position that, since the entire course of time can only be an unbroken activity of the whole original perfection, the final result must be an absolute satisfaction, and similarly each moment, taken in the whole, satisfactory as an approximation.   But this conviction, issuing as it does solely from the religious consciousness, has no need to be introduced into speculative theology exactly as it has been taken up into Christian Dogmatics.   So far as the latter is concerned we must stop at the affirmation that the world is *good*, and can make no use of the formula that it is *the best* ; and this because the former assertion signifies far more than the latter.[2]   The latter expression is connected with the idea (which we have already rejected) of many worlds all originally equally possible with the one which actually came into existence, and also it seeks to represent the entire course of time in the actual world as the result of mediate divine knowledge (the idea of which we have also rejected), so that the whole productive activity of God is assumed to be selective and therefore secondary.

The second doctrine is to be found in the tradition of most peoples—the fable of a Golden Age previous to actual history. The essential element in it is always the belief that the world was then of such a character as to assure satisfaction to man apart from

---

[1] See, among others, Michaelis, *Th. Dogm.*, § 55.　　　[2] Cf. § 54, 2.

any need on his part to develop self-activity. Something similar
—but with the addition that, if this state had endured, man would
not have died—has been found in the brief Old Testament indications of the life of Paradise,[1] which do not, however, indicate an age
but only a relatively short period in the life of the first man. Thus,
first of all, we should have to settle the conflict over interpretation
which has been waged so long, whether actual history is meant to
be recorded there, and hence whether there is a question of a
temporal condition or not. If the narrative is historical it would
as such have no place here, except in so far as such a temporal
condition (it may be held) presupposes as its ground another
original perfection which has been transformed into the one just
described, from which such a temporal process could no longer
follow ; or else, it may be argued, the original perfection described
here underlay the narrative, but now is no longer to be assumed.
The latter view has never been maintained, and would be contradicted by the fact that the historical process nowhere presents
anything but functions of the original perfection as above described.
But the former view must be considered. Now, if it necessarily
implies that the original perfection of the world has not remained
the same, it fails to maintain the unity of the whole world-order
in its relation to the Creation and the continuity of the divine
Preservation. But apart from this undeniable and fundamental
error, it follows further that God approved that initial state even
with respect to that part which was capable of deterioration and
was in fact to deteriorate. Moreover, it seems contradictory that
those fundamental conditions under which the Redeemer was
actually ordained to come into the world and establish the invincible
Kingdom of God should be less perfect than those under which
the first man came into the world, since far greater things were to
come to pass in the former case than in the latter. If now we
examine this alleged primordial state of the world, we shall find
that it is in contradiction with the divine commission to man ; for
man could only attain to dominion over the earth by the development of his powers, and the constitution of the world, which
occasioned this development and which implies a receptivity for
the influence of those developed powers, must be contemporaneous
with the divine command. Lastly, if history is essential to the
fashioning of the world by man, then from this point of view the
narrative belongs solely to pre-history, and its real content is simply

[1] Gen. 2⁸ᶠ·.

that an adaptation of nature for the existence of the human organism preceded all development of human powers, and that on our planet the very significant detrimental differences in this adaptation could only come to light with the dissemination and further development of the human race. And if perhaps it may be concluded also from the narrative that there were at one time no hostile contacts in the animal kingdom [1] and nothing at all injurious or useless to mankind,[2] it does not by any means follow that this applied also outside the place where man originally lived, nor even that later this place lost its peculiar advantages.

If, however, the result of exegetical inquiry should be that no actual history is recounted in this passage, and if the story therefore is to be regarded as a kind of poetry, it would come up for consideration here in so far as it either contained a direct utterance of the religious consciousness or was occasioned by it. Its statements about the origin of sin do not concern us. Even the connexion between sin and evil and sin and death, on which it evidently proceeds, does not in and for itself need to be discussed here ; only, with reference to the doctrine of the perfection of the world set forth above, the following observations should be made. Even if we accepted absolutely the idea that apart from sin there would have been neither evil nor death, it would by no means follow from this that the earth must originally have been adapted to an enduring condition of sinlessness ; evil and death may none the less have been preordained as certainly as God foreknew sin. And other points must be considered. If we think away the gradual decay of organic powers, the possibility that the organism may be destroyed by external forces of nature, and disappearance through death, what we are thinking of is no longer beings of our kind, while yet real human history would only begin when all these things were present. Again, care for the preservation of life and the avoidance of what would disturb it, which is conditioned by mortality, is among the most powerful motives of human development, so that through mortality and the evils which are associated with it more human activities due to our relations with the external world have been developed than could be expected without mortality, and (assuming that the totality of human life increases rather than diminishes) the death of individuals does not lessen the fitness of the world for man's dominion over it, nor is it thereby hindered

---

[1] Gen. 2¹⁹ does not go quite so far.
[2] *Ibid.* ver. 16 ; that is, if the tree (ver. 17) was not in itself harmful.

in the development of its wealth of means of stimulation.   Finally, enduring sinlessness would have stood out far more strongly and conspicuously if man, unimpeded in the development and use of his powers, bore evil, and, combining God-consciousness with love of his race, overcame the impulse to cling to his own life and accepted death.   In view of all this, no reason can well remain for doubting that the original perfection of the world relatively to man was at the beginning no other than what we have here described, and that neither the Old Testament story [1] nor the relevant indications in the writings of the New Testament [2] compel us to hold that man was created immortal, or that, with alteration in his nature, the whole arrangement of the earth relatively to him was altered as well.

SECOND DOCTRINE : THE ORIGINAL PERFECTION OF MAN

§ 60. *The predisposition to God-consciousness, as an inner impulse, includes the consciousness of a faculty of attaining, by means of the human organism, to those states of self-consciousness in which the God-consciousness can realize itself ; and the impulse inseparable therefrom to express the God-consciousness includes in like manner the connexion of the race-consciousness with the personal consciousness ; and both together form man's original perfection.*

1. If the God-consciousness in the form of the feeling of absolute dependence [3] can only become actual in connexion with a sensible determination of self-consciousness, the tendency towards God-consciousness would be altogether nugatory if the condition necessary for it in human life could not be evoked ; and we should be no more able to think of it as actual than in the case of the beasts, because the confused state of man's consciousness would not exhibit the conditions under which alone that feeling could emerge.   Religious experience, however, consists precisely in this, that we are aware of this tendency to God-consciousness as a living impulse ; but such an impulse can only proceed from the true inner nature of the being which it goes to constitute.   Hence, at least in so far as we are religious men, we reckon the whole range

[1] Gen. 2[17].
[2] Rom. 5[12], based on Gen. 2[17], just as little excludes the possibility that Adam may have been created mortal ; and 1 Cor. 15[56] actually indicates death as such as existing before the advent of sin.
[3] Cf. § 5, 1–3.

of those states with which the God-consciousness can unite as belonging to this true inner nature. And as it would be an absolute imperfection of human nature—that is to say, a complete absence of inner coherence—if the tendency were indeed present latently, but could not emerge, so it is an essential element in the perfection of human nature that those states which condition the appearance of the God-consciousness are able to fill the clear and waking life of man onwards from the time when the spiritual functions are developed. And as we consider it an imperfect state of religious life in the individual if many moments of clear sensibly-determined self-consciousness occur without the God-consciousness being combined with them, so we account it part of the original perfection of man that in our clear and waking life a continuous God-consciousness as such is possible ; and on the contrary, we should have to regard it as an essential imperfection if the emergence of the feeling of absolute dependence, though not abrogating any feeling of partial dependence or freedom, were confined as such to separate and scattered moments.

The God-consciousness, moreover, combines not only with those sensible excitations of self-consciousness which express life-enhancements or life-hindrances immediately arising out of the impression of the world, but also with those which accompany the cognitive activities, and finally with those which are connected with every kind of outwardly directed action. Hence all these mental life-functions and the relative disposition of the organism belong together to the original perfection of man, though only in so far as the demand which we make for God-consciousness is conditioned by them, and in such a way that the first place always belongs to it. Thus, first of all, there is the physical basis of spiritual life, *i.e.* the fact that the spirit, become soul in the human body, acts also on the rest of the world in innumerable ways, and asserts its nature, just as the other living forces assert their nature relatively to it, so that life-feeling in general takes shape as the consciousness of interaction ; from which it follows that to the original perfection of man this also belongs, that opposite life-moments, hindrances and furtherances, have one and the same bearing on the excitation of the God-consciousness. Next, there is the intellectual basis of spiritual life, *i.e.* the fact that the spirit by means of sense-impressions can obtain that knowledge of existence which is one element in its own nature, as also knowledge of what we ourselves by our activity can produce in and from existence, and can express this knowledge with actual consciousness in the most varied degrees of general and particular ideas, and that thereby it arrives at the accompanying consciousness of a natural order in connexion with which the God-consciousness develops. Upon the agreement of these ideas and judgments with the being and relations of things depends all the influence of man on external nature which is more than simply instinctive, and also the connexion between knowledge and practical life. But though the knowledge of God, in this sphere, is bound up pre-eminently and fundamentally with the idea of a natural order, the excitation of the God-consciousness is not at all imperilled though certain ideas should not agree with the actual being of the object presented ; as indeed the comprehensive interconnexion of all being would not be mirrored in our idea if we did not assume that so long as the whole of existence is not reflected in our thought every act of thought contains an element of error.

2. With regard to the impulse to express the God-consciousness externally : there is, of course, no ' inner ' which does not become also an ' outer,' and thus there are expressions of the God-consciousness, in which no relation to the race-consciousness can be directly shown. But the question here is of those expressions which aim at fellowship and on which all such fellowship is based. Now the fellowship without which there can for us be no living and vigorous piety is conditioned by these external expressions ; it therefore is conditioned also by the inner union of the race-consciousness and the personal self-consciousness, for as this is the general source of all recognition of others as being of like nature with ourselves, it is also the only source of the presupposition and the ground of the fact that the ' inner ' is known and grasped along with and by means of the ' outer ' ; hence we may justly regard the two thus interrelated as belonging to the original perfection of man. This inclusion of the race-consciousness in the personal self-consciousness and the communicability of the ' inner ' through the ' outer,' which is connected with it, is the fundamental condition or basis of social life, for all human fellowship rests solely upon it ; and even in this wider connexion it belongs here, for, in every other kind of fellowship also, whatever its object, a man's acts, because accompanied by a sensible excitation of self-consciousness, may contain at the same time a communication of his God-consciousness. Nay more, the free and mobile outward life of man must be able in its whole range to serve this external expression and communication of the God-consciousness (though not in the case of each individual

taken singly, but only in combination with others), for otherwise there would be a sensuously stimulated self-consciousness with which the God-consciousness could unite inwardly, but in conjunction with which it could not express itself outwardly ; and thus the range of externalization and communication would be more narrowly limited than that of the inner excitation. Such a discrepancy we should have to call an original imperfection.

3. The statements in our proposition then include all the conditions necessary for the continuous existence of the God-consciousness in every human individual, and also for its communication from one to the other in proportion to the different levels of human fellowship, including also the perfection with which it can be communicated from the Redeemer and through Him to the redeemed : hence the requirements of this section are fulfilled. In the knowledge of the elements of this original perfection as present in every one we find a justification for the original demand that the God-consciousness should exist continuously and universally ; and human nature, repeating itself identically through heredity in every human being, is seen to be sufficient for its realization.[1] We found ourselves obliged to treat the two chief points as one whole complete in itself, which is a fresh justification, in the sphere of the God-consciousness, of a scientific method of treatment which everywhere aims at totality and is impossible on any other terms ; it is justified both for Dogmatics proper, where we have to reduce the whole of religious affections to *loci communes*, and for religious Ethics, where we have to distinguish those types of conduct which show the influence of the God-consciousness on our purposes ; also for Practical Theology in general, which is concerned with the description and distinction of the different forms of fellowship in God-consciousness. This is natural, for the whole procedure of Dogmatics—in which, if we take the word in a rather wider sense than usual, the last-mentioned discipline also is included—rests on what we have here exhibited as the original perfection of man.

§ 61. *Fulness of experience in the sphere of faith is due to the individual development, in virtue of this original perfection of human nature, of each human life brought into existence by procreation. But how, on the same presuppositions, the first men developed, history gives no account, and the hints we*

---

[1] Omnes homines in primo homine sine vitio conditi (Ambrose, *de vocat. Gent.* i. 3).

have on that subject cannot form a religious doctrine in our sense of the word.

1. To understand the fundamental aspects of human life as set forth in the above description of man's original perfection, *i.e.* so that everything is related to the God-consciousness, is undoubtedly a matter of faith ; for it depends entirely on the certainty which accompanies religious experiences, by virtue of which alone all other states of life attain certainty through sharing in those experiences. If, on the contrary, we suppose a man to have religious experiences, but unaccompanied by certainty, so that he can equally well regard them as deceptive or veridical, he will not arrive at the idea of original perfection given above, but will co-ordinate the God-consciousness with other elements of life, or will possibly even take original perfection to consist solely in the possibility of freeing himself from the God-consciousness as a product of human imperfection ; and thus what one experiences as a furtherance another will experience as a hindrance. Now matters of fact in the development of man are never questions of faith but of history, and statements concerning matter of fact, whether general or particular, are not propositions of faith but historical statements, even when, viewed directly, their subject-matter is the state of the God-consciousness in an individual or a community. In this respect there can be no distinction between the first men and ourselves. Everything we know of the actual conditions of the first men and of their course of development, including the manner in which the indwelling tendency to God-consciousness became operative in them without the stimulating influence of tradition, all this is in no sense faith but history—unless we are prepared to alter completely the usage of the word and, say, call history which is mingled with uncertainties, ' faith.' Otherwise ' faith ' would consist simply in historical knowledge, and would be held and disseminated by historical statements and portrayals. That even in their case we should regard as an advance only those conditions which express an increased value of the God-consciousness, is certainly a matter of faith, but of the very same faith as is expressed in the conception of original perfection given above. There could only be specific doctrines of faith concerning the first men in so far as their unique manner of coming into being and of temporal existence might modify the application of our conception to them. Even then we should, of course, always have to maintain that the applica-

tion of our conception is limited to the sphere of procreation, and could leave aside the question what in their case took its place, except in so far as the relation thence arising between them and us altered our God-consciousness in its combination with our race-consciousness. The question arises, then, whether their history has come down to us in such a form that we are compelled to lay down such propositions.

2. Now it is clear that the Old Testament narrative,[1] on which alone we have to depend, is far from putting forward a history of this kind. For even if the question whether this narrative is meant to be taken historically were answered entirely in the affirmative, the particular points which it presents simply take for granted most of what we chiefly want to know about the first men. Especially, for one thing, speech, and the form of consciousness determined by it, the acquisition of which by men after birth is the surest proof that in their case the state of animal-like confusion is already disappearing, is here everywhere assumed ; and in the same way, the God-consciousness appears as already present, and we learn nothing of the mode of its development. Even what is recounted of the converse of God with man, instead of helping the solution of the other problems, is itself a new and still more difficult one. For we learn nothing more exact of the way in which God made Himself intelligible to men, except that bodily form is quite plainly ascribed to Him. But it is equally difficult to see how an idea of God already existing could have been referred to such a phenomenon as its object, or how on occasion of such a phenomenon a true God-consciousness could have arisen. And indeed, even with regard to external conditions, the description of the life of Paradise is only helpful in a negative way, for though the question how man could have supported life from the beginning raises no particular difficulty, no information is given about how the first men spent the time, or of the result in the expansion both of the objective consciousness and of self-consciousness. Even what is said about the naming of the animals [2] leaves us quite uncertain whether the designation had any regard to the relation of the kinds of animals to their species and of the species to the larger classes, and if so, to what extent. The moral situation is equally undefined, for their innocent lack of modesty, as well as their initial obedience to the divine command, admits of the most diverse interpretations. Since, then, besides all this, no measure of time is given, and conse-

---

[1] Gen. 1[26] ff. 2[7]–3[24].　　　　　[2] Gen. 2[19].

quently all materials for forming a historical picture are wanting, we can only say that everything we are told about the first men before the Fall is adequately elucidated by the conception of original perfection which we have proposed.

3. If the narrative is regarded not as history but simply as an ancient attempt to make good the lack of a historical account of the beginnings of the human race, the particular points in it will have inner truth for us in so far as they agree with the conception which we have laid down. But all attempts to form a historical picture of the first beginnings of human existence are bound to fail, because, as we have no experience of an absolute beginning, we have no analogy by which we could make the absolute beginning of rational consciousness intelligible. We have no clear idea even of the consciousness of the child in the first period of life. Yet we cannot miss the fact that in the case of the child the arising of consciousness out of unconsciousness coincides with the detachment and separation of its life from community with the life of the mother, and forthwith the environing spirit, already developed, influences the spirit which is just arriving at conscious thought ; the first man, on the other hand, can only be described as one to whom this means of development was wholly lacking. The formula which accords best with this analogy and with our experience of the conditions of any as yet largely undeveloped human society is that the first men are to be regarded as good-natured grown-up children ; [1] but this is really quite inappropriate and gives us no clear view, for we cannot think of their spiritual development any more than that of the child as proceeding purely from within outwards, and the bodily sustenance of adult primitive man required from the outset activities which we can only conceive as acquired by memory, association, and repetition. If it be suggested that the first man was more like an animal and guided only by instinct, we cannot understand the passage from this condition to one of consciousness and thought without the assistance of a life which was already intelligent, since it would be the beginning of a new kind of existence wholly unconnected with what went before. Attempts have been made to avoid this difficulty by means of two ideas, the grounds of which, at least to some extent, are to be found in the Old Testament narrative. One is the proposition, familiar in many dogmatic systems, that the necessary capacities were from the first present in man by creation, and were capable of extension

[1] Cf. de Wette, *Sittenlehre*, § 38, and *Theol. Zeitschrift*, ii. pp. 84–88.

from what was necessary for the preservation of life further and higher to the genuinely spiritual level. But this really only means that the first condition of man cannot be conceived as different from the later conditions which are determined by previous conditions ; that is to say, an absolutely first condition cannot be conceived at all. Also, if we are unwilling to fall back on instinct, it is unthinkable that there should be a consciousness of these created capacities before they are applied, and again it is inconceivable that, in a genuinely human situation, there should be an impulse which would set them in motion without consciousness of them. Certainly those theologians [1] do not lessen the difficulty (rather they simply return to the starting-point and give a description of the problem more than a solution) who are ready to make assertions about an actual condition of the first man, but at the same time represent the personal perfections which they ascribe to him as mere potentialities, excluding everything which requires previous exercise. The other expedient is as follows : it is supposed that those things which secure for a human being, when born, fellowship with those who are already grown and developed, the newly created man obtained through a revealing and educative fellowship with God or the angels. But if we examine this more closely it leads us back, by one way or another, to the first idea. For if this educative revelation were a purely inward influence, this would be immediately connected with creation itself and indistinguishable from it, and the true and proper life of man would, on this view, begin in much the same way as on the view that there were abilities implanted at creation. If, on the other hand, the fellowship in question is external and mediated through human language, then of course the grown-up child, with this environment, can through speech learn also to think by innate human reason ; but if it is to be set in motion in definite activities demanded by self-preservation, either those higher Beings too must lead a completely human life so as to bring the imitative impulse into play, or else we must assume that the understanding is sufficiently developed to apprehend the teaching and precept which would exert an educative influence.

4. If, then, we are unable to form an intelligible idea of the first states of development of primitive man, and if we cannot point to anything compelling us to modify the application of our conception to them in any special way, there is no reason why we should lay

---

[1] Reinhard, *Dogm.*, §§ 70, 73.

down any special doctrines concerning the first men. All that follows is that we can only exhibit the validity of our conception within the context of earlier and later generations, where human existence begins in the manner with which we are familiar and depends for its development upon human tradition. In this connexion, our certainty of the original perfection of human nature, as set out by us, furnishes ground for the assumption that the first men themselves, when their influence on a second generation began, stood at some quite definite point in the line of development (though a point which we may be unable further to define), and consequently they were in a position to influence the development of the God-consciousness in the next generation ; that is to say, self-communicating piety is as old as the self-propagating human race. This assumption is implied in the consciousness that piety is a universal element of human life.

If, then, following the Mosaic account of the creation, which views all organic beings 'after their kind,'[1] we take the expression of the divine will given there with respect to man[2] not as referring exclusively to the first men in their unique position, but to them only in so far as they were the first instances of the human species, and if we ask whether the designation, 'image of God' (which indisputably denotes the superiority of human nature over the other creatures described), is in harmony with the conception we have set forth, we can only answer 'yes' with great caution. For even though we can describe the living presence of the God-consciousness as a being of God within us, which seems to be something much greater than a resemblance to God, yet this living presence of the God-consciousness is something different. And since this activity of the God-consciousness occurs in us only in connexion with our physical and bodily organism, if we would argue regressively from the likeness or image of God, as it is and has been described here, to God Himself, then we should have to accept one of two alternatives : either the whole world is related to God in the same way as our whole organism is related to the highest spiritual power in us, in which case it would be difficult to see how God could fail to be identical with the world ; or else there is something in God which at least corresponds to our psychical organization, which is largely constituted by the so-called lower psychical forces ; and in this way the idea of God would acquire a strong and really defiling admixture of humanity, and attributes

[1] Gen. 1[11. 21. 24]. [2] Gen. 1[26].

would have to be ascribed to God which can mean nothing when
taken as divine,[1] or else attributes would have to be ascribed to men
which could not be thought of as human.[2]   Here, then, is another
instance of the truth that Biblical expressions, especially when they
do not occur in a purely didactic context, can seldom be adopted in
the terminology of Dogmatics without more ado.   Hence it is not
surprising that many of our theologians, taking what immediately
follows it as the explanation of the divine words regarding ' the
image of God,' have, like the Socinians, connected the divine image
with man's formative and governing relation to external nature
rather than with his own inner being.

The other common phrase, ' original righteousness,' which is
not quite so scriptural, gives rise to other difficulties.   These
difficulties arise not only because righteousness in the ordinary
sense is concerned only with more extended social relations, such as
a first human pair could not possibly have ; it is, in fact, concerned
primarily with the sphere of law proper which, starting from a state
of simple family life, could only reach development in later generations.   But the difficulties in question arise even more because we
are accustomed to include righteousness under the general idea of
virtue ; yet a basal disposition is never called virtue, but only one
which arises through spontaneity.   Here, however, it is a question
of just such a basal disposition, or of one present in man by creation,
from which a development should start such as can relate itself to
divine demands ; and it is a conformity to these demands, achieved
by an active attitude to them, which is so frequently called
' righteousness ' in the Old Testament Scriptures : thus giving rise
to a very undesirable double meaning of the word.   In this way
we should be led back, only too easily, to the idea of created
capacities, a result which could only be avoided by a most definite
explanation that in this connexion the word ' righteousness ' has a
totally different meaning—a meaning which certainly can be traced
back to the usage of common life, inasmuch as we call a thing
' just ' (right) when it corresponds to its definition.   If now we
consider the divine decree ordaining the whole development of the
human race by means of redemption, and the fact that this was
included in the idea of human nature from the beginning, though
unknown to mankind itself, then it will be precisely those attributes

[1] So Quenstedt, *Syst. Theol.*, p. 843, reckons as part of the original perfection *conformitas appetitus sensitivi cum Dei castitate.*

[2] *Ibid.* p. 844 : In corpore primi hominis eluxit imago Dei . . . per im-
passibilitatem.

laid down in the proposition given above on which this capacity for redemption depends.

5. In view of these considerations, it will be felt as very natural that our symbolical documents and, in agreement with them, later teachers of doctrine have wavered in their use of these expressions, sometimes designating by them those original excellences of human nature which lie at the root of all later development [1] and sometimes asserting a definitely perfect condition of the first man, thus laying down doctrines about the first man [2]—this condition being regarded sometimes more as present by creation and some- times as in part acquired. Now if we interpret the first class of passages quoted in such a way that ' nature ' in the second of them is called ' good ' and ' holy ' because the perfections asserted in the first passage develop out of it (as indeed the first passage itself represents them as still in the future), then our proposition makes clear how and why this development takes place. For even the uniform *temperamentum* of the bodily functions can only indicate, on the one hand, the uniformly easy control of the soul over them in every direction ; and on the other hand, of course, there must here be reckoned the resistance, equally adequate on all sides, which the organism offers to external influences, thus always maintaining itself in its original relation. This latter point is not definitely included in our formula, because the power of the God-consciousness does not immediately depend upon it ; rather it shows itself to be so indifferent to the favourable or unfavourable relations of bodily life to external nature that it has often been maintained that piety flourishes best in sickness and poverty. In fact, this sufficiency of the organism, and everything pertaining exclusively to the natural side of man [3] in his conflict with other

---

[1] *Apolog. Conf.* i. (p. 20. Ed. Lücke) inclines in this direction : Justitia originalis habitura erat non solum aequale temperamentum qualitatum corporis, sed etiam haec dona, notitiam Dei certiorem timorem Dei fiduciam Dei, aut certe rectitudinem et vim ista efficiendi ; though even this shows some confusion. And *Solid. Decl.*, p. 643 : In Adamo et Heva *natura* initio pura bona et sancta creata est.

[2] Here belongs *Solid. Decl.*, p. 640, in so far as it calls original sin a privatio concreatae in Paradiso justitiae originalis seu imaginis Dei, ad quam homo initio in veritate sanctitate atque justitia creatus fuerat ; and *Conf. Belg.* xiv. : Credimus Deum ex limo terrae hominem ad imaginem suam bonum scilicet iustum et sanctum creasse, qui proprio arbitrio suam voluntatem ad Dei voluntatem componere et conformem reddere posset. Less clearly, *Conf. Helv.* : Fuit homo ab initio a Deo conditus ad imaginem Dei in iustitia et sanctitate veritatis, bonus et rectus.

[3] Cf. Luther in *Genes.* i. § 187 : ' To this inner perfection was later added the most beautiful and admirable strength and glory of the body and all its members.'

natural forces, would be better dealt with under the heading of the Perfection of the World in relation to mankind, on the same principle as that which led us to discuss human mortality not in the form of the question whether it conflicted with man's proper perfection but rather as the question whether the perfection of the world in relation to man was diminished by it.   With regard especially to the obedience of the lower powers of the soul to the higher (a point which is always reckoned an essential part of original righteousness) the question only arises here, where we are altogether disregarding the actual condition of the first pair as individuals, in so far as there resides in the lower functions a receptivity for the impulses of the higher ; and this not only in the state of quiescence but during their proper life-process.   And this point is, of course, brought out in our proposition, since the activities in which the influence of the God-consciousness takes effect determine all its communications.   But when Augustine understands by the expression ' desire ' [1] simply the proper life-process of these functions, and at the same time holds that it cannot be thought of as co-existing with original righteousness, he seems to be at least as much open to blame as the Pelagians, if they considered the opposition between the lower and higher faculties as man's original condition, and included all acquired perfection under the concept of the removal of that opposition.   For Augustine's opinion presupposes also an original contradiction between the spirit in man and that which is necessary for his animal life.

But this leads us over to the other point of view—namely, the representation of original righteousness or the divine image as an actual condition of the first man.   Now if, on this view, the statement that man was created by God good, righteous, and holy, means no more than that, in opposition to the Pelagian doctrine, the first real state of man could not have been one of sin, we may unreservedly assent.   For sin must have been preceded by knowledge and recognition of the divine will, and in that case it must have been preceded by free activity which was not sinful.   But if what is meant is a real power exercised by the higher faculties over the lower, then (even if we do not conjoin with this the position of Augustine referred to above), the greater this power is taken to be, it is from this point of view impossible to conceive of anything but

---

[1] *Concupiscentia.*   The relevant passages are too many to give in detail, but the use of the word is so varied that it would be hard to decide whether, and if so how far, his doctrine goes beyond the proper bounds.

a growing intensification of that power in the same regard. This is probably the real reason why the Roman Church has explained man's original state of sinlessness, not by the original perfection of human nature, but rather by an extraordinary divine influence—an explanation which clearly implies a Pelagian conception of human nature as such.[1] It may not be quite so harmful in its consequences, but it confuses the idea of original perfection none the less, when our dogmatic theologians maintain that the first pair, in their original condition, were partakers of the Holy Spirit.[2] Thus the attempt to define more closely the primitive condition of the first man seems to lead nowhere, whether he be considered as completely corresponding with what we can recognize in later times as a progressive development of original perfection, or whether he be considered as completely corresponding to what appears to us a retrogressive state. The Pelagians, starting from the second of these presuppositions, gain a double advantage—they admit no original perfection which has been lost, and a progressive development can take place from the point of departure which they accept ; but they incur a double disadvantage—that the good for them is not original, and that the Redeemer appears only as an individual member in the development. The doctrine of the Church, on the other hand, gains a double superiority—it postulates the good as immediately produced by God, and, since with the loss of this condition the development is broken and a new point of departure is needed, the Redeemer can come in as the turning-point ; but it incurs a double disadvantage—the good which was already actual in the phenomenal world has been lost, in spite of the sustaining divine omnipotence, and the sole purpose for which we are tempted to form a picture of the original state of the first man, i.e. in order to have a starting-point for the genetic conception of all that follows, is not attained. Hence we may take it as more to the purpose not to define anything more accurately as regards the condition of the first man, but simply to elicit the ever self-identical original perfection of nature from the higher self-consciousness viewed universally. But if we are to see everything that can develop out of such original perfection all together in a single human instance, it is not to be sought in Adam, in whom it must have again been lost, but in Christ, in whom it has brought gain to all.

---

[1] Frenum extraordinarium. See Bellarmin., de Gratia pr. hom, cap. v.
[2] Melanchth., loc., p. 112 : Adam et Eva erant electi, et tamen revera amiserunt Spiritum Sanctum in lapsu.

SECOND PART OF
THE SYSTEM OF DOCTRINE

SECOND PART

Explication of the facts of the religious self-consciousness, as they are determined by the antithesis.

INTRODUCTION

§ 62. *The God-consciousness described in the foregoing occurs as the actual content of a moment of experience only under the general form of self-consciousness, i.e. the antithesis of pleasure and pain.*

NOTE.—Cf. § 5.

1. The disposition to the God-consciousness can be represented as a continuous impartation of that consciousness, but only in a degree that is infinitely small; with the consequence that the transition to a definite and perceptible magnitude is always dependent on some other fact of consciousness. Now, were such a transition to take place in our self-consciousness apart from the form of the antithesis, *i.e.* neither as an advancement nor as an arrestment of the God-consciousness, it would need to be a transition that was continuous and uniform. This is conceivable if, independently of any other fact of consciousness, the God-consciousness were to rise noticeably above the infinitely small degree just referred to. The condition of the God-consciousness in such a case would be one of constant repression, dull uniformity, any emergence of vitality above a very low average being found only among the other facts of consciousness. A constant uniformity in the God-consciousness, however, is conceivable also in a state of existence where an absolute facility existed of evoking it in its absolute strength from every other fact of consciousness. The condition of the God-consciousness in this case would be that of a blessed uniformity of constant predominance. Clearly, however, our religious consciousness is not such that more and less do not apply to it ; on the contrary, it oscillates between these extremes, sharing, as it does, the variations of our temporal life. True, this more and less, simply as such, may seem to be of the nature of a fluctuating difference rather than of an antithesis. Still, contrariety

of movement creates an antithesis ; for a movement from less to more indicates that the disposition to the God-consciousness is developing with increasing freedom, while one from more to less is an arrestment of it and indicates that other impulses are more powerful.

But now in this as in other provinces of experience (as there is no such state as absolute blessedness or as complete abeyance of the God-consciousness) pleasure and pain are by no means to be regarded as so separate from each other that one of them might in some circumstances actually exist without the other. If, then, the determining power of the God-consciousness is felt to be limited, pain is bound up with it, *i.e.* is present even in the highest pleasure. Whereas, if the consciousness that this power is arrested excites pain, the God-consciousness is nevertheless willed as such a power, and is thereby in and for itself an object of pleasure.

2. If, however, our proposition is to be understood as implying that what emerges in actual consciousness, under whichever form of the antithesis, as God-consciousness is always what has already been described, namely, the feeling of absolute dependence, and that no modification of the God-consciousness can be instanced where this feeling might either be absent or have added to it anything except what is related to and constitutes the antithesis in question ; and if there is taken along with this our former assertion [1] that in the Christian consciousness (the same has always held good, however, of religion moulded by any other form of belief) the feeling of absolute dependence never purely by itself fills a moment of religious experience—then each of the two statements is explained by the other in this way, namely, that what was described in our First Part (taken along with what in other forms of religion develops otherwise out of the fact that, as often as the indwelling God-consciousness really seeks to emerge, it appears either as advanced or arrested in its functioning) likewise constitutes the God-consciousness in its entire range, and that this fact must govern our conception of the whole content of every moment of religious experience, occur where it may. This assertion is challenged mainly on the ground that in our use of the idea of absolute dependence we have annulled every distinction between human freedom and subordinate forms of finite being,[2] while yet the God-consciousness surely (if one's own acceptance of the divine will and one's love to God form part of the God-consciousness) has

---

[1] § 29.　　　　[2] § 49.

a content which relates exclusively to human freedom and presupposes it. These elements, it is held, consequently cannot be
derived from the feeling of absolute dependence, and just as little
from the antithesis mentioned if it refers solely to that feeling. To
dispose of this objection in all its aspects, and thereby to substantiate our assertion with respect at least to all monotheistic
forms of faith, lies outside our present task.

One point, however, common to all forms of faith in so far as
they all participate in the antithesis, may be adduced here. This,
namely, that absolute facility in the development of the God-
consciousness from any given stimulus and in every situation, which
is proposed as the end, is equivalent to constant communion with
God, while every retrograde movement is a turning away from
God. Now if, religion being admittedly an essential element of
life, only communion and not turning away can be willed, the latter
can be received into consciousness only if it is what was originally
in harmony with the divine will. In Christianity this proviso is
enunciated in the most general and fruitful way by the postulation
of redemption as the work and dispensation of God, and hence also
of faith in redemption as conformity to the divine will.

3. Everything related to the Redeemer in the religious consciousness of the Christian is peculiar to the distinctively Christian
articulation of the antithesis under discussion. No proposition,
as we have already said, describing the feeling of absolute dependence apart from this antithesis, can be a description of a religious
moment in its entire content, for in every such moment that feeling
occurs only as a relative turning away from God or turning towards
Him. From these two statements we must go on to assert that
no proposition merely describing the condition of the individual life
with reference to this antithesis is a description of the entire content
of a religious moment, since in every such moment the condition
described must needs manifest itself in the emergence of the
feeling of absolute dependence. In the actual life of the Christian,
therefore, the two are always found in combination : there is no
general God-consciousness which has not bound up with it a relation
to Christ, and no relationship with the Redeemer which has no
bearing on the general God-consciousness. The propositions of the
first part, which lay less direct stress on what is distinctively
Christian, are on that account often treated as Natural Theology of
an original and universally valid kind, and as such are overrated
by those who are themselves less permeated by the distinctive

element in Christianity.   Others, again, underrate these propositions as attainable even apart from Christianity, and will only allow those propositions which express a relation to the Redeemer to rank as specifically Christian.   Both parties are in error.   For the former propositions are in no sense the reflection of a meagre and purely monotheistic God-consciousness, but are abstracted from one which has issued from fellowship with the Redeemer.   Similarly, propositions expressing a relation to Christ are genuinely Christian propositions only in so far as they recognize no other criterion for relationship with the Redeemer than the measure in which the continuity of the God-consciousness is produced thereby ; so that a relationship with Christ, which resulted in the God-consciousness losing its prominence or being, as it were, superseded (because Christ alone and not God had a place in self-consciousness), might indeed be a most intimate one, but strictly speaking it would not belong to the sphere of religion at all.

§ 63. *While in general the manner in which the God-consciousness takes shape in and with the stimulated self-consciousness can be traced only to the action of the individual, the distinctive feature of Christian piety lies in the fact that whatever aliena-tion from God there is in the phases of our experience, we are conscious of it as an action originating in ourselves, which we call Sin ; but whatever fellowship with God there is, we are conscious of it as resting upon a communication from the Redeemer, which we call Grace.*

1. Let us suppose an æsthetic form of faith.[1]   It will reduce both these arrestments and continued developments of the God-consciousness, as indeed every other change in man's experience, to passive states, and represent them consequently as the effects of external influences in such a manner that they will appear simply to be appointed events, while the ideas of merit and guilt will really not apply to them at all.   Accordingly, we may say that the controversy regarding freedom, as it is usually urged in this sphere, is just the controversy as to whether our passive states are to be regarded as subordinate to our active states or *vice versa* ; and that freedom in the latter sense is the universal premiss of all teleological forms of faith, which alone, by starting as they do from the ascendency of spontaneous activity in man, are able to find guilt in all arrestments of the disposition to the God-consciousness,

[1] § 9.

and merit in every progression of it.   More precise determinations, however, of the ' how ' of either are not to be found in the common nature of these forms of faith ; this only is self-evident, namely, that if both arrestment of the impulse to the God-consciousness and quickened development of it are to be equally the act of one and the same individual, and consequently opposites are to be explained by the same cause, then, in relation to the doer, the two must cease to be opposed.

2. In Christian piety as described here there is no such initial difficulty to be surmounted. The description given here, however, is identical with the general exposition put forward above.[1]   For if the feeling of absolute dependence, which was previously in bondage, has been set free only by redemption, the facility with which we are able to graft the God-consciousness on the various sensuous excitations of our self-consciousness also springs solely from the facts of redemption, and is therefore a communicated facility. And if the bondage of the feeling of absolute dependence did not betoken its real absence (for absence would imply the impossibility of such an act as is here designated sin), then in every portion of life that could be regarded as a whole in itself, the God-consciousness too was present in degree even if only as something infinitely small, and thus whenever such a portion of life came to an end there took place an act having relation to the God-consciousness.   Not, however, an act involving the evocation of the God-consciousness as a co-determinant of the moment, i.e. not a turning to God (from which an experience of communion with God always arises of itself), but a turning away from God,[2] so that with the acceptance of such a redemption there is always conjoined a backward look to sin as prior to it. Now the fact that here communion with God rests on an act extraneous to it by no means prevents our bringing Christianity under the general category of teleological forms of faith. For, on the one hand, communication and action are not mutually exclusive, for corporate acts, e.g., have their origin for the most part in a single person, and yet are acts also on the part of the rest ; while, on the other hand, appropriation of redemption is always represented as action, as a laying hold of Christ, or the.like.[3]

---

[1] § 11, 2 and 3.
[2] Cf. Rom. 3²³.   Conf. Aug. xix. : Voluntas . . . avertit se a Deo.
[3] Augsb. Conf. xx. : ' He therefore desires that we should *embrace* the promise of God by faith.' Melanchthon, Loci Comm. Theol. De Vocabulo Fidei : ' Si fides non est fiducia intuens Christum . . . non applicamus nobis eius beneficium.' De Fide : ' Pia mens . . . intelligit hanc misericordiam fide id est fiducia apprehendendam esse.'

In the case, however, of a religious consciousness contrariwise regarding its derangements as coming from elsewhere, but communion with God (into which these do not enter) as proceeding from the individual's own spiritual vitality, the term redemption could be applied (and even that in a very subordinate sense) only to that which sealed up the external sources of the derangements. Redemption through Jesus, however, has never been thought of in this way. And the further we carry the way of looking at things just indicated, then the more the lack of communion with God is taken to be merely fortuitous, the less definitely are sin and grace as such (and as earlier and later) differentiated from each other, and the more does the conception of redemption recede into the distance, till all three disappear together. This disappearance actually occurs when it is assumed that the unity of the sensuous and the higher self-consciousness is the natural basic condition of the individual—a condition in which the absence of the God-consciousness in any particular moment remains merely accidental, something which at once cancels itself out in corporate life, inasmuch as all do not suffer from the same accident at once. This, taken strictly, is the non-Christian view which recognizes no need of redemption ; for in Christianity these two, sin and grace, are valid ideas only on the basis of redemption and on the assumption that it has been appropriated.

3. Moreover, the proposition cannot be taken as implying that in the immediate Christian self-consciousness sin and grace are to be referred to separate moments and to be kept absolutely apart from each other as mutually incompatible. On the contrary, as the energy of the God-consciousness is never at its absolutely highest any more than the engrafting of the God-consciousness on the excitations of the sensuous self-consciousness is ever absolutely constant, there is involved in this circumstance a limiting deficiency of the God-consciousness, which is certainly sinful. Just as little, however, in a truly Christian consciousness can the connexion with redemption be utterly null, for in that case the Christian consciousness would, until the connexion was re-established, be, contrary to what is assumed, non-Christian. And as this connexion proceeds originally from the Redeemer, so His communicated action is implied throughout. Here, accordingly, while the elements we are discussing are antithetic they are only such as in the religious life of the Christian are conjoined in every moment, though always in varied measure.

§ 64. *For the purpose of our exposition, it is necessary to separate the two subjects, so as to treat first of Sin and then of Grace ; and of each in accordance with all the three forms of dogmatic propositions.*

1. In our exposition all doctrines properly so called must be extracted from the Christian religious self-consciousness, *i.e.* the inward experience of Christian people. Since, however, it is the case that every Christian is conscious both of sin and of grace as always combined with each other and never dissociated, we may well be asked what warrant we have for separating them, seeing that if either be described by itself alone what results will not be the description of a Christian consciousness. A description of the sense of sin as the exclusive content even of merely detached portions of life would only amount to a historical sketch, the accuracy of which would require some sort of proof, but could find no verification in the Christian consciousness itself ; such a description would therefore be no doctrine of the faith. Similarly the description of an inherently absolute and continuous efficacy of the God-consciousness would only be an anticipation ; no one could point to such a state as actually brought about in him by redemption ; so that this again would be no doctrine of the faith. Granting both positions (on the understanding that in each case one of the two elements is absolutely excluded), the separation of the two is nevertheless necessary to our exposition ; only we must recognize that it is not met with in any Christian consciousness, but is an arbitrary expedient adopted here with a view simply to greater clarity of thought. For although our dogmatic propositions as a whole represent only the doctrine held to be valid in the Evangelical Church of our time, yet the Christian self-consciousness which they are meant to articulate with the utmost precision is not really confined to any definite period, but is the universal, the always and everywhere self-identical element in the Christian Church—so far, that is to say, as dogmatic propositions do not relate to the *differentiæ* of the Christian communions, as they do not wherever the antithesis of sin and grace is in question. We must accordingly describe the Christian consciousness with reference to its content, composed of these antithetic elements, in such a way that even the first moment of the genesis of the Christian consciousness and everything that in later moments represents the first, may be comprised in our description. Now, in the case of those who are not

born in Christianity but come to accept it, it is obvious that their appropriation of redemption, and therefore of grace, must be preceded by a recognition of their need of redemption ; and this emerges only in connexion with the consciousness of sin. In such persons, accordingly, there is a consciousness of sin anterior to the consciousness of grace ; and since everything sinful in their later life is connected with the sin that was present prior to grace, they have in every moment of their later life the consciousness of sin as of something present in them before grace was there. Nay, this consciousness must be shared without exception even by those who are born within Christendom, were it only in virtue of their corporate feeling, the formula that sin is anterior to grace being simply the expression of the human race's need for redemption and of its relation to Christ. Hence to vindicate our proposition we do not even need to decide whether or not each individual born in Christendom was at first outside of grace for a time, and, like those not so born, attained to grace only after passing through a state characterized exclusively by the consciousness of sin.

2. In pursuance, then, of this course of separating the consciousness of sin and the consciousness of grace in our exposition, we shall first describe by itself that element of the Christian self-consciousness which is more and more to disappear through the action of the other, and which, arising out of man's common condition anterior to the entrance of redemption, likewise represents that condition. Thereafter we shall describe by itself that element which is ever to be less and less limited by the other, and which, arising out of redemption, likewise represents the total efficacy thereof. The separation of these two elements common to all Christian states of mind into which the antithesis has developed is an obvious possibility for the simple reason that otherwise there can scarcely be a full perception of the two implied relations. It is more difficult, however, to show that, and how, the separation can be managed in the other two types of dogmatic propositions without disadvantage to their content. Thus, if, to begin with, we were to speak of the world by itself and not in relation to man, then, first, whether the antithesis in question had unfolded itself in man or not, whatever in the world influences man would always be the same, and there could accordingly be no special relationship between the world and either member of the antithesis. But again, such change as has been wrought in the world by human activity is always as regards the world simply the work of the

whole man, and there least of all differences relating to the God-consciousness would have to be taken into account. But what we have to deal with in this connexion is always simply states of the world in relation to man, and there it is evident that the world will be a different thing to a man according as he apprehends it from the standpoint of a God-consciousness completely paralysed or of one absolutely paramount. It will accordingly be possible to distinguish in the Christian life itself between what in our conception of the world is to be placed to the account of sin, and what to the account of grace. The like holds good also of the results of man's action upon the world as far as these are realities to himself and come within his consciousness. For the more significance he attaches to the antithesis, the more apparent will be to him the homogeneous and self-coherent character of what has proceeded from him because of sin and without the prompting of the God-consciousness, and on the other hand of what, as resulting from the operation of redemption, must bear the impress thereof. Finally, as regards the divine attributes, it is of course evident that statements concerning God cannot issue from a condition of alienation from God, but are only possible when a man is in some sense turned again towards Him ; for all statements concerning God presuppose a turning towards Him. But not even where sin is viewed from the standpoint of a paramount God-consciousness can we conceive of divine attributes that have to do with sin apart from its disappearance as a result of redemption. For since all divine attributes are activities, attributes of the kind in question must be activities making for the maintenance and confirmation of sin ; but to admit such attributes would be to run counter to Christian piety. Similarly, should we assume a divine agency as the source of the God-consciousness but not as developing out of sin and limited by sin, it too could only be formulated in terms of concepts of the divine attributes from which the distinctively Christian character had completely vanished ; so that within the range of this particular type of concept that character would never appear at all. Surely, however, it is natural for Christian piety, seeing as it certainly does in redemption a divine measure, to make statements concerning God that relate to the God-consciousness ; and in fact it will be these very statements which set forth the trend and aim of the divine causality, as reflected in our feeling of absolute dependence in general, so that it is only in combination with them that the ideas underlying our First Part attain to perfect precision and vivid clearness. In order to discover these statements it is certainly quite unnecessary to separate the two members of our antithesis from each other ; yet a correct, and, in view of what has already been said, perhaps a preferable, way of describing the divine activity by means of which the God-consciousness attains to supremacy, will be to ask, first, what divine attributes are to be discerned in the state of sin—though, of course, only in as far as there is therein an expectation of and preparation for redemption ; and then, secondly, to what attributes the growing dominion of the God-consciousness points back, as it comes to be formed out of the state of sin through redemption. Even were these attributes mere abstractions (as would obviously be less true of the latter than of the former), yet, when viewed in combination—just as it is the fusion of the two elements that constitutes the reality of the Christian life—they would yield a truly living representation ; and if we then view them in combination with the divine attributes set forth in our First Part, the exposition of our God-consciousness under this form will be complete.

3. This Second Part of Dogmatics might accordingly be arranged in two ways. Thus we might take the three forms of dogmatic proposition as our primary division, and then under each of them treat first of what relates to sin, and secondly of what relates to grace. Or, again, we might set forth these two elements of our self-consciousness as the main heads, and treat first of sin under all the three forms of proposition, and next of grace in the same way. The latter scheme seems preferable inasmuch as the main division will then be formed by what is found already divided in the immediate Christian self-consciousness. This part of our work will therefore have two aspects, in one of which we shall deal with the consciousness of sin under all the three dogmatic forms, in the other with grace on similar lines.

FIRST ASPECT OF THE ANTITHESIS

EXPLICATION OF THE CONSCIOUSNESS OF SIN

§ 65. *The propositions to be enunciated here must all harmonize with those of the same type in our First Part; but they must also have regard to the propositions of the Second Aspect, which explicate the consciousness of grace, these last being meanwhile held in reserve.*

1. Any attempt to consider the fact of sin purely by itself is at once confronted by an apparent antinomy. Thus were we from our point of view to regard every arrestment of the God-consciousness that takes place merely as the act of man, then, as being a turning away from God, it would be in contradiction with the disposition to the God-consciousness which is present in man as a vital impulse, and is here assumed as such. Equal difficulty would appear to lie in the necessity of the actual existence of sin being consistent with divine omnipotence, since man's turning from God must like all else be ordained by God; for of course man even in the state of sin is involved in the natural order, and it is only in virtue of his position within that order—with the entire range of which the divine causality is co-extensive—that sin can develop in him at all. Again, if there are divine attributes related to sin, indeed, but not in the way of giving it persistence and confirmation, how should even that, which from its very nature ought not to continue, have come into being in association with all that owes its being to the eternally omniscient divine omnipotence? Finally, if sin exists only where there is a powerlessness of the God-consciousness, and if it develops in man in consequence of impressions received from the totality of finite existence, how could this fail to abrogate what we laid down as the original perfection of man and the perfection of the world in relation to him?

2. Although this antinomy can be only apparent (the two sets of propositions alike having their source in our immediate self-consciousness, which as the truth of our being cannot be in contradiction with itself), yet it follows from this relationship that we

are here face to face with a large number of difficulties. For if we are too readily disposed to exclude sin from the range of our absolute dependence on God, we inevitably verge upon Manichæism; while if we seek to reconcile it with the original perfection of man, we shall hardly avoid Pelagianism. It may, in fact, be said that in the development of the Church's doctrine there has been an almost constant wavering between these antagonistic positions. Nevertheless, though this wavering cannot now be brought to rest, and though no formula can be found which would not be felt by some to lean more towards the latter extreme, and by others towards the former, yet in a general way, at least, the second part of our proposition is as well adapted to smooth out the difficulties as the first part of necessity raises them. Thus since in our statements about sin we are to keep in view those still to be made about grace, we may regard sin on the one hand as simply that which would not be unless redemption was to be; or on the other as that which, as it is to disappear, can disappear only through redemption. In the first case we obviate any seemingly inevitable risk of approximating to Manichæism; in the second we can scarcely, except by wantonness, fall into Pelagianism. If, however, the danger indicated is not perpetually to recur in consequence of our having to refer to the terms recognized by the Church, we must claim the right to interpret these terms in such a way as most adequately to secure ourselves against the danger, or else, should they not lend themselves to this, to replace them by others. In order to attain at least to an approximate solution of our problem we must have recourse to one or other of these alternatives under all the three forms.

FIRST SECTION

Sin as a State of Man

§ 66. *We have the consciousness of sin whenever the God-consciousness which forms part of an inner state, or is in some way added to it, determines our self-consciousness as pain ; and therefore we conceive of sin as a positive antagonism of the flesh against the spirit.*

1. Without running counter to our method we cannot at the outset give an objective elucidation of sin, but must revert to the personal self-consciousness which attests an inner state as sin—a procedure all the less open to objection because sin cannot emerge in the life of the Christian apart from such a consciousness. To lack this consciousness would simply be an additional sin, of which, as such, we could not fail subsequently to become conscious. If, then, it is our primary object to ascertain the characteristic element in the consciousness of sinfulness, we ought not, within the sphere of Christian piety, to look for it except in relationship to the God-consciousness, and accordingly the only course open to us is to reckon everything as sin that has arrested the free development of the God-consciousness. Now, if in any particular moment under examination God has formed part of our self-consciousness, but this God-consciousness has not been able to permeate the other active elements therein, thus determining the moment, then sin and the consciousness of sin are simultaneous, and the sensuous self-consciousness by reason of its having been gratified is affected with pleasure, but the higher, owing to the impotence of the God-consciousness, with pain. If, on the other hand, God has not formed part of the moment at all, if, that is to say, the occurrence of the moment excludes the God-consciousness, showing that the God-consciousness cannot make the moment its own, which also means that it cannot be supposed to accord and acquiesce in it, then the consciousness of sin follows on the sin itself. Supposing, however, that the God-consciousness has determined the moment, and that pleasure is present in the higher self-consciousness, still every attendant feeling of effort implies a consciousness of sin—in some

degree, consequently, annulling that pleasure—since we thereby are made aware that if the sensuous elements which have been overcome had been reinforced from without, the God-consciousness would have been unable to determine the moment. In this sense, therefore—but only because there exists a living seed of sin ever ready to burst forth—there is such a thing as an abiding consciousness of sin, now preceding the sin itself as a warning presentiment, now accompanying it as an inward reproof, or following it as penitence. That no God-consciousness, however, should ever be directed at all upon a moment such as that described could only happen if in the person acting there were no relationship between the moment and the class of actions under discussion (in which case he would be in a state of innocence), or if the God-consciousness were no longer active within him (which would be the state of hardening).

2. If we conceive now a state in which the flesh, *i.e.* the totality of the so-called lower powers of the soul, were susceptible only to impulses proceeding from the quarter of the God-consciousness, and were never an independent motive principle, a conflict between the two would not be possible, but we should again have conceived a sinless state. In every moment in this self-consciousness the two powers would be perfectly at one, every moment beginning in the spirit and ending in the spirit, and the flesh serving only as a living intermediary, a healthy organ, and never exhibiting anything not initiated and directed by the spirit, whether as an act of its own or as an intrusive extraneous element in an act proceeding from the spirit. As long, however, as spirit and flesh have not in this sense become one, they co-exist as two powers at issue with each other,[1] and in so far as the spirit presses towards the perfect unity indicated, this state can be characterized only as an incapacity of the spirit. The possibility of this we left aside when treating of the original perfection of man,[2] except that there there those relationships, and no others, had to be brought out which contain in themselves the principles of progressive development. Since, however, the consciousness of sin never exists in the soul of the Christian without the consciousness of the power of redemption,[3] the former is never actually found without its complementary half which we are to describe later, and, if taken by itself alone, represents only that state of a hopeless incapacity in the spirit, which prevails outside the sphere of redemption.

[1] Gal. 5[17], Rom. 7[18-23].   [2] § 60.   [3] Rom. 7[25] 8[2].

This explanation of sin as an arrestment of the determinative power of the spirit, due to the independence of the sensuous functions, is certainly reconcilable with those explanations which describe sin as a turning away from the Creator,[1] though less so with those which interpret sin as a violation of the divine law.[2] But it cannot be of any great consequence to insist on a reconciliation with the latter, for in the sense in which God and the eternal law might be distinguished—as if one could turn away from the latter as from a single and perhaps arbitrary act of God without turning away from Himself—law is not an originally Christian term and must therefore be merged in a higher. We should certainly require to widen it in a very indefinite and arbitrary way if we had to bring under it all that may count as sin not only in deeds, but in thoughts and words. Our explanation, however, unifies this division in the most natural way. For if a thought or word viewed otherwise than as an act did form the content of a moment, it could only incorrectly be called a sin. An interpretation more Christian in its origin, and at the same time directly in keeping with our own, is that which says that sin consists in our desiring what Christ contemns and *vice versa*.[3]

§ 67. *We are conscious of sin as the power and work of a time when the disposition to the God-consciousness had not yet actively emerged in us.*

1. It is in reality already implied, in the relation of this proposition to all that has been said above, that in the period to which the consciousness of sin points back, sin was not present in us in the same way as we are now conscious of it. For in this latter form it can be present only simultaneously with and as related to the God-consciousness. If our God-consciousness is not yet developed, there can be in us no resistance to it, but merely an independent activity of the flesh which, though in time it will quite naturally come to act as a resistance to the spirit, cannot at that stage be regarded as sin in the proper sense, but rather as the germ of sin. This interpretation we apply generally to individual persons in their earliest stages of development, and in exactly the same way to whole peoples and eras. Nevertheless, the proposition is not to be understood as implying that all sin, whatever its content, is to be relegated to that prior time ; it refers only to the state of sin in general.

---

[1] *Conf. Aug.* xix. : Voluntas . . . quae avertit se a Deo.

[2] For others of this type cf. Gerhard, *Loc. Th.* t. v. pp. 2 ff.

[3] Aug., *de vera relig.* 31 : Non enim ullum peccatum committi potest, nisi aut dum appetuntur ea quae ille contemsit, aut fugiuntur quae ille sustinuit.

The functions of the lower life which may come into conflict with
the spirit are not all developed prior to the God-consciousness, but
as they do develop without having the God-consciousness directed
upon them in their initial stages, the same result follows.

2. Resistance, as an activity by which an opposed activity is
to be neutralized, has naturally its degrees of more and less, and
is thus an intensive phenomenon conditioned by time, and when
present in anything that has life advances by repetition in time to
proficiency. Now our proposition goes back to the universal experience that in each individual the flesh manifests itself as a reality
before the spirit comes to be such, the result being, that, as soon as
the spirit enters the sphere of consciousness (and it is involved in
the original perfection of man that the independent activity of
the flesh cannot of itself prevent the ingress of the spirit), resistance takes place, *i.e.* we become conscious also of sin as the God-
consciousness awakes within us. The activity of the spirit, however, not merely in general, as present in the distinctive form of
human life, but also in particular, in its effort to win dominion over
the flesh, is likewise an intensive phenomenon, and, as a living
force, attains by repetition in time to proficiency. Thus the
strength which the spirit gradually acquires is the work and power
of the period subsequent to the awaking of the God-consciousness,
though of course in association with the previously given spiritual
forces to the promptings of which that awaking was due ; while
the strength of the resistance made by the flesh and manifested in
the consciousness of sin, is due to the advantage gained by the
flesh during the prior time,[1] though again, of course, in association
with the corporate life upon which the amount of that advantage
depends. Now if the whole situation subsequent to the awaking
of the God-consciousness could be conceived as a progressive
ascendancy of the spirit over the flesh, self-consciousness could
hardly have such a phase as the consciousness of sin ; and accordingly this phase will be more and more attenuated as that conception becomes dominant, and *vice versa*. We actually find, however,
that our development is always an irregular one, and also that the
spirit is obstructed in its action by the flesh—the circumstance,
indeed, to which our consciousness of sin is due. This irregularity
is twofold. In the first place, the development of the spirit proceeds intermittently through widely separated moments of exceptional illumination and stimulation ; and thus if, after such a

---

[1] Gen. 8:21.

moment, the activity of the spirit should seem less than it was during the moment, or if the stimulation did not from the outset correspond with the illumination, we become conscious of our state as one of sin, since in the actual experience of the moment the flesh overrides the effort of the spirit.[1]   Secondly, we are conscious of the spirit as one, while the flesh is a manifold, and a manifold composed of diverse elements, so that the spirit cannot stand in a uniform relation to it.   Since, however, the spirit's demand is always the same, the spirit itself, wherever it is less able to work effectively, appears as a baffled and defeated force, and the subject therefore as in a state of sin.   The more thoroughly we trace back the state of our spiritual life to a conscious beginning, to a general ' taking command of one's self '—so to call it [2]—which is represented in every decision of the will, then, whenever the act does not correspond with that decision, the more conscious we are of a domination of the flesh, and we cannot do otherwise than trace this back to a time prior to that beginning.

§ 68. *Although sin, as a result of the unequal development of insight and will-power, can be conceived in such a way that its existence does not invalidate the idea of the original perfection of man, still we are bound to regard it as a derangement of our nature.*

1. This proposition would seem to bring the entire life of the spirit under the two contrasted categories of intellect and will, but it is far from being intended here to make light of the third element in our experience, namely, our immediate self-consciousness, which in fact forms the starting-point in every part of our exposition. Indeed, it is precisely the relationship of that self-consciousness to the other two factors that serves as the measure of the disparity in their development.   Let us figure to ourselves the above-mentioned ' taking command of one's self ' in its most general form ; it is simply the discernment of the absolute superiority of those states of mind which combine with the God-consciousness without obstructing it.   That discernment cannot emerge without the individual's appropriating it, and this takes place only through an act of self-consciousness in which the said discernment, as giving approval and recognition, becomes a command.   Now the fact that this excitation of the self-consciousness follows upon the discernment more rapidly than it is able to determine our volitions, constitutes just that inequality along with which sin and the con-

---

[1] Rom. 7[18].   [2] Rom. 7[22].

sciousness of sin are given. It is true that there are two ways in which at the very start we might conceive of this disparity as being removed, and in either case there would be no consciousness of sin. Thus if a man were to attain gradually to a discernment of the relationship of his various inner states to the God-consciousness, but only in the same measure as his recognition thereof could set the will in operation, then for him no consciousness of sin could arise, as indeed he could never imagine a more divine life than that which he actually exhibits at every moment. Similarly, if the antithesis were actually present in its full extent and clearly realized, but the will were uniformly powerful enough to resist every impulse of the flesh, then again a person having this experience could never come to be conscious of sin as his own condition. Neither of these cases, however, occurs in our experience ; in fact we can see quite well why they cannot. Thus—to begin with the second case—the antithesis presents itself to our understanding in the manner of a general pattern or formula which in any particular instance is, so to speak, recognized from afar ; and it is in this way too that the immature begin to receive the said discernment from their elders soon after their own earliest experiences of excitation. But the impulse that the commanding recognition is to give to the will must —just because the flesh has to do with the particular only, and knows nothing of the general—in every given instance be a special one ; and here the flesh has habit on its side as the real law in its members,[1] whereas it is only gradually that the earlier happier moments come to the succour of the spirit. If, however, we turn to the first case, then, while we might perhaps regard this (though, as a matter of fact, we never do find perfect equipoise, but always advance and retreat) as a possibility in a single individual, it could not be so in a communal life. For all would not take the same path, and consequently each would necessarily see in the case of others, and then recognize in his own, something for which at the moment he had not the requisite will-power. Accordingly, since without this disparity—as a counterpart to which we might also imagine a lagging of the intelligence behind the will, though this would be in appearance only—there could arise no consciousness of sin, the latter is to be understood simply as issuing from the former ; indeed, it would be impossible for any one to specify any other mode of attaining to that consciousness. It is along the same lines that we can understand what is unquestionably the most pernicious

[1] Rom. 7[28].

element of all, namely, how the resistance of the flesh reacts upon the intelligence, so that for one thing the intelligence seeks to palliate the inner states thus produced, on the pretext of their being compatible with the God-consciousness ;[1] and for another the God-consciousness, being seized upon when but in germ by the power of the flesh, is altered and disintegrated to such a degree that every state comes to be compatible with some aspect of it, and thus the moral antithesis itself is lost.[2] If on this view idolatry may rightly enough be thought to have the same origin as sin, no less rightly will all anthropopathic ideas of God which attenuate the antithesis or base it on distinctions of human law be regarded as survivals of idolatry.

2. Nevertheless, we are not entitled to say that sin, on the view taken of it here, would conflict with the original perfection of man, and thus annul it. On the contrary, we must rather insist upon the fact that sin in general exists only in so far as there is a consciousness of it ; and this again is always conditioned by a good which must have preceded it and must have been just a result of that original perfection. The ' bad conscience ' which we may have within us is there, for one thing, only because of our seeing the possibility of what is better—a conviction which must accordingly have come to us in a different way ; and for another, because of the mere fact of our *having* a conscience, *i.e.* an inward demand for harmony with the God-consciousness. Hence if in an individual, at a time of life when the God-consciousness could have been developed, or among a people still at an early stage of development, the notion of that ' better ' has not been evolved in similar fashion, we regard their imperfection and the power of the flesh in them not as sin, but as grossness and ignorance. Sin, accordingly, manifests itself only in connexion with and by means of already existent good, and what it obstructs is future good. Similarly, if the consciousness of sin comes about through the experience that the God-consciousness operates less effectively upon a sensuous disposition than upon any other, even in that case, too, it issues from a comparison with a previously existent good. And in point of fact that is confirmed by what forms a counterpart to the foregoing, namely, that a trace of the consciousness of sin lurks even in the most exalted moments of religious experience, just because the God-consciousness does not permeate our whole being uniformly ; and this residuum is carried onwards to the time

[1] Rom. 2[15].   [2] Rom. 1[18. 25].

following, since a moment of that kind cannot leave behind it effects that will be homogeneous at every point. Thus the state of sin over its entire range actually presupposes the original perfection of man, and is indeed dependent upon it ; and, accordingly, just as the latter conception expresses the unity of our development, so sin in turn represents its intermittent and disjointed character, though without in any way abrogating the unity itself.

3. Now if, after having thus found ourselves able to interpret sin in its relation to the original perfection of man, we could likewise become perfectly certain of its inevitability, we should have no choice but to acquiesce in the latter. The most natural thing would then be to say that the consciousness which we characterize as the consciousness of sin, taken in its widest compass and even including the God-consciousness, vitiated as that may be and in its distinctive nature subverted by disruption, is nothing but that consciousness of good still lacking to us which arises within us, as a result of individual acts and inner states. But this view, in nullifying as it does not only the reality of sin but also the need of redemption, leaves so little room anywhere for the peculiar work of a Redeemer that it can scarcely be regarded as a Christian view at all. As a matter of fact, the certainty with which we are aware of the good realized within us in some exceptional moment is at the same time a conviction that we might evade every moment in which the same degree of will-power is not demonstrably present ; while again, every retrograde movement is a derangement of one originally provided for in our nature ; and thus the experience of an abatement in will-power and the consciousness that sin can be avoided, as also the conception of sin as a derangement of our nature, are so far one and the same. In order to affirm, however, that it is possible to obviate entirely the active resistance of the flesh, we require to have an assured belief in a development of power of the God-consciousness that has proceeded continuously from its earliest manifestation to a state of absolute strength, i.e. a condition of human perfection evolved without sin. This certainty is therefore at once the basis of the full consciousness of sin as a derangement of our nature, and of faith in the possibility of redemption by the communication of the spiritual power so attested. For since even our most perfect inner states still retain traces of sin (this is the testimony of the universal consciousness of mankind), then he alone to whom we do not ascribe that common consciousness of sin, and in so far only as we are justified in not so ascribing it (such justifica-

tion being asserted in the above formula itself), can exercise redeem-ing activity.[1]   It is of course true that the consciousness of sin comes from the law,[2] but as the law in the very multitude of its precepts is but an imperfect representation of the good, and even in the unity of an all-embracing maxim does not show how it can be obeyed, the knowledge of sin that arises out of it is ever in some respects incomplete and in some uncertain ; and it is only from the absolute sinlessness and the perfect spiritual power of the Redeemer that we gain the full knowledge of sin.   And our belief that sin is a derangement of human nature rests solely upon the possibility that, on the assumption of the original perfection de-scribed above, the God-consciousness could have developed pro-gressively from the first man to the purity and holiness which it manifests in the Redeemer.

§ 69. *We are conscious of sin partly as having its source in ourselves, partly as having its source outside our own being.*

1. The relation of the various dispositions and activities of sense —a relation varying in a special way with every single person—to the higher activity of the soul is based upon what we may pro-visionally call an innate difference in these dispositions, which serves in part to constitute the peculiar personality of the individual. Such differences, however, we observe being handed on within the same stock, and thus also coalescing when new families are formed from various stocks, while we find them also established among larger human masses as the distinctive characteristics of tribes and peoples.   Hence in virtue of this dependence of the specific con-stitution of the individual life upon a larger common type, as also of the later generations upon the earlier, the sin of the individual has its source in something beyond and prior to his own existence. Hence it is just the same even if such differences are held not to be innate, but to be due to education alone, since the type of education itself is determined by proclivities and experiences which precede in time the life of the learner.   On the other hand, as the swift movement of a sensuous excitation towards its object without ranging itself with the higher self-consciousness is unquestionably the act of the individual, every single sin of the individual must necessarily have its source in himself.

From the one point of view we distinguish between our good nature—for many impulses even of sense do not seek to pass

[1] Rom. 7²⁴ 8².   [2] Rom. 7⁷.

beyond what the spirit itself demands of them—and our evil nature, and we are conscious of each of these as something got and received by us conjointly with others. From the other, we recognize our evil nature as being also our own sin, since, instead of having overcome it by our action, we voluntarily perpetuate it from one moment to another.

2. The fact that one person is more disposed to reflection, his external activity being either on the whole feeble, or, if vigorous, yet crude and ignorant, and that another gives himself to external activities, and, generally speaking, thinks but little, or thinks in a dull and confused way—this, too, we place among the innate differences. True, by the social life around him the former will be drawn into the sphere of activity ; while, as regards the latter, the results of reflection that are accepted in his community will somehow be lodged also in his mind ; but the original idiosyncrasies will continue to operate ; and in the case of the former, dawning piety will combine more easily with his thought, though his modes of action will remain carnal ; while, in the case of the latter, it will be the intelligence that proves refractory ; and thus sin will take a different form in each. Now, in whatever degree such diversity is connected with the disposition natural to each, and in each prior to all action, in the same degree the sin of each, as regards its particular form, will be rooted in something beyond his own life. On the other hand, in so far as every moment (be its content an idea or an action in the narrower sense) owes its occurrence solely to voluntary action—even a moment which, though the God-consciousness has already become active, does not contain that consciousness—the sin of each, as regards its reality, uniformly has its source in himself.

3. It is true also of the development of the sensuous life, which takes place in all men before that of the spiritual, that it does not depend upon the individual alone. The coming of the Ego into this world as a result of conception and birth cannot be regarded by our immediate self-consciousness as our own act—though speculation has sometimes sought to represent this as the primary apostasy, and as due to ourselves. In truth, however, just as the coming of the Ego is, with respect to each later generation, due to the action of the one before it, so the sinful self-assertiveness of sense, proceeding as it does from its earlier development, has a more remote source than the individual's own life. But once the God-consciousness has emerged as a definite and effective agency, and

as capable of growth, then every moment in which it does not manifest itself as such, and with a certain increment of power, even if infinitesimal, in comparison with earlier moments of the same kind, is an arrest upon the higher activity—an arrest originating in the doer himself—and is a veritable sin.

Postscript.—It is this twofold relation, found universally though in varying proportion in all consciousness of sin, that forms the essential and ultimate ground of the fact that the explication of the Christian consciousness of sin in the teaching of the Church falls into the two doctrines of ' original sin '[1] and ' actual sin.'[2] And in fact the true significance of that division emerges clearly from the foregoing exposition. Thus under the one head the state of sin is considered as something received, something we bring with us, prior to any act of our own, yet something in which our own guilt is latent ; under the other, it is set forth as becoming apparent in the sinful acts which are due to the individual himself, but in which the received element brought with us is revealed. The traditional terminology, however, is in every aspect unsatisfactory. Thus, in the second expression (actual sin), the term ' sin ' is, in accordance with common usage, predicated of the real act, but the adjective suggests the misleading idea that original sin is nothing real, or at least that alongside of actual sin there is a type of sin that is merely in seeming or that lies outside the sphere of action. In the first term again, ' original ' (*Erb*) correctly expresses the connexion of the later generations with the earlier, as well as with the process by which the race is preserved ; but the word ' sin ' is misleading, being used here apparently in the same sense as in the other expression ; in which case an earlier source would be predicated only of some actual sins and not of others. Such, however, cannot be the true purport of the expression, since original sin indicates that inherent quality of the acting subject which is a part condition of all his actual sins and is anterior to all action on his part.[3] Hence we might well wish for an alteration in these inexact designations, which besides are not found in Scripture ; but such alteration will have to be introduced with great caution—a process to which the following treatment is meant to contribute ; and if we would avoid breaking the historical continuity of doctrine, and causing fresh misconstructions and misunderstandings, we shall have to carry out the change by means of gradual adjustments.

---

[1] Peccatum originis.   [2] Peccatum actuale.
[3] Peccatum enim originis non est aliquod delictum quod actu perpetratur :

FIRST DOCTRINE: ORIGINAL SIN

§ 70. *The sinfulness that is present in an individual prior to any action of his own, and has its ground outside his own being, is in every case a complete incapacity for good, which can be removed only by the influence of Redemption.*

Conf. Aug. 2 : Docent quod—omnes homines secundum naturam propagati nascuntur . . . sine metu Dei sine fiducia erga Deum et cum concupiscentiâ, quodque hic morbus seu vitium originis vere sit peccatum damnans et afferens nunc quoque aeternam mortem his qui non renascuntur per baptismum et spiritum sanctum.—*Apol. Conf.* 1 : hic locus testatur nos non solum actus sed potentiam seu dona efficiendi timorem et fiduciam erga Deum adimere propagatis secundum carnalem naturam . . . ut cum nominamus concupiscentiam non tantum actus seu fructus intelligamus sed perpetuam naturae inclinationem.—*Conf. Gall.* ix. : Affirmamus quicquid mens humana habet lucis mox fieri tenebras cum de quaerendo Deo agitur, adeo ut sua intelligentia et ratione nullo modo possit ad eum accedere. Item . . . nullam prorsus habet ad bonum appetendum libertatem, nisi quam ex gratia et Dei dono acceperit.—*Expos. Simpl.* viii. : Peccatum autem intelligimus esse nativam illam hominis corruptionem . . . qua concupiscentiis pravis immersi . . . nil boni ex nobis ipsis facere imo ne cogitare quidem possumus.— ix. : proinde nullum est ad bonum homini liberum arbitrium nondum renato.—*Conf. Angl.* x. : Ea est hominis conditio, ut sese naturalibus suis viribus ad fidem convertere et praeparare non possit. Quare absque gratia Dei quae in Christo est ad facienda quae Deo grata sunt nihil valemus.— *Repetit. Conf.* : Et haec depravatio est carere iam luce Dei seu praesentiâ Dei quae in nobis fuisset, et est aversio voluntatis nostrae a Deo . . . et hominem non esse templum Dei sed miseram massam sine Deo et sine iustitia.

1. This idea of a sinfulness present from the first in every human being is in perfect accord with what has been set forth above. For if, even in the life of the man who has been received into fellowship with the redeemed, there is in the strict and precise sense no moment in which the consciousness of sin, as something present and operative, would not form an essential part of his self-consciousness were this latter clearly and fully realized,[1] then a sinfulness which is not completely overcome even by the power of redemption must for that very reason be regarded as in itself literally infinite. And if the disposition to the God-consciousness is thereby obscured and vitiated,[2] then man, just because his God-consciousness, though the best thing in him, is thus polluted and untrustworthy, must be wholly incapable not only of developing, but even of consciously aspiring to, such inner states as would harmonize with the proper

sed intime inhaeret infixum ipsi naturae substantiae et essentiae hominis (*Epitom.*, Art. 1, p. 577, Ed. Rech.).

[1] § 62, 1 ; § 64, 1 and 2. [2] § 8, 2.

aim and object of the said disposition. Hence, as Christian piety traces everything at all connected with the God-consciousness either to sin or to grace,[1] everything in our inner states that is not sin must be attributed to our share in redemption, and this redemption must be regarded as the only thing that can remove the incapacity referred to.

2. We admit then unreservedly this incapacity for good—good being understood here solely as that which is determined by the God-consciousness—between the limiting points of willing and doing,[2] within which all self-activity proper must fall. Yet we must not magnify our congenital sinfulness to such an extent as would involve the denial of man's capacity to appropriate redemption, for that capacity is the very least that can be predicated of that disposition to the God-consciousness which is inherent in man's original perfection.[3] In the light of such a denial nothing would remain of those higher gifts which constitute the prerogative of human nature, and in which everything that distinguishes man from brute must have some share ; these gifts would in fact be so utterly extinct that we should have literally to say that man has been born without human nature—an assertion that contradicts itself as soon as it is made. Again, were we to affirm that the capacity for redemption has been lost,[4] we should come into conflict with our very belief in redemption. The capacity to appropriate the grace offered to us is the indispensable condition of all the operations of that grace, so that, without it, no improvement of man would be possible ; or else to render such improvement possible, we should have to make another assumption—namely, such a new creation of man, he remaining absolutely passive, as alone could produce the capacity in question. But in that case this creative act might equally be applied to the whole process, and man's complete sanctification effected in the same way, so that

---

[1] § 62.   [2] Phil. 2^{13}, cf. 4^{13}.

[3] Cf. *Conf. Belg.* xiv., the two statements : Adeo ut ipsi (homini) tantum exigua illorum (donorum omnium quae a Deo acceperat) vestigia remanserint : and, Nulla enim intelligentia nec voluntas conformis est divinae, nisi quam Christus in illis fuerat operatus.

[4] *Solid. declar.* ii. p. 656 : ita ut in hominis natura post lapsum ante regenerationem ne scintillula quidem spiritualium virium reliqua manserit aut restet, quibus ille ex se ad gratiam Dei praeparare se, aut oblatam gratiam apprehendere aut eius gratiae capax esse possit. This, however, as may be readily discerned, is cancelled (so far at least as it conflicts with our statement) by what follows (p. 771) : Hoc Dei verbum etiam nondum ad Deum conversus externis auribus audire aut legere potest. In eiusmodi enim externis rebus homo adhuc aliquo modo liberum arbitrium habet, ut . . . verbum Dei audire vel non audire possit.

redemption would become superfluous. For these reasons the incapacity spoken of is only to be referred to our personal activity in the narrower and proper sense, and not to our receptivity ; and if anyone chooses to speak of vital inward receiving as the beginning of co-operation, we should not admit unconditionally that original sin debars man from all initiative and co-operation in spiritual things.[1] In fact, however, the work of this vital receptivity is not really initiation ; there must be first of all a drawing-near of what is to be received, and similarly the said working is, strictly, not a co-operation at all, but a yielding of the self to the operation of grace. Our statement, moreover, has in its favour all the invitations of the Redeemer, which in reality were appeals to this receptivity ; and no less the universal practice of the heralds of God's kingdom, who invariably called upon men to receive the grace of God. In fact, even if we start from the assumption of a constantly increasing deterioration of mankind, we must nevertheless acknowledge with Augustine that some element of the original good must still survive in human nature.[2]

3. Even within the sphere of voluntary action, however, thinkers have always taken care to confine the incapacity in question to what Christian piety regards as alone good in the strictest sense. This again takes for granted that there is a distinction of praiseworthy and blameworthy which is quite independent of a man's relationship to redemption ; in fact, just as the unredeemed may have in themselves that which is commendable, so the redeemed are conscious of having acquired it without the aid of grace. Now this whole phase of life may very appropriately be described as ' civil righteousness '—the expression taken in a broad sense. For, to begin with, all that lies nearest to what is determined and effected by the God-consciousness has a communal reference, and evidence that might be brought forward against this will always be merely apparent ; while, again, the mind of the civil community cannot apply the standard of the God-consciousness to the human actions and inward states that bear upon the communal interest, but can at most demand a spirit of patriotism in its highest purity and perfection. This spirit, however, while capable of evoking the most

---

[1] *Solid. declar.*, p. 643 : Repudiantur . . . qui docent . . . hominem ex naturali nativitate adhuc aliquid boni . . . reliquum habere, capacitatem videlicet . . . in rebus spiritualibus aliquid inchoandi operandi aut cooperandi.

[2] *Enchirid.* xii. : Quamdiu itaque natura corrumpitur inest ei bonum quo privetur . . . quocirca bonum consumere corruptio non potest nisi consumendo naturam.

consummate self-renunciation in the individual, is merely the self-love of the nation or the country as a composite person, and may be conjoined with animosity and injustice of all kinds towards those who are outside the group, unless the reverse is dictated by the group's own selfish interest or love of honour—and these, again, are but self-love.   Hence the very best elements of this side of life, so far as they subsist independently of the power of the God-consciousness, can rank only as the mind, wisdom, and righteousness of the flesh.   Still, far too much is conceded, and an important aspect of Christian piety greatly obscured, when the incapacity is restricted to the so-called works of the First Table of the Decalogue on the ground that it is these alone which man cannot perform apart from redemption, and that the works of the Second Table are identical with that civil righteousness of which man is capable even without the aid of God's Spirit.   The truth is rather that the latter works, in any sense in which the Christian can regard them as fulfilling the divine law,[1] are in no sense external or carnal ; they are truly spiritual works, and are possible only in virtue of an efficacious and purified God-consciousness, so that in this respect no distinction can be drawn between duties towards God and duties towards our neighbour.[2]

§ 71. *Original sin, however, is at the same time so really the personal guilt of every individual who shares in it that it is best represented as the corporate act and the corporate guilt of the human race, and that the recognition of it as such is likewise recognition of the universal need of redemption.*

Conf. Aug. ii. : Quodque hic morbus seu vitium originis vere sit peccatum damnans et afferens nunc quoque aeternam mortem his qui non renascuntur.—*Apol. Conf.* i. : Quodsi has tantas vires habet humana natura . . . quorsum opus erit gratiâ Christi ? *Ibid.* ii. : Quia igitur . . . omnes sunt sub peccato . . . ideo data est promissio iustificationis propter Christum.—*Conf. Basil.* viii. : Atque haec lues, quam originalem vocant, genus totum sic pervasit, ut nulla ope nisi divina per Christum curari potuerit.—*Conf. Gall.* xi. : Credimus hoc vitium vere esse peccatum, quod omnes et singulos homines, ne parvulis quidem exceptis adhuc in utero matris delitescentibus, aeternae mortis reos coram Deo peragat.—*Conf. Belg.* xv. : Credimus quod peccatum originis ita foedum et execrabile est coram Deo, ut ad generis humani condemnationem

---

[1] Matt. 22[37-39], supplemented by John 13[34] and Col. 3[23].
[2] We must accordingly adhere to the quite general statement in Melanchthon, *Loc. theol.* (*De lib. arb.*) : Non potest voluntas exuere nascentem nobiscum pravitatem, nec potest legi Dei satisfacere.—(*De pecc.*) : Peccatum originis est in natis ex virili semine amissio lucis in mente et aversio voluntatis a Deo et contumacia cordis ne possint *vere* obedire legi Dei.

sufficiat.—*Art. Smalc.* : Si enim ista (*sc.* hominem posse naturalibus viribus mandata Dei servare) approbantur, Christus frustra mortuus est, cum nullum peccatum aut damnum sit in homine pro quo mori eum oportuerit.—*Conf. Bohem.* iv. : Necessum esse ut omnes norint infirmitatem suam, quodque se ipsos modo nullo servare possint, neque quicquam habere praeter Christum, cuius fiducia sese redimant ac liberent.—*Epitom. Artic.*, p. 575 : Affirmamus quod hanc naturae corruptionem ab ipsa natura nemo nisi solus Deus separare queat.—Reiicimus . . . dogma quo asseritur peccatum originale tantummodo reatum et debitum esse ex alieno delicto . . . in nos derivatum.—*Solid. Decl.*, p. 639 : Et propter hanc corruptionem . . . natura aut persona hominis lege Dei accusatur et condemnatur . . . nisi beneficio meriti Christi ab his malis liberemur.—Melanchth., *Loc.*, p. 94 : Propter quam corruptionem nati sunt rei.

1. In not a few of these symbolical passages, and in many theologians the doctrine of original sin appears to imply that the sinfulness innate in all men, just in so far as received from an external source, is yet in every case the individual's own guilt ; a guilt indeed which involves eternal punishment as its due, so that the greatest possible accumulation of actual sins could add nothing to the penal desert which attaches to everyone on account of this so-called disease. Nor can we regard it as other than natural that the doctrine in this form has been repudiated by many who, to avoid recognizing as guilt anything that lies wholly outside a man's own action, prefer to describe original sin as an evil.

The doctrine, however, is given this incredible turn and acquires its repellent and offensive tone only when, alike against the nature of things, and in opposition to a true and generally recognized principle,[1] original sin is divorced from actual sin. Yet this is not to be understood in the sense that original sin is not guilt until it breaks forth in actual sins, for the mere circumstance that there has been no opportunity for and no outward incentive to sin cannot enhance the spiritual status of man ; it is to be understood rather as implying that in the individual original sin is the sufficient ground of all actual sins, so that only something else outside of him, and not anything new within him, is needed for the generation of actual sin. Original sin is purely a thing received only in the degree in which the individual is not yet spontaneously active, and it ceases to be such in the degree in which that activity is developed. Up to that point, and in that measure, it is rightly termed *originated*,[2] as having its cause outside the individual. None the less,

---

[1] Melanchth., *Loc.*, p. 110 : Itaque semper cum malo originali simul sunt actualia peccata.
[2] Peccatum originis originatum.

as every predisposition in man attains by exercise to proficiency and thereupon grows, so, by the exercise due to the voluntary action of the individual, is there growth in congenital sinfulness. But this growing increment, similar in character to what was originally inherited, namely, a persistent inward ground of sinful actions, though on the one side a result of actual sin, is yet in this respect, as an intensified sinfulness, always anterior to the actual sins emanating from it, and is therefore original sin, though no longer merely 'originated' but individually committed; it is, in fact, like the sin of our first parents which is usually designated by the term *originating original sin*,[1] since it brings forth and increases sin in oneself and others. Since, then, this later sinfulness which has issued from the individual's own action is one and the same with that which was congenital in origin, it follows that, just as the supervening sinfulness has arisen within him from voluntary acts based upon the original sinfulness, so the latter, which in fact falls more and more into the background in comparison with the former, and which always forms his starting-point, does not continue in him, and therefore would not have arisen through him, apart from his will. We are thus justified in calling it the guilt of the individual. From this point of view it may doubtless be said that the foregoing can hold good of human beings only in so far as they themselves have acted, but not in the same sense of children or the unborn. Here certainly there is a distinction not to be overlooked. Since, however, it is an accepted fact that actual sin proceeds unfailingly from original sin, then wherever human life exists, actual sin has its root within, and the link in virtue of which original sin is guilt exists also in the immature, even though as yet it has not manifested itself in time. So that of them it may be said that they will be sinners because of what is already within them. That they are not such in the same sense and degree as those in whom actual sin has become permanent has probably never been seriously questioned, more especially as the reference here is exclusively to guilt. But this difference does not touch congenital sinfulness, and so far as the confessional passages which refer to children are chiefly bent on bringing this out, we can altogether adopt them as our own.

2. Now if the sinfulness which is prior to all action operates in every individual through the sin and sinfulness of others, and if, again, it is transmitted by the voluntary actions of every individual to others and implanted within them, it must be something

---

[1] Peccatum originis originans.

genuinely common to all. Whether, in fact, we regard it as guilt and deed or rather as a spirit and a state, it is in either case common to all ; not something that pertains severally to each individual and exists in relation to him by himself, but in each the work of all, and in all the work of each ; and only in this corporate character, indeed, can it be properly and fully understood. Hence the doctrinal statements that deal with it are not to be regarded as utterances of the individual consciousness, which fall to be treated rather under the doctrine of actual sin, but are utterances of the corporate consciousness. This solidarity means an interdependence of all places and all times in the respect we have in view. The distinctive form of original sin in the individual, as regards its quality, is only a constituent part of the form it takes in the circle to which he immediately belongs, so that, though inexplicable when taken by itself, it points to the other parts as complementary to it. And this relationship runs through all gradations of community— families, clans, tribes, peoples, and races—so that the form of sinfulness in each of these points to that present in the others as its complement ; and the aggregate power of the flesh in its conflict with the spirit (it being the source of everything in human action which is incompatible with the God-consciousness), is intelligible only by reference to the totality of those sharing a common life, and never fully in any one part ; and whatever of that power appears in the single unit, whether personal or composite, is not to be attributed to, or explained by, that unit alone. The like holds good also of time. What appears as the congenital sinfulness of one generation is conditioned by the sinfulness of the previous one, and in turn conditions that of the later ; and only in the whole series of forms thus assumed, as all connected with the progressive development of man, do we find the whole aspect of things denoted by the term, ' original sin.' Moreover, the interconnexion of places and that of times condition each other and indicate dependence on each other. And every man will readily testify that it is only in relation to the totality of things that either the idea of the sinfulness of individuals or his sense of sharing it becomes to him certain and adequate. It is precisely in virtue of this connexion, in fact, that the individual is the representative of the whole race in this regard, for the sinfulness of each points to the sinfulness of all alike in space and time, and also goes to condition that totality both around him and after him.

In this view, moreover, the various expressions used to denote original sin—all of which have a relative truth—most readily find their mutual reconciliation. Thus it can be called guilt [1] with perfect accuracy only when it is regarded simply as meaning the totality of the whole race, since it cannot in similar fashion be the guilt of the individual, so far at least as it has been engendered in him. It is called corruption of one's nature [2] as contrasted with the original perfection, inasmuch as the latter in its true development has to some extent been subverted by original sin ; original defect,[3] inasmuch as it is the source of all individual perversions of the relation between the spirit and the several functions of our sensuous life ; original disease,[4] inasmuch as on its account an element of death is lodged in every action of the spiritual life ; original evil, inasmuch as in the individual it is a persistently operative cause of impediments to life which is independent of his own action. How difficult it is to describe original sin—I will not say wholly, but even partially—as punishment [5] need hardly be emphasized, not only because punishment is always something inflicted while sin can never be inflicted, so that punishment in the person who suffers it must always be that which is not sin ; but also because in every sin for which original sin is supposed to be the penalty original sin itself is always presupposed, and thus in the last resort the punishment would precede the sin.

3. Were the phase of consciousness denoted by the concept of original sinfulness thus far developed not a corporate feeling, but one personal to the individual, it would not have necessarily bound up with it the consciousness of a universal need of redemption ; for each individual would think himself thrown primarily on his own particular group for the increase of his spiritual strength. Hence the denial of the corporate character of original sin and a lower estimate of the redemption wrought by Christ usually go hand in hand. Nor would the connexion of the two things be stronger if the original sinfulness could exist in us without our being conscious of it, since the consciousness of sin would either not emerge in us at all, or would do so only in consequence of each actual sin as it occurred, and be referred to that alone. In such case the individual would primarily be thrown upon his own resources, falling back from his

[1] Reatus.
[2] Corruptio naturae. Another interpretation of this phrase will be referred to later.
[3] Vitium originis.
[4] Morbus originis. On *morbus* and *vitium*, cf. Cicero, *Tusculanae disputationes*, iv. 13, Ern.
[5] *Apol. Conf.* i. : Defectus iustitiae originalis et concupiscentia sunt poenae.

weaker moments to his assumed stronger moments.   This, however, is possible only where the God-consciousness has not evolved at all, or where the disposition towards it has not been aroused by communication—only in a sphere, that is to say, outside Christianity and Christian teaching.   It is only when the God-consciousness has been attained that we acknowledge its pre-eminence among the elements of consciousness and strive for its supremacy ; and when this takes place, the antagonism of the flesh, as a permanent factor determinative of the actuality of individual sins, must also become a fact of consciousness.   Of this antagonism we only gain a clear understanding when we regard it as belonging to our consciousness as universalized to represent that of the human race ; hence we must either abandon all our struggle for the supremacy of the God-consciousness or else recognize our need of a succour lying outside the sphere of that universalized self-consciousness ; which means that for us there will either be a surrender to the absolute futility of any such struggle, or a presentiment of such succour.   We can now see the appropriateness of linking the first consciousness of sin, due to the accession of the God-consciousness, with the first presentiment of redemption.   And how the two have been conjoined in the Protestant Church from the outset is made clear by the passages cited. Equally clear is the connexion between the conviction that powers beyond the existing corporate human consciousness cannot be set in motion on our behalf and in our midst, and the resolve to do one's best (*with* that consciousness but *without* redemption properly so called) to overcome, even if only partially, the antagonism of the flesh.

4. This inherent connexion between the consciousness of a universal original sinfulness and the sense of our need of a redemption is broken and set awry—not without serious detriment to genuine Christian piety—when the idea that original sin ought to be punished is thrust between the two.   If punishment be taken to mean, not the intensification of sin itself—which in a teleological form of faith could be regarded only as further guilt and sin, so that here the connexion specified would not be inherent—but the evil that issues from sin or is ordained as its concomitant, then the sense of our need of redemption as mediated solely by a consciousness of penal desert will not be so pure as that described above.   This is quite clearly the case where penal desert is affirmed solely in view of the punishment itself, and where it is supposed that the fear of punishment will evoke or at least deepen the felt need of redemption

from sin ; for in that case the removal of the state of sin is desired, not with a view to freeing the God-consciousness from obstruction and widening its scope, but in order to secure particular states of the sensuous consciousness and avert their opposites.   One's motive for not willing the antagonism of the flesh, and for willing redemption, would then be merely the sensuous consequences of each, and here accordingly piety in the real sense fades out.   Again, it might be thought that the matter to be considered is not so much punishment itself as one's deserving to be punished, and that the feeling to be stimulated is not so much fear of punishment as the dread of deserving it.   But here, too, the relation to the sensuous is made the standard for the spiritual, the assumption in this case being that if a given individual is not in himself concerned to make the God-consciousness supreme, he may be induced to do so by the consideration that otherwise he will appear as one unworthy of sensuous well-being.   And this view is as great a danger to Christian piety as the other.   It is on these grounds that we have not adopted this idea here.   From the symbolical passages cited, however, we can see how essential it is for them to deduce the need of redemption from the consciousness of sinfulness, but also how easy it is for us, without breaking that connexion, to set aside the irrelevant idea of the penal desert of original sin.   The latter idea will be discussed in its proper place.

§ 72. *While the idea that we have thus developed cannot be applied in precisely the same way to the first human pair, we have no reason for explaining universal sinfulness as due to an alteration in human nature brought about in their person by the first sin.*

1. This proposition, which is merely precautionary and is not meant to settle anything regarding the way in which sin originated in the first human pair, really assumes that, agreeably to our earlier explanation,[1] we are not required to formulate any doctrine, properly so called, upon the subject.   While we can universalize our self-consciousness to represent the consciousness of the whole human race, and thus bring it into connexion with the God-consciousness, yet just because of what in our first parents was definitely and precisely related to the fact that they were not born but created, we cannot include them in that community of consciousness, their consciousness being, so far, the opposite of ours.   It is true that if

[1] Cf. § 15.

the point at issue were their sin during the further course of their life, the diversity would gradually disappear, but it is otherwise with a sinfulness which we assume to be prior to all action. Hence, since we can have no experience in common with our first parents in this regard, and have therefore no testimony of consciousness on the matter to set forth, we have likewise no relevant doctrine to formulate.[1] If, however, we had any knowledge from another source (whether speculative or more historical) as to the relation between sinfulness in them and their nature as created beings, it would of course be necessary to inquire how such knowledge was related to our doctrinal statements ; and, so far as such knowledge was not purely historical, but interwoven with our own presuppositions and theories, precautions could then be taken, as is done here, to prevent the Christian from unwittingly framing doctrines incompatible with his faith. After all, our consciousness of sin and its connexion with the longing for redemption will always remain absolutely the same whatever may have been the circumstances of the first pair, unless it be maintained that so long as the begetting and training of children was their task they had not yet sinned ; for in that case a still larger area would be excluded from the sphere of our universalized self-consciousness, since the elements of original sinfulness might then have come together only by degrees. If, however, it is assumed that they had already sinned at that stage, their earliest offspring might, like ourselves, have a sinfulness existing prior to all action of their own, and derived from a source outside their own being. And this will sufficiently serve our purpose here, even though we thereby gain no clear idea of how that sinfulness passed, and still passes, from the first pair to their posterity. And, after all, no special importance is attached to this point in our symbolical books, which, while tracing the loss of innocence in all later human beings to the rise of sin in the earliest,[2] yet in some cases do not enter upon further explanations as to the nature and mode of this influence, and in others actually renounce the problem.[3]

2. On the other hand, the question how sin originated in our first parents after their God-consciousness had developed is, though not a question arising directly out of the interests of Christian piety, nevertheless a most natural one. Obviously we cannot answer it

---

[1] Cf. § 60, 1.
[2] *Conf. Aug.* ii. ; *Apol. Conf.* i. ; *Conf. Helv.* viii. ; *Conf. Belg.* xv. ; *Art. Smalc.* i.
[3] *Conf. Gall.* x. : Nec putamus necesse esse inquirere, quinam possit hoc peccatum ab uno ad alterum propagari.

in their case with the same assurance as we answer it in our own by propositions elaborated here. To begin with, we cannot frame any clear idea of how in them the sensuous functions gained power before the spiritual ; for the first pair must from the outside have stood upon a level similar to that on which, in those who are born, the spirit already is a power. If, then, we are to regard the God-consciousness as evolving in them from within or by means of a communion with God which we cannot adequately figure to our-selves, no reason can be given why it should have developed more potently and rapidly as an inactive consciousness, but more tardily and feebly as impulse to action. And the less so because, in the case of such a development from within, we have no grounds what-ever for assuming an unequal growth of intelligence and will such as we might find where the two factors received unequal stimulus—the one by communicated ideas, the other from customs already pre-valent. Nor can we imagine any one-sided tendency—except that of sex—inherent in the first pair in this or any other respect, since otherwise the profusion of diverse characters which experience now reveals could not have developed from them as being an epitome of human nature. Since, then, in the nature of things, analogy fails us here, all turns upon the endeavour to elucidate the genesis of sin in the first pair apart from an already existent sinfulness. But whether we take the narrative of the first sin literally or ascribe to it a universal significance, the attempt seems doomed to failure. The prevalent interpretations are that man sinned through the seductions of Satan [1] and by a misuse of his own free will.[2] In the present instance these two factors cannot well be separated com-pletely, for sin is always a misuse of free will. On the other hand, the more we ascribe to the action of Satan, the more nearly the temptation approximates to magic or mere compulsion, and the human act and therefore also the sin are correspondingly less. But again, the less the temptation of Satan, the less is it possible to explain the facts apart from a sinfulness already present, since mis-use of free will by itself is no explanation, but forces us to assume something else as prompting it. Then if we fall back directly upon the suggestions of Satan, these again could not have taken effect unless there was something already present in the soul which implied a certain readiness to pass into sensuous appetite ; and any such

---

[1] *Conf. Belg.* xiv. : verbis et imposturis diaboli aurem praebens. Cf. Gerh., *Loc. Th.*, t. iv. p. 294 sq.

[2] Augustin., *Enchirid.* 30 : Homo libero arbitrio male utens et se perdidit et ipsum.

inclination toward sin must therefore have been present in the first pair before their first sin, else they would not have been liable to temptation. Nor does it avail to break up the first sin into a number of elements with a view to finding some infinitesimal part as its germ ; [1] for when what we have to deal with is a definite act, we must seek for something that will explain the act as a whole. And this we can never find as long as we assume an inner state in which there was no spontaneous activity of the flesh, and the God-consciousness alone held sway ; for in that case no sinful appetite could ever have arisen in the pair themselves, nor could Satan have made them believe that God had forbidden something out of jealousy, but their trust in God must already have been extinguished. But if such trust had died out, they must already have lost the image of God,[2] and sinfulness must already have been present, whether in the form of pride [3] or otherwise. Our last resource would then be to explain the first sin as due to such a misuse of freedom as had no ground whatever in the first man's inward being, *i.e.* to say that he chose the evil without a motive. But either this must have taken place prior to his having had any exercise in the good at all, since even the briefest exercise would have induced a facility which, in the absence of conflicting motives, would necessarily have proved operative, in which case his sin must have been his first free act—the least admissible of all positions ; or else there was an impossibility that repetition of actions should produce any facility in the first pair, and this again would imply that no confirmation in good and no increase in the power of the God-consciousness was possible for them [4]—an idea that conflicts with every view of man's original perfection.

This difficulty of representing to ourselves the emergence of the first sin without assuming a foundation for it in a prior sinfulness is immensely aggravated if we consider the circumstances in which the Mosaic narrative exhibits the first pair. For one thing, it is

[1] Luther, on Gen. 3³, finds the beginning of sin in the fact that Eve tampers with God's word, and adds to God's command the word ' perhaps ' ; as if that would have been a sin unless the emergent wanton appetite had not lain behind it. Others, like Lyra, insist rather upon the sensuous pleasure itself, and regard the act of looking at the tree as the beginning of the sin ; but here a like criticism applies.

[2] Non est anima ad imaginem Dei, in qua Deus non semper est (Ambros. *Hexaëm.* vi. 18).

[3] Augustin., *d. Gen. c. Man.* ii. 22 : Videmus his verbis per superbiam peccatum esse persuasum.

[4] Origen. in *Matth.* x. 11 : Πάλιν τε αὖ οὐκ ἄν, ἀστείας καὶ ἀμεταβλήτου φύσεως ὢν ἀπὸ τοῦ καλοῦ ἀπέστρεφεν ἄν, μετὰ τὸ χρηματίσαι δίκαιος ἐκ τῆς δικαιοσύνης αὐτοῦ, ἐπὶ τὸ ποιῆσαι ἀδικίαν.

almost impossible to conceive of temptation, or of the abuse of free will, amid such simplicity of life, and where the natural wants were so easily satisfied ; since in such a condition of things no single object could have offered an exceptionally strong allurement. And again, it is quite impossible to imagine a direct intercourse with God without an intensified love to God and an increased knowledge of Him which must have preserved our first parents from the influence of foolish illusions. This has indeed been recognized from early times.[1] And, indeed, in view of the ease with which sin might have been avoided, the more literally we accept the narrative, the greater is the propensity to sin which must be assumed as already present. Indirectly this appears to be assumed even by those who assert that God did not will to confirm man in good prior to his voluntary obedience.[2] For, as such confirmation in good must have been a special work of God, and not something effected by the exercise of powers lodged in human nature, this fact, while presupposing the above-mentioned incapacity to acquire facility through exercise, also presupposes that, without such special divine aid, the spiritual energy in man might quite as readily at any moment have proved too weak to meet a sensuous impulse.

3. With this is connected the fact that, apart from the vitiating power exercised even in our condition of innate sinfulness by actual sin in strengthening inclination by habit, nothing of a peculiar or novel nature took place in our first parents as a result of the first sin ;[3] and that what is represented in our symbolical books as such a result must be assumed to have preceded the sin. The understanding must have been involved in an utterly heathen darkness before it could have credited a falsehood to the effect that God grudged man the knowledge of good, and the will must have lacked the energy to resist even the weakest enticement if the mere sight of the forbidden fruit could exert such power over it. In fact, Adam must have been sundered from God before his first sin ; for, when Eve handed him the fruit he ate it without even recalling the divine interdict ; and this presupposes a like corruption of his nature ; for surely incorrupt nature could not have indulged appetite in express

---

[1] Augustin., *de corr. et grat.* xii. : Adam et terrente nullo et insuper contra Dei terrentis imperium libero usus arbitrio non stetit in tanta non peccandi facilitate.

[2] See Gerhard, *Loc. Th.*, t. iv. p. 302.

[3] *Conf. Helv.* ix. : Post lapsum intellectus obscuratus est, voluntas vero ex libera facta est serva.—*Conf. Belg.* xiv. : Homo se ipsum verbis diaboli aurem praebens . . . a Deo, qui vera ipsius erat vita, penitus avulsit totamque naturam suam corrupit.

disobedience to the divine command.   Nor can it fairly be maintained that this reasoning hangs entirely on a literal interpretation of the Mosaic narrative, for, whatever idea we may have of the first sin, we must always assume the priority of some sinful element ; and if we seek to understand that sin genetically, we must follow a method akin to that adopted here.   If, however, human nature in the first pair was the same before the first sin as it appears subsequently alike in them and in their posterity, we cannot say that human nature was changed as a result of the first sin, and the statement of our symbolical books to that effect is one we must depart from.   No one can be asked to believe that in a single individual the nature of the species could be changed and yet that individual remain the same ; for the terms ' individual ' and ' species ' lose their meaning unless everything met with in the individual, whether successively or simultaneously, can be understood from and explained by the nature of the species.   If an individual belonging to a certain species manifests some attribute incompatible with the definition of the species, then either the definition of the species has been wrong from the start and needs to be corrected, or we were misled as to the identity of the individual.   Still less is it possible to suppose that such an alteration of nature should have resulted from an act of the alleged individual as such, since the individual can act only *in accordance with* the nature of his species, but never can act *upon* that nature.   Hence we cannot well hold to the idea under discussion without conceding a share in the matter to the devil ; and if we do this, we find an equal difficulty in avoiding the Manichæan heresy.[1]   For if it is quite certain that an alteration in a determinate nature cannot be effected by that nature itself, the actual alteration can be apportioned between the man and the devil only in this way, that the element of action is ascribed to the latter, and mere passivity, or receptivity, to the former.   But in that case, it must be further admitted that, if the individuals are to remain the same, it is a mere confusion of speech to describe the outcome as merely an alteration of their nature, and that it is more correct to say that the human nature which God originally created was destroyed by the devil through the first sin, when the nature acquired is the work of the devil in the same degree as was the first sin, because the nature created by God so remained purely passive as to allow itself to be completely permeated by the alteration wrought by the devil.   To the view that of course in that case the counter-change to be wrought

[1] Cf. § 22.

by redemption is once more a subversion of preceding nature, little objection can be taken by those who maintain that the present nature of man is incapable even of appropriating redemption.[1] These things, however—alike the passivity of man in the event by which his nature was subverted, and the power ascribed to Satan of subverting the work of God and putting his own work in its place, so as to bring an entire world of human beings under its partial control—are quite unmistakable approaches to Manichæism. And what is said on the other side in order to nullify this adjunct of the Flacian teaching [2] seems to have very little foundation indeed. For, on the one hand, bare possibility is nothing except as there is a transition to actuality, and if man now cannot act otherwise than sinfully and perversely, and such self-determination to evil is the work of Satan, the still remaining work of God, so far as it is actuated by the work of Satan, now subsists only as an instrument of Satan, and is therefore only seemingly the same as it was. On the other hand, if the original work of God consisted not merely in man's ability to think, speak, and act, but also in the free will that sets these capacities in operation, then if free will is lost, the work of God no longer has any existence. To this difficulty of avoiding on the ordinary line of thought everything of a Manichæan character is probably due the hypothesis which, while admitting a change in human nature in consequence of the first sin, still regards it as operating rather in a bodily way.[3] In order to keep clear of the idea that the change, namely, the loss of the power of the God-consciousness, was not prior to the sin, it is not said to have been preceded by any express interdict of God ; but in that case it is not blameworthy in the first pair to have been unwilling to acknowledge the authority of obscure sentiments : and the resolve to suppress these, whatever the occasion of it, could not be reckoned sinful. And thus the spiritual vitiation of man following upon the eating of the forbidden fruit, and brought about by the effect thereof upon the body, would have taken place without sin at all, and universal sinfulness would be attributable to evil—a conclusion which, conflicting as it does with the essence of a teleological type of faith, cannot be regarded as Christian, especially as the administration of

[1] *Solid. Decl.* ii., p. 656.
[2] *Solid. Decl.*, p. 648 : Asserimus id ipsum esse Dei opus, quod homo aliquid cogitare loqui agere operari potest . . . quod vero cogitationes verba facta eius prava sunt . . . hoc originaliter et principaliter est opus Satanae.
[3] Reinhard, *Dogm.*, §§ 75–80.

a material antidote at the right time would have rendered redemption superfluous.

We must accordingly adhere to the position that the idea of a change in human nature entailed by the first sin of the first pair has no place among the propositions which rank as utterances of our Christian consciousness. The less we found cause at a previous stage [1] to ascribe a high degree of religious morality and religious enlightenment to the first pair before their first sin, and the less we are able to explain the first sin as proceeding from a perfectly sinless condition, the more decisively does every reason disappear for admitting that a change in human nature was then produced. The grounds of our renouncing that idea will be all the stronger because it cannot be clearly presented to the mind, and on the one hand merely begets the Manichæan heresy, while on the other it drives many Christians, from mere dread thereof, into the Pelagian heresy, in that they will rather deny the universal incapacity of all men apart from redemption for good than derive that incapacity from such a change. The untenable character of the theory of a change, moreover, becomes specially evident when we go back to the rigid formulæ in which the older dogmaticians gave unqualified expression to the confessional view.[2] Thus the very first statement, namely, ' the person corrupts the nature,' brings out clearly the fact that, in the act in question, if the nature corrupted in consequence of it was good, the person cannot have been good, for good cannot corrupt good ; but if the nature was already bad, its corruption had not been brought about by the action of the person. Similarly on the other alternative : if the person no longer was good (since in corrupting the nature it acted wrongly), while the nature was good still, since it required to be corrupted, then all wrong action on the part of all later individuals must be explicable apart from the hypothesis that their nature had to be corrupted beforehand. In that case all corruption would fall under the third formula, namely, that persons corrupt themselves and one another ; which manifestly is an adequate description of all the sin that ever appears amongst men. Here, however, the nature is kept out of the matter altogether ; whereas, if it is assumed that the nature had already been corrupted, there can be no talk of its corrupting the

---

[1] Cf. § 61.

[2] Quenstedt, *Syst. Theol.*, p. 913 : Tribus autem modis fit peccatum quando persona corrumpit naturam, ut factum ab Adamo et Eva, quando natura corrumpit personam, ut fit in propagatione peccati originis, quando persona corrumpit personam, ut fit in peccatis actualibus.

person, since the person must necessarily have within itself the corruption of the nature. Finally, if the second formula, namely, ' the nature corrupts the person,' is meant to refer to the propagation of original sinfulness, then, while it is true that individuals can only be as their nature is, they are nevertheless such from the first ; and the form of expression is faulty, since they must have been uncorrupt before they could be corrupted. This, in turn, gives rise to fresh doubts about the first formula, for it is inconceivable that the individual person should do more to the nature than the nature to it. Were we to admit, however, and to admit as universally true that the nature corrupts the individual, then since the nature has no existence save in the totality of individuals, a fourth formula would emerge, namely, that the nature corrupts itself ; a statement by the use of which hardly anyone could indicate the thoughts he really had in his mind.

4. If, accordingly, no change in human nature took place in the person of the first pair as a result of their first sin, and what is alleged to have developed from that sin must be assumed to have been in existence before it ; and if this does not apply merely to the case of some particular first sin, but a like situation emerges (whatever the nature of that sin may have been) in the case of every individual ; then the universal sinfulness that precedes every actual sin in the offspring is to be regarded not so much as derived from the first sin of our first parents, but rather as identical with what in them likewise preceded the first sin, so that in committing their first sin they were simply the first-born of sinfulness. It is true that our confessional books adopt the derivation in question,[1] but in such matters we are the less obliged to follow them because our consciousness of universal sinfulness, as set forth above,[2] is something inward and immediate, while that derivation of it gives a purely external account on which the inward in no way depends, and by which it cannot in any way be reinforced. But it is solely on that inward experience that our consciousness of the need of redemption depends ; hence the derivation referred to is in no sense an element of our faith. And as even the confessional books for the most part do not engage in any detailed discussion as to the nature and manner of that derivation,[3] we could not but feel

---

[1] *Conf. Aug.* ii. ; *Apol. Conf.* i. ; *Conf. Helv.* viii. ; *Conf. Belg.* xv. ; *Art. Smalc.* i., etc.
[2] § 70.
[3] The *Conf. Gall.* x. says explicitly : Nec putamus necesse esse inquirere quinam possit hoc peccatum ab uno ad alterum propagari. Similarly Calvin,

a difficulty if the derivation occurred in Scripture in conjunction
with statements of faith properly so called. But the classical
passage usually cited in its support [1] shows nothing of the kind.
The apostle refers to the origin of sin only with a view to
elucidating the doctrine of the restoration of life through Christ,
and the point of comparison is simply that each originates in
and emanates from one. It is true that the apostle sets forth
sin as dependent upon its first occurrence, and thus as something
continuous, so that the whole continuous process of sin was
introduced along with Adam's sin, and if Adam had been able
to refrain from sin, we too could have refrained. Then if we
take also the previous statement, namely, that death passed upon
all men for that all sinned themselves, and observe how Paul, while
he certainly distinguishes between the sin of Adam and that of
those who had not sinned after the likeness of Adam's transgression,
yet, though including all in one condemnation, describes Adam's
contribution thereto as a small thing in comparison with what
Christ had done for the removal of sin ; we see that all this signally
agrees with the idea that corporate sin is the corporate act of the
human race, originating in the first human beings, and can be taken
away only by the activity of Christ, which likewise extends to all
mankind. In similar fashion Paul contrasts Adam and Christ in
another reference ; [2] just as again he testifies that sin arises in us,
and that our mind can be defiled, in the same way as in the case of
Eve ; [3] whence it follows that in going back to the first man for an
explanation of sinfulness, we gain nothing of special importance, and
that in the passages cited the sole concern was to give due weight
to the relation between the earlier and the later dispensation.

We can thus readily dispense with all those artificial theories
which for the most part tend only to lay stress upon the divine
justice in imputing Adam's sin to, and exacting its penalty from, his
posterity. To have done with them is all the more satisfactory
because they (e.g. those which assert that all mankind, as embraced
in Adam's being,[4] participated in his sin) rest upon a particular

---

Instit. ii. 1, 7 : Neque in substantia carnis aut animae causam habet con-
tagio : sed quia a Deo ita fuit ordinatum, ut quae primo homini dona con-
tulerat, ille tam sibi quam suis haberet simul et perderet. From which we
see clearly that Calvin's main concern is to repudiate explanations which
might have links of connexion with non-Christian views.

[1] Rom. 5[12-21].   [2] I Cor. 15[21-22].   [3] 2 Cor. 11[3].

[4] Ambros., in Rom. v. : Manifestum in Adam omnes peccasse quasi in
massa.—Ex eo igitur cuncti peccatores quia ex ipso omnes sumus.—Hieron.,
in Hosea vi. 7 : Et ibi in paradiso omnes praevaricati sunt in me in similitudinem praevaricationis Adam.

theory of the origin of individual souls, while, within our limits, we have neither grounds nor materials for propounding any such theory. Or else (e.g. those which most arbitrarily interpret God's command as a covenant made in the person of Adam with the entire human race, the legal consequences of violating which fall also on his posterity) they bring man's relation to God and God's imputation of sin under the category of a merely external legal relationship, a view which has had a most detrimental effect upon interpretation of the work of redemption. This view is carried to its extremest point when people assume what has often been asserted and is widely current, though quite arbitrary and wholly groundless, that, had our first parents only withstood their first temptation successfully, no second would have been imposed upon them, and they, and we as well, would have remained for ever exempt from all temptation. The truth is rather that the temptation given in the Mosaic narrative is a most trifling one, representing the simplest and most primitive conditions ; and it is in the nature of things that the more variously the powers of man came to be drawn upon, and the more complicated his circumstances became, the more dangerous must his temptations have been ; while again, it seems the very acme of inconsistency to say that the Redeemer could be tempted in His earthly life, but that, if Adam and Eve had been victors in their first conflict, they would have become proof against all temptation. And indeed it is glaringly and intrinsically incompatible with all that we can learn of the divine ways, to suppose that to such an extent God should have made the destiny of the whole human race contingent upon a single moment, the fortunes of which rested with two inexperienced individuals, who, moreover, never dreamt of its having any such importance.

5. If then, on the one hand, we discard the view that a change took place in human nature itself, but, on the other, still maintain that an incapacity for good is the universal state of men, it follows that this incapacity was present in human nature before the first sin, and that accordingly what is now innate sinfulness was something native also to the first pair. This we admit ; yet it must be so construed as to be compatible with the equally inherent original perfection of man, and in such a way that the state of the first human pair is understood to have been throughout analogous to our own, as described above.[1] In no sense, therefore, are we substituting for the idea of a longer or shorter state of perfectly active piety, the idea

[1] Cf. §§ 60, 61, 68.

that the first free act after the awakening of the God-consciousness was sin—a conception already negatived by what has been said above.[1]   The truth is rather that the awakening of the God-consciousness implies also the initiation of the good, which in turn could not remain without consequences [2] that proved operative even after the first sin.   In that case, however, there must have come for our first parents a time when their sensuous nature on one side or another would gain such strength that it could win the mastery as easily as lose it.   For, while we cannot be expected to form a vivid idea of the first man in his necessary diversity from us, yet there are two points in which he resembles us, and to which in him, too, we can fasten the rise of sin.   Thus there was in the first pair, if not the idiosyncrasies of personal constitution, yet the idiosyncrasies of sex ; and, again, while we cannot conceive of the will lagging behind the intelligence precisely as it does in ourselves, yet they were subject (in their simple life possibly in a less degree) to changes of mood amid which such shortcoming of will-power showed itself intermittently on various sides.   In the light of all this, the origin of sin and the consciousness of it become quite intelligible.

Now, while the first appearance of sin in the first pair, due to that original sinfulness, not only was in itself a single and trivial event, but in particular was without any transforming influence upon human nature, yet the growth of sin in consequence of the increase of the human race by ordinary generation had its origin in the first emergence of sin, and therefore in the original sinfulness itself.   And in its relation to redemption this is to be understood in the sense that without the entrance into all mankind of an element free from that sinfulness, nothing could be expected but that the disposition to the God-consciousness inherent in human nature should be constantly vitiated in its action, and everything that was developing spiritually in man ever dragged downwards under the dominion of the flesh.   Finally, as regards the Mosaic narrative : in accordance with the limits which we have assigned to Dogmatics, that science cannot be expected to determine how the said record is to be interpreted, and whether it purports to be history or allegory.   Without encroaching upon the work of exegesis or criticism, however, we can

---

[1] Cf. § 67, 2.

[2] Hugo of St. Victor, *Opp.* iii. 181 : Paradisus est locus inchoantium et in melius proficientium, et ideo ibi solum bonum esse debuit, quia creatura a malo initianda non fuit, non tamen summum.   This implies, of course, that as soon as sin appeared, the state of Paradise must have come to an end altogether.

use the story, as the early theologians did,[1] in illustration of the universal process of the rise of sin as something always and everywhere the same, and it is in this illustrative quality that, for us, the universal significance of the narrative resides.   There we find in Eve, on the one hand, a clear representation of the independent activity and revolt of the sensuous element that develops so readily upon any external incentive by way of opposition to a divine command, and likewise a clear view of how there comes to be conjoined therewith an all too easily effected vitiation of the already developed God-consciousness.   On the other hand, in Adam we see how easily sin is assimilated by imitation even without any overpowering activity of sense, and how this presupposes some degree of forgetfulness of God, traceable possibly to mere lack of thought.   If, moreover, we bring the story into connexion with the ideas of original perfection and original sinfulness as formulated here, by connecting the earlier state with the later, it sets before us in general how outside the sphere of redemption the good develops only alongside what is bad, and how this good includes that knowledge of the distinction between good and evil which is essential to the development of man.   It is plainly indicated in the story that that knowledge was not bestowed prior to the sin, and this can easily be extended into the view that man could only have remained without sin as long as he remained without that knowledge.

6. If, accordingly, for the contrast between an original nature and a changed nature we substitute the idea of a human nature universally and without exception —apart from redemption—the same ; and if, for the contrast between an original righteousness that filled up a period of the first human lives and a sinfulness that emerged in time (an event along with which and in consequence of which that righteousness disappeared), we substitute a timeless original sinfulness always and everywhere inhering in human nature and co-existing with the original perfection given along with it—though in such a way that from the concomitance and development of the two there could issue no active righteousness properly so called, but at best a vacillation between vitiated spiritual efforts and increasing and fully matured sin ; if, finally, for the antithesis between an original guilt and a transmitted guilt we substitute the simple idea of an absolutely common guilt identical for all ; then the confessional formulæ in which this doctrine in its relation to the succeeding one is most

---

[1] Augustin., *de Gen. c. Man.* ii. 21 : Etiam nunc in unoquoque nostrum nil aliud agitur, cum ad peccatum delabitur, quam tunc actum est in illis tribus, serpente, muliere, et viro.

succinctly expressed may be qualified and supplemented as follows. In the first place, we certainly admit a universal imputation of the first sin, an imputation resting upon the belief that to whatever human individual had fallen the lot of being the first, he, too, would have committed the sin. So, too, had the actually first man been one of those born later, he would have added his quota to the deterioration above described, and therefore bears the guilt thereof as does any other. Further, in the doctrine of the Church the first sin of the first man, and that only, is called ' originating original sin,' and the sinful constitution of all other men ' originated original sin '—the bent and inward disposition thus bearing the name of ' sin ' equally with the act itself; but we transfer this to the relation between each earlier generation and the one immediately succeeding it, and maintain that the actual sin of the earlier is always the originating original sin for the later, while the sinfulness of the later generation since it produces the actual sins thereof, is also original sin, while yet as dependent upon the sin of the earlier it is originated, and thus is originated original sin as well. Finally, we make good another defect by applying the distinction of ' originating ' and ' originated ' also to actual sin in its relation to original sin. On the one hand, we use this distinction to set forth the interrelationship of all who are living at one time, the actual sin of those who play a more vigorous and stimulating rôle being the originating, that of the more passive the originated; on the other hand, the collective sin of each generation is in turn originating with respect to the sinfulness of the succeeding one, just as that collective sin itself is rooted in the original sin originated by the earlier. In this compact group of ideas sin in general, and original sin in particular, are seen to be the corporate action and the corporate guilt of the whole human race.

Second Doctrine : Actual Sin

§ 73. *In all men, original sin is always issuing in actual sin.*

Melanchthon, *Loc. Th.*, p. 123 : Semper cum peccato originali sunt peccata actualia. Augustine *c. Julian.*: Lex ista quae est in membris . . . manet in carne mortali . . . quia operatur desideria contra quae dimicant fideles.—*Conf. Gall.* xi. : Dicimus praeterea hanc perversitatem semper edere fructus aliquos malitiae et rebellionis, adeo ut etiam qui sanctitate excellunt quamvis ei resistant, multis tamen infirmitatibus et delictis sint contaminati quamdiu in hoc mundo versantur.

1. This proposition is to be taken in its most universal sense ; it is only as we exclude Him from the context of universal sinfulness

that we acquit even Christ of actual sin. Taken thus universally, however, it is an expression of our Christian consciousness. The more definitely and vividly anyone sets the Redeemer before him, the more he realizes that he is at no moment free from sin. He knows this, however, not simply from his own personal idiosyncrasy, but in a universal way, e.g., inasmuch as he is a constituent portion of humanity as a whole ; i.e. he knows it through his consciousness as enlarged to a racial consciousness, and thus knows it true of others as well as of himself. And this consciousness goes back to that of universal sinfulness ; it is, in fact, simply the latter from another point of view. For the disposition to sin, of which our apprehension is at once inward and timeless, would not be a reality at all unless it were constantly manifesting itself ; and conversely, that which does manifest itself would merely be something adhering to us from without and therefore no sin, unless it formed part of the manifestation and temporal process of original sin. And just as all that is involved in original sin must manifest itself somewhere in the measure in which it is variously distributed among men, so it necessarily has a part in every act (*Bewegung*) of every man in whom it is present and makes some element thereof to be sin in manifestation. Thus throughout the entire range of sinful humanity there is not a single perfectly good action, *i.e.* one that purely expresses the power of the God-consciousness ; nor is there one perfectly pure moment, *i.e.* one in which something does not exist in secret antagonism to the God-consciousness.

2. It would not at all harmonize with this universal consciousness, however, were we to restrict actual sin to those cases in which our sinfulness breaks forth externally in actions perceptible by others as well as by ourselves. Such outbreakings of sin always depend upon external conditions—conditions quite different from those that have brought about this or that definite sinful state. Just as those last, the external solicitations, can evoke only such inner movements as are already prepared for in the personality of the individual, so the sinfulness of one's condition cannot depend upon the occurrence of circumstances favourable or unfavourable to its outward manifestation. In point of fact, the sinfulness of a man's condition is not in itself really aggravated by its finding external expression, for actual sin in the precise sense is present even where the sinful element shows itself only internally, and enters into a moment of consciousness merely as a thought or a

desire.[1] Just as love, as an inward affection, is the fulfilling of the law, since it infallibly manifests itself in outward act on every given opportunity, so, for the same reason, evil desire, though working only within, is already actual sin. And this is a principle which, if we take the term ' desire ' in its widest sense, applies to all actual sin, with the exception perhaps of those cases in which the activity of the God-consciousness seems to be obstructed only by slothfulness ; although these cases, too, may well be traced to a desire that only awaits its opportunity. Any explanation of actual sin, whether more or less general, will be valid only in so far as it teaches that actual sin springs from an underlying sinfulness, and as it can easily be united with the consciousness of the need of redemption.[2]

While we regard the original sinfulness from which all actual sin proceeds as the corporate act and the corporate guilt of the human race—distributed among individuals in respect of place and time not equally and uniformly, but unequally— yet this means no more than that in one individual one type of sin is specially predominant and another less so, while in another individual the case is reversed, according as in each case, conformably with his personal temperament, a weaker enticement only is needed for one kind of sin than for another. It must certainly not be taken to mean that, apart from redemption, any given individual is so well secured by his person- ality against any of the various forms of sin that he could not possibly fall into it. On the contrary, our consciousness testifies in each of us that neither he nor any other, if thrown upon his own resources, has within him a perfect security against any form of evil ; for every observant person discovers in himself so many anticipations and, so to say, germs of all evil that, if only the incentive that must always be added to the original sinfulness in order to produce actual sin could become strong enough, any kind of evil, if not habitually yet in particular cases, might emerge as actual sin.[3]

[1] Actio pugnans cum lege Dei (Melanchthon, *l.c.*) might also denote such a movement, as yet entirely inward.

[2] Hence, the Christian consciousness can least of all be satisfied with theories like that of Reinhard (*Dogmatik*, § 75) : Peccatum est quaevis aber- ratio a modo tenendae verae felicitatis.

[3] Calvin, *Inst.* ii. 3.3 : Omnibus ejusmodi portentis obnoxia est unaquaeque anima.

§ 74. *There is no difference of worth between men in regard to sin,*
apart from the fact that it does not in all stand in the same
relationship to redemption.

1. In harmony with what has been said above, all actual sins
must rank as equal not only in respect of their nature and character,
but also of their origin ; for every such sin is a manifestation of
the universal sinfulness, and represents a victory, though but
momentary or partial, of flesh over spirit.   The determining power
of the God-consciousness, which in sin is obstructed, may of course
be greater or less.   Now if it is greater, then on the one hand the
spiritual life in which it is found as such must be stronger, and in
such a life, by reason of that strength, sin is increasingly in process
of disappearing, and is therefore less.   On the other hand, however,
we may affirm that if the spiritual strength is greater, the resistance
of the flesh that overcomes it must be stronger, and therefore the
sin greater.   Since, therefore, from different points of view we get
opposite results as to the one and the same case of sin, we must
either regard all sins as equal, because from opposite points of view
each is at once greater and less ; or we must first combine the two
points of view, whereupon we find that the determination of the
sinful quality of single moments becomes feasible only by reference
to the condition of the acting subject as a whole, *i.e.* his state as
one in which sinfulness is on the increase or on the wane—which,
within the sphere of the Christian consciousness, means by reference
to the individual's state of grace, precisely as our proposition
affirms.   Apart from this, however, and each moment being taken
by itself, it remains true that what gives a moment the character of
sin is the self-centred activity of the flesh, whereas the content of the
sin does not enable us to differentiate ; for all activities of the flesh
are good when subservient to the spirit, and all are evil when
severed from it.   The same result follows when we note that the
amount of sin is greater, the slighter the outward solicitations
which need to be overcome.   For these, too, are not the same for
everyone ; to a more experienced subject a particular solicitation
may be insignificant which to others is strong and urgent.   Doubtless, therefore, there are greater and lesser sins, though for us they
are so only with respect to the efficacy of redemption ; and, accordingly, Church teaching has rightly excluded from this sphere the
doctrine of the equality of all sins.[1]   Taken by itself, however, the

---

[1] *Conf. et Expos. simpl.* viii. : Fatemur etiam peccata non esse aequalia,
licet ex eodem corruptionis et incredulitatis fonte exoriantur.   Melanchth.,

doctrine might possibly be defended. Hence most of the ordinary classifications of sin, disregarding as they do the relationship to redemption, assert a distinction among sins as concerns their form and appearance, but do not assert a difference in their proper quality as sins.

2. Surveying the diversities of actual sin with a view to arranging them in distinct groups, we encounter at the outset the two principal forms which are associated with the two main elements of original sinfulness ; [1] thus actual sin may be either more *an expression of appetite* or more a positive obscuration, i.e. *a vitiation, of the God-consciousness*. We cannot wholly separate the two, for the one ever evokes the other ; thus when in any social group, some definite form of appetite breaks out predominantly, it is presently followed by a transformation of the God-consciousness as a means of cloaking the discordance. So Paul [2] explains how each of the two aggravates the other ; and if we imagine the two at their climax—the superstitious frenzy that heaps up all the products of idolatrous error, and the passionate frenzy of unbridled lust—and if each of them inevitably seems equally deserving of condemnation, it is clear that they must have been equal in their original action and reaction upon each other.

As regards the division into outward and inward sins, what was said above [3] with a view to setting aside this distinction might be open at most to the following objection. The external accomplishment of an act of sin occupies a divisible portion of time, and for the most part can be resolved into a succession of moments. Now just as it is obvious that, if a reaction of the God-consciousness takes place during that time, a different quality emerges, so the sinful quality of an action—other things being equal—is the more aggravated the longer the interval in which no such reaction supervenes. What follows from this, however, is simply that there are some sinful acts that point to a greater power of sin than others ; but in no sense does it follow that anyone is incapable of committing acts of the same sinful quality, though not of the same kind as these. On the other hand, it remains true that in every individual there are inward stirrings, sinful or akin to sin, which never take shape as outward sins because at bottom and even inwardly they are the workings of others' thoughts and excitations rather than his own,

---

Loc. Th. p. 126 : Ac stoicae illae disputationes execrandae sunt, quas servant aliqui disputantes omnia peccata aequalia esse.

[1] *Apol. Conf.* i. (from Hugo of St. Victor) : Originale peccatum est ignorantia in mente et concupiscentia in carne.

[2] Rom. I[21-26].   [3] In section 2 of the foregoing paragraph.

and thus belong to the communal life rather than to the individual himself.   But there will be no one whose life exhibits these only, and when we discount them the distinction between outward and inward sins is seen to be fortuitous rather than essential.

Again, when a distinction is drawn between intentional and un-intentional sins, it is customary to regard the former as in general the greater.   But this is wrong.   Unintentional sins, so far as they are really actions and not mere consequences,[1] are sins either of ignorance or of impetuosity.   But if the ignorance is due to a defective estimate of the ethical significance of our actions generally, or the impetuosity due to a passionate tendency of one kind or another ; and if, on the other hand, a transient incapacity during an instant peculiarly unfavourable to one's resisting a sensuous impulse can be thought of as a completely isolated moment having no subse-quent results ; then intentional sins of the latter type will be lesser than unintentional sins of the former type.   If, accordingly, some-times the one class may be greater, and sometimes the other, the two, considered in themselves, are equal.

The most important division of sins in the present reference is unquestionably that of mortal and venial sins ; yet as these terms do not themselves involve a rigorous antithesis, it is difficult to say what the distinction really means.   Some thinkers ascribe to them the very sense which is indicated in our proposition as constituting the only tenable distinction ;[2] in which case we should have to dis-cuss only how far the idea of punishment must have a place in the definition or not.   Certainly, such interpretations make it quite clear that otherwise the distinction rests solely on the relationship of the acting subject to redemption.   But this agreement seems once more to vanish when it is likewise asserted that even those who have been brought within the scope of redemption can commit mortal sins, but that the redemptive link is thereby severed [3]—

---

[1] In the latter case they would not be sins at all, and in view of this some qualification must be applied to the principle found in Melanchth., *Loc. Th.*, p. 117: Nihil est peccatum nisi sit voluntarium.   Haec sententia de civilibus delictis tradita est . . . sed non transferendum est hoc dictum ad doctrinam Evangelii de peccato.

[2] Melanchth., *op. cit.*, p. 332 : Haec mala in renatis sunt . . . sed quia persona accepta est . . . fiunt huic personae haec mala venialia peccata ; and p. 123 : actualia peccata quae in non renatis omnia sunt mortalia.   The most definite statement of this view is found in Baumgarten, *Theol. Str.* ii. 484 : Since, however, we do not admit this, namely, that *mortalia* and *venialia* are to be distinguished by a *discrimen objectivum*, but rather take the relation-ship of the person concerned to the reconciliation brought by Christ as the ground of distinction, etc.

[3] Melanchth., *op. cit.*, p. 124 : Necesse est autem discernere peccata quae

a view the possibility of accepting which cannot be discussed here.

As, however, the possibility of restoring the redemptive tie must not be excluded, we are brought back, on the one hand, to the older definition, according to which only those non-venial sins are absolutely mortal in the interval between which and death no restoration of the redemptive link takes place ; [1] while, on the other, we must now make a distinction amongst venial sins themselves, since even mortal sins under certain conditions become venial ; and thus the intrinsic distinction is lost. If to this we add the fact that the sin against the Holy Spirit is thought by many to be a sin which renders impossible any restoration of the link with redemption, then, instead of a simple antithesis we get the following gradation. Sins in themselves venial are those of the forgiven which can hardly be avoided in the present life,[2] and always carry their remission with them ; [3] moreover, all the sins of the unforgiven become venial should the unforgiven be converted, as also all intentional sins of the redeemed, should they return to grace. Mortal sins again, strictly so called,[4] are those of the two last-named groups should the connexion with redemption not be respectively effected or restored ; while the only absolutely mortal sin—assuming that the exegesis is correct—is that against the Holy Spirit. Obviously, however, the difference between sins in themselves venial (requiring as they do repentance and prayer for pardon) and the mortal sins of the forgiven (which become venial if by repentance the forgiven again attain to the temporarily lost state of grace), is the less pronounced the shorter the interval between the lapse and the recovery. Indeed, in the light of the qualification ' against conscience,' this difference might be traced back to that between intentional and unintentional sins. Since, however, even in the state of grace the power of the will always lags behind the intelligence even though the knowledge of the sinfulness of one's ordinary states becomes deeper,

in renatis in hac vita manent ab illis peccatis, propter quae amittuntur gratia et fides.

[1] Augustine, *de Corr. et Grat.* 35 : Ego autem id esse dico peccatum ad mortem, fidem quae per dilectionem operatur deserere usque ad mortem.

[2] Augustine, *de Spir. et Litt.* 48 : non impediunt a vita aeterna iustum quaedum peccata venialia, sine quibus haec vita non ducitur.

[3] Baumgarten, *loc. cit.* : For, although we say that they are called *venialia* because they always carry remission with them . . .

[4] Melanchthon, *loc. cit.* : Est igitur actuale mortale in labente post reconciliationem actio interior vel exterior pugnans cum lege Dei facta contra conscientiam. p. 276 : nec potest stare cum malo proposito contra conscientiam fides.

it follows that intentional sins will occur which, being as they are associated with progress, cannot bring about a complete lapse from grace. Ignoring this aspect of progress, some rashly contend that the regenerate can no longer sin knowingly—'knowing' implying at all events the lowest degree of 'intentional'; whereas all we are entitled to say (on the analogy of what was said regarding the relationship of the individual man to his nature) is that he cannot by a single act (an act, moreover, not exempt from the influence of divine grace) wholly dispossess himself of this state of grace. In the last resort, accordingly, there is no essential distinction except that which is based upon the relations of the acting subject to redemption. As regards the sin against the Holy Spirit, that no doubt would form a species by itself; but as long as the interpretation of the passages upon which the conception rests [1] is in dispute, Dogmatics must leave the ascertainment of the facts to the exegetes—just as it must leave to the pastoral office the handling of the case where a man believes himself guilty of the sin, and cannot presume to decide either what the sin is or in whom it is found. In general, however, it must repudiate the suggestion that there may be a sin which, though repented of in view of redemption, yet cannot be forgiven, as setting a limit to the universality of redemption.

3. A like result follows from a closer study of those gradations of human states relatively to sin which, taken directly from passages of Scripture, or indirectly from popular exposition, have passed into Dogmatics. Thus the state of *freedom*,[2] in contrast to that of *bondage*, is taken to be that in which (conceived in its ideal form) only sin in itself venial is to be found, this being due to a link with redemption so stable and vital that unintentional sins in such a life always are less grave than any intentional sin. The very term 'bondage,' however, as applied to the state in which sin is predominant implies that the man, by reason of his inward recognition of the God-consciousness, is not fulfilling the demands of the flesh with entire acquiescence. But if we reflect that freedom, as a consequence of the link with redemption, can grow only out of a state of bondage, we can see how freedom, in its gradual development through exercise, will still continue to exhibit traces of bondage. From the state of bondage, again, it is customary to distinguish as still worse the states of self-assurance, hypocrisy, and hardening. But if there should supervene a state worse than bondage, the inward recognition just referred to must needs have been utterly

---

[1] Matt. 12^31, Luke 12^10.   [2] Rom. 6^18-22 8^2.

stifled. Yet, since even in the state of freedom it momentarily
falls silent, when sins of impetuosity are done, such silence could
only serve to introduce an altogether distinct state if it could be
regarded as continuous, and the inner voice as irretrievably extinguished ; and this is in fact the sense of the term *hardening* [1]—a
state which manifests itself most distinctly in a conscious and fixed
will not to give effect to the God-consciousness. This condition,
however, can never be more than approximated to, for the disposition to the God-consciousness is a constituent element of human
nature,[2] so that, even in such a vitiation of that consciousness as
ascribes human vices to the gods, the soul is never wholly without
a dim sense of the presence of something incompatible with the
God-consciousness. But were we to assume that that consciousness
is dead beyond recall,[3] and thus that the hardened soul is altogether
impervious to grace, we should be placing a particularistic limitation
on the sphere of redemption. The consciousness of the divine law,
accordingly, cannot be wholly wanting except when the God-
consciousness has not developed, *i.e.* at a period prior to the state
of bondage. If in the individual soul the development is obstructed
by the power of the sensuous, this may be a state of brutishness ;
but that, too, would belong to the state of bondage, for the obstruc-
tive element is identical with that which impedes the efficacy of
what has already developed. The states of *self-assurance* and
hypocrisy,[4] lying between the two extremes of freedom and hardening, do not stand in markedly different relations to these extremes,
nor are they at all mutually exclusive ; they really belong to the
state of bondage, and are compatible with all its various degrees,
except the bondage present to a minor extent in the state of freedom.
Here too, then, we ultimately have only the antithesis of freedom
and bondage, and these in turn simply reflect the two diverse
relations to redemption.

4. The distinction amongst sins which our proposition sets forth
as the only essential one, if we also take account of the relationship
of actual sin to original sinfulness, can be most definitely expressed

---

[1] Reinhard's explanation in *Dogm.* § 88, ' Conditio hominis qui diutius
peccando tandem desiit propositis ad virtutem incitamentis moveri,' requires to
be brought closer to the standpoint of religion, but even so would come to the
same thing.
[2] Augustine, *de Spir. et Litt.* 48 : Nam remanserat utique id, quod anima
hominis nisi rationalis esse non potest ; ita ibi etiam lex Dei non ex omni
parte deleta per iniustitiam.
[3] This is certainly not implied either in Heb. 3[8-13] (taken in relation to
Ex. 17[7]) or in 2 Cor. 3[14].
[4] Cf., amongst others, Reinhard, *loc. cit.*

as follows. The actual sin of those who have been brought into permanent connexion with the power of redemption is no longer ' originating ' in themselves, or, through their ill-doing, in others. It has been vanquished by the energy of the God-consciousness implanted in them personally and spontaneously, so that where it still shows itself it is seen to be on the wane, and has no further contaminating power. Hence the sins of the regenerate are such as do not obstruct the spiritual life either in themselves or in the community. On the other hand, the sins of the unregenerate are always ' originating,' not only in the individuals themselves, since every sin adds to the force of habit and thus to the vitiation of the God-consciousness, but also beyond themselves, since like instigates like, and the vitiated God-consciousness spreads and establishes itself by communication to others. Thus whatever element of spiritual life may exist in a society still outside the sphere of redemption, and may seek to expand and rise from lower stages to higher, whether in political life or in science and art, has its progress constantly thwarted by such sin, and dragged back into the whirlpool, so that the sin may be truly said to be detrimental to the spiritual life of the community, or in other words to rob the community of spiritual life. If we incline to abrogate this antithesis, and assume merely a difference between a larger freedom in some and a lesser freedom in others without reference to a definite point of demarcation at which a bondage characterized by a mere presentiment of freedom passes into a freedom merely showing traces of bondage, we shall thereby be abandoning the attitude of at least the stricter type of Christianity, and our position, in virtue of its Pelagian tendency, would at last merge in naturalism, for once that antithesis has been surrendered, redemption would come to have no distinctive inner effect whatever. Such effect, however, is so palpably present everywhere in Holy Scripture as an ultimate fact of consciousness, that it is unnecessary to go back to particular expressions and formulæ, such as ' being buried in the death of Christ,' or ' the new creature,' or in the contrast between the carnal and the spiritual man. If, however, we thought of describing the latter contrast as one between a state in which sin still persists and a state in which everything is sin, we should thereby warp the facts, since there is no hard-and-fast distinction between the two ; and, besides, it would be unduly harsh to stigmatize as sin everything noble and beautiful that has developed in heathenism. Here we can only seek to supply what is defective in that statement of the antithesis.   We say then, in harmony with what was argued above, that in all good works of the regenerate there remains some form of venial sin, but it is, so to speak, merely the shadow of sin, that is— if we consider the inward state as a whole—the not-willed but actually repudiated after-effect of the force of habit, which can only be overcome by degrees.   On the other hand, in the sins of the natural man, which as such are not yet forgiven, there is always the now deeper and now fainter shadow of the good, namely, an acquiescent presentiment or imagining of a state free from inward conflict ;   only a shadow, it is true, because these imaginings never take practical shape or become permanently effective.   So, too, in heathenism the communal life, principally because of the vitiated God-consciousness with which it was necessarily bound up, was never able to produce anything higher.   Similarly in the unen-lightened man who has only an outward connexion with Christianity we may indeed trace many a Christian feature, which nevertheless is not in him a thing of living power, but merely the reflection of what is present as a reality in others.

SECOND SECTION

THE CONSTITUTION OF THE WORLD IN RELATION TO SIN

§ 75. *Once sin is present in man, he finds also in the world, as his sphere, persistent causes of hindrance to his life, i.e. evils. This section, accordingly, will deal with the Doctrine of Evil.*

1. It is clear that in a system of doctrine the world cannot come under discussion at all except as it is related to man. Even though, in consequence of sin, the world were to suffer a change outside the human relation, new elements being introduced or the old modified, this could have no place whatever in Dogmatics. Only incidentally, therefore, and only because the idea of such a change is frequently brought into religious teaching, do we need to state that this is a wholly untenable idea, deduced from certain Mosaic passages [1] on quite insufficient grounds. Even in its relation to man, in fact, the world can only assume different characteristics in the manner indicated in our proposition—partly by its appearing different to him, and partly because the results of sin dissolve the original harmony between the world and man. Thus the conception of the original perfection of the world,[2] if brought into relation to the original perfection of man, does not imply that the world is the domain of evil. No doubt there must always have been a relative opposition, making itself felt with varying intensity, between the existent as externally given and the corporeal life of human individuals, otherwise human beings could not have been mortal; [3] but as long as every moment of human activity might have been a product of the original perfection of man, every moment being determined by the God-consciousness, and all the sensuous and bodily aspects of life being brought into in exclusive relation to it, that opposition could never have been construed by the corporate consciousness as an obstruction to life, since it could not in any sense act as an inhibition of the God-consciousness, but at most would give a different form to its effects. This holds good even of natural death and the bodily afflictions that precede it in the shape of disease and debility; for what can no longer serve the guiding

---

[1] Gen. 3[14. 16-18].   [2] Cf. § 59.   [3] On this, cf. § 59.

and determining higher consciousness, is not willed. Hence it is not by death, but, as Scripture says, by the fear of death, that we are subject to bondage.[1] If, however, the predominant factor is not the God-consciousness but the flesh, every impression made by the world upon us and involving an obstruction of our bodily and temporal life must be reckoned as an evil, and the more so, the more definitely the moment of experience terminates solely in the flesh apart from the higher consciousness ; the reason being that there is then a repression of the only principle which could in such a case restore the harmony. Since, then, the relative opposition between the external world and the temporal life of man is an inevitable and universal fact, sin involves evil of the first type indicated above ; the world, that is, appears otherwise to man than it would have appeared had he had no sin. As regards the second type, which must primarily have its source in human activity akin to sin, it is obvious that an activity that was purely and simply an expression of man's original perfection could never turn out to be a hindrance to the spiritual life. For, even if such activity, through the error and against the intention of the agent, were to turn out a hindrance, though only to the life of sense, then, since along with this would necessarily go an incentive to correct the error, it would not be regarded as an evil. Just as little again could the action of one person prove a hindrance to another's life, since, in virtue of the God-consciousness that was supreme in all, each could not but acquiesce in the other's every action. But if that supremacy is done away, there emerges opposition between the individual beings, and what is a furtherance to one will often for that very reason become a hindrance to another. So that here, too, evil arises only with sin, but, given sin, it arises inevitably.

2. Now, anything that gives rise to obstructions in human life so far as it is independent of human action, we call *natural* evil ; while what in bringing about such obstructions is really due to human action, we call *social* evil. The latter term is preferable to ' moral ' evil ; for if we say ' moral ' we suggest that the bad also as such (*das Böse*) is subsumed under the concept of evil.[2] It is true that social evils too presuppose sin ; what in one person issues from sin becomes an evil for another, and probably for himself as well ; but precisely on that account it seems the more necessary to insist, even by our use of terms, on the essential difference in the reference involved in the two. The above division may not look

---

[1] Heb. 2[16].   [2] Cf. § 48, 1.

quite satisfactory, since, *e.g.*, disease may in many cases be a natural, and in other cases a social, evil (this ambiguity being inherent in general terms) ; indeed, we must often regard as one and the same evil what should be ascribed partly to the one source and partly to the other, and it would perhaps, therefore, be more accurate to say that all evils arise from the two elements together or from one of the two. Still, the main fact remains unaltered, namely, the different way in which the two kinds of evil stand related to sin. Both kinds, however, when viewed from the standpoint of the original perfection of the world,[1] are evils only because they either diminish the wealth of stimuli which further men's development or make the world less tractable to human effort. Of the former class are the evils of scarcity and want, of the latter those of oppression and antagonism ; and everything that from our point of view may be regarded as evil, together with all the deadening and derangement of our spiritual powers in consequence of sin, must be traceable to these two types.

3. As summarizing the foregoing, our proposition implies, first, that without sin there would be nothing in the world that could properly be considered an evil, but that whatever is directly bound up with the transitoriness of human life would be apprehended as at most an unavoidable imperfection, and the operations of natural forces which impede the efforts of men as but incentives to bring these forces more fully under human control. Secondly, it is implied that the measure in which sin is present is the measure in which evil is present, so that, just as the human race is the proper sphere of sin, and sin the corporate act of the race, so the whole world in its relation to man is the proper sphere of evil, and evil the corporate suffering of the race. Finally, the proposition signifies that, apart from such evil, there is no other consequence of sin that bears upon the relationship of the world to man, and that our religious consciousness makes no claim to substantiate the theory of some sort of magical effect which sin at its first appearance must have produced upon the world as a whole.

§ 76. *All evil is to be regarded as the punishment of sin, but only social evil as directly such, and natural evil as only indirectly.*

1. It would be altogether contrary to this proposition to admit only such a connexion between evil and sin, as implied that evil was the original and sin the derivative, *i.e.* that it was the obstruc-

[1] Cf. § 59.

tions to man's sensuous life that first evoked in him the bad, and repressed his God-consciousness. Such things are often enough said in particular cases, and the morally bad derived from natural imperfection, physical or psychical. Were it really so, however, the Christian consciousness would necessarily be in conflict with itself ; for to see an obstruction of life in any moment of experience in which there was a disturbance merely of the sensuous consciousness would of itself argue an impotence in the God-consciousness, and therefore sin. The said theory, therefore, can hold good only of an individual case as such, certain evils favouring the development of certain forms of sin, but only because these evils themselves have had their source in sin. To advance the view as universally and exclusively true, however, would imply that the ultimate ground of sin lies wholly outside human activity, in an original ordainment of evil independent of such activity ; and this would mean that sin was not the collective act of the human race, but in the first instance the work of external nature, where evil was supposed to have its basis, and ultimately a divine appointment. This view, however, would not only take us beyond distinctly Christian ground—since redemption would then be essentially an emancipation from evil—but it would carry us out of the sphere of the teleological, *i.e.* the distinctively ethical religions, into that of æsthetic or of nature-religion, where the guiding hope would be merely that a joyous emergence of the God-consciousness might possibly take place once we had become prosperous and happy.

In opposition to all this we record our consciousness that in the admitted connexion between sin and evil, sin is ultimately always the primary and original element, and evil the derivative and secondary. For the term ' punishment ' implies, first, an evil actually existing in relation to some preceding badness (*Böse*). This does not indeed exhaust the connotation of the term, and when we use it in its true sense we really refer the said connexion to an originator, and ascribe it to a free action on his part ; and it is either in an improper sense, or because we actually refer the connexion to the divine causality, that we apply the term punishment to an evil that, instead of being inflicted upon a wrong-doer, rather befalls him. Our formulated statement is accordingly the expression of our religious consciousness in so far as we refer that connexion to the absolutely living and active divine causality as described above, and do not seek to involve that causality in any particular way in the antithesis of free and necessitated. And for that very reason this consciousness, of which probably no one can divest himself, is essentially different from the partly one-sided and partly perverted mode of it found in Judaism, and still more in heathenism ; for, when that ordained connexion between sin and evil is divorced from the universal world-order and the system of nature, and is represented as something individual and unequal in its incidence, or is referred to some superinduced change in the Supreme Being, we have a view which rests upon a vitiated God-consciousness, and thus itself is of the nature of sin.

2. In distinguishing here between social evils and natural evils we are proceeding upon the fact that the former alone are dependent upon sin directly. It might no doubt be argued that the expressions ' due to human activity ' and ' due to sin ' do not mean the same thing, since the root of evil is often not sin so much as error. Nevertheless, when we try to conceive of an error absolutely free from guilt, we find that the range of such errors is much narrower than is usually supposed, so that, strictly speaking, we have to fall back, not upon free human action at all, but upon merely passive states which in reality belong to our natural imperfection. Evils which could be explained in this way, because not due to sin, would in fact fall into the category not of social but of natural evils.

The connexion of the latter group with sin, again, is only an indirect one ; for death and pain, or at least analogous natural maladjustments of the individual life to its environment, are found where no sin exists. Natural evils, therefore, objectively considered, do not arise from sin ; but as man, were he without sin, would not feel what are merely hindrances of sensuous functions as evils, the very fact that he does so feel them is due to sin, and hence that type of evil, subjectively considered, is a penalty of sin. That even the most serious maladjustments of this kind, considered purely by themselves and from the standpoint of man's natural perfection, are not punishments, but incentives rather to the development of the spirit, is taught by Christ Himself with reference to the man born blind ; [1] for what He says there regarding His own special miraculous power is susceptible of universal application. Even if we probe still more deeply, and assert that the obstructions to our life, taken purely by themselves and before they become evils through sin, are nevertheless rooted in the same evil as sin was said above to be,[2] in the temporal frame and the spatial individualization of existence, upon which the beginnings of all sin depend ; yet,

[1] John 9[3].   [2] § 69.

even as thus connected in their common origin, sin would for us still be first and evil second, as certainly as man is primarily an acting subject, and his activity not wholly dependent upon his passive states.

3. As the value of the Mosaic narrative must be estimated in view of the fact that there can be no proper history of the first man, and as a state of being which offered him abundant enjoyment without effort on his part can be no genuine representation of the original perfection of the world, it is possible that the true significance of that symbolic narrative may be seen in its relation to the contrasted states. Thus the fact that, when man after the Fall had to till the ground in the sweat of his brow—this in itself being no evil, and therefore not a penalty of sin—the tilled ground brought forth thorns and thistles for him, is certainly meant to indicate that nature's opposition to man's moulding handiwork is to be thought of only in connexion with sin. Similarly, the fact that death, hitherto unknown to him, is put before him as the recompense of transgression, and that the first case of death is represented as the outcome of sin, seems to indicate that it is through sin alone that natural imperfections come to be incorporated with social evils. Now, as the Pauline account [1] of the relationship of death, and thus of all secondary natural evils, to sin turns wholly upon that symbolical narrative, and can only be interpreted in the light of it, it too (precisely on the analogy of sin) depicts the evil which befell the first pair after the Fall as ' originating orginal evil,' and this again can be applied to every contribution which the individual in consequence of his sin makes to the deterioration of the world.

§ 77. *The dependence of evil upon sin, however, can be empirically established only as we consider a communal life in its entirety ; on no account must the evils affecting the individual be referred to his sin as their cause.*

1. If sin as an organic whole can be rightly understood only as the corporate action of the human race, its causal action relatively to evil can only be understood from the same point of view. In fact, the most definite expression of this conviction lies, for each of us, in the general statement that throughout the human race as a whole, increase of sin is necessarily attended by a corresponding increase of evil (though as the effects of sin naturally ensue only by degrees, it is often the children and grandchildren who first suffer for the sins of the fathers),[2] and that, in like manner, as sin

---

[1] Rom. 5[12ff.].   [2] Ex. 20[5].

diminishes, so will evil diminish. As the intercourse, however, of the human race is even yet relatively limited, and many groups, being in a manner outside the range of the sins of other groups, form enclosed wholes by themselves, the same principle will hold good of these as well. Following up this line, we shall next be able to say of every nation, and indeed of every social class in it, so far as it seems to stand by itself, that the measure of its sin will be also the measure of the evil it suffers. Nor does this strict correspondence with sin apply to social evils only; for since large bodies of men not seldom affect one another precisely as natural forces do, and external nature obstructs the common efforts of all, these influences are, in every large association of human beings, felt the more intensely as evil, the more deeply it is involved in sin; and, in fact, even common evils not seldom acquire their peculiar cast and character from the nature of the sin that predominates in the society. All this becomes unmistakably clear only when we have in view a circle of homogeneous communal life not too small in extent.

2. Now it would indicate not only a limited and erroneous but a dangerous point of view—even if a view deeply rooted in Judaism and Greek heathenism—were we to make a similar affirmation regarding the individual, namely, that for each the measure of his sin is the measure of the evil that befalls him. For the very conception of the community and fellowship of human life implies, as indeed follows all but self-evidently from the manner in which sin produces evil, that quite possibly only the merest fraction of the common evil may fall upon the author of much of the common depravity. Accordingly, to refer first to natural evils, we find Christ explicitly declaring that, on the one hand, those operations of nature in which the original perfection of the world is most clearly shown are by divine appointment not less active where there is sin than where there is righteousness; [1] and on the other, that natural evils, [2] and accidental evils such as might almost be identified therewith, [3] are assuredly not linked to the sin of the individual—so far as we can isolate it—in such a way as to warrant our measuring his sin by the evil he suffers. And even if we go back to the view that sinfulness and natural imperfections spring from a common root, yet the individual's share in the one seems to be quite independent of his share in the other. Only in this way, indeed, can our assumption hold good without subverting the completeness and constancy of the natural order. Again, as regards social evils: were these to be

[1] Matt. 5⁴⁶.　　　[2] John 9³.　　　[3] Luke 13⁵.

apportioned to each individual according to his share in the collective wrong-doing, we should often, as by some magic process, have to find justice in injustice.[1] In point of fact, Christ warns His disciples of persecution and suffering in their work for the Kingdom of God, but not assuredly in proportion to their sin. How indeed could such a supposition be squared with the idea—an idea pervading the New Testament, and, if rightly understood, essential to Christianity —that within a common sphere of sin it is possible for one to suffer for the rest, so that the evil due to the sin of many may all converge upon one, and that penal suffering may fall pre-eminently upon one who is himself most free from the common guilt and most resolute in his battle with sin ?

Postscript.—From the point now reached, we find it possible to estimate a position which I would characterize broadly as the Cynical, but which has been maintained repeatedly and in various forms in Christian times—namely, that all evils have sprung from our social life and from men's endeavours, by combining their forces, to explore and dominate nature more effectively, and that in the so-called state of nature these evils would virtually not have emerged at all. In one aspect, this view seems to be a mere corollary of our proposition. For since in social life the individual may have to suffer for the many, it is impossible that evil could be the same in the solitary state as it is in society. Clearly, too, the less a man is inclined to activity, and therefore the less in touch with other men and with external nature, the less exposed will he be to the evils that result from such contact. If this view, however, is advanced, not as a mere observation, but as counsel and warning to the effect that a man would do well to act less in order to suffer less, it conflicts with the spirit of Christianity in that it commends the maxim of the slothful servant, and finds a higher ideal in being passive than in being spontaneously active.

POSTSCRIPT TO THIS DOCTRINE

§ 78. *The consciousness of this connexion does not demand a passive endurance of evil on account of sin ; nor does it entail an endeavour either to bring about evil because of sin, or on the other hand to do away with evil in itself.*

1. This proposition, since it does not more exactly determine anything in regard to the origin of the consciousness already eluci-

---

[1] Cf. Luke 13[1-3].

dated, or further define or analyse its non-active content, can only be dealt with here as an addendum.   But as the proposition has to do with the issues of that consciousness in so far as the latter may express itself in an impulse to deeds that react upon it, it is strictly one that verges upon the sphere of Christian Ethics.   At the same time it is not taken from that sphere.   A system of Christian Ethics formulated independently, *i.e.* not simply in relation to a definite existing system of Christian doctrine, or as a series of practical corollaries drawn from such a system, would hardly be capable of directly combining the points which our proposition summarizes. On the contrary, the question whether the Christian consciousness enjoins a passive acceptance of all evil, or whether, on the other hand, every other task imposed upon us should be laid aside until some evil that we suffer from has been got rid of ; or again, the question whether a positive system of penal law is directly derived from religion, and whether the sense of one's own sin should induce one to bring evil upon oneself, would all emerge at quite different points in Christian Ethics.   What entitles our proposition to a place here is its distinctively dogmatic combination of the points concerned.

2. In every instant of suffering the consciousness of the connexion between evil and sin is present, and is indeed combined in the unity of the moment along with our God-consciousness ; this association of our feeling of absolute dependence with our state of suffering constitutes the mood of religious submission, which is thus an essential element of piety, but an element which wholly disappears if we regard the said connexion as non-existent or as of minor importance, and in face of our present difficulties in life look for corresponding ameliorations in the future.   Similarly, should this submission develop into something more positive, and should we become willing that evil should continue or unwilling that it should cease (on the pretext of not desiring to infringe the desires of God or to be found in opposition to Him), then our submission would not be grounded upon the connexion in question.   Queer fancies of this type, due to misconception, have always been repudiated by the Christian Church, which has always set itself here against superstition and fanaticism.   For the continuance of evil could assuredly not be willed as a hindrance to life, since every such hindrance tends to restrict on one side or another the activity that flows from the God-consciousness.   And still less in the sphere of redemption, within which we confidently hope sin will disappear, could we desire

the continuance of evil, since, evil and sin being connected, we should in that case either desire the continuance of sin itself or else not desire the realization of that hope. On the other hand, it is no less certain that the Christian consciousness could never give rise to a moment of activity specially directed towards the cessation of suffering as such—partly, of course, because such a moment would really be determined by the interests of the lower side of life, and partly because (since, in view of the aforesaid connexion, suffering necessarily evokes the consciousness of sin) it is a disposition hostile to sin itself that needs to be aroused. And at the same time, as every restriction of spontaneous activity implies a still defective domination over nature, we are confronted with the task of making that domination effective. These, then, would be the two consistent and practical results flowing from our sense of the connexion of sin and suffering, whereas every activity directed against suffering in itself would, precisely because of the end in view, be a sensuous one, and also would only too easily take on a character of passionate vehemence.

Further, there is thus exposed the unchristian or rather the wholly irreligious nature of a certain other view—namely, that it is evil alone which, from the outset, has evoked all the human activity that goes to subjugate nature and to form social life. For if that activity has been directed solely against evil, and has accordingly sprung up only as a reaction against depressive influences without any spontaneity, then this whole phase of life will be of a purely sensuous kind, and will draw no incentive from the God-consciousness. On such terms the truth would lie with those who think that religion does not express itself in outward acts at all, and who so divorce that entire sphere of things (as merely secular and purely a matter of necessity) from the province of religion, as to make an irremediable cleavage in life.

3. Finally, if on the one hand sin is essentially a corporate thing, since every sin emanating from an individual implies the guilt of others, so that corporate evil can be related only to corporate sin, and on the other hand every increase of sin must be regarded as of itself entailing an increase of evil; then our consciousness of this divinely ordained connexion can furnish no grounds for our bringing about evil as a result of observed sin; for by its very nature such procedure could not but interfere with the divine ordinance in question. Whether there may, however, not be other grounds for doing so is, of course, not the question here.

THIRD SECTION

§ 79. *Divine attributes relating to the consciousness of sin, even if
only through the fact that redemption is conditioned by sin,
can only be established if at the same time we regard God as
the Author of sin.*

1. To begin with, it is certain that we can arrive at ideas of
divine attributes only by combining the content of our self-consciousness with the absolute divine causality that corresponds to
our feeling of absolute dependence. That in this manner we trace
the annulment of sin by redemption to the divine causality is a fact
that we may premise as given universally in the Christian consciousness. But divine attributes that were there conceived as
operative would of course be operative primarily in redemption,
and it is only through redemption that they would be related to sin.
Now, if in relation to sin there are divine activities other than those
concerned in its removal, the existence of sin must in some sense be
due to the divine causality, and that causality must be determined
in a special way with respect to sin's existence. We have already [1]
discussed the fact that, in general, sin as an act, besides having
always a basis in the natural order (this term being taken here as
connoting the historical as well), also comes under the co-operative
agency of God; but this points only to the creative and preservative
omnipotence of God. If, nevertheless, because sin does exist and
in so far as it exists, we feel bound to posit a special divine activity
bearing upon it, we must not forget that in thus considering the
consciousness of sin *per se*, we are moving in the region of the
abstract, and should therefore err were we to look for divine activities
bearing upon sin purely by itself. On the other hand, as regards
sin in its relation to redemption, we must—if this section is to have
any subject-matter at all—be able somehow to show that sin does
actually exist in virtue of certain special divine activities; and what
is more, we must do so, keeping in mind the fact that we have

[1] See § 48.

already ruled out as inadmissible any distinction in the divine causality between causing and permitting, or between creating and preserving.

2. Our task, accordingly, is to answer the question whether and how far God can be regarded as the author of sin—sin too as such (not merely, that is, as regards the material element in sinful action)—yet always of sin as linked with redemption. If an affirmative answer can be given, there will then be divine attributes in virtue of which sin is ordained by God—not indeed sin in itself, but in so far as redemption likewise is due to Him. These attributes then will have as their counterpart those which we shall have to look for under the like condition in the second division of this Part —those, namely, in virtue of which God is the Author of redemption, not in itself, however, but in so far as sin too is due to Him. The conceptions of the divine attributes to be formulated here will accordingly, on the one hand, be posited only on the assumption of their being interwoven with those that come to us from an examination of the consciousness of grace ; for we assume it beforehand to be out of the question that the two sets of conceptions could in reality be so distinct as the mutual opposition of the two elements of our Christian consciousness, when considered thus abstractly, suggests. On the other hand, the divine attributes in question are to be conceived of as attaching to the divine omnipotence only as this has been described as the eternally omnipresent, for this is the most general expression of that feeling of absolute dependence which is regarded here as forming the basis of this first aspect of the antithesis.

§ 80. *As in our self-consciousness sin and grace are opposed to each other, God cannot be thought of as the Author of sin in the same sense as that in which He is the Author of redemption. But as we never have a consciousness of grace without a consciousness of sin, we must also assert that the existence of sin alongside of grace is ordained for us by God.*

1. If to the power of the God-consciousness in our souls, just because we are conscious of it as not due to our own agency, we give the name ' grace ' and (abstracting from the universal divine co-operation without which sin itself were impossible) ascribe to it a special divine impartation ; and if, again, the content of a moment which lacks the determining activity of the God-consciousness, just because we are conscious of it as an act of our own cut off from that

divine impartation, is termed ' sin '—this of itself justifies the first part of our proposition. The universal co-operation of God is the same in either domain, but in the case of sin there is lacking that specific divine impartation which gives to every approach to salvation the character of grace. It might, of course, be said that as the disappearance of sin is uniformly proportionate to the inflow of grace, the relation between the two resembles that between two species of animals one of which preys upon the other, the two continuing in that relationship as ordained for both by one and the same divine will. This, however, would be tantamount to denying the specific divine impartation in question, and to affirming that redemption is effected solely by the spontaneous efforts of man, so that in the sphere of grace the human factor would be related to the divine co-operation precisely as in that of sin. But while such a view need not be regarded as in itself unchristian, since it might still leave room for the influence of the specific activity of the Redeemer, it nevertheless would not be the doctrine recognized by the Church and therefore expressive of the Church's corporate feeling. Accordingly, if the antithesis in our self-consciousness really implies a special divine impartation, the question what divine activity in turn underlies the fact of sin as such, *i.e.* as that which evokes redemption, can be answered only by saying that no evidence exists of any such activity.

2. No less true, however, is the second half of our proposition. We are conscious of the said communicated power of being determined by the God-consciousness always and only as co-existing with an incapacity of our own that reveals itself as a co-determining factor, and we also know that, while the power overcomes the resistance, it nevertheless leaves it still there. Hence we can conceive of the divine will that imparts the power only as at the same time having in it something which entails that sin even in the process of disappearing should continue to exist side by side with grace.[1] For if the divine will without any such latent strain were wholly directed against sin, the latter of necessity would vanish altogether and at once. Now, the second part of our proposition rests wholly upon the assumption that everywhere human evil exists only as attached to good, and sin only as attached to grace. Were it possible to speak of a type of sin absolutely unconnected with

---

[1] Melanchthon, *Loc.*, p. 121 : Respondeo de renatis adultis omnes concedere coguntur reliqua esse peccata. Cf. 1 John 1[8].—*Conf. Anglic.* xv. : Sed nos reliqui etiam baptizati et in Christo regenerati in multis tamen offendimus omnes.

redemption, we should certainly not have to assume a divine activity directed to the existence of such sin. But if it is the case that the state of hardening is, strictly, not a human state at all,[1] no such type of sin really exists either within the narrower sphere of Christianity, where everyone is brought into some kind of connexion with redemption, or outside that sphere, where even the most impotent and vitiated God-consciousness belongs to a corporate life that at the same time comprises a morally higher element which finds expression in precept and law ; and, as a matter of fact, every such corporate life, imperfect and sinful as it may be, has yet, in virtue of its presentiments and aspirations, an inward link with redemption.   Least of all, however, can we imagine that sin could have a place in the creative dispensation of God apart from redemption, since in the divine will bearing upon the existence of the whole human race the two are ordained to stand in relationship to each other. For the mere fact that the emergence of sin preceded the advent of redemption in no sense implies that sin was ordained and willed purely for itself ; on the contrary, the very statement that the Redeemer appeared when the fulness of the time was come [2] makes it quite clear that from the beginning everything had been set in relation to His appearing.   And if we add the fact that the sin which persists outside direct connexion with redemption never ceases to generate more sin, and that redemption often begins to operate only after sin has attained to a certain degree, we need have no misgiving in saying that God is also the Author of sin—of sin, however, only as related to redemption.

3. The antinomy in these two statements, both of which are expressions of our religious consciousness, is all the more difficult to resolve because it is not in two different relations that they are severally predicated ; on the contrary, both are postulated in respect of one and the same relation, namely, as we trace the potency of the God-consciousness to a special divine impartation. It is true both statements are derived solely from the consciousness of the Christian who has been brought into the actual fellowship of redemption, and in this narrower field the antinomy appears easy of solution if we say that, as sin is in fact present and continues to exist prior to redemption, and as the divine impartation can operate only in the forms of human life, we must infer that in the narrower sphere sin can be overcome even by divine grace only in a time-process. We cannot, however, claim to have dealt successfully

[1] Cf. § 74, 3.   [2] Gal. 4[4].

with our problem unless we also bring the presence of sin in the human race as a whole into connexion with our God-consciousness. Precisely because the narrower sphere is in process of constant expansion—and that, moreover, in virtue (under God) of the labours of the forgiven—we cannot but have that outer field constantly in view. In this reference, accordingly, our race-consciousness finds expression solely in the antithesis between the Kingdom of God and the world, and this again represents in the most general way both the antithesis of sin and grace and their co-existence ; so that in this necessary universalization of our consciousness we meet again with the same antinomy, which accordingly must be solved for the universalized consciousness as well.

4. Now every attempt to solve the antinomy by accepting one statement and rejecting the other leads inevitably to a result incompatible with the character of Christianity, drawing us, in fact, into either the Pelagian or the Manichæan heresy. We fall into the latter when we put the first half of our proposition in such a way as entirely to exclude the second. Thus if sin is in no sense grounded in a divine volition and is nevertheless held to be a real act, we must assume another will so far completely independent of the divine will as to be itself the ultimate ground of all sin as such. Nor will it matter greatly whether this will is the human will itself or another ; for, if we still assume, what is certainly given in our self-consciousness, the co-existence of sin and grace in the same individual, that state of things can be regarded only as a conflict of these two antithetic wills, which means that every activity of the flesh would be an overcoming of the divine will—a view implying in any case that the divine omnipotence is circumscribed, and therefore abrogated, and that the feeling of absolute dependence is proclaimed an illusion. Or, again, were we, contrary to all inward experience, to advance the opposed and clearly fanatical statement that the influx of divine grace involves the complete disappearance of sin proper, only a semblance of it being left behind, then wherever real sin still existed the divine omnipotence would still be excluded from the entire sphere of free action as such, and the two spheres— that of the divine will and that of its antithesis—would stand opposed to each other, even externally, in the most rigorous fashion.

Just as certainly, however, we should fall into the Pelagian heresy were we to admit the validity of the second part only of our proposition, and so do away with all distinction in the divine causality, which would thus be identical alike in the activities of the flesh and the energy of the God-consciousness. In that case the spontaneous activity of man must be the same throughout ; the antithesis between our native incapacity and the imparted energy of the God-consciousness would disappear ; and, since the most powerful element in us, equally with the power of the flesh, would be the outcome of our own activity, the consciousness of incapacity that forms part of our inward experience can indicate only a transitional and even now evanescent state of the social life of mankind. In such an indistinguishable ' more or less ' of flesh and spirit, redemption inevitably comes to occupy a very insecure position, and it is virtually a matter of accident how much or how little special influence is ascribed to the Redeemer, whether more as the Author of redemption or as its occasion. This attenuation of the specific difference between Redeemer and redeemed—this, as we might almost call it, merely figurative use of the term ' grace '—marks the Pelagian heresy. Pelagianism, therefore, on the one hand sacrifices the practical religious interest (which postulates somewhere a perfectly pure impulse) to the theoretical (which demands that every vital activity shall have the same relation to the divine causality), and on the other feebly and through mere stolidity surrenders all hope of perfect satisfaction. Manichæism in turn is a surrender of the theoretical religious interest in the reality of the divine omnipotence, in favour of the practical interest attaching to the idea that evil is real in the most unqualified sense, so as all the more to bring out the necessity that the perfect good should counteract it redemptively. And this, too, is to despair of reconciling the existence of sin with the divine omnipotence.

§ 81. *If ecclesiastical doctrine seeks to solve this antinomy by the proposition that God is not the Author of sin, but that sin is grounded in human freedom, then this must be supplemented by the statement that God has ordained that the continually imperfect triumph of the spirit should become sin to us.*

Conf. Aug. 19 : Tametsi Deus creat et adiuvat naturam, tamen causa peccati est voluntas malorum videlicet diaboli et impiorum, quae non adjuvante Deo avertit se ad alias res.—*Sol. Decl.*, p. 647 : Neque Deus est creator vel autor peccati.—Melanchthon, *Loc.*, p. 72 : Non igitur Deus causa est peccati, nec peccatum est res condita aut ordinata a Deo. P. 76 : peccatum ortum est a voluntate diaboli et hominis, nec factum est Deo volente.—*Exp. Simpl.* viii. : scientes . . . mala non esse quae fiunt respectu providentiae Dei voluntatis et potestatis Dei, sed respectu Satanae et voluntatis nostrae voluntati Dei repugnantis.—*Conf. Hungar.* (Ed. Aug., p. 251) : Sicut impossibile est contrarie inter se pugnantia . . . causam efficientem formalemque esse posse sibi contrariorum . . . ita impossibile est Deum, qui est lux, justitia . . . causam esse tenebrarum peccati . . . sed horum omnium causa Satanas et homines sunt.   Quaecunque enim Deus prohibet et propter quae damnat facere ex se et per se non potest.

1. The use of the terms 'Creator' and 'creation,' as bearing upon sin, was made possible only through that scholastic misuse of abstract terms which gave to the controversy about original sin the peculiar turn represented by the question whether it was a substance or an accident.   That usage, however, is as it stands quite inadmissible, since sin is not an independent entity, and does not form an independent process.   And just as little—least of all if we distinguish between 'creation' and 'preservation'—can we apply the said terms to the sinful nature, since that nature does not start with sin, but sin first makes its appearance in the course of life.   If, however, we still keep to the statement that God is not the Cause or the Author of sin, we find that such denial, taken strictly, involves two distinct ideas, one of which stands out more prominently in the first two, the other in the last two, citations given above.

The first is that, as in God thought and creation are one,[1] and as sin cannot be a divine thought or purpose, there cannot be in God any creative will in relation to sin or the sinful nature.   But the same might be said of every finite nature.   The sinful nature is a blending of the being and not-being of the God-consciousness, but in the same way every finite nature is a blending of being and not-being ; and not-being can no more than sin be the divine purpose.   Yet in relation to every finite nature there is a creative divine will—not, however, as something existing purely by itself, but as comprised in the will that creates the finite God-consciousness in its entirety, and thus embraces redemption likewise.   Hence the first or negative clause of the Church's doctrine requires modification in the sense that the negation is not to be taken as implying that sin must be referred to another creative will which is actually such in the same sense as God is Creator in general, i.e. in virtue of a timeless eternal causality ; for, were the negation so taken, the same would hold good in every case of individual differentiated being, and ultimately therefore of the entire aggregate of such. In that case we should be forced to choose between a demiurge— distinct from God—as the creator of the world, who created also the sinful nature as such, and an evil primordial being—opposed to God

[1] § 40, 1 and § 55.

—in whom lay the timeless causality of sin, but who must also have been the creator of finite being, and that not merely in part, as some have idly said, but wholly.[1] From this point of view, accordingly, we are shut up to the choice between saying that for sin there is no eternal causality at all, and finding that eternal causality in God.

A transition from the first main idea of our proposition to the second is found, however, in the theory that traces the sinful state in its entirety to the loss of the God-consciousness originally imparted to human nature by God Himself.[2] Thus, while generally the cessation of anything must be due to the same divine will from which it took its rise—otherwise, indeed, there would be no finite being at all—yet it would seem that there must be a difference in the case of the God-consciousness, the cessation of which, *i.e.* of the presence of God in man, could not be due to the divine causality. Now this plea might no doubt hold good were sin a complete cessation of the God-consciousness, and if the sinful nature were wholly sin. But in the sinful nature the bad exists only correlatively with the good, and no moment is occupied exclusively by sin; for sin actually presupposes the God-consciousness, so that the sinful nature always retains the presence of God as something imparted, though only in the most limited degree. Hence in this respect, too, the limitation of the God-consciousness, as well as its impartation, may be grounded in one and the same divine will.

The second thought taken as starting-point is that God cannot possibly have brought about, and therefore cannot be the Author of, what He Himself forbids. Now we must of course admit that the will of God which commands other beings, though we call it will, is not identical with His efficient will.[3] For the divine command does not manifest itself in addition as a will that, in all cases falling under the command, effects what is in conformity with it; in fact, the Scripture actually says that the commanding will of God does not of itself secure obedience,[4] and we are all clearly

---

[1] It is quite clear that in bringing the devil into the matter our confessional documents had not this in view. For they regard the devil as coming under the same category as man, namely, that of a free finite being, so that his sin, too, is to be thought of as grounded in his freedom, and his relation to human sin is by no means to be regarded as prejudicing the fact that man's sin is grounded in his own freedom. Thus the introduction of the devil brings no Manichæan element whatever into the Church's doctrine, especially as that heresy is none the more easily obviated if we leave the devil out of account.

[2] Cf. § 72.

[3] Calvin., *Inst.* i. 18. 4: Perperam enim miscetur cum praecepto voluntas, quam longissime ab illo differre innumeris exemplis constat.

[4] Rom. 7[8f. 16-18].

conscious of the difference between the state in which what is given us is only the commanding will of God, and that in which God's efficient will is added as well.[1]   And we are quite as clearly conscious that the difference between the will of God as commanding and His will as accomplishing what is commanded is altogether unlike that, *e.g.*, in the narrative of the creation, between God's utterance of this fiat and the will that carries it out.   A further reason why the commanding will of God is not as such an operative will is that sin is committed only where there exists a commanding divine will to which some active impulse is the opposition.   For if sin be committed by one who thinks he is fulfilling the divine will, then what is sin is not the act itself, but only the mistaken thought, and even this is sin only where it has arisen in antagonism to God's commanding will.   This holds good likewise when sin is committed inadvertently.   Thus all sin lying between the extremes of innocence and hardening [2] presupposes the consciousness of a commanding will.   Now, though the commanding is not identical with the efficient will, yet the latter cannot be opposed to the former ; for the prohibition could not be genuine if God Himself brought the transgression of it to pass.   Here, however, we must not forget that the divine commanding will was posited solely as an absolutely perfect will, to which accordingly even what is effected in us by divine grace as efficient divine will never wholly corresponds.   If then this shortcoming in us be described as sin still clinging to us,[3] then even from this point of view the negative part of the Church's doctrine will require modification.   We must say that the negation is to be understood only in the sense that a want of conformity to the commanding will of God can none the less be brought about by His efficient will, and that so far sin is grounded in the divine causality.

2. As regards the second or affirmative part of the Church's doctrine, it is no doubt perfectly accurate ; but we cannot regard it as fitted to nullify those limitations of the first part which we had to claim on behalf of our religious consciousness.   It is, in fact, only in view of these limitations that we are able to interpret the combination of both facts in the sense that sin, so far as there is no divine causality for it, is not grounded in human freedom either. This is the only conclusion that agrees with the relationship we have formulated between the divine eternal causality and the temporal and finite causality.[4]   But the fact of sin's being grounded in our

[1] Phil. 2[13].   [2] Cf. § 66, 1 ; § 74, 3.   [3] Cf. § 63, 3.   [4] Cf. § 51, 1.

freedom is all the more compatible with its being rooted likewise in the divine causality because, with regard to the feeling of absolute dependence, we recognize no difference between the greater and the less activity of temporal causality.[1] It is only the temporal cause that is stated in this part, and the statement is first and foremost intended to obviate the idea that, if no divine causality can be assumed for sin, the consciousness of sin is a mere delusion. Sin is therefore referred to that highest degree of inward activity which constitutes the distinctive element in our being. What then is here asserted is that in the whole range of life between the inward state of the Redeemer, in whom no break in the supremacy of the God-consciousness could issue from His highest spiritual activity, and those states of human disorder in which the spiritual functions are brought under the power of disease, and responsibility ceases owing to a lack of freedom, free self-development is always attended by sin. Hence if this whole form of existence—the life of the natural man—subsists in virtue of divine appointment, sin, as proceeding from human freedom, has also a place in that appointment.

Next, our proposition affirms for the sphere of finite causality as well, that we cannot truly regard ourselves as merely passive and extraneously determined in our acts of sin.[2] The very phrase ' freedom of the will ' conveys a denial of all external necessity, and indicates the very essence of conscious life—the fact, namely, that no external influence determines our total condition in such a way that the reaction too is determined and given, but every excitation really receives its determinate quality from the inmost core of our own life, from which quality, again, proceeds the reaction, so that the sin proceeding from that core is in every case the act of the sinner and of no other. In like manner, the expression ' freedom of the will ' negatives the idea that the individual is in all cases pre-determined by the common nature of man. In reality, the common elements of our nature are the results of a process of development, and the expression in question marks out each individual as *ab initio* distinct and apart from all others. Hence no one can transfer the guilt from himself to common human nature ; a man's particular sinful self-determinations are his own acts, alike whether they issue from the sinfulness that is part and parcel of the principle of his individual will, or whether by means of them that sinfulness itself becomes more and more confirmed in

[1] Cf. § 49.   [2] Cf. Gen. 3[12. 13].

him.   None of these cases of determination, however, excludes the possibility of sin being related to the divine causality.

Besides, the proposition must only be interpreted in a sense compatible with the fact that sin is a state of bondage.[1] If the bondage ceases when redemption begins to operate—a process that cannot be conceived as independent of divine causality— but in such a manner that the operation annuls the bondage only by degrees, and is therefore permanently limited in scope by it, then we are again shut up to the conclusion that the sin which is rooted in a freedom thus linked with impotence is as such ordained by God—unless, indeed, we are positively to assume that divine action can be limited by what does not depend upon the divine causality.

3. Since then the Church doctrine, as an accurate expression of our self-consciousness, does not exclude the possibility of God's being in some sense the Author of sin, and since we are drawn by opposed interests to both alternatives ; then in seeking to solve this apparent antinomy we have no choice—if we are to keep the divine omnipotence unlimited and unabridged—than to assert that sin, in so far as it cannot be grounded in the divine causality, cannot in that measure exist for God, but that, in so far as the consciousness of our sin is a true element of our being, and sin therefore a reality, it is ordained by God as that which makes redemption necessary.   The more closely these two things are capable of being unified in the sphere of actual fact—in the same way as the diverse elements of our Christian consciousness form a unity within us— and the more definitely we can keep them apart in our thinking, so that neither will seem to involve the contrary of the other, the more completely shall we find all difficulties disappear, and that without our either in Manichæan fashion ascribing to sin a reality independent of and opposed to God, or with the Pelagians mini-mizing and by degrees annulling the antithesis of sin and grace. Now the latter part of the Church's formula asserts the reality of sin as our own act, while the first declares that sin is not brought about by God.   If then, with that formula, and with the problem still set us, we collate the passages cited from the confessional documents, we note that certain of these bring out that the temporal source of sin lies in human freedom, while they do not say that sin involves a divine eternal causality as well ; in others, again, what comes out is that sin cannot have its source in the divine will,

[1] Cf. § 74.

though they do not assert that, in so far as such a source is actually lacking, it does not exist for God. Now the more fully those one-sided views are both developed, the more do the difficulties increase, and we must either resort to over-subtle distinctions in which our immediate religious self-consciousness does not recognize itself, and which cannot be combined in a single organic view, or else we must renounce all deeper inquiry, and so arrest the development of theology.

In endeavouring, therefore, to obviate this one-sidedness by combining the two points of view, we ask first—starting with the former group—what is that element in sin for which, so far as it is rooted in human freedom, we might look to find also an eternal divine causality? Well, in every distinct moment of sin there is for one thing the manifestation of a sensuous natural impulse, in which of course the eternal divine causality is implicated; and, for another, we posit the God-consciousness as capable of being related to that impulse—else there would be no question of sin at all—and the God-consciousness of course goes back to the divine causality in the primordial revelation. But these two elements taken together do not constitute sin; it follows that so far this divine causality does not bear directly upon the sin. In so far as the sin consisted in the impotence of the God-consciousness, it would be a mere negative, *i.e.* something that could be neither a divine thought nor the result of a divine act;[1] however, a mere negation of power does not amount to sin, and, in fact, the mind is never satisfied to have sin explained as simply a defect.[2] The defect becomes sin for us only in virtue of the fact that the God-consciousness, impotent against the sensuous impulse, disavows as consciousness of the divine will that state of defect, whether simultaneously or before or after; for, without such disavowal, which is simply the recognition of a commanding or prohibiting divine will, there is no sin. We shall accordingly be able to say that, as the recognition of the commanding will is wrought in us by God, the fact that the inefficacy of the God-consciousness becomes sin in us is likewise wrought by Him, and indeed wrought with a view to redemption.[3] For the consciousness of an as yet meagre potency of the God-consciousness would be that of a state that must needs be transcended, but the consciousness of a state in which

---

[1] Melanchthon, *Loci. Th.*, p. m. 76 : Etsi enim sustentat naturam, tamen defectus illi in mente non efficiuntur ab ipso.
[2] Cf. § 68.   [3] Gal. 3[22].

there is antagonism to the divine will is a consciousness of something that must be wholly annulled.

Taking up now the other standpoint, let us ask what meaning compatible with sin's being our own act we can give to the idea that sin is not brought about by God.　If sin is not to be attributed to the divine causality on the alleged ground of its being a negation, we must bear in mind that, in accordance with what has been said above, it shares that feature with all finite being, and may therefore be none the less our own act, as finitude is the very stuff of our experience ; yet negation too is eternally wrought by God within and along with the whole development of the God-consciousness. Again, if the reason why there can be no divine causality for sin is that it is out of harmony with the commanding will of God, let us remember that it has this in common with all the good that is indubitably originated by God, to which sin is always attached, as indeed it is present in association with all good whatever ; and even so it is still our own act, as yet out of connexion with redemption.[1] Only if sin were a thing absolutely contradictory to the commanding will of God, such as would utterly annul sin in us, would it be impossible to think of the efficient will of God as related to sin. Sin, however, is never such, else it would imply the state of absolute hardening which, as we have seen, does not lie within the human sphere at all.　Hence our supplementary clause is fully justified, for it is through the commanding will of God present within us that the impotence of the God-consciousness becomes sin for us.　By that will, accordingly—though it may be impossible to ascribe any particular act of sin to a divine causality specially pertaining to it —sin has been ordained by God, not indeed sin in and of itself, but sin merely in relation to redemption ; for otherwise redemption itself could not have been ordained.

4. Nevertheless, if it be held that sin arose out of a sinless state of morally perfect activity, we must concede that our proposition does not solve the difficulties.　On the assumption of a state of that kind, we must either have recourse to the theory of such a withdrawal of God's hand as would imply a special divine act veritably giving rise to sin, or else we must represent sin as a revolt—surely

---

[1] Only in this sense can we accept the formula of the *Augsburg Confession* : voluntas non adjuvante Deo avertit se ad alias res.　The original German phrase, which, however, has been altered in the revised German Confession, certainly points to a more positive sense : alsbald so Gott die Hand abgethan (' as soon as God withdraws His hand ').　For this withdrawal of God's hand, as a special divine act, would then be the primary condition of sin.

least explicable in such a state—directed towards the complete sub-version of the commanding will of God. Hence thinkers who proceed on that assumption usually resort to the idea that, as God is not the Author of sin, and nevertheless sin actually exists, it exists by His ' permission.' A term such as this, however, derived as it is from human government and its conditions, is admissible only in a sphere of divided causation. But eternal causality is like no other, and all temporal causality must be uniformly related to it. More confusing still than the idea of permission, however, is the hypothesis that, though God may have ordained sin, He ordained it only as an indispensable means to wider ends of high moment, making the evils consequent upon sin a source of more than countervailing gain, and through Christ completely effacing the mischief of sin itself.[1] But quite apart from the fact that the antithesis of means and end cannot exist for a purely creative and all-creating will, we could not well imagine a more fallacious way of presenting Christianity than to say that Christ came only to make good the mischief arising from sin, while God, looking to the manifold gains to come thereby, could not dispense with sin itself. As against this, our own theory is that sin was ordained only in view of redemption, and that accordingly redemption shows forth as the gain bound up with sin ; in comparison with which there can be no question whatever of mischief due to sin, for the merely gradual and imperfect unfolding of the power of the God-consciousness is one of the necessary conditions of the human stage of existence.

§ 82. *What has been said concerning the divine causality with regard to sin holds good also with regard to evil, in virtue of its connexion with sin.*

Sol. Decl., p. 641 : Poenae vero peccati originalis, quas Deus filiis Adae ratione huius peccati imposuit, hae sunt, mors, aeterna damnatio et praeter has aliae corporales spirituales temporales atque aeternae aerumnae et miseriae. P. 819 : Ut enim Deus non est causa peccati, ita etiam non est poenae.—*Conf. Bohem.* iv. : Insuper docent, omnia incommoda et adflictiones quibus hic quatimur conflictamurque meritissimo iure a Deo ob peccata hominibus infligi.

1. The parallelism expressed in this proposition is for the most part recognized and assented to, but it is only sparingly dealt with in the symbolic documents, and seldom consistently developed in the systems of doctrine. This is more or less due to the fact that the treatment of the subject has had mixed up with it two irrelevant

[1] Cf. Reinhard, *Dogm.* § 75.

matters, and these we would eliminate at once. To begin with, everywhere in the discussion we meet with the misleading assumption that God has conjoined evil with sin in the purely arbitrary fashion exemplified in the penalties of human law ; and with this, again, has been combined the idea of eternal penal suffering—a procedure which, though compatible with the assumption just indicated, we for our part cannot follow, since we are here concerned only with what is given in our self-consciousness, and as yet we lack all the data for the discussion of the latter problem. Just as little, however, have we any occasion to suggest the idea of an arbitrary penal law instituted by God. Were we to apply the previously cited Mosaic passages [1] to this point, we should also have to make room for the fantastic notion that the nature of the physical world had been changed by the entrance of sin. In the economy of the world, resting as it does upon the divine causality, it is impossible that one thing should be more and another less arbitrary ; everything is equally arbitrary, or else equally not so.

2. Now, keeping to what is given in our self-consciousness on the matter, we find there two opposed interpretations of evil. One is that we ascribe evil to ourselves as the consequence of our sins, thereby denying that God is the Author of evil in the same sense as He is the Author of the original perfection of the world ; and this view is amply justified by the fact that the latter conception implies, not that the world is the domain of evil, but rather that everything involved in the relative antagonism between our own life and other things operates merely as a stimulus. The other interpretation is that we acquiesce in all the evils of life as the expression of a divine decree passed upon us. Now, this acquiescence justifies itself most completely in those cases where we can regard evils affecting us as linked up with the atoning sufferings of Christ —as indeed all fellowship with Christ must be capable of being regarded as a fellowship in His sufferings. Observe, however, that the said evils, if viewed purely and exclusively in this light, could not really be regarded as evils in which we must simply acquiesce, but would rather be calls and incentives to a definite spiritual activity—challenges to be embraced with joy. Since, however, we are at the same time conscious of evil, and the said interpretation is also applied in cases where there is no special link between that evil and our participation in Christ's redemptive work ; this clearly implies the assumption that evil as such has its origin in God—not

[1] Gen. 3^14. 16-18 ; cf. § 75, I.

indeed evil taken purely by itself, but only in its relation to sin, as that which alone runs counter to the simple and unqualified interpretation of the hindrances of our sense-life as being but incentives to action.   Here again therefore the true solution is to be found, not in the view that, as evil is grounded in our freedom through the medium of sin, it is not derived from God, but rather in the view that, as we posit everywhere the eternal along with the temporal causality, evil likewise, just in so far as it is grounded in our freedom, is at the same time ordained by God, while if it is not ordained by God, it cannot properly exist at all.   It cannot be grounded in God in so far as it takes the form of a conflict of finite beings, for these are ordained by God not in their particularity, but solely in their mutual dependence and measure.   So far therefore it does not really exist, but is for us merely a semblance arising from our way of isolating things.   God has ordained, however, that the natural imperfections are regarded by us as evil in proportion as the God-consciousness is not yet dominant within us, as also that sin develops into social evil in proportion as it is dominant, while at the same time both sin and evil are likewise grounded in our freedom.

3. The two facts, however—that connexion of evil with sin which is grounded in our freedom, and the divine causation of evil in relation to sin—become explicable only when we look at sin as corporate action and at evil as corporate suffering.   The individual cannot say, except incidentally, that the evils from which he suffers are traceable to his own freedom ; the truth is that wherever the sin is with which evil is linked, there too is the freedom from which it issues.   But as no sin belongs exclusively to the individual, the said connexion can be exhibited only in the context of a corporate life, and that the more clearly the more independent and self-contained this corporate life is.   Taken strictly, therefore, even this explanation only covers those whose existence is due to natural generation and who depend upon a corporate life from the outset ; whereas, with regard to the first human being, considered by himself, it is difficult to represent the divine causality present in evil as combined with the fact that evil originated in his own freedom ; and the difficulty is all the greater the more necessary we find it to assume an initial condition free from natural imperfections.   In that case it is, in fact, hardly possible to avoid the thought of an arbitrary decree of God linking evil with sin—and indeed the attempt to explain our present human evils from the natural properties of the forbidden fruit does not evade it either ; in which case

the confessional statement quoted above can claim no sort of validity.

Postscript.—We can exhibit divine attributes only as modes of the divine causality ; it follows that, were God in no sense the Author of sin and evil, there could be no divine attributes in virtue of which sin and evil would exist.　If, however, we have satisfactorily proved the existence of that causality, we must also enunciate divine attributes or modes of action of a peculiar type and distinct from those hitherto laid down—all the more that sin and evil are on the one hand ordained by God, and on the other are to be done away by redemption.　Now, if we had to formulate the concepts of these attributes for the first time, we might hesitate as to whether it were better to propose two—one for sin and the other for evil— or one only, since evil depends solely upon sin.　But in point of fact, the religious consciousness has long ago attained to clearness about this situation, and has expressed this aspect of the divine causality in the twin concepts of holiness and justice.　This might doubtless be criticized on the ground that in our ordinary language the former concept does not relate to sin alone so much as to the antithesis between good and bad, and similarly the latter not so much to evil alone as to the antithesis between reward and punishment.　But in fact the two terms, especially the first, have been defined and explained in so many other ways as well, and even— reward and punishment being simply the outflow of the divine pleasure and displeasure—brought so close to each other in meaning, that the following discussion of them will best show how relevant they are at our present stage, and how no other meaning can be held to than that which we shall attach to them here.

First Doctrine.　God is Holy

§ 83. *By the holiness of God we understand that divine causality through which in all corporate human life conscience is found conjoined with the need of redemption.*

1. We use the term ' conscience ' to express the fact that all modes of activity issuing from our God-consciousness and subject to its prompting confront us as moral demands, not indeed theoretically, but asserting themselves in our self-consciousness in such a way that any deviation of our conduct from them is apprehended as a hindrance of life, and therefore as sin.　In thus limiting our attention to the God-consciousness, we are true to the spirit of our theology

generally.   We may certainly assume as a known fact that conscience
is elsewhere explained by a corresponding relation to the idea of the
good ; here we have but to say in passing that the two explanations
are in no real sense different.   Thus, if it ever were to occur that
under the idea of the good the natural conscience made other
demands than in the same community are insisted on by the God-
consciousness prevailing there, so that the two were in conflict, we
should simply have to attribute the fact to a defect in their development or in their application, just as we do where the natural conscience in any one region or period is not identical with that of
another, or where different forms of faith differ in the moral demands
they make.   In the Evangelical (Protestant) Church, however, we
are not troubled with any such conflict, for there it is readily admitted that the modes of action emanating from our God-consciousness are identical with those developed from the idea of the good.
Now we need give no proof of the fact that, wherever these demands
or a law of this kind is referred to the God-consciousness, conscience
also is very markedly traced to divine causality, and, as the voice of
God within, is held to be an original revelation of God ; it is one of
those inward experiences which we may assume to be universal in
this sphere.   None the less, conscience is not identical with the fact
of the God-consciousness in man, as constituting the original perfection of his nature ; for apart from the discrepancy between the
form of the God-consciousness as understanding and its emergence
as will, and indeed apart from this discrepancy as combined with a
tendency to agreement, there would be no conscience at all ; and
similarly apart from conscience, nothing that results from that discrepancy would be sin for us.   Thus the divine causality, in virtue
of which conscience exists, falls wholly within the sphere of the
antinomy in which we now live, and is no less certainly the divine
causality through which sin exists, though for us it is owing to
conscience alone that a given state, and that as something due only
to ourselves, becomes sin.[1]   And if in addition to this causality,
and to the universal co-agency of God we were to postulate another
divine causality as the ground of sin, we should have to assume two
divine activities antagonistic to each other.   It follows, therefore,
that the causality we have postulated is the whole and sole divine
causality which sin as such implies.

2. Now if our explanation signifies that conscience is present

---

[1] Cf. I Pet. I[14-16], where the holiness of God is associated with the
demand that we should no longer live according to our lusts in ignorance.

only along with the need of redemption, then while this is certainly the purely Christian account of the matter, it must not be taken to mean that we would assume the presence of conscience only where the need of redemption is recognized ; on the contrary, treating here as we do of the divine causality, we start from the assumption that redemption through Christ is ordained for the whole human race, and that all mankind are in the state of needing redemption. If, instead of that state, we were to imagine a gradual development in the power of the God-consciousness, then, while even there we might find the discrepancy above referred to, yet, as progress would in that case approximate very closely to the practice of an art, the laying down of a demand such as conscience makes would be superfluous—just as art of every kind develops without any such demand ; indeed, as conscience always entails pain, it would be a piece of cruelty. In point of fact, it is with a view to redemption that men are in common held under the power of conscience, which always involves the sense of their incapacity ; and so, too, later, it is because conscience still continues to stimulate the sense of sin within them that they are held steadily to redemption. If, however, we could ever think of the will as being perfectly at one with the God-consciousness, so that nothing was striven after but what was prompted by the latter, then—granted that the still remaining defects of performance were due solely to the mental or bodily organism subserving the will—conscience in its distinctive character would cease to exist. Hence, too—to speak here only incidentally or provisionally—if we think it an adequate description of the inward state of the Redeemer to say that He had at all times a perfectly satisfied conscience, we must take the phrase as meaning a conscience that was always silent, so that He can have had a conscience only in the form of fellow-feeling, and not as something personally His own.

What we have said partly explains why we find the proper sphere of conscience in corporate life. For, granted that a single generation of men were to attain to the consummate strength and purity of will above referred to, it would of necessity influence the succeeding generation by awaking conscience in the adolescent ; and the same thing would apply to the greater differences in development within a single generation. On the other hand, a conscience manifesting itself solely in each individual by himself would be too variable to secure the certainty of its judgments and of their being attributable to the divine causality. The true conscience, however, emerging in a society as the same thing in all and for all, is law—primarily moral law, though ever finding outward expression in civil law. Thus the holiness of God is the divine causality that legislates in the corporate life of man, and since the law, especially as traced to its inward source, is always for us the absolutely holy, and the whole historical process is ordained by this divine causality, no exception can well be taken to our regarding that causality as a distinctive divine attribute, or to our designating it exclusively by the name 'holiness.'

3. The customary and popular interpretation of the term as used in the liturgical and homiletical field, however, is that the holiness of God consists in His being well-pleased with what is good and displeased with what is bad. That interpretation may be understood in two ways. Its implication is doubtless that the terms 'good' and 'bad' are predicates of the actions of free finite beings.[1] But as taken so, the interpretation can only be given a place in scientific discourse with great modifications. Pleasure and displeasure in their very antithesis always imply an element of passivity, and unless this is eliminated, the attribute of holiness will involve some disturbance of our feeling of absolute dependence, since a divine state would then be determined by human action, and thus the relation between God and man so far become one of reciprocity. Again, the attribute as so interpreted would be a purely inward and quiescent one—such indeed as our immediate religious consciousness gives us no occasion to postulate. Both points might no doubt be disposed of if, of these human states of pleasure and displeasure, we transferred to God only the active aspect, namely, their outward manifestation in the effort to effect or prevent something. But as we find this twofold aim only in redemption, and as it would be altogether a departure from the usage of the Church to say that redemption is grounded principally in the divine holiness, then, unless we are to surrender the term altogether, we must again come back to the view that the manifestation of the divine displeasure, if detached from the effectuation of the good, is simply the effectuation of this displeasure in the acting subject by means of conscience and law. If, however, the interpretation is taken to mean that God's pleasure in the good and displeasure with the bad form the basis of His creative activity and determine it,[2] it follows that the bad, in-

[1] Henke, *Lineam.*, p. 66: Deus ab omni labe et vitio purissimus, omnis pravi osor irreconciliabilis, boni rectique amantissimus.

[2] As indicated by Mosheim, *Th. Dogm.* i. p. 292: Sanctitas est immutabile propositum voluntatis Dei perfectionibus suis congruenter agendi; and

asmuch as being the object of displeasure it is opposed to the good, cannot exist, and so cannot be regarded as a thought of God ; [1] in other words, there is no reality in, nor any divine idea of, the bad. This we may lay down without misgiving, with the necessary consequence that in the same sense finite being cannot from itself generate the bad,[2] *i.e.* that the bad as an actual antithesis to the good has no existence at all, and that therefore that displeasure with the bad which is wrought in us by the divine causality is, strictly speaking, only our own displeasure in the fact that the effective power of the God-consciousness falls short of the clearness of our apprehension. Thus what is tenable in both interpretations, when taken together, corresponds exactly with what we have laid down, and we are in this way able to refer the conception of God's holiness directly to His omnipotence and omniscience, and regard these as holy.   With this, again, agree those other interpretations which ascribe to God's holiness the function of demanding from His creatures what is perfectly good ; [3] for that demand is made upon them only in virtue of the law or the moral feeling implanted in them.   Some of these interpretations bring into the conception the inward purity of God as the ground of the demand ; such of them, however, as confine themselves to that purity, or go back even to God's perfect self-love,[4] while they might be relevant in a speculative or a so-called natural theology, have no place in a systematic statement of Christian doctrine.

SECOND DOCTRINE.   GOD IS JUST

§ 84. *The justice of God is that divine causality through which in the state of universal sinfulness there is ordained a connexion between evil and actual sin.*

1. This interpretation undeniably is much narrower and more limited than that yielded by the method of other theologians, and therefore requires special vindication.   To begin with, here too

---

Ammon, *Summa Theol. Chr.*, p. 92 : Consensus voluntatis liberrimae perfectissimus cum legibus intellectus sapientissimi.

[1] Cf. § 55, 1.   [2] Cf. § 67, 2.

[3] Quenstedt, *Syst. Th.* i. p. 420 : Sanctitas Dei est summa omnisque omnino labis aut vitii expers in Deo puritas munditiem et puritatem debitam exigens a creaturis.

[4] Buddeus, *Instit.*, p. 252 : Quando Deus se ipsum amore purissimo amare concipitur ut simul ab omni imperfectione secretus censeatur amor ille vocatur sanctitas.—Something similar was said by Hilary, on Psalm cxliv. ; he would take the divine holiness as signifying especially the non-existence of all self-seeking elements in God.

use is made of the position that justice is of two kinds, namely, legislative (or distributive) and retributive. The former of these, however, cannot be brought under our definition at all. In fact, the thinkers referred to seem to have forgotten that the terms 'law' and 'justice' always imply a relation to something given. Human legislation and distribution can be just, and may be said to be just, only in view of an already given situation to which it is attached and upon which it is based. Divine legislation and distribution, however, is primordial and creative; it is that from which existent things themselves and their relationships all alike proceed, which needs nothing to attach itself to, and which in its perfection accordingly cannot be described as justice at all, but would more aptly be designated wisdom [1]—a divine attribute that we cannot deal with till a later stage. Hence the divine justice can be retributive only. But even of retributive justice our interpretation covers only the half; for the term is used to denote not only the punishment of wickedness, but also the rewarding of goodness, while our definition has nothing to say of a connexion between well-being and the power of the God-consciousness, but refers only to that between evil and sin—precisely that connexion, in fact, which we call punishment. Now we might concede the omission, and even excuse it as involved in the very process of abstraction in which we are engaged when discussing one element of our Christian consciousness, namely, the consciousness of sin, and for the time putting aside the other; but at most we should thereby be exposing an inconvenience of our method, which here forces us to split a divine attribute in two. In point of fact, however, our Christian consciousness recognizes no reward proceeding from the divine justice; anything that might possibly be called reward is for us something unmerited, and attributable to the divine grace.[2] The rewarding side of the divine justice can have no other object than Christ,[3] and Him only as one who is different from all other men. From our own religious consciousness, therefore, we can know only of God's punitive

---

[1] Something of this kind seems to have been in the minds of the theologians who apply the term 'internal' justice to the divine holiness, while to justice itself they give the name 'external' justice. On that view, it is holiness itself that is the legislative activity of God; or else, if external justice is in turn divided into legislative and retributive, the former refers to holiness as the supreme perfection that constitutes the ground of law, the latter to holiness as displeasure at what is bad.

[2] Rom. 4⁴·¹⁶; cf. Matt. 20¹⁴·¹⁵. While in 2 Tim. 4⁸ the conferring of the reward is ascribed to God as judge, yet He is there represented rather as an umpire—a symbol that is not relevant here.

[3] Phil. 2⁹⁻¹⁰, Heb. 2⁹⁻¹⁰.

justice ; His rewarding relatively to ourselves we must simply leave out of account. For while Christ Himself seems more often and more variously to portray the rewarding action of God,[1] yet the increase of a man's powers and the expansion of his field of action—two things, be it noted, corresponding exactly to each other—are no more a reward in the proper sense (*i.e.* one that might be contrasted with evil as conjoined with sin) than·the increase of wickedness could in the proper sense rank as a punishment.

2. Now, if the conception of divine justice has to do only with the connexion of evil with sin, it would surely seem natural that it can apply solely to the sphere of sin ; and in that case the postscript (p. 341) may well appear superfluous. It is clear that if we formed part of a sinless corporate life we should never have an idea of this side of the divine causality at all, for it is only through our consciousness of sin that we come to the idea of the divine justice. The term itself, however, likewise implies that as sin diminishes the connexion between sin and evil is done away in an equal degree ; and done away, moreover, quite independently of whether there is any change in the material side of man's condition ; and this abrogation, *i.e.* the forgiveness of sin, falls under the very same divine causality ;[2] for it is in this that the recompense of Christ lies. Our restriction of the connexion itself to actual sin rests partly on the fact that, as the original sinfulness still remains unchanged in the corporate life of man, the connexion with evil could not possibly be annulled were it due to that sinfulness ; partly also on the fact that the connexion exists only in so far as it has a place in our consciousness, while the consciousness of the original sinfulness exists in us only in and along with actual sin. Moreover, it is only with actual sin that we must connect not merely the existence of social evil—for it is only definite sinful tendencies of individuals which in corporate life develop into persistent causes of hindrance —but the fact that natural imperfections are regarded as evils. Hence in the measure.that sin is done away, not only does evil occur no more, but even the sin which has become actual operates no longer as a hindrance to life, but as a helpful incentive.[3] The formation and annulment of the connexion of sin and evil, accordingly, involves two things : first, that the entire constitution of the world, in so far as evil depends upon it, is related in the most

---

[1] Matt. 25^{21}.
[2] Hence in 1 John 1^9 forgiveness too is attributed to God's justice.
[3] Rom. 8^{28}.

definite way to human freedom as that in which sin is grounded ; and secondly, that in our consciousness the two are connected not merely occasionally, but essentially and universally. Since therefore the divine justice, thus regarded, is a form of the divine causality that remains self-identical throughout our whole experience, and covers the whole province of finite intelligence known to us, so that, together with the form of the divine causality treated in the foregoing paragraph, it regulates everything that upon this side of our antithesis bears upon the ethical, we seem to be perfectly justified in setting it forth as a distinct divine attribute.

To deal now with the first element in the attribute, namely, the relation of the entire world-order to human freedom ; it will be universally admitted that the relation in question is to be found only in a corporate life. Only to the extent that such a corporate life is a unity complete in itself, and most perfectly therefore in human life considered as an integral whole, does this divine causality reveal itself in such a world-order that the hindrances to life that issue from sin cannot be averted or removed by any circumstances of the external world, however favourable. On the other hand, if we regard the individual as the proper object of the divine justice, we degrade that attribute to the status of a mere counterpart of civil justice, which we so often feel to be injustice. In fact, if we are determined to see the consummate justice of God only in the punishment of every particular offence—or, let us say, in the rewarding of every particular virtue or perfect act of virtue on the part of an individual—then as, e.g., intemperance and falsehood are clearly not always punished by contempt or disease, and as, moreover, the very same evil which, falling upon one person, is interpreted as the punishment of his sin, may also fall upon others to whom without grave injustice we could not attribute the same sin, we find ourselves in a difficulty from which we can hardly escape except by asserting that the divine justice cannot fully reveal itself here below but will attain to completeness only in the life to come. That is an idea which—though attempts have been made to clear it of the charge of involving God Himself in a temporal process— only puts the difficulty further away, for we have no evidence of such disparity of suffering there as would counterbalance the disparities between doing and suffering here. If, however, we posit the idea of a corporate penalty along with that of a corporate guilt, we reach a complete vindication of the principle that all sin is reflected in evil, and that all evil can be explained by sin ; and this is precisely the connexion set forth above.

As regards the second element, namely, that in our consciousness this connexion between sin and evil is actually and even universally made—this is really the consciousness of penal desert, which in the human mind is as truly the creation of the divine justice as conscience is the creation of the divine holiness. The universality of that consciousness, however, manifests itself most unmistakably in the fact that domestic, civil, and social penalties everywhere flow from it, and indeed represent an affirmation of the connexion between sin and evil, just as the gradual mitigation of these penalties in consequence of the progressive disappearance of sin from corporate life represents the abrogation of it ; both features thus appearing as conjoined in the divine justice.

3. The classification of penalties as natural and arbitrary—a classification which indeed could not be fully demonstrated or applied in the realm of finite and temporal causation—is one which we find here no reason whatever to adopt. In point of fact natural penalties, grounded as they are in the creative and regulative divine causality, are arbitrary in the only sense in which that word can be applied to God ; while those which we might most properly call arbitrary, namely, the evils that do not correspond to the actions of those affected by them, are in reality natural ; for this non-equivalence has its source in the world-order as a whole. With a different usage of the terms, again, we apply the adjective ' natural ' to the penalties determined by the relation of the world-order to our freedom, while those that flow from human freedom itself we designate ' arbitrary.' But if we regard both kinds as divine, the distinction disappears ; for penalties inflicted by man, no less than the other group, take place in accordance with the divinely ordained spiritual development of mankind. In fact, the two kinds, as being equally of divine appointment, are essentially correlative and complementary ; for the ' arbitrary ' without the ' natural ' would lack reality, and the latter without the former would lack significance. Of penalties in the future life it is here impossible to say anything whatever ; nor can we determine how far they are to be regarded as ' arbitrary ' rather than ' natural,' or *vice versa*. The idea of these penalties is not taken directly from our self-consciousness ; and only in another section of our work shall we be able to inquire how the distinctively Christian form of this pre-Christian and widely diffused idea is related to a universal ground or reason which we

must certainly assume to exist, and, again, how far it is possible in this matter to go back to the conception of divine justice, whether interpreted as here or otherwise.

The case is different with certain other classifications sometimes applied to the subject, *e.g.* those based upon the various purposes of punishment. (1) To begin with, it seems clear that penalties cannot be ordained by God as reformative. Thus, suppose that an excess of sensuousness is counteracted only by means of sensuous feeling itself, then, *e.g.*, an appeal to fear as against pleasure cannot possibly issue in a higher energy of the God-consciousness and a greater freedom of the spirit ; indeed, all that could be effected in this way would be such a fresh distribution of sensuous motives as would, in accordance with the individual's nature, be felt as less disagreeable. It is also obvious that if the God-consciousness could be strengthened by punishment, a system of divine penalties as perfect as possible could have been made to serve instead of redemption. (2) We have, secondly, just as little right to suppose that the purpose of divine punishment is merely vengeful or retributive. Fundamentally, badness (or wrong) and evil are incommensurable ; it is only when a bad action brings evil upon another person that it is commensurable with a retributive evil. But this retributive evil is inflicted only in so far as the injured person regards his pleasure in the suffering of the injurer as removing or assuaging his own pain. Hence under the conditions of antiquity it is the custom everywhere that a penal evil can be bought off by conferring some other pleasure on the injured person. It was partly in this practice that the criminal jurisdiction of the State took its rise, replacing the vendetta by milder measures. Divine penalties of such a type, however, could be believed in only at a very primitive stage of development —a stage at which the Deity is still thought of as susceptible to irritation, and as not above feeling an injury or having other passive states ; and what has all along been preached, sometimes with apparent profundity, regarding the mysterious nature of the divine wrath and the fundamental necessity of divine retribution, cannot be made clear to the mind. And we can leave the matter there all the more confidently because (3) the consciousness of deserving punishment, as superinduced in us by divine justice, is fully explained by the remaining purpose of punishment, namely, to prevent or to deter. Punishment is, in fact, that which must of necessity be interposed wherever and in so far as the power of the God-consciousness is as yet inactive in the sinner, its object being to prevent his dominant sensuous tendencies from meanwhile attaining complete mastery through mere unchecked habit. Further, what is said, with reference to the Mosaic legislation, as to the people's being kept solidly together under the law applies generally to all criminal jurisdiction among all peoples, and equally to the natural penalties set forth also in the Mosaic legislation. Hence it is only relatively to the dispensation of redemption, and in so far as redemption has still to become operative, that the divine justice can be fully understood.

4. From what has just been said we see, on the one hand, how clearly the divine holiness and the divine justice are connected, and, on the other, how necessary it is to keep them separate. They are connected in the most intimate way as expressions of the divine causality as bearing upon sin in its relation to redemption. On the very same principle, according to which we say of sin that in the sense in which it cannot have its cause in God it cannot exist at all, we say of evil that if it cannot be grounded in God, *i.e.* if it be a real negation of the original perfection of the world for man, it likewise cannot exist at all. Similarly, just as with regard to sin, so too with regard to evil, we assert that so far as it is real, it must have its source in the divine causality. And, again, just as the consciousness of sin as necessarily entailing penalty—a consciousness due to the divine justice—is possible only on the assumption that conscience is due to the divine holiness, so, without that consciousness of penal liability, conscience would have no means of gaining a secure hold in any human soul still under the dominion of the flesh, and thus no means of generating there a consciousness of the need of redemption. But for the same reason it is also necessary that the distinction of the two concepts should be maintained here where, though we are dealing with elements of the religious consciousness which are provisionally abstracted from redemption, we must nevertheless premise the fact of redemption as that on which everything turns. For suppose matters brought to the point that both the natural imperfections and the sins of the world were no longer evils to us, but merely incentives ; that we therefore felt nothing at all to be evil in relation to ourselves, and that accordingly the justice of God was not immediately present even in our own purely personal religious experience ; yet we should still require conscience, and should therefore constantly revive within us the consciousness of God's holiness. Similarly, even while we still need both, we keep them rigorously apart. For our displeasure with what is bad, *i.e.* the reflection in us of God's holiness, is absolutely pure and satisfy-

ing only when not affected by anticipations of punishment ; and the consciousness of penal desert is so firmly rooted in our corporate sense that we always acquiesce in punishment, even although our personal moral feeling regarding any particular occasion of it has been entirely corrected and purified, and our will has completely escaped from the bondage it implies.   Precisely on this account, therefore, that form of the God-consciousness (*i.e.* the concept of divine justice) is no more transient in us than the form represented by the conception of the divine holiness, for it permanently conserves the same truth for our corporate sense, to which, in fact, it is in its origin specially related.   Were it, however, to be said that the two conceptions, having to do merely with the natural imperfection of man, would apart from that sphere be nothing at all in God, and even within that sphere would cease to be of valid application as soon as the said imperfection was finally done away, and that accordingly they are not divine attributes in the same sense as those dealt with in the first part of our system—we should reply as follows.   First of all, the same would hold good of the divine attributes which are subsequently to be developed from the second aspect of the antithesis, for to these also it is essential that they refer back to the first aspect ; and, in fact, the same objection might be made to all the so-called moral attributes of God so far as they have any reference to the antithesis at all.   But we have never attached great importance to these mere general phrases ; so I shall only call attention to these special considerations bearing on the conceptions of the two attributes before us.   First, as regards God's holiness : apart from its implication of that in virtue of which sin does not exist for God, and from the fact that it forms so far a general characteristic of God's consciousness of His works, and so of His omnipresence and omniscience, holiness is an essential element in our consciousness of God, for we can be cognizant of the absolute power of the God-consciousness only as we are cognizant of the state of sin as removed by redemption.   The same is true also of the divine justice, since the Redeemer's merit is only the other side of sin's desert of punishment, and just as the former has always been present in the latter as a premonition of it, so the latter will always be present in the former as recollection.   And no less is the relation of God's government of the world to our freedom one with its relation to redemption, while this whole interrelated system of the spiritual and the sensuous is the domain of what is accordingly the equally omnipresent and eternal justice of God.

§ 85. *To attribute mercy to God is more appropriate to the language of preaching and poetry than to that of dogmatic theology.*

1. For one thing, preaching and poetry can afford to be less precise in their use of anthropopathic terms. And mercy is certainly such a term in a pre-eminent degree, since in the human sphere we apply it exclusively to a state of feeling specially evoked by the sufferings of others and finding outlet in acts of relief. Such helpful ministration is, no doubt, an ethical activity, but here it is conditioned by a sensuous sympathy, namely, the pain produced in us by hampered conditions in the lives of others ; and, in fact, if the help tendered does not spring from such a feeling we do not call it mercy. In this sense mercy is the counterpart of ' kindness,' *i.e.* the helpfulness in which the correlative sensuous sympathy, namely, pleasure in some furtherance of life in the case of others, plays a part ; and here, too, help given without such feeling behind it would not be called kindness. Thus neither of these qualities, as so understood, can be applied to God without our bringing Him under the antithesis of the agreeable and the disagreeable. And even if we were to overlook this and use the two terms solely of the respective acts of helpfulness, yet it would be out of keeping with the character of teleological (ethical) religions were we to admit, in a rigorously formulated system of doctrine, a divine causality bent upon a sensuous furtherance of life simply as such. Nor can the difficulty of finding a place for the conception of mercy in God be due to our looking for it at this particular stage of our inquiry. For, as mercy obviously presupposes evil and the consciousness of evil, the discussion of it could not well come before that of evil ; while, again, as mercy always implies some degree of separateness between the two parties involved—for within a closer group, as between father and children, we do not speak of mercy—the objects of God's mercy cannot be those who are already enjoying, and in so far as they are enjoying, their part in redemption.

2. Again, from a somewhat different point of view, the merciful God is for the most part contrasted with the jealous God. Now, as wrath and jealousy have obviously to do with offence and sin, mercy would in such case be the repression of jealousy by compassion. If, accordingly, we once more set aside the fact that this involves an emotional state, and think only of the withholding of punishment,

we must nevertheless here too set aside the idea that the punishment which is related to redemption is revoked merely on the ground of pain or defect experienced by some other. Thus, these eliminations having been made, all that remains is God's readiness to remit the punishment altogether. Yet, even so, we cannot allow mercy to rank as a distinct attribute, since we have ascribed that remission as well as the enactment of the penalty to the divine justice. Should this procedure be regarded as wrong, however, and mercy in the sense indicated be taken after all as a distinct attribute, then mercy and justice would each delimit the other. Where justice ceased, mercy would begin, and *vice versa*—a relation that cannot subsist between divine attributes. It is true that the classical passage for the use of the word in the New Testament [1] best agrees with that interpretation, for kindness to the unthankful is the suppression of jealousy by compassion. But the point of Christ's saying is the demand made upon the hearers, and in speaking of self-discipline it was natural that the analogous element in God to which He directed their minds should there be referred to by the same term.

[1] Lk. 6[35f].

SECOND ASPECT OF THE ANTITHESIS:
EXPLICATION OF THE CONSCIOUSNESS OF GRACE

INTRODUCTION

§ 86. *The more distinctly conscious we become that the misery involved in our natural state cannot be removed either by the recognition that sin is inevitable, or by the assumption that it is decreasing of itself, the higher becomes the value we place upon Redemption.*

1. Unmistakable evidences of the consciousness of this insufficiency are to be found in almost all other religions, from the lowest to the highest. They all prescribe either sacrifices and purifications, or mortifications and penances, or both. Manifestly these are all devices for getting rid temporarily of the misery caused by sin, in the different forms which it assumes in different religions. By the degree in which this is actually effected, the more believing man is distinguished from the less believing. For, with the exception of those sacrifices which have no relation at all to evil, all sacrifices and purifications—unless we are to suppose that they come simply from an utterly confused superstition—are based upon the conviction that both the admissions referred to in the proposition need to be accompanied by an acknowledgment in the form of an act, it may be only a symbolical act, in order to get rid of the misery. But in a teleological religion this is not permissible. Such a religion sets down as a fact the ineffectiveness of the God-consciousness itself, and so finds here only a contradiction from which no effect can proceed; all that can be done is to admit the state of sin.[1] Mortifications and arbitrary exercises are less symbolical, and have in a greater degree a real content; their purpose everywhere doubtless is to exhibit power over the flesh by means of actions the demand for which does not arise of itself in the ordinary course of life; to supplement, that is, in some way the imperfect manifestation of this power in the demands which life makes of itself. This would be superfluous if the inevitableness of sin itself sufficiently gave peace of mind. Moreover, the wildest superstition

[1] That this is the sense of Heb. 10^{1-3} is not open to doubt.

355

reveals itself wherever these exercises are not so treated as to correspond to the given situation. But since in the life of any society demands are evolved every moment which it is our duty to fulfil, these arbitrary supplementary activities, by taking up time, inevitably prevent the full performance of duty. Thus through the very activities which are supposed to get rid of the misery, new misery is created.

But, even quite apart from the question whether performances of both kinds are not usually designed rather to avert punishment than to remove guilt, their futility as means to peace of mind is obvious. Hence every unsatisfied longing which still remains in spite of them is the expression of an inclination towards Christianity; it indicates the likelihood that a Redeemer, in whom is offered not the shadow but the reality, will be accepted.

2. Let us now consider the religious consciousness of the Christian. It is composed of the consciousness of sin which we have expounded above, and the consciousness of grace which we have still to expound but which we assume to be familiar. In it, too, we find both elements. First, the recognition that sin is inevitable for us, in so far at least as that it is not in our power at any particular moment to be sinless. But no less, the assumption that it is growing less, since this is essentially involved in the consciousness that the strength of our God-consciousness is growing greater. But in spite of this connexion these two elements belong not to the consciousness of grace, or that by which the misery is taken away, but on the contrary to the consciousness of sin, or to the misery itself. For to be conscious that the disappearance of sin is a thing of the future is the same thing as to have it still actually present; and, more completely still, the consciousness of its inevitableness is also that of its power over us. Both therefore indicate our need of redemption, and so cannot carry in themselves the removal of the misery—that would require that it should be established and provable in some special way that the consciousness of sin can be taken away by means of itself.

Let us suppose, on the other hand, that the misery has been removed from some other side; and add, further, that even the consciousness that sin must inevitably remain while it is gradually disappearing does not hinder the removal of the misery: just on that account the worth of the removal is the greater. But this can be rightly recognized only if we consider both elements in the natural condition of man as he shares in the corporate life of sin.

In this condition the opinion that sin, because inevitable, does not involve guilt or deserve punishment cannot be derived from the God-consciousness ; rather would this have first to be destroyed, that is, the consciousness that God is holy and righteous would have to be rooted out—which would be a new guilt. Just as little can we deduce the absence of guilt and of liability to punishment by asserting that the future already exists in the present, the disappearance of sin in its continuance. For if we are to go beyond the present content of our self-consciousness, we are just as much entitled, indeed we are equally constrained, to say that our present consciousness will be continued in our future consciousness, and with it the misery. So we are bound to maintain that all such statements as that God forgives sin because it is inevitable, if only it is decreasing, can never establish that removal of the misery of which they would persuade us. They always come back to a forgiveness of sin, arbitrarily, by ourselves ; and, at best, they are a recourse to the divine compassion,[1] but without first positing redemption, and so also without reconciling compassion with righteousness. For even if we admit that in the natural state there does occur an increase in the strength of the God-consciousness, even if it is only in so far as it co-operates in the effort after civil righteousness :[2] it must result from this that the more sin decreases the sharper becomes the feeling for right and wrong. Consequently no increasing satisfaction arises—which is the only thing which could legitimately offer any guarantee for the removal of the misery. And here it is to be observed that those who think to remove the misery in this way, without redemption, are least in agreement on the question whether human life on the whole is developing towards a greater perfection (so that brutality, where it has once been overcome, does not return), or whether the race is destined, partially, by whatever revolutions it may be, to be continually thrown back, to begin its career all over again.

3. If, nevertheless, such presentations of the forgiveness of sins secure acceptance as Christian, what is specifically Christian must have been long since, and in many quarters, displaced, before conceptions so little Christian could creep in ; or it must have been supposed that the effectiveness of redemption begins only after the misery has already been removed. But this is the less arguable inasmuch as peace of mind presupposes a decrease of sin, and consequently an increase of activity pleasing to God. So that to exhibit

----

[1] Cf. § 85, 2.　　　　　　　　　　[2] Cf. § 70, 2 and 3.

this, and to evoke it, would then be no part of the Redeemer's work. Yet it is possible, on the other hand, that even a truly Christian piety may have come to regard this matter in so unchristian an aspect only because it wished to oppose false conceptions of the way in which the misery is removed by redemption, by setting forth another explanation, which at least makes room for the fact that the activity of the God-consciousness, out of which the decrease of sin arises, is determined by the Redeemer. Coming nearest to this false peace, and therefore attributing the lowest imaginable value to redemption, is the view that an increasing activity of the God-consciousness is possible without any special divine help, developing simply out of the natural state of man ; but that, in spite of the inevitableness of sin, sinners would have no right to be at peace regarding the sin still remaining without a special divine assurance about it—so that in essence the Redeemer is represented only as the herald of this divine promise. It does not need to be stated how little historical justification there is for this view in the Christian Church ; it need only be remarked how little reason can be advanced for the demand that we should believe in one who does no more than announce forgiveness, and how difficult it is to understand why such an assurance should have been given only after so long a time and in such a way. From this lowest value on, the felt content of redemption grows the greater, the greater the share attributed to the Redeemer in the cessation of the misery as well as in the rise of what approximates state of blessedness.

§ 87. *We are conscious of all approximations to the state of blessedness which occur in the Christian life as being grounded in a new divinely-effected corporate life, which works in opposition to the corporate life of sin and the misery which develops in it.*

1. This proposition is not to be regarded as a complete statement of specifically Christian piety, since in it no mention is made of the fact that every approximation to the state of blessedness essentially includes a relation to Christ. But it does undeniably express the content of the consciousness of divine grace, as it stands in antithesis to the consciousness of sin. For approximation to the condition of blessedness is the real opposite of the misery, and this approximation is accepted as divine grace in the same sense and degree in which the corporate life in which such elements of experience become ours is posited as due to divine agency.

Consequently all further exposition of what is specifically Christian can easily be attached to this proposition. The relation between approximation to blessedness and removal of misery may, it is true, be presented in a twofold way. First, it may be held that not the slightest approximation to blessedness can occur so long as there is even the slightest misery present, which is as much as to say, so long as sin, and with it evil (or *vice versa*), still occurs in the sphere of human life. This is the view of those who choose to regard the world, even under the influence of redemption, as nothing but a vale of woe ; fortunately they never work out their view consistently. This view, according to which (if we take it strictly) all the effects of redemption can be developed only beyond this present life, will not be advocated here, as is at once clear from the wording of the proposition, in which the beginning of blessedness is attributed to the new corporate life simply in virtue of its opposition to the corporate life of sin—the latter still persisting in the sphere of its activity. But further, that conception does not express the truth of the Christian consciousness as it has been witnessed to from the beginning.[1] Rather, there is always in the God-consciousness, whatever its strength, a blessedness corresponding to that strength ; and even in its beginnings this blessedness removes the misery, though, of course, this can arise again with sin, but only to be again removed.[2] So that we can completely equate the two aspects, and say that the same condition is the removal of misery (when we regard man in his relation to the corporate life of sin), and the beginning of blessedness (so far as he belongs to the new corporate life).

2. In indicating only in a quite general way the place of these approximations in the Christian life we wish to begin with to forestall all one-sided conceptions, which suggest that such approximations can only occur in the form of particular activities or states, and that they are confined, say, to the moments of devotional meditation or ascetic practices. On the contrary, there is an element of blessedness in moments of meditation only when they pass over into thought or act, and in ascetic practices only in so far as they are not properly, or at least not exclusively, ascetic, but are in some way connected with our ordinary vocational activity. The element of blessedness exists just as much in moments of activity proper and of thought proper, though in the former only in so far as they do not proceed from such motives as have their roots altogether

---

[1] John 1¹⁶, 1 John 3¹⁴, ²¹, Phil. 4⁴.   [2] Cf. § 74, 1.

in the world-consciousness or in such as satisfy mere civil righteousness ; and similarly, it is not present in the latter in so far as they
merely develop the world-consciousness : but in both only in so far
as they have their ground in the God-consciousness, newly awakened
to life.   Without this the religious man cannot experience a growing
blessedness.

3. If now anyone maintains that our proposition, taken by itself,
really applies equally well to all forms of faith, provided only they
involve a fellowship, this is true only in so far as thereby there is
laid upon them the duty of proving that their corporate life is due
to divine agency.   But this by no means assumes that there is a
difference between the growing blessedness which then began to develop in the Christian fellowship and that which proceeded directly
from Christ Himself.   We shall come immediately to the point that
to regard our corporate life as divinely-created, and to derive it
from Christ as a divinely-given One, are the same thing ; just so, at
that time, to believe that Jesus was the Christ, and to believe that
the Kingdom of God (that is, the new corporate life which was to be
created by God) had come, were the same thing.   Consequently, all
developing blessedness had its ground in this corporate life.   Just as
little can one regard it as an approximation to the Roman Catholic
point of view, that this change in the personal state should be
ascribed directly to the common or corporate life.   We cannot as yet
bring out here its real antagonism to the Roman Catholic view ;
that must wait until we come to describe more closely, on the one
hand, the process in detail ; on the other, the nature of the community.   And so the proposition as such is one which applies equally
to the most various conceptions of Christianity.   Two things only
it excludes.   First, the idea that one can share in the redemption
and be made blessed through Christ outside the corporate life which
He instituted, as if a Christian could dispense with the latter and
be with Christ, as it were, alone.   This separatism disregards the
fact that what owes its origin to divine agency can nevertheless
be received only as it appears in history, and also can continue to
function only as a historical entity.   We can therefore only describe
it as fanatical ; it can, in self-consistency, only arise sporadically,
and so must also continually disappear again.   It destroys the
essence of Christianity by postulating an activity of Christ which is
not mediated in time and space ; and at the same time it so isolates
itself that what has been achieved in it can have no continuing
influence.   The second thing excluded is the supposition that,

without the introduction of any new factor, and within the corporate life of sin itself, the better individuals could attain to such an approximation to blessedness as would remove the misery. If this idea be taken strictly, then either another purpose must be assumed for the appearance of Christ, quite apart from the blessedness of man (in which case this would, at any rate, not be a religious purpose) ; or it would have no specific purpose at all (in which case it would be wrong to name anything after Christ). From our standpoint, the only verdict of the Christian consciousness on this supposition must be that it is based upon an inadequate consciousness of sin. For if sin be posited as corporate act and corporate guilt, then, not only is every activity of the individual involved in the production and renewal of sin, however strong an opposition to individual sins it may include, but also every combination even of the relatively best individuals remains only an organization within the corporate life of sin itself. On the other hand, if the supposition is not to be taken strictly, then it may be Christian in the measure in which it regards Christ as a new factor in the situation, and the corporate life as one formed out of the corporate life of sin.

§ 88. *In this corporate life which goes back to the influence of Jesus, redemption is effected by Him through the communication of His sinless perfection.*

1. At the present time it cannot be maintained that this way of understanding redemption is the only one which is current in the Protestant Church. And we by no means wish to refuse to recognize as Protestant Christians those who do not accept the idea of such a communication, provided only that they trace every approximation to blessedness back to Christ, and seek to find it in a fellowship which makes it a principle that, for redemption, nothing need be sought beyond His influence, and also that nothing in that influence is to be neglected. We, however, hold to this conception as the original one, taken over from the primitive Church into our Church, and at the same time as that which most definitely excludes all sneaking complacence, and alone consorts with the stricter interpretation of the corporate life of sinfulness, as may be clearly seen from what immediately precedes. The two things hang together in the closest way. The less specific and absolute perfection we ascribe to the Founder of the new corporate life, while at the same time expecting nothing new that goes beyond Him, the easier must it seem to us to overcome what demanded of Him no greater equipment.

And the less importance we attach to what proceeds from the natural state of man, the less occasion there is to postulate anything specifically different in Him who inaugurates the better state. For the development of the one view—and this is all that is required of a system of doctrine, for that the view should become more generally accepted can be only the result of its presentation—does not require that the other should be refuted, but only that the relation which exists between them should be clearly set forth again at its most significant points. Just as little can there be any question here of proofs in the proper sense. Not, of course, because Protestant theology, as an undertaking within the Protestant Church, itself presupposes the Protestant faith, but because no single modification of it is capable of proof ; it is simply a statement with regard to the stronger or weaker impression which one fact makes in comparison with another. Examples of such differences occur everywhere in the field of history, and always so that it is possible for everyone to be firmly convinced that his impression is the right one, while yet no one can prove its rightness.

2. We set aside, then, all thought of proof. Even of proof from Scripture—not only because of the ambiguity of most of its statements, but because in that way we could prove only the assertion that this is the original form of the Christian faith. Even so, what we must not omit here remains difficult enough ; and that is, to unfold the way in which this faith originated, along with its content. That is, we must show, without recourse to compulsion by means of miracle or prophecy (which is a thing alien to faith), how the conviction could arise, both originally and now, that Jesus possessed a sinless perfection, and that there is a communication of this perfection in the fellowship founded by Him. For it is obvious that in the certainty regarding these two points (and certainty about the one involves a related and parallel certainty about the other), there is removal of the misery and growing blessedness. First, then, our proposition is by no means to be understood as asserting that at a time when the consciousness of sin was powerfully aroused, both as a personal and as a corporate consciousness, in many minds, it was only necessary that an exceptional moral excellence should be adequately manifested in a public life, for the sinless perfection longed for as the only possible help to be attributed to such an individual—a view which might be expressed by saying that it was faith that made Jesus the Redeemer. For in such faith the arbitrary decision of the believer would have become

more marked on every transference of it, since it would not have been supported by the original impression made by His person ; and consequently the certainty would have become less. Gradually the thought would more and more have gained ground that another might come, to whom that conception might be transferred with better right. So that in this way there could only arise a decreasing faith in Jesus, and thus an increasing unbelief. And the only remedy for this would be, that the immediate impression made by the community should be such that sinless perfection could be claimed for it, and then, for its sake, for its founder also. It would not be enough even, that the pure and perfect potency of the God-consciousness should have been actually present in Jesus, but faith in it nevertheless only the work of that longing, eager for satisfaction. For even so He would have been made Redeemer by believers.[1] On the contrary, our proposition depends upon the assumption that the very recognition of that perfection was its own work, so that it is just as possible that in some persons the full consciousness of sin and the longing which goes with it are first aroused by means of that recognition,[2] as that in others they are already present. It is only in this way, too, that we can regard the founding of the new corporate life as something more than a special act, without which that exceptional peculiarity could still have existed in Jesus. Rather, just as the latter could have been manifested only in act, so the former is its essential work.

If, however, the faith of the later generations, and consequently of our own, is to be the same as the original one and not a different faith—and in the latter case, not only would the unity of the Christian Church be imperilled, but also all references to the original testimonies of the faith—then it must still be possible to have the same experiences ; and the recognition of the sinless perfection in Jesus Christ, definitely constraining us to the new corporate life, must in the same way be still His work. But there is given to us, instead of His personal influence, only that of His fellowship, in so far as even the picture of Him which is found in the Bible also originated in the community and is perpetuated in it. Our proposition, therefore, depends upon the assumption that this influence of the fellowship in producing a like faith is none other than the influence of the personal perfection of Jesus Himself.[3]

3. It is no less difficult to expound the second part of our

---

[1] Contrary to the claim of Christ, John 15[16].
[2] Cf. § 14, 2.   [3] Cf. § 14, 1.

proposition, namely, that in the corporate life founded by Christ there is a communication of His sinless perfection ; while we attribute this to no single individual in the fellowship except Christ. For, since those who companied with Christ are no longer with us, and we cannot concede to any group of individuals, however well they may have been selected to complement each other, the right to lay down dogmas, that is, rules of faith or life, with any claim whatsoever to infallibility or enduring validity ; since, on the contrary, our historical interpretation is based upon the view that the influence of distinguished individuals upon the mass is to be thought of as declining : where and of what sort are we to suppose this communication to be ? If we regard the mass as a whole, it manifestly shares so largely in the general sinfulness, and this at certain times so saliently and in such specially heightened measure, that it is doubtful whether there is less of this sinfulness at any one point rather than another, and whether it might not therefore have been better for the shaping of human affairs if Christianity had not become such a widely spread historical force. Against these objections, brought forward with much plausibility by its opponents, faith alone can prevail ; it must consequently assume that all this represents only the non-existence of the new corporate life, and so the existence of the sinful life in which the new really exists but only in hidden fashion. Thus our proposition depends upon the assumption that in the Christian fellowship, outwardly so constituted, there is still that communication of the absolutely potent God-consciousness in Christ as a thing which is inward, and yet. since faith can rest upon nothing except an impression received, capable of being experienced. This experience is made up of two elements, one of which belongs to the personal consciousness, the other to the common consciousness. The former is that the individual even to-day receives from the picture of Christ, which exists in the community as at once a corporate act and a corporate possession, the impression of the sinless perfection of Jesus, which becomes for him at the same time the perfect consciousness of sin and the removal of the misery. And this is already in itself a communication of that perfection. The second element is that in all those aberrations of the Christian Church, however much they may resemble the sinful corporate life, there is still a tendency issuing from that perfection ; a tendency which in every manifestation—nay, constantly even in the setting up of the concepts of truth and goodness —falls more or less a prey to non-existence, but which in its deepest inwardness, or as an impulse, corresponds to its origin, and consequently, in spite of all reactions, will also increasingly make itself manifest.   And this impulse given by His historical life, an impulse which, regarded from within, is perfectly pure, is, just like the first element, a true and effective communication of the perfection of Christ.

4. In the corporate life of sinfulness sin propagates itself naturally, so that an unhindered potency of the God-consciousness in Jesus cannot be understood simply as a product of that life.   This God-consciousness, manifesting itself in this potency, can have come into existence only outside the sinful corporate life.   And since the whole human race is included in this sinful corporate life, we must believe that this God-consciousness had a supernatural origin, though only in the sense which has been postulated above.[1] So, too, in relation to the Redeemer Himself, the new corporate life is no miracle, but simply the supernatural becoming natural, since every exceptional force attracts mass to itself and holds it fast. But in relation to the corporate life of sinfulness, which hitherto had included everything and dominated every formation, the new is something that has come into being supernaturally.   The same is true of the passage of every individual from the old corporate life into the new.   In relation to the new creation itself such a passage is not supernatural ; such effects follow as of course from its nature. But it is something which has come about supernaturally, so far as its relation to the earlier life of this individual is concerned.

To sum up : in this whole matter we posit, on the one side, an initial divine activity which is supernatural, but at the same time a vital human receptivity in virtue of which alone that supernatural can become a natural fact of history.   This is the link which connects the corporate life before the appearance of the Redeemer with that which exists in the fellowship with the Redeemer, so as adequately to bring out the identity of human nature in both.   And so, in this whole context, the appearance of the Redeemer in the midst of this natural development is no longer a supernatural emergence of a new stage of development, but simply one conditioned by that which precedes—though certainly its connexion with the former is to be found only in the unity of the divine thought.

§ 89. *In the sense in which it can be said that sin is not ordained by God and does not exist for Him,*[2] *the term Redemption would*

---

[1] Cf. § 13, 1.   [2] Cf. § 81.

*not be suitable for this new communication of a powerful
God-consciousness. And so from that point of view the
appearance of Christ and the institution of this new corporate
life would have to be regarded as the completion, only now
accomplished, of the creation of human nature.*

1. It requires no further explanation, that the conception of
redemption is related in the closest way to the consciousness of
sin, and that when it is used as an expression for the complete work
of Christ, there is included along with the removal of the misery,
which alone is properly described as redemption, a growing blessedness as well. For that reason alone the expression is inadequate,
and an unsuitable one in this respect, that a word is used for the
whole (the imparting of blessedness) which properly applies only
to the beginning of it. But there is no objection to its use if this is
understood. For it is certain that in our Christian consciousness
the divine grace as such is always thought of in connexion with
sin ; while sin itself is always conceived of as including our inability to do what our God-consciousness requires us to strive after.
So nothing in the divine grace is overlooked if it is described as the
removal of sin, in so far as sin is that inability. But if the expression
is to be used not only for the effect, but also for the purpose, of the
appearance of Christ, in so far as that appearance is ordained of
God, then, since we cannot separate it from its connexion with sin
and the consciousness of sin, this is only possible in so far as we can
regard the consciousness of sin as ordained of God. How far this
is possible has already [1] been explained, but it now becomes clearer
—God has ordained that the earlier insuperable impotence of the
God-consciousness shall become for us, as our own act, the consciousness of sin, in order to intensify that longing without which
even the endowment possessed by Jesus would have met with no
living faculty for the reception of what He communicates. But,
on the other hand, that God is not the creator of sin is, not only
strictly true, but also the definite teaching of the Church. The
ground for this assertion is best expressed in the formula that evil
cannot be a creative thought of God. It follows that the term redemption is not so suitable to describe the divine decree as it is to
describe the effect of the decree, for the Almighty cannot ordain one
thing for the sake of another which He has not ordained. From this
standpoint, which is also that of the Church, no better expression

[1] Cf. § 80.

apparently can be found for the divine decree than a Biblical one
which at the same time indicates the effect as a whole. As everything which has been brought into human life through Christ is presented as a new creation,[1] so Christ Himself is the Second Adam, the
beginner and originator of this more perfect human life, or the completion of the creation of man. This at the same time indicates
in the most definite way that it was impossible to attain to this
higher life out of the natural order which had its beginning in Adam.

2. That this formula is exactly equivalent in meaning to the
first, and attributes to Jesus, as the One in whom the human creation
is perfected, the same peculiar dignity and character as does the
other when it is fully understood, need not be set forth at length.
For this Second Adam is altogether like all those who are descended
from the first, only that from the outset He has an absolutely potent
God-consciousness. With this He enters the existing historical
order of human nature, in virtue of a creative divine causality. It
follows that, according to the law of this order, His higher perfection must work in a stimulating and communicative way upon the
nature which is like His own, in the first place to bring to perfection
the consciousness of sinfulness by contrast with itself, and then
also to remove the misery, by assimilation to itself. Now this
Second Adam, though He does not belong to the former order, but
in relation to it has come into being supernaturally, is yet placed
in the historical order, and that too as an individual man. So in
His whole activity He stands under the law of historical development, and that activity is brought to perfection through gradual
expansion, from the point at which He appears, over the whole.

That in this way the creation of man is, as it were, divided into
two stages has analogies enough in history,[2] and also it has always
been asserted of the material creation whenever the distinction has
been made between a first and a second creation. At the same
time this formula serves as a corrective to the confusions which arise
only too easily from improper use of the others. How easily the
view recurs which was already attacked by Paul,[3] that sin is wholesome, if it is true that it was on account of sin that Christ had to be
sent, and so the imparting of blessedness depends upon sin ! Moreover, when considered more closely, this formula is a more precise
and direct expression of our Christian self-consciousness than the
first. For to begin with, certainly the most exact term for the

[1] 2 Cor. 5[17].   [2] Here, too, belongs what has been said above, § 13, 1.
[3] Rom. 6[1].

condition outside fellowship with Christ is consciousness of sin and of need of redemption, inasmuch as and so far as this too is ordained by God.   But in fellowship with Christ everything which belongs to a sinfulness no longer productive, is also, just for that reason, no longer in the same sense a consciousness of sin, because it is no longer a being fleshly-minded, but simply an incapacity for what has only just come to be ; and the consciousness of the Redeemer is the consciousness of One who makes us strong.[1]

3. But in the case of this expression also the demand certainly cannot be set aside that here again the conception of creation must be referred back to that of preservation.   Not only is the man Jesus called the Second Adam, which can only mean the second Created One, but also all those born again are called the new creation, and thus that is represented as a creation which, quite correctly, we describe as originally a preservation, that is, as a preservation of the ever-prevailing power of Christ for redemption and blessing : but conversely, the appearance of Christ Himself is to be regarded as a preservation, that is, as a preservation of the receptivity, implanted in human nature from the beginning and perpetually developing further, which enables it to take into itself such an absolute potency of the God-consciousness.   For although at the first creation of the human race only the imperfect state of human nature was manifested, yet eternally the appearance of the Redeemer was already involved in that.   So that, in whatever sense its fulfilment has to be conceived, the unity of the divine decree comes out with equal clearness whether we say that God ordained sin for men relatively to redemption, or that He put human nature under the law of earthly existence in the sense that, just as the sensuous self-consciousness developed first in each individual, while the God-consciousness came only later, and up to a point gradually took possession of the sensuous self-consciousness and subjugated it, so too the God-consciousness in the race to begin with was inadequate and impotent, and only later broke forth in perfection in Christ, from whom it continually extends its authority, and proves its power to bring peace and blessedness to men.

Further, from this standpoint the relation of Christ to those who lived before His appearance, or who are separated by distance from the corporate life inspired by Him—always an important question for Christian thought—becomes clearer.   If the first stage in creation is ordained by God only in view of the second, obviously the

----

[1] Phil. 4[13].

same must be true of everything that forms part of the same natural
order with it.   Accordingly, in the ordaining view of God everything which belongs to the first period of the world must have a
share in the relation to the Redeemer.   At the same time it appears
the more natural that this otherwise hidden relation should become
specially evident at particular points, which is just the assumption
that prompts a search for types and prophecies.

§ 90. *The propositions which work out, according to the three points
of view given in § 30, the content of the consciousness of grace
here presented, also complete the system of Christian doctrine
within the limits here prescribed for it.*

1. In elaborating, in what follows, this content, we shall hold to
these three forms.   In itself, there is no objection to the first and
original one, and it is obvious that with a method of procedure
which is in any degree correct nothing of any significance in Christian
doctrine can escape our notice.   But it is difficult to see how we
are to distinguish between the first, or the direct description of the
gracious state of the redeemed, and the second, or the description
of what has come into the world through redemption.   For this
last is simply the corporate life founded by Christ and its relation
to that part of the world of men which finds itself excluded therefrom.   The gracious state of the redeemed, again, is simply their
activity just in this corporate life and the way in which they are
affected by the opposition which still exists to it ; so that the two
spheres seem to be exactly the same.   Connected with this is the
fact that here it is less clear that the description of the state must
come first.   For, on the one hand, it is only out of this new corporate
life that the communication of the divine grace comes to each individual, and so it seems necessary that this should be recognized
first.   Yet, on the other hand, the corporate life is made up of the
redeemed as such, and it seems impossible to understand if we have
not first considered the peculiar quality of these.   None the less
both difficulties disappear at once when we come to look into the
matter more closely.   It is true that the corporate life consists
solely of redeemed individuals, but it has its significance for the
world only through its organization.   Considered as an organization it belongs to the second form of presentation.   The state of the
individuals as such, on the other hand, as contrasted with their
state in the corporate life of sinfulness, is to be worked out rather
from the first standpoint.   And if in doing so we must in a certain

sense presuppose acquaintance with the corporate life, yet it is not a dogmatic knowledge of it. Nor indeed can it be maintained that such acquaintance is really presupposed, since that state of grace was called into being, along with the corporate life, or indeed before it, by the first proclamation of the Gospel. Thus both methods of presentation are possible, and can be kept apart, even though mutual relations between them are inevitable.

2. Finally, as regards the divine attributes which are to be dealt with in the last section, it would be a very strong objection to the propriety of our whole disposition of the subject if, after we had completed the argument, there still remained divine attributes which represent a factor in our Christian self-consciousness, yet can be definitely distinguished from those with which we have been dealing. So for the present we refuse to admit this, and on the contrary regard it as a good sign that we have reduced the large number of indefinite terms denoting attributes to a smaller number of clear formulæ, and also have definitely excluded all that is merely speculative. The event must show whether we have really done this. But here we have not only to supply what before was lacking, but also, as we have remarked above,[1] to give their full content (since we are only now for the first time moving in the sphere of the potent God-consciousness) to all those manifestations of the feeling of absolute dependence which could only be indefinitely described in the first part. For in Christianity it is only relatively to the Kingdom of God that we are conscious of the divine omnipotence and eternity, as well as of the attributes which depend upon them. It is another question whether in fact the whole doctrine of God which answers to the Christian faith can be dealt with simply by an enumeration of the divine attributes, and whether we ought not rather in addition to set forth the significance of the divine decrees. But this question arises only if we take cognizance of other treatments of Christian doctrine. For a proposition indicative of a divine decree is not as such an expression of the immediate self-consciousness. But if we can bring rightly and completely into consciousness what has come into the world through redemption, then we shall thereby have given the content of the divine decrees also.

[1] § 29, 1 and p. 272.

FIRST SECTION

The State of the Christian as conscious of the Divine Grace

§ 91. *We have fellowship with God* [1] *only in a living fellowship with the Redeemer, such that in it His absolutely sinless perfection and blessedness represent a free spontaneous activity, while the recipient's need of redemption represents a free assimilative receptivity.*

1. This is the basic consciousness that each Christian has of his own state of grace, even where the most dissimilar views of Christianity prevail. The consciousness of one who in no degree relates the potency of the God-consciousness which he finds in himself to Jesus is not Christian at all; while, if he does so relate it, but without in any degree recognizing the contrast noted in our proposition, then, since he finds in himself, not merely no sin, but not even imperfection, and is altogether spontaneous and independent in his activity, he must have left the state of grace behind him, and have himself become a Christ. If, on the other hand, a man relates his state, as touching fellowship with God, to Jesus, but without finding in himself any living receptivity for Him, then he certainly believes in Christ in so far as he assumes Him to possess a saving influence, but as yet he does not find himself a recipient of grace, for he cannot have experienced any change through Christ. For there can be no change in a living being without his own activity; hence, without such activity—that is, in a purely passive way—no influence exerted by another can really be received. Or again, if a man's own activity were one of opposition, if it were simply resistance, then the grace would necessarily have been imparted against his will, that is, by compulsion, and so would not be blessedness. Thus all real vital fellowship with Christ, in which He is in any sense taken as Redeemer, depends on the fact that living receptivity for His influence is *already* present, and *continues* to be present. And this holds true equally for every moment and

---

[1] Cf. § 63.

degree ; for, once arrived at the limit, the connexion would necessarily break off of itself.

But it cannot be denied that our proposition leaves plenty of scope for the most various interpretations of this relationship, provided they all keep within the limits laid down. One man may regard the relationship as absolutely the same at all moments, so that all the influences already felt in no way alter its character ; another may believe that in the recipient of grace there gradually arises a co-operative self-activity, so that the new Ego considered in its self-identity is a self-active entity and more and more develops itself in that character, and only the person as such, considered as the subject of change, is the seat of pure receptivity ; for which reason he is conscious of the potency of the God-consciousness as something constantly his own, though of course derived from Christ. Indeed, if we go back to the distinction between the personal self-consciousness and the common consciousness and accept our proposition as expressing the common Christian consciousness, but add that every adult Christian can and ought to be conscious of himself personally as free and self-active in the Kingdom of God, while at the same time he has only become such within the corporate life whose consciousness is rightly defined in our proposition—this view also would lie within the limits stated. But, of course, these views are not all equally current in the Church.

2. If then a statement such as we have given is equally valid for all elements, however widely they may differ, within the corporate life founded by Christ, it indicates only one possible division of our subject-matter. We must first explain how in virtue of this consciousness we conceive the Redeemer, next how we conceive the redeemed. The order fixes itself, for whatever in the state of the Christian contrasts with his former state in the fellowship of sinfulness can only be explained by the influence of the Redeemer. Hence the content of this section falls into two divisions. To the first belong all propositions concerning Christ which are immediate expressions of our Christian self-consciousness. If any teaching concerning Christ is given in other treatments of Protestant doctrine, but not here, that omission is not an arbitrary judgment on our part but sure internal evidence that such teaching is lacking in purely dogmatic content, and for that reason possessed only of a subordinate explanatory or subsidiary value (for if it *could* have come in under our plan, it would assuredly by our method

have found a place for itself). The second division must contain all propositions which directly ·describe the relation of grace to sinfulness in the human soul, and this as mediated by the entrance of the Redeemer. This division was, above,[1] marked off from the second section ; accordingly, we must include here everything by means of which the individual obtains and takes a share in the Christian fellowship—only, however, so far as it is regarded as his personal quality or mode of action.

[1] § 90, 1.

§ 92. *The peculiar activity and the exclusive dignity of the Redeemer imply each other, and are inseparably one in the self-consciousness of believers.*

1. Whether we prefer to call Christ the Redeemer, or to regard Him as the one in Whom the creation of human nature, which up to this point had existed only in a provisional state, was perfected, each of these points of view means only that we ascribe to Him a peculiar activity, and that in connexion with a peculiar spiritual content of His person. For if His influence is only of the same kind as that of others, even if it is ever so much more complete and inclusive, then its result also, that is, the salvation of mankind, would be a work common to Him and the others, although His share might be the greater ; and there would be, not one Redeemer over against the redeemed, but many, of whom one would only be the First among those like Him. Nor would the human creation then be completed through Him, but through all of those redeemers together, who, in so far as their work implies in them a peculiar quality of nature, are all alike distinguished from the rest of mankind. It would be just the same, if His activity were indeed peculiar to Himself, but this less in virtue of an inner quality belonging to Him than of a peculiar position in which He had been put. The second form of expression, that the human creation had been completed in Him, would then be altogether without content, since it would be more natural to suppose that there are many like Him, only they did not happen to occupy the same position. In that case He would not even be properly Redeemer, even though it could be said that mankind had been redeemed through His act or His suffering, as the case might be. For the result, namely, salvation, could not be something communicated from Him (since He had nothing peculiar to Himself) ; it could only have been occasioned or released by Him.

Just as little could the approximation to the condition of blessedness be traced to Him, if He had indeed had an exclusive dignity, but had remained passive in it, and had exercised no influence corresponding to it. For (apart from the fact that it is incomprehensible how His contemporaries, and we after them, should ever have come to attribute such an influence to Him, especially when the manner of His appearance was what it was), supposing that the blessedness could have been communicated merely through men's observing this dignity, although there were united with it no influence acting on others, then in the observers there must have been something more than receptivity ; His appearance would have to be regarded rather as merely the occasion for this idea, spontaneously produced by themselves.

2. Thus the approximation to blessedness, out of the state of misery, cannot be explained as a fact mediated through Jesus, by reference to either of these elements without the other. It follows, therefore, that they must be most intimately related and mutually determined. So that it is vain to attribute to the Redeemer a higher dignity than the activity at the same time ascribed to Him demands, since nothing is explained by this surplus of dignity. It is equally vain to attribute to Him a greater activity than follows naturally from the dignity which one is ready to allow to Him, since whatever results from this surplus of activity cannot be traced to Him in the same sense as the rest. Therefore every doctrine of Christ is inconsistent, in which this equality (of dignity and activity) is not essential, whether it seeks to disguise the detraction from the dignity by praising in Him great but really alien activities, or, conversely, seeks to compensate for the lesser influence which it allows Him by highly exalting Him, yet in a fashion which leads to no result.

3. If we hold fast to this rule, we could treat the whole doctrine of Christ either as that of His activity, for then the dignity must naturally follow from that, or as that of His dignity, for the activity must then result of itself. This is indicated by the two general formulæ above. For that the creation of human nature has been completed in His person is in and by itself only a description of His dignity, greater or less, according as the difference between the condition before and after is regarded as greater or less ; but the activity follows of itself, if indeed the creation is to continue to exist. Again, that He is the Redeemer similarly describes His activity, but the dignity follows of itself to just the same degree. Nevertheless, it is not advisable to choose one of these methods of treatment to the exclusion of the other ; this would involve at once both giving up the (traditional) language of the Church, and making a

comparison between our statements and other treatments of doctrine more difficult. Some of the churchly formulæ deal with the activity of Christ ; others are concerned with His dignity ; hence the strongest assurance that the two classes agree is to be found in the fact that the subject should be treated separately from both standpoints. The more what is peculiar in each of them is related to the other, the more probable it is that the propositions which are laid down reproduce with purity an original self-consciousness. The common measure of both, namely, the extent to which activity and dignity are embraced in one presentation, is to be found in the first place in the presentation of the result in individual lives, and next in the presentation of the Church, which must be just as complete a revelation of the dignity of the Redeemer as the world is a complete revelation of the attributes of God.

This division falls accordingly into two doctrines—that of the Person of Christ, and that of His Work. These two are quite different so far as the individual propositions are concerned, but their total content is the same ; from each point of view the content both of the second division and of the second section may be regarded as that which came to pass through Christ.

FIRST DOCTRINE : THE PERSON OF CHRIST

§ 93. *If the spontaneity of the new corporate life is original in the Redeemer and proceeds from Him alone, then as an historical individual He must have been at the same time ideal (i.e. the ideal must have become completely historical in Him), and each historical moment of His experience must at the same time have borne within it the ideal.*

1. If the peculiar dignity of the Redeemer can be measured only by His total activity as resting upon that dignity, while this activity can be seen in its completeness only in the corporate life He founded ; if, further, on the one hand, all other religious communities are destined to pass over into this one, so that all religious life existing apart from this is imperfect, whereas in this there is perfection ; if, on the other hand, this life itself, at all times and even in its highest development, has no other relation to the Redeemer than that which has been indicated above,[1] so that it can be all that it is only in virtue of its susceptibility to His influence : then the dignity of the Redeemer must be thought of in such a way that He is capable of achieving this. But inasmuch as His activity, so far as we can relate it directly and exclusively to His person, is to be considered in the first place in His public life, but in this life there are no conspicuous isolated acts which definitely stood out in separation from the rest of it, the true manifestation of His dignity, which is identical with His activity in the founding of a community, lies not in isolated moments, but in the whole course of His life. These are the two truths which, in our proposition, are not simply laid down but are also fully and at every point related to each other.

2. Now, if we live in the Christian fellowship, with the conviction which is common to all Christians, that no more perfect form of the God-consciousness lies in front of the human race, and that any new form would simply be a retrograde step ; and, further, that every increase in the activity of the God-consciousness within the Christian fellowship proceeds, not from any newly-added power,

[1] § 91.

377

but always and only from an ever-active susceptibility to His influence, clearly every given state of this corporate life must remain no more than an approximation to that which exists in the Redeemer Himself ; and just this is what we understand by His ideal dignity. But this corporate life is not concerned with the multifarious relationships of human life—as though Christ must have been ideal for all knowledge or all art and skill which have been developed in human society—but only with the capacity of the God-consciousness to give the impulse to all life's experiences and to determine them. Hence we do not make the ideality of the Redeemer cover more than this. To this, it is true, it might still be objected that, since the potency of the God-consciousness in the corporate life itself remains always imperfect at best, we must certainly attribute an *exemplary* (*vorbildliche*) dignity to the Redeemer, but *ideality* (*Urbildlichkeit*) (which, properly, asserts the existence of the concept itself), that is, absolute perfection, is not necessarily to be attributed to Him, not even according to the principle laid down above, for it is not necessary to explain the result, which always remains imperfect. Rather, it might be argued, this is the fundamental exaggeration into which believers fall when they regard Christ in the mirror of their own imperfection ; and this exaggeration continually perpetuates itself in the same manner, since believers in all ages read into Jesus whatever they are able to conceive as ideal in this sphere. But in this connexion there are two things to be observed. First, that on this view (if clearly realized) there must be developed at least a wish—for the absolutely perfect is always at least an object of aspiration—the more the individual subordinates his personal consciousness to the God-consciousness, even a hope, that some day the human race, if only in its noblest and best, will pass beyond Christ and leave Him behind. But this clearly marks the end of Christian faith, which on the contrary knows no other way to a pure conception of the ideal than an ever-deepening understanding of Christ. If, on the other hand, this consequence is not consciously realized, or is definitely rejected, then this limitation of the ideal to the merely exemplary can only be a misunderstood rule of prudence, the apparent ground for which will reveal itself later. Second, we must reflect, on the one hand, that as soon as we grant the possibility of a continued progress in the potency of the God-consciousness, while denying that its perfection exists anywhere, we can also no longer maintain that the creation of man has been or will be completed, since undoubtedly in progress thus continual perfection remains always only a bare possibility. And this would be to assert less of man than of other creatures—for it may be said of all more limited kinds of being that their concept is perfectly realized in the totality of individuals, which complete each other. But this cannot hold of a species which develops itself freely, if the perfection of an essential vital function be posited in the concept but actually found in no individual ; for perfection cannot be obtained by adding together things that are imperfect. And, on the other hand, it is to be considered how difficult it would necessarily be to indicate a difference between a true ideal and such an example in which there at the same time resides the power to produce every possible advance in the totality. For productivity belongs only to the concept of the ideal and not to that of the exemplary. We must conclude, then, that ideality is the only appropriate expression for the exclusive personal dignity of Christ.

With regard to the above statement, however, that the thought either of desire or of ability to go beyond Christ marks the end of the Christian faith, here, too, it is not easy to distinguish, among the various conceptions of it which leave room for the perfectibility of Christianity, between those which, although they do not seem so, nevertheless are still Christian, and those which are not, yet wish to pass as such. Everyone recognizes that there is a great difference between two classes. There are those who say it is not only possible but our duty to go beyond much of what Christ taught His disciples, because He Himself (since human thought is impossible without words) was seriously hindered by the imperfection of language from giving real expression to the innermost content of His spiritual being in clearly defined thoughts ; and the same, it may be held, is true in another sense of His actions also, in which the relations by which they were determined, and therefore imperfection, are always reflected. This, however, does not prevent us from attributing to Him absolute ideality in His inner being, in the sense that that inner being may always transcend its manifestation, and what is manifested be only an ever more perfect presentation of it. But there is another class : those who are of opinion that Christ is no more even in His inner being than could be manifested of it, while the fellowship of doctrine and life which takes its origin from Christ, with the testimonies to Him which it preserves, has in virtue of special divine guidance so fortunate an organization that both doctrine and life can easily be re-modelled in accordance with any more perfect ideal which later generations might conceive, without the fellowship needing to lose its historical identity, so that the necessity of founding new religious fellowships has been for all time done away. A single step more, and even the first presuppositions of the Christian faith will be removed ; and that step may quite consistently be taken. For if Christ was so much under the constraint of what was necessarily involved in His appearance in history, then both He Himself, and His whole achievement as well, must be capable of being explained simply by what was historically given Him. That is, Christianity in its entirety can be explained by Judaism at the stage of development which it had then reached—the stage at which it was possible for a man like Jesus to be born of it. Accordingly, Christianity was nothing but a new development of Judaism, though a development saturated with foreign philosophies then current, and Jesus was nothing but a more or less original and revolutionary reformer of the Jewish law.

3. But however certain it may be that the source of such a corporate life, continually advancing in the power of its God-consciousness, can lie only in the ideal, it is not on that account any easier to understand just how the ideal can have been revealed and manifested in a truly historically-conditioned individual. Even generally considered, we are compelled to keep the two ideas separate, and, whether we are speaking of works of art or of the forms of nature, we regard each separate one only as a complement of the rest and as requiring completion by them. But if sin is posited as a corporate act of the human race, what possibility then remains that an ideal individual could have developed out of this corporate life ? The way of escape, which suggests that the ideal might be produced by human thought and transferred more or less arbitrarily to Jesus, is already cut off. In that case Christianity would be founded upon an imperfect ideal ; it would therefore have to give up its claim to take up into itself all forms of faith and to develop out of itself more and more perfection and blessedness. But if our aim is to make room in human nature before Christ, and apart from Him, for the power of producing within itself a pure and perfect ideal—then human nature, since there is a natural connexion between reason and will, cannot have been in a condition of universal sinfulness. Hence, if the man Jesus was really ideal, or if the ideal became historical and actual in Him—the one expression means the same as the other—in

order to establish a new corporate life within the old and out of it, then certainly He must have entered into the corporate life of sinfulness, but He cannot have come out of it, but must be recognized in it as a miraculous fact (*eine wunderbare Erscheinung*), and yet (in harmony with the analogies established above)[1] only in the meaning of the word ' miracle ' which has here once for all been determined. His peculiar spiritual content, that is, cannot be explained by the content of the human environment to which He belonged, but only by the universal source of spiritual life in virtue of a creative divine act in which, as an absolute maximum, the conception of man as the subject of the God-consciousness comes to completion.   But since we can never properly understand the beginnings of life, full justice is done to the demand for the perfect historicity of this perfect ideal, if, from then on, He developed in the same way as all others, so that from birth on His powers gradually unfolded, and, from the zero point of His appearance onwards, were developed to completeness in the order natural to the human race.   This applies also to His God-consciousness, with which we are here specially concerned ; which certainly, in the case of others as little as in His, is infused by education—the germ of it is found originally in all—but which in Him too, as in all, had to develop gradually in human fashion into a really manifest consciousness, and antecedently was only present as a germ, although in a certain sense always present as an active power.   So even during this period of development, after it had actually become a consciousness, it could exert its influence over the sensuous self-consciousness only in the measure in which the various functions of the latter had already emerged, and thus, even regarded from this side, it appeared as itself something that was only gradually unfolding to its full extent.   If we make the mistake of thinking that, on account of His ideal nature, we must deny this and assume that from the very beginnings of His life He carried the God-consciousness as such within Himself—then from the very outset He must have been conscious of Himself as an Ego ; indeed (the deduction is very simple), He must have been master of language from the first, at least so far as its more abstract part is concerned, and before He ever spoke ; thus His whole earliest childhood must have been mere appearance.   This excludes the thought of a true human life and quite definitely adopts the error of Docetism ; and on these terms we should have to separate in time that in which Christ is like all men from what in Him is ideal, allotting to the former the whole

[1] § 13, 1.

period of development up to the beginning of mature manhood, and only then allowing the ideal to come in over and above. But this latter is then inconceivable without an absolute miracle. Nay more, sin too would then, at that earlier stage, be at least possible in Him, and therefore also certainly actually present, even if only in the faintest degree ; and thus Jesus would be Redeemer and redeemed in one person—with all the further consequences of that.

The pure historicity of the person of the Redeemer, however, involves also this fact, that He could develop only in a certain similarity with His surroundings, that is, in general after the manner of His people. For since mind and understanding drew their nourishment solely from this surrounding world, and His free self-activity too had in this world its determined place, even His God-consciousness, however original its higher powers, could only express or communicate itself in ideas which He had appropriated from this sphere, and in actions which as to their possibility were predetermined in it.[1] If we wished to deny this dependence of development upon surroundings, we should logically have to assume an empirical omniscience in Christ, in virtue of which all human forms of thought, as well as languages, would have been equally familiar to Him, so that He would have lived in whatever is true and right in each of these just as much as in that of His native land. We should also have to add the same omniscience relatively to the various human relationships and their management. And this, too, would mean the loss of true humanity.

4. Further, whatever is involved in the ideality of the contents of His personal spiritual life must also be compatible with this purely human conception of His historical existence. Thus, in the first place, His development must be thought of as wholly free from everything which we have to conceive as conflict. For it is not possible that, where an inner conflict has ever at any time taken place, the traces of it should ever disappear completely. Just as little could the ideal have been recognized as present where even the slightest traces of this conflict betrayed themselves. The power with which the God-consciousness, so far as it was developed at each particular moment, determined that moment could never have been in doubt, or disturbed by the memory of an earlier conflict. Nor could He ever have found Himself in a condition through which a conflict could have been

[1] It will doubtless be generally recognized that this is implied in the statement in Gal. 4⁴, that Christ was made under the law.

occasioned in the future, that is, there could have been in Him, even from the beginning, no inequality in the relation of the various functions of sensuous human nature to the God-consciousness. Thus at every moment even of His period of development He must have been free from everything by which the rise of sin in the individual is conditioned.[1] Two things, further, are quite well possible together : first, that all powers, both the lower ones which were to be mastered and the controlling higher ones, emerged only in gradual development, so that the latter were able to dominate the former only in the measure of their development ; and, secondly, that the domination itself was nevertheless at each moment complete in the sense that nothing was ever able to find a place in the sense-nature which did not instantly take its place as an instrument of the spirit, so that no impression was taken up merely sensuously into the innermost consciousness and elaborated apart from God-consciousness into an element of life, nor did any action, that can really be regarded as such, and as a real whole, ever proceed solely from the sense-nature and not from the God-consciousness. What we could lay down above [2] only as a possibility, namely, a sinless development of a human individual life, must have become actual in the person of the Redeemer in virtue of this undisturbed identity of the relationship, so that we can represent the growth of His personality from earliest childhood on to the fulness of manhood as a continuous transition from the condition of purest innocence to one of purely spiritual fulness of power, which is far removed from anything which we call virtue. For in the condition of innocence there is an activity of the God-consciousness, but only an indirect one, which, though still latently, restrains every movement in the sense-experience which must develop into opposition. The nearest approximation to this, which not seldom occurs in our experience, we usually call ' a happy childlike nature.' The adult fulness of power, on the other hand, although its growth is gradual and the result of practice, is distinguished from virtue in this respect, that it is not the result of a conflict, inasmuch as it does not need to be worked out either through error or through sin, nor even through an inclination to either. And this purity must on no account be regarded as a consequence of outward protection, but must have its ground in the Man Himself, that is, in the higher God-consciousness implanted in Him originally. Otherwise, since such outward protection depends upon the actions of others, the ideal in Him

Cf. §§ 67–69. [2] § 68, 1.

would be produced rather than productive, and He Himself would be just as much the first from the totality redeemed, as afterwards Himself the Redeemer.

Secondly, so far as what is conditioned by race in His person is concerned, Christ could hardly be a complete man if His personality were not determined by this factor ; but such determination in no way concerns the real principle of His life but only the organism. Racial peculiarity is in no way the type of His self-activity ; it is only the type of His receptivity for the self-activity of the spirit ; nor can it have been like a repelling or exclusive principle in Him, but must have been united with the freest and most unclouded appreciation of everything human, and with the recognition of the identity of nature and also of spirit in all human forms ; also it must have been without any effort to extend what in Him was racial beyond its appointed limits. And it is only when we have guarded ourselves thus that we can say that the racial too in Him is ideally determined, both in itself and in its relation to the whole of human nature.

5. Here we can only call attention in passing and by anticipation to the influence which this conception of the ideality of the Redeemer in the perfectly natural historicity of His career exercises on all the Christian doctrines current in the Church, all of which must be formulated differently if that conception more or less is given up. To begin with, the fact that all doctrines and precepts developed in the Christian Church have universal authority only through their being traced back to Christ, has no other ground than His perfect ideality in everything connected with the power of the God-consciousness. In so far as this is set aside, there must be conceded a possibility of doctrines and precepts arising in the sphere of piety which go beyond the utterances of Christ. Similarly, the preaching of the written word, in so far as it contains only glorification of Christ, and the sacrament of the altar, can be regarded as permanent institutions in the Christian Church only if we premise that the whole development and maintenance of Christian piety must always proceed from vital fellowship with Christ. Nor could Christ be presented as a universal example unless His relation to all original differences in individuals were uniform—for otherwise He would necessarily be more of an example for some than for others. This only becomes possible through His ideality. But just as little could He be a universal example, unless every moment of His life were

ideal. Otherwise it would be necessary first to distinguish the ideal from the non-ideal, which could only be done according to an external law, which (it follows) would be superior to Him. That law would come in, unless (as His ideality implies) what is racially determined in Him had been limited ; otherwise we should have to consent to adopt into the Christian norm of life all that is simply Jewish in His life. Moreover, these points, cardinal for the Christian fellowship, are not doctrines which became current only through later developments ; they are the original doctrines of His disciples, closely bound up with the way in which they applied to Jesus the idea of the Messiah, and such as are easily brought into connexion with His own utterances, so far as these are accessible to us.

§ 94. *The Redeemer, then, is like all men in virtue of the identity of human nature, but distinguished from them all by the constant potency of His God-consciousness, which was a veritable existence of God in Him.*

1. That the Redeemer should be entirely free from all sinfulness is no objection at all to the complete identity of human nature in Him and others, for we have already [1] laid down that sin is so little an essential part of the being of man that we can never regard it as anything else than a disturbance of nature. It follows that the possibility of a sinless development is in itself not incongruous with the idea of human nature ; indeed, this possibility is involved, and recognized, in the consciousness of sin as guilt, as that is universally understood. This likeness, however, is to be understood in such a general sense that even the first man before the first sin stood no nearer the Redeemer, and was like Him in no higher sense, than all other men. For if even in the life of the first man we must assume a time when sin had not yet appeared, yet every first appearance of sin leads back to a sinful preparation.[2] But the Redeemer too shared in the same vicissitudes of life, without which we can hardly imagine the entrance of sin at a definite moment even in Adam, for they are essential to human nature. Furthermore, the first man was originally free from all the contagious influences of a sinful society, while the Redeemer had to enter into the corporate life when it had already advanced far in deterioration, so that it would hardly be possible to attribute His sinlessness to external protection—which we certainly must somehow admit in the case of the first man, if we would not involve ourselves in contradictions.

[1] § 68, above.   [2] Cf. § 72.

Of the Redeemer, on the contrary, we must hold that the ground of His sinlessness was not external to Himself, but that it was a sinlessness essentially grounded in Himself, if He was to take away, through what He was in Himself, the sinfulness of the corporate life. Therefore, so far as sin is concerned, Christ differs no less from the first man than from all others.

The identity of human nature further involves this, that the manner in which Christ differs from all others also has its place in this identity. This would not be the case if it were not involved in human nature that individuals, so far as the measure of the different functions is concerned, are originally different from each other, so that to every separate corporate life (regarded in space as well as in time) there belong those who are more and less gifted ; and we only arrive at the truth of life when we thus correlate those who differ from each other. In the same way, therefore, all those who in any respect give character to an age or a district are bound up with those over whom (as being defective in that particular respect) they extend an educative influence, even as Christ is bound up with those whom His preponderatingly powerful God-consciousness links to the corporate life thus indicated. The greater the difference, and the more specific the activity, the more must these also have established themselves against the hindering influences of a worthless environment, and they can be understood only by reference to this self-differentiating quality of human nature,[1] not by reference to the group in which they stand ; although by divine right they belong to it, as the Redeemer does to the whole race.

2. But in admitting that what is peculiar in the Redeemer's kind of activity belongs to a general aspect of human nature, we by no means wish to reduce this activity, and the personal dignity by which it is conditioned, to the same measure as that of others. The simple fact that faith in Christ postulates a relation on His part to the whole race, while everything analogous is valid only for definite individual times and places, is sufficient to prove this. For no one has yet succeeded, in any sphere of science or art, and no one will ever succeed, in establishing himself as head, universally animating and sufficient for the whole human race.

For this peculiar dignity of Christ, however, in the sense in which we have already referred back the ideality of His person to this spiritual function of the God-consciousness implanted in the self-consciousness, the terms of our proposition alone are adequate ; for

[1] Cf. § 13.

to ascribe to Christ an absolutely powerful God-consciousness, and to attribute to Him an existence of God in Him, are exactly the same thing. The expression, 'the existence of God in anyone,' can only express the relation of the omnipresence of God to this one. Now since God's existence can only be apprehended as pure activity, while every individualized existence is merely an intermingling of activity and passivity—the activity being always found apportioned to this passivity in every other individualized existence—there is, so far, no existence of God in any individual thing, but only an existence of God in the world. And only if the passive conditions are not purely passive, but mediated through vital receptivity, and this receptivity confronts the totality of finite existence (so far, *i.e.*, as we can say of the individual as a living creature that, in virtue of the universal reciprocity, it in itself represents the world), could we suppose an existence of God in it. Hence this clearly does not hold of what is individualized as an unconscious thing ; for since an unconscious thing brings no living receptivity to meet all the forces of consciousness it cannot represent these forces in itself. But just as little and for the same reason can what is conscious but not intelligent represent them, so that it is only in the rational individual that an existence of God can be admitted. How far this is also true similarly and without distinction if we regard reason as functioning in objective consciousness lies outside our investigation. But so far as the rational self-consciousness is concerned, it is certain that the God-consciousness which (along with the self-consciousness) belongs to human nature originally, before the Redeemer and apart from all connexion with Him, cannot fittingly be called an existence of God in us, not only because it was not a pure God-consciousness (either in polytheism or even in Jewish monotheism, which was everywhere tinctured with materialistic conceptions, whether cruder or finer), but also because, such as it was, it did not assert itself as activity, but in these religions was always dominated by the sensuous self-consciousness. If, then, it was able neither to portray God purely and with real adequacy in thought, nor yet to exhibit itself as pure activity, it cannot be represented as an existence of God in us. But just as the unconscious forces of nature and non-rational life become a revelation of God to us only so far as we bring that conception with us, so also that darkened and imperfect God-consciousness by itself is not an existence of God in human nature, but only in so far as we bring Christ with us in thought and relate it to Him. So

that originally it is found nowhere but in Him, and He is the only
' other ' in which there is an existence of God in the proper sense,
so far, that is, as we posit the God-consciousness in His self-consciousness as continually and exclusively determining every moment,
and consequently also this perfect indwelling of the Supreme
Being as His peculiar being and His inmost self.   Indeed, working
backwards we must now say, if it is only through Him that the human
God-consciousness becomes an existence of God in human nature,
and only through the rational nature that the totality of finite powers
can become an existence of God in the world, that in truth He alone
mediates all existence of God in the world and all revelation of God
through the world, in so far as He bears within Himself the whole
new creation which contains and develops the potency of the God-
consciousness.

3. But if as a person of this kind He needs to have the whole
human development in common with us, so that even this existence
of God must in Him have had a development in time, and as the
most spiritual element in His personality could only emerge into
manifestation after the lower functions ; yet He cannot have entered
life as one for whom the foundations of sin had already been laid
before His being began to be manifested.   We have envisaged this
earlier establishment of sin for all of us,[1] without entering upon
natural-scientific investigations into the origin of the individual
life, and the coming together in us (if we may use the phrase) of
soul and body, but simply by holding to the general facts of experience ; so here, too, we seek to combine with these facts only the
relatively supernatural, which we have already admitted in general
for the entrance of the Redeemer into the world.

The origin of every human life may be regarded in a twofold
manner, as issuing from the narrow circle of descent and society
to which it immediately belongs, and as a fact of human nature in
general.   The more definitely the weaknesses of that narrow circle
repeat themselves in an individual, the more valid becomes the
first point of view.   The more the individual by the kind and degree
of his gifts transcends that circle, and the more he exhibits what is
new within it, the more we are thrown back upon the other explanation.   This means that the beginning of Jesus' life cannot in any
way be explained by the first factor, but only and exclusively by
the second ; so that from the beginning He must have been free from
every influence from earlier generations which disseminated sin

[1] Cf. § 69.

and disturbed the inner God-consciousness, and He can only be understood as an original act of human nature, *i.e.* as an act of human nature as not affected by sin. The beginning of His life was also a new implanting of the God-consciousness which creates receptivity in human nature ; hence this content and that manner of origin are in such a close relation that they mutually condition and explain each other. That new implanting came to be through the beginning of His life, and therefore that beginning must have transcended every detrimental influence of His immediate circle ; and because it was such an original and sin-free act of nature, a filling of His nature with God-consciousness became possible as its result. So that upon this relation too the fullest light is thrown if we regard the beginning of the life of Jesus as the completed creation of human nature. The appearance of the first man con- stituted at the same time the physical life of the human race ; the appearance of the Second Adam constituted for this nature a new spiritual life, which communicates and develops itself by spiritual fecundation. And as in the former its originality (which is the condition of the appearance of human nature) and its having emerged from creative divine activity are the same thing, so also in the Redeemer both are the same—His spiritual originality, set free from every prejudicial influence of natural descent, and that existence of God in Him which also proves itself creative. If the impartation of the Spirit to human nature which was made in the first Adam was insufficient, in that the spirit remained sunk in sensuousness and barely glanced forth clearly at moments as a presentiment of something better, and if the work of creation has only been completed. through the second and equally original impartation to the Second Adam, yet both events go back to one undivided eternal divine decree and form, even in a higher sense, only one and the same natural system, though one unattainable by us.

§ 95. *The ecclesiastical formulæ concerning the Person of Christ need to be subjected to continual criticism.*

1. The ecclesiastical formulæ are, on the one hand, products of controversy, in that, although the original consciousness was the same in all, yet the thought expressive of it took different forms with different thinkers, according as they linked their presentation of what was new to one or another of the existing conceptions. In this way it was possible for Jewish or heathen elements or pre-

suppositions to creep in, even though it were unconsciously, and to evoke corrective opposition. Even the later development of the original formulæ partly took the same road, in order to guard against misunderstandings which might arise from rhetorical or poetic expressions in doctrinal language ; partly it proceeded with that over-subtlety which was later · brought to perfection in Scholasticism, and which, utterly disregarding the true interests of Dogmatic, propounded difficult questions simply for the sake of definitions. The result inevitably was that Dogmatic was over-loaded with a multitude of definitions, which have absolutely no other relation to the immediate Christian self-consciousness than that indicated by the history of controversy. The realization of this has produced in some minds a distaste for everything which had a controversial origin ; they will only admit such expressions as lie outside all controversy and obviate in advance, wherever possible, all future controversy ; they are in the keenest antagonism to the tendency of others, who want to retain everything now existing just as it has come to be. So that without a process of elimination and compromise neither adjustment nor progress is possible.

2. For this unavoidable critical process, two rules (in view of the opposing parties) must be adopted. The rule for the one party is this : a thing no longer really exists, but becomes mere matter of history, when it can exercise no further activity owing to the situation to which it properly belonged being no longer present. The rule for the other party is this : if we go back to formulæ which are simple, but just on account of their simplicity are too indefinite for didactic purposes, we gain a merely apparent satisfaction, which lasts only until the disagreement which has remained hidden under the identity of the formula breaks out somewhere or other. The task of the critical process is to hold the ecclesiastical formulæ to strict agreement with the foregoing analysis of our Christian self-consciousness, in order, partly, to judge how far they agree with it at least in essentials, partly (with regard to individual points), to inquire how much of the current form of expression is to be retained, and how much, on the other hand, had better be given up, either because it is an imperfect solution of the problem or because it is an addition not in itself essential, and harmful because the occasion of persistent misunderstandings.

§ 96. First Theorem.—In Jesus Christ divine nature and human nature were combined into one person.

Augsb. Conf., Art. 3 : That the two natures, divine and human, inseparably united in one person are One Christ.—*Conf. Angl.* ii. (p. 127 [1]) : ita ut duae naturae divina et humana integre atque perfecte in unitate personae fuerint inseparabiliter coniunctae, ex quibus est unus Christus, etc.— *Expos. simpl.* xi. : Agnoscimus ergo in uno atque eodem domino nostro duas naturas divinam et humanam, et has dicimus conjunctas et unitas esse . . . in una persona, ita ut unum Christum . . . veneremur . . . juxta divinam naturam patri juxta humanam vero nobis hominibus consubstantialem. —*Conf. Gallic.* xv. p. 116 : Credimus in una eademque persona, quae est Jesus Christus, vere et inseparabiliter duas illas naturas sic esse conjunctas ut etiam sint unitae.—*Conf. Helv.* xi. p. 96 : Hic Christus . . . cum . . . totum hominem anima et corpore constantem assumsisset, in una individuaque persona duas sed impermixtas naturas—frater noster factus est.—*Sol. decl.* viii. : Credimus iam in una illa indivisa persona Christi duas esse distinctas naturas divinam videlicet quae ab aeterno est, et humanam quae in tempore assumta est in unitatem personae filii Dei.—*Symb. Nic.* : 'Ιησοῦν Χριστὸν, τὸν ἐκ τοῦ πατρὸς γεννηθέντα πρὸ πάντων τῶν αἰώνων . . . θεὸν ἀληθινόν . . . τὸν δι' ἡμᾶς . . . κατελθόντα . . . καὶ σαρκωθέντα, etc.   *Symb. Quic.* 28, 29: . . . Quia dominus noster Jesus Christus dei filius Deus pariter et homo est. Deus est ex substantia patris ante secula genitus, homo ex substantia matris in seculo natus.

1. Although only a few of the credal passages quoted here indicate the object of this presentation of the unique personality of the Redeemer, yet it is unmistakable that the tendency is the same as in the propositions so far laid down, namely, to describe Christ in such a way (*frater, consubstantialis nobis*) that in the new corporate life a vital fellowship between us and Him shall be possible, and, at the same time, that the existence of God in Him shall be expressed in the clearest possible way ; from which it follows at once that the most unconditional adoration and brotherly comradeship are united in our relation to Him. With this we are in complete agreement. Yet, on the other hand, there is almost nothing in the execution of this aim against which protest must not be raised, whether we regard the scientific character of the expression or its suitability for ecclesiastical use.

With regard to the first : to begin with, we must warn the reader against the very confusing description of the subject that results when the expression ' Jesus Christ ' is used, to indicate not only the subject of the union of the two natures (at which point the first

[1] The page-numbers for the Reformed Confessions refer to the *Augusti Corpus* etc.

four passages properly stop), but also the divine nature of the Redeemer from all eternity before its union with the human nature ; so that this union no longer appears as an element that goes to constitute the person, Jesus Christ, but rather as an act of this person Himself. This confusion has, most glaringly, passed over from the two passages drawn from the ancient creeds into the Helvetic Confession.[1] But the New Testament knows nothing of this usage ; even the expression ' Son of God ' it uses (when it speaks independently) only of the subject of this union,[2] and not of the divine element in it before the union. So our proposition has held to what is correct. The expression ' Jesus Christ ' itself only became a single proper name originally through misuse (though this happened very early), since properly Christ is only the description of the real dignity added to the proper name ; but even in the combination it is obvious that the historical and the ideal are both comprised. But far worse than this ambiguous description of the subject is this (which cannot possibly be justified on any strictly scientific investigation), that the expression ' nature ' is used indifferently for the divine and the human. Any other expression that was used indifferently of both would lead one to suspect that such a formula was bound to become the source of many confusions. For how can divine and human be thus brought together under any single conception, as if they could both be more exact determinations, coordinated to each other, of one and the same universal ? Indeed, even divine spirit and human spirit could not without confusion be brought together in this way. But the word ' nature ' is particularly ill-adapted for such a common use, even if we leave Latin and Greek etymology completely out of account and simply take our stand on our own use of the word. For in one sense we actually oppose God and nature to one another, and hence in this sense cannot attribute a nature to God. Nature in this sense is for us the summary of all finite existence, or, as in the opposition of nature and history, the summary of all that is corporeal, and that goes back to what is elementary, in its various and discrete phenomena, in which all that we so describe is mutually conditioned. Over against this divided and conditioned we set God as the unconditioned and the absolutely simple. But just for this reason we

---

[1] The *Belgic Confession*, too, shares in the same confusion, x. p. 176 : Necesse itaque e··m qui Deus sermo filius et Jesus Christus nominatur jam tum extitisse cum ab ipso omnia crearentur.

[2] No one, we may suppose, will cite John 1¹⁸ or 17⁸ as instances against this assertion.

cannot attribute a nature to God in the other sense. For always, whether we use the word generally, as when we speak of animal and vegetable nature, or of an individual, as when we say that a person has a noble or an ignoble nature, always we use it solely of a limited existence, standing in opposition to something else, an existence in which active and passive are bound up together, and which is revealed in a variety of appearances, in the latter case of individuals, in the former of vital factors. And upon closer consideration it is hardly to be denied that this expression, if we go back to the original Greek word,[1] bears in itself traces of heathen influence, though possibly of unconscious influence. For in polytheism, which represents the Godhead as no less split up and divided than finite existence appears to us, the word 'nature' has certainly the same meaning in the expression *divine nature* as it has elsewhere. The fact ought to have been a warning, that the heathen sages themselves had already risen above this imperfect representation of God, and said of Him that He was to be thought of as beyond all existence and being.

It is no better with the relation which is here set forth between nature and person. For in utter contradiction to the use elsewhere, according to which the same nature belongs to many individuals or persons, here one person is to share in two quite different natures. Now if 'person' indicates a constant unity of life, but 'nature' a sum of ways of action or laws, according to which conditions of life vary and are included within a fixed range, how can the unity of life coexist with the duality of natures, unless the one gives way to the other, if the one exhibits a larger and the other a narrower range, or unless they melt into each other, both systems of ways of action and laws really becoming one in the one life?—if indeed we are speaking of a person, *i.e.* of an Ego which is the same in all the consecutive moments of its existence. The attempt to make clear this unity along with the duality naturally but seldom results in anything else than a demonstration of the possibility of a formula made up by combining indications out of which it is impossible to construct a figure. On the other hand, as soon as the same writer avoids this formula of two natures, he not seldom says something which one can follow, and of which the figure can

---

[1] φύσις. This censure seems also to fall on a writing which is merely deutero-canonical, for in 2 Pet. 1⁴ the expression is found, θείας φύσεως κοινωνοί. But the immediate context of itself shows that these words cannot be taken so precisely as must be done in the case we are dealing with, where an important dogmatic definition is in question.

be drawn (*nachzeichnen*).[1] Hence all the results of the endeavour to achieve a living presentation of the unity of the divine and the human in Christ, ever since it was tied down to this expression, have always vacillated between the opposite errors of mixing the two natures to form a third which would be neither of them, neither divine nor human, or of keeping the two natures separate, but either neglecting the unity of the person in order to separate the two natures more distinctly, or, in order to keep firm hold of the unity of the person, disturbing the necessary balance, and making one nature less important than the other and limited by it. The same thing comes out even in the vacillation between the expressions 'connexion' and 'union'—in the latter there is a tendency to wipe out the difference of the natures, while the former makes the unity of the person doubtful. The utter fruitlessness of this way of presenting the matter becomes particularly clear in the treatment of the question whether Christ as one person formed out of two natures had also two wills according to the number of the natures, or only one according to the number of the person. For if Christ had only one will, then the divine nature is incomplete if this is a human will ; and the human nature, if it is a divine will. But if Christ has two wills, then the unity of the person is no more than apparent, even if we try to conserve it by saying that the two wills always will the same thing. For what this results in is only agreement, not unity ; and, in fact, to answer the problem thus is to return to the division of Christ. And one or the other will is always simply a superfluous accompaniment of the other, whether it be the divine will that accompanies the human or *vice versa*. And manifestly, as we are accustomed to take reason and will together the same question may be raised with regard to the reason ; then all that has just been said repeats itself, since each nature is incomplete without the reason that belongs to it, and a unity of the person is as little compatible with such a twofold reason as with a twofold will ; and it is equally unthinkable that a divine reason, which as omniscient sees everything at once, should think the same as a human reason, which only knows separate things one after the other and as a result of the other, and that a human will, which always strives only for separate ends and one for the sake of the

---

[1] Cf. Joann. Damasc. iii. 19 : ἀλλ' οὐκ ἀνάγκη τὰς ἀλλήλαις ἑνωθείσας φύσεις καθ' ὑπόστασιν ἑκάστην ἰδίαν κεκτῆσθαι ὑπόστασιν. δύνανται γὰρ εἰς μίαν συνδραμοῦσαι ὑπόστασιν μήτε ἀνυπόστατοι εἶναι μήτε ἰδιάζουσαν ἑκάστη ἔχειν ὑπόστασιν, ἀλλὰ μίαν καὶ τὴν αὐτὴν ἀμφότεραι,—and iii. 2 : λόγος σαρκὶ ἐψυχωμένη καὶ ἐν αὐτῷ τὸ εἶναι λαχούσῃ ἑνωθεὶς καθ' ὑπόστασιν.

other, should will the same as a divine will, whose object can be nothing but the whole world in the totality of its development.

Finally, for the scientific perfection of dogmatic terminology it is also necessary that related doctrines should be capable of easy comprehension in their relations to each other ; if so, the way in which this formula is related to the formulæ of the doctrine of the Trinity is no great recommendation of it.   There the expression ' unity of nature' alongside of the trinity of Persons has been avoided, and ' unity of essence ' used instead.   But, however praiseworthy this may be, since the term ' essence ' is certainly much more appropriate to the Godhead than the term ' nature,' yet the question inevitably arises what the relation is between what in Christ we call His divine nature and that unity of essence which is common to all three Persons of the Trinity, and whether each of the three Persons, outside their participation in the Divine Essence, has also a nature of its own as well, or whether this is a peculiarity of the Second Person.   No satisfactory answer to this is to be found either here or in the doctrine of the Trinity.   But the matter becomes still more confused through the introduction in the Dogmatic of the whole Western Church of another usage of the word ' Person,' according to which, in the one case, we have three Persons in one Essence and in the other one Person out of two natures.   If now we carry over into the doctrine of the Trinity the explanations which are usually given of the word ' Person ' in the doctrine of Christ—and there is sufficient reason for this, since it is asserted that Christ did not become a Person only through the union of the two natures, but the Son of God only took up human nature into His Person— then the three Persons must have an independent anterior existence in themselves ; and if each Person is also a nature,[1] we come almost inevitably to three divine natures for the three divine Persons in the one Divine Essence.   If, on the other hand, the same word ' Person ' means something different in the one doctrine from what it means in the other, so that in the Person of Christ we have still another Person in the other sense of the word, the confusion is just as great.

2. It lies in the nature of the case, that after this formula had once secured recognition as the foundation for all other definitions regarding the Person of Christ, an involved and artificial mode of procedure was inevitable if terms so indefensible were to be kept as innocuous as possible.   The almost inevitable consequence was

[1] The formulæ here are taken from Reinhard, *Dogmatik*, § 92, p. 347.

that, as this foundation itself contains an apparent contradiction, the whole development was bound to resolve itself into a disproof of this reproach couched in a series of negative terms—terms which no more express or reproduce the actual content of our immediate impression than they contain a knowledge of Christ in the form of intuition—that is, of objective consciousness (though indeed it would be less of a recommendation to us than to others if they *could* do this last). Accordingly we are compelled to put a very low estimate upon the value of this theory for ecclesiastical use. It cannot give any guidance in the proper preaching of Christ, for it takes a purely negative form ; at most it might serve homiletical diction as a test of whether in the glorification or the vivid presentation of Christ elements may not have been introduced which transgress the prescribed limits. But even in this connexion the definitions of the Schools have long since become a dead letter in which no one any longer can find refuge. For the devotional phraseology even of the most orthodox teachers, in so far as they are not content simply to hand on the letter of tradition but aim at edification and confirmation in a living faith, is so remote from the terminology of the schools that it would hardly be possible to find any current terms to bridge the gulf. No less unfruitful does this development appear when we regard the divergent opinions which prevail among us, some of them docetic in character, since they identify the Redeemer so closely with God that the truth of His humanity is obscured ; some of them Ebionite, inasmuch as they leave no room for any essential distinction between Christ and an exceptional man. They are utterly unsuitable for use in determining in either direction the boundary between what is Christian but appears unchristian, whether owing to its own *gaucherie* or to the misrepresentation of opponents, and what has ceased to be Christian altogether, because it is naturalistic or fanatical.

3. It must be remembered, further, that in the original construction of Protestant theology nothing was done for this article—the old formulæ were simply repeated. For although the question was at once taken up again on one particular side in the controversies between the two Protestant parties, this could not lead to a complete new revision, since the matter arose only *à propos* of another point in dispute ; nor did what on this occasion was actually established secure symbolical recognition anywhere within the sphere of the Augsburg Confession. And so, if Dogmatics are to be ever more completely purged of scholasticism, the task remains of construct-

ing a scientific statement of this particular doctrine also, in which
the impression of the peculiar dignity of the Redeemer that we have
obtained from the testimonies borne to Him shall not be reflected
merely in negative formulæ, and which at the same time (at least
as much as with other dogmatic definitions) shall approximate to
what can be presented to Christian congregations in religious teaching. We hope that above [1] we have laid the foundation for such a
revision, which attempts so to define the mutual relations of the
divine and the human in the Redeemer, that both the expressions,
divine nature and the duality of natures in the same Person (which,
to say the least, are exceedingly inconvenient) shall be altogether
avoided. For if the distinction between the Redeemer and us
others is established in such a way that, instead of being obscured
and powerless as in us, the God-consciousness in Him was absolutely
clear and determined each moment, to the exclusion of all else, so
that it must be regarded as a continual living presence, and withal a
real existence of God in Him, then, in virtue of this difference, there
is in Him everything that we need, and, in virtue of His likeness to
us, limited only by His utter sinlessness, this is all in Him in such a
way that we can lay hold of it. That is to say, the existence of God
in the Redeemer is posited as the innermost fundamental power
within Him, from which every activity proceeds and which holds
every element together ; everything human (in Him) forms only
the organism for this fundamental power, and is related to it as the
system which both receives and represents it, just as in us all other
powers are related to the intelligence.[2] If this form of expression
is very different from that of the language of the Schools as used
hitherto, yet it rests equally upon the Pauline phrase ' God was in
Christ ' and the Johannine ' the Word became flesh ' ; for ' Word ' is
the activity of God expressed in the form of consciousness, and
' flesh ' is a general expression for the organic. In so far as all
human activity of the Redeemer depends, as a connected whole,
upon this existence of God in Him and represents it, the expression
(that in the Redeemer God became man) is justified as true exclusively of Him ; and similarly every moment of His existence, so far
as it can be isolated, presents just such a new incarnation and
incarnatedness of God, because always and everywhere all that is
human in Him springs out of that divine. And it would be difficult

---

[1] § 94.
[2] Precisely as in the *Symbol. Quic.* 25 : Nam sicut anima rationalis et
caro unus est homo, ita et Deus et homo unus est Christus.

for anyone to prove that there is anything docetic or Ebionite in this description. It could be called Ebionite only by one who feels that he must insist upon an empirical emergence of divine properties if he is to recognize a superhuman element in the Redeemer ; and the only thing that could be regarded as docetic is that in the Redeemer the God-consciousness is not imperfect. But neither objection would find any support even in the letter of the accepted ecclesiastical doctrine. Hence even in dealing with the ecclesiastical propositions now to follow, our criticism must be related to the form of statement just given, in order at each point to show how far the intention of these propositions agrees in meaning with our form of statement, and how far the unsuitability and difficulty of those formulæ has, on the one hand, prevented the exposition from answering fully to the intention, and on the other has given scope for subtle inanities.

§ 97. *Second Theorem.—In the uniting of the divine nature with the human, the divine alone was active or self-imparting, and the human alone passive or in process of being assumed ; but during the state of union every activity was a common activity of both natures.*

1. If we take an objective view of the task of presenting Christ clearly as such a unity of both natures, it is natural and indeed inevitable that we should separate from one another the act of union and the state of union. For the former was only the beginning of the Person of Christ as it came to manifestation in the world, and accordingly must be expressed by a reference to the previous non-existence of that Person ; while the latter, as the specific existence of the Person, must be described by a formula which is equally appropriate to all moments of it. But for our task the description of the first beginning, since we are not directly affected by it, seems a work of supererogation. This accordingly is better omitted : such exercises are always of doubtful value. Thus the inclusion of this theorem calls for special justification. But, in the first place, it is quite in order to refer back to its beginnings such a difference as that between Christ and all other men, because it does make a difference if it is recognized as original ; and, again, the expression must be quite differently phrased if the difference is a later accession and hence only a subsequent condition of a person originally entirely like ourselves. And since if we reproduce the impression made

upon us we cannot but deny the latter suggestion, the necessity arises of presenting the first moment also as continuous with every later one. And so both the theorems set forth above, while they definitely insist on the distinction between beginning and further career, must be understood only as they merge in each other. For, on the one hand, the beginning of the Person is at the same time the beginning of its activity ; on the other, every moment so far as it can be isolated and considered in itself is a new coming into being of this specific personality. And as every activity of Christ must exemplify the same relation as that which marks the act of union (which, indeed, is only a union for such activities), that is, that the impulse springs from the divine nature ; so also conversely the act of union must exemplify the same relation as that through which every activity of Christ exists (since every activity is only an individual manifestation of this union)—that is, that both natures work together into one. By this canon alone must both the formulæ presented in our theorem be judged and applied, as well as all others which appear elsewhere and are derived from them.

2. There are manifold objections to the expression by which it is sought to describe more nearly the active participation of the divine nature in that act of union—namely, that in it the divine nature has assumed the human into the unity of its Person.[1] Not only on account of the expression ' divine nature,' but, in the first place, because it makes the personality of Christ altogether dependent upon the personality of the second Person in the Divine Essence. For since the Sabellians denied this, but yet believed no less than orthodox Christians in the union of the divine with the human in Christ, it seems an injustice to all who may perhaps approximate to the Sabellian view to attach the expression for this belief to the orthodox Trinitarian doctrine : especially as the original faith-constituting impression made upon the disciples, even as they grasped it in thought and reproduced it, was not connected with any knowledge of a Trinity. But the worst is, that the human nature in this way can only become a Person in the sense in which this is true of a Person in the Trinity, so that we are confronted with the dilemma, that either the three Persons must, like human persons, be individuals existing independently by themselves,

---

[1] Reinhard's phrasing is particularly infelicitous (*Dogm.* § 91) : Qui (filius Dei) cum natura *quadam* humana quam sibi adiunxerit unam efficiat personam.

or Christ as man was not such an independent individual—an assertion which gives us a completely docetic picture of Him. It is, therefore, much safer (as it is also analogous to the origin and development of faith) to establish the doctrine of Christ independently of that doctrine of the Trinity. It is true that even our first proposition might still be regarded as docetic—as if, that is to say, the truth of the human nature in Christ were already lost when we say that in the origin of the Person of Christ the human nature was altogether passive, since obviously in the origin of every other human person it takes an active part, in that its body-forming power shapes itself into a new unity of human existence in the completeness of all vital functions. But if we call to our help the canon set forth above, according to which the act of the union also must have been once a common activity of both—of the self-imparting Divine Essence,[1] and of the human nature appointed to be assumed by it—then the position is that the human nature certainly cannot have been active in being assumed by the divine, in such a way that (to put it so) the being of God in Christ was developed out of the human nature, or even in such a way that there was in the human nature a capacity to draw down the divine to itself; only the possibility was innate in it (and must have remained in it intact even during the dominion of sin) of being assumed into such a union with the divine, but this possibility is far from being either capacity or activity. On the other hand, in accordance with our canon we must add that the human nature can have been assumed by the divine only as engaged in a person-forming activity, since the divine activity is not person-forming in the way of generation. In speaking, therefore, of the origin of the specific personality of Christ, that is, of the implanting of the divine in the human nature, it must be said that in this the latter was only receptive and could only take a passive part, since no person-forming activity of human nature apart from any activity of the divine nature could ever have produced anything but an ordinary human person. But in so far as Christ none the less was also a perfectly human person, the formation of this person also must have been an act of the human nature ; and so the whole process must have been a common act of the two natures. This is recognized by all dogmatic theologians who, rejecting the opinion that the body of Christ was completely formed

[1] In the proposition itself, even after expressing unqualified disapproval of the term ' divine nature,' I allowed it to stand, purely for convenience' sake. But here in the detailed discussion that consideration is irrelevant, and hence I have reverted to the simplest term.

in a single moment,[1] or that in essentials it came down from heaven with the divine,[2] reckon the gradual formation of the organism from the first beginnings of life onwards as part of the truth of the human nature of Christ. But during this development the human nature was not altogether passive ; hence there was also a physical activity of this nature at the first beginnings of life *alongside of* its merely passive attitude relatively to the divine activity.

On the other hand, doubts of an altogether opposite kind might be raised against a special divine activity in the origin of the Person of Christ, namely, that this activity must either have occurred in time (which conflicts with the first canon, that God must remain outside every temporal medium), or it would not have been a special and immediate activity (in which case the already admitted supernatural quality would again be endangered). So we see how either of two errors could be chosen even by those of genuinely Christian temper. In order to avoid entangling the Eternal in temporality, one may decide to make it a condition in presenting the peculiar dignity of Christ that it must be possible to regard Him like any other person as a product of the human nature. And in order at the same time to leave room all the more assuredly for an immediate divine activity, one might propose the view that even the humanity of Christ did not begin at any particular time—an interpretation which necessarily borders on docetism and threatens the true historicity of Christ no less than the opposite view does His ideality. But vacillation between these two views will be altogether avoided if it be admitted that the uniting divine activity is also an eternal activity, but that, as in God there is no distinction between resolve and activity, this eternal activity means for us simply a divine decree, identical as such with the decree to create man and included therein ; but the aspect of this decree which is turned towards us as activity, or its manifestation in the actual beginning of the life of the Redeemer, through which that eternal decree realized itself, as at a single point of space so also at a moment of time, is temporal. So that the temporality has reference purely to the person-forming activity of the human nature, during which

---

[1] Joann. Damasc. iii. 2 : καὶ τότε ἐπεσκίασεν ἐπ᾽ αὐτὴν ἡ τοῦ θεοῦ . . . ἐνυπόστατος σοφία καὶ δύναμις, ὁ υἱὸς τοῦ θεοῦ . . . καὶ συνέπηξεν ἑαυτῷ . . . σάρκα ἐψυχωμένην . . . οὐ ταῖς κατὰ μικρὸν προσθήκαις ἀπαρτιζομένου τοῦ σχήματος, ἀλλ᾽ ὑφ᾽ ἕν τελειωθέντος. On the other point, see Athanas., *ad Epict.* (ed. Patav.), i. p. 731 : πόθεν δὲ πάλιν ἡρεύξαντό τινες ἴσην ἀσέβειαν . . . ὥστε εἰπεῖν, μὴ νεώτερον εἶναι τὸ σῶμα τῆς τοῦ λόγου θεότητος ἀλλὰ συναΐδιον αὐτῷ διὰ παντὸς γεγενῆσθαι, ἐπειδὴ ἐκ τῆς οὐσίας τῆς σοφίας συνέστη.

[2] See Gerhard, *loc.* iii. p. 421.

it was taken up into the union ; and we can with equal justice say that Christ even as a human person was ever coming to be simultaneously with the world itself.[1]

The presentation of this act of union and of the relation of the two natures in the union involves two other formulæ, one asserting the *impersonality* of the human nature in Christ before its union with the divine ; the other affirming His *supernatural conception*.

With regard to the first of these, the statement that the human nature of Christ in itself is *impersonal*, or that it has no subsistence of its own, but subsists only through the divine, is, in this scholastic dress, very clumsy and obscure. It is not an easily solved problem, to think of something as the human nature of Christ and yet as impersonal, since the nature in which we all share can only be called the nature of an individual in so far as it has become personal in him. But if we go into the idea, there must arise the new difficulty, how, in view of this impersonality, the human nature in Christ can fail to be more imperfect in Him than in us all ? But this confusion disappears when the matter is rightly conceived. The term ' human nature ' can properly mean only this life-form as a unity, as in essence it is person-forming and has its existence in the changing course of personal life. Hence the origin of each individual of our species is to be regarded as an act which human nature as a living force brings about by itself. The meaning is this—that since by this act there could be given to a person at the start only the germ of the imperfect and obscure God-consciousness, not the absolutely powerful God-consciousness itself, while in the Person of Christ this last must have been included in the development right from the very beginnings of life, therefore without the accession of the uniting divine activity the Person of Christ would not have come into being. But the expression remains an unfortunate one, that the human nature of Christ would have been impersonal—all that it means is that the human nature would not have become this personality of Christ, but that that divine influence upon the human nature is at one and the same time the incarnation of God in human consciousness and the formation of the human nature into the personality of Christ. In the same way, the ex-

[1] Of the two terms employed by the Greek Fathers for this act of union, ἐνσάρκωσις is much to be preferred to ἐνσωμάτωσις. The latter in part admits of the idea that the λόγος was implanted in a body already complete, in part the idea that the λόγος was only allied to a body, but Himself took the place of the soul. Neither idea is present in ἐνσάρκωσις. Hence, where the subject is handled properly, this term and the corresponding ' incarnatio ' are much more common than ' corporatio ' and ἐνσωμάτωσις.

pression 'this human nature would have remained impersonal'
(which likewise is only apparently negative) merely indicates the
permanency of that same divine influence and of whatever follows
from it in the Person of Christ. But the formula was shaped with
special reference to those who hold that the Word was united with
the Person of Jesus only long after His Person had reached maturity
—and who therefore assume a personality for His human nature
apart from this union.

It is involved in this formula that in the origin of the Person of
Christ a supernatural activity was operative. The second formula
agrees with it, in that it adds to this yet another *supernatural*
element—namely, the complete exclusion of the male activity *in the
conception of Christ*. For this is a second element : the being of
God in Christ cannot possibly be explained by the fact that no male
activity had any share in His conception. This position must
be considered from a twofold point of view : first, with reference to
the available New Testament testimonies on the subject ; next, with
reference to its dogmatic value. Those stories [1] are never again
referred to in the further course of the history of Christ ; nor does
any apostolic passage appeal to them. They conflict with the two
genealogies of Christ, which go back to Joseph in a simple and
straightforward way without taking any account of these stories.
So far as John is concerned, they conflict not only with his silence
concerning the fact itself, but also with the way in which he relates,
without any corrective remark, that Jesus was called the son of
Joseph by His countrymen and acquaintances.[2] The same sort of
thing is also found in both Matthew and Luke.[3] Anyone who
takes the stories of a Virgin Birth as literally exact has of course one
miracle more to stand for ; but probably no one will wish to maintain that such acceptance of them introduces into our faith an
element at variance with its true nature—though certainly those
who delight in parallels between these birth-narratives and the
various Jewish and heathen legends of the supernatural conception
of distinguished men go as far as they can in that direction. On
the other hand, others have doubts about basing a doctrine, in these
circumstances, solely upon these stories, and even, it may be, about
setting it up as an indispensable part of the creed. They rather
find themselves constrained to conclude from the available evidence
that among the original followers of Christ no great value was

---

[1] Matt. 1[18-25] and Luke 1[31-34].
[2] John 6[42].   [3] Matt. 13[55], Luke 4[22].

attached to this circumstance, nor was there any quite fixed and generally recognized tradition on the subject. And if they do so, we are bound to grant them that it is quite possible to believe in Christ as Redeemer without believing in His supernatural conception in this sense.

So far as the second point of view is concerned—that of the dogmatic value of this belief—first, not only are the passages in the ancient creeds [1] so expressed that they betray virtually no trace of a dogmatic purpose, but the same is true also of the modern creeds borrowed from them. [2] The additions made in the latter to the expressions sometimes adopted from the old creeds, sometimes presupposed as accepted, [3] have at most here and there a slight dogmatic colouring, either with reference to original sin or to the implanting of the divine in human nature—the only points on account of which the fact can have importance for the Christian faith. A closer consideration will show, however, that it is without any real bearing upon either question. For we have already claimed that the Person of Christ is supernatural, in our sense of the term, in both these relations ; and thus, although this was not definitely expressed, it has been indicated that no adequate explanation of His origin can be found in an act of the person-forming power of human nature, mediated through a double-sided sexual activity. For, as has been said above, [4] the sinfulness of every individual has its root in the previous generation. It follows that the Redeemer could not come into being through natural procreation, since He must not Himself belong to the corporate life of sinfulness. The same is true also with regard to the other point. For the reproductive power of the species cannot be adequate to produce an individual through whom something is to be introduced, for the first time, into the species, which was never in it before. For that it is necessary to

---

[1] *Symb. rom.* : τὸν γεννηθέντα ἐκ πνεύματος ἁγίου καὶ Μαρίας τῆς παρθένου· qui natus est de spiritu sancto ex Maria virgine.—*Symb. Nic. Const.* : σαρκωθέντα ἐκ πνεύματος ἁγίου καὶ Μαρίας τῆς παρθένου καὶ ἐνανθρωπήσαντα.

[2] *Conf. Aug.* 8 : natus ex virgine Maria.—*Exp. simpl.* xi. p. 26 : non ex viri coitu sed conceptum purissime ex spiritu sancto et natum ex Maria *semper virgine.*—*Conf. Helv.* xi. p. 96 : carnem . . . ex intacta virgine Maria, spiritu cooperante, sumens.—*Conf. Gallic.* xiv. p. 116 : cuius caro sit vere *semen Abrahae et Davidis,* quamvis arcana et incomprehensibili spiritus sancti virtute fuerit suo tempore in utero beatae illius virginis concepta.—*Conf. Anglic.* ii. p. 127 : in utero beatae virginis ex illius substantia *naturam humanam* assumsit. —*Conf. Belg.* xviii. p. 180 : conceptus in utero beatae virginis Mariae idque *virtute* spiritus sancti absque viri opere.

[3] Even where the subject is not mentioned at all, as in the *Symb. Quic.* and the *Conf. Hungar.*, no definite intention need be suspected.

[4] See § 69.

postulate, in addition to this reproductive power, a creative activity combined with the human activity ; only thus can the influence of the sexual activity in procreation be neutralized—an influence which would involve participation in the universal sinfulness. In this sense everyone who assumes in the Redeemer a natural sinlessness and a new creation through the union of the divine with the human, postulates a supernatural conception as well. But where natural procreation is inadequate, there its partial neutralization must also be inadequate. For the being of God in a life cannot be explained by its origin from a virgin without sexual intercourse ; and equally the absence of any paternal share in the new life cannot free that life from participation in the corporate life of sinfulness so long as the maternal share remains altogether what it is by nature. And so before long the complementary idea was formed, that in the same way Mary too must have been free from inherited sinfulness. But for one thing, the same affirmation must be made, and for the same reason, about the mother of Mary, and so right back through the generations. And for another, in so far as every psychical factor has also its physical counterpart, every actual sin of Mary must have exercised an influence upon the child so long as its life was enclosed within hers. Since, therefore, there is no doctrine or tradition of a continuous series of mothers who were conceived, and who remained, without sin, the absence of the male share in the begetting of the Redeemer is in both connexions inadequate ; and consequently the assumption of a Virgin Birth is superfluous. Consequently everything rests upon the higher influence which, as a creative divine activity, could alter both the paternal and the maternal influence in such a way that all ground for sinfulness was removed, and this although procreation was perfectly natural—as indeed only this creative divine activity could avail to give completeness to the natural imperfection of the child who was begotten. The general idea of a supernatural conception remains, therefore, essential and necessary, if the specific pre-eminence of the Redeemer is to remain undiminished. But the more precise definition of this supernatural conception as one in which there was no male activity has no connexion of any kind with the essential elements in the peculiar dignity of the Redeemer ; and hence, in and by itself, is no constituent part of Christian doctrine. Whoever accepts this definition, therefore, accepts it only on the ground of the narratives involving it contained in the New Testament writings ; hence belief in it, like belief in many matters of fact which have just as little necessary connexion with the dignity and the work of the Redeemer, belongs solely to the doctrine of Scripture ; and everyone has to reach a decision about it by the proper application of those principles of criticism and interpretation which approve themselves to Him. But anyone who accepts a supernatural conception in our sense of the term can hardly, at least, find any reason in the supernatural element which they contain for denying the historical character of these narratives, or for departing from the literal interpretation of them. Similarly anyone who cannot accept them as literally and historically true is still quite free to hold to the doctrine proper of the supernatural conception. But if it is superfluous to set up a doctrine of the Virgin Birth proper, it is also inadvisable to do so, for this involves one all too easily in investigations of a purely scientific character which lie quite outside our sphere.[1]

And now in order to avoid misunderstanding, it is necessary to say only this further about a conception which has come to prevail everywhere in Christendom. First, this physiologically supernatural element does not, in itself, imply what we demand of the divine influence in the conception of the Redeemer ; nor has it any influence upon the racial character of Jesus' personality—it neither abolishes, in itself, that which carries with it a participation in sinfulness, nor does it rob Him of what belongs to His historicity. Secondly, for the same reasons, we must avoid spinning out the notion, which, as we have seen, has no other basis than the Gospel narratives, further than these narratives require ; hence the assertion that Mary remained a virgin is to be rejected as completely baseless. Thirdly, the notion must not be based upon—and just as little made the basis of—a condemnation of the sexual impulse, as if its satisfaction were something sinful and productive of sin. Lastly, even if we take the narratives literally and in a historical sense, we must not assume that their terminology is pedantically exact ; in particular, we must keep in mind that the angel could not then speak to Mary of the Holy Spirit in the more precise New Testament sense.[2] Therefore all ingenious explanations as to why this activity is attributed specially to the Holy Spirit are out of place.[3] But only completely uninitiated persons could, in spite of the clear distinc-

---

[1] Consider, *e.g.*, the expressions italicized in the quotations given above from the creeds.

[2] Joann. Damasc., rightly understood, agrees with this (i. 19, iii. 11) τῇ μὲν ἐνσαρκώσει τοῦ λόγου οὔτε ὁ πατὴρ οὔτε τὸ πνεῦμα κατ᾽ οὐδένα λόγον κεκοινώνηκεν εἰ μὴ κατ᾽ εὐδοκίαν, although elsewhere he speaks differently and less precisely.

[3] Cf. Gerh., *loc.* iii. p. 416, whose explanations depend principally upon Hilarius, *de fid. trin.* ii.

tion always made by the teachers of the Church,[1] so confuse the relation as to call Jesus the son of the Holy Spirit.

3. The second formula of our proposition, which describes the state of union of the two natures, can also be rightly understood only by the help of the canon we have laid down. Otherwise it would be easy to regard the association of the two natures as one on equal terms ; and, since an absolute equilibrium between them cannot be assumed, also to suppose an occasional preponderance on the side of the human nature. The nature of the association, however, must at every moment be such that the activity proceeds from the being of God in Christ, and the human nature is only taken up into association with it. If we think here of the antithesis—and it must certainly not be overlooked—between predominantly active and predominantly passive moments in human life, we might well be apprehensive that we are still losing, in this way, the completeness of the human nature in Christ, since of course passive states cannot proceed from the divine in Him, from which yet everything must proceed—and so passive states would necessarily be lacking in Him. To take this point now in its widest reference, we find one passive condition posited as necessary, almost as constant, in Christ, so that in a sense all His actions depend upon it—namely, sympathy with the condition of men ; yet at the same time in everything which proceeded from this we shall most distinctly recognize the impulse of the reconciling being of God in Christ ; which accordingly seems to be conditioned by a passive state which could only take its rise in the human nature. Now if that were really the case, and Christ could have come to all those actions, and therefore strictly speaking to the whole work of redemption, only through an almost accidental feeling [i.e. sympathy], then inevitably our whole idea of the Redeemer would thereby become something different from that which up till now we have represented to ourselves. But our canon also compels us to think of the human nature of Christ in such feelings, not as moved for and through itself, but only as taken up into association with an activity of the divine in Christ. Now this 'divine' is the divine love in Christ which, once and for all or in every moment—whichever expression be chosen—gave direction to His feelings for the spiritual conditions of men. In virtue of these feelings, and in consequence of them, there then arose the impulse to particular helpful acts. So that in this interrelation every original activity belongs solely to the divine, and

---

[1] Many passages in Gerh., loc. cit.

everything passive solely to the human. For even the human activities conditioned by those impulses carry in themselves the quality of passivity. There must certainly, however, have been, even in the life of Christ, other passive states which did not proceed from any spiritual impulse, but only from the natural connexion of the human organism with external nature. Now to these states we must, also in accordance with our canon, apply the formula originally intended only for the act of union, that the human nature is not the personal nature of Christ before it has been taken up into union with the divine. For all such states were still impersonal so long as they were simply passive ; but their assumption into the innermost personal consciousness and their permeation by a divine impulse were so entirely one and the same thing that before such permeation they would have been assumed only as an external and alien element. So that, to sum up, we may say that there can have been no active state in Christ which, regarded as existing for itself, did not arise from the being of God in Him, and was not perfected by the human nature ; and similarly no passive state whose transformation into activity—which first made it a personal state—did not follow the same course.

Against this, of course, the objection might be urged, that if we distinguish individual moments, and ascribe to the divine in Christ the rise of all the activities which follow each other thus in time, then this divine in Christ, in contradiction to what can properly be asserted of a being of God, is being described as a temporal thing, with an activity which arises and passes away. But this difficulty too is resolved if, carrying further (under the guidance of our canon) the answer already [1] given to the same objection with regard to the act of union, we say that even during the union the Divine Essence in Christ retained its identity, only becoming active in temporal fashion, and that only that side of this activity is temporal which had already become human and passed over into the sphere of outward appearance. So that in Christ Himself the original assumptive divine activity and the divine activity during the union are not to be distinguished ; but all activities, in so far as distinguishable in time, are simply developments of the human activities. Every outward activity of Christ, whether it is to be regarded rather as an activity of the intellect or as one of the will, was in its aspect of human growth a result of the temporal development ; and only in so far as all emergent activity of Christ is to be regarded thus can we

[1] In 2 of this section.

rightly ascribe to Him a perfect human soul, but a soul inwardly impelled by this special being of God in Him, which, retaining its unchangeable identity, permeates that soul in the variety of its functions and moments, as that variety continually develops.[1] This, too, is the meaning of the phrase of the Schools, that *the union is a personal one.* It is not a special nature which comes into being in this way, one which could and must be distinguished from other human existence ; what comes into existence through the being of God in Christ is all perfectly human, and in its totality constitutes a unity, the unity of a natural life-story, in which everything that emerges is purely human, and one thing can be deduced from another, since every moment presupposes those which have gone before, yet in which everything can be completely understood only upon the presupposition of that union through which alone this Person could come into being, so that every moment also reveals the divine in Christ as that which conditions it. And if, after all that has been said, we define the spheres of our two propositions in relation to each other, then we shall have to say that the first applies exclusively to the very earliest beginning of the existence of Christ when the life was coming into being as a simple entity, and consequently that it holds only of the time before the historical appearance of Christ. And similarly the latter applies exclusively after this appearance ; for only when the human element is absolutely complete, and there is no more growth in its coexistence with the being of God in Him, can it be purely co-operative in its action. And so it is comprehensible that for the time filled by this historical appearance there should be two different modes of interpretation, which, although quite consistent with each other, yet when their true relation is not recognized, seem to be incompatible. One of these pays such exclusive attention throughout to the initiatory divine factor that it is in danger of losing sight altogether of the human context ; the other attempts everywhere to grasp the human context so completely that it comes near losing sight of the underlying divine factor.

4. In agreement with both formulæ of our proposition are, further, the old canons—they have only a negative but no real

[1] The same view is expressed, among others, by Joann. Dam., if only he be rightly understood (iii. 7 ; p. 215 seq.) : 'Ιστέον δὲ, ὡς εἰ καὶ περιχωρεῖν ἐν ἀλλήλαις τὰς τοῦ κυρίου φύσεις φαμὲν, ἀλλ' οἴδαμεν ὅπως ἐκ τῆς θείας φύσεως ἡ περιχώρησις γέγονεν· αὕτη μὲν γὰρ διὰ πάντων διήκει καθὼς βούλεται καὶ περιχωρεῖ, δι αὐτῆς δὲ οὐδέν. καὶ αὕτη μὲν τῶν οἰκείων αὐχημάτων τῇ σαρκὶ μεταδίδωσι (of which more below) μένουσα αὐτὴ ἀπαθής, καὶ τῶν τῆς σαρκὸς παθῶν (to which everything temporal belongs) ἀμέτοχος.

positive value—which as a result of the discussions in the Councils are expounded even in the oldest systematic treatises.[1] It is obvious that underlying the earliest threefold statement of the points in question [2] is the idea that the divine nature in Christ cannot in any way be separated from the human nature in Him, so as to permit of the sundering of the two. Every such separation, even if in accordance with these formulæ it were understood only in a temporal or spatial sense, could still be only a separation of the activities ; and if such a separation were possible, then there would have to be in Christ, on the one hand, human activities in no way dependent upon the impulse of the divine, and on the other, divine activities which would have nowhere betrayed themselves in His human nature. But these could have given no proof of their derivation from the act of union, since they would bear in themselves no similarity to this ; accordingly these formulæ exclude just what our canon also excludes. The other threefold statement [3] quite clearly has the purpose of rejecting any idea of an alteration of one nature by the other. Through any such alteration—which of course could only have proceeded from the human nature—the divine would have become something conditioned in space and time ; and similarly, if the human had been altered by the divine, the Person would have lost its identity with the rest of the human race. In neither case would there have been a union of the divine with the human. Here too the aim, therefore, is the same as that which guides us in seeking to understand the divine factor in the union in the only way which is compatible with the integrity of the human, and *vice versa*. None the less, these two formulæ are not for us to-day ; they are altogether based upon the conception of divinity as a nature, which can only serve to introduce confusion everywhere.

It is time that, along with these negative formulæ, we consigned to the history of dogma also the extremely empty and formal theory, that propositions about Christ, to be correct, must be differently constructed according as we are speaking of the whole Person of Christ, or only of one of the two natures. Such rules, if they are to be normative for the language of edification, imposing the limits within which it must move, could only be of value in times of heresy-hunting ; but heresy-hunting in this form is hardly likely to recur. In general, we must recognize that we are no longer

---

[1] *E.g.* Joann. Dam. iii. 3 ff.   [2] ἀχωρίστως, ἀδιαιρέτως, and ἀδιαστάτως.
[3] ἀναλλοιώτως, ἀτρέπτως, and ἀσυγχύτως.

at the same stage as the men of these far-off days, when the more exact technical terminology was only being gradually developed out of the popular presentations of eminent men. Now that the system of doctrine has been completed, and development within the Schools goes its own way, Christian preachers must have the freedom granted to the poets, to make use of terms which cannot find a place in the terminology of technical theology, provided that in their immediate context, from which they must not be torn, they are unobjectionable, and that they involve nothing which would lessen the dignity of the Redeemer or offend people's feeling for that dignity. If, on the other hand, these rules are meant to be used only in technical theology itself, in order that at every point it may more easily determine whether individual formulæ are or are not consistent with the general propositions, then they depend too much upon the use of the expression ' nature,' for the divine as well as for the human, to be useful when once that mode of expression has been abandoned. And we possess a far better canon in the formula that in Christ the creation of man first reaches completion. For what distinguishes Christ from all others is that which is innermost in Him ; hence the indwelling being of God in Him must be related to the whole human nature in the same way as that which previously was innermost was related to the whole human organism—an analogy which, even if not clearly expressed, runs through the whole foregoing presentation of the subject.

5. It follows at once from the character of the being of God in Christ as now set forth, and from the necessity of ceasing to treat the Supreme Being as a nature, as well as from our previous teaching on the divine attributes, that the theory of a mutual communicatión of the attributes of the two natures to one another also is to be banished from the system of doctrine, and handed over to the history of doctrine. For in so far as we arrive at our ideas of divine attributes only by analogy, the attribution of these to human nature, if that nature is not to be destroyed by the infinity of these attributes, is merely an assertion of absolute human excellence. But on the other hand, in so far as each particular attribute is simply a negation of the essence of man, and it is only when viewed all together as one that they can represent the Divine Essence, it is impossible to predicate of human nature even the individual features of this collective view. For example, if we were to attribute to human nature the identity of omniscience and omnipotence, so that one and the same omniscient omnipotence and

omnipotent omniscience of the divine nature should have permeated the assumed human nature,[1] as heat permeates iron, then during this communication nothing human could have been left in Christ, since everything human is essentially a negation of omniscient omnipotence. If in consequence we fall back upon regarding the divine attributes as altogether or for the most part quiescent— though the former alternative alone is consistent, not even the miracles being traced to an exceptional activity of the divine attributes [2]—the emptiness of this whole theory comes out most clearly. For since divine attributes are simply activities, in what consists the communication of these when they are inactive ? Moreover, in that case the union of the natures would altogether cease to be a dogmatic idea in the stricter sense, for it cannot possibly be a statement regarding an impression received from Christ, since the quiescent attributes cannot make themselves perceptible even indirectly. It is the same with the communication of human attributes to the divine nature. On the one hand, all statements regarding our God-consciousness are just such an attribution, inasmuch as all divine attributes are drawn, by analogy, from human. But apart from this, it would necessarily mean the negation of the Divine Essence, if to the divine nature there were to be ascribed any human quality (and in any way) which had to be excluded in the original formation of our conceptions of divine attributes. If, for example, to the divine nature there were to be communicated anything human in the way of capacity for suffering, in such a communication no room is left for anything divine ; nay, every notable human excellence, even, is a diminution of the capacity for suffering, and even what most inwardly resembles the divine in man does not so much suffer as give its activity a re-active form. It has been believed that the capacity for suffering must be attributed even to the divine nature in Christ, partly on the ground that otherwise redemptive power would be lacking to His suffering ; [3] not only, however, has this older assertions against it,[4] but equally it depends, as we shall show later, upon wrong ideas

---

[1] See *Sol. decl.*, p. 778 : cum tota divinitatis plenitudo in Christo habitet ut in proprio suo corpore etiam . . . in assumpta humana natura divinam suam virtutem exerceat . . . idque ea quodammodo ratione qua . . . ignis in ferro candente agit.

[2] See Reinh., *Dogm.*, § 97, 2 and 6.

[3] *Sol. decl.*, p. 771 : Si enim persuaderi mihi patiar ut credam solam humanam naturam pro me passam esse, profecto Christus mihi non magni pretii salvator erit, sed ipse tandem salvatore eget.

[4] Joann. Dam. iii. 7 : αὕτη μὲν (ἡ θεία φύσις) τῶν οἰκείων αὐχημάτων τῇ σαρκὶ μεταδίδωσι μένουσα αὐτὴ ἀπαθὴς, καὶ τῶν τῆς σαρκὸς παθῶν ἀμέτοχος.

of the work of redemption.   And so it might well be said that this doctrine of the mutual communication of attributes, truly and completely worked out, must cancel again the union of the two natures, since in virtue of that communication each nature would cease to be what it is.   The rejection of this theory, however, by no means involves a preferring the Reformed school to the Lutheran. For if the former speaks, instead,[1] of contrasted attributes of two natures in one person, it is rightly met with the objection that it is dividing Christ, since contrasted things cannot be one, nor can the natures be one either, if their attributes are held apart.   But the other school is chargeable with a similar division.   For if the communication is to be a real one, then through it there arise in each nature two kinds of activities, which cannot really form a series—e.g. in the human nature of Christ there would have to be ideational activities both in the manner of a limited con-sciousness and in that of the communicated omniscience.   Both doctrines, therefore, are equally to be rejected, since they both depend upon the false idea of a divine nature to which it is possible to ascribe a group of attributes.

§ 98. *Third Theorem.—Christ was distinguished from all other men by His essential sinlessness and His absolute perfection.*

1. By essential sinlessness we are to understand a sinlessness which has its adequate ground within His personality itself, so that it would have been altogether the same whatever the outward relations might have been (and among outward relations we may include also whatever belongs to the body).   This expression at least sets forth with sufficient definiteness the point at issue, since it follows from what has been said that this inner ground can be none other than the union of the divine and the human in His Person.   That which in individual cases we experience immediately we must conceive to be possible also in general.   We have imme-diate experience of the fact that by a favourable combination of cir-cumstances sin, even inward sin, may be prevented from becoming actual.   But this happens in such a way that therein we not only remain conscious of ourselves as sinful men, but are even confirmed in this consciousness through this very perception, for it implies a recognition that in our case the *inner* ground for the prevention of sin is lacking.   Such sinlessness, which in comparison with essential

---

[1] *Conf. Gall.* xv. p. 116 : manente tamen unaquaque illarum naturarum in sua distincta proprietate, etc.   Similarly, *Conf. Belg.* xix.

sinlessness is no more than accidental, would therefore not express the peculiar excellence of the Redeemer ; and not only so, but where the inward possibility of sinning is posited, there too is posited in addition at least an infinitely small amount of the reality of sin, in the form of tendency. So that one who can be content with such accidental sinlessness in the Redeemer may also let pass actual sin in Him, provided it does not make itself so perceptible [1] that someone for a moment might claim superiority to Christ. At the same time, the usual formulæ of technical theology do not mark the distinction with the required sharpness, and the quarrel which has been waged between them seems a perfectly empty one. It is true that the formula, *potuit non peccare*, asserts the essential pre-eminence of Christ, if taken as affirming a contrast to the state of all other men. For these, one and all, can never not-sin ; sin creeps into everything—which, strictly speaking, must then have been the case with Christ also (to the extent of the infinitely small amount referred to above), if a real possibility of sinning is ascribed to Him. But the formula does not express that pre-eminence, as soon as it is taken to mean something different from the other formula, *non potuit peccare* ; for when made a contrast to this it involves the possibility of sinning. But exactly the same holds true of the latter formula ; it too may be used by one who is only assuming a general divine protection exerted over the Redeemer. Thus it too corresponds to the content of our formula only if it be taken as the equivalent of the first in the sense indicated.

But, even on the basis of our formula, it remains difficult to determine what it excludes from Christ, and that in such wise as to preserve intact all that must belong to Him in virtue of His likeness to us. And this point is indisputably one from which it must be possible to develop much that is essential for Christian ethics ; for everything depends on determining the point where sin begins. A special difficulty arises here from the fact that even in the earliest documents of the faith it is asserted that Christ was tempted in all points, a statement which in the light of the conclusion reached above [2] involves sin in Him, if we take it as meaning that there was even an infinitely small element of struggle involved. On the other hand, susceptibility to the contrast of the pleasurable and the painful belongs to the reality of human nature, so that it must be possible for pleasure and pain to exist in a sinless way, and the beginning of sin must lie between the moment at which pleasure

---

[1] John 8[46].   [2] Cf. § 93, 4.

and pain exist in this sinless way and that at which struggle begins. If, at the same time, we remember that in Christ every impulse must have been determined by the God-consciousness, it follows that in Him, too, pleasure and pain must have been possible, but not so that they determined the impulse ; that is, they must have been present only as the result of an impulse which was determined in the manner appropriate to Him. They *are* such results when as sensation or feeling they remain wholly within the limits of the quiescent consciousness, but not when they pass over into desire or repulsion. Now temptation consists just in the approximation of these two, and Christ can have been tempted without prejudice to His essential sinlessness only if pleasure and pain came to Him as intensified sensation, while His essential sinlessness explains why they never could become anything more than symptoms of a state, but without any determinative or co-determinative power ; but not if they came so that the transition from the one sort to the other ever really took place.[1] Only, as this rule must hold good for every moment of Christ's life without exception, it must be observed that this way of expressing it is applicable only to a developed consciousness, and that the childhood of Christ as well can only have had the character of perfect innocence if this rule held good then also in proportion to the stage of development reached at the moment. So that in respect of sin Christ was at all times equally different from all other men, and at all times equally essentially free from sin.

It belongs further to this sinlessness, that Christ can neither have originated real error Himself, or even have accepted the error of others with real conviction, and as well-established truth. Nor is it necessary to restrict this principle to the sphere of His proper vocation ; only we must hold fast to the distinction between the acceptance and the propagation of ideas which were definitely maintained by others (in regard to these one neither makes any investigation nor accepts any responsibility), and the forming of a judgment which in some connexion thereafter determines one's mode of action. In the latter case, error always presupposes either a precipitancy which nothing but irrelevant motives could have

---

[1] In the treatment of this question I could take no special account of the story of the Temptation, for to me it is impossible to regard it as historical. Obviously its content, taken literally, is such that in comparison Christ must often have been much more strongly tempted in the course of His active life. And hence the narrator is by no means to be blamed who indicates (Luke 4[13]) that this is not to be regarded as for Him the end of all temptation.

occasioned, or an obscured sense of truth which partly has its basis in the universal sinfulness, but partly too is in each single case bound up with the special sinfulness of the individual.

Closely connected with this doctrine of the essential sinlessness of Christ is the idea of the *natural immortality* of Christ—namely, that Christ would not have been subject to death in virtue of His human nature ; an idea which has not, it is true, been fixed by being included in any of the creeds, nor is really based on passages in the Bible,[1] but yet has found very general acceptance. But the only basis for the conception is that when death is regarded as the wages of sin, he who is free from all connexion with sin must also have been free from the dominion of death. When we take into account what has already been said above [2] about the natural immortality of Adam and the connexion of all natural evils with sin, nothing more can be inferred from the sinlessness of Christ than that death can have been no evil for Christ. We must hold to this position, and instead of the idea in question take our side with those who acknowledge that immortality was conferred upon Christ's human nature only with the Resurrection.[3] All the more that mortality and the capacity for physical suffering are so closely connected that such a natural immortality in Christ would make the capacity of human nature in His Person for suffering a mere empty phrase, and no great worth could be attached to His physical sufferings without self-contradiction.

Yet this idea is not represented as simply an inference from the sinlessness of Christ ; it is held that it alone reveals to us the true significance of all the statements which set forth His death as a voluntary one, and thus brings out fully the higher significance of His suffering and death. But precisely from this point of view the idea is a highly dubious one. For one who cannot naturally die cannot be put to death by force either ; it would therefore have been necessary that Christ by a miracle should first have made Himself mortal, in order that it should be possible to put Him to death ; so that His death would have been, almost directly, His own act.

2. Now so far as the *absolute perfection* of His human nature during the period of His manhood is concerned, special emphasis is very often laid upon intellectual and physical excellence, especially

[1] What Christ Himself says in John 10[17-18] expresses, not a physical, but a social and ethical relation.
[2] Cf. § 59, *Postscript*.
[3] *Conf. Belg.* xix. p. 181 : et quamvis eidem naturae immortalitatem resurrectione sua dederit, etc.

in the older treatments of the subject.   But—since here no records come to our aid which would transform every such proposition into a historical one, and so remove it from the sphere of doctrine altogether—it may well be doubted whether the impression which we receive from Christ is sufficient to justify us in postulating for Him qualities which we cannot deduce from the union of the divine with the human nature.   Only one thing can be said if we deduce the temporal appearance of this creative activity, as an individual fact, from the general divine ordination.   And this is that, just as the Redeemer could appear only at a particular time and only out of the midst of this people, so, too, the divine activity would not have assumed the human nature and created the Person of the Redeemer in such a way that any deformity could have resulted. It is natural enough, therefore, to ascribe to the Redeemer a physical ideality also ; but since the physical aspect of His appearance was to be of no significance in itself, but only as the organ of that union, the ideality must be restricted solely to this.   From this assumption, and from the undisturbed and continuous influence of a pure will, there is to be inferred only a healthiness which is equally remote from a disproportionate strength or dominance of individual physical functions and from morbid weakness, inasmuch as by both of these the balanced aptitude of the organism for all demands of the will is impaired.   To this accordingly we must restrict ourselves, and all the more reject all prying questions,[1] because our ideas of the relation between body and soul are still open to important corrections.   And thus, if the ancients have not seldom something to say about the beauty of the Redeemer,[2] this is an idea which lies very near the frontier which we must not touch, and we may disregard it as an unconscious after-effect of heathen notions.

§ 99. *The facts of the Resurrection and the Ascension of Christ, and the prediction of His Return to Judgment, cannot be laid down as properly constituent parts of the doctrine of His Person.*

1. When we compare with the canon for dogmatic statements

---

[1] It is a divine provision, certainly of the highest significance, but not sufficiently recognized, that neither a trustworthy tradition regarding the external aspect of Christ's person, nor an authentic picture of it, has come down to us. For the same reason, we may be sure, we lack an exact description of His manner of life and a connected narrative of the events of His career.

[2] *E.g.* Chrysost., *in ep. ad Col. Homil.* viii. : οὕτως ἦν καλὸς, ὡς οὐδὲ εἶναι εἰπεῖν.

laid down above,[1] the propositions, on the one hand, concerning
the Person of Christ which we have so far set forth, and on the
other the statements contained in the oldest creeds [2] expressing
these facts (*i.e.* Resurrection, Ascension, and Judgment), it will
be seen that the former correspond to both the requirements insisted on, and the latter to neither. For if the redeeming efficacy
of Christ depends upon the being of God in Him, and faith in
Him is grounded upon the impression that such a being of God
indwells Him, then it is impossible to prove any immediate connexion between these facts and that doctrine. The disciples
recognized in Him the Son of God without having the faintest
premonition of His resurrection and ascension, and we too may
say the same of ourselves ; moreover neither the spiritual presence
which He promised nor all that He said about His enduring influence upon those who remained behind is mediated through either of
these two facts. This may well depend upon His sitting at the
right hand of God—by which, however, since the expression may
be strictly an impossible one, we must understand simply the
peculiar and incomparable dignity of Christ, raised above all conflict
—but not upon a visible resurrection or ascension, since of course
Christ could have been raised to glory even without these intermediate steps ; and if so, it is impossible to see in what relation
both these can stand to the redeeming efficacy of Christ. It is
true, on the one hand, Paul seems to attribute to the resurrection,
just as much as to the death, a share of its own in redemption ; [3]
yet on the other, the way in which he brings it forward as a guarantee
of our own resurrection [4] shows that he in no sense thinks of it as
having an exclusive connexion with the peculiar being of God in
Christ. Also, it is never adduced as an evidence of the divine
indwelling in Christ ; for it is everywhere ascribed, not to Himself,
but to God.[5] No more does John adduce the visible ascension as a
proof of the higher dignity of Christ. Hence we may safely credit
everyone who is familiar with dogmatic statements with a recognition of the fact that the right impression of Christ can be, and has
been, present in its fulness without a knowledge of these facts.

So far as the Return to Judgment is concerned, we can treat of

[1] Cf. § 29, 3.
[2] *Symb. Nic.*: καὶ ἀναστάντα ἐν τῇ τρίτῃ ἡμέρᾳ κατὰ τὰς γραφάς· καὶ ἀνελθόντα
εἰς τοὺς οὐρανοὺς καὶ καθεζόμενον ἐκ δεξιῶν τοῦ πατρὸς· καὶ πάλιν ἐρχόμενον μετὰ δόξης
κρῖναι ζῶντας καὶ νεκρούς.
[3] Rom. 4[25].   [4] 1 Cor. 15[13. 16].
[5] Acts 2[24] 3[5] 4[10] 10[40], Rom. 4[24], 1 Cor. 6[14] 15[15], 2 Cor. 4[14].

the doctrinal significance of this idea only at a later point. Here it need only be remarked that although the Judgment, in so far as we regard it as a transferable divine act, is so closely bound up with the work of redemption that it is not easy to think that God could hand it over to any but the Redeemer, yet this implies nothing greater in the Person of Christ than already we ascribe to Him apart from this ; and in any case it does not really belong to the work of redemption itself, since of course those who believe do not come into judgment. But considered as the Return of Christ it is connected with the ascension as its counterpart. Just as the latter is only an accidental form for effecting the sitting at the right hand of God, so also the promise of return is only an accidental form for the satisfaction of the longing to be united with Christ. And just as the incomprehensible and miraculous in the ascension cannot be made dependent on the divine in Christ, which reveals itself as the impulse to all His free actions, and since the ascension is nowhere presented as His act, no more can the miraculous in the Return depend upon it. So that the dissimilarity between our propositions above (those, that is to say, which we have recognized as such) and these assertions must be clear to everyone.

It is somewhat different with Christ's so-called Descent into Hell.[1] This—according to its dominant idea—would certainly belong to His redemptive activities if only we could regard it as a fact. It would then have to be regarded as an exercise of His prophetic and high-priestly office towards those who had died before His appearance. But for one thing the only passage which seems to treat of this descent [2] is far from including anything of the kind, and for another the transaction, even with this extended interpretation of the passage, would not correspond to the task to be accomplished, as we are bound to understand it. For all those also who have died since His appearance without having heard the preaching of the Gospel have the same claims as the others. Moreover, the expressions used in that passage in no way compel us to assume such an otherwise unattested fact, any more than they fix the time at which it is supposed to have happened. For these reasons the Descent has been completely omitted from our proposition.

2. Belief in these facts, accordingly, is no independent element in the original faith in Christ, of such a kind that we could not

---

[1] *Symb. Rom.* : κατελθόντα εἰς τὰ κάτωτα only in one Greek, but in several old Latin copies ; *Symb. Quic.* 36 : descendit ad inferos.
[2] 1 Pet. 3[19]. Eph. 4[9] should certainly not be adduced here.

accept Him as Redeemer or recognize the being of God in Him, if we did not know that He had risen from the dead and ascended to heaven, or if He had not promised that He would return for judgment.   Further, this belief is not to be derived from those original elements ; we cannot conclude that because God was in Christ He must have risen from the dead and ascended into heaven, or that because He was essentially sinless He must come again to act as Judge.   Rather they are accepted only because they are found in the Scriptures ; and all that can be required of any Protestant Christian is that he shall believe them in so far as they seem to him to be adequately attested.   Here the sacred writers are to be regarded only as reporters ; accordingly belief in these statements belongs, immediately and originally, rather to the doctrine of Scripture than to the doctrine of the Person of Christ.   Yet an indirect connexion with that doctrine is not to be denied to such belief, in so far, that is, as our judgment about the disciples as original reporters reacts upon our judgment about the Redeemer.   Anyone, for example, who, in view of the miraculous element involved, and to avoid accepting the resurrection of Christ as literal fact, prefers to suppose that the disciples were deceived and took an inward experience for an outward, ascribes to them such weakness of intellect that not only is their whole testimony to Christ thereby rendered unreliable, but also Christ, in choosing for Himself such witnesses, cannot have known what is in men.[1]   Or, if we suppose that He Himself wished or arranged that they should be constrained to regard an inner experience as outward perception, then He Himself would be an originator of error, and all moral conceptions would be thrown into confusion if such a higher dignity as His were compatible with this.   With the ascension it is different, so far at least as we have no adequate reason for maintaining that we have before us a direct report from an eyewitness of what actually happened, and least of all from an apostolic eyewitness.   If, nevertheless, it is affirmed that Christ did rise from the dead, but was not taken up into heaven, but lived in concealment for an indeterminate time, so that He must have arranged something which could be regarded as an ascension to heaven, then the case is just the same as with the resurrection.   Least closely connected with the doctrine of the Person of Christ proper is the promise of His Return, especially as it is promised for the sake of an office to be fulfilled, and so far would belong to the next section, if only that office were one directly

[1] John 2[25].

belonging to His vocation as Redeemer. Only if exegesis brought out clearly that a time had been fixed for this Return which has now long since elapsed, or if it were described in a way whose impossibility we could prove, would this necessarily react, if not on the doctrine of the Scriptures, yet certainly on that of the Person of Christ.

Postscript to this Doctrine.—The presentation of the Person of Christ given above, first in our own quite independent form of expression, then in closer connexion with the accepted forms of the Church, is, in essentials, so widespread and so long current in the Christian Church, that it must be regarded as the general faith of Christians. All the more that even many of those who content themselves with a lesser idea of the Redeemer reject this dominant view only because they are suspicious of the miraculous in general —whether they overlook the distinction which we have laid down,[1] or reject it—or because they believe that along with it they must accept a doctrine of the Trinity which is offensive to them on account of its polytheistic complexion. It is therefore to be hoped that many will find it easier to accept, in a freer presentation, a view by which they are repelled when they find it invested in hard scholastic forms.

It cannot, however, be definitely proved that the same form of doctrine prevailed universally in Christendom where the same faith about the relation to the Redeemer underlay it, the reason being that neither understanding nor terminology had sufficiently developed for that. Also it is undeniable that alongside this view of the Redeemer other different and lesser ones were current in Christendom very early. For both these reasons the question cannot be avoided whether the view of the Church can really be vindicated as the original one by statements of Christ Himself and of the Apostles, or whether they are right who assert that it is a view which arose later. Here it must be premised, that even supposing the originality of our doctrine were not proved, it still would not follow that it is false or arbitrarily invented, provided only that those original testimonies are not demonstrably at variance with it. But the question itself, it must be admitted, is so complicated that it cannot be decided in a manner which could win general acceptance, so long as, on the one hand, the most various opinions exist alongside each other as to the way in which the New Testament writings came into existence and as to who their authors were, and,

[1] Cf. § 13.

on the other hand, exegetical methods are so various and so arbitrary. So long as it is possible to dispute interminably over the meaning of particular passages, it is useless to have recourse to particular sayings of Christ's own to prove His essential sinlessness [1] or the being of God in Him.[2]   But anyone who in the interpretation of particular passages is not content merely with a sense in harmony with his own theory, but keeps an open mind for a true impression of the whole, will scarcely be able to ascribe to the sayings of Christ about His relation to men and to His Father [3] (having regard to the way in which they complete and pervade each other) a lesser content than that set forth in our propositions, although perhaps not precisely in the sense of the ecclesiastical formulæ relating to the doctrine of the Trinity.   And at the same time these sayings are not of such a kind that they destroy the reality of Christ's human existence, as if in His temporal consciousness He had, say, a recollection of a separate existence of the divine in Him, before His incarnation.[4]

In entire agreement with this is the double appellation, Son of Man and Son of God, which Christ gives to Himself.   For He could not have given Himself the first name, if He had not been conscious of sharing completely in the same human nature as others ; but it would have been meaningless to claim it specially for Himself, if He had not had a reason for doing so which others could not adduce— if, that is, the name had not had a pregnant meaning, which was meant to indicate a difference between Him and all others.[5]   Similarly the connexion between the appellation Son of God and what Christ says about His relation to His Father shows that He did not use it of Himself in the same sense in which it had already been used of others [6]—as indeed is clearly involved in the expression ' only-begotten ' which comes from Christ Himself.[7]   Only if we destroy this natural connexion between two designations which manifestly refer to each other, will it become easier to admit lesser

---

[1] John 8[46].   [2] John 10[30-38].
[3] John 5[17. 21. 26] 8[24. 36] 14[11. 20] 17[10. 21-23].
[4] An indication of this sort might be found in John 17[5], but John 5[19. 20] makes this interpretation almost impossible.   But even apart from that it would be open to suspicion, because the petition has remained unfulfilled, since in spite of all the labour expended no one has yet reached a clear consciousness on the matter, and no one ever will.
[5] It is a strange idea that this designation was intended to refute the popular opinion that no one would know whence the Messiah came ; not less strange is the other, that it was intended to refer to a vision in Daniel (7[13]) where one *like* a Son of man—manifestly by contrast with the beasts mentioned earlier—comes in the clouds of heaven before the Ancient of days.
[6] Compare especially John 10[35ff.].
[7] John 3[16].

interpretations and to associate them with Ebionite theories. While, on the other hand, those passages in which a high degree of grief is ascribed to Christ,[1] or in which something is told of Him which seems to imply passionate excitement,[2] are really only details which —so far from being evidence against His sinlessness, or incompatible with the being of God in Him—manifestly caused no one to doubt Him, because everyone habitually interprets such individual moments in harmony with the total impression he has already received. So they serve only to remind us that faith in Jesus as Redeemer was not based on details, but develops out of a total impression—from which it follows only that there are no details in existence which could have prevented that impression. But that the faith even in the first generation of His disciples had the same content as we have set forth here, is proved, not only by the most various testimonies which ascribe to Christ perfect purity [3] and fulness of power,[4] but also by the way in which Paul describes Him, in contrast with Adam, as the originator of a new human worth, and by the Johannine presentation of the λόγος, as well as by the theory set forth in the Epistle to the Hebrews.

Now of course even these testimonies could be weakened by artificial interpretations, by tearing them out of their context and combining them with what is irrelevant. But it is not sufficient to show merely that this expression and that other may have less significance ; it must also be made clear how it can have come about that an ordinary relation was described in extraordinary and inappropriate terms, and how the original sense of these was so early lost in the tradition. So long as this cannot be done better than it is by entirely arbitrary hypotheses, the belief will probably hold the field that the faith of the Church is also the original faith and is founded upon the sayings of Christ about Himself.

Now if this is in general the sufficiently clear result of an examination of Scripture, our Dogmatic can not only easily dispense with the whole arsenal of particular statements which have been set forth under various rubrics [5] as proving the being of God in Christ, but put them aside all the more readily that they give no help in presenting the subject in the best way, but rather hide what is important and certain under what is untrustworthy. For what is the use of ascribing divine titles to Christ, if He Himself calls attention to an

---

[1] Matt. 26[37], Luke 19[41].   [2] John 11[33, 38].
[3] 2 Cor. 5[21], 1 Pet. 2[22], Heb. 1[3] 7[26-27] 9[14].   [4] Phil. 4[13].
[5] ὀνομαστικῶς, ἰδιωματικῶς, ἐνεργητικῶς, and λατρευτικῶς.

improper use of the word ' God ' [John 10$^{34-36}$] ?   But appellations
which express the unity of the divine and the human in so definite
and unambiguous a way as the later ' God-man ' do not occur in
Scripture ; all the predicates which can be cited in this connexion
are more or less uncertain in meaning.[1] So, too, as far as the divine
attributes are concerned, it is natural that, since Christ is always
spoken of as a man, only such attributes are ascribed to Him as
express exalted humanity, so that it is easy to explain them as
nothing but very permissible hyperbolical expressions.   Since,
further, it is difficult to distinguish between worship in the strict
sense and the utterances of a deep, but not properly divine, adoration, if we were to proceed on that line everything would depend
upon the divine activities asserted of Christ.   But creation and preservation are only ascribed to Christ [2] in such a way that it must
remain doubtful whether they do not mean that He is active cause
only in so far as He is final cause.   Finally, in the Resurrection and
the Last Judgment, Christ is everywhere distinguished from God,
for He appears only as a deputy with full powers, and hence His
power is represented as resting in the Father, just as the appointment proceeds from the Father originally.   Exactly the same is true
of the sending of the Spirit, which Christ ascribes, now to Himself,
now to the Father, who sends it at His request.[3] So that without
those great supreme testimonies all these details would have little
effect.

[1] It is obvious that no reference can be made here to the miraculous signs
of the Old Testament, heavenly voices and appearances, by which the Son of
God is to be recognized.   For in any case they could have nothing to say
about the Person of Christ ; at most they might have to be considered ἀpropos
of the doctrine of the Trinity.
[2] 1 Cor. 8⁶, Col. 1$^{15-17}$, Heb. 1⁴.
[3] Luke 24^{49} and John 15$^{2.\ 6}$; cf. John 14$^{16.\ 36}$.

SECOND DOCTRINE : THE WORK OF CHRIST

§ 100. *The Redeemer assumes believers into the power of His God-consciousness,[1] and this is His redemptive activity.*

1. In virtue of the teleological character of Christian piety, both the imperfect stage of the higher life, as also the challenge of it, appear in our self-consciousness as facts due to our own individual action—though we do not feel responsible for the latter in the same way as for the former. In virtue, however, of the peculiar character of Christianity this challenge is also apprehended in our self-consciousness as the act of the Redeemer.[2] These two points of view can be reconciled only by supposing that this challenge is the act of the Redeemer become our own act. And this, accordingly, is the best way of expressing the common element in the Christian consciousness of the divine grace. Hence, from this point of view, the peculiar work of the Redeemer would first be to evoke this act in us. But if we regard the matter more closely, it is clear that what we have thus described is in every case an act both of the Redeemer and of the redeemed. The original activity of the Redeemer, therefore, which belongs to Him alone, and which precedes all activity of our own in this challenge, would be that by means of which He assumes us into this fellowship of His activity and His life. The continuance of that fellowship, accordingly, constitutes the essence of the state of grace ; the new corporate life is the sphere within which Christ produces this act ; in it is revealed the continuous activity of His sinless perfection.

But His act in us can never be anything but the act of His sinlessness and perfection as conditioned by the being of God in Him. And so these too in addition must become ours, because otherwise it would not be His act that became ours. Now the individual life of each one of us is passed in the consciousness of sin and imperfection. Hence we can know the fellowship of the Redeemer only in so far as we are not conscious of our own individual life ; as impulses flow to us from Him, we find that in Him from which everything proceeds to be the source of our activity also—a common possession,

---

[1] Cf. § 88.   [2] Cf. § 63, 1 and 2.

as it were. This too is the meaning of all those passages in Scripture which speak of Christ being and living in us,[1] of being dead to sin,[2] of putting off the old and putting on the new man.[3] But Christ can only direct His God-consciousness against sin in so far as He enters into the corporate life of man and sympathetically shares the consciousness of sin, but shares it as something He is to overcome.[4] This very consciousness of sin as something to be overcome becomes the principle of our activity in the action which He evokes in us. But our own immediate experience in being thus assumed into the fellowship of Christ will be explained in the first Doctrine of the second main Division, which deals with forgiveness. And the further development of this fellowship in time, through a series of common actions, is the subject of the second Doctrine, dealing with sanctification. Here we have only to explain more exactly what the Redeemer does and how He accomplishes it.

2. All Christ's activity, then, proceeds from the being of God in Him. And we know no divine activity except that of creation, which includes that of preservation, or, conversely, that of preservation, which includes that of creation. So we shall have to regard Christ's activity too in the same way. We do not, however, exclude the soul of man from creation, in spite of the fact that the creation of such a free agent and the continued freedom of a being created in the context of a greater whole is something which we cannot expect to understand ; all that we can do is to recognize the fact. The same is true of the creative activity of Christ, which is entirely concerned with the sphere of freedom. For His assumptive activity is a creative one, yet what it produces is altogether free. Now the being of God in Him as an active principle is timeless and eternal, yet its expressions are all conditioned by the form of human life. It follows that He can influence what is free only in accordance with the manner in which it enters into His sphere of living influence, and only in accordance with the nature of the free. The activity by which He assumes us into fellowship with Him is, therefore, a creative production in us of the will to assume Him into ourselves, or rather—since it is only receptiveness for His activity as involved in the impartation [5]—only our assent to the influence of His activity. But it is a condition of that activity of the Redeemer that the individuals should enter the sphere of

---

[1] Gal. 2[20], Rom. 8[10], John 17[23], 2 Cor. 13[5].
[2] Rom. 6[2. 6. 11], 1 Pet. 2[24].
[3] Col. 3[10], Eph. 4[22. 24].   [4] John 16[33].   [5] John 16[19].

His historical influence, where they become aware of Him in His self-revelation. Now this assent can only be conceived as conditioned by the consciousness of sin ; yet it is not necessary that this should precede entrance into the sphere of the Redeemer. Rather it may just as well arise within that sphere as the effect of the Redeemer's self-revelation, as indeed it certainly does come to full clarity only as we contemplate His sinless perfection. Accordingly, the original activity of the Redeemer is best conceived as a pervasive influence which is received by its object in virtue of the free movement with which he turns himself to its attraction, just as we ascribe an attractive power to everyone to whose educative intellectual influence we gladly submit ourselves. Now, if every activity of the Redeemer proceeds from the being of God in Him, and if in the formation of the Redeemer's Person the only active power was the creative divine activity which established itself as the being of God in Him, then also His every activity may be regarded as a continuation of that person-forming divine influence upon human nature. For the pervasive activity of Christ cannot establish itself in an individual without becoming person-forming in him too, for now all his activities are differently determined through the working of Christ in him, and even all impressions are differently received—which means that the personal self-consciousness too becomes altogether different. And just as creation is not concerned simply with individuals (as if each creation of an individual had been a special act), but it is the world that was created, and every individual as such was created only in and with the whole, for the rest not less than for itself, in the same way the activity of the Redeemer too is world-forming, and its object is human nature, in the totality of which the powerful God-consciousness is to be implanted as a new vital principle. He takes possession of the individuals relatively to the whole, wherever He finds those in whom His activity does not merely remain, but from whom, moving on, it can work upon others through the revelation of His life. And thus the total effective influence of Christ is only the continuation of the creative divine activity out of which the Person of Christ arose. For this, too, was directed towards human nature as a whole, in which that being of God was to exist, but in such a way that its effects are mediated through the life of Christ, as its most original organ, for all human nature that has already become personal in the natural sense, in proportion as it allows itself to be brought into spiritual touch with that life and its self-perpetuating organism. And this in order that the former personality may be slain and human nature, in vital fellowship with Christ, be formed into persons in the totality of that higher life.

Let us now look at the corporate life, or at the fellowship of the individual with the Redeemer. We may best describe its beginning, since it is conditioned by a free acceptance, by the term *calling*—the whole official activity of Christ began with just such a call. But the share of the Redeemer in the common life, viewed as continuing, we are fully justified in calling *soul-bestowal* (*Beseelung*), primarily with reference to the corporate life—as indeed the Church is called His Body. In just the same way Christ is to be the soul also in the individual fellowship, and each individual the organism through which the soul works. The two things are related as in Christ the divine activity present in the act of union is related to that activity in the state of union, and as in God the activity of creation is related to that of preservation. Only that here it is still clearer how each moment of a common activity can be regarded also as a calling, and likewise how the calling proper can be regarded as soul-bestowal. But this formula, too, we shall employ in another place.

3. This exposition is based entirely on the inner experience of the believer ; its only purpose is to describe and elucidate that experience. Naturally, therefore, it can make no claim to be a proof that things must have been so ; in the sphere of experience such proof is only possible where mathematics can be used, which is certainly not the case here. Our purpose is simply to show that the perfect satisfaction to which we aspire can only be truly contained in the Christian's consciousness of his relation to Christ in so far as that consciousness expresses the kind of relation which has been described here. If this content be lacking in the Christian consciousness, then either the perfect satisfaction must come from some other quarter, or it does not exist at all, and we must be content with an indefinite appeasement of conscience, such as may be found without any Redeemer ; and in that case there would be no special possession of divine grace in Christianity at all. Now these negations cannot be logically refuted ; they can only be removed by actual facts : we must seek to bring doubters to the same experience as we have had.

Now such a presentation of the redeeming activity of Christ as has been given here, which exhibits it as the establishment of a new life common to Him and us (original in Him, in us new and derived), is usually called by those who have not had the experience, 'mystical.' This expression is so extremely vague that it seems better to avoid it. But if we are willing to keep so close to its original use as to understand by it what belongs to the circle of doctrines which only a few share, but for others are a mystery, then we may accept it. Provided that we recognize that no one can be received into this circle arbitrarily, because doctrines are only expressions of inward experiences—whoever has these experiences *ipso facto* belongs to the circle ; whoever has not, cannot come in at all. But an analogy to this relation may be pointed out in a sphere which is universally familiar. As contrasted with the condition of things existing before there was any law, the civil community within a defined area is a higher vital potency. Let us now suppose that some person for the first time combines a naturally cohesive group into a civil community (legend tells of such cases in plenty) ; what happens is that the idea of the state first comes to consciousness in him, and takes possession of his personality as its immediate dwelling-place. Then he assumes the rest into the living fellowship of the idea. He does so by making them clearly conscious of the unsatisfactoriness of their present condition by effective speech. The power remains with the founder of forming in them the idea which is the innermost principle of his own life, and of assuming them into the fellowship of that life. The result is, not only that there arises among them a new corporate life, in complete contrast to the old, but also that each of them becomes in himself a new person—that is to say, a citizen. And everything resulting from this is the corporate life—developing variously with the process of time, yet remaining essentially the same—of this idea which emerged at that particular point of time, but was always predestined in the nature of that particular racial stock. The analogy might be pushed even further, to points of which we shall speak later. But even this presentation of it will seem mystical to those who admit only a meagre and inferior conception of the civic state.

Let us be content, then, that our view of the matter should be called mystical in this sense ; naturally everything to be derived from this main point will be called mystical too. But just as this mystical view can substantiate its claim to be the original one, so too it claims to be the true mean between two others, of which I shall call the one the magical way, and the other the empirical. The former admits, of course, that the activity of Christ is redemptive, but denies that the communication of His perfection is dependent on the founding of a community; it results, they maintain, from His immediate influence upon the individual: and for this some take the written word to be a necessary means, others do not. The latter show themselves the more consistent, but the more completely they cut themselves loose from everything originating in the community the more obvious becomes the magical character of their view. This magical character lies in an influence not mediated by anything natural, yet attributed to a person. This is completely at variance with the maxim everywhere underlying our presentation, that the beginning of the Kingdom of God is a supernatural thing, which, however, becomes natural as soon as it emerges into manifestation; for this other view makes every significant moment a supernatural one. Further, this view is completely separatist in type, for it makes the corporate life a purely accidental thing; and it comes very near being docetic as well. For if Christ exerted influence in any such way as this—as a person, it is true, but only as a heavenly person without earthly presence, though in a truly personal way—then it would have been possible for Him to work in just the same way at any time, and His real personal appearance in history was only a superfluous adjunct. But those who likewise assume an immediate personal influence, but mediate it through the word and the fellowship, are less magical only if they attribute to these the power of evoking a mood in which the individual becomes susceptible to that personal influence. They are more magical still, if these natural elements have the power of disposing Christ to exert His influence; for then their efficacy is exactly like that attributed to magic spells. The contrary empirical view also, it is true, admits a redemptive activity on the part of Christ, but one which is held to consist only in bringing about an increasing perfection in us; and this cannot properly occur otherwise than in the forms of teaching and example. These forms are general; there is nothing distinctive in them. Even suppose it admitted that Christ is distinguished from others who contribute in the same way to our improvement, by the pure perfection of His teaching and His example, yet if all that is achieved in us is something imperfect, there remains nothing but to forgo the idea of redemption in the proper sense—that is, as the removal of sin—and, in view of the consciousness of sin still remaining even in our growing perfection, to pacify ourselves with a general appeal to the divine compassion. Now, teaching and example effect no more

than such a growing perfection, and this appeal to the divine
compassion occurs even apart from Christ. It must therefore be
admitted that His appearance, in so far as intended to be something special, would in that case be in vain. At most it might be
said that by His teaching He brought men to the point of giving up
the effort, previously universal, to offer God substitutes for the
perfection they lacked. But since the uselessness of this effort can
be demonstrated, already in our natural intelligence we have the
divine certainty of this, and had no need to obtain it elsewhere.
And probably this view is chiefly to blame for the claim of philosophy to set itself above faith and to treat faith as merely a transitional stage. But we cannot rest satisfied with the consciousness of
growing perfection, for that belongs just as much to the consciousness of sin as to that of grace, and hence cannot contain what is
peculiarly Christian. But, for the Christian, nothing belongs to
the consciousness of grace unless it is traced to the Redeemer as its
cause, and therefore it must always be a different thing in His case
from what it is in the case of others—naturally, since it is bound up
with something else, namely, the peculiar redemptive activity of
Christ.

§ 101. *The Redeemer assumes the believers into the fellowship of His
unclouded blessedness, and this is His reconciling activity.*

1. If this assumption into the fellowship of Christ's blessedness
were independent of the assumption into the power of His God-
consciousness, or even if the former were to follow from the latter,
the teleological nature of Christianity would be changed. But
just as in God blessedness and omnipotence are balanced, mutually
conditioned, and yet also independent of each other, so also in
the Person of Christ blessedness and the power of the God-consciousness must be balanced in the same way, one conditioning
the other and each independent of the other. Accordingly we can
say that it must be the same with the effective influence of Christ.
Either this must be simply admitted, or else there must be two
contrasted ways of regarding Christianity, complementary to each
other, one of them presenting it as an effort after blessedness for
the sake of the power of the God-consciousness, the other *vice
versa*. But since the effective influence of Christ arises only in so
far as a receptivity or a longing for it pre-exists in its object, so
the reconciling activity can only manifest itself as a consequence of
the redemptive activity because the consciousness of sin, in itself

and not as a source of evil, forms the necessary basis of that longing, inasmuch as in the case of the individual evil is not connected with sin. So if we think of the Redeemer's activity as an influence upon the individual, we are bound to make the reconciling factor follow upon the redemptive and issue from it. But we equate the two thus far, that the communication of blessedness no less than the communication of perfection is given immediately in the assumption into vital fellowship with Christ.

2. Now in view of the exact parallel between this proposition and the preceding one, so that regarded in and by themselves they might fittingly have been run together into one, this seems hardly to need explanation. On the one hand, every activity in Christ proceeded from the being of God in Him, and this activity was never hindered by any resistance of His human nature. Similarly, the hindrances to His activity never determined any moment of His life until the perception of them had been taken up into His inmost self-consciousness, which was so completely one with His powerful God-consciousness that they could appear in it only as belonging to the temporal form of the perfect effectiveness of His being. On the other hand, it was still less possible that hindrances arising out of His own natural or social life could be taken up in this innermost consciousness as hindrances ; they could be no more than indications of the direction set for His activity. Similarly, the redeemed man too, since he has been assumed into the vital fellowship of Christ, is never filled with the consciousness of any evil, for it cannot touch or hinder the life which he shares with Christ. All hindrances to life, natural and social, come to him even in this region only as indications. They are not taken away, as if he were to be, or could be, without pain and free from suffering, for Christ also knew pain and suffered in the same way. Only the pains and sufferings do not mean simple misery, for they do not as such penetrate into the inmost life. And this holds good also of his consciousness of the sin still occurring in his life. It cannot have its source in his new life ; he refers it therefore only to the corporate life of general sinfulness, which still has a place in him. Not that it is not pain and suffering, so far as he clings to his own personality ; but it reaches the life of Christ in him only as an indication of what he has to do ; consequently there is in it no misery. The assumption into vital fellowship with Christ, therefore, dissolves the connexion between sin and evil, since morally

the two are no longer related to each other, even if from the merely natural point of view the one is the consequence of the other. Morally, however, each of them by itself is regarded solely in relation to the task of the new life. Hence, just as the redemptive activity of Christ brings about for all believers a corporate activity corresponding to the being of God in Christ, so the reconciling element, that is, the blessedness of the being of God in Him, brings about for all believers, as for each separately, a corporate feeling of blessedness. Therein, too, their former personality dies, so far as it meant a self-enclosed life of feeling within a sensuous vital unity, to which all sympathetic feeling for others and for the whole was subordinated. But what remains as the self-identity of the person is the peculiar way of apprehending and perceiving, which as individualized intelligence so works itself into the new common life that relatively to this factor also the activity of Christ is person-forming, in that an old man is put off and a new man is put on. Here too, if we wish to note similarities between the activity of Christ in forming the new corporate life and the divine activity in forming the personality of Christ, we shall be able to distinguish a first moment, which corresponds to the act of union as first beginning, and as such can only look back to what preceded, and a second, which represents the state of union, and, as expressing continuance, also looks forward to the future. Now here the beginning is the disappearance of the old man, and so also of the old reference of all evil to sin, that is, the disappearance of the consciousness of deserving punishment. Consequently the first thing in the reconciling aspect is the forgiveness of sins.[1] For in the unity of life with Christ all relation to the law ceases, since the general movement contrary to sin, proceeding from Him, begins.[2] But the state of union is the real possession of blessedness in the consciousness that Christ in us is the centre of our life, and this in such a way that this possession exists solely as His gift, which, since we receive it simply by His will that we should have it, is His blessing and His peace. But the same thing is true here again, that each moment or aspect may at the same time be regarded in accordance with the formula of the other. For in the first moment the whole development is already implicitly contained, but at the same time in every later moment the first persists ; for the fact that this possession of blessedness is pervaded throughout by sin (a fact which our recurrence to Christ makes it all the more

[1] Rom. 8¹, 1 John 1⁸· ⁹ 2¹· ².   [2] Gal. 2¹⁹⁻²¹ 5²²⁻²⁴.

impossible for us to overlook) always points on in turn to the forgiveness of sins.

3. Obviously our proposition is mystical in the same sense as the previous one, and its truth also can only be proved in experience. But in the same sense it too stands intermediate between a magical view, which destroys all naturalness in the continuous activity of Christ, and an empirical, which reduces it altogether to the level of ordinary daily experience, and thus does not make its supernatural beginning and its distinctive peculiarity the fundamental things in it.

The latter view likewise starts from the connexion between sin and evil, and rightly infers that when sin is taken away so also is evil. But since this connexion principally holds good for social evil alone, and is exact even for this only if we consider a large corporate life as a rounded whole, whereas in every individual part of that life inward improvement may well be accompanied by increasing evil, because of its connexion with the rest, the growing improvement of the individual can furnish no guarantee at all that he is being set free from evil and cannot form a basis of blessedness. Even along with increasing perfection the fact remains not only that he encounters hindrances to life, but that they are such as in the light of the sin still present in him have the aspect of punishment. It follows that this reconciliation only very accidentally takes the form of enjoyment and possession ; in essence it can never be set forth as more than hope. But in either form it is not, so far as content is concerned, anything peculiarly Christian, nor can it as enjoyment have a greater strength, or as hope possess a higher degree of certainty, within Christianity than without. And how slight this is everywhere, history clearly shows. For, altogether apart from Christianity, the dispute is constantly recurring as to whether evil in the world is really growing less, or only changing its form while in sum remaining what it has ever been. Not only so, but within the Christian Church itself the same doubt constantly reappears, and this the more strongly the less experience there is of the enjoyment of the unclouded blessedness of Christ, and the more recourse is had to that general hope. And, quite contrary to Christ's own assurance,[1] that blessedness is relegated to the life beyond time, and thus clearly declared to be independent of the gradual improvement. But in that case Christ has part in our blessedness or salvation only through His influence upon this pro-

[1] John 5²⁴.

gressive improvement, which means that a specific difference between Him and other men is of little importance.

Only those views of Christ's reconciling activity appear to be magical which make the impartation of His blessedness independent of assumption into vital fellowship with Him. This means that the forgiveness of sins is made to depend upon the punishment which Christ suffered, and the blessedness of men itself is presented as a reward which God offers to Christ for the suffering of that punishment. Not, of course, that the thought of our blessedness as a rewarding of Christ is altogether to be rejected—on the contrary, we shall have to speak of that later. Nor that all connexion between the suffering of Christ and the forgiveness of sins is to be denied. But both ideas become magical when blessedness and forgiveness are not mediated through vital fellowship with Christ. For within this fellowship the impartation of blessedness, as explained above, is a natural one ; whereas without this the rewarding of Christ is nothing but divine arbitrariness. And this in itself is always something magical, but it is especially so when something so absolutely inward as blessedness is supposed to have been brought about externally, without any inner basis. For if it is independent of life in Christ, then, since man does not have the source of blessedness in himself, it can only have been infused into each separate individual somehow or other from without. In no less magical a way is the forgiveness of sins achieved, if the consciousness of deserving punishment is supposed to cease because the punishment has been borne by another. That in this way the expectation of punishment might be taken away is conceivable ; but this is merely the sensuous element in the forgiveness of sins. The properly ethical element, the consciousness of deserving punishment, would still remain. And this therefore would have to disappear as if conjured away, without any reason. And to what extent something even of this view has passed over into Church doctrine is a question we shall have to discuss below.

4. Now if we compare the connected view here set forth with the two alternative views which have just been cited, they certainly suggest the reflection that in our view, the suffering of Christ has nothing to say, so that there has not even been an opportunity to raise the question whether, and to what extent, it belongs to redemption or to reconciliation. But the only conclusion to be drawn from this postponement of the question is that no reason existed for adducing it as a primitive element either in the one

place or in the other. And this is so far correct, that otherwise no complete assumption into vital fellowship with Christ, such as makes redemption and reconciliation completely intelligible, would have been possible before the suffering and death of Christ. As an element of secondary importance, however, it belongs to both ; immediately to reconciliation, and to redemption only mediately. The activity of Christ in founding the new corporate life could really emerge in its perfect fulness—although belief in this perfection could exist even apart from this—only if it yielded to no opposition, not even to that which succeeded in destroying His person. Here, accordingly, the perfection does not lie properly and immediately in the suffering itself, but only in His giving up of Himself to it. And of this it is only, as it were, a magical caricature, if we isolate this climax, leave out of account the foundation of the corporate life, and regard this giving up of Himself to suffering for suffering's sake as the real sum-total of Christ's redemptive activity. But so far as reconciliation is concerned, our exposition makes it obvious that, in order to effect assumption into the fellowship of His blessedness, the longing of those who were conscious of their misery must first be drawn to Christ through the impression they had received of His blessedness. And here too the situation is that belief in this blessedness might be present even apart from this, but that none the less His blessedness emerged in its perfect fulness only in that it was not overcome even by the full tide of suffering. The more so that this suffering arose out of the opposition of sin, and that therefore the Redeemer's sympathy with misery, ever present, though without disturbing His blessedness, from the time of His entrance into the corporate life of sin, had here to enter on its greatest phase. And here it is not the giving up of Himself to suffering, as something that forms part of the redemptive activity, but the suffering itself which is the full confirmation of belief in the Redeemer's blessedness. But here again it is only a magical caricature of this which, completely overlooking the necessity of an imperturbable blessedness in Christ, finds the reconciling power of His suffering precisely in the fact that He willingly gave up even His blessedness, and experienced, even if only for moments, real misery. So far as Church doctrine is not wholly free from this idea either, we shall return to the matter below.

The climax of His suffering, we hold then, was sympathy with misery. This, however, at once involves the further conclusion that no suffering which is not bound up with the redemptive activity of Christ can be regarded as belonging to reconciliation, because suffering of that sort would also have no connexion with the Redeemer's opposition to misery, and so it could belong to the reconciliation only in a magical way. Now Christ's sufferings can be thought of in this connexion with His redemptive activity only when regarded as a whole and a unity ; to separate out any particular element and ascribe to it a peculiar reconciling value, is not merely trifling allegory if done in teaching, and worthless sentimentality in poetry ; probably it is also seldom free from a defiling admixture of superstition. Least of all is it proper to ascribe such a special reconciling value to His physical sufferings ; and that for two reasons. On the one hand, these sufferings in themselves have only the loosest connexion with His reaction against sin. On the other hand, our own experience teaches us that an ordinary ethical development and robust piety have as their reward the almost complete overcoming of physical sufferings in the presence of a glad spiritual self-consciousness, whether personal or corporate. Certainly they can never suppress that consciousness, nor make a moment of blessedness any less blessed. But in order that the exposition just given may serve as an all-round test in scrutinizing Church formulæ, it must be brought into relation to our general formula of the creation of human nature as completed through Christ, so as to convince ourselves that in this twofold activity of Christ such creation is really fully accomplished. For whatever in human nature is assumed into vital fellowship with Christ is assumed into the fellowship of an activity solely determined by the power of the God-consciousness, therefore adequate to every new experience and extracting from it all it has to yield. It is at the same time assumed into the fellowship of a satisfaction which rests in that activity and which cannot be disturbed by any outside influence. Now that each assumption of this sort is simply a continuation of the same creative act which first manifested itself in time by the formation of Christ's Person ; that each increase in the intensity of this new life relatively to the disappearing corporate life of sinfulness is also such a continuation, must now be clear ; and that in this new life man achieves the destiny originally appointed for him, and that nothing beyond this can be conceived or attempted for a nature such as ours—all this requires no further exposition.

However exactly this presentation of the subject may correspond

to the immediate consciousness of the Christian, so that it recognizes
itself in it, still it is inevitable that, as it stands half-way between
the empirical and the magical interpretations, it should be mistaken
by each of these for the opposite one. For, on the one hand, since
a spiritual thing like the foundation of a corporate life must be
spiritually achieved, and there is no spiritual influence but the
presentation of oneself in word and deed, the Redeemer could only
enter into our corporate life by means of such self-presentation,
thereby attracting men to Himself and making them one with Himself. Now to warn those who lean to the side of magic, this touch-
stone must be kept before them, whether their conception really
agrees with the possibility of conceiving the effective influence of
Christ under this historical natural form. And nothing is easier
than for them to misunderstand this, and to imagine that Christ
must work simply in the ordinary human way as teacher and example, the divine in Him being altogether left out of account. But
on the other hand, the distinction between such a Christ and Christ
as we here understand Him, can only be made plain by reference to
' Christ in us,' whereas the relation of teacher and pupil, like that
of pattern and imitation, must always remain an external one. If,
however, those who lean to the empirical view were asked whether
they too had a real experience of vital fellowship with Christ, they
would only too easily misunderstand the question, and suppose
that they were being asked to assent to the objectionable magic
view. For that reason we shall leave wide room on both sides open,
not only for the Christian Church as a whole, but also for the Protestant Church, in which all these differences are present, in order
that, wherever there is a recognition of Christ—and the danger
of letting this go is just as great on the side of the magical
extreme as on that of the empirical—and so long as such an
extreme has not yet been reached, we may always be able to
maintain fellowship, and by means of it bring all ever nearer
to the centre.

§ 102. *Church doctrine divides the whole activity of Christ into three
offices, the prophetic, the priestly, and the kingly.*

1. At first sight this division has against it the appearance
of being very arbitrary. It looks as if from the great number
of Biblical expressions used by Christ Himself one in particular
had been chosen and the others set aside, and to this one two others
added, which were used, not by Christ Himself, but only by His

disciples.[1] If then pictorial expressions are to be used at all, unquestionably the picture of the Shepherd, which was used by Christ Himself and repeated by Peter, has a better right (it will be said) than the expressions ' High Priest ' and ' Prophet.' Now if this really were the case—that out of a number of equally justifiable expressions, all of them pictorial, these had been selected, more or less by accident—then it would be surprising (since pictorial expressions are always hard to define, and therefore in a dialectical discussion almost inevitably involve great inconveniences) that such a presentation had been able to maintain itself for so long without being supplanted by some other even if it were one no less arbitrary ; and not only so, but one would reasonably hesitate to make any further use of this form of expression in a strictly theological treatment. But these expressions are not to be put on one level with other pictorial expressions ; manifestly their purpose is to be sought in the comparison they indicate between the achievements of Christ in the corporate life founded by Him and those by which in the Jewish people the theocracy was represented and held together, and this comparison is not even to-day to be neglected in the system of doctrine. For even if it is equally true that this presentation is rather characteristic of the earliest formative period of the faith (when it certainly was necessary to bring the anti-Jewish element in Christianity into evidence under the Jewish form itself) than fitted to be a persistent type of doctrine, this would only mean that these forms alone cannot suffice for us. When we have, however, developed the subject in our own way, as above, on the basis of our own Christian experience, it is still worth while to preserve a continuity with those original presentations, for the first theoretical interpretation of Christianity was based upon a comparison of the new Kingdom of God with the old. And so we have to show that our conception is in agreement with that which the earlier Christians formed for themselves, when they represented the offices of Christ as new and intensified forms of those through which in the old covenant the divine government was revealed.

2. Of course we are here concerned rather with the idea of these authorities [prophet, priest, and king] in Judaism than with

---

[1] Apart from the Epistle to the Hebrews, the conception of the ' High Priest ' occurs (but only indirectly) in Paul (Rom. 5[11]), and in Peter (1 Pet. 2[21]), and in John (1 John 2[1]); Christ calls Himself a prophet in Luke 13[33], and less directly in similar passages.

their historical development. The kings were properly the representatives of the God of Israel; to them the government was entrusted, in order that the people might be held together and the common life, where necessary, renewed and purified. The priests were the guardians of the temple and the shrines, and presided over the immediate relation of the people to God, bringing requests and offerings before Him, and bringing back from God forgiveness and blessing. The prophets were men specially called and sent forth by God, belonging to both sides, God and man, and mediating between them, but not so constantly as the priests. For although there were schools of the prophets, yet there was no uninterrupted succession of prophets in the narrower sense. In the hour of need the prophet arose, now from the ranks of either kings or priests, now from the midst of the people, with a message of warning when one of the appointed authorities had erred from the right path, of revival when the original spirit threatened to be extinguished by the dead letter. Now in order to make clear the relation of the Kingdom of heaven to this earthly theocracy, Christ, on whom alone the Kingdom rests, is represented as uniting all these three offices in Himself. The meaning of this is that in this Kingdom of God (which, it is always understood, is not of this world) the establishment and maintenance of the fellowship of each individual with God, and the maintenance and direction of the fellowship of all members with one another, are not separate achievements but the same; and further, that these activities and the free dominion of the Spirit in knowledge and doctrine do not spring from a different source but from the same.

3. Now in what way the whole redemptive and reconciling activity of Christ, as just described,[1] is completely reproduced in terms of these three offices, can be shown only in the exposition which follows. But so much at least we can point out here and now—that if we ascribe to the Redeemer only one of these three functions, and neglect the others, or, alternatively, completely exclude one of them, then that harmony between the old covenant and the new is destroyed, and the peculiar quality of Christianity is endangered. For to claim for Christ the prophetic office alone means limiting His effective influence to teaching and admonition relatively to a form of life already in existence either before Him or apart from Him, and to a relation to God already established apart from Him at some other point; and on such an interpretation the

1 §§ 100 and 101.

peculiar element in Christianity is seriously overshadowed. It is just the same if we ascribe to Him the two formative activities, but exclude Him from the prophetic activity, with its character of direct spiritual stimulation. For then one cannot see how, if the power of the living word is to have no share in the work, the Kingdom of God can arise except in some magical way. If, on the other hand, we exclude the kingly office, then the other two taken together, though certainly they unite each redeemed individual closely to the Redeemer, yet supply no relation to a corporate life, and so produce only an unpleasing and even, when more closely observed, an unchristian separatism. Lastly, if the high-priestly office is passed over, but the other two retained, then the prophetic activity could be related only to the kingly, and consequently, if we are to remain true to the original type, all religious content would be lacking. On the other hand, if Christ be represented solely as High Priest, it would be almost impossible to avoid the magical conception of His influence. Similarly, if we retain only the kingly dignity, and think of Christ solely as forming and directing the Church, the immediate relation of the individual to the Redeemer would be endangered, and we should have strayed in the direction of the Roman Church, which makes this relation dependent at once upon the Church and upon those who direct its government. Now where there is revealed an interdependence of this sort, there is also a presumption that what is so bound up together is also complete.

§ 103. *First Theorem.—The prophetic office of Christ consists in teaching, prophesying, and working miracles.*

1. These three activities also constituted the dignity of the Old Testament prophets. Certainly the essential thing was always stimulus by means of teaching and admonition ; but in all important instances, where the teaching had some definite occasion, it at once became prophecy (since the idea of the divine retribution was dominant), now threatening, now promising, in agreement with the original type created when the law was given. But since the prophets never appeared except in connexion with crimes or public misfortunes, which might be supposed always to involve the guilt of those to whom they had to speak, they required, in default of an outward vocation to which they might have appealed, some special proof of their authority. Hence miracles were expected or assumed as a token of their divine mission. It was only

the absence of this third mark of a prophet that made it possible for the Baptist to say that he was no prophet,[1] in spite of his very definite divine vocation. For he certainly had taught and prophesied,[2] but the gift of miracles had not been granted him,[3] and hence he would not be troubled with a useless question about it.

In Christ these three signs of a prophet did not follow one from the other ; all three were one from the very outset. For the preaching of the Kingdom of God was both teaching and prophecy, and the Kingdom of God itself is properly the miracle accomplished by Christ ; but since its fulfilment began simultaneously with the preaching, all three elements were present in one and the same germ, and we can differentiate them only as this germ develops further.

2. That the prophetic voice had fallen silent was a fact which had long been generally admitted when Jesus appeared. Instead, there was then a tradition of doctrine in the schools of the scribes. This made no claim to be anything more than tradition ; it was gradually extended by the subtle combinations of distinguished scholars, and in connexion with it there was also an official practice of teaching in the synagogues. But Christ could not belong to any of the sects into which the scribes were divided ; as little could He undertake any official activity which would have involved Him in other duties, and have limited Him in a way incompatible with His appointed work. But since, outside the activity of the scribes, there was complete freedom of teaching, He was able to come before the people in a regular way, as soon as He had reached the age required by custom. Thus no exception to His competence to teach could be taken by any public authority. The *teaching office* of Christ, therefore, means only His determination to make the fullest possible use of this freedom. Thus for Him no other occasion was needed for any particular act of teaching than the presence, individually or in groups, of those who were anxious to be taught ; His conversation was all of the nature of teaching, so far as the subject and the conditions permitted. And to this extent it must certainly be admitted that Christ taught, in this wider sense, even before His public ministry began ; still, that He taught publicly as a boy remains a mistaken view, and one entirely without foundation in the Gospel story,[4] but resembling the apocryphal stories. Similarly, there is really only one Gospel

---

[1] John 1²¹.   [2] Matt. 3¹⁰· ¹⁴· ¹⁷.
[3] John 10⁴¹.   [4] Luke 2⁴⁶· ⁴⁷.

testimony [1] which connects the beginning of His public appearance with His reception of the baptism of John ; and the explanation which Jesus Himself gives of this circumstance forbids the supposition that by this baptism He became something which He had not been before, or that He received an authority or a consecration which was not already His. The former supposition is incompatible with belief in the originality of the divine in His person ; and for the latter there is no external authority of any kind in the rite instituted by John. The only value, therefore, which we can attribute to this transaction is that it helps us to understand His public appearance historically : He marked His more open transition from seclusion to public life by an act of confession which inevitably evoked a more definite opinion about Him, to which He was able to attach His teaching. For the people His work as a teacher came to an end with His arrest, but for the disciples only with His ascension. It seems to have been His chief work in the days of the resurrection, partly to expound the Scripture to His disciples, without doubt establishing the way in which they were afterwards to make use of it among their people ; partly also to complete His injunctions as to the corporate life deriving from Him, and so to establish that life more securely. It is obvious, therefore, how essentially this teaching activity on Christ's part belonged to the redemptive activity described above. But so far as the *source* of the teaching is concerned, that of the prophets' teaching (although their participation in teaching came to them in the form of a special divine call) was always simply the law ; their calling was entirely concerned with the relation between God and the people, and the end to which they worked was a purely national one. Now it was part of Christ's regard for the law not to destroy the law ; hence He recognized and affirmed the national obligation towards it. Nevertheless, just as His inspiration was not a transient one, dependent on individual occasions supplied by the state of the people, and just as He is not to be regarded as merely a product of human nature in a specifically national form, so too the inner development of His thoughts could not be dependent on the law. Moreover, to regard His teaching as a purification and a development of the ethics current among the people, springing out of universal human reason, is part of the empirical conception we have rejected. Rather, the source of His teaching was the absolutely original revelation of God in Him. In Him the contrast

[1] Luke 4[14] ; but compare also Acts 1[21, 22].

between learning and teaching was only the contrast between the influence of the divine principle in Him upon the receptivity of His spiritual organ (so as to yield a pure apprehension of the human conditions confronting Him in their bearing on man's relation to God) and the influence of the same principle upon the spontaneity of His spiritual organ. But since receptivity always involves spontaneity, His teaching was already forming itself imperceptibly in His learning ; and this first development of His own thought was already the source of His astonishing questions.[1] Naturally, however, after spontaneity had gained the upper hand, and teaching had come to be His constant preoccupation, the law no less than the Messianic hopes was the point of connexion at which He developed His preaching of the new corporate life to be founded by Him—the Kingdom of God.

Hence, if the *content* of Christ's teaching is to be specially stated here (although in point of fact our task throughout has been simply to expound that teaching), then here also we should first have to recur to the prophetic element. The prophet felt it incumbent on him to do full justice by his preaching to the impulse which he felt had come to him from God, and to pass on its full content to his hearers—always a limited and definite task. In the same way, Christ's self-determination to teach was the task of satisfying fully the powerful (which also means the creative) God-consciousness, as it took shape in His spiritual organ, and of so reproducing it in His teaching that thereby the assumption of men into His fellowship might be effected. No other measure is applicable here of the success of His teaching, and consequently of its perfection. Naturally His discourses were sometimes more general in character, sometimes more detailed ; sometimes they were more the pure outflowing of what was in Him, sometimes they had a closer bearing on some outward occasion ; and the attempt has for long been made to distinguish the more essential from the more subordinate and accidental, though in very different ways. We can only say that everything is essential so far as it is connected with His self-presentation, for it was only by the proclamation of His peculiar dignity that men could really be invited to enter into the fellowship offered them. And so these three parts are inseparable from one another as constituting the essence of His teaching—the doctrine of His Person, which is at the same time, in its outward aspect, the doctrine of His calling, or of the communication of eternal life in the Kingdom

---

[1] Luke 2⁴⁷.

of God, and in its inward aspect, the doctrine of His relation to Him Who had sent Him, or of God as His Father, revealing Himself to Him and through Him. So that everything which belongs to His high-priestly and kingly office must likewise appear in His teaching, since He proclaimed His mission to raise men to fellowship with God and to rule spiritually. And only that is accidental in His teaching which contains least of this, and keeps most to the historical situation, and bears on the given national factor. To emphasize the latter above the former leads very easily to a dangerous distinction between a teaching *of* Christ and a teaching *about* Christ (as something merely additional), and undeniably imperils what is specifically Christian, as if all that is involved were some improvements upon natural ethics and natural theology —which, besides, are represented as if human reason must have found them out by itself. But with this proviso, there is room enough for Christians of different temperaments to hold for their own use predominantly to one or another of these elements.

But further, this original revelation of God in Christ is so adequate and also so inexhaustible, that, so far as this first aspect is concerned, Christ is manifestly at once the climax and the end of all prophecy. No presentation of our relationship to God can arise outside the sphere in which Christ is recognized, which would not fall short of that revelation ; nor can any possible advance within the Christian Church ever bring us to the point either of perceiving anything imperfect in the teaching of Christ Himself, for which we could substitute something better, or of conceiving anything which aids man's understanding of his relation to God more spiritually, more profoundly, or more perfectly than Christ has done. Indeed, with the assumption that Christian doctrine is capable of being perfected in a way which implies our transcending Christ, the assumption of Christ's peculiar dignity would have to be given up. Even the most admirable later achievements in this sphere can never be more than a correct development of what lies undeveloped in His utterances, as we possess them, or, as the connexion of thought assures us, must even then have been before His mind. Now if Christ is the climax of all prophecy because of the perfection of His preaching, proceeding from a divine impulse, He is so also because even as teacher He is not one among many of His like. And He is the end of all prophecy, because no new teaching can arise which, after His, would not be false ; that is to say, from now on all true teaching in this sphere goes back, not to Moses and the law, but to the Son. He is also the end of prophecy for this reason, that now there can be no such thing as an independent personal inspiration, but only a being inspired by Him.

This only remains to be said, that, like the teaching of the prophets, His too was always the direct utterance of His whole being, hence not to be separated from the total impression His being made. And from this it follows for His teaching, that (since His inspiration was not transient but constant) every utterance of His moved spirit in speech and accompanying expression contains elements of teaching, and serves as confirmation of His teaching proper, inasmuch as it bears witness to the being of God in Him.

3. The prediction of the Old Testament prophets, so far as we can form conclusions about the whole from what remains to us, was of two kinds. One kind was special prediction, directed to an individual event ; since it rested upon the two chief concepts of the Jewish religion, the divine election of the people and divine retribution, it was for the most part hypothetical, and formed an addition to teaching which conveyed warning, encouragement, and comfort, in accordance with the spirit of the law. The other kind rose above the individual event to an exposition of the universal, and as such claimed absolute value—this was Messianic prediction. The first kind was a foretelling in the proper sense ; in its more or less definite assertions it attained now a higher, and now a lower degree of accuracy. In Messianic prophecy, the individual assertions, more or less, are nothing but an external vesture, so that it often remains uncertain whether this point or that does or does not really belong to the prediction itself. But its essence consists in this, that it spoke of the future of God's true messenger. The idea of that messenger could be grasped by individuals only in limited fashion, by each in his own way ; but rightly understood it always involved the end of those two Jewish conceptions of retribution and election. Now Christ, as the Messiah appearing in person, could only predict messianically concerning what had not yet appeared but would be fulfilled by means of the same activity as that from which the prediction itself proceeded ; that is, He could predict only concerning the further development of His Kingdom or its completion. Hence this prediction was precisely the same thing as His teaching ; in this sense He prophesied without foretelling.[1] But neither could He foretell the merely accidental, for everything so to be described is without value in

[1] Acts 1⁷.

His Kingdom, and thus could not be the object either of investigation or of premonition. He could foretell, therefore, only the end of such institutions as rested upon those limited concepts of election and retribution ; and this He did, not hypothetically, but with the perfect accuracy belonging to His infallible perfection. His certainty in this foretelling, indeed, must be identical with the certainty of His own mission. In both connexions, therefore, Christ is the climax of prophecy. And just as He is the climax, so too He is the end. For essential prophecy has now been completely fulfilled, since the Spirit has been poured out ; nothing essential can be thought of which is still lacking to the kingdom of God ; to point forward to anything new which is still to occur would necessarily be to preach another gospel. It is just the same with the foretelling. Apostolic prediction—what there is of it [1]—we can regard only as an interpretation or an echo of Christ's prediction ; there was only one occasion for it which did not yet exist in His time—namely, the application to hostile heathendom of prophecies similar to those which He had uttered against Judaism. For the rest, along with those limited concepts there disappeared the basis and support for all prophecy such as is attached exclusively to a heightened excitation of the devout soul. All that remains is such prophecy as can arise from an intelligent and comprehensive view of human relations and from a true and deep sympathy. But to no prediction, whatever its content, and however great its accuracy, and however wonderfully the pictures of an excited faculty of premonition may occasionally come true, can we ascribe a sacred character.

If this proposition has not hitherto received such definite doctrinal expression in the Protestant Church as in consistency it has been given here, perhaps such expression is also more necessary now than before, and in all likelihood it will meet with little opposition in the Church itself. And this, not only because it essentially belongs to the naturalization of the Kingdom of God in the world, but because the whole previous practice of our Church shows that it invariably regards any claim to the gift of prophecy as symptomatic of fanaticism. For us at present, therefore, it remains only to interpret the prophecies of Christ and the Apostles. But that is a task which can only be done in accordance with the rules of the art of interpretation, not with an arbitrariness which would be justified

[1] I do not include here the Revelation of John ; I cannot admit its apostolic origin.

only in the measure in which it itself was prophecy. But all fore-tellings, both those derived from the historical sense and those derived from inexplicable capacities for premonition, must be left to the natural science of mind.

4. Although it was laid down that even wonders and signs were not to protect the prophet who spoke against Jehovah and His law,[1] yet this very fact makes it clear that when people thought of a prophet they always thought also of wonders and signs.[2] With reference to the Redeemer, we might of course [3] surmise it to be natural in a higher order of things that He should have even miraculous powers at His command ; but from this comparison with the Jewish prophets it is clear in what sense Christ Himself and His disciples could appeal to His miracles, and yet why Christ, when signs and wonders were demanded of Him, refused to do them. For even the wonders of the prophets were not intended to evoke faith in their Messianic prophecies, and could not do so ; their purpose was to evoke faith in their conditional predictions in order to induce people to do what had to be done. But Christ gave no such conditional predictions about Himself, and faith in His relation to the Messianic idea was meant to proceed solely from the direct impression made by His Person.[4] That is why Christ never availed Himself of His miraculous powers in any definite connexion with the demands He made or His statements about Himself,[5] but (in the same way as everyone avails himself of his natural powers) according as opportunity offered of doing good by them.

In those days the true recognition of Christ might in individual instances be evoked by miracles ; elsewhere it found a confirmation in them ; but it might never be properly based upon them. Hence for us, so far as our faith is concerned, they cannot but be altogether superfluous. For miracles can only direct the spiritual need to a definite object in virtue of their immediate impressiveness, or, if it has already been directed thither, justify this inner relation in an external way.[6] This impressiveness, however, is lost in pro-portion as the person who is to believe is at a distance from the miracle itself in space and time. What takes the place of miracles for our time is our historical knowledge of the character, as well as of the scope and the duration, of Christ's spiritual achievements.

---

[1] Deut. 13[1-5].   [2] See above (§ 103. 1).
[3] Cf. § 14, *Postscript*, pp. 70 ff.   [4] Matt. 16[16], John 1[14. 16] 4[42] 6[68. 69] 7[25. 26].
[5] Even John 11[42] is no exception to this, although I cannot argue the point here.
[6] This last must also be the sense of John 20[30. 31].

In this we have an advantage over the contemporaries of the Redeemer, and a witness whose power increases exactly in proportion
as the impressiveness of the miracles is lost. But what does this
mean except that our attention is directed away from the individual,
more physical, miracles to the general spiritual miracle, which
begins with the person of the Redeemer and is completed with the
completion of His Kingdom ? Our faith in the external miracles
wrought by Christ, as deeds which were not wrought by Him in
accordance with rules learned anywhere, and whose success cannot
be traced to natural laws recognized by us as valid for all time—
this faith belongs not so much to our faith in Christ directly as to
our faith in Scripture.

For we cannot include these phenomena in the field of nature
familiar to us without having recourse to presuppositions such that
the trustworthiness of the whole body of our records concerning
Christ is imperilled.[1]   And this conviction will probably be the result
of the controversy now being waged on this question, and as a conviction will be the more living and the more universal the greater
the candour and the intelligence with which the controversy is
carried on.

If we confine ourselves to these individual miracles, then we
cannot make it so clear as we did in the case of teaching and prophecy
that Christ is also the climax of miraculous activity. For in Christ's
miracles we have nothing which definitely raises them, in and by
themselves, above other similar miracles of which we have stories
from many various times and places. But if we consider the total
spiritual miracle, then we must declare Him to be the climax, all
the more definitely that we recognize that—apart from Him—this
total spiritual miracle could not have been achieved by all the powers
of spiritual nature as we know it. But equally certainly Christ is
also the end of miracle. For the surer it is that by Christ redemption
has been completed, so that whatever is yet in store for the human
race, so far as fellowship with God is concerned, is to be regarded
only as a further development of Christ's work, not as a new revelation, the more reason we have for rejecting everything that claims
to offer miraculous evidence for a new achievement in the sphere
of spiritual life. Only new natural epochs—or even new historical
epochs, so long as they are not in the sphere of religion—could still
be announced by miracles ; and in that case to pass judgment
on such miracles is purely a matter for natural science.

[1] Cf. § 99.

On this point too we can scarcely say there is a fixed doctrine in the Protestant Church. Yet Luther's words [1] on the matter show clearly enough that he did not regard the great change in the Church which he helped to bring about (in spite of the fact that, at least in a subordinate sense, it was the beginning of a new corporate life) as a point of development such that it needed to be supported by the power of working miracles. Also this doctrine has the support of a maxim which we may regard as having become dominant in the Protestant Church by tacit agreement, namely, that we assume the presence of superstition wherever new miracles are represented and believed to have occurred for the confirmation of Christianity. Against this it might be objected that our proposition certainly cannot be admitted strictly and literally, since the miracles of the disciples of Christ were just as well attested as His own, and He manifestly bequeathed to them His power of working miracles. And since (it might be argued) it can in no sense be proved that these miraculous gifts were suddenly to die out with the death of the Apostles, so much anyhow is certain, that Christ Himself did not claim to be the end of miraculous powers, while it must be left undecided whether these gifts really have gradually died out, or whether perhaps they do not still persist in the Church, or at least revive periodically. To this the answer is that the same thing holds true of the miracles of the Apostles as of their prophecies, and that Christ transmitted to them the power of working miracles only as a sign to accompany the earliest preaching. Even if it cannot be strictly proved that the Church's power of working miracles has died out (and this the Roman Church denies), yet in general it is undeniable that, in view of the great advantage in power and civilization which the Christian peoples possess over the non-Christian, almost without exception, the preachers of to-day do not need such signs. And in every individual case it will always be possible to show that alleged miracles, whatever spiritual aim may be ascribed to them, would always be inadequate to it, and consequently that they are superfluous. Indeed, the Roman Church itself, by the manner in which in one case it limits miracles, and in another scrutinizes them, betrays no great confidence in the principle which it sets up.

[1] 'The same signs as the Apostles did might easily happen even to-day if there were any need' (*W.A.* xi. pp. 1294, 1339).

§ 104. *Second Theorem.—The priestly office of Christ includes His perfect fulfilment of the law* (i.e. *His active obedience*), *His atoning death* (i.e. *His passive obedience*), *and His intercession with the Father for believers.*

1. The difficulty of presenting the total activity of Christ under these forms of the old covenant occurs chiefly in this section. For one thing, the analogy between that part of the effective influence of Christ which must be assigned to this section, if a place is to be found for it at all, and the functions of the High Priest, is less conspicuous. For another, many aspects of the functions of the High Priest, which must be paralleled in Christ, reveal themselves in activities of the Redeemer which one would be more inclined to assign to one of the other two offices. Thus the extraordinary, but most significant, function of the High Priest, that of receiving instructions from Jehovah in the Holy of Holies, has no direct analogy in the work of Christ. In so far as Christ received from His Father all instructions which He imparted to His followers,[1] this must be reckoned chiefly to His prophetic activity. The benedictions which the High Priest pronounced over the people remind us of what we have already ascribed to the reconciling activity of Christ, but Church doctrine does not expressly include it in that activity. Yet since the benediction of Christ cannot be simply a wish, but must be a real gift, His benediction must be involved in His governing and directing activity; indeed, the Epistle to the Hebrews undoubtedly conceives of a kingly activity in addition to the high-priestly. So there remain only symbolical actions. Among these the functions of the Day of Atonement are the most impressive. But we cannot think of relating any of these to the special functions of Christ which have just been mentioned. While if we regard the High Priest as being at the same time the head of the priesthood, so that its performances are traceable to him, then he would be the agent of the people with Jehovah, and this would be completely expressed by the idea of representation. On the other hand, nothing is said directly about a legal perfection of the High Priest, and the atoning death of Christ, regarded as a sacrifice, has nothing corresponding to it. So far as the first point is concerned, two things should be kept in mind. First, that personal physical perfection was essential in the High Priest. The nearest direct parallel to this in the doctrine of the person of Christ

[1] John 7[16] 8[26] 17[8].

is, of course, His sinless perfection. And second, and chiefly, that
before the High Priest entered upon the official performances of the
Day of Atonement—and to these, as his most characteristic duties,
we must pay particular attention—he had to purify himself in
many different ways, and to bring a sin-offering for himself and his
house, in virtue of which he was then held to be legally perfect.
And so far as the other point is concerned, the fact that Christ
offered *Himself* is to be disregarded in this connexion. For in so far
as He Himself was the offering, He is to be compared to the sacri-
ficial animal. Not only is this mode of expression found in various
places in the Bible,[1] but this twofold reference has also passed over
into confessional documents,[2] so that it is the more necessary for us
to distinguish the two aspects from each other ; and yet here we
should have to think of Christ principally as the sacrificer, not as the
offering. As the sacrificer, however, He is active, and His suffering
can be only an accompaniment, and can have its ground solely
in sympathy with sin, which of course we may also presuppose
in the High Priest, especially in his acts of atonement. Yet here a
new difficulty arises, namely, that both the active and the passive
obedience of Christ belong entirely to His self-presentation, and
consequently to His prophetic office ; just as His intercession or
representation, since it cannot be thought of as lacking in effect,
seems to coincide wholly with His government. Here too, then,
we shall have to make a distinction on both sides, and set forth the
representation of Christ here only in so far as it is something different
from His government, and His twofold obedience only in so far as
it is something different from His self-presentation or His proclamation of the divine will by word and deed.

2. If we begin by dividing the obedience of Christ into active
and passive, we are by no means to imagine that these two are
so divided that they occupied different parts of His life, as is
commonly supposed—that the passive obedience began only with
His arrest, while the active had expressed itself from the beginning
of His public life up to that point. For not only can there be no
suffering at all without reaction, which is always activity ; we have
already established the special conclusion with regard to Christ,[3]

---

[1] Eph. 5[2], Heb. 9[26].

[2] Maneat ergo hoc in causa, quod sola mors Christi est vere propitiatorium
sacrificium (*Apol. Conf.* p. 255). Oblatio Christi semel facta, perfecta est
redemtio propitiatio et satisfactio pro omnibus peccatis (*Conf. Angl.* xxxi.
p. 138). Similarly *Conf. Tetrap.* xix. p. 354 ; *Declar. Thorun.* p. 425.

[3] See § 94, 2.

that we can separate off no moment in His life which does not contain His powerful God-consciousness, and that this can manifest itself only as activity—activity which, even where it appears as reaction (and this of course it does in His sufferings proper), could never be anything else than the most perfect fulfilment of the divine will ; as indeed His perfect submission, without complaisance on the one side, or bitterness or ill-humour on the other, is the crown of His active obedience. Similarly, there is never any activity without some definite occasion — which always presupposes a passive state ; and just as little is there ever any activity without limits to what is effected by it—and these limitations also are felt as suffering. Now both those occasions and those limitations came to Christ out of the corporate life of universal sinfulness ; and thus every instance of opposition which He experienced during His active life, every snare of His adversaries, and equally the in-difference with which many passed Him by, became for Him suffer-ing, because in it He had a sympathetic feeling of the world's sin, and thus carried that sin ; so that this suffering accompanied Him throughout His whole life. Looked at more closely, then, active and passive obedience were bound up with each other at every moment. The one term, therefore, describes simply the condition, pleasing and completely satisfying to God, in which Christ was receptive towards everything which came to Him from the corporate life of sin, in that He accepted everything solely as it was related to the task to be discharged by means of the potency of his God-consciousness, in the most perfect and the purest way. The other describes the parallel condition of His self-activity relatively to everything which it was incumbent on Him to do for the corporate life which He had come to call into being—the meaning of all this being that He never conceived any other purpose than this. But both receptivity and self-activity, and hence both active and passive obedience, were present in all the moments of Christ's life. The action of Christ without the suffering could not have been re-demptive, nor the suffering without the action reconciling ; and on that account redemption cannot be ascribed to the active obedience alone, nor reconciliation to the passive obedience alone, but both to both.

3. In comparing Christ, as regards His active obedience as thus defined, with the High Priest, we must, of course, consider only the original institution of this office, not what it degenerated into in reality. The High Priest, in virtue alike of his setting-apart and

of the seclusion of his life in the precincts of the temple, was very favourably situated. It was not easy for him to neglect anything pertinent to his calling, nor was anything likely to be demanded of him which was out of keeping with his dignity and thus apt to injure it. Also it was much easier for him than for anyone else to keep clear of ceremonial defilements. These privileges had to be granted to human weakness if, in relation to his people, he was to represent even symbolically that which Christ actually was in relation to men. For the people were in constant danger, indeed almost in constant consciousness, of defilement. But the High Priest through his setting-apart was relieved of all worldly affairs, and even of the most natural duties, if to fulfil them involved even a slight defilement. It was his function to represent the pure man, who as such was alone authorized to officiate at the yearly sacrifice of atonement, by way of supplement to all the sacrifices which the people were ceaselessly offering through the priesthood as a whole. Thus the people, living at a greater or less distance from the temple, seemed to itself to be living also at a greater distance from God—a distance which was only temporarily lessened by the alternation of the times of divine service and those of ordinary business. But the function of the High Priest was to counterbalance these fluctuating movements by remaining constantly in the immediate neighbourhood of the temple, even although he actually entered it only at prescribed times and for prescribed purposes. Now just this is the essential thing in the high-priestly significance of the active obedience of Christ. For that it is His action alone which completely corresponds to the divine will, and gives pure and full expression to the dominion of the God-consciousness in human nature—this is the basis of our relationship to Him ; and on the recognition of this everything specifically Christian is based. What this implies is that, apart from connexion with Christ, no individual man, nor yet any part of the corporate life of men is at any time, in and for itself, righteous before God or an object of His good pleasure. And just as of the whole Jewish people the High Priest alone appeared immediately before God, and God saw the whole people as it were only in him, so Christ too is our High Priest because God sees us, not each of us for himself, but only in Christ. In living fellowship with Christ no one wishes to be anything for himself, nor yet to be regarded by God as anything. Each one wishes to appear only as animated by Christ, and as a part of His work which is still in process of development ;

so that even that which has not yet been altogether united with Him is still related to the same animating principle, because it is yet to be animated by Him some day. Thus, just as the High Priest was then, so Christ is now, the One who presents us pure before God in virtue of His own perfect fulfilment of the divine will. Because of His life in us, the impulse to the fulfilling of that will is also active in us, so that in this connexion with Him we too are objects of the divine good pleasure. This is the meaning (characteristic of our view, and from a Christian standpoint unobjectionable) of the often misunderstood expression, that Christ's obedience is our righteousness, or that His righteousness is imputed to us.[1] Such an expression is very easy to misunderstand, and it certainly cannot be thoroughly defended except on the assumption of a common life—which for that matter is also most definitely assumed in the conception of the High Priest. Thus we are also enabled to distinguish the prophetic value of Christ's obedience from the high-priestly. To the prophetic office of Christ belongs everything which is proclamation, and so self-presentation as well, not in words only, but also in deed. This, however, is addressed to men in view of their opposition to Christ, in order to make them susceptible of union with Him. Hence the obedience of Christ in this aspect of it is held up [2] even for all who are in the Church, and bears on the distinction between Christ and them which still persists. But the high-priestly value of His obedience relates to His union with us, in so far, that is, as in virtue of the vital fellowship existing between Him and us His pure will to fulfil the divine will is active in us also, and we therefore share His perfection, if not in execution, at least in impulse.[3] Our union with Him, accordingly, although it never attains more than relative manifestation, is yet recognized by God as absolute and eternal, and is affirmed as such in our faith.

There are only two things in the ordinary presentation against which we must still be on our guard. First, the active obedience of Christ must not be presented as the perfect fulfilment of the divine *law*. For law always denotes a distinction and a severance between a higher will which commands, and an imperfect will

---

[1] Eam ob causam ipsius obedientia . . . qua nostra causa sponte se legi subjecit, eamque implevit, nobis ad iustitiam imputatur (*Sol. decl.*, p. 585). Jesus Christus nobis imputans omnia sua merita, et tam multa sancta opera, quae praestitit pro nobis ac nostro loco est nostra iustitia (*Conf. Belg.* xxii. p. 183).

[2] Phil. 2 5-8, 1 Pet. 2 21.

[3] Cf. § 88, 3.

which is subordinate to it.   In this sense the claim must certainly
be made for Christ that He was not subject to the law, since, even
if in view of the two natures a twofold will be ascribed to Him, yet
the two even so must be in complete agreement.[1]   But just as
little can it be said that He willingly subjected Himself to the law ;
for not even willingly could He bring Himself so to differ from the
divine will that it could become a law for Him.   The active obedience of Christ was rather His perfect fulfilment of the *divine will*.[2]
But if what is in question is the Mosaic law, in so far as it chiefly
prescribed performances and abstentions, then to this He certainly
was subject so far as His personality was concerned,[3] so that it
cannot be said that He undertook its fulfilment willingly.   But
the high-priestly worth of His obedience could not have consisted
in this alone, except in so far as it was part of His fulfilment of the
divine will.   The second point is this, that if we are to express
ourselves with any accuracy we cannot say, either, that Christ
fulfilled the divine will *in our place* or *for our advantage*.   That is
to say, He cannot have done so *in our place* in the sense that we
are thereby relieved from the necessity of fulfilling it.   No Christian
mind could possibly desire this, nor has sound doctrine ever asserted
it.   Indeed, Christ's highest achievement consists in this, that He so
animates us that we ourselves are led to an ever more perfect
fulfilment of the divine will.[4]   Not only so ; but He cannot have
done it in the sense that the failure to please God which is present
in us in and for ourselves, should or could, as it were, be covered by
Christ's doing more than was necessary to please Him.   For only
that which is perfect can stand before God ;   hence even Christ
Himself had (to put it so) nothing to spare, which could be distributed among us, whether we regard the completeness of His fulfilment in outward acts (which, moreover, for reasons which will
emerge more clearly later, would be quite un-Protestant) or whether
we regard only the purity of the inward sentiment.

Neither can He have fulfilled the divine will in any way *for our
advantage*, as if by the obedience of Christ, considered in and for
itself, anything were achieved for us or changed in relation to us.
The true view is that the total obedience—δικαίωμα—of Christ
avails for our advantage only in so far as through it our assumption
into vital fellowship with Him is brought about, and in that fellow-

---

[1] But this, of course, is not what is meant in *Sol. decl.*, p. 605 : tam non
fuit legi subjectus, quam non fuit passioni et morti obnoxius, quia dominus
legis erat.
[2] John 4³¹ 5¹⁹. ³⁰ 6³⁸.   [3] Gal. 4⁴.   [4] John 15². ⁵. ⁸. ¹¹.

ship we are moved by Him, that is, His motive principle becomes ours also—just as we also share in condemnation for Adam's sin only in so far as we, being in natural life-fellowship with him and moved in the same way, all sin ourselves.[1]

4. We come now to the *passive obedience* of Christ. It has already been stated above that the resemblance to the High Priest is here only a very general one. So we cannot use it to explain the connexion between the passive obedience of Christ and His redeeming and reconciling activity, especially since nothing is said about the High Priest enduring evil, while this is assumed to be the important element in the passive obedience of Christ, with the result that His feeling as sacrificer and His suffering as sacrificed or as sacrifice are confused. If for the present we allow this confusion, we are thrown back upon the fact that in every human society, so far as it can be regarded as a self-enclosed whole, there is as much evil as sin ; and that while the evil is certainly the punishment of the sin, yet each individual does not wholly and exclusively suffer precisely the evil which is connected with his personal sin.[2] Therefore it can be said, in every case in which anyone suffers evil not connected with his own sin, that he suffers punishment for others ; and as the causality of this sin has now exhausted itself, these others, in virtue of his punishment, can no longer be affected by the evil. Now in order that Christ should assume us into the fellowship of His life, it was necessary that He should first have entered into our fellowship. He without sin, so that no evil could arise from the presence of sin in Him, must enter into the fellowship of the sinful life where, along with and as a fruit of sin, evil is constantly arising. Hence it must be said of Him, that His suffering in this fellowship, if occasioned by sin—and from merely natural evils He never suffered—was suffered for those with whom He stood in fellowship, that is, for the whole human race, to which He belongs, not only because no particular fellowship within the human race can be completely isolated, but also by His own deliberate choice. Not only was the distinction between Jews and Gentiles abolished, in real fact, alike by His manifestation as ideal man and more particularly in His consciousness ; but for one thing His activity had already, at least indirectly, a bearing on the Gentiles, and for another thing, and especially in the last days of His life, He was surrounded by Judaism and heathendom, as political and religious authorities, causing His suffering, and representing

[1] Rom. 5[12. 18].   [2] Cf. § 77.

the sin of the whole world. If we abstract from those evils which did not properly have any high-priestly character, and regard only the suffering which He experienced as High Priest, it is obvious that the sympathy with sin, conditioned as it is in Him as human experience by this situation, must have been brought to its climax in this alliance of the two chief classes of sinners against His sinless personality. Now just as this sympathy with human guilt and liability to punishment was the initiatory motive in redemption (as every definite human activity is preceded by a determining impression), so too the highest degree of just this sympathy was the direct inspiration of the greatest moment in the work of redemption. And as victory over sin rose out of this,[1] and along with sin its connexion with evil has also been overcome, by the substitution of equivalents we may say that through the suffering of Christ punishment is abolished, because in the fellowship of His blessed life even the evil which is in process of disappearing is no longer at least regarded as punishment.[2]

What has now been set forth is the real meaning of the statements that Christ by His willing surrender of Himself to suffering and death satisfied the divine justice, as that which had ordained the connexion between sin and evil, and thus set us free from the punishment of sin.[3] Everywhere within the specific sphere of Christianity this is easily intelligible and easily defensible, though the statements are often criticized from without. And from this presentation it must be possible to deduce whatever in the way of appropriation of Christ's suffering (as distinct from its exemplary value, which belongs to His prophetic office) has proved fruitful in Christian piety. Even that form of the doctrine which sometimes appears one-sided, and which concentrates the whole power of redemption almost exclusively in the suffering of Christ, and so finds satisfaction in this alone, may readily be understood in this light. For in His suffering unto death, occasioned by His steadfastness, there is manifested to us an absolutely self-denying love ; and in this there is represented to us with perfect vividness the way in which God was in Him to reconcile the world to Himself, just as it

---

[1] John 12²⁴. [2] Rom. 8²⁸.

[3] Deus ergo propter solum Christum *passum* et resuscitatum propitius est peccatis nostris, etc. (*Expos. simpl.* xv. p. 41). Hunc . . . credimus . . . unica sui ipsius oblatione Deo . . . pro nostris . . . peccatis satisfecisse . . . sicque morte sua triumphum egisse, etc. (*Conf. Mylhus.* iv. p. 104). Profitemur quod . . . anima et corpore passus est, ut pro populi peccatis plane satisfaceret, etc. (*Conf. Scot.* ix. p. 149). Ad haec passus mortuus et sepultus, ut pro me satisfaceret meamque culpam persolveret (*Catech. maj.*, p. 495).

is in His suffering that we feel most perfectly how imperturbable was His blessedness. Hence it may be said that the conviction both of His holiness and of His blessedness always comes to us primarily as we lose ourselves in the thought of His suffering. And just as the active obedience of Christ has its properly high-priestly value chiefly in the fact that God regards us in Christ as partners in His obedience, so the high-priestly value of His passive obedience consists chiefly in this, that we see God in Christ, and envisage Christ as the most immediate partaker in the eternal love which sent Him forth and fitted Him for His task.

Although it seems now hardly necessary to stay to compare this simple presentation with those artificial constructions [1] which never tire of bringing together all sorts of reasons to prove the necessity or the appropriateness of Jesus' suffering and death, yet there still remain serious misunderstandings which we must dispose of. The first is this, that although it is in a specially impressive way from His suffering that we gain a true understanding of Christ, yet this is no justification for the triviality of the so-called ' wounds-theology,' once very widespread but now almost obsolete, which thought to find the deep import of the suffering of Christ in its sensuous details, and hence, for the sake of allegorical trivialities, broke up into details the totality of Christ's suffering. Underlying this was a confusion of thought ; what can only be attributed to Christ as a sacrifice or victim was transferred to His high-priestly dignity. The victim has no independent activity ; it is completely passive in everything which happens to it. So Christ too was perfectly passive in respect of those details of His suffering as to which He had no choice, and which consequently are not to be regarded as being for Him significant elements in experience. The second misunderstanding is to take the formula, that through the suffering of Christ the punishment of sin is taken away—a formula perfectly correct when interpreted as explained above—to mean that He bore the punishment, that is, that His suffering was equal to the sum of the evils constituting the amount of the punishment for the sins of the human race, since otherwise the divine righteousness would not have been satisfied. From which it naturally follows, since the total sin of the human race cannot be reckoned anything less than infinite, that the suffering also was infinite. If now the suffering of Christ and His death, although limited to a definite space of time and relative to a capacity for suffering infinitely diminished

---

[1] Among others, Reinhard, *Dogm.*, §§ 107 and 108, pp. 401 ff.

by His higher spiritual power, is thus to be equated to the total of human suffering for sin, postulated as infinite, then it is scarcely possible to avoid the supplementary assumption that the divine nature in Him also shared in the suffering.[1] This presentation of the matter, contradicting as it does the incapacity of the divine nature for suffering (a truth long recognized even in this doctrine), certainly can offer no defence to any serious attack by its opponents. But this misunderstanding only reaches its height in the view that the suffering of Christ is a transference of punishment in the still more exact sense that God (who nevertheless, according to the doctrine of the Church itself, is not in general the Author of punishment) appointed His suffering for the Redeemer as punishment, so that Christ is supposed to have felt the primary and most direct punishment of sin, namely, the divine wrath, as striking Him and resting upon Him. This theory, on the one hand, deprives the human consciousness of Christ of all human truth, by regarding as His personal self-consciousness what from the nature of the case could in Him be only sympathy.[2] And, on the other hand, it is obviously based on the assumption that there is an absolute necessity in the divine punishment, without any regard to the natural connexion of punishment with moral evil. This again can hardly be divorced from a conception of the divine righteousness which has been transferred to God from the crudest human conditions. Now if we take these two elements together, as they are united in the phrase *vicarious satisfaction*, we must surely admit that it is not fitting to stamp it as *the* phrase in which these aspects of the high-priestly work of Christ should be comprised. But perhaps the protest against this expression (which, of course, has already been attacked on many sides, yet continues to be the expression current in the Church) cannot be set forth more effectively than by demon-

---

[1] This is expressed, not obscurely, in the whole context of the passage quoted above from the *Sol. decl.*, p. 696, although throughout, so far as words are concerned, the proposition that the divine nature does not suffer is not abrogated. For it is at the same time maintained that the human nature became capable of suffering this only through its union with the divine, which is the same as saying, through the divine. With this, further, agrees the fact that this credal document—which of course is open to serious criticism—also teaches practically the opposite of the view here set forth : Reiicimus . . . quod fides non respiciat tantum obedientiam Christi, sed divinam ipsius naturam, quatenus videlicet ea in nobis habitet et operetur, et quod per hanc inhabitationem nostra coram Deo peccata tegantur (p. 697).

[2] It has given me much pleasure to read that the late J. J. Hess, too, could not bring himself to regard the passage Matt. 27[46] as a description by Christ of His own state of misery, but only as the first words of the Psalm, quoted with reference to what follows.

strating how it would have to be reinterpreted if it is to be accepted
at all.   Instead of taking it as a single expression which refers
equally both to the active and to the passive obedience—as it claims
to do—we must divide it up, and apply ' vicarious ' only to the
passive, and ' satisfaction ' only to the active obedience.   For Christ
certainly made *satisfaction* for us by becoming, through His total
action, not only the beginning of redemption in time, but also the
eternally inexhaustible source, adequate for every further development, of a spiritual and blessed life.   But this satisfaction is in no
sense ' vicarious ' ;   it could not have been expected of us that we
should be able to begin this life for ourselves, nor does the act of
Christ set us free from the necessity of pursuing this spiritual life
by our own endeavour in fellowship with Him.   On the other hand,
the suffering of Christ is certainly *vicarious*, and that with respect
to both its elements.   For He had sympathy with sin in perfect
measure even in regard to those who had not yet themselves become
miserable through consciousness of it.   While the evils which He
suffered were vicarious in this general sense, that one in whom there
is no moral evil ought not to suffer ;   hence when he does experience
evil, *he* is struck instead of those in whom the moral evil is.   But
this ' vicarious ' quality in no way makes ' satisfaction ' ;   so far as
the first element is concerned, because those who are not yet miserable must first become so in order to be able to be received by Christ ;
so far as the other element is concerned, because it does not exclude
other suffering of the same sort.   Rather, all those who are assumed
into the fellowship of Christ's life are called to share the fellowship
of His suffering,[1] until the time when sin has been completely overcome and through suffering satisfaction has been made in the corporate life of humanity.   Until then all suffering, even on the part of
one who is only relatively innocent, always has a vicarious character.
If, however, we wish to regard these two aspects of the high-priestly
office of Christ in their indivisibility (that is, so far as it is possible
to include the suffering under the activity), then we may turn the
expression about, and call Christ our *satisfying representative* : in
the sense, first, that in virtue of His ideal dignity He so represents,
in His redemptive activity, the perfecting of human nature, that in
virtue of our having become one with Him God sees and regards
the totality of believers only in Him ;   and, second, that His sympathy with sin, which was strong enough to stimulate a redemptive
activity sufficient for the assumption of all men into His vital

[1] Matt. 10$^{24-28}$, John 15$^{18-21}$.

fellowship, and the absolute power of which is most perfectly exhibited in His free surrender of Himself to death, perpetually serves to make complete and perfect our imperfect consciousness of sin. It was just like the complementary sacrifice of the High Priest : that had special reference to those trespasses which had not been consciously recognized, so that his sympathy, regarded as the source of his action, took the place of that consciousness, and the people then felt themselves as free from all anxiety about divine punishment for the sins they had committed as if each one himself had fulfilled everything that the law required where there was consciousness of sin.

Only one misunderstanding still remains to be guarded against at this point ; we must not set forth Christ's surrender of Himself to death as a free decision on His part in any other sense than that which is here taken as fundamental, namely, that His self-surrender was identical with His persistence in redemptive activity. For otherwise the suffering of Christ, so far as it must be regarded as His own act, appears arbitrary, because in that case He must simply have appointed Himself to the suffering as such ; and that which, if regarded as a divine ordinance, would be that irrational necessity of retribution which we have already disposed of, would, as the free act of Christ, be an arbitrary self-torture—a pattern for the arbitrary mortifications of the Roman Church, by the transference of which it is possible for one person to set another free from punishment. But in addition to this, we should still need to take precautions—and it is impossible to see how our precautions could be successful—lest the example of Christ might be taken to afford a justification of voluntary death, even of the sort which is absolutely unchristian. For if we wish to assert the reality of human moral nature in Christ, we must not ascribe to Him, even in this connexion, any other rules of conduct than such as we have to recognize as valid for us all ; otherwise there would be a danger that His life would cease to be an example, and consequently that it would cease to be an ideal. Thus, so far as self-preservation is a duty at all, it must be true of Christ also that if He foresaw His death, and if there was any means of avoiding it without dereliction of duty, He was bound to make use of it, as He had done previously.[1] The only thing He was *not* bound to do was to ask for the help of angels,[2] or in this struggle to call to His aid any miraculous power. He must therefore have

---

[1] Luke 4[30], John 8[59].   [2] Matt. 26[53].

accepted it as a duty involved in His vocation to appear in the holy
city for this feast, in spite of the foreknowledge He possessed ; [1]
and beyond question it was an element in the development of this
great crisis that Christ met His death in His zeal for His vocation
relatively to His Father's law, just as truly as His opponents
—at least the best among them—condemned Him to death in their
professional zeal for the law.　If, nevertheless, we wish to regard
even this from the standpoint of the divine decree, then we must
concede that it behoved the Perfecter of faith to die a death which
should be not simply an occurrence, but at the same time a deed
in the highest sense of the word, in order that in this too He might
proclaim the full dominion of the spirit over the flesh.　By a natural
death, whether due to accidental illness or the result of the weakness of old age, this could have become evident only accidentally
and in a lesser degree.　But this danger, too, of presenting the voluntary character of Jesus' death in a doubtful light, will best be avoided
by keeping to the method we have hitherto followed, and making
real use of it.　For the atoning sacrifice of the High Priest was
also a free action, though a professional one, on the one side conditioned by the sin of the people, and on the other following an
established divine ordinance without arbitrariness of any kind.

5. Finally, Christ's *representation* of us before God, if we take
the word in its usual meaning (that is, as either, more generally,
the direction of another's business, or, more specifically, and more
in the dominant Biblical sense, the bringing of the wishes of another
before a third party and urging him to grant them), seems hardly
to be at all separable from His kingly office.　For how can that
which Christ is thought of as obtaining from His Father be separated
from that which He Himself as king brings about, and determines by
laws and ordinances of government ?　If then the phrase is to have
any reality, if it is not as an undefined middle term to introduce
confusion into our treatment, it must be confined to things which
either do not belong at all, or at least do not wholly belong, to
the Kingdom of Christ ; either this, or as a part of His activity
it too must have been carried on during His earthly life, just like
other parts—otherwise He would not have been a perfect High
Priest.　The New Testament passages upon which the use of the
term is chiefly based [2] give little definite guidance, since it is not

---

[1] Matt. 16²¹ and elsewhere ; cf. John 11⁷⁻⁹ ; cf. ver. 56.
[2] Rom. 8³⁴, Heb. 7²⁵, 1 John 2¹ ; but it is to be noticed that both the
expressions found here, ὑπερεντυγχάνειν and παράκλητος, are also used elsewhere
of the Holy Spirit,

clear that in all of them the reference is to the High Priest ; they seem rather to proceed from different points of view. Hence we had better keep to the conception of the high-priestly function, and bring in chiefly His appearing before God on our behalf.[1] And, if in doing so the distinction mentioned above is observed, then the representation will consist chiefly of two things : Christ appears before the Father, first, to establish our fellowship with Him, and then, further, to support our prayer before the Father. For the Kingdom of Christ extends only over those who have already been assumed into vital fellowship with Him ; while the gradual addition of individuals to this realm depends upon the divine Providence with regard to them. But just as in general this fellowship is sought for us by Christ, and is granted by God for His sake, so it is not only in His high-priestly prayer that we have the memorable fact of this representation ; that is indicated also in everything which He says about His prayer,[2] not even excluding statements which seem to be contradictory, and also in what is said about His prayer by others.[3] As regards the rest, if we proceed wholly on the principle that whatever does not belong to the Kingdom of God must also be excluded from the subjects of our prayer,[4] then in the spiritual sphere there are some things which are not so exclusively spiritual in character that they are not also interwoven with the general world order, and some which are not entirely determined by the general rules and ordinances properly to be deduced from the kingly dignity of Christ. And when He bids us pray to the Father ourselves, the fact that it is to be prayer in His name involves the certainty of a co-operation on the part of Christ which hallows our prayer by purifying and perfecting our consciousness of God. Now this co-operation is His representation of us, in the sense that it is only through Him that our prayer comes acceptably and effectively before God. In virtue, therefore, of that relation to us which is based upon His peculiar dignity, He remains the representative of the whole human race, for, like the High Priest, He brings our prayer before God and conveys to us the divine blessings. Faith in that part of this work which lies beyond Christ's earthly career is in no sense dependent on knowledge—which is denied us—of the character of His exalted life, but only on the

---

[1] Heb. 9[24].
[2] John 14[16] 16[26] 17[9], Luke 22[32].
[3] Luke 6[12] and elsewhere ; Heb. 5[7].
[4] Matt. 6[33].

content and dignity of His personality in relation to God and to us, as these have been set forth above.

6. Now just as, in accordance with all that has been said, Christ is the climax of the priesthood, and far beyond all comparison even with the High Priest, so He is also the end of all priesthood. For that which is the essential thing in the conception of priesthood, that of which every earlier priesthood was only an imperfect indication, has been given absolutely and once for all in Christ ; for He is the most perfect mediator for all time between God and every individual part of the human race, of which no one, in and for himself, could be in any sense an object for God, nor could enter into any connexion with Him. Hence, now that the true and eternal priesthood is known, there is no place for any arbitrarily devised priesthood—a mere copy of the real—nor for any further sacrifice : all human institutions of this sort are abolished. But at the same time, the high-priesthood of Christ has passed over to the fellowship of the faithful, so that Christians as a whole are called a priestly nation.[1] Two things are clearly involved in this. First, that among themselves all distinction between priests and laity is abolished. Even the Apostles never claim for themselves anything that can properly be called priestly, so that the revival of the priesthood in the Church must be viewed as one of the greatest misapprehensions. But second, Christendom as a whole, as the human race already united to the Redeemer, stands to the rest of humanity in the relation in which the priests stood to the laity. For it is only in so far as there exists a real vital fellowship with Christ at least in one part of the race that there is also a relationship between Him and the rest. Hence in this sense the Christian community, as inseparable from Christ, appears before God for the whole race and represents it. On the other hand, there can be no talk at all of any special intercession and representation on the part of individuals in the community of the perfected.[2] Similarly, all the activity of Christendom as a whole on behalf of the Gospel belongs to the active obedience of Christ, but nothing follows from this as to a meritoriousness of individual good works done by the faithful. The same is true also of all sufferings for the sake of the Gospel in the widest sense : they belong to the atoning suffering of

---

[1] 1 Pet. 2⁹.
[2] Credimus quoniam Jesus Christus datus est nobis unicus advocatus . . . quicquid homines de mortuorum sanctorum intercessione commenti sunt nihil aliud esse quam fraudem et fallacias satanae, ut homines a recta precandi forma abduceret (*Conf. Gallic.* xxiv. p. 119).

Christ,[1] but nothing follows from this as to arbitrary mortifications —any more than there was anything arbitrary in Christ's suffering. Hence Christ remains the end of the priesthood, for all this is high-priestly only in so far as it is really at the same time Christ's doing and suffering. These last-mentioned inferences—and they are perfectly natural—ought surely of themselves to suffice to secure its place in our system for a mode of presentation which has been attacked by almost all modern dogmatic theologians since Ernesti.[2]

§ 105. *Third Theorem.*—*The kingly office of Christ consists in the fact that everything which the community of believers requires for its well-being continually proceeds from Him.*

1. The term ' king ' has, and had in the time of Christ, many meanings ; and there is a great difference between its strict official use and its vague polite use. It is, therefore, impossible to base our presentation upon an exegetical decision on the questions in what sense Christ was asked whether He was a king,[3] and whether He answered in the same sense or another. Rather we must keep to the recollection, not yet extinct, that the conception of king was opposed on the one hand to that of a tyrant, whose power was just as unlimited, but not natural ; and on the other hand, to that of the authorities of a society, who possessed only a limited and delegated power, conferred on them by the governed themselves. A tyranny, on the other hand, always involved the possibility, not to say the assumption, that the power which had been arbitrarily seized was also selfish, and might have other aims than the free development and the natural prosperity of those over whom it was exercised. In contrast with both, the lordship of Christ is as unlimited as that of the animating principle always is when it is neither outwardly hindered nor inwardly weakened. Moreover, it is in the interest of those over whom it is exercised, as obviously follows from the facts that it is nothing but the lordship of that element whose weakness in themselves men deplore, and that submission to His lordship must always be voluntary. But the kingly power has this in common with the other two, that its object cannot be an individual as such, but only a society, and the individual only in so far as he belongs to the society. Individuals, then, submit voluntarily to the lordship of Christ ; but in so doing they at the same time enter a society to which they did not previously

---

[1] 2 Cor. 1[5] 4[10].   [2] See his *Diss. de triplici munere Christi.*
[3] John 18[33], Matt. 27[11].

belong. So that, in attributing a kingly dignity to Christ, we are *eo ipso* declaring ourselves definitely opposed to the contention that Christ did not intend to found an organic community, but that the society of believers came into being, or was formed, later, without His injunction. But since, at the same time, no one enters this community except by submitting himself to Christ's lordship, it follows that Christ Himself initiated this Kingdom, and is thus without any predecessor in His kingly dignity.

Christ Himself, however, indicates still another contrast, when He describes His Kingdom as not of this world, and so distinguishes it in yet another way from both those others. This negative description involves in the first place that His kingly power is not immediately concerned with the disposal and arrangement of the things of this world—which means that nothing remains as the immediate sphere of His kingship but the inner life of men individually and in their relation to each other. It involves further, that for the exercise of His lordship He makes use of no means which are dependent upon the things of this world, *i.e.* of no constraint which requires superiority in material forces, nor yet of enticements or threatenings of any kind which require support of that kind and make a merely sensuous appeal—for that, too, belongs to this world. But this is by no means to say that the kingly power of Christ began only after He had been raised above the earth, still less—as might be held—that it covers only His exalted life ; He Himself says, not that He will be a king, but that He is one ; and not only did He prove Himself a king during His earthly life—by giving laws for His community, by sending out His servants for its extension, by imposing rules of conduct and giving directions as to the way in which His commanding will should be carried out [1]—but His kingly power is and remains everywhere and always the same. For those laws and directions do not grow old, but remain valid, with undiminished force, in the Church of Christ ; and if for the future He refers His disciples to His spiritual presence, yet even that does not make a distinction between different times. For even His original influence was purely spiritual, and was mediated through His bodily appearance not otherwise than even now His spiritual presence is mediated through the written Word and the picture it contains of His being and influence—so that even now His directive control is not simply a mediate and derived one. So that, keeping in mind what was said

---

[1] Matt. 10^{5-14} 18^{15-20} 28^{19-20}.

above, we may say that His government of us bears the same relation to our activity in His name as His representation of us does to our prayer in His name.   Indeed, it is also obvious that since He stands to the totality of believers in exactly the same relation as the divine nature in Him does to the human, animating and taking it up into the fellowship of the original life, His lordship too is in the strictest sense a sole lordship, for no one else is in a position to share it. Thus, just as Christ has no predecessor in the society governed by Him, but is its original founder, so too He has in it no successor and no representative.   For He exercises His lordship through ordinances which He Himself established,[1] and has Himself declared these to be sufficient,[2] so that nothing is now necessary but the right application of these ; and to apply them is the common task of those who are ruled by Christ, just because they are His subjects. Even if at any time they could transfer this task, either to one individual or to several—though of course they could not do so without giving up their vital relation to Christ—yet any such individual would be only their representative, and not a representative of Christ.[3]   So that among believers there is nowhere any lordship other than His alone.

2. The difficulty in regard to this part of the work of Christ consists especially in defining aright the kingly power of Christ in relation to the general divine government (a difficulty which cannot be overlooked once the subject is somewhat more closely scrutinized from a *theoretical* point of view), and further in defining it aright relatively to secular government (a difficulty which at once emerges in the *practical* treatment of the question).

The customary division of the Kingdom of Christ into the kingdom of power, the kingdom of grace, and the kingdom of glory helps us little.   We have first to break it up so as to comprehend under the two latter the proper object of Christ's kingly activity, namely, the world which has become participant in redemption, while under the kingdom of power we understand the world as such, and in itself.   But in taking this position, we seem to lend ourselves to the extravagant notion that there belonged to Christ a kingdom of power, as it were, before the kingdom of grace, and independent of it. Now, to say the least, such a kingdom could not possibly belong to His redemptive activity ; and if the Apostles knew of such a

---

[1] Eph. 4[11-16].   [2] Matt. 21[20], John 15[9, 10] 17[4].
[3] *Expos. simpl.* xvii. p. 50 : Ecclesia non potest ullum aliud habere caput quam Christum . . . Nam ut ecclesia corpus est spirituale, ita caput habeat sibi congruens spirituale utique oportet.

kingdom belonging to the Word,[1] it must have been a knowledge which, because unconnected with redemption, could not belong to Christian piety either. Anyone who thinks it necessary to interpret the expressions which they use with reference to Christ as the Word made flesh, the God-man and the Redeemer,[2] or which Christ uses of Himself,[3] as if they attributed to Him the governance of the whole world, involves himself in a contradiction, not only with all the passages in which Christ Himself offers petitions to the Father and refers to what the Father has retained in His own power, but also with all passages which express His intention to establish an immediate relationship, both of petition and response, between believers and the Father. It is true that occasionally there is to be found even within the Protestant Church a form of doctrine, and here and there, in conjunction with it, even a type of Church service which leaves room (all the prayers being addressed solely to Christ) only for a relationship of believers to Christ, to the exclusion of the Father. But we must, with Scripture and very much more with the Church, pronounce this a dubious innovation. If, however, this rock is to be avoided, by the power of Christ we can understand only that power which begins with the kingdom of grace and is essentially included in it. And this itself is a power over the world only in so far as believers are taken out of the midst of the world, and the fellowship of believers or the kingdom of Christ can increase only as the world (as the antithesis of the Church) decreases, and its members are gradually transformed into members of the Church, so that evil is overcome and the sphere of redemption enlarged. But even this is a power of Christ over the world which proceeds only from the kingdom of grace, *i.e.* it exists in virtue of the influence of the command to preach given by Christ and perpetually valid in the Church. On the other hand, what part of the world, or what individual, becomes ripe for the fruitfulness of this preaching before other parts, or before other individuals, is a matter belonging to the kingdom of power, which the Father has retained for Himself.[4] Accordingly, the only things which remain subject to Christ's direct control are the forces of redemption implanted in the Church ; and it would be a rather unfruitful distinction, and not even correctly described, if we called His Kingdom a kingdom of grace in so far as these forces show themselves effective in a purely inward way, for sanctification and edification,

---

[1] John 1[2. 3].
[3] Matt. 11[27] 28[18] ; cf. John 17[5. 22. 24].
[2] Heb. 1[2. 3].
[4] Acts 1[7], John 6[44].

and a kingdom of power in so far as they are employed in the overcoming of the world ; for these two things it is quite impossible to separate from each other. The distinction, however, between the kingdom of grace and the kingdom of glory is usually taken to be that the latter follows upon the former, so soon as all Christ's subjects have been placed in full possession of all the benefits won for them, and no longer have any contact with the world—an assumption which we shall consider more closely later. Here it need only be remarked, with reference to the kingly dignity of Christ, that if the assumption is taken strictly then there can be no other activity in this Kingdom than one of expressive representation, in which case the exercise of a general directive power is reduced to a minimum. Hence we can certainly regard it as a glory of Christ that He has no more to suffer, even in sympathy, with the whole body of believers, because it has been finished and perfected ; but in no sense is this a condition which should be described as a Kingdom. Thus there remains only the one kingdom of grace as Christ's true kingdom, as indeed it is the only one a consciousness of which really emerges in our moods of devotion, the only one of which we require knowledge for our guidance, because our active faith must be directed towards it. The two other terms in the customary division we can use only to determine the scope of this very kingdom of grace. In calling it a kingdom of power we are asserting, not only that the extension of the influence of Christ over the human race knows no limits, and that no people is able to offer it a permanently effective opposition, but also that there is no stage of purity and perfection which does not belong to Christ's Kingdom. And in calling it a kingdom of glory we are confessing our belief —of course in connexion with that highest purity and perfection, only approximately given in experience—in an unlimited approximation to the absolute blessedness to be found in Christ alone.

So far as the distinction between the kingly power of Christ and civil government is concerned, it would seem, after what has been said, that nothing is easier than to distinguish exactly between the two in conception. For civil government is unquestionably an institution which belongs to the general divine government of the world,[1] and even by His own declaration is accordingly as such alien to Christ's Kingdom. On the other hand, civil government is a legal thing, and exists everywhere, even where there is no

[1] Rom. 13[1, 2].

Christian religion. Hence, since it springs out of the corporate life of sinfulness, and everywhere presupposes this (for of course for the sanction of its laws it reckons upon the force of sensuous motives), it cannot as such have the slightest authority in the Kingdom of Christ. On this view the two powers seem to be held entirely apart from each other, so that the sole lordship of Christ in His Kingdom remains secure although His followers conduct themselves in worldly affairs in accordance with the regulations of the secular government, and regard everything that comes to them from it as coming from the divine government of the world.[1] But how greatly the situation is altered as soon as we think of the secular government as exercised by Christians over Christians, is clearly to be seen in the fact that, on the one side, the Church has attempted to control the secular government in the name of Christ, while on the other, the Christian magistracy as such has claimed for itself the right to regulate the affairs of the society of believers. In order not to introduce at this point anything which belongs to Christian Ethics—from which even the theological principles of Church Law must be derived—the only question we shall here have to propound is whether the Kingdom of Christ is changed in extent through the entrance of this new material relationship. Now it is certainly true that Christ must completely control the society of believers, and consequently that every member of the society must show himself, wholly and in every part of his life, to be governed by Christ. But since this depends entirely upon the inner vital relationship in which each individual stands to Christ, and since there can be no representative who exercises the kingly office of Christ in His name, this simply means that everyone, whether magistrate or private citizen, has to seek in the directions given by Christ, not indeed right directions for his conduct under civil government (for this is always a matter of the art of politics), but certainly the right temper of mind even in this relationship. On the other hand, it also remains true that no one can exert influence upon the society of believers except in the measure in which he is a pre-eminent instrument of Christ's kingly power,[2] since otherwise the sole lordship of Christ would be imperilled. And this

---

[1] *Aug. Conf.* xvi. : Quia Evangelium tradit iustitiam aeternam cordis, interim non dissipat politiam aut oeconomiam, sed maxime postulat conservare tanquam ordinationes Dei et in talibus ordinationibus exercere caritatem.

[2] This is also the basis of the rule of Peter, Acts 1[21], and of the procedure of the Church as related in Gal. 2[7 9].

does not at all depend on his outward vocation ; [1] one who is called
as a bond-servant is not therefore a bond-servant in the society, but
a freedman of the Lord, and similarly he who is called as a lord does
not therefore become a lord in the society, but only a bond-servant
of Christ like everyone else.[2]   So that the civil contrast between
magistrate and private citizen loses all significance in the Church ;
it makes no difference to a man's relationship to the kingly power
of Christ.

3. In this way, then, we have separated the kingly power of
Christ, on the one hand, from the power which the Father has retained for Himself, while on the other we have set it beyond all the
resources of the civil power.   The latter is undoubtedly the way in
which what Luther called ' the two swords ' should be kept separate
from each other.   We may therefore say of this part also of the
work of Christ, as of the former ones, that He is the climax and the
end of all spiritual kingship ; and this will hold true in and for itself
as well as relatively to this separation.   In and for itself we must
compare His lordship with every other purely spiritual power, and
all the relationships of master and scholars, pattern and imitators,
law-giver and law-receivers, we must put far below it—they stand
on a vastly lower level, and are only concerned with individual
parts of the life of the human spirit.   The same is true of the
founders of other religions, who neither evoked a temper of mind
opposed to former habits and customs, as Christ did (rather they
accommodated themselves to these in various ways), nor, as Christ
did, called the whole human race under their lordship.   In the
same way He is the end of all such kingship, for there is just as
little possibility of a similar kingdom after His,[3] as there is that a
similar one should now exist or should ever have existed alongside
of it.   But He is both climax and end, only in so far as the above-
mentioned separation is maintained.   For it is part alike of the
purity and of the perfection of His spiritual power that sensuous
motives can have no share whatever in it.   That is why Christianity
is neither a political religion nor a religious state or a theocracy.
The former are those religious fellowships which are regarded as
the institutions of a particular civil society, and which rest upon
the assumption that the religion is derived from civil legislation, or

---

[1] *Expos. simpl.* xxx. p. 91 : Si magistratus sit amicus adeoque membrum
ecclesiae, utilissimum excellentissimumque membrum est, quod ei permultum
prodesse eamque peroptime iuvare potest.

[2] I Cor. 7[22].

[3] Heb. 12[27] : even I Cor. 15[28] does not contradict this.

is related as a subordinate movement to the same higher impulse which first called the civil organization into being, so that for the sake of the civil society its members also unite in a religious fellowship, which therefore is animated by the common spirit of the society and by patriotism—these being ' fleshly motives ' in the Scriptural sense. Theocracies, on the other hand, are religious fellowships which as such have subordinated the civil society to themselves ; in which consequently political ambition aims at preeminence within the religious fellowship, and there is the underlying assumption that the religious society, or the divine revelation upon which it rests, was able to call into being the civil society— which in this sense is possible only for religious fellowships which are nationally limited. To both, then, political religions as well as theocracies, Christ puts an end through the purely spiritual lordship of His God-consciousness ; and the stronger and the more extensive His Kingdom becomes, the more definite becomes the severance between Church and State, so that in the proper outward separation —which, of course, may take very different forms—their agreement is ever more perfectly worked out.

Postscript to this Division.—Only after we have concluded our treatment of the whole of the doctrine of Christ are we in a position to see what kind of meaning is to be given to the two contrasted *states of humiliation and exaltation* ascribed to Him. For these expressions, when taken as precisely as a place in the system must involve, cannot be applied either to the relationships of the Person by itself, or of the Work by itself, nor to the relationship of the Work to the Person. In the first place, the term ' humiliation,' taken strictly, presupposes a higher being which existed previously. But what this is, we cannot discover, so long as we abide by the unity of the Person. It may rightly be called an exaltation, that Christ became the first-fruits of the resurrection, and sits at the right hand of God ; and in comparison His earthly condition may be called a lower one—but not a humiliation, for the Person of Christ began only when He became man. On such terms the Person of Christ is divided, and since the divine in Him is regarded as something special existing from eternity, its descent to earth takes on the appearance of a humiliation. But to the absolutely highest and eternal — which necessarily remains always self-identical — no humiliation can possibly be attributed. It would follow from this that, from the same point of view, the indwelling of the Holy Spirit in the fellowship of believers must also be a humiliation—all the more that human nature in us is not pure and sinless as it was in the Person of Christ. Nay more, in view of the omnipresence of God in all finite creatures, creation itself would be a humiliation ; and this, although the glorification of God is actually given as the purpose of creation. But if we accept the term ' humiliation ' instead of the more exact ' state of lowliness,' but hold fast to the unity of the Person, even so the antithesis reveals itself as a mere deception, or at least as merely an appearance for others but not a reality for Christ Himself. For how can one have been conscious of the lowliness of His state who speaks of His relationship to God the Father in such a way [1] that even to be set at His right hand could not be regarded as an exaltation ? If, further, we think of the customary conception of the two natures and of a mutual impartation of the attributes of each, we cannot refer the humiliation to the union of the two natures (for that remains even if the humanity of Christ be exalted to the right hand of God), but only to the divine nature, either in so far as it refrains from the use of its attributes, or in so far as along with them it must accept those of the human nature. Now the latter circumstance remains unaltered in the state of exaltation as well. For since the distance between God and every finite being is infinite, it remains unchanged whether we think of humanity in its present state or in advanced development. The former has only slightly more plausibility. For if (and this is involved in this mode of presentation) even in the state of lowliness exceptions to the non-use of divine attributes occurred in virtue of the free will of Christ,[2] then of course the renouncement of them itself must have been voluntary. Indeed, we must assert this, even without any regard to exceptions ; for no compulsion can be laid upon the divine nature. In fact, we must rather say that a compulsion to make use of those attributes against His free will would have been a humiliation. But we cannot imagine that even in the state of exaltation Christ makes a more complete use of them. For if all the attributes of the divine nature are active without intermission in the human nature, then all activities of the human nature must be at rest without intermission ; which is the same as saying that so far as its activity was concerned the human nature was absorbed by the divine, and there remained only its passive aspect—and this is quite contrary to the original assumption. But how, again, could we conceive an un-

---

[1] John 1⁵¹ 4³⁴ 5¹⁷. ²⁰ff· 6⁵⁷ 8²⁹ 10³⁰. ³⁶, etc. etc.
[2] *Sol. decl.*, p. 767 : divinam suam majestatem pro liberrima voluntate quando et quomodo ipsi visum fuit etiam in statu exinanitionis manifestavit.

interrupted use of the divine qualities, if we are really to think of Christ as representing us before the Father, and making requests for us in view of sin—that is, as sympathetically sharing in the conflicts of the warring Church ? So that even here there remains only a less or more, which cannot justify the use of such expressions. And it hardly need be said that this antithesis cannot be related to the functions of Christ either. For even if we were to say that the kingly function is by far the highest, even so the prophetic and the priestly were next to it, and were not opposed to it as lowly functions—for it was in no lowly attitude that Christ exercised the prophetic activity.

If now, in view of the complete untenability of this formula, we inquire what its origin was, the answer is that its only basis is a passage of Scripture,[1] whose devotional and—when we regard the whole context—rhetorical character indicates no intention that the expressions used should be set up as a fixed didactic formula. Besides, it would follow from this passage that the exaltation of Christ is simply a reward appointed Him by God for the humiliation, without direct connexion either with His peculiar dignity or with the completion of His work. But the way in which Paul here sets up Christ as an example is quite compatible with the view that his starting-point was simply the appearance of lowliness in Christ's life as well as in His death. In the transmission of doctrine, accordingly, we are perfectly entitled to set this formula aside ; it may justly be entrusted to history for safe keeping.

---

[1] Phil. 2$^{6\text{-}9}$. None of the other passages cited in this connexion contributes anything to the question.

Second Division: The Manner in which Fellowship with
the Perfection and Blessedness of the Redeemer
expresses Itself in the Individual Soul

§ 106. *The self-consciousness characterizing those assumed into living
fellowship with Christ may be set forth under both conceptions,
Regeneration and Sanctification.*

1. If it be the essence of redemption that the God-consciousness
already present in human nature, though feeble and repressed,
becomes stimulated and made dominant by the entrance of the
living influence of Christ, the individual on whom this influence is
exercised attains a religious personality not his before. Before this
the God-consciousness was evinced only casually in isolated flashes,
never kindling to a steady flame. The God-consciousness was not
in a position to take constant control of the various elements of
life. Even those elements actually controlled by it were in fact
always quickly submerged by elements of a contrary nature; whereas
a devout personality must be taken to mean one in which every
mainly passive element is part of the relation to the God-consciousness produced by the influence of the Redeemer; and every active
element is due to an impulse of the same God-consciousness. Life
thus comes under a different formula, making it a life that is new;
hence the phrases 'a new man,' 'a new creature,'[1] which bear the
same sense as our phrase 'a new personality.' This new life of
course presents itself as something in process of becoming, for the
individual identity persists and the new life can only, as it were,
be grafted on to the old. And yet the situation in which the new
life is present as something in process of becoming, when related in
memory to the situation in which it was not present at all, can be
attached and bound together with the old into one continuous
personal life only by assuming a turning-point at which the continuity
of the old ceased, and that of the new began to be in process of
becoming. This is the essence of the conception 'regeneration.'
Similarly from another point of view the growing continuity of the
new life in which the elements answering to its formula are more

[1] 2 Cor. 5^{17}, Eph. 4^{24}.

476

and more integrated and the elements representing the old life recur ever more feebly and rarely is denoted by the expression 'sanctification.'

If now in this connexion we recall what was said before, namely, that the relation of Christ to the rest of humanity is exactly the same as the relation within His personality of its divine to its human element, we may add that these two conceptions, regeneration and sanctification, set forth just the same distinction as between the act of uniting and the state of union ; except that in that instance first of all one Person originated intact, and so the state of union too was an unbroken continuity, and an uninterrupted diffusion through the human nature ; which would, accordingly, happen in this instance too were it not that, through the identity of the subject with the earlier personality, elements from the life of sinfulness are still present as a hindrance. And as in that former instance one could not exist without the other, so here we cannot isolate regeneration or sanctification.

2. The formulation of this division being thus generally justified, we need only add to what has already been said [1] one remark about the order adopted. The part which has just been concluded, dealing with the kingly office of Christ, might of itself have led in the most natural way to a description of the new corporate life over which He holds sway ; and as the incitements that bring about this assumption into living fellowship with Christ come to each man only from this corporate life, and as the sanctification of each depends on the effective influence upon him of the whole, this doctrine might very well have been treated in the next section. But the other arrangement is equally correct. For, the entrance of Christ into humanity being its second creation, humanity thus becomes a new creature, and one may regard this entrance as also the regeneration of the human race, which to be sure only actually comes to pass in the form of the regeneration of individuals. And as the community of believers in its true essence consists only of the totality of the sanctified elements of all who are assumed into living fellowship with Christ, so again the sanctification of the individual includes everything by which the fellowship is constituted and maintained and extended. In view of this symmetrical interlocking, the order taken justifies itself for one reason, because while individuals are indeed originally laid hold of by Christ, yet at the same time it is always by an influence of Christ Himself,

[1] Above, § 90, 1 and § 91, 2.

mediated by His spiritual presence in the Word, that individuals are assumed into the fellowship of the new life ; but, above all, because the earlier place is more suitable for what in one aspect relates back to the old corporate life of general sinfulness but in another aspect lies at the base of the new common life under grace. This double reference holds for both of the conceptions to be discussed in this Division.   While regeneration is for the individual the turning-point at which the earlier life as it were breaks off and the new begins, it can also be regarded as the vanishing of the old life in a fashion explicable only by the redeeming activity of Christ, which, be it noted, takes effect in such wise that simultaneously therewith the power of the new life is implanted in the soul.   The treatment of the theme has therefore both a backward reference to the previous division of the subject and an anticipation of the main lines of the next Section, where the power of the new life is considered as the common spirit which animates the whole.   Sanctification also has two aspects : from one point of view it is measured by the degree in which the common sinfulness is more or less rapidly overcome in the individual soul ; from the other it is measured by the relation of the individual soul to the new corporate life in the service of which it makes more or less rapid progress.

First Doctrine : Regeneration

§ 107. *Assumption into living fellowship with Christ, regarded as a man's changed relation to God, is his Justification ; regarded as a changed form of life, it is his Conversion.*

1. Seeing that we are here concerned simply with the situation of the individual in his transition from the corporate life of sinfulness to a living fellowship with Christ, we must use this situation to explain the necessary connexion of the two elements just specified. ' Form of life ' is to be understood simply as the fashion in which the time-elements of life happen and arrange themselves ; and self-consciousness is viewed as passing into action, that is to say, as basis of the will.   In the condition left behind, the stirrings of a self-consciousness suffused with a consciousness of God were never determinative of the will, being but casual and fleeting ; the sensuous consciousness alone was determinative.   When life is linked to Christ it is the other way about, and this change is expressed by the term ' conversion.'   As a matter of fact, our relation to God is really an affair of the quiescent self-consciousness, looking

at itself reflected in thought and finding a consciousness of God included there. Now we know that only one relationship to the divine holiness and righteousness is proper to the corporate life of sinfulness, namely, the self-consciousness of guilt and merited punishment.[1] Obviously this relation must vanish at the very beginning of living fellowship with Christ, and not at some later stage of its development towards perfection, for the two are contradictory ; there can be no true consciousness of fellowship with Christ as long as that other consciousness persists.

It is clear also that the two elements cannot be held separate in such a manner that a conversion could even be imagined without justification, or a justification without conversion. Justification would then be a resolve to forgive oneself on the ground that sin is unavoidable, a vanishing of the old relation to God without any new relation taking its place, and therefore not really justification at all but a complete cessation of the God-consciousness within the self-consciousness—that is, hardening. A new relation can arise only through the union with Christ which effects conversion too. Equally inconceivable is a new direction of the will, based on becoming one with Christ, in which the consciousness of guilt and punishability persists. The new man would then have to remain altogether unconscious, or, to put it otherwise, there would have to be an assumption into fellowship with the perfection of Christ that did not include fellowship with His blessedness. If this ever seems to happen, the explanation is either that the consciousness of guilt is merely a delusive carrying-forward of past feelings into the present, or that ' conversion ' has been a mere desire to become better by one's own resources, without any genuine living fellowship with Christ. Conversion and justification, being thus utterly inseparable, must also be regarded as happening simultaneously, and each is the infallible criterion of the other.

2. In the fuller treatment of these matters much diversity is found in the text-books, identical expressions being taken by different writers in different senses ; and the present writer may be open to the charge that he, too, chooses his terms arbitrarily. For, to compare the expressions ' regeneration ' and ' conversion,' there is no real indication that the second conception is just a part of the first ; it is quite as legitimate to put it the other way about. Still less is there anything in the expression ' justification ' pointing to the beginning of a new form of life ; if we consider that the

[1] Cf. §§ 83 and 84.

condition being superseded is one governed by law, the expression rather suggests that this condition is to continue than that it is to lapse. Moreover, other expressions as significant and as scriptural as conversion might also put in a claim to be preferred; and in view of the great wealth of expression, mainly pictorial, of which Biblical writers [1] avail themselves in this connexion, variation is unavoidable. The important matter is the exact exposition of the actual meaning of the expressions rather than any particular choice of words. The choice made here is justifiable on the one hand because regeneration expresses in the most definite way the beginning of a consistent life; and on the other hand because the relation to the past, which in the general expression 'regeneration' falls very much into the background, comes to be the ruling consideration in the more particularized expressions 'conversion' and 'justification.' The use of the word 'conversion' for the transformation, the right-about-turn to better things, makes evident that it is the beginning of a new page, a new order in contrast to the old. Justification, too, presupposes something in respect of which a person is justified; and since no error is possible to the Supreme Being it must be assumed that something has happened to a man between his former and his present state by which the divine displeasure has been removed and without which he could not have become the object of divine favour. However, it seems inadvisable to introduce still other figurative expressions from the Bible; for without a fine-spun and unprofitably lengthy discussion one could not distinguish all the various aspects of what is, after all, only a momentary point of departure; not to speak of the fact that enlightenment and renewal can be used just as well of what is continuous and permanent, and referred to the sphere of sanctification.

The order seems, in view of the symmetry of the definition, a matter of entire indifference; many considerations, however, make it more convenient to begin with conversion.

First Theorem : Conversion

§ 108. *Conversion, the beginning of the new life in fellowship with Christ, makes itself known in each individual by Repentance, which consists in the combination of regret and change of*

---

[1] *E.g.* 'enlightenment,' Eph. 3⁹ 5¹⁴, Heb. 6¹⁻⁶; 'renewal,' Eph. 4²³, Tit. 3⁵ Heb. 6⁶.

heart ; and by Faith, which consists in the appropriation of the perfection and blessedness of Christ.

Conf. Aug. xii. : Constat autem poenitentia proprie his duabus partibus, altera est contritio seu terrores incussi conscientiae agnito peccato, altera est fides.—*Apol. Conf.* v. : Nos igitur constituimus duas partes poenitentiae videlicet contritionem et fidem. Si quis volet addere tertiam videlicet . . . mutationem totius vitae ac morum in melius non refragabimur.—*Expos. simpl.* xiv. p. 36 : Per poenitentiam autem intelligimus mentis in homine peccatore resipiscentiam verbo evangelii et spiritu s. excitatam fideque vera acceptam, qua protinus homo agnatam sibi corruptionem peccataque omnia sua . . . agnoscit ac de his ex corde dolet, eademque coram Deo deplorat et . . . execratur cogitans iam sedulo de emendatione. Et haec quidem est vera poenitentia, sincera nimirum ad Deum et omne bonum conversio, sedula vero a diabolo et omni malo aversio. Diserte vero dicimus hanc poenitentiam merum esse Dei donum et non virium nostrarum opus.—*Ibid.* xv. p. 48 : Qua propter loquimur in hac causa . . . de fide viva vivificanteque, quae propter Christum quem comprehendit viva est.—*Repetit. Conf.* p. 147 (Twesten): Ostendimus supra, fide significari fiduciam acquiescentem in filio Dei, propter quem recipimur et placemus.—Melanchth., *loc. s. t. de voc. fides* : Fides est fiducia applicans nobis beneficium Christi . . . fiducia est motus in voluntate, quo voluntas in Christo acquiescit.—*Ibid.* : Quibuscunque verbis alii uti volent, rem retinere cupimus.

I. The definition found in these citations from confessional literature certainly does not appear to tally with that given formally here ; for the word *pœnitentia* rather corresponds merely to repentance—that is, to only one part of conversion ; and in the Swiss Confession the word *conversio*, which corresponds to our word conversion, expresses only one part of it, namely, *pœnitentia*. And even if we enter the caveat that although turning away from evil is not explicitly mentioned, it is understood to be implied, still these two together—turning away from evil and turning to God and the good—include only that part of conversion which we define as change of heart. It must be noted, too, that while *aversio* and *conversio* taken together are here regarded as equivalent to the whole experience, yet, in fact, this experience is already reckoned to include both the painful recognition of sin which precedes the turning away, and the faith which precedes the turning towards, so that turning away and turning towards do not really give a complete account of the matter. In the *Augsburg Confession*, besides faith we meet only contrition, equivalent to our regret. But in the *Apology* ' change for the better ' is added, which of course in its permanent aspect means sanctification, but, regarded as a new beginning, has its place here and corresponds to our expression ' change of heart.' If we gather all the elements of the Con-

fessions together, the general result is identical with our own statement. Our general definition is sufficiently justified by prevalent
devotional usage, and certainly is greatly to be preferred to the
expression *pœnitentia* or repentance, because that word has no
definite reference to the actual beginning of a new form of life, and
also because it sounds very awkward to hear faith (a word that we
obviously use in exactly the same sense as the Confessions) reckoned
as a part of repentance. And indeed we find the expressions
' repentance ' and ' conversion ' made interchangeable in other places
in the *Apology*.[1] Another point of difference is best seen in certain
passages in the confessional documents where contrition and faith
as the two constituents of conversion are alluded to as ' mortification '
and ' revival.' [2] Clearly ' mortification ' here is regret or contrition
and ' revival ' is faith ; but if so, no notice is taken of what we have
called change of heart. Nevertheless, no genuine laying hold of
Christ in faith is even conceivable without such an alteration in the
innermost aspirations and endeavours, nor any contrition other than
a passing wave of emotion ; and so in both connexions change
of heart too is silently taken for granted. Lastly, it must be
emphasized that our general expression ' conversion,' as well as the
narrower terms ' repentance,' ' regret,' and ' change of heart,' are all
employed in Church usage, not only as denoting what happens at the
beginning of the new life, but also for what occurs in the course of
the new life in connexion with the sin that still remains. All the
same, it follows from the explanations previously given [3] that there
must be a very great difference between what constitutes turning
away from sin in the two differing cases of one who is not yet, and
one who already is, in fellowship with the Redeemer. In the latter
case, the connexion with the Redeemer and the correspondingly
changed disposition may become clouded over and less effective, but
neither is utterly lost. In their case no sin can come to consciousness unaccompanied by regret, yet they do not require to begin the
new life all over again, nor is change of heart in the strictest sense
necessary. On the other hand, in regard to faith, it is clear that
faith is a permanently enduring state of mind, and that at this
point in the treatment of the doctrine of conversion, strictly under-

---

[1] See p. 168 : Ostendendum est quod scriptura in *poenitentia* seu *conversione* has duas partes ponit.

[2] *Apol. Conf., ibid.*: Paulus fere ubique cum describit conversionem, facit
has duas partes mortificationem et vivificationem . . . sunt ergo hae duae
partes contritio et fides.

[3] § 74.

stood, only the origin of faith is in question. For appropriation, taking possession,[1] is a single act ; whereas faith in its duration is the resulting, abiding consciousness of being in possession. Thus the beginning of divinely created faith essentially belongs to conversion ; its duration is the constant basis of the new life. Thus, even though treating regeneration and sanctification more or less separately, we begin by bringing out their necessary interconnexion, and the continuity of the divine action throughout the whole course of the new creation.

The Roman Church does not count faith as an element in conversion, but puts in its stead confession and satisfaction, in spite of the fact that confession, rightly understood, is included in regret, and that satisfaction is a sheer impossibility. The reason lies partly in her doctrine of the Church and partly in the different sense in which the Church uses the word ' faith,' understanding by it only the divinely imparted and humanly accepted knowledge of man's destiny ; its assertion being accordingly that faith precedes repentance and conversion.[2] This difference of language is unfortunate, increasing, of course, the difficulty of comparing clearly the points of divergence ; and it is unfortunate too that in ordinary life this same word ' faith ' is so often used for a conviction that is without either influence on the will or adequate foundation. Nevertheless, we cannot let the word drop, but must rather maintain all the more strenuously its well-won title. The justice of our own usage is easily demonstrable. The expression has become established among us as the translation of the word by which the original language of Scripture defines the inward condition of one who feels content and strong in fellowship with Christ. Moreover, the controversy with the Roman Church about good works has given the word an additional historical value for us.

2. Repentance and faith, then, are to be taken as covering the whole experience of conversion. Now, since every turning-point is at once the end of one movement and the beginning of the reverse, in these two things, taken together, existence in the common life of sin ceases, and existence in fellowship with Christ begins. Since some activity of the self is an essential element in both, and opposed

---

[1] *Expos. simpl.* xv. p. 42 : fides Christum recipit.

[2] *Catech. Rom. praef.* 27 : Cum enim finis qui ad beatitudinem homini propositus est altior sit, quam ut humana mentis acie perspici possit, necesse ei erat ipsius a Deo cognitionem accipere. Haec vero cognitio nihil aliud est nisi fides.—*Ibid.* p. II. de poenit. 8 : Verum in eo quem poenitet, fides poenitentiam antecedat necesse est . . . ex quo fit, ut nullo modo poenitentiae pars recte dici possit.

activities cannot accompany, but must succeed one another, the turning-point must be a twofold inactivity, a state of being no longer active in one direction and not yet active in another. In the spiritually living existence of the subject nothing is left in place of the vanishing activity except its inert echo in feeling, and nothing is present in respect of the activity not yet begun except inert anticipation of it in desire. The first is regret—which certainly expresses an existence in fellowship with sin, an existence, however, in which there is no activity of the self—for where regret is, the regretted condition has been abjured—but simply the retention in consciousness of something that is past. At every moment in which it is no more than an approach to complete transition, this consciousness witnesses to a disturbance and obstruction of life proper, and is felt as pain. The regret that goes with conversion, relating not to particulars but to a general condition, and abjuring that condition finally is, considered apart from everything else, the purest and most perfect pain, which, if allowed to reach its limit, might bring life itself to an end.[1] This is to be noted, however, that regret arising out of the knowledge of sin given by the law is not the same as that directly appertaining to conversion. The law, after its wont, goes into particulars, and the regret evoked by it is only regret for particular motions and affections and not for the general condition and its deepest cause. Nor is there anything in this connexion out of which a new and opposite movement of life might develop. The outcome of such regret is therefore death or despair. However large the previous experience of this regret may have been the true conversion-regret must always eventually arise out of the vision of the perfection of Christ, and this beginning of regeneration must be due to Christ's redeeming activity. It is only on this view of repentance and faith that their interconnexion is clear, their origin thus being the same. Christ awakens a wholly perfect regret just in so far as His self-imparting perfection meets us in all its truth, which is what happens at the dawn of faith. And Christ can, in fact, lay hold of us in His receiving activity only if and when His soul-stirring exhibition of Himself to us leads us to abjure utterly our previous condition. In the same way, regret and faith being directly interdependent, the beginning is present of existence in living fellowship with Christ. For our attitude here

---

[1] *Apol. Conf.* v. p. 169 : Mortificatio significat veros terrores quos sustinere natura non posset, nisi erigeretur fide. Ita hic (Col. 2[11]) exspoliationem corporis peccatorum vocat, quam nos usitate dicimus contritionem, quia in illis doloribus concupiscentia naturalis expurgatur.

cannot be different from that of the human nature of Christ in its act of uniting with the quiescent consciousness of being accepted. This attitude is not only originally joyful and—unlike regret—uplifting,[1] but it includes also in its steady progress a stimulation of the will, and develops into an activity of the will ; and so with the dawn of faith conversion is complete. Still, in between that quiescent consciousness and real activity there comes desire, in two interconnected forms. There remains over from regret the con-tinual abjuration of the fellowship of the sinful life, and there is also the desire to receive the impulses that come from Christ. This desire, acting in two directions, is the change of heart effected by Christ which binds regret and faith together and represents the true unity of conversion. One may include the negative ray of desire along with regret in the concept repentance, and count the positive ray as a part of revival, or one may with equal justice give desire a middle place of its own.

Regret that lies outside Christianity and has no reference to the consciousness of God is beyond the scope of our discussion. But within the sphere of Christian piety, if we carry our examination further back into the common life of sinfulness, we find many sorts of regret. Such regrets, too, can be traced back more or less directly to the vision of Christ, and are not always limited to some particular, but may show genuine pain at the general human state of sinfulness as illustrated in one's own person ; but they do not develop into a continuous inward movement amounting to the dawn of living faith. All the same such stimulations, arising as they do from the influence of the common Christian life, even though they are only an unconnected and casually-appearing mixture of elements, are to be regarded as divinely caused, and indeed involved in the divine ordinance which places all men in relation to the Redeemer ; and in this sense such a condition is ascribed to *the prevenient grace of God*.[2] In the same way a change of heart may appear before it is permanently bound up with con-version ; and, all the more because the insight which rejects former desires is looking back to the figure and teaching of Christ, this too is to be regarded as a work of preparatory grace. Nor do we find such regret and change of heart always separately ; they may be

---

[1] *Ibid.* : Et vivificatio intelligi debet . . . consolatio quae vere sustentat fugientem vitam in contritione.

[2] This is never more than an inexact phrase, for according to our general formula all divine grace is always prevenient ; and it would be more correct to say ' preparatory.'

related to one another without losing their preparatory character. The higher character which both possess is only recognized from the simultaneous dawning of faith ; and perfect and *effective* divine grace is seen only in the union of all three—regret, change of heart, and faith. There are similar preliminary approximations to faith. For, even when the perfection of the Redeemer is not recognized as more than human, it would be wrong to regard as an adverse judgment of human reason such a sense of its compelling power as sets Him on a different plane from other sages or God-gifted men, and such a satisfaction in the idea of His Kingdom as sets it high above other earthly aims. A presentiment of His higher dignity may be already implied in this, and an inward surrender may arise out of it. This, too, is a gracious work of preparation, and of faith also it is true that its higher character, as it dawns, is recognizable only in its unity with the other elements of conversion.

From all this it follows naturally that since imperfect regret and change of heart may quite easily occur even when the soul has conceived a higher idea of the Redeemer, conversion cannot be distinguished either in and for itself, or by any particular mark, from the effects of preparatory grace. Only gradually can each consciousness reach certainty for itself, and its peace of heart become fixed. Even approximations to faith are bound to have an influence on conduct indistinguishable with any certainty from the beginnings of sanctification, because in accordance with the laws of organic nature the true life of Christ in us announces itself at first only in weak and intermittent impulses, and then gradually a unified activity emerges. The only marks we can point to are steady progress in sanctification taken in its full meaning, and active participation in the extension of Christ's Kingdom. What is incomplete is usually in its very nature fluctuating. And it is scarcely thinkable that a man should be received into unity of life with Christ without very soon actively proving himself an instrument of His redeeming activity. When therefore the Redeemer calls the decisive working of divine grace a new birth, we must take part of the meaning to be that just as in the natural life birth is not the absolute beginning, so here a period of hidden life precedes it, and at first even the newly-born life remains unconscious, only gradually learning to know itself as a real personality in a new world. Keeping to the illustration given us by the Redeemer Himself, we must rest assured that even though neither we nor others can point out the very beginning of our new life, and its moment in time is as little to be determined as the point in space from which the wind begins to blow, still the fact of the distinction between the new life and the old remains, and of our share in the new we become ever more certain.

3. The idea that every Christian must be able to point to the very time and place of his conversion is accordingly an arbitrary and presumptuous restriction of divine grace, and can only cause confusion. In its most definite form it is found in the assertion of an otherwise worthy party in the Church that every true Christian must be able to allege, as the beginning of his state of grace, a penitential crisis of soul, that is to say, a surging up of regret to the limit of despairing self-abhorrence, followed by a feeling of divine grace reaching to the limit of inexpressible felicity ; all steadfastness of heart being mere illusion, and all evidences of sanctification deceitful works of men. This view never became part of the general teaching of the Church ; it is no more than a dubious aberration. In this connexion two points can be made here. In the first place, the true change of heart, complete because covering all the ground from regret to faith, need by no means invariably spring from a flood of regret that almost wrecks the whole being by its painful emotion. On the one hand, the capacity of people for emotion is very various. What to an insusceptible nature is a very intense degree of excitement seems but a trifle to one more emotionally constituted, and in this respect the same person differs from time to time. In such a matter no definition or summary statement is possible. On the other hand, the experiences recorded in the autobiographies of many religious men show that even if a shattering storm of feeling occur which is reckoned by themselves to be the moment of their conversion, often enough they sink back again into a state of futility and uncertainty ; and so the supposed value of that moment seems entirely doubtful. Even in these cases steadfastness of soul comes only gradually. Further, self-abasement being not a pure judgment but also feeling must as the spiritual side of regret be distinguished from pain, its sensuous side, and these may stand in very various relations to each other. One practised in the estimation of sensuous susceptibilities may have the strictest and profoundest judgment of self-abasement without any corresponding intensity of feeling. So, on the one hand, care must be taken, if intensity of feeling gives a predominantly sensuous colouring to the whole condition, lest regret,

being not yet pure and in its inmost fibre free from sensuous admixture, may thereby be unfitted to have life-giving faith as its immediate result. And, on the other hand, the oftener and more strongly such imperfect regret occurs before conversion, the easier it is for the relation between self-abasement and pain to take a quite different form within genuine repentance. The very thing that evokes the utter self-abasement to which faith and the positive pole of change of heart attach themselves, may be allowed a place only as a kind of memory of former suffering and a shadowy image of already felt pain. This is new evidence of the inadmissibility of the demand that everyone must be able to distinguish, in the phenomena of consciousness, between the working of grace as initiating the new life and the preparatory work of grace. Hence we can concede the reality of this conception of an agonizing crisis of repentance only as denoting the whole change of conditions, from the first challenging and preparatory effects of grace on to the unchangeable fixing of the heart in faith. Whether these are spread over a longer or compressed into a shorter interval, and how far during this period particular oscillations may differ in amplitude, and whether the final oscillation must be the largest—all these questions are left quite undetermined.

The second point we can determine is this. A constituent part of living fellowship with Christ is a share in His blessedness. This too, then, must be included from the very beginning in the dawn of faith ; all the more because the unblessedness that clings to regret can be relieved only by its opposite, namely, blessedness. The two chief elements in conversion can still be very closely linked together, and even in perfect regret no great pain need be felt. Thus many and various relations are possible between the pain of repentance and the joy of conscious fellowship with Christ ; among them this one, that if a glorious outpouring of joy be found along with a faint measure of sorrow, the suffering may become almost imperceptible. Undeniably there are types of conversion which seem to be mainly a happy rescue from despair. But there are others in which no such agonizing crisis occurs, and which are experienced as an almost unalloyed blessing from above, the painful element in regret being suppressed to a point just short of actual disappearance.

4. Although some teachers in English and German Churches have recently declared that no conversion whatever is needed in the case of those born in the bosom of the Christian Church and

already as children received into its fellowship, since they are already members of the body of Christ and recipients of regeneration in baptism, we must in accordance with almost the whole trend of our discussion withhold our agreement. For everything we said regarding the original cause of the beginning of sin in man holds good just as much about those born within the Christian Church as about others. The former, too, reveal a tendency to drag down the divine, which of course influences them like others through the Christian community, to the sphere of the sensuous. It may, indeed, be fitly said that in Christian children sensuous representations of the divine spontaneously develop, sometimes of the pagan, idly frivolous kind, sometimes Judaic and gloomily fearful. If, therefore, in spite of infant baptism, sin thus shows its power in them, they need conversion as much as anyone born outside the Church. The only difference really present is that in the case of others it is a matter of chance how and when the gospel call reaches their ears, whereas Christian children are already called in virtue of their standing in a natural and orderly relation to the working of divine grace. This in no way invalidates the natural order we described, namely, the sequence of preparatory and quickening grace ; and where this order obtains conversion takes place. Furthermore, the opinion referred to finds at most an apparent support in our confessional statements ; fundamentally they are in entire agreement with our position. This may be seen partly in the fact that they never raise any distinction in connexion with the doctrine of conversion, between those born inside and outside the Church,[1] and partly because they expressly ascribe to our baptism only the beginning of the divine work of grace.[2] That the same effect occurs within the Church even without previous baptism is evident from the facts about persons baptized in heart alone. It is true that some passages seem to approach more nearly to the opinion in dispute.[3] But if we recall how differently they speak of regeneration, saying that in it the Holy Spirit opens our eyes to the

---

[1] Compare, in the *Apology for the Augsburg Confession*, the whole treatment of the conceptions repentance, confession, and satisfaction.

[2] *Apol. Conf.* i. : Addidit etiam (Lutherus) de materiali quod spiritus sanctus datus per baptismum *incipit* mortificare concupiscentiam et novos motus creat (and obviously only *incipit creare*) in homine.—*Ibid.* iv. : Igitur necesse est baptizare parvulos, ut applicetur iis promissio salutis.

[3] *Expos. simpl.* xx. : Assignantur haec omnia baptismo. Nam intus regeneramur purificamur et renovamur a Deo per spiritum sanctum, foris autem accipimus obsignationem, etc. — *Conf. Gallic.* xxxv. p. 123 : Quamvis baptismus sit fidei et resipiscentiae sacramentum, tamen . . . affirmamus . . . infantes . . . esse baptizandos.

understanding of divine mysteries,[1] and that sanctification begins with regeneration, it is clear that they are really seeking to connect with regeneration the original baptism of adults who asked for it, and only loosely by indulgence let their statement serve for infant baptism too. Nowhere in the testimony of such Churches is anything more intended than what Calvin [2] himself has said. With him indeed we have been in pretty close agreement ; his phrase ' seed of repentance and faith ' might have been our text.

It is evident enough that one can all too easily lapse unawares into the region of magic, if regeneration be brought into connexion with our particular method of administering the sacrament of baptism. We need only look at the answer we should have to give to the question how, in our commonly adopted practice of the rite, the receiving activity of Christ and the passive condition of him who is received are related to one another.

5. As regards the first of these, we again become conscious of an inconvenience in our arrangement, for in the public teaching of the Church regeneration is usually ascribed to the Divine Spirit, of whom we have not yet treated, and, to mention what we have already said would be our next topic, the divine activity in justification is usually ascribed to God the Father. But here again we must recall our fundamental proposition, that the whole procedure in redemption, the same for all races, Jew and Gentile, is also the same for all ages, and that the essential identity of redemption and of the Christian fellowship would be imperilled if our faith had either another content or another origin—the one implies the other—than it had in the case of the first disciples. If faith arises in the same way, conversion must happen in the same way. Now in the first disciples both were effected by the Word in its widest sense, that is, by the whole prophetic activity of Christ. And we must be able to understand this that we have in common with them, if need be without a doctrine of the Holy Spirit, just as the disciples understood their own condition without any such doctrine. The constant factor is above all the divine power of the Word—taking the expression in its widest sense—by which conversion is still effected and faith still arises. The difference is simply that the self-revelation of Christ is now mediated by those who preach Him ; but they

---

[1] *Expos. simpl.* ix. : In regeneratione intellectus illuminatur per Spiritum sanctum ut et mysteria et voluntatem Dei intelligat.

[2] *Institutt.* ix. 16. 20 : Baptizantur in futuram poenitentiam et fidem, quae etsi nondum in illis formatae sunt, arcana tamen spiritus operatione utriusque semen in illis latet.

being appropriated by Him as His instruments, the activity really proceeds from Him and is essentially His own. This is definitely and uncompromisingly asserted in most of our Confessions, though with references to the Holy Spirit which will become clear to us only later in our discussion.[1] If other passages [2] seem to be less convincing, still they draw attention to exceptions which when looked at more closely are only apparent. For if one ventures to make a merely relative separation between the Word itself and the public ministry of the Word, and to recall that all Christians are summoned to a common ministry of the Word, it is with a view to affirming boldly that no example can be given of conversion apart from the mediation of the Word : and we need cherish no misgiving that to assert this strenuously is to limit the divine omnipotence. For the second creative act is recognized as a work of the divine omnipotence just because only through the power revealed in it the business of conversion is carried through in all believers. The miracle of the appearance of Christ, who could Himself work only in the form of the Word, would be insufficient if some had to be converted otherwise than through influences proceeding from Him ; indeed, in that case they would not be included in the priestly intercession of Christ.[3] Again, if it were possible that Christ should reveal Himself to some immediately and inwardly without the Word, this could happen to all ; which would amount to redemption through the mere idea of the Redeemer,

[1] *Augsb. Conf.* v : To win such faith God has appointed preaching, by means of which the Holy Spirit awakens and comforts the heart and imparts faith.—*Art. Smalc.* vii. : Constanter tenendum est Deum nemini spiritum vel gratiam suam largiri nisi per verbum et cum verbo externo et praecedente : and it is here to be remarked that the communication of the Spirit is described as a consequence or result—ut ita praemuniamus nos contra Enthusiastas, qui iactitant se ante verbum et sine verbo spiritum habere.— *Expos. simpl.* xiv. : Per poenitentiam autem intelligimus mentis in homine peccatore resipiscentiam, verbo evangelii et spiritu sancto excitatam. *Ibid.* xvi. : Haec autem fides merum est Dei donum, quod solus Deus ex gratia sua . . . donat, et quidem per Spiritum sanctum mediante praedicatione Evangelii.—*Conf. Gall.* xxv. : Credimus quoniam non nisi per Evangelium fimus Christi compotes.—*Conf. Belg.* xxiv. : Credimus veram hanc fidem per auditum verbi Dei et Spiritus sancti operationem homini insitam eum regenerare.

[2] *Expos. simpl.* i. : Quamquam enim nemo veniat ad Christum, nisi qui trahatur a patre ac intus illuminetur per spiritum sanctum, scimus tamen Deum omnino velle praedicari verbum Dei. Equidem potuisset per spiritum sanctum suum aut per ministerium angeli instituisse Cornelium, etc.—Agnoscimus interim Deum illuminare posse homines etiam sine externo ministerio, etc.—*Conf. Helv.* xiv. : Quae (ecclesia) externis . . . ritibus ab ipso Christo institutis et verbi Dei . . . publicâ disciplinâ . . . ita construitur, ut in hanc sine his nemo *nisi singulari Dei privilegio* censeatur.

[3] John 17²⁰.

making the actual appearance of Christ superfluous. For the
present day this is the specially relevant reason for the position we
take, which has behind it the whole apostolic usage and the express
witness of Scripture,[1] and is no mere design of strengthening our
case in opposition to certain visionaries. All the same, this statement was needed in order to expose fully the danger of fanaticism
on this point. For if it be allowed that there are divine workings
of converting grace in no actual historical relation to the personal
efficacy of Christ (even though it is as workings of Christ that they
come to consciousness), there would be no security that this inward
mystic Christ was identical with the historical Christ. Every
exposition of the matter, therefore, which deprives the Word of
its sole place in conversion not only wipes out all lines of demarcation (for then everyone with unrestrained caprice can profess that
anything and everything is Christian and due to Christ), but also
dissolves all fellowship ; for every individual, who is inwardly
and independently enlightened, must also be perfectly complete
in himself, with no inducement to, or need of, fellowship. All
essentially separatist tendencies spring from ideas of this kind. The
influence of Christ, therefore, consists solely in the human communication of the Word, in so far as that communication embodies
Christ's word and continues the indwelling divine power of Christ
Himself. This is in perfect accord with the truth that, in the consciousness of a person in the grip of conversion, every sense of
human intermediation vanishes, and Christ is realized as immediately present in all His redeeming and atoning activity, prophetic,
priestly, and kingly. In this sense everything that in any way
contributes to conversion, from the first impression made on the
soul by the preaching of Christ on to its final establishment in faith,
is the work of Christ. These divine workings of grace are supernatural in so far as they depend upon and actually proceed from
the being of God in the Person of Christ. At the same time, being
historical and formative of history, they are natural in so far as
they have a general natural connexion with the historical life
of Christ ; and in detail each working that establishes a new
personality is bound up in its efficacy with the historical totality
of Christ's effects.

6. As regards the state of the subject himself during conversion,
we may take conversion to be the moment at which the entry into
living fellowship with Christ is complete. This moment is the

[1] Rom. 10[17], Tit. 1[3].

beginning of a higher form of life which only Christ can communicate, because only in Him is it originally present.   It seems obvious, then, that here no causal agency can be attributed to the person who is being taken up into fellowship, for the higher form cannot be in any way derived from lower stages of life as present either in the individual or in a group of people yet to be converted.   On the other hand, if we remember that the converted person, both afterwards within the living fellowship of Christ and even beforehand in the common life of sin, is, as an individual of reasonable perceptions, spontaneously active, and that in general there is never in any living being a complete moment wholly devoid of spontaneous activity, two questions are inevitable.   The first is : How is the ordinary natural action of the subject going on at the moment of conversion related to the work of Christ which produces change of heart and faith ?   The second is : How is the presupposed passive condition during conversion related to the spontaneous activity which ensues in fellowship with Christ ?

In regard to the first question, we may, without abandoning our fundamental assumption, regard the natural spontaneous action of the subject in that moment as non-co-operative.   All that preparatory grace has already brought to pass within him of course co-operates, but this is itself part of the divine work of grace and not of his own action.[1]   Anything proceeding purely from his own inner life could co-operate only so far as the efficacy of divine grace was actually conditioned by these activities of his own.   It cannot indeed be denied that this may happen.   For the Word through which the influence of Christ is mediated can mediate only by making an impression on men, and for this the activity of his sense-faculties as well as of the inner functions of his consciousness is required.   In so far as the activity of all these functions depends on the free will of man, the capacity of apprehension must therefore be allowed to exist in his natural condition.[2]   But as regards what

---

[1] *Sol. decl.*, p. 674 : Ex his consequitur, quam primum Spir. s. per verbum et sacramenta opus suum regenerationis et renovationis in nobis *inchoavit,* quod revera tunc per virtutem Spir. s. cooperari possimus ac debeamus.—Hoc vero ipsum non est ex nostris carnalibus et naturalibus viribus, sed ex novis illis viribus, quae Spir. s. in nobis in conversione inchoavit.   What is said expressly of the period after conversion holds good all the more for the period preceding it.—*Ibid.*, p. 681 : . . . hominem ex se ipso aut naturalibus suis viribus non posse aliquid conferre vel adjumentum adferre ad suam conversionem.

[2] *Ibid.*, p. 671 : In eiusmodi enim externis rebus homo adhuc etiam post lapsum aliquo modo liberum arbitrium habet, ut . . . verbum Dei audire vel non audire possit.

happens after the Word has made its impression on the soul, in the attainment of its aim for men, here we cannot concede man's natural co-operation. Even the consent accompanying the reception of the Divine Word, as far as it is directed to what is essential and characteristic in it, can be ascribed only to the antecedent work of grace. On the other hand, if it should be held that the natural activity which goes on during Christ's working of conversion is of the nature of resistance, it must be, if not disapproval, at least indifference ; that is to say, the activity remains directed to other matters, and as far as the operation of Christ is concerned, negligible. If conversion is effected during such a condition it is certainly not in virtue of the Word so received. To assume an entire lack of relation between man's personal activity and the higher operation of Christ therefore yields no satisfactory result, and the problem remains to find room for an activity in real relation to the work of Christ, and yet neither co-operation nor resistance. If now we take as starting-point that organic co-operation which we admitted to go on before apprehension of the Word, and that minimum of opposition consisting in the direction of the will to other things, which we rejected, it is clear that the two cannot coexist. That co-operation of the mental organism in the reception of the Word implies a consent of the will ; and this is just a surrender to the operation of Christ or giving rein to a lively susceptibility thereto. This middle stage, to which we have recourse in all similar cases— a passive condition, yet including that minimum of spontaneous activity which belong to every complete moment—meets the conditions of the problem perfectly. The solution, however, is invalidated if this susceptibility be again divided into active and passive, and only the latter allowed as applicable to our case ; for then one would simultaneously have to find room for another spontaneous activity, and the whole difficulty would return.[1]

Let us now go back to the other question. Since the whole life of the Redeemer, because solely determined by the being of God in Him, is activity, and not passivity, it is clear that in fellowship with His life no moment can be purely passive, because everything in it that proceeds from Him and becomes an impulse is necessarily activity. Spontaneous activity in living fellowship with Christ begins in the moment of being received into His fellowship. There

[1] Cf., *inter alia*, Gerhard, t. v. p. 113, and *Sol. decl.*, p. 662 : Et hoc ipsum vocat (Lutherus) capacitatem non activam sed passivam, which are not really Luther's words.

is no interval.   Conversion may be said to be just the evocation of this spontaneous activity in union with Christ.   The lively susceptibility passes into quickened spontaneous activity.   Every heightening of that lively susceptibility is a work of preparatory grace.   The grace that effects conversion changes it into quickened spontaneous activity.   If we trace this element backwards from the point at which it first appears already heightened by the preparatory work of grace, and ask in what the first beginning of life has consisted by which it can be differentiated from pure passivity, we can only point to that desire for fellowship with God, never entirely extinguished, though pushed back to the very frontiers of consciousness, which is part of the original perfection of human nature.   As this is what we regard as the first point of attachment for every operation of divine grace, the only thing we are ruling out is a passivity that would be entirely foreign to human nature, in virtue of which a person would resemble a lifeless object in the matter of conversion,[1] and we are saying nothing about that in our Christian self-consciousness which we ascribe to the grace of God in Christ.   For mere desire is not an act ; it is but the anticipatory feeling of an act that may possibly happen if a certain impulse occurs later.   It is exactly what shows itself as the feeling of need for redemption, a feeling without which there could be no dissatisfaction with the common state of sinfulness, but only a universal complacent recognition of the inevitability of sin.   Hence this desire is simply the ineradicable residuum in human nature of the original impartation of the divine which makes human nature what it is, and not in itself but only in so far as it is stirred up to some definite degree of strength does it give rise to the contrast between nature and grace.   Indeed, the parallel between the beginning of the divine life in us and the incarnation of the Redeemer comes out here too.   In Him the passivity of His human nature in that moment was just such a lively susceptibility to an absolutely powerful consciousness of God, accompanied by a desire to be thus seized and determined, which became changed through the creative act into a spontaneous activity constituting a personality.   In the same way our desire is heightened in conversion by the self-communication of Christ till it becomes a spontaneous activity of the self that constitutes a coherent new life.

---

[1] *Sol. decl.*, p. 662 : Antequam autem homo per Spir. s. . . . . regeneratur . . . ex sese ad conversionem nihil . . . cooperari potest, nec plus quam lapis truncus aut limus.

SECOND THEOREM : JUSTIFICATION

§ 109. *God's justifying of one who is converted to Him includes the forgiving of his sins, and the recognizing of him as a child of God. This transformation of his relation to God, however, follows only in so far as he has true faith in the Redeemer.*

Augsb. Conf. iv. : ' And it is taught that we attain the forgiveness of sins and are counted just before God out of grace for Christ's sake through faith.'— *Conf. Tetrap.* iii. : . . . nostri hanc totam (iustificationem) divinae benevolentiae Christique merito acceptam referendam solaque fide percipi docuerunt.—*Expos. simpl.* xv. : Iustificare significat peccata remittere, a culpa et poena absolvere in gratiam recipere et iustum pronunciare. . . . Certissimum est autem omnes nos . . . iustificari solius Christi gratiâ, et nullo nostro merito aut respectu . . . Quoniam vero iustificationem hanc recipimus non per ulla opera sed per fidem . . . ideo docemus . . . hominem iustificari sola fide in Christum.—*Conf. Gallic.* xviii : Credimus totam nostram iustitiam positam esse in peccatorum nostrorum remissione, quae sit etiam . . . unica nostra felicitas. Itaque . . . insitâ Jesu Christi obedientiâ acquiescimus, quae quidem nobis imputatur, tum ut tegantur omnia nostra peccata, tum etiam ut gratiam coram Deo nanciscamur.—*Ibid.* xx. : Credimus nos sola fide fieri huius iustitiae participes. . . . Itaque iustitia quam fide obtinemus pendet a gratuitis promissionibus, quibus nos a se diligi Deus declarat et certificatur.—*Conf. Belg.* xxii. : Interim proprie loquendo nequaquam intelligimus ipsam fidem esse quae nos iustificat, ut quae sit duntaxat instrumentum, quo Christum iustitiam nostram apprehendimus.—*Ibid.* xxxiii. : Credimus nostram beatitudinem sitam esse in peccatorum nostrorum propter Jesum Christum remissione atque in ea iustitiam nostram coram Deo contineri.—John 1[12], Gal. 3[26] 4[5].

1. In the treatment of this subject, too, the language of the Confessions cited is not quite consistent, and so the diction of our proposition does not conform to that of every quotation. Some, like us, use the word ' justification ' for the larger conception ; others use for that ' forgiveness of sins,' understanding by that phrase the whole state of blessedness, and accordingly counting justification, if it is to be regarded as something additional, as a special element therein. In this connexion it is evident that forgiveness in itself is just the removal of something negative, and therefore can be no full description of complete blessedness. Indeed, from our point of view, strictly speaking, one relation to God is abolished but no other established, unless indeed an earlier relation had come into existence ; otherwise, though one has forgiven the other, both remain as far apart as ever. The term ' justification,' however, applied to the same experience has, as bearing on inquiry into what happens, a more positive sound, leaving aside for the moment the question of accuracy. It is therefore better fitted either, as in the *Augsburg*

Confession, to describe a positive element accompanying that negative one, or, as is preferred here, to describe the whole, and leave a place for a positive element alongside of forgiveness. This method of description has been chosen because, where sin has to be presumed, an act of justification (however it comes about) must include forgiveness ; at the same time, since justification includes something more than forgiveness, this too has to be specified. This several Confessions express positively, but the others in a rather indeterminate and inconvenient fashion, by ' attaining grace,' ' received into grace '—indeterminate, because the content of the additional factor is not explained ; and inconvenient, because the same expression ' grace,' used everywhere in this connexion for the divine activity itself, is thus made to signify merely its result. Our designation of this positive element is unquestionably more exact, but (even though works on Dogmatics frequently use the terms ' sonship ' or ' adoption ') it is in this connexion so little an accepted credal definition that we need to point back to passages in which its content has been established in the most precise way and in the same connexion. Our designation has, indeed, this drawback, that it is in verbal agreement neither with the ordinary nor with the other and more special expression ; but this difficulty vanishes as soon as the actual interrelations of the subject are understood.

The Roman Church differs entirely from the Protestant in its use of the expression ' justification ' : instead of something correlated to conversion, and therefore included in regeneration, it makes ' justification ' mean something more general than these, including both them and sanctification. If we recall how, on the other hand, the existence of faith is placed anterior to conversion, we can perceive how the two things go together : faith and justification are kept as far apart as possible, in order the more easily to show man's justification to be dependent on his sanctification. But even apart from this, it cannot be advisable virtually to abolish the difference between the divine work on man and the divine work in man. The previous life void of divine influence is what is here given in experience, and we are faced by the task of rightly distinguishing the turning-point which is the source of everything later from the results that flow from it.

2. For the self-consciousness at rest in contemplation, justification is the same thing that conversion is for the self-consciousness passing into movement of will ; an analogy is therefore to be

expected between the two aspects of both. Repentance, as the self-consciousness moved by the consciousness of sin, comes to rest in forgiveness in the same way as the faith which from its birth is active through love is in thought the consciousness of being a child of God, and as this itself is identical with the consciousness of living fellowship with Christ. That this is not to be interpreted as meaning that forgiveness could precede faith is stated in the theorem itself : it means simply that forgiveness, like repentance, denotes the end of the old state ; as also being a child of God, like faith, expresses the character of the new. Each, of course, like both elements of conversion, is dependent on the whole activity of Christ, but directly and for itself expresses merely the relation of the man to God. In the common life of sinfulness the individual as a human being has no other relation to God except (in view of His holiness and justice) a consciousness of being guilty before Him and meriting punishment. It is obvious that this consciousness must cease as soon as, through and along with faith, living fellowship with Christ begins.[1] If we ask how this happens, the easiest answer certainly is that the longer and more uninterruptedly we are under the sway of Christ, the sooner do we forget sin, because it no longer emerges ; and if sin does not come into consciousness, neither does the sense of guilt and of deserving punishment. Yet, for one thing, this would be to place the change in our relation to God at the end of the process of sanctification, during which the sense of deserving punishment and therefore the lack of blessedness would continue. And besides, the forgetting of guilt is not the consciousness of forgiveness ; for even if this last is no more than the abolishing of a previous consciousness, it is also a real consciousness in which the memory of sin is an essential factor.

If, however, justification and conversion are simultaneous, forgiveness must be our present possession, even while sin and the consciousness of it are also present. But if the relation of sin to the holiness and justice of God is to cease, it and the consciousness of it must be transformed. Now, one who has let himself be taken up into living fellowship with Christ is, in so far as he has been thus appropriated, a new man ; and both are one and the same consciousness. Sin in the new man is no longer active ; it is only the after-effect of the old man. The new man thus no longer takes sin to be his own ; he indeed labours against it as something foreign to him. The consciousness of guilt is thus abolished. His penal

[1] Cf. § 107, 1.

desert must vanish with this ; while for the rest, there lies in living fellowship with Christ, immediately and not just as a vague something in the future, a readiness for and a right to fellowship with the sufferings of Christ, which make it impossible for him to keep regarding social and still less natural evils as punishment,[1] or to go on fearing future punishment—impossible, for he is at the same time received into the fellowship of the kingly office of Christ. Thus, owing to faith, the consciousness of sin will become the consciousness of forgiveness of sin. And in regard to the second element of conversion, Christ cannot live in us without His relation to His Father being formed in us also and making us sharers in His sonship ; this is the power to be children of God that flows from Him, and it includes the guarantee of sanctification. For it is the children's right to be brought up to a free, active share in the home-life ; and it is the law of childhood that through the shared life the likeness of the father develops in the child.

The two elements are therefore inseparable. Divine adoption would be nothing without forgiveness, for to deserve punishment begets fear, and fear slavery. And forgiveness without adoption would not fix a settled relation to God. The two, however, in their indissoluble connexion, constitute that complete transformation of the relation to God which, as bound up with the putting off the old man, is forgiveness, and as bound up with the putting on the new man is adoption. The two are so mutually conditioned that either can be regarded as first in order. One can say if one likes that the feeling of the old life must first be wiped out before the new life can begin to take shape ; but just as well that only in the new life is found the right and the power to throw off the old. It is equally true to assert that after a man is forgiven he is made a child of God, and that after he is received among God's children he obtains the forgiveness of sins.

3. This exposition of the matter is indeed readily liable to the misconstruction that each man justifies himself, although in point of fact it traces everything back to the influence of Christ. But truly, deriving justification entirely as it does from conversion, it would appear to ascribe both justification and conversion wholly to Christ and so to harmonize completely with the view that the two elements of regeneration are related to one another as sharing respectively in the perfection and in the blessedness of Christ, and are thus referred entirely to Him. That is a position for which an

[1] Rom. 8[22. 35-39].

exact confessional basis can be found,[1] although it certainly diverges far from the prevailing fashion of basing justification alone on a divine activity and attributes both forgiveness and adoption in a special way to God.[2] The same thing is demanded by our own method of statement, where justification is described as a change in the relation to God. For in that, of course, an activity of God is implied, and man can be conceived only as passive. In regard to this last point we have already put ourselves in harmony with the prevailing view by not ascribing everything in this connexion to the activity of the convert, even though it be an activity conditioned and evoked by Christ (as if justification were a part of sanctification or its result), but by deriving it entirely from the influence of Christ producing faith in man's living susceptibility. In regard to the first point, however, we have to see how the formula of a divine act of justification stands related to what has been said.

In this connexion it is clear, first, that we cannot conceive this divine activity as independent of the agency of Christ in conversion, as if one might exist without the other. This follows from the position already taken, that justification itself and conversion are interdependent ; just as in the Church formula which declares faith to be the receptive organ for this act of justification, which it could not be if the act were not received.[3] In devotional poetry and prose this connexion is usually set forth in its bearing on the intercession of Christ, as if Christ indicated to God those in whom He had wrought faith and urged Him to give them their share in forgiveness and adoption. This is of course a very poetic manner of putting things, for it is materializing things greatly to imagine Christ pointing out something to God. But neither in this positive nor in the other negative formula is there any dependence of the divine activity on the activity of Christ or its result, not even in the intermediate form of its being motived by Christ. For the decision as to *who* is to attain to conversion and *when* we have already

---

[1] *Conf. Belg.* xx. : Necessarium est enim aut omnia quae ad salutem nostram requiruntur in Jesu Christo non esse, aut si in eo sunt omnia, tum eum, qui fide Jesum possidet, totam salutem habere.

[2] This is also scriptural, if we venture to assume that the expression ' justify,' as here expounded, corresponds to the Pauline δικαιῶσαι; this comes out most strikingly in Rom. 8[33].

[3] Confessional formulæ, too, state this inseparability, though often hesitatingly, and in language the content of which becomes clear only after a careful comparison, e.g. *Expos. simpl.* xv. : Itaque iustificationis beneficium non partimur partim *gratiae Dei vel Christo* partim nobis . . . sed in solidum *gratiae Dei in Christo* per fidem tribuimus.

assigned, not to the realm of grace, making it depend on Christ, but to the realm of power, making it depend on God ; which is the Father's drawing men to the Son.

In the second place, if we would as far as possible avoid figurative language and speak in exact dogmatic terms, we can as little here as elsewhere admit an act in time eventuating at a particular moment or an act directed upon an individual. All that can be individual or temporal is the effect of a divine act or decree, not the act or decree itself. Only in so far as the dogmatic treatment makes its starting-point the self-consciousness of the individual, and therefore in this case the consciousness of an alteration in the relation to God, can we think of the justifying action of God as bearing on the individual. Because everyone connects this alteration with others involved in it, that bearing appears simultaneous with these others ; but only thus far and in this respect is such an individualizing and temporalizing of divine activity permissible. It must never be regarded as something in and for itself, as if the justification of each individual rested on a distinct and separate divine decree—not even though it should be described as determined from all eternity and only passing into reality at a fixed point in time.[1] There is only one eternal and universal decree justifying men for Christ's sake. This decree, moreover, is the same as that which sent Christ on His mission, for otherwise that mission would have been conceived and determined by God without its consequences. And once more, the decree that sent Christ forth is one with the decree creating the human race, for in Christ first human nature is brought to perfection. Indeed, since thought and will, will and action are not to be sundered in God, all this is one divine act designed to alter our relation to God ; its temporal manifestation is seen in the incarnation of Christ from which the whole new creation proceeds, and in which it has its starting-point. Thenceforward the promulgation in time of this divine act is really a continuous one, but in its effects it appears to us in as many points separated and (as it were) strung out from one another, as there are different people whose union with Christ is accomplished.

Turning now to justification in its two elements, we must similarly say that to admit an individual decree of forgiveness and adoption would be to subject God to the antithesis of abstract and concrete, or universal and particular, since the decree of redemption

[1] Cf. Gerhard, iv. p. 147.

is just the universal in its two particular bearings. Besides, the consciousness of guilt and of penal desert being ordained for men by God only in relation to redemption, that is, only as something which everywhere and for everyone vanishes with the entrance of redemption into his life, no special decree or act is necessary for its cessation. All that is needful is that the consciousness of its cessation should arise in the individual. How this happens in connexion with conversion has been shown. Similarly with reference to adoption, it is already implied in the divine decree of redemption or of the new creation of human nature that God is gracious to the human race in His Son ; hence an individual act making the individual an object of the divine love is not necessary. All that is needful is that the consciousness of this relation should arise in the individual ; and this happens in the way already described. Thus we have to posit only one universal justifying divine act bearing on redemption, and this realizes itself gradually in time.

In the third place and finally, we cannot pass over the fact that this exposition seems to conceal one other divergence from the view prevailing in our Church. For in our Church the divine act is regarded as declaratory ; the converted man ' is declared just ' by God ; and in such an exposition no room at all seems to be left for this phrase which indicates the opposition between our own Church and the Roman. But the truth is this. The phrase in question certainly goes back to what is here denied, namely, a multiplicity of divine justifying acts or decrees. For in regard to a single universal decree it is not easy to conceive how it could be declaratory in particular cases. God ordained the Redeemer because through Him sin was to be taken away and men become children of God. But in God thought and will are one. He expresses thought by deed, and through preaching the deed propagates the thought. A special act, therefore, by which God—so we should have to state the matter—declared to Himself what He in another act performs, would be an utterly empty thing. This form of representation, so common in the Old Testament, is simply one of its anthropomorphisms. Looked at more closely, however, any individual declaratory act is in the same case. It cannot as such prevent a recurrence of the consciousness of being concerned in the production of sin, and to that extent would be vain. So also would be a declaration of sonship ; for that is not in itself capable of preventing a man from being conscious of sharing in enmity to

God. Such an act attains reality only as combined with the influence of Christ in effecting conversion. But this also being traceable to the universal divine ordinance, the declaratory act is again merged in the creative act. Since, however, with faith there arises a simultaneous consciousness of forgiveness and of adoption, it is quite right to say that every act of conversion is for the man himself a declaration of the universal divine decree to justify for Christ's sake. But as regards our relation to the Roman Church, it is only superficially that our opposition to it seems to lie in this point of the declaratory character of the divine justifying act, and that Church will assuredly be very far from accepting the mode in which this character is here denied. For we still hold to this, that a man is justified as soon as faith has been wrought in him ; [1] the interest of Rome, on the contrary, is to establish that this takes place afterwards by means of good works.

4. The final point in regard to this distinctively Protestant doctrine that we are justified by faith—that is, that the application of the universal divine justifying act to the individual is bound up with and conditioned by the dawn of faith—is this. The doctrine is all the more necessary if justification be conceived as a purely declaratory act. Otherwise colour might be lent to the notion that a man has redemption assigned to him in a method which is arbitrary —a method, that is, which, as far as he himself is concerned, is baseless. Yet even if we do not sunder the effective and the declaratory, it is needful to fix the point when, and the manner how, the justifying divine act completes itself in man. On this our theorem makes these pronouncements.

The first is that although once forgiveness and adoption exist, the man is the object of divine favour and love, this does not happen until he lays hold believingly on Christ.[2] This does not in the least mean that previously he was the object of divine displeasure and wrath, for there is no such object. But the word ' overlooked ' [English A.V. ' winked at '], used in another connexion, has here its specific sense, inasmuch as for God the individual is not previously a personality at all in this reference, but merely a part of the mass out of which persons come to exist through

---

[1] *Conf. Belg.* xxiv. : Fide utique in Christum iustificamur, et quidem priusquam bona opera praestiterimus.—*Apol. Conf.* ii. : . . . quod fides sit ipsa iustitia, qua coram Deo iusti reputamur . . . quia accipit promissionem . . . seu quia sentit quod Christus sit nobis factus a Deo sapientia iustitia sanctificatio et redemtio.

[2] Atqui extra controversiam est neminem a Deo extra Christum diligi (Calv., *Institt.* iii. ii. 32).

the continuance of the creative act from which came the Redeemer.[1]

But since faith arises only through the agency of Christ, it is clearly implied in our theorem that no natural constitution of man, nothing that takes shape in him independently of the whole series of gracious workings mediated by Christ, alters his relation to God, or effects his justification, and that no merit of any kind avails for this. From this it follows immediately that before justification all men are equal before God, despite the inequalities of their sins or their good works ; this is in harmony with the self-consciousness of everyone who finds himself in fellowship with Christ, as he reviews his former share in the common life of sin.

The second point is this. Since, as has been laid down, sharing in the blessedness of Christ is involved in justification, as sharing in His perfection is involved in conversion, and since faith needs no supplement, it follows that faith gives blessedness (saves), and indeed in such wise that the blessedness cannot be increased from any quarter, *i.e.* faith *alone* saves. For anything that could increase the blessedness could have originated it. This blessedness indeed is such that only in the smallest degree does it admit of maxima or minima, but as far as possible is constant. For just as the union of the divine with the human nature in Christ remained the same through all experience and development, so our union with Christ in faith remains always the same.

On the other hand—and this is the third pronouncement—our exposition of the facts certainly does not lead up to the customary formulæ that faith is the *causa instrumentalis*, or the ὄργανον ληπτικὸν of justification. These formulæ, liable to many mis-understandings, are not greatly fitted to throw light upon the subject. A productive cause has no place as an essential constituent in the course of the series of activities for which it is employed. Having done its part, it is laid aside. But faith abideth always. A receptive organ, on the other hand, belongs to the sphere of nature ; and the above formula might give the impression that faith is something which everyone has to produce in order that divine grace may become effective ; whereas we bring with us nothing except our living susceptibility, which is the real receptive organ. It is perhaps this formula that has betrayed many theologians into

---

[1] Sola gratia redemtos discernit a perditis, quos in unam perditionis concreverat massam ab origine ducta causa communis (Augustin., *Enchir.* xxix.).

maintaining the position that faith must be our own work, and that only when this work has been accomplished can the operation of divine grace begin.

SECOND DOCTRINE : SANCTIFICATION

§ 110. *In living fellowship with Christ the natural powers of the regenerate are put at His disposal, whereby there is produced a life akin to His perfection and blessedness ; and this is the state of Sanctification.*

1. The retention of the term ' sanctification ' is justified because it is scriptural. But as it depends on a rather indefinite concept of the holy, a concept which divergent interpretations and usages have made yet more intricate, a still further exposition is necessary if it is to be used in Dogmatics. The first etymological consideration that has to be taken into account is the Old Testament use of the word for everything separated from ordinary social life and devoted to some use relating to God. This relation to God, however, makes no difference in any activity due to an impulse proceeding from Christ ; for since it is produced by the absolutely powerful God-consciousness of Christ, it of itself includes severance from participation in the common sinful life. And fellowship being essential to human nature, this of itself supplies a basis for an active tendency to a new common life ; just as, owing to its Old Testament use noted above, the expression carries with it the priestly dignity of all Christians and represents the new common life as a spiritual temple. So that the state of sanctification too may be regarded as service in this temple. This close connexion with characteristically Christian ideas makes the retention of the old term in the vocabulary of Dogmatics all the more desirable in view of the temptation at this point to snatch at expressions which tend to obscure what is peculiarly Christian in the spirit of the new life, and make it harder to distinguish the Christian development from a gradual attainment of perfection along purely natural lines.

The second consideration is the connexion of the term with holiness as a Divine attribute ; for of course we hold by the interpretation of this given above.[1] It is, however, also clear that the regenerate man, through the manner of life that we are now going to describe in more detail, develops a conscience also in others, in

---

[1] Cf. § 83.

proportion as all his activities diverge from what happens in the common sinful life.

In both its aspects, however, we cannot call this condition holiness—that is, being holy—but sanctification, which means becoming holy, sanctifying oneself ; which we call sanctification, because it is a striving for holiness. If the meaning were being holy, it would imply that a complete transformation had occurred at the moment of regeneration, every link with the sinful common life entirely ceasing, and the whole nature being completely and instantaneously penetrated by the life of Christ and brought under His sway. This change would then be all a part of regeneration, and there would be no doctrine to state about what later develops out of it.

Sanctification, then, being understood to be progressive—so that the content of time-experience becomes from the turning-point of regeneration ever further removed from what preceded that crisis, and ever approximates more to pure harmony with the impulse issuing from Christ, and therefore to indistinguishability from Christ Himself—we have the two points of view from which sanctification has to be considered.

2. First then, if we compare the state of one who is in process of being sanctified with what existed before regeneration, it is preferable to dwell not on points of difference from the moments in which the mastery of sinfulness was earlier manifested, but rather on the difference from those moments which previously came under preparatory grace. These preparatory workings we cannot limit to approximations to repentance and faith in thought and emotion ; they are also to be seen in action ; for it is contrary to nature that lively thoughts and strong feelings should have no influence on concurrent actions—stronger or weaker, of course, in proportion to their affinity. Indeed, it is possible that with the frequent repetition of similar influences, the active effects occur more and more easily and become habits. In each separate case, however, the impulse to the alteration of action comes from without and remains effective only for so long as the momentary emotion endures ; it is not in a position to reproduce itself from within, as witness the common feeling of having under external compulsion done something quite foreign to one's nature. Such actions are not the doer's own ; they belong to an external life that is showing its power within him. Deeds therefore which resemble those of the state of sanctification, but are not rooted in the regeneration of the doer, are properly

deeds of the Christian common life exercising its power over the individual. It is thus also with habits formed in the same way, as is best seen by reference to the illustration used in Scripture about strangers and fellow-citizens.[1] The latter out of the inner power of their common indwelling characteristic spirit establish law and custom among themselves, and thus their acts are wholly in character. Strangers have no part in the formation of either ; they have no formative power in themselves and merely accommodate themselves to custom, acting in many ways according to it even when no demand has been made on them. But if they return to their own country where these foreign influences no longer surround them, they divest themselves with the utmost ease of every adopted habit. It is therefore not the form, and still less the numerical value of separate actions or series of actions that differentiates the state of sanctification from the condition before regeneration. It is the fact that unwillingness to remain in the common life in which sin is ever being propagated has become a power of repulsion, constantly at work in the form of an essential tendency of being, while in itself this is but the consequence of having surrendered to the receptive influence of Christ ; a surrender which throughout the entire sphere of spontaneous activity has consolidated itself as a steadfast willingness to be controlled by Him.

This is still the only tenable distinction if, conversely, we look back on the old life from the standpoint of the new. That strength of the God-consciousness is not original ; it is a gift which becomes ours only after sin has developed its power ; and what has emerged in time can be removed in time only by its opposite. Hence not merely is approximation to the goal delayed by the fact that what have become habitual and therefore often and easily provoked sins have to be countered by the aforesaid power of repulsion, but inasmuch as the sinfulness of each has a ground in existence prior to him and external to him, his sin cannot be perfectly blotted out, but remains always something in process of disappearance. In so far as it has not yet disappeared, it may make itself visible, and acts will occur within the state of sanctification similar to those common before regeneration, where what emerges is the power of the sinful common life, whereas the traces of preparatory grace lie deeply hidden. Nay more ; since even in sanctification growth does not take place without a preliminary struggle between the old man and the new, this struggle cannot at any point in its whole

[1] Eph. 2[19].

course be viewed as an even advance to increase in the power of the one and decrease in the power of the other. By the influence of the sinful common life around us our own sinfulness is constantly being stirred up again. In itself it might be steadily limited by the growth of the new man, but this cannot equally be said of the reinforcements it receives from without. At least in view of the variegated changes in this sphere, where in the most irregular and unforeseen ways the individual life is held in grip, more firmly or more slackly, by the common sinful life, it could only be explained by a special miracle, and not by the ordinary course of divine grace among men, if in that struggle there were not special moments when the power of sin came out more strongly than in the earlier moments. Even after regeneration, then, many and varied conditions appear, among others repentance, and this by no means always merely in the form of slight compunction for trifles. But this repentance is distinguished from every previous repentance by the fixed inward resolution to be no longer under the power of sin, and is to be conceived as a vanishing quantity in the same way as the repentance which, so long as even in obedience some opposition to the impulses proceeding from Christ makes itself felt, accompanies all actions which appear as fruits of this obedience, yet also show traces of opposition. Even if these intermittent evidences of the continued presence of sin make particular instants, as compared with others, seem relapses, none the less a settled consciousness remains that the longer the series of such fluctuations observed, the greater is the advance seen to be on the whole, and that the certainty of faith as an understanding of what union with Christ means and as a delight in that union is always increasing, so that in the powers put at Christ's disposal sin can never win fresh ground, while all the time it is being dislodged from its former positions. It is chiefly by this fact, that sin can win no new ground, that the state of sanctification is most definitely distinguished from all that went before.

3. If now, on the other hand, we consider how this condition approximates to likeness to Christ, there has above been drawn a boundary line which it is not given to us to overstep. From the beginning of His incarnation onwards Christ developed in every way naturally yet constantly and uninterruptedly in organic union with the indwelling principle of His life, and in its service. To no other who brings with him a personality that has shared the common life of sinfulness is this vouchsafed. This difference from Christ

must, strictly speaking, be there at every moment, and it will come into actual consciousness in proportion to the clarity of our self-consciousness in relation to the divine—that is, our illumination. For wherever there is imperfection, especially such as not merely represents the form of development in time, but is a real imperfection touching the relation between deed and motive, there will also be a basis for the recollection, and to that extent for an actual realization, of the old life ; and therefore even in moments really involving an advance in likeness to Christ, there will also exist a consciousness of sin. But this does not prevent union with Christ from being operative in every moment of the state of sanctification ; and thus at every moment that life merits the description given in our proposition.

This is already involved in the analogy suggested—namely, that regeneration may be regarded as the divine act of union with human nature and sanctification as the state constituted by that union. Just as that act of union would have been an empty illusion had it not produced an enduring state of living union in which the two elements were inseparable, the human nature in all its performances proving itself the instrument of the divine power, so the activity of divine power in Christ that in regeneration flows out from Him and unites individuals to Himself would be nothing at all, would be indistinguishable from the most fleeting and superficial impulses, and as far as possible from being the end of the old life and the beginning of the new, unless that act showed itself operative in every moment in time, making every moment a recapitulation of the first, and, as it were, a being laid hold of afresh by the receptive activity of Christ—every moment thus including in itself a new determination to live not for self but in fellowship with Christ. Taken together, these two things involve the sinless perfection of Christ and, for the introspective self-consciousness, His blessedness. To make clear here, too, the limits of the likeness and the difference, we shall have to distinguish a constant and a variable within this growing correspondence between the elements of our life and the impulses proceeding from Christ. Viewed as a renewal of regeneration every moment is like every other, and is a participation in the perfection and blessedness of Christ ; for without this no reception into fellowship with Him is possible. This constant is in its one aspect the ever self-renewed willing of the Kingdom of God, on which every single act and resolve of Christ was based. In its other aspect it is the consciousness of the union of the Divine Essence with human nature through Christ, as was the case in Christ in every detail of His self-consciousness. All this is participation in blessedness, since union with the Supreme Being is absolute satisfaction ; it is equally participation in sinless perfection, for the kingdom of God excludes all sin, yet includes strength for all good. The variable factor, *i.e.* everything else occurring as a particular item in the life of the regenerate, lies within the limits so drawn. Particular actions show in their execution more or less sin, and so do particular purposes. The actual individual self-consciousness bears witness to this in many a moment of sorrow, where the sorrow is assuaged by the simultaneous presence of the constant factor. At other moments the self-consciousness is a joy that passes into humility because its only right to exist is found in what assuages the sorrow lying so near it.

Any further doctrine there is to formulate concerning the state of sanctification must bear upon this antithesis between the element that belongs to the starting-point and the element that belongs to the goal.

First Theorem : The Sins of the Regenerate

§ 111. *Since they are continually being combated, the sins of those in the state of sanctification always carry their forgiveness with them and have no power to annul the divine grace of regeneration.*

1. Taking together the two propositions just laid down, namely, that in the state of sanctification no new sins develop, and that in all moments, in all acts and works, even in the best and likest to Christ, some trace of sin exists belonging to the former state,[1] it becomes clear that in the state of sanctification there can be no sin which could make regeneration nugatory. For every sinful act includes a resistance on the part of the new man, albeit not a persistent or successful resistance ; and therefore in such acts, just as much as in those where the old man is overborne, the new man is seen to be active, and therefore still alive. It is, of course, only in moments of defeat that anyone has ever fancied that the state of grace might be lost ; yet in this region there is no definite contrast between defeat and victory, but only a distinction of less or more in which no definite point can be fixed at which the result begins to be

---

[1] *Expos. simpl.* xvi. : Sunt multa praeterea indigna Deo, et imperfecta plurima inveniuntur in operibus etiam sanctorum.—*Conf. Belg.* xxiv. : Nullum enim opus facere possumus, quod non est carnis vitio pollutum.

fatal. If we do seek to establish such a contrast, pronouncing this a sinful act and that a good work, we are merely naming it by its preponderating quality. In some cases, indeed, the difference seems almost infinite ; yet if the sin be the deed of a regenerate man, it cannot be the same sin as a sin ever so like it in the unregenerate ; if only for this reason, that in it as in his good works a constant element is present. Everyone who observes himself or others will note acts which fluctuate between the two descriptions, and cases in which it is adventitious circumstances that tip the balance one way or the other, making the same action at one time a good work though on the point of becoming a sin, and at another time a sin instead of a good work. The state of grace cannot possibly be lost in the first case and not in the second. The principle we here go by, namely, that in the state of sanctification no new sin can develop, seems rather indefinite. No action is quite identical with any previous action, and it is not every sin that is a novelty. The labelling, therefore, of any given action as novel seems to depend on a rather arbitrary estimate of the degree in which it is to be regarded as akin or similar to previous actions—a point of which, strictly speaking, a man can judge only for himself. This, and no more, can be laid down in general terms. Taking regeneration in the sense we have given it, and assuming that only subsequent to it a sense-function develops which previously was latent, or that relations are formed so entirely new that they awaken an echo in those elements of our being in which sin previously resided, everyone must confess that it is inconceivable that such a function or such relations should develop in sinful fashion. And in the same way, if in an individual we conceive of any function or relation whatsoever which by personal idiosyncrasy or the influence of training and social morality, was kept so constantly pure even before regeneration that no sin ever arose out of it, it is unthinkable that after regeneration sin should effect an entrance at that point. What follows is clear enough. In every case where sin appears to have entered we must say either that the sin is not really new, but belongs to a former period and has simply been revived ; or else that regeneration has not been of a right and true kind, inasmuch as sinfulness has borne new fruit.

Also from another point of view we must reject the proposition contradictory of ours. The assertion that a regenerate man, though a new man, might by an act lose the grace of regeneration stands in the closest connexion with the idea already rejected, that our first parent could by an act lose the characteristics he still had while acting. If the reply be made that grace is not lost by the act of the new man, but by his not acting, this again conflicts with the assumption that regeneration is the beginning of the life of Christ in us, a life which necessarily is action. In fact, it is evident, just as before, that however such a destructive action might be conceived, the grace of regeneration would have to have been lost previously. Indeed, loyalty to the concept of regeneration permits us another analogy. It would be through the co-operation of the very impulses proceeding from Christ that a man would have to proclaim his severance from living fellowship with Christ, just as, in the case of the Evil Spirit, it was through the very powers that made him most akin to God that he broke away from that relation —the same result following in each case.

Finally, if we return to the problem of how we are definitely to differentiate the condition of sanctification (whether it can be lost or not) from the condition obtaining within the common life of sinfulness (though under the influence of preparatory grace), the problem forces us to make a distinction between the work of divine grace on men and in and through men. If the latter be not a purely momentary thing, ever ebbing again, and equivalent to no more than inspiration, it goes without saying that it must be continuous ; for if even this work of grace could be imagined as ceasing, its duration, whether long or short, would always make it a mere inspiration. The proposition contradictory of ours, therefore, must choose between a self-effected alteration of man's own nature, and a voluntary self-withdrawal of divine grace previous to the decisive action, just as before the fall of man a withdrawal is supposed to have taken place of an extraordinary, restraining divine grace. It seems impossible, therefore, that the doctrine opposed to ours can in this conceptual form be derived from the self-consciousness of one who is conscious of divine grace. For even if we concede that a moment of regeneration is not capable of being definitely isolated in perceptible self-consciousness, and also that the assurance of a form of life antagonistic to the former condition does not at once supervene, still we must agree that in actual experience the manifestations of the new life become ever more continuous, and that confidence in the endurance of this living union with Christ thus becomes more and more a feature of the perceptible self-consciousness, for in spite of all fluctuations an increasing sway of the life of Christ over the flesh marks out the state of sanctification

This natural confidence answering to the fact of regeneration can be expressed in thought only by the first half of our theorem, and not by its contradictory.

2. Even though they are backed by teachers of repute, and have made their way into more than one confessional document, the opposing formulæ, that faith may be lost,[1] that justification may be lost, and that grace may be lost,[2] have the less claim on our acceptance that other credal statements clearly expressing the confidence of our theorem are (in part explicitly, in part by implication) on our side.[3]

If we compare these differing statements with one another, certain facts emerge. First, the concept of falling away and the fallen, and the intrusion of a reference to baptism show that the formulæ opposed to ours are connected with old ecclesiastical decisions which rightly stood out against a harsh desire to exclude certain people. But those falling away, lapsing outwardly from the faith and forsaking the Church, had not necessarily lost faith inwardly : they abjured only outwardly through fear : that is to say, it was merely in courage they were imperfect. Nor were the

---

[1] *Epit. artic.* iv. : Credimus . . . cum dicitur renatos bene operari libero et spontaneo spiritu, id non ita accipiendum esse, quod . . . nihilominus tamen fidem retineat (scil. homo renatus) etiamsi in peccatis ex proposito perseveret.—*Ibid.* : reprobamus dogma illud, quod fides in Christum non amittatur . . . etiamsi (homo) sciens volensque peccet.

[2] Melanchth., *loc.* pp. 124 and 276: Necesse est autem discernere peccata quae in renatis in hac vita manent ab illis peccatis, propter quae amittuntur gratia et fides . . . est igitur actuale mortale in labente post reconciliationem actio interior vel exterior pugnans cum lege Dei facta contra conscientiam—nec potest stare cum malo proposito contra conscientiam fides.—*Augs. Conf.* xii. : '. . . . that those who have sinned after baptism can always, if they are converted, receive forgiveness. . . . Hereby those are repudiated who teach that such as have once become religious can never fall away.'—*Declar. Thorun.* xi. p. 421 : Quasi statuamus semel iustificatos Dei gratiam eiusve certitudinem . . . non posse amittere quamvis in peccatis pro lubitu volutentur. Cum contra potius doceamus, ipsos etiam renatos quoties in peccata contra conscientiam recidunt, in iisque aliquamdiu perseverant, nec fidem vivam nec Dei gratiam iustificantem nedum eius certitudinem . . . pro illo tempore retinere, etc.—Reinh., *Dogm.*, § 127, is careful to take the main proposition, ipsum tamen justificationis decretum in Deo mutabile non est, along with that (*ibid.* 2.) that a man can be justified more than once in his life. For as often as he receives faith once more after the occurrence of a moral lapse the decretum justificans related to this faith must again take place in God. See § 128 : . . . iustificatio . . . neglecta fide iterum potest amitti.

[3] *Expos. simpl.* xvi. : Eadem (fides) retinet nos in officio.—*Conf. Gall.* xxi. : . . . . credimus fidem electis dari, ut non semel tantum in rectam viam introducantur, quin potius ut in ea ad extremum usque pergant.—*Sol. decl.*, p. 802: Deus proposuit se iustificatos etiam in multiplici et varia ipsorum infirmitate . . . defensurum . . . et si lapsi fuerint, manum suppositurum ut ad vitam conserventur.—Augustine's sentence is relevant at this point : Ego autem id esse dico peccatum ad mortem, fidem quae per dilectionem operatur deserere usque ad mortem (*De corr. et grat.* 35).

baptized all regenerate then any more than now. Such, therefore, as forsook Christianity, to enjoy perhaps more sensual freedom, had not been completely laid hold of and were not yet possessed of genuine faith and justification. Secondly, as soon as this same concept 'falling away' is applied to our present circumstances in the same sense that it involves loss of faith or justification, the question what sort of sin it is that occasions this loss is answered in very different ways. To sin with knowledge and with will, to sin deliberately, and to continue in deliberate sin, are widely different.[1] Taking the two extremes, the first belongs to that fluctuating less or more found in everyone who is in the state of sanctification, where even the imperfection of a good work is often enough known and willed ; the second, deliberate continuance in a knowing and complete resistance, is obviously a case where regeneration has been only apparent. Thirdly, it is beyond doubt that if the doctrine of the inadmissibility of justifying divine grace (or, better expressed, the absolute trustworthiness of such grace) has not become an accepted dogma of the Church, this is entirely due to the controversy with the Roman Church and the polemic against fanatical sects ; as indeed every dogmatic proposition which cannot be made good by analysis of the Christian self-consciousness must have its basis either in speculation or in some similarly external ground. This is clear enough for the further reason that it also covers the case of one continuing in sin deliberately. The fanatical caricature of this doctrine, which rests solely on an inward certainty of feeling, and enlarges the thesis by inverting it and giving it the form that whatever the regenerate man does is right or at least permissible, is quite familiar, but finds no support in the formula here adopted. So, too, the inference that the Roman Church seeks to draw from the doctrine of justification by faith is amply guarded against by our presupposition that the regenerate continuously struggles against sin. As for the wanton abuse of the doctrine, there is just as much excuse for it in the doctrine that one can always be converted again if one falls from grace as in the doctrine that the sins which may be committed by a regenerate man do not annul his state of grace. It is, however, much more in accord with our line of argument to meet the objection in view by saying that one who seeks such a subterfuge does not really want to struggle against sin and is therefore not regenerate ; this whole doctrine has nothing whatever to do with his case. No ground therefore remains for seeking to improve upon the simple

[1] See above, § 74.

unforced utterance of the evangelical Christian self-consciousness by a preamble made up of additions untenable in themselves and confusing in their effect.

3. Neither is the declaration that in the state of sanctification sins always carry their forgiveness with them intended to mean that the regenerate man is conscious of forgiveness while he is sinning, or that he sins in and with this consciousness ; the sin must come to consciousness as an accomplished fact and as accompanied by repentance ; for forgiveness and repentance are mutually dependent. But this is certain, that resistance, even if not fortunate and victorious, is a presage of repentance, and hence too of the consciousness of forgiveness.   The real meaning is simply that what is true of the concept of justification as a whole is true of this particular part of it.   The gracious forgiveness of sins is not an individual decree or act bearing on the single life, nor is it merely declaratory ; it is one that emancipates from the sphere of guilt and penal desert, and one that is general—being fulfilled, indeed, at some point of time for each individual, but being then really fulfilled, and needing no repetition.   For the divine omniscience cannot in the act of forgiving sins regard them as altogether blotted out at the moment of regeneration, but only as gradually vanishing.   If conversion be this turning-point, yet so that sin none the less reappears later, then even subsequent to it there must in consciousness be a relation to this act, though naturally an altered relation.   In the life under the dominion of common sinfulness, sin is common guilt, and sins are not reckoned separately to individuals ; each has his share in the common guilt and nothing is separately forgiven him.   In the state of sanctification the converse is the case.   Redemption is possible only in the form of a common life, and sin has its basis, strictly speaking, not in this common life, but only in the individual, in so far as he still has something in him of the old common life of sin.   His is therefore not a guilt appertaining to the common life but to him as an individual, and it is so reckoned.   It is only an apparent contradiction that sins are reckoned to him, and are yet always forgiven ; not only because forgiveness itself is always a kind of reckoning, but because it is the only kind of reckoning that enters here.   Sins are reckoned personally to the natural person who has passed out of the sinful common life into the new life, and indeed more personally to him than to one who still belongs to the old common life ; they are not reckoned to the new man who, identifying himself with the whole through the feeling of com-

munity, does not carry in himself the sense of guilt. They are forgiven him because they can be reckoned only to the old man that he no longer is. Hence also he has the consciousness of forgiveness as soon as he is conscious of himself as being within the new common life. For in virtue of his willing the Kingdom of God and repudiating sin the continuity of the new life has not been interrupted, having always produced simultaneously some degree of resistance to sin. It is self-evident that this consciousness, in whatever degree it may be felt, cannot be simultaneous with sinning, that the repudiation of sin can make itself felt only after the event, and that the consciousness of forgiveness presupposes regret.

4. Since in dealing with the subject one can hardly avoid diverging into Christian Ethics, less might be said here about the struggle with sin itself, were it not that in this connexion too misunderstandings have arisen. It has now been made quite clear that in the state of sanctification the danger each is in of falling into sin comes from those departments of the sensuous life which before regeneration had exercised most power, and has its seat in those relations where habits in accordance with inclination were most easily formed. This sphere, within which lie the enticements which always are hardest to resist entirely, is the sphere of temptation for the individual. Now in everyone the activity of the life of Christ, issuing from His will for the Kingdom of God, defines itself by the demands that meet him in virtue of his position within the common life. That will takes shape in certain fixed aims ; and these come to constitute a continuous will as the law of Christian morality begins to embrace the whole of life. Hence the sphere of temptation must lie within this sphere of vocation, taking that word in its widest sense. There can be no struggle against our own sin other than the struggle against the sin we actually encounter in the course of our activity in the Kingdom of God ; and any action taken against such sin is part of this activity. The struggle therefore consists simply in this, that we seek to reject or conquer the temptations that arise in the course of this activity; and this formula must cover the whole campaign against whatever sins are possible within the varying course of the state of sanctification. Otherwise two differing yet parallel demands would arise, neither of which at any given moment could be fulfilled without infringing on the other. Both points can be made clear, as follows. The right use of divine forgiveness is conditioned in every case by the struggle against sin ; but the right use of divine adoption by which, within the state

of sanctification, even after sin, that is to say at every moment (for there is always some sin remaining), one can still say he is a child of God, is conditioned by the liveliness and activity of faith. And since forgiveness and adoption are one and the same, what conditions each must also be one and the same. There is therefore no such thing as a struggle at random against possible future sins, which could only mean the suppression or weakening of sensuous powers developed in a natural way, and injury to them as instruments of the spirit. Nor are there exercises in repentance consisting of special acts which do not arise out of our business in the Kingdom of God. Still less is there room for an arbitrary flight from the sphere of temptation which would be at the same time a flight from the sphere of duty ; no such step could issue from our being taken up into living fellowship with Christ. Fellowship with Him is always a fellowship with His mission to the world, and this such a withdrawal would contradict. What remains as the one right course, is resistance to the temptations that actually occur.

SECOND THEOREM : THE GOOD WORKS OF THE REGENERATE

§ 112. *The good works of the regenerate are natural effects of faith, and as such are objects of divine good pleasure.*

Apol. Conf. iii. : Deinde docemus, quomodo Deo placeat, si quid fit, videlicet non quia legi satisfacimus, sed quia sumus in Christo.—*Artic. Smalc.* xiii. : Hanc fidem sequuntur bona opera. Et quod in illis pollutum et imperfectum est, pro peccato et defectu non censetur, idque etiam propter Christum : atque ita totus homo, cum quoad personam suam tum quoad opera sua iustus et sanctus est. . . . Dicimus praeterea, ubi non sequuntur bona opera, ibi fidem esse falsam.—*Expos. simpl.* xvi. : Docemus enim vere bona opera enasci ex viva fide . . . et à fidelibus fieri secundum voluntatem vel regulam verbi Dei. . . . Etenim non probantur Deo opera et nostro arbitrio delecti cultus, . . . placent vero approbanturque a Deo quae a nobis fiunt per fidem, quia illi placent Deo propter fidem in Christum, quia faciunt opera bona . . . docemus Deum bona operantibus amplam dare mercedem. . . . Referimus tamen hanc mercedem non ad meritum hominis accipientis.—*Conf. Mylhus.* viii. : . . . quamvis haec (fides) per opera caritatis se sine intermissione exerceat . . . attamen iustitiam et satisfactionem pro peccatis nostris non tribuimus operibus quae fidei fructus sunt.—*Conf. Belg.* xxiv. : Atque haec opera, quae a bona fidei radice proficiscuntur, coram Deo bona eique accepta sunt. . . . Facimus igitur bona quidem opera, sed neutiquam ut iis promereamur. . . . Interim tamen non negamus Deum bona opera remunerari. —*Conf. Angl.* xiv. : Opera, quae supererogationis appellant, non possunt sine arrogantia et impietate praedicari.

1. The discussions, so common in our confessional documents and in all older expositions of doctrine, of the idea that good works

are not necessary for justification, we must regard as irrelevant to the subject ; for if even the first point in the doctrine of regeneration be conceded, the idea is such as could occur to no one. Justification and conversion are mutually conditioned ; hence as conversion cannot be conditioned by good works, neither is justification. And it would be odd to put the further question whether eternal life and blessedness are conditioned by good works. Both begin along with faith, for both are included in what we have seen to be the constant element existing in the soul from the moment of regeneration onwards. We cannot argue this particular point with anyone who dissents ; we should first have to refute him on other points. Anyone who holds that good works are necessary to blessedness, because for him faith is mere knowledge, is using a different vocabulary from ours, or holding an entirely different doctrine of redemption.

The most remarkable misconception, however, is that which, in the course of this controversy, has led to the extravagant position that good works are injurious to salvation—a position only half-heartedly surrendered, as if there might be something in it, if only the proposition were defined more closely and with more propriety,[1] so as to avoid all offence. The fact is, that works which would be injurious if a man put his trust in them would not be good works at all in our sense. Anyone who does truly good works has blessedness already in his faith, and therefore cannot find himself wanting first to rely upon his works.

On the other hand, the positive statement that good works are the natural effect of faith is so closely bound up with all that has been said above that it needs no explanation. Allowing ourselves to be taken up into living fellowship with Christ, we are laid hold of by the union of the divine with the human nature in His Person, and consent to this becomes a constant and active will to maintain and extend this union. Anything this will produces is a good work, were it only an incipient resistance to sin. Thus it is a needless anxiety that wants to deny that faith is conserved or retained by good works.[2] If we imagine the retention of faith as if its implanting were something transitory (which it really is not, any more than

---

[1] *Epit. Artic.* iv. : Repudiamus . . . *nudam* hanc offendiculi plenam . . . phrasin, bona opera noxia esse ad salutem. See also what immediately follows.

[2] *Ibid.* : Credimus fidem in nobis conservari aut retineri non per opera, sed tantum per Spiritum Dei. The latter remark is not yet relevant, but is quite true. All the same, the Holy Spirit has no other way of giving strength to faith than by activity in works.

any act of recognition), then we can only conceive the life of faith as a series of moments in which faith is always the same and unaltered. But it is impossible to conceive two moments of faith thus separated from one another without the first producing a good work before the second has come into existence. Hence the retention of faith, if for the moment we speak of such a thing, is always mediated by good works. The right thing to say is this, that our union with Christ in faith is, though not as completely, yet quite as essentially, an active obedience as His life was an active obedience of the human nature to the indwelling being of God within Him ; and our reception into living fellowship with Him is the fruitful germ of all good works in the same way as the act of uniting was in His case the germ of all redeeming activity. This may also be expressed by saying that the regenerate cannot but do good works in virtue of faith ; and it is surely a vain misunderstanding thereupon to interject the question : Are good works also free ? To ask that involves the assumption that the weakest will, though the will most easily forced to change, is the most free, and that the hero of faith, who does not know how to describe his condition better than by saying that he ' can do no other,' is not free. The whole living susceptibility which is the condition of men in conversion is clearly a free condition ; so is the will for the Kingdom of God arising from conversion, for there is no will without freedom. To be continuously and receptively open to the influence of Christ, and continuously active in will for His Kingdom, is the life-process of the new man.

2. Connected with this is the question how far the good works of the regenerate man are his own in such a sense that they can be *reckoned to him*. We shall disregard to begin with the part of the question which concerns the possibility of reward, and first answer that which concerns the authorship of good works. If we recall at this point the fact that there is no redemption which does not establish a new common life to which everyone appropriating redemption essentially belongs, two questions arise : How far do the good works belong to the individual doing them or to Christ ? And how far to the community or to the individual ? In regard to the first question it is self-evident that in virtue of the living fellowship existing between them, what belongs to Christ in a good work cannot be separated from what belongs to the individual ; for this would be to dissolve the fellowship. A formula, however, has to be found which will bring out the participation of both.

Now conversion is the beginning of sanctification, and in it Christ alone is active, the individual being merely in a state of living susceptibility ; yet in conversion the new life comes into being. Hence every moment of active faith must be ascribed to Christ in so far as the analogy with its commencement holds good, that is, in so far as in that moment new life comes into being or is enhanced ; in short, in so far as it contains progress. For if we could ourselves make the new life grow, we could make it begin. But as in that turning-point the new man came into being, and the will for the Kingdom of God thus arising is our own will, every moment in the activity of faith is to be ascribed to us and is our work, in so far as it is an expression of this implanted will. To call the divine grace in sanctification co-operative grace on this account is an incorrect expression, even apart from its unhappy suggestion that grace is thus assigned a secondary place in the authorship of good works. For the fact is not that divine grace is working along with what is a good work of our own, but that divine grace has here been at work from the beginning, and what is its own it effects by itself. The expression, however, intends to make out a third kind of grace in addition to preparatory and effectual grace, and especially to indicate that the regenerate man has become spontaneously active. This intention is undoubtedly right, but since this third kind is no less effectual than the second, a different word would describe it better than co-operative. Now while this formula obviously applies primarily only to the determination of the will (for in the execution of the act imperfection and sin are always present, and they cannot therefore be ascribed to Christ), it has already been allowed that even in particular resolves something impure may mingle ; hence we shall have to confine it to whatever in a good work is of the nature of progress. If, however, we consider the relation of the individual to the Christian common life, everything shows as absolutely common ; and it would be a misconceived interest to try to define the participation of each in the common activity.

3. From all this it is very easy to understand in what sense good works are the object of divine good-pleasure. The actual deeds, as they come into view, cannot be so, for they are at the same time good works and sins. The object of good-pleasure is only that element in them which is an activity of faith and an expression of our living fellowship with Christ. Thus it is only the love in our good works that is pleasing to God, this being, in the will for the

Kingdom of God, at once love to men and love to Christ and love to God ; while at the same time it is Christ's love working in and through us. Now, since what is sometimes there and sometimes not cannot be an object of divine good-pleasure, this latter must rest especially on the element that remains constant through all moments in the state of sanctification, while also it draws to itself and assimilates what is changing. It is therefore quite right to say that it is really only the person, and the person only as God regards him in Christ, that is the object of divine good-pleasure ; the works are so regarded merely for the person's sake. This consciousness, necessarily involved in the will for the Kingdom of God, is the blessedness which accompanies that will.

In this light, the question whether God rewards good works appears very superfluous. What is our own feeling ? If sonship is involved in regeneration, and blessedness in sonship, can the regenerate man desire or obtain a further reward ? He already possesses the implicit guarantee for every advance in sanctification. Nor can he desire any ; for inward spirit and reward cannot really be related to each other ; and besides, the works are sin too, and merit no reward. This is why it is rightly held that the state of grace leaves no room for reward. It is quite improper to give the name ' reward ' to a widening of one's circle of influence, or, what is the same thing, an enhancement of one's powers ; that merely offers us a further opportunity of doing things for which a reward is given. As a matter of fact, in all the citations from Confessions which admit the idea of reward, one has the feeling that they are only half convinced. There is all the less reason for conceding the point that the idea of reward can be no motive to progress in sanctification.

4. Although we have already made a distinction in the activities of faith between what is an expression of our actual condition, and what constitutes an advance, this cannot be stretched to mean that there are two kinds of good works—those that spring from existing powers, and those that increase power. There are not two kinds. If there were, we should be entangled in an interminable and insoluble struggle. We should have to try at every moment to do some work of each kind, and yet one of the new kinds would always have to be postponed to the other. It can be shown, rather, that in this sphere there can be no actions specially aimed at enhancing our powers. With faith the will for the Kingdom of God has come into existence. This creates for every believer,

in view of his individual situation in the world, challenges to activity in the Kingdom of God, answering to the powers at his command and his knowledge of the conditions by which he is surrounded. The sum-total of these relations constitutes his sphere of vocation, the idea of which is intimately bound up with his will for the Kingdom of God : and all the good works of each individual must lie within this sphere ; nothing outside vocation can be a good work. At certain periods of life and in certain relations, acts directed towards the discipline and the enhancement of power are part of a man's vocation, and are justified on that score ; but real discipline and enhancement of power is found in the actual pursuit of one's vocation, as is the case with all finite spiritual powers ; and the more we consider the inner meaning of things, the more we shall see that there can be no other way of it. For the power of faith cannot be strengthened by special acts not prompted by Christ, while those which He does prompt belong essentially to vocation, and go to achieve something for the Kingdom of God. Just because there are sinful ways, as well as ways well-pleasing to God, of enhancing spiritual and sensuous powers, we must see to it that everything that may be done for this end is justifiable as an act of vocation. Accordingly, if by means of grace we understand such activities as advance sanctification, and by good works the fruits of sanctification, it follows that we recognize no means of grace but such as are at the same time good works, and that all good works must likewise be means of grace. There are no purely ascetic acts, nor are there arbitrary good works—that is, good works lying outside our vocation. Still less are there any such as, after he had done justice to his vocation, a man might do by way of supplement.

5. If the foregoing is the essence of sanctification, so that all activity in the Kingdom of God and every inward development of personality proceeds from the living power of faith and its action through love, it can hardly be more than an accident of memory if at this point a question crops up as to the necessity and use of law, in whatever sense that term be taken. Something like legislation will always exist in Christian life in order in certain spheres to guide the actions of those who lack insight. This is where civil law and the regulations applying to every kind of art and handi-craft come in. Such legislation is a good work in so far as it has its basis in love ; and since it is a proceeding that involves and makes large demands on spiritual powers, it is also a means of grace. But

to law itself we can concede no value in the sphere of sanctification, for love always is, and does, much more than law can be or do. Law does not even suffice to produce the recognition of sin in those who are being sanctified, for in itself it does not pierce behind the outward act to the inward mood and temper. In Christ we have a far more perfect means of recognizing sin. And Paul [1] himself no longer grants even this necessity for law once faith has been revealed. Still less can law hold before us the goal of sanctification. That goal can only be behaviour [2] exhibiting in all its details the strength and purity of inward disposition, and law, as a collection of separate precepts,[3] can never let us see this. Paul therefore cites as works of the Spirit things that cannot be defined or measured by any law, for to call propositions expressive of the inward spirit commandments is a most inaccurate form of language. The two commandments cited [4] by Christ as containing the whole law are not really commands. Nor do even they set forth the goal of sanctification in its full purity, for they exhibit love to God and love to our neighbour as two separate things alongside of each other. As for Christ's one commandment,[5] He really means by calling it so to contrast it with the whole law of commandments : for His is no command ; its real analogy [6] is found in His own redeeming love.

Hence one may justly say that in the Christian Church it is neither necessary nor advisable to begin instruction about sin, and still less about sanctification, with the Decalogue. In either case, this can only lead to imperfect and superficial ideas. Even though one endeavours to import into the Decalogue all kinds of things that are not there, such a method is for one thing an opportune illustration of bad, arbitrary exegesis ; and besides, the same result can be more easily and logically derived from the moral

---

[1] Gal. 3^{25} 5^{18}, even though he here speaks of the flesh lusting against the spirit.

[2] Eph. 4^{13}, where we are expressly pointed to the standard set by Christ.

[3] νόμος ἐντολῶν ἐν δόγμασι (Eph. 2^{15}).—Sol. decl. vi. : observandum est, quando de bonis operibus agitur, quae legi Dei sunt conformia . . . quod hoc loco vocabulum legis unam tantum rem significat : immutabilem scilicet voluntatem Dei, secundum quam homines omnes vitae suae rationes instituere debeant.—In this whole discussion, de tertio usu legis, which, contrary to our own view, upholds the notion of law within Christendom, we best see the inexactitude of the idea underlying it, and the sort of confusion it inevitably sets up.

[4] Matt. $22^{37\text{ff.}}$.   [5] John 15^{12}.

[6] Conf. Gall. xxiii. : Credimus omnes legis figuras adventu Jesu Christi sublatas esse, quamvis earum veritas et substantia nobis in eo constat, in quo sunt omnes impletae.

law of reason as developed under the influence of Christianity—
a law which formulates, not acts, but modes of action.[1] Christian
Ethics, however, will answer much better to its true relation to
Dogmatics, and so to its own immediate purpose, if it drops the
imperative mood altogether, and simply gives an all-round description of how men live within the Kingdom of God.

[1] One cannot say with truth of any law : Lex inculcat . . . esse voluntatem
et mandatum Dei ut in nova vita ambulemus.   Here obviously the Mosaic Law
is meant.

SECOND SECTION

The Constitution of the World in Relation to Redemption

§ 113. *All that comes to exist in the world through redemption is embraced in the fellowship of believers, within which all regenerate people are always found. This section, therefore, contains the doctrine of the Christian Church.*

1. In reckoning the two expressions—the fellowship of believers and the Christian Church—as equivalent, our proposition seems to be in opposition to the Roman Symbol ; but neither earlier versions of the latter nor the Nicene Creed know anything of using the two side by side yet with a distinction. What is evident is that fellowship may be taken in a narrower or a wider sense. For, if the regenerate find themselves already within it, they must have belonged to it even before regeneration, though obviously in a different sense from actual believers. If this were not so, no accession to or extension of the Church could be imagined except by an absolute breach of continuity—that is, in a way unknown to history. But the truth is that the new life of each individual springs from that of the community, while the life of the community springs from no other individual life than that of the Redeemer. We must therefore hold that the totality of those who live in the state of sanctification is the inner fellowship ; the totality of those on whom preparatory grace is at work is the outer fellowship, from which by regeneration members pass to the inner, and then keep helping to extend the wider circle. It would, however, be quite a novel and merely confusing use of terms to try to assign the two expressions in question respectively to the two forms of fellowship.

Further, no particular form of fellowship is here definitely asserted or excluded ; every form, perfect and imperfect, that has ever been or that may yet appear, is included. This, and this only, is assumed, that wherever regenerate persons are within reach of each other, some kind of fellowship between them is bound to arise. For if they are in contact, their witness to the faith must in part overlap, and must necessarily involve mutual recognition and a common understanding as to their operation within the common area. What was stated at the beginning of our treatment [1] of the consciousness of grace, namely, that it always proceeds from a common life, was meant exclusively in this far-reaching sense ; but now that very statement finds for the first time its full explanation. For if, when regenerate, we did not find ourselves already within a common life, but had to set out to discover or constitute it, that would mean that just the most decisive of all the works of grace was not based on a life in common.

2. The more closely our proposition stands connected with that just cited (§ 87), the more difficult does it seem to make it harmonize with the dictum that our dogmatic propositions should express only what is identical in primitive Christian piety and in our own. For how did men find themselves to be already within the fellowship, who received Christ in faith as the result of His personal influence ? On this point we remark that a collective need for redemption and expectation of it already existed, which was prepared to recognize the contrast between itself and One who came offering help. Thus the outer fellowship arose simultaneously with the public appearance of Christ. The power to form the inner was in Him alone, until gradually the inner took shape from the outer, first of all in the disciples who constantly accompanied Him. As to the question that may be interjected, whether Christ had in fact any intention of founding such a fellowship, it is clear enough that He could not have exercised any activity whatever of an attractive and therefore redemptive kind, without such a fellowship arising. Hence there is not the least need to prove when and how He actually did found it. The self-organizing faculty recognizably present in every spiritual relation belongs to the natural form assumed by the supernatural in Christ ; and the essence of the resulting organization must be explicable, partly by the influence of Christ on individuals who thus become His instruments, and partly by His peculiar dignity, which is to be manifested in this organization over against the world. The above question, however, is explained by inward experiences seemingly due to the immediate influence of Christ unconditioned by the fellowship ; and, from an opposite point of view, by the need to guard against collisions between different fellowships within the same circle—on which account also men sometimes wish to recognize only civil society, but not religious. On this point what is needful has already been said ; [2] also upon the relation to civil

[1] § 87.					[2] §§ 100 and 105.

society of the individuals who are bound up with Christ.[1]   And as no redeeming work can take effect on individuals without a fellowship arising, this fellowship cannot consist in anything else than all the factors belonging to the state of sanctification of all under grace.

3. The Christian self-consciousness expressed in our proposition is the general form, determined by our faith in Christ, taken by our fellow-feeling with human things and circumstances.   This becomes all the clearer if we combine with it the corresponding negative expression.   For if, leaving redemption out of account, the world is, relatively to humanity, the place of original perfection of men and things which yet has become the place of sin and evil ; and if, with the appearance of Christ a new thing has entered the world, the antithesis of the old ; it follows that only that part of the world which is united to the Christian Church is for us the place of attained perfection, or of the good, and—relatively to quiescent self-consciousness—the place of blessedness.   This is so, not in virtue of the original perfection of human nature and the natural order, though of course it is thus conditioned, but in virtue solely of the sinless perfection and blessedness which has come in with Christ and communicates itself through Him.   With this goes the converse,[2] that the world, so far as it is outside this fellowship of Christ, is always, in spite of that original perfection, the place of evil and sin.   No one, therefore, can be surprised to find at this point the proposition that salvation or blessedness is in the Church alone, and that, since blessedness cannot enter from without, but can be found within the Church only by being brought into existence there, the Church alone saves.   For the rest, it is self-evident that the antithesis between what is realized in the world by redemption and all the rest of the world is acute in proportion to the completeness with which the peculiar dignity of Christ and the full content of redemption is apprehended.   It disappears or loses itself in a vague distinction between better and worse only where the contrast between Christ and sinful man is similarly obliterated or toned down.

4. This, too, affords the best proof that our proposition is simply an utterance of the Christian self-consciousness.   For if the Christian Church were in its essential nature an object of outward perception, that perception might be passed on without involving attachment to the fellowship.   But the fact is that those who do not share our faith in Christ do not recognize the Christian fellowship in its antithesis to the world.   Wherever the feeling of need of redemption

---

[1] § 106, 2.   [2] Gal. 1[4], 1 John 5[19].

is entirely suppressed, the Christian Church is misconstrued all round ; and the two attitudes develop *pari passu*. With the first stirrings of preparatory grace in consciousness, there comes a presentiment of the divine origin of the Christian Church ; and with a living faith in Christ awakens also a belief that the Kingdom of God is actually present in the fellowship of believers. On the other hand, an unalterable hostility to the Christian Church is symptomatic of the highest stage of insusceptibility to redemption ; and this hostility hardly admits even of outward reverence for the person of Christ. But faith in the Christian Church as the Kingdom of God not only implies that it will ever endure in antithesis to the world, but also—the fellowship having grown to such dimensions out of small beginnings, and being inconceivable except as ever at work—contains the hope that the Church will increase and the world opposed to it decrease. For the incarnation of Christ means for human nature in general what regeneration is for the individual. And just as sanctification is the progressive domination of the various functions, coming with time to consist less and less of fragmentary details and more and more to be a whole, with all its parts integrally connected and lending mutual support, so too the fellowship organizes itself here also out of the separate redemptive activities and becomes more and more co-operative and interactive. This organization must increasingly overpower the unorganized mass to which it is opposed.

§ 114. *In a comprehensive summary of what our Christian self-consciousness has to say about the fellowship of believers, we
must first treat of the origin of the Church, the way in which
it takes shape and disengages itself from the world ; then the
way in which the Church maintains itself in antithesis to
the world ; and finally the abrogation of this antithesis, or
the prospect of the Church's consummation.*

1. These three points certainly do not seem to have the same relation to our Christian self-consciousness. The second is the sphere of everyday experience ; our spiritual life proceeds within the limits of this antithesis. In proportion as we know how to distinguish within ourselves between what appertains to the fellowship of believers and what still appertains to the world, our Christian common feeling will rightly separate, in what happens around us, what belongs to the Church and to the world. This all contributes to our propositions concerning the maintenance of the Church

co-existently with the world.   Propositions even with the same content would be inadmissible if drawn from other quarters.   As in individuals the distinction between what belongs to sin and to grace is drawn, not from the outward aspect of the act open to perception, but from the constitution of the inward motives, so affirmations concerning the Christian Church can be rightly made only by those who know its inner life through personal participation in it.   The affirmations of our self-consciousness, however, about the consummation of the Church, if indeed there are any, are certainly only most unreliable ones ; and as to the origin of the Church only historical evidence can be accepted, with which we cannot deal here. To begin then with this last point : the Christian fellowship gradually expands as individuals and masses are incorporated into association with Christ.   The general fact has been established that the new life of the individual arises out of the common life within the outer circle of which it lies.   And this holds good also of the new life of the first disciples, when as yet the power of the inner circle was entirely confined to Christ.   The origin of the Christian Church is thus the same thing as happens daily before our eyes. On the principle that the redeeming activity must lay hold of everything gradually, it is of no consequence that we should establish a technical rule for the exact how and why of this expansion.   Rather, since at any one moment the redeeming activity is reaching out from the community to cover a far larger number than are at that time actually led to conversion, our starting-point must be a right grasp of the distinction between the converted and all the rest ; to have this is to understand the beginnings of the Church.   Here certainly we have a self-consciousness which has to be grasped in thought, namely, the antithesis which is established in our fellow-feeling and sympathy between the previous inclusion of all in the common state of sinfulness, and the new differentiation between those under grace and others.   As regards the consummation of the Church : if we go by personal experience, all that is given in our self-consciousness is, we must grant, just growth in sanctification, without any presentiment that an entire harmony of all our faculties, and the consummation of the individual life as an instrument of Christ's life in us, will, after the old man has been completely eradicated, finally emerge.   In the same way, if we go by corporate feeling, the Church only confronts us as something growing out of the world and gradually, of itself, expelling the world—the presentiment of the consummation being always held up by the indestructible element of sympathy due to the fact that the old man is always born again with each new individual. Thus the consummation of the Church, even as a presentiment, requires as a condition that the propagation of the race should cease : it therefore founders on the rock of our racial consciousness ; and it looks as if everything put forward as Christian doctrine on this point must derive from some other source than the Christian self-consciousness. In that case it would have no right to a definite place in our exposition, but, resting as it must on an objective consciousness, could, in view of its source, come in only in subordinate wise.[1] Yet two points may still be noted in this reference. For one thing, we are far from being in a position fully to realize as a presentiment the alternative conception of an advance asymptotically approaching the consummation in infinite time, an advance always limited by the appearance of new generations ; nor does this conception supply what is lacking in the presentiment of the imperfect sanctification of our own self at the end of life. And in the second place, even if this presentiment cannot in itself furnish any doctrine in our sense, because it is not an isolable moment of self-consciousness, still the admission of it can yield a proof, as the other form of infinite approximation cannot, that we have rightly appreciated what underlies it and the doctrine of the maintenance of the Church, namely, the essential nature of the Kingdom of God. The proof is that the truth of the exposition holds good even in an attempt to consider the Church in itself apart from its antithesis to the world ; to this extent this attempt is necessary and natural.

2. Between these three main divisions of the subject there is an analogous dissimilarity, not to be overlooked, which may be put thus. In discussing the second we find ourselves entirely, and all but exclusively, within the sphere of the redeeming activity of Christ, for this is the actual boundary of the Kingdom of Christ.[2] Yet if we were to conceive the absolute consummation extensively as well as intensively, the dissimilarity between Him and us would be entirely abrogated, and His lordship would cease.[3] This is an additional confirmation of the view that this is not matter for Christian doctrine in the strictest sense of the word. Especially as in the consummation itself no sense of need can be supposed to persist in self-consciousness, so that the consummation can be

---

[1] Cf. our former treatment of the facts of the resurrection and ascension of Christ.

[2] Cf. § 105.   [3] 1 John 3².

regarded as specifically Christian only in so far as it remains the consummation of a common life dependent on Christ. And while presumably in this consummation natural changes would be involved which lie outside the sphere of the kingly dominion of Christ and belong to the divine government of the world, yet about this bodily side of the matter—which would be the point at issue—we have here nothing to say. Hence, take it how we will, we find ourselves here at the limit of Christian doctrine, and can say nothing definite without overstepping it. So too with regard to the emergence of the Christian Church, alike at its beginning and all the way along. For while the power of the Divine Word and of the Love that seeks the salvation of men remains always the same in the great inward act of preaching, the difference in its efficacy rests on different conditions of susceptibility ; and this again depends on the circumstances in which the divine government of the world places different persons. This cannot but seem very natural ; for in the passing of either individuals or masses from the world into the Church the divine government of the world plays a part and necessarily in the form of activity. Hence our sympathetic appreciation of the matter would be very incomplete if it did not accept the difference that arises as resulting from the divine government of the world. At this point, however, we must bring in another element, to supplement a defect in our previous exposition. We formerly considered the activity of the Redeemer and its operation in the soul of the individual apart from the life of the community ; and thus later, in the doctrine of sanctification, it was still possible for us to consider the individual merely as a separate being, acting independently in living fellowship with Christ. Now of course it is by the very same act that the individual is regenerated and that he becomes a spontaneously active member of the Christian Church. But this second aspect of the matter we previously ignored : hence we must now discuss that act anew and independently of our earlier exposition, in view of the fact that it forms the basis of the relation of the individual to the larger whole. And here our attention is at once focused on the most definite thing in our whole self-consciousness, where we always distinguish and combine both things— our independent personality in living fellowship with Christ, and our life as an integral constituent of a whole.

From both points of view the doctrine of the Church, in its continuous existence alongside of the world, is the essential kernel of this whole section. Hence it is appropriate to establish this doctrine first, and then to treat the other two subjects more by the way of appendix. In adopting the order natural to an historical review, we shall attain greater vividness and simplify many problems.

FIRST DIVISION : THE ORIGIN OF THE CHURCH

§ 115. *The Christian Church takes shape through the coming together of regenerate individuals to form a system of mutual inter-action and co-operation.*

1. In the light of the practice of the Protestant Church for the strengthening of its fellowship, whether by the reception of the instructed youth of the community and by mission work, or in the transfer of individual members from other Christian communions, our proposition certainly gives right expression to the prevailing sentiment and practical methods. The practical methods are always determined with reference to regeneration ; in each case, naturally, in accordance with the manner in which this conception is understood ; and thus (though in most cases one cannot as yet be certain on the point) the prevailing assumption is that regenera-tion has come about. At least the freer a community is within its own sphere, the more strictly will it insist that those about whose regeneration there are good reasons for misgiving are not to be received as members. This would not be necessary, and indeed would be inexpedient, if those received were only being introduced into a communion where preparatory grace was at work. Now with regeneration there is always imparted a strong will for the Kingdom of God. It must therefore be a conviction common both to receivers and received, that all exert the same kind of activity ; and since, belonging to the same locality, they have the same sphere of influence, every such act raises the problem afresh of ordering this common activity aright. That at the same time a mutual influence is provided for, is due not only to the fact that in each there remains much of the world, against which the common activity of the rest must be brought to bear ; but also to the fact that, as none credits himself with a complete and perfect apprehension of Christ, each individual regards that of others as complementary to his own ; and so a mutual and reciprocal presentation results. From this everything must be derivable that can be represented as an element in the life of the Church.

2. It seems harder, certainly, to apply all this to the original emergence of the fellowship emanating from Christ. But if we

recur to the fact that already, when the activity of Christ began, there was a fellowship of those who waited for the fulfilment of their Messianic hopes, while we certainly do not assert that this was the Christian Church before Christ, yet it was a religious fellowship ; there was an interchange of kindred impulses of the spirit and community in all things relating thereto. Now when several of its members came to recognize Christ, they felt no reason to dissolve their fellowship. But as it had now gained a relation to Christ which could not but create a mutual influence among them in the sense explained, they came at the same time to exercise a combined influence upon their fellow-members who had not yet attained to the recognition of Christ. These latter thus formed the outer circle, receiving from the first the preparatory operations of grace, in contrast to the inner circle from which these operations proceeded all the more forcibly that they were exactly adapted to the situation. This combined influence, however, remained subordinate and fragmentary as long as a common susceptibility to the influence of Christ was the predominant factor in their association. In this respect we may say that although a number of regenerate persons were there, yet as long as Christ's personal activity lasted, the Church remained unconstituted, merely latent in the association of these individuals with Him.

§ 116. *The origin of the Church becomes clear through the two doctrines of Election and Communication of the Holy Spirit.*

1. Were it not for the connexion already established, it might perhaps seem strange to find these two conceptions thus put side by side, for they do not sound as if they were at all related ; and as regards their meaning, the idea of election does not seem any more closely bound up with the communication of the Holy Spirit than with, say, conversion or justification. Now, however, it cannot surprise us. The first conception has to do with what, as was argued, in the origin of the Church, is matter of the divine government of the world, namely, the fact that those who are to form the Church must be separated out from the world. This, then, is how we view the origin of the Church, when we look backwards to the region from which its members come. The second conception has to do with what, in the individual, is the basis of the continuity of the Church's co-operation and interaction. Now since this constitutes the very essence of the Christian Church, this conception gives the view of the Church's origin which looks forward to

the common life so arising. This common life can attain and keep true vital unity, like that of a coherent or so-called moral personality, only through the identity of that which stirs and strives in each and every individual. Through this principle, therefore, communicated to individuals as elect, the whole life and work of the Church must be explicable.

The two conceptions, however, have this in common, that they do not fit the situation in which the effective power of the new life was not as yet communicated to others, but existed solely in Christ ; except in the sense in which it may be said also of Christ that He was elect, and that He possessed the Holy Spirit. Really, however, this is to assume the antithesis between the outer circle, which is the area of the preparatory operations of grace, and the inner circle from which these operations proceed. For those who are drawn within the first circle by the preaching of the gospel are not usually, in the language of the Bible or of the Church, termed ' elect,' unless it is as a result of the arrangements of the divine government of the world that they are thus differentiated from the rest. They are termed ' called,' and the other term is left for those who through regeneration are brought into the inner circle. Similarly, of this inner circle the Holy Spirit is the bond by means of which the influences exerted by individuals upon those in the outer circle form a unity, and their mutual interaction becomes, as it were, an organic system. As to the ' called,' however, we do not regard the Holy Spirit as having yet been communicated to them, or dwelling in and moving them.

2. Now, as regards the term ' election ' as applied first of all to the individual, the real problem is the same. All men for us are in the state of common sinfulness, in which everything is common guilt. All thus are absolutely equal : none has any advantage in reference to the new life communicated by Christ. All are first drawn within the circle of preparatory grace ; but, for one thing, the differences between them which thus arise are not attributable to themselves ; and for another, there is favour shown already in the fact that some are called and others are not. Hence for this discussion we can take both together, election and the calling that precedes and relates to it. Thus everywhere, in the light of the partial success and partial failure of preaching, we can see a preference of some to others introduced by the divine government of the world without any ground for it in the persons themselves ; and this can be followed out, in large things and small, not only

in this sphere but also in others, which, however, lie beyond the scope of our present subject.   If we conceive the incarnation of Christ as the beginning of the regeneration of the whole human race, then the erection of a permanent place for the preaching of the Gospel amongst a people through the instrumentality of the firstfruits from its own midst is the beginning of that people's regeneration.   Such a nation, then, has an advantage over those among whom the voice of preaching has had no effect.   But we cannot ascribe this to a difference in merit in nations any more than in individuals.   In the case of individuals the same thing happens, whether they have come in from outside or have been born within the outer circle of the fellowship.   Now we certainly ascribe this to a divine ordinance, as the Redeemer Himself did ; [1] it is equally our part to acquiesce in it, for otherwise we should be (and that, too, in our moral consciousness) in contradiction to our God-consciousness.   But we have no reason for doing so except that we rest in the will of God ; about which all that we can say is, that it was not determined by the merits of anyone, so that the issue cannot be regarded in the one event as reward or in the other as punishment.   For our feelings, as in the conception of election, everything else remains wholly undefined.

3. After what has been said, the expression ' Holy Spirit ' must be understood to mean the vital unity of the Christian fellowship as a moral personality ;   and this, since everything strictly legal has already been excluded, we might denote by the phrase, its *common spirit*.   Accordingly, it should not really be necessary again to give the explicit assurance that by the phrase we mean to describe exactly what even in Scripture is called the Holy Spirit and the Spirit of God and the Spirit of Christ, and in our Church doctrine is also presented as the third Person in the Godhead.   That we have not here to deal with this last point is at once evident from our arrangement of this whole treatise.

But in the Christian Church, as individual influences no longer proceed directly from Christ, something divine must exist.   This something we call accordingly the Being of God in it, and it is this which continues within the Church the communication of the perfection and blessedness of Christ.   All this, already indicated in a preliminary way, will be more precisely expounded later. Already it is apparent that the communication of the sinless perfection and blessedness which, as an absolute and continuous willing

---

[1] John 6[14].

of the Kingdom of God, is the innermost impulse of the individual, must also be the common spirit of the whole, or there could be no common spirit at all. Were there any other than this, that impulse would be subordinate to it and thus to what is less perfect than itself ; in every corporate life all that is personal must be subordinated to the common spirit. On the other hand, if there were no common spirit, the Christian Church would be no true common or corporate life ; yet this is what it has professed to be from the beginning as regards the divine Spirit dwelling in it, and this is how it has been accepted in the self-consciousness of every effective member. This will for the Kingdom of God is the vital unity of the whole, and its common spirit in each individual ; in virtue of its inwardness, it is in the whole an absolutely powerful God-consciousness, and thus the being of God therein, but conditioned by the being of God in Christ.

First Doctrine : Election

§ 117. *In accordance with the laws of the divine government of the world, so long as the human race continues on earth, all those living at any one time can never be uniformly taken up into the kingdom of God founded by Christ.*

1. By ' uniformly ' here is not meant an equality in the strength of faith or in the degree in which all the natural powers are put at the disposal of the common will : for in that sense the proposition would be quite obvious ; it would occur to no one to desiderate such an equality. The absence of uniformity refers to the definite distinction between the inner and outer circles of the Christian fellowship. Now all other fellowships of faith are destined to pass into the Christian fellowship ; and if we assume that those born within the fellowship in due time come under the influence of preparatory grace, a time can be imagined when all whose consciousness has reached the necessary point of development will belong to that outer circle. But in this there is not involved any share in the perfection and blessedness of Christ. Hence these are definitely distinguished from the spontaneously active members of the fellowship. This tallies exactly with the distinction already drawn between calling and election. Two points are involved here, both to be regarded (the one more definitely, the other also in some measure) as laws of the divine government of the world. One such law obviously is, that what proceeds from a single point spreads only gradually over the whole area. Less obvious perhaps

is this, that the state of grace cannot be inborn, but that even Christian children at birth essentially resemble all other sons of Adam. Any difference would be an exception not explicable by the fundamental fact of Christianity : it would be a new, independent miracle ; and, besides, it would shatter the conception of race.

2. Even suppose that Christ, when He made a beginning of preaching the Kingdom of God with a reference to His own Person, had everywhere found an equal feeling of need for redemption ; yet in one respect, relatively to His Person, some would have been prepared by the Baptist, others not ; and in another respect, relatively to His interpretation of the Kingdom of God, some were specially wedded to the existing idea, and thus disposed to reject His, while others were not. Thus He could not but exert His influence with the most varied degrees of effectiveness : indeed, though always within definite limits,[1] He at times moved about and widened the circle of His preaching, and at other times tarried in one place to consolidate His work. Nay, even where He was asked to depart,[2] that fact must have worked to the unmerited disadvantages of many who would otherwise have come naturally to join Him. But all this is rooted in the divine government of the world. And we find the same absence of uniformity in connexion with the subsequent preaching of apostolic times and on to the present day. For the tendency to enlarge the Church outwardly— a tendency which dwells in the whole body but especially appears in individuals—is in itself quite uniform, proceeding as it does from the equality of all in the state of sinfulness ; but in practice it is subordinated, partly to the social circumstances that must offer a point of attachment, partly to that secret attraction and repulsion [3] which equally with these circumstances are subject to the divine government of the world. It could not be otherwise if the supernatural in Christ is to become natural, and the Church to take shape as a natural historical phenomenon.

3. If we consider the propagation of the Church from one generation to another, here too we find that the regeneration of individuals is bound up with the natural circumstance (also rooted in the divine government of the world) that every two successive generations overlap. A similar absence of uniformity thus arises, as each person sooner or later arrives within this inner circle among different and more or less suitable surroundings and influences. Thus two things always happen. Among those living within the

---

[1] Matt. 15²⁴.　　　　　[2] Matt. 8³⁴.　　　　　[3] Acts 16⁶⁻¹⁰.

circle of the Church there are in every period many who do not yet belong to it ; and of these it will be possible to say that they might already have been members of the Church if their path in life had been otherwise guided. Of course in any given nation a long series of generations, living on the whole in the state of sanctification, has an influence on those that follow, as natural tendencies to passion are mitigated ; yet this never is more than an improved form of general sinfulness, and at some point self-knowledge and penitence must enter. Yet we grant that if an early and corresponding recognition of the Redeemer also ensues, a time can be imagined in which (although the birth of body and of spirit never coincide in time, and nature and grace never cease to be distinguishable) the development of living faith is as nearly as possible coincident with the first development of moral ideas and sentiments. Such a time is the nearest possible approximation to the human development of Christ. In such a situation, each will attain far earlier to the possession and enjoyment of his appropriate share in the higher life. Yet even so differences will remain, such that some will as yet have failed to attain to enjoyment though their companions of the same age have long possessed it.

4. While we denote this ordinance by the phrase ' divine election,' because we hold firmly that its final ground lies in the divine good-pleasure, this does not hinder us from inquiring by what this divine good-pleasure is determined. Especially as we are not in a position to say that God makes no distinctions, but that some human wills place hindrances in the way ; for at first the will itself develops gradually, not without being influenced by external relations, until it reaches a greater or smaller degree of excitability. Paul long ago broke ground in this inquiry,[1] and tried to formulate the law by which the apostolic Church to begin with filled up with those who previously were heathen, while the great majority of the Jewish people remained outside. The demand for such an investigation has become still more pressing since whole peoples have accepted Christianity, of whom a considerable proportion at least attained regeneration, while on the other hand many a member of nations long Christian remained provisionally excluded from that inner circle. There is besides the fact that the end of life is appointed so differently for different people. To many born in the Christian Church who have already experienced many operations of preparatory grace, it comes before these im-

[1] Rom. 10 and 11.

pressions can be gathered up and intensified in regeneration so as
to constitute the beginning of a spiritual life. Many are called
away, their length of life divinely fixed, from places where the
gospel has only just begun to be heard. Thus obviously it is
the divine government of the world which appoints that many—
whether many or few really make no difference, since their attitude
to the proffer of divine grace is in any case the same—die unregenerate simply because the course of their life is run. We
cannot say, then, that God has definitely not willed this ; for it
has its basis in the relation between the order of nature dependent
on Him and His decree of redemption through Christ, which to us
is equally matter of inward certainty. We cannot therefore resist
the conclusion that if God had not willed this definitely and unconditionally, He would either have established a different order of
nature for human life, or a different way of salvation for the human
spirit. His ordinance being of such a nature, we are of course called
upon to accept even this divine will as consciously as possible and
without inward dissent.

§ 118. *While Christian sympathy is not disquieted by the earlier and
later adoption of one and another individual into the fellowship of redemption, yet on the other hand there does remain
an insoluble discord if, on the assumption of survival after
death, we are to think of a part of the human race as entirely
excluded from this fellowship.*[1]

1. Regarding ourselves as members of the Church over against
the world, with these two elements in our self-consciousness, the
consciousness of sin and the consciousness of grace, we find that in
virtue of the latter, in which we are given perfect certainty of the
divine decree for our blessedness, we stand opposed to all those in
whom this consciousness has not yet developed. On the other
hand, in virtue of the consciousness of sin we are on exactly the
same footing as they ; for the consciousness of forgiveness belongs
to the other element, and yet keeps ever present to our minds that
original something which belongs to the consciousness of a nature
in which all share. If therefore that equal natural incapacity
out of which, in everyone, the consciousness of the need for redemption may spring, is in one case reinforced, but in another left
to itself, in one case absorbed into the revelation of the divine decree

[1] Once for all in connexion with this doctrine I refer the reader to my
treatise on ' Election.'

of pardon, but in another not so absorbed—this non-uniformity within the same human race (no section of which is definitely distinguished from any other in respect of the divine activity of Christ) is of such a kind that to accept it we must either again reduce our God-consciousness to a mere idiosyncrasy, or else attach much less value to the difference between those blessed by grace and others, almost making it a merely accidental more or less. Otherwise the blessedness springing from the consciousness of grace would of necessity be swallowed up in the sympathetic feeling of unblessedness that accompanies humiliation.

All this takes on a quite different aspect as soon as we venture to hold that at each particular point this antithesis is merely a vanishing one, so that everyone still outside this fellowship will some time or another be laid hold of by the divine operations of grace and brought within it. In that case there is no longer a cleavage in our race-consciousness ; the merely gradual passage of individuals into the full enjoyment of redemption is for our race-consciousness just what the gradual progress of sanctification is for our personal self-consciousness, namely, the natural form necessarily taken by the divine activity as it works itself out historically and, as we have seen, the inevitable condition of all activity in time of the Word made flesh.

Any possible objection to this is met by the two following considerations. The *first* is an application we make of the proposition stated above, namely, that the incarnation of Christ is analogous to the regeneration of the whole race considered as a unity. No one can say that it would have been better for the whole race if Christ had been born sooner, and the new spiritual common life sooner begun. It would certainly have been better had it been possible for this new life to emerge in the same purity and power at an earlier date. But when we read that ' when the fulness of the time was come ' Christ was born,[1] this means that the divine fore-ordination concerning the whole human race and the special determination of the point in time when the Redeemer should be manifested are so much a single indivisible revelation of divine omnipotence that the spiritual life conditioned by this determination of time is certainly also the absolutely greatest, and gives expression to the entire idea of the essential nature of humanity. Now the same thing can be said of the individual. Each man, when his time is fully come, is regenerated ; and then his new life.

[1] Gal. 4⁴.

conditioned by this fixation of time, is, however late its appearance, an absolute maximum, and fully expresses the entire idea of his personality, dependent as this is on its position within the race as a whole.   In harmony with this belief, therefore, we cannot imagine, even of an individual, that it would have been better for him to have been regenerated earlier.   Nor is there any reason to fear that this will lead to slackness in witnessing to Christ, or undermine training and teaching, on the ground that it is useless to press the gospel on people before their time is come.   This has been clearly shown by Augustine,[1] and no such application of the doctrine will readily be made seriously by anyone who is truly being sanctified, that is to say, it will not be entertained by anyone who is capable of bearing witness or taking part in teaching and training. For one thing, such a person is moved by an inner impulse [2] irrespectively of any distinct result he may anticipate ; and for another, he is well aware that the gracious operations of the Spirit that issue from every regenerate person are a *sine qua non* of the regeneration of each when his time is fully come.

The *second* consideration is an application of the truth that in regeneration each person becomes a new creature.   If that is so, sympathetic concern about a regeneration that occurred too late is meaningless, for there is nothing originally present to think about ; just as it would be a waste of pity, on the assumption of a creation of the world in time, to sigh that it was not created sooner.   And even if someone inclined to say that for him the earlier period is not a void but a horror, yet this horror vanishes in the certainty of the forgiveness of sins just as completely whether that period was long or short.   And although such a regret may occasionally be felt on the ground that the new life cannot now endure so long as if it had developed sooner, this too is a mere delusion, revealing a lack of acquaintance with the nature of the new life.   For that life is in itself eternal, and gains no increment by the duration of time.   No one who is maturely sanctified has such feelings ; they belong to a morbid condition.   Only beginners can be troubled by such afterpains, and when peace comes they die away of themselves ; so that there is no reason why we should take account of them in the sphere of doctrine.   Rather must the earliest to be regenerated and the latest each count himself of the same worth as the other, even though in the one case it happened in the morning of childhood, and in the other only after a long course of experience.   For while

---

[1] Throughout in his *De correptione et gratia*.   [2] 2 Cor. 5[14. 10].

the one represents a more exact model of the original union of the Divine with human personality, the other gives a better picture of the ultimate penetration of the entire human nature by the redeeming power of Christ, involving as that power does the total effective influence of all those previously regenerated. Every appearance of difference must more and more vanish as a common feeling and common spirit gets the upper hand in both, leaving each to appropriate all that is the other's. There is no ground to fear that this will occasion any indifference towards the operations of preparatory grace, or lead men to put off repentance and conversion to the indefinite future. Anyone desiring to take this course is not putting off conversion because of anything in Christian doctrine, but because even yet he wants to have a share in the common life of sin more than in the Kingdom of God. To withhold this doctrine from such a man is no help to him ; we must find what will awaken his longing for the Kingdom of God.

Summing up, we may conclude that if only everyone who has lagged behind us is some time or another taken up into living fellowship with Christ, our sympathetic concern can accept the fact with perfect satisfaction without any contradiction arising between it and our God-consciousness.

2. It is self-evident, however, that these considerations are no longer applicable, once we come to think of a portion of our race as destined to be entirely shut out from this fellowship and the higher state dependent thereon. Nor can the idea be admitted (here we are strictly in accord with all that we have just been saying) that we may make a distinction according as we do or do not assume a future life. For if this life as such is eternal, the possession and the deprivation of it cannot be thrown into greater contrast by raising the question of its endless or insignificant duration, if it be the case that one does attain the blessedness in which alone life's value lies, and another does not. Assuming this for the moment, the discord can be resolved only in one of the two following ways. We may justify the concurrent existence of such equality and inequality between ourselves and others and try to trace it back to a law ; and this would show the opposition indicated to be an illusion. Or we may explain as an illusion one of the two—either the original equality, or the inequality due to the divine assignment.

As regards the first point, two arguments may be tried. To begin with, if equality is the original appointed plan for human nature, but inequality of the kind noted just as much results from the plan, contradiction between the two can only be stated in the form of some censure of the appointed plan ; which is meaningless, for unless we were men we should not be at all.   But the inequality that first arises through the intervention of Christ cannot have its seat in the human nature underlying the common life of sinfulness, unless, contrary to our assumptions, we go back to Pelagian principles, and admit either powers of attraction in one class of people or powers of repulsion in the other.   And apart from this, we should still be thrown back upon an inequality in the distribution of endowments that can have its basis only in the divine good-pleasure.   Conversely, if the equality is held to have the same basis as the inequality, namely, the divine plan of salvation, this means that in respect of redemption God has put all men under sin, although only for some does redemption accrue.   In that case, the reception of the one and the exclusion of the other has its ground in such divine arbitrariness, that we must rightly describe the ordinance as sheer caprice.   And even if the concurrent existence of the equality and inequality can be thus made conceivable, yet those who, to our advantage, are rejected, are and inevitably remain objects of sympathy ; and the more our race-consciousness equals our personal consciousness, this sympathy extinguishes the blessedness belonging to the latter, for it is a fellow-feeling with misery. An escape from this difficulty and a faultless solution of it have been thought to lie in the hypothesis that the plan of salvation, which is the ground both of the equality of incapacity and the inequality of help received, is intended to bring home to one class the divine mercy and to the other the divine justice,[1] so that within the human race there might be given a complete divine manifestation in both respects : justice toward the lost and mercy toward the saved. Against this, however, it may be pointed out that the solution does not cover the special case in which divine justice also would be completely manifested if all that is possible through redemption were actually realized ; for then it would show itself compensatory toward Christ, but punitive toward all as long as they belonged to the common life of sinfulness.   We cannot, however, concede in general that the revelation of divine attributes is pieced-out or

---

[1] *Conf. Gallic.* xii. : Credimus ex hac corruptione . . . deum alios quidem eripere, quos . . . in Jesu Christo elegit : alios vero in ea corruptione et damnatione relinquere, in quibus iustitiam suam demonstret, sicut in aliis divitias misericordiae suae declaret.—*Conf. Belg.* xvi. : Credimus . . . deum se . . . demonstrasse . . . misericordem et iustum. Misericordem quidem eos . . . servando, quos . . . elegit . . . iustum vero reliquos in . . . perditione . . . relinquendo.

partial ; for then they would be limited, and God would be an unlimited Being with limited attributes.   Justice and mercy must not
exclude one another.   Mercy in the case of the same people must
show itself as justice.   And in thought this is incompatible with
the permanent exclusion of some from the communicated blessedness of Christ.

Thus all that remains is the second line of thought, namely, that
one of the two, either the equality or the inequality of the two
sections of mankind, should be explained as an illusion.   But the
inequality between those taken up into living fellowship with Christ
and those excluded from it cannot possibly be regarded as an illusion
without sacrificing the essential content of our Christian consciousness.   It is otherwise with regard to the equality which we find in
the consciousness of sin.   This would be an illusion if there were
really an original inequality in men, that is, if from the very beginning
there were a cleavage in humanity.   For once we realize this, the
contradiction vanishes, those originally not on the same footing as
ourselves not being possible objects of our sympathy, and the unity
of human nature as hitherto understood being a delusion.   But if
it is then supposed that only in the one class and not in the other
is there a sensitiveness and susceptibility for divine grace, or that
only in the one class and not in the other is there an invincible
opposition to divine grace, we land in assumptions leading to
Manicheanism which are just as much opposed to our interpretation
as the Pelagian assumptions above referred to.   Indeed, redemption
itself then takes on a quite different form.   For Christ would then
really have come only to develop and bring to light an already
existing disparity ; His real function becomes that of judge, and
what may be called redemption is merely the form of one side of
this function.   There is thus no way of resolving this discord if on
the ground of our Christian consciousness we must accept the fact
that part of our race is utterly excluded.   If our proposition indicates that the discord would be greater on the assumption prevailing
throughout the Christian Church of personal survival after death
than if we could adopt the opposite view, the reason is simply this.
In the present life, while we do recognize the state of grace as a
communication of the perfection and blessedness of Christ, it is this
merely in innermost principle : for if, in anyone under grace, his
total self-consciousness in time be considered, it is always found to
include also a consciousness of sin.   The inequality is therefore not
present for others, because in the only thing that is open to their

observation, namely, the temporal consciousness, they recognize merely a distinction of less and more, and of this they think less, the less they have been captured by the operations of preparatory grace. On the other hand, when we take the life beyond into account, we have then to conceive of a complete development of blessedness and woe, which means that the antithesis is stretched to its utmost ; and the more even now we are pre-occupied with the anticipation of the future life the deeper must our sympathy be with a future of woe, and therefore the harsher the discord.

3. There is a certain affinity between the thought of this last paragraph and two other attempts to solve the problem. One, while admitting the survival of those who attain to the communication of Christ's blessedness, holds that the excluded perish utterly at death, so that they are only to be considered as physically like children who die ere it is theirs to enjoy the light of day. This indeed lessens the inequality, for a brief unhappiness offers a smaller contrast than an endless woe. But apart from the point that this makes redemption primarily the cause of immortality, thus attri-buting to it a physical effect foreign to its nature and definition (since otherwise here too we should have a fundamental cleavage in human nature), still there remains the particularizing character of a redemption which can only secure for some both blessedness and immortality, but not for all. The other attempt seeks to lessen the inequality on a different side, conceding that after the present life even the unregenerate may attain, by a faithful use of the natural light that was given them, to a certain perfection and happiness, if only a subordinate degree. They would only be excluded from a higher stage.[1] But in that case one cannot see why they should not stay, or receive a place, within the sphere of preparatory grace, and why this grace should not sooner or later reach its goal. Other-wise redemption remains particularized in this case also, and we are once more confronted (in a new form) by a divine caprice that makes perfect harmony impossible.

In the light of these explanations, the following theorems of Church doctrine have now to be more closely defined and reviewed.

[1] Cf. Reinhard, *Dogmatik*, § 116, 3.

FIRST THEOREM : PREDESTINATION

§ 119. *The election of those who are justified is a divine predestination to salvation in Christ.*

Conf. Saxon., Twest., p. 157 : Utrumque certissimum sit agentem poeni-tentiam propter filium Dei gratis fide accipere remissionem peccatorum et iustificationem et hunc esse haeredem vitae aeternae.—*Ibid.*, p. 162 : Vult deus intelligi, genus humanum a deo conditum esse . . . non ad aeternum exitium, sed ut colligat sibi in genere humano ecclesiam, cui in omni aeternitate communicet suam sapientiam bonitatem et laetitiam.—*Expos. simpl.* x. : Deus ab aeterno praedestinavit vel elegit libere . . . sanctos quos vult salvos facere in Christe . . . Ergo non sine medio, sed in Christo . . . nos elegit deus, ut qui jam sunt in Christo insiti per fidem, illi ipsi etiam sint electi, reprobi vero qui sunt extra Christum.—*Conf. Angl.* xvii. : Prae-destinatio ad vitam est aeternum dei propositum, quo . . . constanter decrevit, eos quos in Christo elegit . . . per Christum ad aeternam salutem adducere.—*Sol. decl.* xi. : Praedestinatio pertinet tantum ad filios dei, qui ad aeternam vitam consequendam electi et ordinati sunt.—*Conf. March.* : '. . . that God the Almighty . . . has chosen and ordained to eternal life all who thus steadfastly believe on Christ. . . . Thus too has God according to His strict justice from eternity passed over all who do not believe in Christ, and prepared for them the eternal fire of hell.'

1. Let us consider the self-consciousness we possess as regenerate persons in this aspect. From the very beginning of our progress in sanctification, it is one with our feeling of absolute dependence, and is bound up with that feeling not only in so far as we are con-scious of our activity in the Kingdom of God as an activity divinely produced by means of Christ's mission, but also in so far as the course of each man's progress is one with the position assigned him in the general context of human relationships. The natural ex-pression for this fact is to say that the ordinance according to which redemption realizes itself in each life is one and the same thing with the carrying out of the divine government of the world in respect of that person. This holds not only for the period subse-quent to regeneration, but also for the previous period spent under the influences of preparatory grace (which equally belongs to the realization of his redemption), and therefore also to the moment of regeneration which binds these two periods together. The self-consciousness that thus expresses itself is, however, not a personal and merely individual consciousness, but the common feeling of all who find themselves within the circle of Christ's influence. It is therefore correctly extended to all who may be approaching the point of being drawn into this circle. If then the very same thing holds good of them at the moment of their regeneration, it follows

that the individual's being drawn, each in his turn, into the fellowship of Christ is simply the result of the fact that the justifying
divine activity is in manifestation determined by, and forms part
of, the general government of the world. It would be contrary to
this if anyone were to assert that his conversion and sanctification
would have taken place in the same way and at the same time, even
if his course in life had lain in a quite different environment. How
our proposition is in harmony with the consciousness of freedom
has already been shown,[1] and in that inference it might also have
been stated thus : that the manner and the time of each individual's regeneration is determined by what is peculiar to his own
inner life, that is, his freedom, and by his relations to the natural
and historical development of justifying divine grace, that is, his
place in the world. Primarily, then, the kingdom of grace or of
the Son is absolutely one in origin with the kingdom of omniscient
omnipotence, or of the Father :[2] and since the whole government
of the world is, like the world itself, eternal in God, nothing happens
in the kingdom of grace without divine fore-ordination. This
therefore is given from the start in and through the self-consciousness of those under grace : and whether they choose to say that
their state is a work of divine grace in Christ, or that it is a consequence of divine fore-ordination, the one statement in thought
implies the other.

2. But as regards those we find outside the fellowship of Christ
—they cannot so affect us as to give us reasonable cause to make
any statement about them in this connexion. We are indeed
aware that the preaching of Christ which continually sounds forth
from the Church is a living and not unfruitful influence : we see
the operations of preparatory grace thus beginning in individuals :
we see these individuals going on to become members of the Church
whose advancing sanctification leaves no doubt as to their justification ; thus in their case also the divine fore-ordination is revealed.
But about those in whom these operations have not appeared we
have no ground for anything more than this negative statement,
describing simply their relations, up to that point, to the Kingdom
of God and the operations of grace issuing therefrom.[3] As regards
divine fore-ordination, this involves only what has been already

---

[1] § 4, § 46, § 49.
[2] *Sol. decl.* xi. : Pater enim trahit hominem virtute spiritus sui juxta
ordinem a se decretum et institutum.
[3] So in Acts 2[41] and 13[18] it is certainly not meant that of those who did not
then believe, none could possibly become believers at some later time.

explained,[1] namely, that there are always some in whom as yet it
has not attained its aim—that is, the initiation of blessedness in
Christ. But by this path we can never arrive at the idea that for
them, or some of them, there is a fore-ordination of an opposite
kind. That 'many are called and few are chosen'[2] holds true
at every particular turn in the preaching of the Kingdom of God,
and at every time, which means at the present time ; and so one
has always a right to say that the majority are *not yet* to be regarded
as chosen—not, that is to say, at the present time. For naturally
at any particular moment the majority are being held in reserve
for some later moment ; this is in accordance with the order of the
divine decree, since in every process of development in time there
is necessarily a successiveness even of what is originally simultaneous. Only in this limited sense, therefore—that is, only at each
point where we can make a comparison between those laid hold of
by sanctification and those not yet laid hold of—ought we to say
that God omits or passes over some, and that He rejects those He
passes over, and hence that election always and only appears with
reprobation as its foil.[3] From the position we take, the term ' pass
over ' is the most fitting ; it merely negatives a definite act, not as
if those passed over were outside all divine activity and all divine
decree, but this activity (by reason of the total divine order) takes
shape so entirely in remote inner and outer preparations that they
appear to us to be passed over. Those not yet included are for us
just this undefined element. Not possessing spiritual personality,
they are sunk in the mass of the sinful common life, and as long as
in their case the divine fore-ordination does not come to light, they
are just where the whole Church was to begin with. On this
account we can never cease to regard them as objects of the same
divine activity that gathered the Church together, and as embraced
along with us all under the same divine fore-ordination. And
since we have denied the possibility of any relapse from fellowship
with Christ into the common life of sin, whereby that fellowship
were wholly abjured, and have declared this an illusion, it follows
that no divine fore-ordination can be admitted as a result of
which the individual would be lost to fellowship with Christ.
Thus we may reasonably persist in holding this single divine

---

[1] Cf. § 117.　　　　　　　　　　　　　　[2] Matt. 22[14].

[3] . . . quando ipsa electio, nisi reprobationi opposita, non staret (Calv.,
Instit. III. xxiii. I). Only he does not take it in our limited sense, but rather
says roundly that this limitation, for which the reason is given above, is
brought in *inscite nimis et pueriliter.*

fore-ordination to blessedness, by which the origin of the Church is ordered.

3. It is therefore only as it were in an appendix, not here strictly relevant, that we can deal with the other idea of there being a two-fold fore-ordination—on the one hand to blessedness, on the other to damnation.[1] The only point of attachment for it in the foregoing discussion is the possibility of death intervening in some individual case before fore-ordination has fulfilled itself. Suppose an individual in whom noteworthy influences of preparatory grace are to be seen, but about whom it may be equally certain that he is not yet in the state of sanctification ; then it is very natural to think that it is in virtue of a divine ordinance that he did not attain to fellowship with Christ and the enjoyment of blessedness. If, however, we proceed on the definite assumption that all belonging to the human race are eventually taken up into living fellowship with Christ, there is nothing for it but this single divine fore-ordination. We infer from it that for such an one this fore-ordination has not been fulfilled during his lifetime, but not by any means that a different fore-ordination is being fulfilled by his death ; rather, the state in which he dies is only an intermediate state. Such is the faith in Christ which ascribes to Him a claim and power over the whole human race, without at the same time needing to admit any blind divine preference, and in which there is encountered no contradiction between the end in view in the divine plan of salvation and the result accomplished by the divine government of the world. But as soon as people proceed on the opposite assumption (as is obviously done in our Confessions),[2] namely, that death is the end of the divine gracious working, the proposition given above ceases to be a fitting statement ; and, if everything is to be neat and logical, we must admit a fore-ordination by which some are predestined to damnation, as others to blessedness. If, however, even on this assumption, it is still urged that the fore-ordination only holds of those who are saved, the others being simply passed over or left where they are, we must reply that, if the only conceivable meaning of fore-ordination is a divine decree that

[1] Calv., *Institt.* III. xxi. 5 : Praedestinationem qua deus alios in spem vitae adoptat, alios adiudicat aeternae morti, nemo . . . simpliciter negare audet.—Non enim pari conditione creantur omnes, sed aliis vita aeterna aliis damnatio aeterna praeordinatur. Itaque prout in alterutrum finem quisque conditus est, ita vel ad vitam vel ad mortem praedestinatum dicimus.

[2] So, too, Melanchthon, *loc. d. praed.*, when he says : Deus volens non perire totum genus humanum *semper* propter filium . . . vocat . . . et recipit assentientes, means by this only the time ante novissimum diem.

conducts man to his very end,[1] this is an impossible view at least
without forced artificiality. Similarly when, identifying fore-
ordination with election, some deny that there is any fore-ordination
in respect of the wicked, but merely foreknowledge [2]—as if a
foreknown passing-over were not also a fore-ordination. For if
it be asserted that the individual persons elected are fore-ordained,[3]
it follows, if the rest are merely covered by foreknowledge, that in
respect of them there is no divine will at all. And even if it be
ever so strongly argued that electing fore-ordination is not to be
considered as something wholly abstract, but as taking place in
Christ, it none the less follows, if in Christ some cannot be elect
but merely passed over, that the universality of redemption must
be limited in proportion. To sum up, the only possible conclusion
is that if—on the presupposition that for those who die outside
fellowship with Christ there is no further possibility of entrance
into it—it is yet desired to assert that the excluded are simply
passed over, they must then be regarded as not having any existence at all. Now this is quite right if the whole proposition be
taken as dealing with the sphere of the new creation, for in that
sphere the excluded persons are not to be found. But then on that
view even the elect are not there to begin with, but only after each
comes to be in his own time and according to his own fore-ordination ; and the expression ' fore-ordination ' cannot then be applied
to real individuals. Indeed, the proposition would have to run as
follows. *There is a single divine fore-ordination, according to which
the totality of the new creation is called into being out of the general
mass of the human race.*[4] In itself this formula is equally adapted
to all assumptions—to that according to which the non-elect perish
at death, to our own, and to that with which we are now dealing.
All that our assumption adds to it is this, that the totality of the
new creation is equal to the general mass ; what the first adds is
that the general mass eventually becomes equal to the totality of

---

[1] Praedestinationem vocamus aeternum dei decretum, quo apud se
constitutum habuit quid de *unoquoque* homine fieri vellet (Calv., *Instit.*
III. xxiii. 5.

[2] *Sol. decl.* xi. : Aeterna vero electio seu praedestinatio dei ad salutem
non simul ad bonos et ad malos pertinet,—and all that follows.

[3] *Sol. decl.* xi. : Et quidem deus illo suo consilio non tantum in genere
salutem suorum procuravit, verum etiam omnes et singulas personas electorum
. . . ad salutem elegit.

[4] At this point the Augustinian formula already cited is entirely apposite :
Sola gratia redemtos discernit a perditis, quos in unam perditionis concreverat
massam ab origine ducta causa communis (*Enchir.* xxix.). To suit our purpose, we have to alter this only slightly, as follows : Praedestinatio discernit
redemtos a communi perditionis massa.

the new creation ; the last, on the other hand, lets the general mass remain the more extensive. But in harmony with this one must also say of the redeeming power of Christ that it suffices to save from common ruin the totality of the new creation contained in the human race. And a composite formula is always unsound which gives foreknowledge a wider compass than fore-ordination, for no such disparity can exist. God always predetermines the condition just as He foresees that which is conditioned ; and it follows that if He foresees what is conditioned, namely, the lostness of men, and (speaking very humanly) does not alter what conditions it, namely, the particular constitution of the individual in its rela-tion to his position in the course of the spread of the gospel, then He has also fore-ordained what is conditioned. If the one conception be applied to individuals of both sections of mankind, so must the other. In one section individuals are both foreknown and fore-ordained as elements of the mass out of which the children of the Kingdom are to be formed. In the other they are foreknown and fore-ordained as the new creatures that are to be formed out of the mass. Hence the formula suggested as a way out of the difficulty would still deviate from the Confessions of both divisions of the Protestant Church. For, as both definitely agree in excluding one section of the human race, so they agree also in referring the ex-pression ' fore-ordination ' to the individual in his whole actuality ; and if the matter is to end there, the logicality of Calvin's formula incontestably ought to be preferred. The assumption on which it rests has certainly become more and more generally accepted in the Church, but whether it is a necessary or optional assumption is a point to be discussed only when we come to treat of the con-summation of the Church, and not here, where we are dealing with its origin.

SECOND THEOREM : THE GROUNDS OF ELECTION

§ 120. *Election, viewed as influencing the divine government of the world, is grounded in the faith of the elect, foreseen by God : viewed as rooted in the divine government of the world, it is solely determined by the divine good-pleasure.*

Canon. Dordr., Art. ix. : Eadem haec electio facta est non ex praevisa fide.—Art. x. : Causa vero huius gratuitae electionis est solum Dei bene-placitum.—*Conf. March.* : ' That God . . . purely of grace . . . has ordained to eternal life and elected all who thus steadfastly believe in Christ, His own know and understand right well.' Note that (thanks to Prince

Sigismund) it is repudiated as Pelagian that God has elected some, simply on account of the faith He foresaw.—*Colloq. Lips.*, p. 404 (Brandb. and Hess.) : 'That God . . . in Jesus Christ . . . has elected some whom He . . . leads to faith in Christ and renews and preserves in the same to the end.'—(Kursax) : 'That God had chosen from eternity those whom He saw . . . would believe in Christ and continue in faith to their end . . . and that He found no cause or occasion for this choice in the elect themselves.'

1. The antithesis set up here relatively to election applies quite generally to all free actions. Every such action contributes something to the further course of the divine government of the world ; for everything within range of it would be more or less different if *it* were different. At the same time every act is also in its determined place in time and space the result of the divine government of the world in its course up to that point. The consideration of election from this point of view, however, rests on the fact that the Kingdom of God and the divine procedure in its harvesting and propagation is represented as a special divine activity by itself, apart from the divine government of the world in general, and that then (all men on account of sin being originally equal in respect of redemption) the question arises why one is chosen and not another. We have the same title and reason to raise this question, whether the view that all are elect is adopted or not ; though in the first case a more exact expression would be : 'Why is one already, and another not yet regenerated ? ' Now looking back upon what was formerly said about the supernatural becoming natural, this can only be decided in the light of nature ; and all we can say is that if any one is regenerated, it can be then inferred that in his case the preaching of the gospel at its maximum of power and the maximum of his susceptibility must have coincided in time. But the answer gives no satisfaction, for this again depends on conditions that are under divine control. And if at this point the question is again raised why circumstances were so controlled that one was regenerated and another not, we must either seek the ground for the determination absolutely at the beginning, before there was anything at all, which means holding firmly to belief in a divine good-pleasure ; or else we must seek it at the end, in the final result, which means that we hold firmly to a divine foreknowledge. Obviously, however, these two are not separable. For there is no foreknowledge in God that is not connected with a divine good-pleasure ; [1] and just as little is there a good-pleasure in any particular thing apart from its entire con-

[1] Cf. § 55, 1.

text, which in the case of everything temporal necessarily includes foreknowledge. In the credal passages quoted, however, and in other similar passages, there is on this point a remarkable hesitation. Good-pleasure and foreknowledge are contrasted ; yet what has been excluded is almost always brought in again by way of some cautious formula. The form of our proposition is meant to do away with this uncertainty and confusion.

2. If the moments of regeneration are chiefly to be regarded as extending the union of the divine with the human nature, and the justifying divine activity as the temporal and particularized continuation of the general act of union begun in the incarnation of Christ, we must admit that the divine procedure will follow the same rule in the one case as in the other. Therefore if the question be ventured, why then for this union with human nature there was chosen precisely Jesus of Nazareth, or rather (since it was only through this union that He became what He was) why exactly this and no other person-creating act of human nature was chosen, at exactly this time—the question must be capable of being answered in a quite analogous way. If we recall that this act was itself a becoming natural of the supernatural, and if we remember the kind of effects that were to proceed from it, we cannot answer in any other way than this : that time and place were chosen as the absolutely best, that is as yielding the maximum operative effect. Now to answer the question thus is obviously to postulate foreseen faith as the ground of individual election. For by the same rule they must be chosen, and the time of their conversion determined, so as to make their share in the furtherance of the work of redemption the greatest possible. In the same way, if we take a large view of election not merely as the determination of the order in which individuals are regenerated, but as the election of nations to have the gospel firmly rooted in their midst, this too will be determined in just such a way as to attain the extensive and intensive maximum for the whole course of the historical development. But everything that the individual or a community can do by word or deed for the extension of the Kingdom of God, being a continuation of, and therefore included in, the prophetic activity of Christ, may be summed up in the terms ' proclamation ' or ' preaching.' And preaching, in this meaning and compass, springs from,[1] and is the natural utterance of, faith. It is thus quite the same thing whether we say that the divine election is

[1] Rom. 10^{17}, 2 Cor. 4^{13}.

determined through the foreseen efficaciousness of preaching, or through the foreseen occurrence of the maximum power of faith.

It is true all the same that in the common use of the formula this moment of regeneration is what is least prominent, and what is stressed is the permanence and steadiness of faith rather than its active power. But the inadequacy of the formula taken in this restricted sense must strike everyone. On this reading it does not get right back to the idea of the Kingdom of God, or to the origin of the Church, which, according to the Scripture passage [1] that forms the basis of most discussions of the subject, is the natural point at which the question arises. In fact, an entirely atomistic view of the work of redemption underlies the whole position, if it is always and only the individual as such that is spoken of ; and no such limitation can possibly yield a right view. This becomes very clear if along with this formula we take two others which are supposed to explain and support it. First, it follows from the formula that if some are not elected at all, they are those in whom effectual grace would not in any case have had firm root. But it is also said of them that God has determined to harden and reject those who persist in repelling His word.[2] If the combination of these formulæ is to lead anywhere, it must be possible to prove a difference between the natural aversion which is the ground of non-election and the antipathy caused by God which is its result. The impossibility of this makes the formula useless, whether as a canon for the investigation of Christian history, or for conducting fruitful self-examination. On the other hand, if, after stating that God elects those whom He sees to be such as will continue in faith, it be also said that He has determined to strengthen and confirm those whom He elects, it is equally impossible to define a difference and boundary line between the former merely foreseen steadfastness, and the latter, which is imparted by God Himself. If, however, it is the intention of the formula to avoid every imputation of Pelagianism, and therefore to reckon the former too as divinely effected (there being no foreknowledge in God that is not operative), the final conclusion is that God has elected only those whom He has also determined to strengthen in faith. Now this is an altogether empty formula, unless one is conceiving faith as also including its operative effect. The same holds good of the more modest formula that

---

[1] Rom. 10 and 11.

[2] *Sol. decl.* xi. : In codem suo consilio decrevit, quod eos qui per verbum vocati illud repudiant . . . et obstinati in illa contumacia perseverant, indurare reprobare et aeternae damnatione devovere velit.

regard to faith cannot be excluded from the divine decree of election.[1]

No one, however, will desire to stretch the application of our first formula so far as to insist on our proving that the maximum fruit of redemption could have been secured only by just exactly the course of election which as a matter of fact has gone to edify the Church. No proof is possible, for there is no alternative with which the comparison can be made. Hence what we have in this formula is faith speaking about what is fundamental to the conception of history and to true self-scrutiny.

3. The answer, however, which has just been given in reference to what can be regarded as divine election in the incarnation of Christ may also be traced back to the second formula of our proposition. For if we say that that point was chosen from which the maximum of efficacy could develop, it may also be said that that point only had this peculiarity because the general situation had become just what it was. But this situation divine guidance might have made different, and then a different point would have had this peculiarity. Christ therefore was determined as He was, only because, and in so far as, everything as a whole was determined in a certain way ; and conversely, everything as a whole was only so determined, because, and in so far as, Christ was determined in a certain way. To say this is obviously to take our stand upon the divine good-pleasure, and to say that the determination in both cases is what it is simply through the divine good-pleasure. Indeed, whenever we form an inclusive idea of natural causality as a self-enclosed whole and go back to its basis in the divine causality, we can reach no ground of determination for the latter except the divine good-pleasure. Just as the whole world was so ordered by God that He could say it was all very good, that is, in accordance with His good-pleasure, and as the individual is in this regard not separable from his connexion with the rest of being—so, viewing the Kingdom of God as a self-enclosed whole, we can only say that, as it is, it is simply determined through the divine good-pleasure. And everything appertaining to it is so determined—Christ as He actually is, and the whole actual inward manifold of the human race in space and time, out of which through Christ the Kingdom of God is formed. There is, of course, nothing to hinder it being also said that the order in which the relationship

[1] Dicimus fidei intuitum decreto electionis esse includendum (Gerh., iv. p. 207).

to Christ comes to be realized in each individual case conforms to that manifold, and is determined by it ; but in that case it must also be possible to say, conversely, that the manifold of the human race conforms to that order, and is determined with relation to it so that, within it, redemption through Christ develops on precisely this scale and in this order. Both statements are equally true, and at the same time, because standing in contrast, they are equally false. Summing up everything, therefore, all that can rightly be said is that both, in their relation to one another, and also each by itself, are in the above sense ordered according to the divine good-pleasure. It has been well-pleasing to God that human nature should show itself in this determined multiplicity of thus determined individual beings ; and no other ground for it can be given. For every other explanation would involve conditioning assumptions ; and these in turn would always themselves be conditioned by the all-embracing divine good-pleasure. Similarly it has been His good-pleasure to make the dispensation of human affairs perfect through Christ. He might from the very beginning have arranged the whole march of the human race differently ; only it would then have been a different human race, for when once one thing is fixed, everything else is fixed along with it in just one way. Every attempted logical proof of the necessity of redemption in this form assumes something the necessity of which itself requires similar proof. For the religious there is no path of escape from this circle of necessities, each leading back to and conditioned by the others, except by way of this one all-inclusive divine good-pleasure. Accordingly, all that remains to us is the task of linking up at every point this divine good-pleasure (which is necessarily implicit in our God-consciousness) with what we perceive of the actual course of the work of redemption, and of resting trustfully upon it, however we may be moved by what happens. Indeed, faith in Christ is itself nothing else than sharing in this divine good-pleasure which abides on Christ and the salvation grounded in Him ; and the consciousness of divine grace, or the peace of God in the redeemed heart, is nothing else than just this quiet acceptance of the divine good-pleasure in respect of the arrangement of events which led to oneself being taken up into the sphere of redemption. Just as in the world in general we meet with the most manifold gradation of life, from the lowest and most imperfect forms up to the highest and most perfect, and cannot doubt but that this very multiplicity is the richest fulfilment, in time and space, of the divine good-pleasure ; and as such gradations also occur within the sphere of human nature : so within the sphere of spiritual life resulting from redemption we shall readily expect all that lies between the greatest and the least, and find peace in regarding all this abundance, linked up in living fellowship, as the object of the divine good-pleasure.

4. We have already seen how these grounds of election are arrived at, and how they seem to be in opposition to one another because they have opposite points of departure. The previous exposition will have removed this apparent contradiction, as our proposition requires, by exhibiting it in formulæ which have an equivalent content, but merely are construed from different angles, so that in accepting the one there is no necessity to reject the other. But it is only possible to show them thus to be in agreement, if both are freed from untenable elements attracted in large measure by their very opposition. What has to be detached from the first is any appearance of the divine decree being dependent on what would obviously be a human kind of foreknowledge on the part of God, the object of which would then be independent of the divine decree, whereas in fact that decree must be guided by His fore-knowledge. For if a determination of the divine decree by faith foreseen be opposed to a determination by the free divine good-pleasure, the inference is hardly to be avoided that faith is grounded, independently of the divine influence, in the free will of man ; and this semblance of Pelagianism cannot be removed by any kind of artificial qualifications, so as to leave the formula any definite content at all. As against this, what we say is that faith foreseen determines the divine decree in so far as it has been the divine good-pleasure to allow to issue from this point such an activity in behalf of the Kingdom of God as is conditioned by precisely this strength and timeousness of faith. The other formula, to the effect that the divine good-pleasure draws on one person and leaves another behind, if set up in contrast to the first, seems only too easily to imply favouritism to the one and repression of the other ; and this in such wise that on such a beginning the end must follow, no matter what may happen in between. There is thus an appearance of divine caprice in an unconditioned divine decree concerning in-dividuals, as though it meant an urgent support of the one person with irresistible aid and a predetermined abandonment of the other ; and this is so difficult to guard against without the whole formula falling to pieces, that the simplest plan is just to accept it. As against this, our exposition knows of no unconditioned divine

decree regarding the individual, for all individuals are mutually conditioned ; it knows only a single unconditioned decree by which the whole, as an undivided system, is what it is in virtue of the divine good-pleasure.   Not at all as if the individual has somehow some kind of existence apart from this divine decree, which then simply does or does not save him.   On the contrary, each individual comes into existence only because and in so far as an element of just such a kind, and of such active powers, is given a place in the whole, in accordance with the divine good-pleasure.   Each, therefore, is fashioned in readiness to become a member of the Christian fellowship, because he is foreseen as a believer.   If now we view our two formulas in combination, they contain two rules by which these disadvantageous inferences are made impossible.   The first is that no individual becomes anything whatever for himself, alone and apart from his place in the whole, in consequence of a special divine decree relating to him.   In the second place, viewed as part of the general context of things, everything, and in particular the way in which redemption is realized, is the perfect manifestation at once of the divine good-pleasure and of the divine omnipotence.

Postscript to this Doctrine.—From the point at which we have arrived let us return once more to the assumption that a section of the human race remains shut out for ever from the sphere of redemption, or (to express it as it touches most closely the proper content of our doctrines) that the Christian Church only arises out of the human race in such wise that a section of mankind is for ever lost to it.   On the one hand, it cannot be denied that at this point a perfect acquiescence in the divine good-pleasure is hard to attain, for racial and personal consciousness are here affected by contrary emotions, and the resulting inevitable and ever-renewed sadness is such as to prevent an unalloyed communication of the blessedness of Christ.   And another problem arises, namely, how so to conceive the matter that human nature shall still remain identical in all. Of course if in Manichæan fashion we are prepared to make a cleavage in human nature, that sadness must die out, since the others are no longer our fellows in the old sense.   On the other hand, unless our Christian self-consciousness is to be essentially modified, the almost equally insoluble problem arises how so to conceive this as that nevertheless Christ is still sent not only to, but also for, the whole human race.   This is only the case if it be admitted that at some time or another some trace of His activity actually makes itself felt in everyone.   But it is easy to see that the difficulty is of a

very different sort according as we are dealing with those who have
already experienced the influences of the Christian Church, or
with those who have remained outside all connexion with it. It
may therefore be advisable to make a corresponding distinction
within the assumption itself. As regards the former class no
incapacity for redemption must in any sense be ascribed to them ;
rather, as often as some operation of preparatory grace has been
vouchsafed to them up to the point of communication, they have
already and by that very fact become instruments for spreading the
Kingdom of God ; for every such communication bears witness to
the grace of God in Christ. But the less we are in a position instantly
to mark a man's transition to the state of sanctification, and must
be careful to recognize the possibility of an imperceptible occurrence
of regeneration no less than of a sudden one, the more we are compelled to recognize, with regard to all who already belong outwardly
to the Christian fellowship, the wisdom of the caution that we
should not lightly reckon anyone among the rejected ; [1] so that
there is no conceivable case to which the assumption we are discussing can be confidently applied. As regards those outside the
Church, it is an essential of our faith that every nation will sooner
or later become Christian, as indeed this was Paul's hope for his
own people, which had so often obstinately refused the divine
grace. In so far therefore as we view the individual in his national
idiosyncrasy, reckoning the spirit he thus shares an essential element
in his personality, to that extent we may say that he bears within
himself this predetermination to blessedness. This holds good the
more as he himself possesses more of those qualities of the common
spirit to which, in his race, the acceptance of faith can attach itself,
and the less as he possesses more of those qualities on which the
race's procrastinating resistance depends. This more and less,
obviously corresponding to the faith foreseen, means for us of
course simply this : that the same people, if alive at the time when
the gospel first appeared among their nation, would have been laid
hold of by it, one man at the very outset, another at some later stage.
None the less, from the fact that out of these circumstances we can
only construct a formula which expresses nothing real, it does not
follow that it could have no other significance in the divine fore-
ordination (even without our having on this account to take refuge
in the *scientia media* of God) : for in those individuals these qualities

---

[1] *Expos. simpl.* x. : Bene sperandum tamen est de omnibus, neque temere
probis quisquam est adnumerandus.

are real. Rather, if all in this fashion are included in the divine fore-ordination to blessedness, then the high-priestly dignity of Christ for the first time comes out in its whole efficacy—an efficacy which implies that God regards all men only in Christ. This very point can be applied also to the previously considered case. So that at least this result clearly emerges, that if we take the universality of redemption in its whole range (which cannot really be conceived without this high-priestly dignity of Christ and all its consequences), then we must also take fore-ordination to blessedness quite universally ; and that limits can be imposed on neither without curtailing the other.

SECOND DOCTRINE : THE COMMUNICATION OF THE HOLY SPIRIT

§ 121. *All who are living in the state of sanctification feel an inward impulse to become more and more one in their common co-operative activity and reciprocal influence, and are conscious of this as the common Spirit of the new corporate life founded by Christ.*

1. This fact itself is expressed in the most definite way in all the scriptural accounts of the first planting of the Christian Church ; and the favourable impression made on non-Christians is always represented as due to this unity ; [1] and this quality of fellowship is brought into the closest connexion with the new life of every individual. Indeed, all informing pictures of the Christian fellowship agree in describing every individual as an integral constituent of the whole, and attributing everything to one spirit moving in, and animating, the whole.[2] And if adherents of the twofold separatist tendency already frequently censured, the naturalistic and the fanatical or visionary, should wish to object that this properly holds good only of the first period of the Christian Church and is by no means essential to it, but must more and more die out, since every reason for thus holding together drops away when once the new life is firmly established and can perfect itself out of the common source in each individual by himself, they may be answered as follows.

In the first place, that which can cease or fall into the background through the gradual strengthening of individuals is only one element in one half of what our proposition affirms ; it is only that element

---

[1] Acts 1[13ff.]. 2[42ff.]. 4[32ff.]. 5[12-14] 9[31].
[2] Rom. 12[3-6], 1 Cor. 12[4ff.], Eph. 2[17-22] 4[16], 1 Pet. 2[5-10].

of the reciprocal influence which comes under the analogy[1] of teaching and learning, or of imparting and receiving. For if any-one is properly taught of God he does not require someone else to teach him. This element in fellowship is also, in one particular respect, always on the way to cessation [2]—if, that is, one is always in contact with the same people. But as new persons are always arriving, this element in fellowship also runs on ; those who were previously receivers now imparting, as givers, to later comers. And this mutual influence has a further element, namely, a reciprocity of impartation and comprehension among equals. This is based on the fact that, owing to varied personal idiosyncrasies, the new life itself is something different in every case ; and every-one, just as he would fain take Christ wholly to himself, strives also to take to himself as far as possible all that Christ has effected ; and thus again each is moved by Christ (as he personally conceives Him) to manifest the power of Christ working in him, which indeed is what happens in all the good works of the regenerate. Still less does the other element, the co-operative activity, ever tend to cease. On the contrary, it is bound to be facilitated and to expand in proportion as the new life gains strength in each. And obviously, in proportion as the will for the Kingdom of God originated simul-taneously with living faith in Christ is more definitely formed within each and develops into a system of purposes, so will each necessarily appropriate the help of all kindred forces. And thus, through this interweaving of what is co-operative and what is reciprocal, and in virtue of the identity of the new life in all, there arises a disposition to a common work or undertaking—a work that can be carried forward approximatingly towards its goal only by means of the conjunction of every power and activity ; a work which would by no means cease though the whole human race were received into the fellowship of redemption, because it ever remains as in itself an infinite and ever-changing exemplification of what is common in the individual and what is individual in the common. For this is the essential thing in the life of a people ; and it is as a people, or a household of God,[3] that Christians have always wished to be regarded.

In the second place, there are, it is true, in this regard two opposite kinds of human association : those which of themselves tend to come to an end, and within which therefore no increasing unity is striven for ; and those which seek to persist, in which

[1] John 6[15].   [2] Eph. 4[11-13].   [3] Eph. 2[19] Tit. 2[14], 1 Pet. 2[9].

therefore the mitigation of differences must be an object, and unity must be held fast. The former are always merely accidental. Partly they are those which by their very nature can be given neither definite form nor definite limits, as in all associations within a free society, though even there under certain circumstances something like a common spirit comes to exist ; partly they are those formed solely in connexion with some particular joint-undertaking without any inward unity of spirit, in such a way that each is left free to seek his own personal ends. · It may be there are even religious fellowships approaching this in character ; of the Christian fellowship it certainly does not hold true. For what each recognizes in the other is a common love to Christ ; and this supplies a unifying principle that is uninterruptedly at work.

2. If now we denote this striving for unity by the expression ' common spirit,' we mean by this exactly what we mean in any earthly system of government, namely, the common bent found in all who constitute together a moral personality, to seek the advancement of this whole ; and this is at the same time the characteristic love found in each for every other. Hence up to this point no objection can easily be made to our proposition. But if one compares its content as there explained with the heading, and rightly infers thence that this common spirit is meant as the Holy Spirit, and the communication of it as the communication of the Holy Spirit, then the suspicion may easily arise that the expression Holy Spirit ' is being taken in an entirely different sense from that given it in Scripture. But the thought-forms that have arisen owing to the place of the Holy Spirit in the doctrine of the Trinity (partly to explain it, partly to refute it, as, for example, when the Holy Spirit is represented as a separate higher Being, indeed, but only a created one) ought none of them to be taken as equivalent to New Testament statements, which as a matter of fact represent the Holy Spirit to us as always and only in believers. He is promised to the whole community,[1] and where an original communication of the Spirit is spoken of, it comes by a single act to a multitude of people,[2] who eo ipso become an organic whole, who are urged on to like activity and stand in for each other. In all, however, He is represented as being one and the same, the various effects produced by Him in various people being distinguished from Himself as His gifts.[3] And this is not meant as if merely to indicate an advantage or superiority which some individuals possess ; which would natur-

---

[1] John 16[7ff.], Acts 1[4, 5].   [2] John 20[22, 23], Acts 2[4].   [3] 1 Cor. 12[4].

ally mean that the Spirit was a particular quality of the personality of each, resembling and generically the same as the quality of anyone else's ; which is how we conceive the matter in the case of special talents and perfections. No : on the one hand the Spirit is represented as a true unity through which the multitude of Christians also become a unity and the many individual personalities become a true common life or moral personality ; and, on the other hand, the Spirit is not assigned to people as it were in a random and unconnected fashion—a phenomenon here one moment and gone the next. The presence of the Spirit rather is the condition of anyone's sharing in the common life ; [1] for, only when this common spirit of the whole begins to show itself at work in a given person can it be known that he is a constituent part of the whole ; [2] just as if anyone joins himself to the whole, it can be taken as certain that he will receive a communication of the Holy Spirit.[3] Now in the sphere of thought there has always been controversy over questions of this kind, as to how far what exists in many is still one, or whether and in what degree it can be rightly said that an idea or a motion of the will common to many is one, or is something particular in each. Here we do not have to decide such differences of opinion, whether on their own account or because we had prematurely represented one view or the other as incompatible with this element of the Christian faith. We prefer not to enter on this field at all, but merely to lay down two points as expressions of our Christian self-consciousness. The first is that the unity of the Spirit is to be understood in the same sense as the unity which everyone attributes to the characteristic form taken by human nature in a nation ; even those who ascribe being only to the separate individual may still say that each man's personality is the national character modified by the original basis of his own nature. Similarly, we say that the new life of each is an activity of this common spirit manifested in the same fashion in all others, an activity conditioned by the state in which regeneration finds him ; and the Christian Church is one through this one Spirit in the same way that a nation is one through the national character common to and identical in all. The second point is that this common spirit is also one, because in all derived from one and the same source, namely, Christ ; for everyone is conscious of the communication of the Spirit as being connected in the closest fashion with the rise of faith in him, and everyone recognizes that the same is true for all

---

[1] I Cor. 12³, Rom. 8⁹.   [2] Acts 10⁴⁷, 19². [3] Acts 2³⁸.

the others. For faith only comes by preaching, and preaching always goes back to Christ's commission and is therefore derived from Him. And as in Christ Himself everything proceeds from the Divine within Him, so also does this communication, which becomes in everyone the power of the new life, a power not different in each, but the same in all.

3. Another possible objection is this. Starting from the point that all other religious fellowships are destined to lose themselves in Christianity, and hence that all nations are destined to pass over into the Christian fellowship, the common spirit of the Christian Church would then be the common spirit of the human race. Now by analogy with the common spirit of a nation such a thing as this latter must exist, and we do not know how to describe it otherwise than by the expressions, racial consciousness, or love of humanity as a species. But in that case the race is one in the same sense as the Church is one, and as there cannot be two living unities for the same whole, what we wish to denote by the expression 'Holy Spirit' would be exactly the same thing as the racial consciousness. This would mean either that the latter was something supernatural, which no one would desire to maintain, or that the former must be natural, and if derived from Christ, then from the human in Him. This would make the communication of the Holy Spirit nothing more than the awakening by Christ of a pure racial consciousness. For the subject about to be dealt with, this is the most logical form of the view which regards the awakening and expansion of a universal love to men as the proper and essential fruit of the appearance of Christ. To us, however, not only is it certain that our participation in the Holy Spirit really belongs to the things which we are conscious of having had imparted to us by Christ, but also that in Christ everything derives from the absolute and exclusive power of His God-consciousness. And if on the other hand we take into account our self-consciousness as still betraying our participation in the common life of sinfulness, we find in it such a variety of interests belonging to the merely individual though also enlarged personality that the pure racial consciousness cannot prevail as a practical motive any more than could a law of morality couched in different terms ; it merely serves as a barrier against personal and social selfishness. Of course it was first through Christ (as Founder of a society which is capable of embracing all men, and which, while attaching individuals to itself, looks simply to the fact of their being human) that the racial consciousness, along with the

God-consciousness and with the same object in view, has become a
powerful practical motive. But just for this reason, this power is
no mere natural principle that would have developed of itself out
of human nature as human nature would have remained without
Christ. On the contrary, we recognize it for the most authentic
expression of the Holy Spirit as a consciousness of the need to be
redeemed that is alike in all, and of the capacity, alike in all, to be
taken up into living fellowship with Christ ; and the universal love
of humanity we know only as one and the same thing with the will
for the Kingdom of God in its widest compass. It is only in this
sense that for us the common spirit of the Christian Church, and
every Christian's universal love for men as a love alike for those
who have already become citizens of the Kingdom of God and for
those to whom this experience is yet to come, are the same One
Holy Spirit.

§ 122. *Only after the departure of Christ from earth was it possible
for the Holy Spirit, as this common spirit, to be fully communicated and received.*

1. Let us compare this proposition with what is most often
taught on this point and is stated not only when the subject is dealt
with in presence of a congregation, but predominantly in the public
teaching given, where the procession of the Holy Spirit is indeed
set forth in the doctrine of the Trinity as timeless and eternal, but
the outpouring of the Spirit, as the beginning of His activity within
the Christian Church, is connected with the event of Pentecost.
The first point needing defence is this, that as has at least been
indicated in our argument, the Holy Spirit must already have been
at work, even though incompletely. Now it certainly is true that
Christ Himself makes His going away a condition of the sending
of the Spirit ; [1] but it is equally true that He Himself communicated
the Spirit to them before His final departure from earth,[2] and indeed
that He even assumed that the Spirit had been already present
with them ; for whatever is a divine revelation in the soul relatively
to Christ [3] is also a work of the Spirit. Now these various statements are not easily to be harmonized, unless what Christ is said to
have expected at His Ascension in Jerusalem [4] was simply a complete filling with the Spirit. If now we start from the position that
the Holy Spirit is the inmost vital power of the Christian Church as
a whole, we must go back to the two most elemental aspects of life,

---

[1] John 16[7].   [2] John 20[22].   [3] Matt. 16[17].   [4] Acts 1[4, 5, 8].

the living susceptibility and the free spontaneous activity ; for these together, in their reciprocal relations, are that by which life is constituted—life being the more complete and the more fully developed, the larger the sphere covered by each of the two, and the more exact their mutual correspondence. In company with Christ the susceptibility of the disciples developed, and in their steady apprehension of what He offered to them there was laid the foundation of their future effectiveness as workers for the Kingdom of God. Hence, as they related their apprehension entirely to the Kingdom of God preached by Christ, each recognized this susceptibility in the others as the very same thing, grounded and upheld in the same way in them all. There came to be among them a fellowship in apprehension, and as face to face with Christ each was able to represent the rest in question and answer,[1] this susceptibility revealed itself as an essential factor in the common spirit. In this sense the right apprehension of Christ is itself ascribed to the Holy Spirit.[2] On the other hand, they had at that time no really spontaneous activity of their own. What Christ suggested to them in that line was practice, not performance proper, and just for that reason it was not free activity, but one that needed on each occasion a new special impetus. One step in the transition towards complete spontaneity is shown in the communication of the Spirit, just referred to, in the forty days after the Resurrection. For the right binding and loosing of sin is in the main just an expression of a fully formed susceptibility for what relates to the Kingdom of God. This expression, however, is inconceivable except as having a reaction on those whose sins are bound or loosed ; it therefore marks a transition to free spontaneous activity ; and obviously the susceptibility reveals itself most distinctly as the common spirit in expressions which presumably are unanimous.

2. The common spirit was, however, as yet incomplete ; hence during the personal presence of Christ there can have been no completely common life representing at that time the Kingdom of God. And this, as a matter of fact, was the case. For the more a common life depends on an individual life, the less is it an existence in common. In part it is so far not equipped for permanent identity amid the changes of death and birth ; in part a common life ought to be one whole, but not an individual person. The more all depend on one, each receiving his impetus from him, the more all are merely his tools or members, and the whole is just the enlargement of this

---

[1] Matt. 16¹⁶, John 14⁸· ⁹· ¹¹ff·.   [2] I Cor. 12³.

one personality.   Or if we consider the multiplicity of individual lives, the whole is really more like a household or a school than an existence in common.   The ancients viewed the State in which all are unconditionally subject to the will of an individual, as an enlarged household, where various living tools move at the command of one master ; and school for us means a spiritual life in common which entirely depends on the thinking power and art of making disciples possessed by an individual, who puts a common stamp on them all.   In this sense, of course, Christ's life in company with His disciples was both a household and a school.   But a house is scattered on the master's death, and if its members are not caught up in some new bond, they disperse.   So, too, in a school, if no other common motive comes to replace the original thirst for learning and personal attachment, no further progress takes place after the master's death, and the previous bond of union gradually dissolves. We find the disciples in the mood thus to disperse after Christ's death, and up to the time of His Ascension their life together was so much interrupted and decreased as to become quite formless.   But even when Christ was alive it could not but be that each felt mainly dependent on Him, and sought to receive from Him ; no one of them all considered himself ripe for free spontaneous activity in the Kingdom of God yet to be formed.

3. If we do not wish to insist that the Holy Spirit is a divine communication of a quite specific kind, which though conditioned by Christ is yet not thus homogeneous with His earlier influence, it is certainly possible to argue that the distinction here sought to be drawn is untenable.   For according to our own statements, in the living fellowship of the regenerate with Christ everything derives from Him, which means that, strictly speaking, there is to be found in every Christian only susceptibility, not spontaneous activity. And hence, it may be said, the life in common is no more now than then a common existence ; for the spontaneous activity then as now was wholly in Christ, and believers' life together even yet is just the mutual impartation of what each has received from Christ. But to this it must be rejoined that when formerly we studied the way redemption is realized in the case solely of the individual by himself, that was an incomplete view of the matter, and at the moment we safeguarded ourselves by a reference to what we are now considering.   We said that *ab initio* preparatory operations of grace arising out of the common existence reach everyone.   The statement that everything in the regenerate derives from Christ

held good of the communication of His sinless perfection, which simply consists in a pure will directed to the Kingdom of God ; in particular aims and purposes this is no longer present.   If therefore we ask how our particular aims arise out of that pure will, the answer is that it happens only in the common life.   They no longer come to anyone directly from Christ ; no one is given a special command by Christ, as was the case with the disciples.   But as no isolated individual can achieve anything in the Kingdom of God, so no one can really form any purpose but one in which he foresees that he will have the support of others and of which the germ is therefore already present in others.   And again, through every such common movement only so much progress will actually be made as has a true common consciousness behind it.   Here therefore there is more in the individual than susceptibility, and his really spontaneous energetic activity is more than the activity of Christ merely passing through him.   But the common spirit expressed in this spontaneous activity is only the Holy Spirit in so far as the activity it induces is a prolongation of Christ's own activity.   And no more than in Christ's lifetime is the individual's susceptibility open merely to what proceeds directly from Christ ; it is also a susceptibility to the spontaneous activity of others.

If now we wish to apply here the general canon that everything essentially connected with our participation in redemption must be the same in us as in the first disciples, we shall say that as long as all spontaneous activity was in Christ alone, but in them mere susceptibility, the Kingdom of God in the narrower sense was confined to Christ alone—the disciples representing only the outer circle of the preparatory workings of grace, where there is nothing but susceptibility.   And just as then in the disciples, so now in everyone the reminiscent apprehension of Christ must grow into a spontaneous imitation of Him.   This common spontaneous activity —which indwells all and in each is kept right by the influence of all, and prolongs the personal action of Christ—in its unity and identity we have full right to call the common spirit of the Christian Church ; it corresponds to all that Christ promised by the Holy Spirit and to everything that is represented as the Spirit's working. Taking everything together, we are thus able to say how it was that after Christ's departure the disciples' common apprehension of Christ changed into a spontaneous prolongation of His fellowship-forming activity, and how it was only through this activity so related to the fixed apprehension of Christ becoming the imperishable common spirit, that the Christian Church arose. So, too, everyone within the circle of preparatory grace, who through the influence of Christian life upon him and in the activity of others flowing through him, possesses this Christian common spirit merely in the form of susceptibility, must, when through faith the rule of the Kingdom of God has been established in his life, refashion his attitude to the apprehension of Christ accepted within the common life into a spontaneous activity of this kind ; and this is the communication of the divine Spirit. If now the justifying divine activity be conceived under the form of particular divine actions, we should have to say that now this communication is in each case, as it were, the latest element or stage of this activity ; in the lifetime of Christ this final act was, so to speak, put off until after His departure from the earth. But as we do not admit the reality of any individual and temporal divine acts, we are not compelled to adopt any such paradoxical formula ; and we shall state the parallel between the first disciples and ourselves equally well if we say that already, even when Christ was with them, and just because they were taken up into living fellowship with Him, they had the principle of the new life, and had it not merely as susceptibility but also as spontaneous activity ; although as long as Christ was with them it took the form exclusively of a continuous desire to receive from Him, and therefore only afterwards could become truly common and manifest itself as Holy Spirit. It is these aspects that are described with more precision in the following theorems.

§ 123. *First Theorem.—The Holy Spirit is the union of the Divine Essence with human nature in the form of the common Spirit animating the life in common of believers.*

1. When in connexion with the doctrines of Christ we were discussing the union in Him of the divine with the human, we put entirely aside the question whether or not this divine, apart from its union with human nature, was something special, as being the second Person in the Godhead, and something relatively distinct in the Divine Essence. So here too, in proposing a similar formula for the Holy Spirit, we must (although the Trinity is now completely before us) in the same way leave this consideration out of account. What we have to treat here is simply this relation between the highest Essence and human nature, in so far as in its operations it meets us within our Christian self-consciousness. Since these operations are fully expounded only in the next division, and the

content of the following section has already been prescribed for us, a summary view of these relations in the doctrine of the Trinity can only be given at the close of our whole exposition. But in advance we must here make a different point. Our discussion is not in the least meant to embrace all the passages in our Holy Scriptures where this expression occurs, or all the ways in which it is used in dogmatic works. Here we have only to do with the Holy Spirit in the Christian Church, and do not raise the question whether, as used apart from this relation, the expression means the same thing or not. But this is equivalent to saying that the Holy Spirit here discussed is not the same as the Spirit to whom a participation in the creation of the material world is ascribed,[1] or the Spirit whose indwelling is the cause of all sorts of extraordinary talents,[2] or even the Spirit mentioned in connexion with the incarnation of Christ, at least so far as a physical effect is there ascribed to Him,[3] even though, strictly speaking, a connexion with the Christian Church does exist here. Indeed, we even put aside the common way of speaking of the Holy Spirit as already active in the prophets before the appearance of Christ,[4] so as not to feel compelled to identify the common spirit of the Jewish theocracy and that of the Christian Church. And here, however much the letter of Scripture may seem to contradict us, the spirit of the New Testament is on our side. In Christ's promises of the Holy Spirit of truth [5] there is nowhere the slightest whisper that this Something had been present earlier and had vanished only temporarily, or indeed that He is anything at all except as He is for the disciples of Christ. Otherwise the disciples would obviously have been prophets, and Christ could hardly have said that prophecy ended with John.[6]

2. If now (provisionally leaving on one side what we have established in the two last propositions) we return to the point that in the Church from the beginning, and therefore already in the New Testament, all the powers at work in the Christian Church— and not merely the miraculous gifts, which in this connexion are quite accidental—are traced to the Holy Spirit ; [7] and if we ask what is thus supposed to have been present from the very start, the following admissions have to be made.

First, these powers are not to be found outside of the Christian Church, and hence they neither arise from the general constitution

---

[1] Gen. 1^2, Ps. 33^6 ; cf. Augustin., *de Gen. ad litt.* cap. 4.
[2] Ex. 31^{2-5}.   [3] Matt. 1^{18}, Luke 1^{35}.
[4] Isa. 34^{16} 61^1, Mic. 3^8.   [5] John $14^{16,17}$ 16^{7ff}.
[6] Matt. 11^{13}, Luke 16^{16}.   [7] 1 Cor. 12, Eph. 1^{17}, 2 Tim. 1^7.

of human nature (which would make Christ superfluous) nor from any other divine arrangement.[1] Second, this Spirit is not something supernatural and mysterious though not immediately divine, a higher yet created essence putting itself in secret ways into relation with men. The Church has properly rejected this in the same way and on the same grounds as all representations of Christ with an Arian bias. For as in Christ, too, the human would be no more human if we had to conceive it united with a higher nature in one person, so our own life and the life of other believers would no longer seem to be humanly interconnected if we had to conceive our consciousness and action as determined by the influence of a superhuman nature. Third, the Holy Spirit is not something that, although divine, is not united with the human nature, but only somehow influences it from without. For whatever enters us from without does so only through the senses and never becomes more than an occasion for our action. What action is to follow on this occasion is determined from within, and only this, and not the former region of the senses, is the sphere of the Holy Spirit. That occasions are given us from without does not preclude the unity of our self-consciousness and self-determination. But this unity would at once be dissolved if determinations were given from without. And if there are passages in Scripture largely influenced by prophetic language that in terms seem clearly to assert such an external influence,[2] these have the letter of other passages quite as definitely against them.[3] There is indeed no way of imagining how the Spirit's gifts could be within us,[4] and He Himself remain without, or how He is to influence us from without except through human speech and significant action—which just means that He is already within, and influencing, someone else. And the man *on* whom the Spirit works is not thereby made a participator in the Spirit. Only one *in* whom and *through* whom He works [5] has received the Spirit. Thus in everyone He brings His gifts to pass, and we are not conscious of the gifts as inward, but the power that effects them as outward: what we do is to distinguish him *on* whom the Holy Spirit is still at work, as thus being one in whom no gift is yet produced, from one within the state of sanctification, *in* whom the Holy Spirit is producing gifts.[6] Thus, as Scripture also says, we are conscious both of the Spirit and of His gifts as some-

---

[1] Gal. 3[2-5].   [2] Acts 1[5] 2[3] 8[29, 39] 10[19, 44].
[3] Mark 13[11], Rom. 8[9, 11], 1 Cor. 6[19], Gal. 4[6], Jas. 4[5].
[4] 1 Cor. 12[7].   [5] Acts 10[44-47].   [6] Gal. 5[22], Eph. 5[9].

thing inward ; of the gifts as being different in different individuals, but of the Spirit being one in different people in spite of the difference of gifts. This explains the testimony of the first possessors of the Holy Spirit, who describe Him as a specific divine efficacious working in believers, though not one to be separated from the recognition of the being of God in Christ. The two things are strictly interdependent. For if in the Person of Christ nothing divine had entered into human nature, while there were something divine in the gifts of the Holy Spirit, then this divine element could not proceed from Christ, but would have to be communicated individually in some utterly miraculous fashion. In that case, however, it would always be thus communicable, although, on account of the absolute arbitrariness of the proceeding, no such supposed possessor of the Spirit would be able to make any claim whatever to be recognized as such by others. Thus all reciprocal influence and co-operative activity would be abolished, and everyone who had the Spirit would have Him all by himself ; an idea that the Church repudiated from the very first as contradicting its self-consciousness. If, on the other hand, something divine did really enter human nature through Christ, but did not remain in human nature on earth after the disappearance of His Person, then nothing could remain in human nature of that which in Christ was dependent on the being of God in Him ; and so there would be no communication of the sinless perfection and untroubled blessedness of Christ.

3. That the testimony of the first disciples agrees with what has been stated in the two last propositions concerning our consciousness is clear ; and all that remains is to justify by means of both of them the language of the proposition we are now discussing. Now if the Holy Spirit is an effective spiritual power in the souls of believers, we must either represent Him as bound up with their human nature, or we shall have to surrender the unity of their being, if on the one hand they are such that in them human nature shows itself in operation, and on the other, such that in them the Holy Spirit is acting in separation from human nature. To adopt such a view would produce so entire a dualism within human life that it could never be maintained. The theory of a definite activity of the Holy Spirit has indeed been carried to this extreme, not, however, when this supposed activity was still taking place, but only long after it had ceased. All that remains to explain is the fact that this union is realized in the form of a

common spirit. Now everything (even in human nature viewed apart from redemption) that as spiritual power is absolutely the same in all individuals of a race and is incapable of any individualizing modification, and above all, reason, we regard as something not varied according to the individual, but as in all and in each the same. Now if we separate the Spirit from the gifts, which are of course individually modified and personal, then the Spirit is, in all who share in Him, one and the same, without being increased when the participants multiply, or being diminished when they grow fewer, and without being anything whatever in one that He is not in another ; except that, still being the same, He shows Himself stronger in one, and it may be weaker in another. He is, however, not only one in all in so far as His life and work in one cannot be distinguished from His life and work in another, but as already explained, because, as no one can attain the new life except in and through the fellowship, he has his share in the Holy Spirit, not in his personal self-consciousness viewed by itself, but only in so far as he is conscious of his being part of this whole—that is, he shares the Spirit as a common consciousness. Hence also the union of the divine with the human nature in believers is not a person-forming union, otherwise it would be indistinguishable from the union of the natures in Christ, and the distinction between Redeemer and redeemed would be lost. If we consider the individual as existing in an inborn and hereditary common life, no such distinction obtains there, as the formula stated above shows.[1] But if the reference be to the common life into which the individual only enters after his personality has reached a certain point of development, it cannot in that case be said that the personality is simply the common spirit taking a specific form, though more and more it comes to be just that. If we could isolate the new life of the individual that begins with regeneration and construct it by itself, then we should certainly be able to describe it as a life absolutely determined by the Holy Spirit, and the new creature would simply be the Holy Spirit Himself in conscious possession of this specific complex of natural human powers. But as a matter of fact, the new life is not a self-identical whole and does not uniformly penetrate the entire organism of the personality. On the contrary, the person, the continuous unity of self-consciousness, is a mingled separation and union of the divine and the human ; and even if someone were actually to reach the point of having the

[1] § 121, 2.

new life diffuse itself over his entire essence, yet the portion of his life spent before his regeneration would still form part of his personality. Finally, the divine activity constituting the new life in the individual is common spirit for this additional reason, that it is in each without regard to personal peculiarities, provided only he belongs to the fellowship through the influence of which his regeneration was conditioned, and out of which, by preaching in the widest sense of the word, this new life was transmitted to him, exactly as it took shape in the disciples through the power of the self-communicating life of Christ ; partly, too, because it only takes possession of the individual with a view to fellowship, and moulds him solely for one end—in order that, and in the manner that, it may best work through him for the whole.

§ 124. *Second Theorem.*—*Every regenerate person partakes of the Holy Spirit, so that there is no living fellowship with Christ without an indwelling of the Holy Spirit, and* vice versa.

1. Up to this point the question as to how redemption is realized in the human soul has been answered by saying that it happens through being taken up into living fellowship with Christ. Now the demand is made that everyone must partake of the Holy Spirit. This, however, is not at all to be understood as meaning that the experience is actually in two parts, and that some new and special thing happens to a regenerate person when he becomes a partaker in the Holy Spirit. Neither in fact nor in point of time are the two things to be distinguished, but in strictness we must say that everyone, as regenerate, also receives a share in the Holy Spirit. For being taken up into living fellowship with Christ includes at the same time being conscious both of our sonship with God and of the Lordship of Christ ; and both in Scripture are ascribed to the indwelling of the Holy Spirit.[1] We therefore cannot imagine how one could exist were the other absent. If, to indulge in a flight of fancy, we suppose that we could find ourselves placed in a similar common life representative of the Kingdom of God, and led by the Holy Spirit as its common spirit, with only this difference that we knew nothing of any such Founder as Christ is ; yet we should not, when contrasting that condition and the sinful common life, be able to derive the first from the second ; and at the same time, since in all the members of that common life sin, while not willed, is yet present, we should have to hold that the

---

[1] 1 Cor. 12³, Gal. 4⁶.

sinful common life is not something grounded within itself (that is to say, something such as it was in its first origin), for otherwise it must have been capable of originating in the same way also at other points. This, we remark in passing, is also the reason why those who start from so imperfect and partial a divine revelation always so easily recognize one another, even in their hostility. So long, therefore, as we do not admit that other similar kingdoms of God may arise independently of the Christian Church at other times or places, we are compelled to accept for it a single origin outside of the common life of sin, from which the divine communication found within it is derived. Membership in this common life therefore means at the same time being set within the sphere of operation of the sole Founder. Thus we find expressed the belief that such an outpouring of the Spirit would only have been possible after the appearance of the Son of God, and on the basis of His personal influence ; and this carries with it the implication that our participation in that Spirit and our own bond with the living influence of Christ are one and the same thing.

On the other side, the same thing holds good. If we begin with Christ and hold to the proposition that the union of the Divine with His human personality was at the same time an enrichment of human nature as a whole, it follows not only in general that even after His departure this union must continue, but also (since this continuation is to proceed from the union itself) that wherever it exists there must be a bond with Christ, and *vice versa*. And since after the departure of Christ the enlarged range of connexion with Him can only proceed from the fellowship of believers, these three facts—being drawn by that union into the fellowship of believers, having a share in the Holy Spirit, and being drawn into living fellowship with Christ—must simply mean one and the same thing.

2. In this connexion it is very natural to ask what is the relation between the two expressions used by the same apostle, that Christ liveth in us, and that we are led by the Spirit.[1] When the same Apostle says that those who are led by the Spirit are God's children, either he is contradicting (and that no one can believe) him who says that those who have received Christ are God's children, or else here too these two things, the life of Christ in us and the leading of the Holy Spirit in us, are one, both within that third thing, being children of God. Either there are two different kinds of children of God (which we should all deny as much as Paul or John), or else

[1] Gal. 2[20], Rom. 8[14].

these two things are the same.   If we are to answer the question
from the connexion in which the expressions are used in the Church,
we notice to begin with that the second is peculiar and characteristic
in a higher degree than the first, and has therefore obtained a
larger place in the language of the Schools and in the usage of
devotional religion which attributes special value to what is easily
understood.   On the other hand, the first is very far from prominent
in the language of the Schools, and has won a special place in the
devotional vocabulary usually known as 'mystical.'   Now, if we consider that the Holy Spirit is also called the Spirit of Christ, it follows
at once that we say more particularly in one context that the Spirit
of Another lives in us, and in a different context that the Other
Himself lives in us, without intending to mean anything different
by the two phrases.   Indeed, in any case nothing different could be
meant.   If we add the thought of the union of the Divine and the
human in Christ, obviously the human can be in us only as a rightly
apprehended picture or representation, but the Divine as a powerful
impulse, even although in us it does not, as in Him, exclusively
determine our whole personality, but only works in and along with
His rightly apprehended picture, which again can only take shape
in our minds in the measure of truth and perfection in which the
Divine glorifies it before our thought.   But just this is the work of
the Holy Spirit—to bring Christ into memory and glorify Him in us.
Thus however they are regarded, the two things are one and the same.

The same result is reached if we compare the content of the two
expressions with reference to the effects they indicate.   If we conceive ourselves as perfectly within the living fellowship of Christ,
then all our actions can be regarded as His.   But the Holy Spirit
also, when leading us through the knowledge of Christ into all
truth, cannot possibly lead us to any other actions than those in
which Christ can be recognized ; the fruits of the Spirit are therefore nothing but the virtues of Christ.   To recognize in our souls
any leading of the divine Spirit which could not be brought into
connexion with what Christ's words and life have conveyed to us
as His way of acting, is to open the door to every sort of visionary
fanaticism that the Protestant Church from the very start has most
steadily opposed.   The leading of the Holy Spirit is never other
than a divine incitement to realize the standard of what Christ, in
virtue of the being of God in Him, humanly was and did.   And the
life of Christ in us is nothing but activity in behalf of the Kingdom
of God which embraces men all together in the grasp of the love

flowing from Him ; that is, it is the power of the Christian common spirit.

From this it is also clear how, if to believe in Christ and to have Christ living in one are the same thing, it may be said on the one hand that the Holy Spirit produces faith, and on the other hand that the Holy Spirit comes through faith.[1] For through the activity of those who already have a share in the Spirit, He effects faith in others who are brought by them to recognize what is divine and saving in Christ ; in these, thereby, the Holy Spirit becomes the moving principle. And so, since the Divine Essence was bound up with the human person of Christ, but is now (His directly personal influence having ceased) no longer personally operative in any individual, but henceforward manifests itself actively in the fellowship of believers as their common spirit, this is just the way in which the work of redemption is continued and extended in the Church.

3. If then in content the two aforesaid expressions mean the same thing, we must not censure either those Christians who prefer to describe their experiences in the sphere of grace as the immediate being and life of Christ within them, nor those who rather (and almost exclusively) find the explanation of their new life in the indwelling of the Spirit of God. Dogmatic terminology is bound not only to keep both forms, but also to point out the appropriate way of using each, so as to indicate the dangers of a one-sided use ; and this in order that the former, believing themselves to enjoy the immediate influence of Christ, may not break away from the fellowship, or the latter fancy that the Spirit active in the fellowship could carry them on when severed from Christ or lead them beyond Him.

It is difficult, however, to leave this subject without raising the question whether the outpouring of the Spirit is to be conceived as a new divine revelation, and one which, although conditioned by the incarnation of Christ, yet in its characteristic nature is equally original, or whether it is not rather a fact not merely dependent on the appearance of Christ, but its natural consequence. In the latter case the appearance of Christ would be, in the sense already indicated, the one and only supernatural foundation of Christianity ; and following on this the whole further development of the spiritual life would issue naturally from that one source. In the former case, the original outpouring of the Spirit would be a second miracle of the same kind, and equally essential. The question is, of course, not one for Dogmatics in the narrowest sense,

[1] 1 Cor. 14³, Gal. 3⁵. ¹⁴.

since we cannot decide it from our Christian self-consciousness ; for to-day the communication of the Holy Spirit to the individual presents itself to each as a natural effect of the presence and activity of the Spirit in the whole formed by the Christian fellowship. But this implies that the acceptance of the former view would have to be based on quite irrefutable testimony. Now the phenomena of Pentecost [1] of course bear distinctly enough the mark of the miraculous. But, for one thing, later communications of the Spirit through preaching (and this is quite analogous to our present situation) are described in exactly the same way and with emphasis on the identity of the phenomena ; [2] so that in this case the miraculous does not belong to the essence of the matter, and we can argue thence that it did not at Pentecost either. On the other hand, it is difficult to assert that the Pentecostal outpouring was the first communication of the Spirit to the disciples, for we are told that already on an earlier occasion Christ had communicated the Spirit to them,[3] and neither the language used nor the treatment of it in the creeds permits us to regard it as a mere promise. On every account, therefore, we do well here to regard the miraculous as not of the essence of the matter but as belonging to the circumstances of the time, and leave the whole question to exegesis. But apart from these accompanying phenomena, the communication of the Spirit cannot be any more or less a miracle in one case than in another ; and in this connexion it may be said that while the gradual dissemination of the Spirit may be in no case a miracle, if regarded as the effect of the living power of the Church, and was no miracle when effected by the living power of Christ, it always is a miracle if regarded as a sudden leap from partially aroused susceptibility into a common and coherent spontaneous activity. As such it broke forth on the day of Pentecost, bearing in token of this originality the miraculous in its train ; and even to-day, in similar cases, the more conversion appears to be something sudden, the more are we inclined to regard anomalous accompanying circumstances as miraculous in character.

§ 125. *Third Theorem.—The Christian Church, animated by the Holy Spirit, is in its purity and integrity the perfect image of the Redeemer, and each regenerate individual is an indispensable constituent of this fellowship.*

1. Fixing our attention on the Redeemer in the maturity of His human life, we see in the totality of His powers an organism

---

[1] Acts 2²⁸·.   [2] Acts 10⁴⁷ 11¹⁵.   [3] John 20²².

adequate to the impulses proceeding from the being of God within Him. The individual as regenerate can never in this respect be regarded even as an image of Him, because the condition of varied sinfulness in which divine grace found him does not permit of an exact correspondence in the relationship of his psychical capacities to the impulses of the Spirit. But if the Christian Church is a true common life, a unified or, as we say, a moral personality though not indeed an inherited or natural one, it cannot on this latter account be the same as a personality arising from the person-forming activity of Nature, for in the two cases growth and decay are related in very different fashion ; but none the less it can and must be an image of such a personality. For since the Divine Essence is one and everywhere self-identical, then, even if its mode of being in the individual, Christ, and in the common life is not the same, it follows that the impulses proceeding from it must be the same in both cases. Hence the modes both of comprehension and of action are the same in the Church as in the Redeemer, because there are present in every member, and therefore in the whole, the very same powers which in Christ's case were taken up into unity with the divine principle. Such an aggregate of human powers in a certain sense exists in every organized mass of people, where the most important contrasts which human life offers are ordinarily found side by side. In the primitive Church, too, in spite of its limited size, the same truth was exemplified by the fact that it very quickly spread among Jews and pagans, and thus included what in this respect was the most significant contrast of all, with the result that thus every further development through the inclusion of minor contrasts was prepared for and introduced. If, however, we are seeking the image in its true perfection, we must regard the Church in its absolute purity and integrity. Manifestly we see its purity only if what we view as an element of the Church is not the entire life of regenerate individuals, even subsequently to regeneration, but only that in their life which constitutes its good works, and not that which belongs to its sins. It follows at once that the absolute integrity of the Church is only to be seen in the totality of the human race. For just as in the first pair (viewed as the common ancestors of all) there can be imagined no distinct differences of temperament or constitution simply because it was from them that all differences, whether climatic or more individual, were to develop, and therefore their perfect image is found only in the fundamental types of all human races taken

together, and of all the tribes into which they are subdivided—
which tribes again are completely represented only by the totality
of all the individual beings belonging to them—so too is it in regard
to Christ as the actually given spiritual archetype and original.
If we recall our explanations regarding His sinless perfection on the
one hand and the basis of the sinfulness of all others on the other
hand, it follows that each individual is not merely in each of his
individual characteristics an imperfect image ; even considered as
a whole he is an image of a one-sided and partial kind, which requires
to be supplemented on every side. From this it follows of itself
that the perfect image of Christ is only to be found in the sum-total
of all the forms of spiritual life based on the varieties of natural
foundation ; for it is only so that one-sided tendencies fully supplement each other, and the imperfections compatible with one are
cancelled by the others. We reach the same result if we regard the
work of Christ rather than His Person, and in that relation view the
Church as an organic body, equipped for a sum-total of activities
in which the perfection of each vital function is conditioned by the
integrity of the various members.[1] For various functions can be
properly apportioned only if the apportionment is based on a
variety of gifts, and this again, if it is to arise in a natural way,
presumes a variety present in the personal living unity. In this
way the two facts harmonize well, that the Church is called the
body of Christ, ruled by the Head,[2] and that the more it becomes
externally complete and inwardly perfect, the more it is also said
to become the image of Christ.[3]

2. From this there now follows the second half of our proposition. In reference to this last point it can indeed be said without
hesitation that everything any single person contributes by his
activity to the maintenance and growth of the whole can only be
replaced by the concurrence of several others, else Christ would
have been wrong in saying of each that he was all the same an
unprofitable servant.[4] Yet, in reference to what was said earlier,
in spite of all his imperfection and one-sidedness every individual,
as a subordinate unit in the whole, is a part irreplaceable by any
other. For even in the sphere of the new man there are several
fundamental forms, corresponding to what are national peculiarities in the natural man ; and each of these fundamental types
includes a multitude of subordinate varieties which we can neither
count nor measure, but which nevertheless our Christian senti-

[1] 1 Cor. 12. [2] Eph. 1²³, Col. 1¹⁹. [3] Eph. 4¹³, 1 John 3². [4] Luke 17¹⁰.

ment (just as in the natural sphere our race-consciousness does) compels us to regard as integral and each a whole by itself. And for this we find a justification not only in the Biblical figures already cited, but also in the recognition we are commanded to give all such peculiarities, without limit or exception.[1] Accordingly, we must say also of the development of the Christian fellowship in time that nothing would happen in the Church as it does, unless each individual were what he is. With this is connected the fact that everything in it is common action and common work, therefore common merit and common guilt ; not manifested in individuals, however, in quite the same ways. Accordingly, the Church only gradually attains to be the perfect image of Christ, and the divine ordinance seen in the gradual addition of individual members and the widening compass of the whole can be expressed in the formula that the advance comes about in such a way that not only is the whole, at every particular moment viewed by itself, as complete and inclusive as possible, but also each moment contains within itself a basis for the largest possible integration in the moment succeeding. At the same time this is only grasped by faith and can never be proved by experience.

Postscript to this Division.—The immediately foregoing discussion concludes our treatment of the many points that have emerged, some of them indirectly related to the previous doctrine, others directly ; a parallel having been shown to exist between the relations of the doctrine of regeneration to the present doctrine and to the preceding one, there can be nothing strange in our thus grouping them together under one Division. Rather it must appear quite natural that the elect are elected to receive the communication of the Spirit. At the same time, this discussion forms the transition to the next Division. In the present Division, we could mention no more than the communication of the Holy Spirit ; in the next, since the Church can be preserved only by the same principle to which it owes its origin and renewal, the continuous operation of the Holy Spirit will be described as we deal with the fundamental features of the Church's life. What will then be set forth will be identical with the content of the doctrine of sanctification in the same sense that the subject-matter just treated of is identical with the content of the doctrine of regeneration.

[1] I Cor. 12[19-26].

§ 126. *The fellowship of believers, animated by the Holy Spirit,
remains ever self-identical in its attitude to Christ and to
this Spirit, but in its relation to the world it is subject to
change and variation.*

1. If the fellowship of believers, as an historical body within
the human race, is to exist and persist in continuous activity, it
must unite in itself two things—a self-identical element, whereby
it remains the same amid change, and a mutable element, in which
the identity finds expression.   If we consider it merely in its co-
existence with the rest of contemporary human life, summarily
described in Scripture as ' the world,' we might apparently say
that the Church can just as well be known by its difference from
the world as the world can by its difference from the Church.   And
certainly amongst believers there are not wanting those who think
that they and their like are recognizable chiefly from the fact that
they are not what the world is.   This, however, is a view inclining
equally to separatism and to legalistic righteousness.   For the
sinful common life, with the exception of the feeling of need surviving in the mass of men (a feeling which constitutes the Church's
elemental claim upon the world and strictly is characteristic of
the Church itself), is really nullity and a purely negative thing ; as
has been made sufficiently clear by our whole account of sin.[1]
Hence it is quite true that the world, as being formless and confused, can be recognized by believers from the fact that it is excluded from a share in the being of the Church.   But the converse
does not hold.   The usage of Scripture in entitling ' world ' that
part of the human race which is not yet Church is very natural,
for the whole human race had been so described, and this particular
part only remained what the whole had always been ; unfortunately, however, it may easily give rise to the impression that the
world in this sense is as much a whole as the Church is.   Whereas,
in fact, it is only an aggregate of individual elements which in many
respects are antagonistic to each other, and which unite only in
accidental and temporary ways.   This erroneous impression is
only heightened when the Church, as it confronts the world, is
constantly described as a ' little flock '—that is, as also being on
its side an aggregate, and one of no importance.   It would therefore be best that this use of the term ' world ' should disappear

[1] §§ 65 ff.

from the devotional field and be kept for the field of Dogmatics, where its true significance can be more easily defined and conserved.

The self-identity of the Christian Church, however, can cover no more than the fact that the mode in which the divine exists in the human ever remains the same, and that the goal also remains the same to which the Church throughout all its movements is seeking to approximate. In Christ also the union of the divine with the human was ever the same ; and, since in His case there can be no question of approximation, the adaptation of what in Him underwent human development to the divine impulse in Him was the same too ; but all else was determined in accordance with the laws of the temporal by His position in the world. Similarly, the relation of the Holy Spirit to the Church as its common spirit remains the same, and the Church is ever self-identical as the *locus* of the Spirit in the human race, as also in this further respect that it is always to the same likeness of Christ that the Church is striving to be conformed.

Turning to the mutable, however, we note that even in Christ, though strife and conflict were absent, this element was not as such determined by the divine in Him—the divine being incapable of any temporal determination—but by the human nature conjoined to it. So, too, in the case of the Church, the mutable as such is not determined by the Holy Spirit but by human nature, on which and through which the Spirit works. Now if we apply the term ' world ' to human nature in the whole extent in which it is not determined by the Holy Spirit, we may also say that everything mutable in the Church is as such determined by the world, but not uniformly. For whatever has been or is gradually being realized in man through the Holy Spirit is as it is because the world, operated on by the Holy Spirit, was as it was. In all gifts of the Spirit there is re-cognizable a definite basis in human nature, causing it inevitably to take the form it does, and throughout the entire development of the new man the kind and the degree of progress depends on the development of nature in the person concerned and on the char-acter of his environment. Similarly, the form which the Christian fellowship takes in a particular nation depends on that nation's peculiar characteristics, for otherwise no reason could be found in the Holy Spirit why it should impress on the Christian fellowship different forms in different places. All this has its ground of determination in the world owing to the law that Christianity must develop as a force in history, and the world as it appears in Christianity is the world as it has been seized upon and permeated by the Holy Spirit. On the other hand, everything that exists within the Church because it is found in those through whom the Holy Spirit works, yet is not due to the Spirit's action, is determined by the world as opposed to the Spirit, and represents the encroachment of the world upon the Church's sphere. This includes not merely what may in a stricter sense be called the sins of the regenerate, but also every hampering and distorting influence which their sinfulness opposes to the Holy Spirit's action, as well as all mistaken and perverse elements that may find their way into the religious consciousness. Now it is true that all such things are in process of disappearing, but they constantly revive as often as the Holy Spirit takes possession of a new field ; just as both things, the signs of having been apprehended by the Spirit and of resistance thereto, are equally found in the sphere of the preparatory operations of grace. The same is true of such differences in the Christian fellowship as are due to the diversities of human nature. Not only is what arises thence, in consequence of the sinfulness persisting in the Church, destined to disappear, but the closer the fellowship is the more will each seek what is his neighbour's and take it up into his own life, with the natural result that differences are correspondingly lessened. But while this happens more or less in each generation, the next is none the less confronted by an undiminished task.

2. If the self-identical element in the Christian Church be considered simply by itself, as something which in a way may be regarded as a manifold, it forms the subject of the disciplines of Christian Dogmatics and Christian Ethics. For if we wish to exhibit that likeness of Christ to which we are ever more striving to approximate, we find it in the outlines of the Christian life laid down in the latter discipline, including as one of its integral parts the development of the Christian consciousness. And if we wish to exhibit the self-identity of the Christian Church as the *locus* of the Holy Spirit, we must present it as inclusive of the truth into which the Holy Spirit alone can lead. Both, however, can only be presented with differences of time and space ; so that all we can say is that in these disciplines and their adjuncts what we are really trying to express is this self-identical element, yet for this purpose we have only these variable means of expression. The same, however, holds true of all aspects of Christian life, in so far as they are based on the truth taught by the Spirit and contain features of Christ's likeness. But the totality of these aspects is just the historical reality of the

Christian Church throughout its whole career, and to this we should have to resort for material if we wished to exhibit the changing and mutable element ; and this we cannot do without at the same time bringing in what is unchanging and self-identical. This is the more evident because the efforts which give rise to these varying forms of Dogmatics and Ethics are all themselves a minor part of the Church's history. Thus neither element can be exhibited apart from the other. If the attempt were made to set forth the self-identical and invariable element in Christianity in complete abstraction from the historical, it would scarcely be distinguishable from the undertaking of people who imagine that they are expounding Christianity when in point of fact what they offer is pure speculation. And if anyone tried to present solely the variable in Christian history in complete abstraction from the self-identical, his aim would apparently be the same as that of people who, penetrating no further than the outer husk of things, permit us to see in the history of the Church nothing but the complex and pernicious play of blinded passion.

The two aspects or elements, then, cannot be exhibited apart from each other without making the real nature of the Church unrecognizable ; on the other hand, we cannot here treat of both together in the way just indicated. Consequently, in the doctrine of the Church in its coexistence with the world, we can only state first those chief activities through the continuous exercise of which the temporal development of this whole really becomes the development of the Christian Church, and which thus form its essential and invariable features. Thereafter we shall treat of those characteristics of the fellowship whereby during its coexistence with the world it is distinguishable from that which it can only become even in appearance after this hampering antithesis between Church and world has passed away, but which—as being the same under both forms—inwardly viewed it already is. The former invariable element is due to the fact that the Church can only persist and reach its perfection through that to which it owes its very existence ; the latter variable element, however, being conditioned by the world, is chiefly traceable to the material which the world offers to the instreaming influence of the principle by which the Church is constituted. This division of the subject, therefore, falls into two halves—one of which comprises the essential and (in spite of its co-existence with the world) immutable features of the Church, while the other sets forth the mutable element which belongs to the Church in virtue of its coexistence with the world.

First Half: The Essential and Invariable Features of the Church

§ 127. *The Christian fellowship, in spite of the mutability inseparable from its coexistence with the world, is, nevertheless, always and everywhere self-identical, inasmuch, first, as the witness to Christ remains in it ever the same, and this is found in* Holy Scripture *and in the* Ministry of the Word of God ; *inasmuch, secondly, as the formation and maintenance of living fellowship with Christ rests upon the same ordinances of Christ, and these are* Baptism *and the* Lord's Supper ; *inasmuch, finally, as the reciprocal influence of the whole on the individual, and of individuals on the whole, is always uniformly ordered, and this is seen in the* Power of the Keys *and in* Prayer in the Name of Jesus.

1. To begin with, we must put aside the objection which asks how the unity and identity of the Church can rest upon these features, every one of which is a subject of controversy, several of which indeed have assumed such different forms in different parts of Christendom as to give rise to special and mutually exclusive communions, while others are totally rejected by particular communions which still claim to be recognized as Christian. In the first place, this is merely a very direct confirmation of what was said above, namely, that it is impossible to exhibit either of the two elements wholly apart from the other. Nay, if we go by what was indicated in the Introduction regarding the relations between Catholicism and Protestantism, it will seem entirely natural that on almost all these subjects Evangelical teaching must find itself in opposition to Roman. The same is true of several smaller communions which in essence certainly are Protestant, and which in their antagonism to the Roman Church leave us far behind. But here we must distinguish between what is inward and what is outward. For no Christian communion will admit that any such body can exist apart from witness to Christ, in the sense that what is essential in such witness must everywhere be the same, any more than it could exist without a continuous living fellowship with Christ, implying a bond between the changing generations due to

their sharing the newly arisen life.   Further, wherever it is possible
to speak of a perfect fellowship resting upon a common spirit, we
must also assume a reciprocal influence of the whole and individuals
on each other.   In part, therefore, differences only concern the way
in which the outward is conformed to the inward ; in part they
consist in varying ideas as to the necessity and exact character of
the connexion which must always exist between the inward and an
outward possessing some particular form or other.   With regard
to these differences, the most important point is this, that we should
judge correctly whether they are rooted in the spatial and temporal
variations found in man's spiritual nature, or are to be viewed as
defects, because due to encroachments of the world upon the
Church.   The latter sort are to be resisted the more stoutly in proportion as such encroachments invade the innermost sanctuary of
the Church ; the former cancel each other where there is mutual
recognition.

2. Thereafter some explanations will have to be given of the
relationships in which the Church institutions named above are
placed in our statement, and the way in which they are combined.
If we start from the principle that our Christianity ought to be the
same as that of the Apostles, our Christianity too must be generated
by the personal influences of Christ, for spiritual states depend on
the mode of their origination.   These influences, however, cannot
now emanate from Him directly, for in that case they could not
be recognized with such certainty as having emanated from Him
supernaturally as to need no confirmatory proof of their identity
with those felt by the Apostles, to which, as we have them in the
New Testament representations of Christ's personality, we have
always to return.   Apart from these influences no activity for the
Kingdom of God could have been evoked even in the disciples by
the imparting of the Holy Spirit ; hence the influence of these representations of Christ will always be an indispensable pre-condition
of the Holy Spirit being imparted.   This principle, it is true,
scarcely appears to cover the whole of the New Testament, nor need
all that is taught on the subject be developed from it.   But leaving
this last point to be dealt with later, on the former it may be said
that for the purpose stated not even the fixed written letter of the
New Testament appears to be necessary ; the further possibility of
oral propagation must be admitted, for no more can be guaranteed
than the unimpaired identity of the tradition.   And so far we can
agree that the actual form in which the personality of Christ is set

before us does not belong unconditionally to the *esse* but rather to the *bene esse* of the Church. As regards the larger and not strictly evangelistic part of the New Testament writings, they furnish proof on the one hand that the Church-forming self-activity which He promised to men really flowed from the impressions left by Christ Himself and from the witness He bade the disciples give ; and in this sense they are the source of what we now possess. On the other hand, they form a supplement to those direct utterances of Christ ; for we can argue back from the ordinances and actions of the disciples to teachings and injunctions of Christ as their source. Scripture, however, as we actually have it—each single book and the whole collection as a treasure preserved for all later generations of the Church—is invariably a work of the Holy Spirit as the common spirit of the Church, and is only one special instance of the witness to Christ described in general terms in the paragraph we are expounding. For oral and written teaching and narrative concerning Christ were originally the same, and only differed by accident. Scripture now stands by itself, for its preservation unchanged guarantees in a special manner the identity of our witness to Christ with that originally given. Yet it would be a mere lifeless possession if this preservation were not an ever-renewed self-activity of the Church, which reveals itself also in living witness to Christ that either goes back to Scripture or harmonizes with Scripture in meaning and spirit. And this witness alone, taken universally as the duty and calling of every member of the Church—and viewed provisionally apart from definite forms of any kind—is what is understood here by the phrase ' the Ministry of the Word of God.' But taken in this general sense and thus related to each other, these two first features of the Church are essential ; for otherwise faith could only be evoked by direct influences [of Christ], in which case we could look for no identity and could have no guarantee of truth. This Ministry, however, by no means acts only on the outside world ; in its operation within the Church equally it is an organic structure, traceable to Christ Himself, for the communication of life and power.

For the same reason, namely, that we have nothing more to expect from unmediated personal influences of Christ, the linking-up of living fellowship with Christ, and its renewal, must come from the Church and be traceable to its actions ; but only to such actions as must also be regarded as activities of Christ—lest Christ should be thought to play a merely passive rôle, and be overshadowed by the Church. And this communal character is the peculiarity of both sacraments. For although baptism as originally instituted was not the first beginning of contact between the Church and the individual, yet it is only through baptism that all that precedes receives such confirmation as thereby to inaugurate a continuous and conscious living fellowship with Christ. And while the Lord's Supper is not the only means of maintaining living fellowship with Christ—and provisionally we are not regarding it here as an isolable action which even in isolation has a specific effect—yet we take it as being the highest of its kind, and subsume under it every other enjoyment of Christ as either an approximation to it or a prolongation of it. Hence we here keep more to this underlying idea than to outward forms in which the idea is realized.

In like manner, the entire influence of the whole fellowship on the individual is concentrated in the forgiveness of sin. For in view of the relationship obtaining between the sins of the regenerate and their good works, these last can be recognized only in the measure in which the sin still clinging to them is removed. But good works are at once the fruit and the seed of the gifts of the Spirit developing in each life, so that the forgiveness of sin first assigns them their place in the fellowship of believers. Finally, as regards Prayer in the Name of Jesus, representing as it does the influence of individuals on the whole, apart from which a whole animated by a common spirit and in that sense self-contained could manifest no progress—there can be no Prayer in the Name of Jesus except in connexion with the things of His Kingdom. Hence its efficacy, promised by Christ even to the smallest gathering of individuals, secures their influence upon the whole. If we regard such prayer as representing all influences of the kind, this rests on the assumption, self-evident to every Christian, that prayer necessarily includes and presupposes personal activity in bringing about what is prayed for. Thus without the two last-named features, there could be in the common life neither order nor progress and success.

3. That we have here given a complete view of the elements on which the unity and identity of the Christian Church rest in every time and place is best seen if we recur to the relation of the Church to Christ. On the one hand, as the organism of Christ—which is what Scripture means by calling it His Body—it is related to Christ as the outward to the inward, so that in its essential activities it must also be a reflection of the activities of Christ. And since the effects produced by it are simply the gradual realization

of redemption in the world, its activities must likewise be a continuation of the activities of Christ Himself. These we have reduced to the scheme of the Threefold Office ; and in the same way
it must be possible to show that the three offices of Christ are
reflected and carried on in the essential activities of the Church
as stated above.

Prayer in the Name of Jesus, embracing as it does the full
vocational activity of each individual Christian, is a reflection of
Christ's kingly activity, both as it is in itself and as concerns the
relation between His rule and that of the Father. It is the latter,
inasmuch as it concludes with the reverently submissive utterance
of the thoughts of each regarding the extension of the Kingdom of
God or the assaults of the world. It is the former, inasmuch as it
comprehends all purposes flowing from the energies of the God-
consciousness. And in the Power of the Keys there is attached to
the forgiveness of sins, rightly understood, all that has to do with
Church order and the estimate of persons in the Church which flows
from the common consciousness. Thus we have here the continuation of that kingly activity of Christ which began with His choice
of the disciples and His giving of ordinances for the fellowship that
was to be.

Further, since the prophetic activity of Christ consists in His
self-presentation and His invitation to enter the Kingdom of God,
the Holy Scriptures are the permanent reflection of His prophetic
activity, inasmuch as in their composition and preservation, regarded as the work of the Church, they form the most direct exhibition of Christ. The Ministry of the Word we cannot but regard as
also a continuation of His prophetic work, for it essentially consists
in the applied presentation of Christ and invitation in His name.

If, finally, the essential element in Christ's priestly office—to
distinguish this as clearly as possible from the prophetic and kingly
offices—lies supremely in this, that He mediates the fellowship of
men with God, there will be no difficulty in acknowledging that
both sacraments have a relation thereto. In this sense, that baptism
owing to its more symbolical character is related more as a reflection,
the Lord's Supper owing to its more real content as a continuation.

This arrangement also shows that everything essentially belonging to Christ's activity has its reflection and continuation in the
Church, for the first three features pertain to His redemptive, the
other three to His reconciling, activity. Nor in our Evangelical
interpretation of Christianity shall we have to indicate any other

feature of the Church which could claim to stand on the same level as these institutions. On the contrary, we shall neither place tradition beside Scripture nor subordinate the Ministry of the Word to any kind of symbolical rites ; we shall neither acquiesce in the multiplication of sacraments nor by attributing magical effects to them destroy the analogy they bear to the other features of the Church ; we shall neither limit Prayer in the Name of Jesus by invocation of the saints nor permit any special representation of Christ—whether individual or collegial—to usurp the place of the Power of the Keys.

First Doctrine : Holy Scripture

§ 128. *The authority of Holy Scripture cannot be the foundation of faith in Christ ; rather must the latter be presupposed before a peculiar authority can be granted to Holy Scripture.*

1. The polemical first part of this proposition is solely due to the fact that what we here deny is actually asserted. Possibly as a matter of fact it is more widely held than definitely stated, for all text-books and Confessions which put the doctrine of Scripture as the source of Christian faith in the foreground seem distinctly to favour this view. Hence it is necessary thoroughly to expose the underlying misconception. If faith in Jesus as the Christ or as the Son of God and the Redeemer of men is to be based on the authority of Scripture, the question arises how this authority itself is to be based ; for obviously the thing must be so done as to impress the conviction on unbelieving hearts, so that they too may by this path come to faith in the Redeemer. Now if we have no point of departure but ordinary reason, the divine authority of Scripture to begin with must admit of being proved on grounds of reason alone ; and as against this two points must be kept in mind. First, this always involves a critical and scientific use of the understanding of which not all are capable ; on this theory, therefore, only those so gifted can attain to faith in an original and genuine way, while all others would merely have faith at second-hand and on the authority of the experts. Now even in the sphere of faith we might accept such a graded distinction if we were speaking of insight into doctrine or a correct judgment upon different doctrinal interpretations ; but to accept it with regard to the possession of genuinely saving faith is incongruous with that equality of all Christians which the Evangelical Church proclaims, and would, as in the Church

of Rome, demand from the laity an unqualified and submissive trust in those who alone have access to the grounds of faith. For the right to the Word of God, which we grant to all Christian people, and the zeal with which we seek to maintain it in vital circulation, has nothing to do with the idea that each individual ought to be able to prove that the books of Scripture contain a divine revelation. Secondly, if such proof could be given and if faith could be established in this fashion—if, that is to say, faith, given a certain degree of culture, could be implanted by argument—then on such terms faith might exist in people who feel absolutely no need of redemption, that is quite apart from repentance and change of mind ; which means that, having originated in this way, it would not be genuine, living faith at all. In other words, a conviction of this kind, gained through demonstrative proof, would in itself have no value, for of itself it would not result in true living fellowship with Christ. But where the need of redemption is really felt, the faith that makes alive may spring even from a message about Christ which is in no way bound up with the conviction that the books of Scripture possess a special character, but may rest on any other sort of witness that is accompanied by real perception of Christ's spiritual power—may rest, that is, simply on oral tradition.

2. With respect to the grounds of faith, then, we can admit no distinction between different classes. And no more can we admit a distinction between different periods of time ; the grounds of faith must be the same for us as for the first Christians. If it be said that in their case, from the Apostles onward, their grounds of faith sprang from their belief in Scripture, that is, in the Old Testament and especially in the prophecies of Christ it contains, we need only add to what was said above on this point that although the Apostles, at the outset of their connexion with Jesus, do describe Him as the Figure whom the prophets foretold, it is impossible to take this as meaning that they had been led to faith in Him by the study of these prophecies and by the comparison of their contents with what they saw and heard in Jesus. On the contrary, it was a direct impression which awakened faith in souls prepared by the testimony of the Baptist, and their description of Jesus was only an expression of this faith combined with their faith in the prophets. Even in their preaching they took the same line. There they first express their faith communicatively by recurring to Jesus' words and deeds ; then they adduce prophetic testimonies in confirmation,

And just as their faith sprang from Christ's preaching of Himself, so in the case of others faith sprang from the preaching of Christ by the Apostles and many more. The New Testament writings are such a preaching come down to us, hence faith springs from them too ; but in no sense conditionally on the acceptance of a special doctrine about these writings, as having had their origin in special divine revelation or inspiration. On the contrary, faith might arise in the same way though no more survived than testimonies of which it had to be admitted that, in addition to Christ's essential witness to Himself and the original preaching of His disciples, they also contained much in detail that had been misinterpreted, or inaccurately grasped, or set in a wrong light owing to confusions of memory.

Thus, in order to attain to faith, we need no such doctrine of Scripture, and the attempt to force unbelievers into faith by means of it has had no success. It follows that, just as the Apostles already had faith before they arrived at that condition of mind, other than faith itself, in which they were able to take a share in producing the New Testament, in our case too faith must preexist before, by reading the New Testament, we are led to postulate a special condition of the apostolic mind in which its books were written, and a resulting special character of the books themselves. A doctrine of this kind can only be made credible to those who already are believers.

3. Hence throughout the whole of the foregoing exposition of faith we have assumed no more than faith itself, present in a feeling of need (in whatever source that feeling may have originated), and Scripture we have adduced only as expressing the same faith in detail ; and it is only now that for the first time we are treating of Scripture in its natural connexion with the Christian Church and considering the question of its difference from other books. None the less, the old method, whether used in Confessions or in text-books, of placing the doctrine of Scripture first is not wholly censurable, if by Scripture proof of doctrine nothing more be meant than showing that a proposition so proved gives expression to an original and authentic element in Christian piety, and if precautions be taken to avoid the impression that a doctrine must belong to Christianity because it is contained in Scripture, whereas in point of fact it is only contained in Scripture because it belongs to Christianity. Were we to rest content with the former position, Dogmatic Theology would continue to be a mere aggregate

of detached propositions, the inner connexion of which was left obscure. Either, its relation to the common faith of the Church would then be what has already been indicated ; true and complete certainty of faith would only exist where there was ability to prove the divinity of Scripture, while all who lacked this degree of scientific culture would believe simply on authority ; and thus piety would spring from, and depend on, science. Or, where the laity break away and base their faith on their experience, rejoicing in its vitality, the scientific exposition of faith would become something which, for the fellowship of the Church, is empty and worthless. Hence for the purpose of our argument it was important to get its true aim quite clear, independently of Scripture ; and only to bring in the doctrine of Scripture at a point where its proper authority can be plainly seen to rest on the relation between the self-identical and the mutable and in its true connexion with the other essential features of the Church.

§ 129. *The Holy Scriptures of the New Testament are, on the one hand, the first member in the series, ever since continued, of presentations of the Christian Faith ; on the other hand, they are the norm for all succeeding presentations.*

1. That the Holy Scriptures are the first member in the series in question implies that the succeeding members are homogeneous with the first ; and this holds true alike of form and content. The New Testament writings are usually divided into historical and doctrinal books ; this, however, is really correct only if the division is based not on the subject-matter preponderant in each case, but on the outward form. In the historical books the discourses of Christ and the Apostles form a very important part, and the apostolic letters with few exceptions are only intelligible in so far as either they contain historical elements or we can form from them a picture of the historical situation. Whether we retain this division or discard it and look more at the form of particular elements in these books, we can only say that all that has approved itself in the way of oral presentation of Christian piety in later ages of the Church has kept within the lines of these original forms, or is attached to them as an explanatory accompaniment. Even religious poetry, in the lyrical form which alone is genuinely churchly, has its germ in the New Testament ; on the other hand, all explanatory and systematizing works, which as presentations of Christian piety have less originality and independence, are only aids to the under-

standing of the original testimonies or compilations drawn from them.

As regards content, however, the general rule is first of all to be applied that in every kind of fellowship the individual element approves itself only in so far as it gives expression to the common spirit. Here too, accordingly, everything of the kind which persists in influence alongside of Holy Scripture we must regard as homogeneous with Scripture ; while nothing that does not persist can be given a place in the series.

2. But if in the historical development of the Christian Church redemption is being ever more completely realized in time, and the Holy Spirit is thus pervading the whole ever more perfectly, it looks as if the first of this or any other series cannot be the norm for all succeeding members ; for in any such development each later member must be more perfect than the preceding. There is truth in this, but only when we are comparing two whole phases of the development, each in its entirety. If we consider the Church during the Apostolic Age as a unity, its thinking as a whole cannot supply a norm for that of later ages. For owing to its naturally most unequal distribution of the divine Spirit, as well as to the further fact that not everyone was equally productive in religious ideas even in the measure of his participation in the common spirit, it was very easily possible (since Jewish and pagan views and maxims were still uneradicated and their antagonism to the Christian spirit could only be recognized gradually) that expositions of religion might be produced which, strictly speaking, were rather Judaism or paganism coloured by Christianity than Christianity itself, *i.e.* were, if considered as Christian, in the highest degree impure. Contemporary with all this very imperfect material, however, were the presentations given in preaching by the immediate disciples of Christ. In their case, the danger of an unconsciously debasing influence from their previous Jewish forms of thought and life on the presentation of Christianity by word and act was averted, in proportion as they had stood near to Christ, by the purifying influence of their living memory of Christ as a whole. Thereby every idea which had attained that clearness in consciousness which must precede oral exposition, was at once forced to betray any antagonism it might have to the spirit of Christ's life and teaching. This holds good, in the first place, of their narratives of Christ's words and deeds, which fixed the standard that was to have the widest purifying influence. But it

also holds pre-eminently of all that the Apostles taught and ordained
for Christian churches, as acting in Christ's name ; though it must
not be forgotten that even when acting merely as individuals, each
of them found not only his complement but his corrective in one
of the other Apostles.[1] Thus in the Apostolic Age what is most
perfect and what is most imperfect stood side by side as *canonical*
and *apocryphal* (both these words taken in the sense indicated by
the discussion above)—two extremes which can never reappear in
the same form in any later age.   Church presentations of Christianity could not but diverge ever more widely from the apocryphal,
since the influence of foreign elements on the Church decreased—
even though in matters of detail there were ever new accretions
from the realm of Judaism—in proportion as the bulk of Christians
came to be born and nurtured in the bosom of the Church.   On the
other hand, the Church could never again reproduce the canonical,
for the living intuition of Christ was never again able to ward off
all debasing influences in the same direct fashion, but only deriva-
tively through the Scriptures and hence in dependence on them.
If then we take both together—canonical and apocryphal—the
Apostolic Age itself comes under the general rule ; the influence of
the canonical evidently becomes surer and wider as the apocryphal
disappears even in outlying parts of the Church ; thus viewed as a
whole, the later presentation is also the more perfect.   On the other
hand, if we take the canonical by itself, it has an authority normative
for all later times.   Such authority we do not ascribe uniformly
to every part of our Holy Scriptures, but only in proportion as the
writers attained to the condition just described, so that casual
expressions and what are merely side-thoughts do not possess the
same degree of normativeness as belongs to whatever may at each
point be the main subject.   Nor is it meant that every later presentation must be uniformly derived from the Canon or be germin-
ally contained in it from the first.   For since the Spirit was poured
out on all flesh, no age can be without its own originality in Christian
thinking.   Yet, on the one hand, nothing can be regarded as a pure
product of the Christian Spirit except so far as it can be shown to
be in harmony with the original products ; on the other, no later
product possesses equal authority with the original writings
when it is a question of guaranteeing the Christian character
of some particular presentation or of exposing its unchristian
elements.

[1] Cf. Gal. 2[11ff.].

§ 130. *First Theorem.—The individual books of the New Testament
are inspired by the Holy Spirit, and the collection of them
took place under the guidance of the Holy Spirit.*

Conf. Helv. i.: Scriptura canonica, verbum Dei Spiritu s. tradita et . . .
mundo proposita, etc.—*Conf. Gall.* v.: Credimus verbum his libris compre-
hensum ab uno Deo esse profectum.—*Conf. Scot.* xviii.: Spiritus dei per
quem s. scripturae litteris sunt mandatae.—*Conf. Belg.* iii.: Confitemur
sanctos Dei viros divino afflatos spiritu locutos esse. Postea vero Deus
. . . servis suis mandavit, ut sua illa oracula scriptis consignarent.—*Decl.
Thor.*: Profitemur . . . nos amplecti sacras canonicas . . . scripturas . . .
instinctu spiritus s. primitus scriptas, etc.

1. It is not easy to assign exact limits of meaning to the ecclesiastical term ' inspiration ' in general, and here we merely wish to
make some preliminary observations before entering on a special
discussion of the subject. The word $\theta\epsilon\acuteo\pi\nu\epsilon\upsilon\sigma\tau\sigma$, which is used of
the Old Testament writings,[1] and which historically constitutes the
most definite basis of usage, may very easily lead to a conception
of the Holy Spirit as occupying a relation to the writer which has
special reference to the act of writing but is otherwise non-existent.
This suggestion attaches less to the phrase $\upsilon\pi\grave{o}$ $\pi\nu\epsilon\acute\upsilon\mu\alpha\tau\sigma$ $\acute\alpha\gamma\acutei\sigma\upsilon$
$\phi\epsilon\rho\acuteo\mu\epsilon\nu\sigma\iota$.[2] Here the interpretation that these men were always
so ' moved,' speaking and writing in what was thus a permanent
state, is in itself quite as natural as one to the effect that they were
only ' moved ' to speak and write. Since the ecclesiastical term
is not strictly scriptural and is, besides, figurative, it is necessary
to define it by relation to cognate terms, which also describe ways
of arriving at ideas. Here on the one side what is known by
inspiration along with what is learnt stands over against what is
excogitated, the latter being that which proceeds entirely from a
man's own activity as contrasted with what is due to influence
coming from without. On the other side, again, stands what is
known by inspiration in contrast to what is learnt ; the latter is
derived from external communication, while the former, being as it
is original in the eyes of others, depends for its emergence solely on
inward communication. Hence the presentation of what has been
learnt may approximate to any extent to the merely mechanical,
whereas in the forthcoming of what is known by inspiration there
may be manifested the whole freedom of personal productivity.

The general custom of calling Holy Scripture as such ' Revelation,' however, leads frequently to the two ideas being treated as

[1] 2 Tim. 3[16].   [2] 2 Pet. 1[21].

interchangeable, which cannot fail to produce confusion. For if this is taken to mean that the sacred writers, being under inspiration, were informed of the content of what they wrote in a special divine manner, there is no foundation for any such statement, whether we consider the act of composing a sacred book itself or the excitation of thought preceding or underlying it. All that they teach derives from Christ ; hence in Christ Himself must be the original divine bestowal of all that the Holy Scriptures contain— not, however, in isolated particulars, by way of inspiration, but as a single indivisible bestowal of knowledge out of which the particulars evolve organically. Thus the speaking and writing of the Apostles as moved by the Spirit was simply a communication drawn from the divine revelation in Christ.

Our paragraph, however, ascribes to the Holy Spirit not merely the composition of the individual books, but also their collection to form the New Testament Canon, and in referring to the latter point it employs a different expression. This distinction is primarily due to the fact that we regard the composition of a book as the voluntary act of an individual, whereas the formation of the Canon is the result of a many-sided collaboration and controversy within the Church ; so that it becomes impossible to ascribe uniformly to the Holy Spirit all the factors contributing thereto. These two expressions will not be interpreted by everyone precisely in our sense ; some will be content to assert merely a guiding influence of the Spirit even in the matter of composition ; others will hold that even in the collection of the books the influence of the Spirit amounted to inspiration.

2. If now we go back to the conception of the Holy Spirit as the common spirit of the Church, and hence the source of all spiritual gifts and good works, it follows that all thinking, so far as it pertains to the Kingdom of God, must be traced back to and inspired by the Spirit. This holds good of the thinking of the Apostolic Age as inclusive of the two opposites—the apocryphal and the canonical ; in this sense, that in the former only isolated traces of connexion with the common life of Christians derive from the Spirit, while in the latter His activity is merely more closely delimited by the individual in whom He is working, with scarcely any weakening or alteration ; yet so that in no case the difference between the individual and Christ is cancelled. While the interval between the apocryphal and the canonical is filled by gradual stages, the action of the Spirit is most profound and concen-

trated within the circle of those singled out by Peter, with the assent of the whole community,[1] as men who had companied with Christ from shortly after the start of His public life. For the individual members of this apostolic class, as we may call it, were so much regarded as being on an equality with each other that without offence to conscience the number of the original Apostles could be filled up from among them by simple lot ; their steadfastness was a guarantee alike of the purity of their zeal and of their full understanding. But even within their circle no one can miss the important difference between aspects of personality that affect merely the private life of individuals and such as could be employed in the control of Christian affairs. It is with reference to the former that even in Apostles human nature most easily betrays itself, while in the latter sphere there could not but be a keener intention to let the Spirit of the whole exert an exclusive rule. Hence what is here spoken or done can be described as inspired in a much stricter and more definite sense. On the other hand, we should recklessly break up the unity of life characteristic of these apostolic men if, in order to bring out emphatically the inspiration of the Holy Scriptures, we were to assert that they were less animated and moved by the Holy Spirit in other parts of their apostolic office than in the act of writing, or in the composition of writings (also concerned with the service of the churches) which were not destined to be included in the Canon ; or again that they enjoyed His aid very much more in the public addresses or parts of addresses which were eventually preserved in the Acts of the Apostles than at any other time ; or that this difference, with or without their knowledge, was to be explained by the fact that over and above their immediate purpose these writings were meant to have a bearing on all subsequent ages. Thus the peculiar inspiration of the Apostles is not something that belongs exclusively to the books of the New Testament. These books only share in it ; and inspiration in this narrower sense, conditioned as it is by the purity and completeness of the apostolic grasp of Christianity, covers the whole of the official apostolic activity thence derived.

If we consider the inspiration of Scripture in this context as a special portion of the official life of the Apostles which in general was guided by inspiration, we shall hardly need to raise all those

---

[1] Acts 1[21ff.] ; cf. John 15[27]. Paul does not belong to this circle, and if the Church has never regarded him as the inferior of the other Apostles in respect of inspiration, it thereby ascribes to him the same prerogatives as to them, although in a sense he had acquired them in a different way.

difficult questions about the extent of inspiration which so long have been answered solely in a manner that removed the whole subject from the domain of experiential insight. Nothing but an utterly dead scholasticism could try to draw lines of demarcation anywhere on the pathway lying between the first impulse to write and the actually written word, or wish to represent the written word in its bare externality as a special product of inspiration. The natural standard here is the analogy of the doctrine of Christ's Person ; at least, if we start with the fact that in the vocational life of the Apostles the whole activity of the common spirit ruling in the Church approximated as closely as possible to the person-forming union of the Divine Essence with human nature which constituted the Person of Christ (this without prejudice to the specific difference that obtains between the two modes of union), and that only in the light of this standard can what is outward in the actions of the Apostles be regarded as partially different in origin from the inward it was meant to express. This being assumed, it at once follows that we must reject the suggestion that in virtue of their divine inspiration the sacred books demand a hermeneutical and critical treatment different from one guided by the rules which obtain elsewhere. This at the same time disposes of all other difficulties.

3. If the inspiration of Scripture be thus traced to the influence of the Holy Spirit on the official activities of the Apostles, it might easily appear as though this held good merely for the doctrinal but not for the historical books, since what is in question in the latter case is not the communication of the writer's own thoughts ; everything depends rather on the sifting and arrangement of exact recollections. But for one thing the thoughts of the Apostles were to be no more than developments of what Christ had said, and these sayings, being elicited by special circumstances, could only be fully understood in their historical context. And this clearly means that a pure and complete apprehension of the various aspects of Christ's life is an essential precondition of the Apostles' official action as a whole. At the same time it is impossible to conceive of any incident in Christ's public life as wholly unaccompanied by quickening and instructive speech ; all His actions were presentations of Himself, and as such were fruitful for His proclamation of the Kingdom of God. Yet these incidents could be interpreted in very different ways ; they could be so interpreted by some observers that the resulting natural impression helped them to

recognize Christ's divine dignity ; by others they could be interpreted so perversely as to yield an impression which was apocryphal
and distorted and could even be used as proof against His Messianic
position. Thus the correctest view of the facts of Christ's life—
traceable in a certain sense directly to the divine Spirit—we naturally find in just that circle of people who had followed Christ's
public life with the growing confidence that in Him they had found
the Promised One, so that in the same circle both things are inseparably united—the right view of Christ and the right development of His teaching and precepts. For the same reason it was
afterwards a matter of the utmost importance for the whole Church
to ascertain and select the right memories of Christ's life, asking
how each supposed memory agreed with the view of the Kingdom
of God He had brought. Hence we must conceive the memory of
the Apostles subserviently to this general aim as also under the
influence of the Holy Spirit ; nor can we in this respect make any
distinction between the apostolic teachings and the evangelical
narratives ; indeed, we find the Apostles themselves narrating
both orally and in writing. Even though their teaching arose out
of definite official relationships, that is to say, out of their vocational
action in the narrower sense, yet narration too sprang from an
effort to promote the good of the whole Church, *i.e.* from their
vocational action in the wider sense. This has no bearing on the
question whether evangelistic narration was a special Church
function, whether co-ordinate with or subordinate to the preaching
of the Apostles. But the reproduction of memories, be it oral or
written, can never quite be separated from historical composition,
as may be seen from the narration even of one isolated fact ; and
the effort to exhibit the Redeemer in His habit as He lived is also
the work of the Spirit of truth, and only so far as it is so can such
narrative have a place in Holy Scripture. If, on the other hand,
we consider that what happened first was the communication of
just such isolated narratives, their collection in wholes like our
Gospels following later, we must concede both possibilities—that
the narrator presents only what he himself had experienced in this
or that connexion, and that with his personal experiences he mingles
what he has heard credibly from others ; nay more, that one who
himself had had no experience in the matter might yet, moved
by the same impulse and the same Spirit, put together material
which he had derived from the pure and original knowledge of
others as fruitfully as an original witness could have done. If

what was principally needed was the right selection and arrangement of historical facts already to hand, the influence of the Holy
Spirit in and throughout such work is entirely analogous to His
influence in the selection of individual books for the Canon.

4. Lastly, we have to consider the part taken by the Holy
Spirit in the collection of these books. Here the first difference
which must strike everyone is this, that although all the particular
books in the collection belong to the Apostolic Age, the actual
collection of them certainly does not ; we cannot therefore have
had handed down to us any strictly apostolic indication of what is
canonical and normative. In discriminating, therefore, we can
hardly use any analogy but this, that we should conceive of the
Spirit as ruling and guiding in the thought-world of the whole
Christian body just as each individual does in his own. Every man
knows how to distinguish his own noteworthy thoughts, and how
so to preserve them that he can count on bringing them up later
in his mind : the rest he puts aside partly for later elaboration ;
others he simply disregards and leaves it a matter merely of accident
whether they ever again present themselves to his mind or not.
Indeed, he may occasionally reject some of his ideas entirely, either
just when they occur or later. Similarly, the faithful preservation
of the apostolic writings is the work of the Spirit of God acknowledging His own products ; He distinguishes what is to remain
unchangeable from what has in many respects undergone transformation in the later development of Christian doctrine. On the
other hand, He rejects the apocryphal in part immediately on its
appearance, and partly He ensures that both this sort of product
and the taste for it shall gradually disappear from the Church.
The one apparent difficulty is this, that in history certain books
underwent varying vicissitudes ; at first they were accepted as
canonical and later were rejected as uncanonical, or *vice versa*.
But for one thing what changed here was not the judgment of the
whole Church ; rather a book which had been accepted in one
region and rejected in another was later universally accepted or
universally rejected. And much might well be thought worthy of
rejection for the Church organized as a great unity or in combination
with the other books, which was acceptable or the reverse in isolated
communities and judged merely by its own influence. On the
other hand, this proves no more than that Holy Scripture *as a
collection* came into existence only gradually and by approximation.
The same influence reveals itself even yet in the Church's careful

estimate of the different grades of normative authority to be conceded to particular portions of Scripture, as also in decisions regarding all sorts of *lacunæ* and interpolations ; so that the judgment of
the Church is only approximating ever more closely to a complete
expulsion of the apocryphal and the pure preservation of the
canonical. The influence directly stimulating this approximation
guides also the whole course of procedure, and that influence is
simply the Holy Spirit ruling in the Church. But all vacillations
of judgment, everything that makes approximation more difficult,
can have no other source than the influence which is exerted on the
Church by the world.

Hence if it is sought to distinguish in this connexion between
points that have been decided once for all and others which the
Church might yet take up, we cannot be too cautious. As history
shows, the sense for the truly apostolic is a gift of the Spirit that is
gradually increasing in the Church ; hence at an early stage much
may, through the mistakes of individuals, have crept into the
sacred books which a later age can recognize as uncanonical and
definitely prove to be so. But even as regards the collection as a
whole, the mere fact that ever since it has existed in the Church
as a collection, and has always retained its identity as such, is no
guarantee that its limits have been irrevocably fixed. Its fixation
(which we have the less right to regard as an absolute miracle or an
altogether isolated work of the Holy Spirit that we are not entirely
ignorant of how it came about) must rather be viewed as but one
incident in a process which can only be fully vindicated through
its ever-renewed confirmation as the Church perseveres in its task of
inquiry, but otherwise is liable to correction. Hence even though
the Canon is fixed in many Confessions of our Church,[1] this ought
not to prevent further unrestricted investigation of the matter ;
critical inquiry must ever anew test the individual writings of
Scripture with a view to decide whether they rightly keep their
place in the sacred collection. Doubt of the genuine can only
issue in ever greater certainty. Even the fact that writings undeniably apostolic and others approximately so have perished is no
argument to the contrary, for we are entitled to believe that nothing
essential to the preservation and well-being of the Church has thus
been lost. We are at least equally entitled to believe that it can
only promote the welfare of the Church if Holy Scripture be distinguished clearly from what does not belong to it.

[1] *Conf. Gall.* iii, ; *Conf. Angl.* vi. ; *Conf. Belg.* iv,

§ 131. *Second Theorem.—As regards their origin the New Testament Scriptures are authentic, and as a norm for Christian Doctrine they are sufficient.*

Art. Smalc. ii. : Regulam autem aliam habemus, ut videlicet verbum Dei condat articulos fidei et praeterea nemo, ne angelus quidem.—*Conf. Gall.* iv. : Hos libros agnoscimus esse canonicos, id est, ut fidei nostrae normam et regulam habemus, idque non tantum ex communi ecclesiae consensu, sed etiam multo magis ex testimonio et intrinseca Spiritus sancti persuasione.—*Expos. simpl.* i. : Credimus . . . scripturas canonicas . . . ipsum verum esse verbum Dei, et auctoritatem sufficientem ex semetipsis non ex hominibus habere. . . . Et in hac scriptura . . . habet . . . ecclesia plenissime exposita, quaecunque pertinent cum ad salvificam fidem tum ad vitam Deo placentem recte informandam.—*Conf. Angl.* vi. : Scriptura sacra continet omnia quae ad salutem sunt necessaria, ita ut quicquid in ea nec legitur, neque inde probari potest, non sit a quoquam exigendum ut tamquam articulus fidei credatur.—*Conf. Belg.* vii. : Credimus sacram hanc scripturam Dei voluntatem perfecte complecti, et quodcunque . . . credi necesse est, in illa sufficienter edoceri. . . . Idcirco toto animo reiicimus quicquid cum certissima hac regula non convenit.—*Conf. March.* ii. : 'At the beginning . . . they confess that they hold . . . the true infallible and solely saving Word of God as it . . . is contained in the Holy Bible, which is and ought to be the one standard for all believers . . . which is perfect and sufficient for salvation and for the decision of all religious controversy, and abides for ever.'

1. From the foregoing explanation it follows that the authoritative character of Scripture does not in the least depend on each book having been written by the particular person to whom it is ascribed. A book might, owing to a later judgment, be wrongly attributed to a certain author in all the surviving MSS., and in this sense be unauthentic, and yet it might belong to the circle where alone we can expect to find canonical writings and hence would none the less remain an integral part of Holy Scripture. Nay more, at its very first appearance a writing (owing to a fiction permitted by the author's moral sense and sanctioned by the feeling of his contemporaries) might have borne in its title the name of someone other than its real author, and yet a book of this character might be an authentic part of the Bible. It is only if such a self-description were positively intended to mislead that the book could not be recognized as fitted to supplement the normative presentation of Christianity. Hence even if many of the doubts that have been raised as to the correct statement of authors' names should be confirmed, we should have no right, much less would it be our duty, to expel those books from the Canon.

There is, however, no way of forming a list of authors to whom

particular books must belong in order to be canonical, or of indicating a class of persons all of whose productions would have a right to
canonicity.   On the contrary, if even now writings should be discovered which were attributable with the highest degree of human
certainty to an immediate disciple of Christ or even to an Apostle,
we should not without more ado incorporate them in the New
Testament, but at most attach them to it as an appendix.   Not
even the early Church—especially as it is unable to prove apostolic
sanction for the separate books [1]—can bind us by its decisions,
even had such decisions about the Canon been unanimous ; hence
the first part of our theorem can scarcely be taken as expressing
anything more precise than what is indicated in the confessional
statements quoted above, namely, that we trust universal Christian
experience as the testimony of the Holy Spirit that the Canon we
have received from Church tradition has not by deceit or ignorance
had introduced into it such constituent parts as belong to either an
apocryphal or an heretically suspect zone of Christianity, to which
such pre-eminent dignity could not be ascribed without danger.
But in saying so we concede that not all the books of the New
Testament are equally fitted, by content and form, to vindicate
their place in the Canon.

    Since, however, this fixation of the Canon was arrived at only
gradually, and we know besides that the imperfections and errors
present in the Church could only gradually be brought to light and
removed by the action of the Holy Spirit, we must show our trust
by practising the greatest freedom as well as the strictest con-
scientiousness in our treatment of the Canon.   This means, first,
that all inquiries intended to ascertain the authors of the books we
have, and the genuineness or the reverse of particular passages, must
pursue an unhampered course, and that no doubts which may
arise should either be accepted by unfriendly prejudice or rejected
without scrutiny.   Not only is this a part of a complete knowledge
of Scripture ; it is not without influence on the interpretation and
the use of individual passages.   It means, secondly, that we refuse
to be perverted from the purest hermeneutical methods, as would
be the case if we knowingly preferred to put an artificial interpretation on a passage rather than construe it in a sense suggestive of a
less pure view of Christian faith.   Under no other circumstances

---

[1] The accounts given by Irenæus, iii. 1, and Eusebius, H.E. ii. 15, iii. 24,
39, v. 8, and elsewhere, are bound, as time goes on, to be less and less regarded
as based on trustworthy information.

could we take the credit of being as actively engaged (though within a smaller field of controversial questions and with better equipment and a more cultivated sense) in the discrimination of Scripture as those were who first made the decisive selection of Holy Scripture out of the whole mass of early Christian writings.

2. To understand the second half of our paragraph in its whole range, we must first go back to the influence originally exerted by the writings of the New Testament. The doctrinal books were meant to bear upon the actual circumstances of Christian people, so that the utterances of the Apostles went to form both the dominant ideas and the purposes of believers ; the historical books were meant simply to rehearse the similarly influential words and deeds of Christ and the Apostles. Hence they must become the regulative type for our religious thinking, from which it is not of its own motion to depart. And when Holy Scripture is described as ' sufficient ' in this regard, what is meant is that through our use of Scripture the Holy Spirit can lead us into all truth, as it led the Apostles and others who enjoyed Christ's direct teaching. So that if one day there should exist in the Church a complete reflection of Christ's living knowledge of God, we may with perfect justice regard this as the fruit of Scripture, without any addition of foreign elements having had to come in. Of course the effects of what was due to the previous action of Scripture are here reckoned to the account of Scripture itself. Thus it is as representing each individual's personal understanding of Scripture that, in the measure of his command of thought and speech, his true expressions of Christian piety take shape. And the interpretation of Christian faith which validates itself in each age as having been evoked by Scripture is the development, suited to that moment, of the genuine original interpretation of Christ and His work, and constitutes the common Christian orthodoxy for that time and place.

To this constitutive influence of Scripture, the second or critical influence—and when we speak of the normative place of Scripture, it is often this alone we have in view—is related in a merely subordinate way ; almost, so to speak, as its shadow. True, we can imagine thinking which is independent of the action of the Holy Spirit through Scripture and yet is religious in its content as well as Christian in its original roots, yet the results of which are trivial and infertile, or erroneous and all but heretical. All such thinking, originating as it does in the immature or confused state of mind of those who receive and develop it, must be tested by Scripture, and can only prove that at least it means to be Christian by seeking to base itself on Scripture and so acknowledging the test. But clearly this critical aspect of the normative use of Scripture must decrease as the productive increases, and as the perfected understanding of Scripture renders its misinterpretation more difficult.

As regards the scientific expression of Christian faith in Dogmatic proper, it is no doubt undertaken solely by persons of a scientific turn ; but they are always persons who desire to be instruments of the Spirit that acts in and through Scripture, in systematizing what is fragmentary in scriptural expressions and in harmonizing different presentations—the original ones and those directed against Judaism and Paganism—with each other, and in supplementing one by another. Here too, therefore, the productive, normative power of Scripture is shown, although in itself Scripture scarcely even suggests the distinction between a more popular and a more scientific terminology. On the other hand, strong suspicion cannot but be felt of a Dogmatic which, after pursuing its own line all along, objects to anything more than a critical use of Scripture for the purpose of proving that certain isolated details in its structure can be paralleled from the Bible and that no part of the system contradicts the language of Scripture properly understood. Only, it ought not to be demanded even in the former case that each individual dogmatic *locus* must be represented in Scripture by a passage specially devoted to it.

3. If we take strictly the phrase that Scripture as norm is sufficient, it follows that Scripture can contain nothing superfluous. What is superfluous is confusing and hence of no more than negative value ; also it tempts the mind into comparisons that lead nowhere. But Scripture does contain much that is little more than repetition, indeed frequent repetition, of what is said elsewhere, and this appearance of superfluity is all the more curious when contrasted with the lack of it in a dogmatic system apparently just as incomplete. This, however, is to be expected from the nature of the case, for Scripture did not come into existence all at once ; and in this regard our paragraph gives expression to the conviction, which is fundamental to the right use of Scripture and is ever anew confirmed by a sound hermeneutical method, that repetitions in the historical books are all the better guarantee of the authenticity of tradition, while quite possibly they may supplement each other. The same holds of repeated discussions of the same topics in the doctrinal books. For, even assuming that in different passages the

writer was not dealing with different situations and relationships, the identity of the Spirit in varied circumstances and individuals is thereby attested all the more powerfully.

§ 132. *Postscript to this Doctrine.—The Old Testament Scriptures owe their place in our Bible partly to the appeals the New Testament Scriptures make to them, partly to the historical connexion of Christian worship with the Jewish Synagogue ; but the Old Testament Scriptures do not on that account share the normative dignity or the inspiration of the New.*

1. Our exposition of this doctrine diverges from custom in this respect, that in the two theorems the New Testament writings alone were treated of ; and this postscript has to justify this divergence and give it clear expression. Intentionally, however, it is announced as a postscript, because it is merely polemical and therefore will have lost its relevance as soon as the difference between the two Testaments is generally recognized. That time is as yet apparently distant, and in a Church system it would be correspondingly hazardous to include, as a theorem proper, a proposition of so dissentient a character. Especially as the same view is dominant outside the Schools ; very often, and sometimes even by emphatic preference, Old Testament passages are made the basis of Christian exhortation, and the New Testament seemingly is allowed an influence merely proportional to its size. This is done from opposite motives alike by people who attach less value to the distinctive features of Christianity and by those who recognize it alone and exclusively as charged with redemptive power. It is only to the latter that we seek to justify our position ; the former are outside our province.

2. As regards the inspiration of the Old Testament writings, we must first of all distinguish between the Law and the Prophets. If the Apostle is right in representing the Law as, although a divine ordinance, yet something that came in between the promise to Abraham's seed and its fulfilment,[1] and in asserting further that the Law lacks the power of the Spirit from which the Christian life must flow,[2] then it cannot well be maintained that the Law was inspired by the same Spirit of which the same Apostle says that it is no longer communicated through the Law and its works,[3] but God sends it into our hearts only through our connexion with Christ. Similarly, nowhere and in no sense does Christ represent

[1] Gal. 3[19].   [2] Rom. 7[6ff.] and 8[3].   [3] Gal. 3[2].

the sending of the Spirit, with whose witness He combines the witness of the disciples,[1] as the return of what had been there already and had merely disappeared for a while. But on the Law there depend all the historical books subsequent to its being given. For if Messianic prophecy as that which has most affinity with Christianity be confronted with the Law as that which has least, no one will venture to hold that what the Jewish historical books contain is the history of Messianic prophecy rather than of the Law. Nay, even in the prophetic books most of the contents relate to the legal dispensation and the circumstances of the people as such, and the Spirit in which they originate is simply the spirit of the people ; it is therefore not the Christian Spirit, which as One Spirit was to break down the wall of partition between this people and all others. So that only Messianic prophecy would remain as capable of sharing in inspiration in our sense. But if we consider that it is only at isolated moments that the prophets rise to inspiration, and that it is only in this reference that the Spirit moving and animating them is called holy,[2] our conclusion surely must be that this title is merely given in an inexact sense, to indicate that this common spirit, bound up as it was with a conscious need of redemption, and revealing itself in the premonition of a more inward and spiritual Reign of God, carried in itself, and could kindle and sustain even outside itself, the highest receptivity for the Holy Spirit.

Let us inquire, secondly, as to the normative dignity of the Old Testament, first of all in the productive sense. Here it cannot on the whole be denied that the religious sense of Evangelical Christians recognizes in the main a great difference between the two Testaments. Even the noblest Psalms always contain something which Christian piety is unable to appropriate as a perfectly pure expression of itself, so that it is only after deluding ourselves by unconscious additions and subtractions that we can suppose we are able to gather a Christian doctrine of God out of the Prophets and the Psalms. On the other hand, a strong inclination to the use of Old Testament texts in expressing pious feeling is almost invariably accompanied by a legalistic style of thought or a slavish worship of the letter. Lastly, as regards the critical aspect of the normative use of Scripture, probably there are few Christian doctrines which at a certain period it was not attempted to prove by Old Testament passages. But how was it really possible that in an age merely of premonition any truth connected with the doctrine of redemption

---

[1] John 14²⁶ and 15²⁶. ²⁷.　　　　　　　　[2] 2 Pet. 1²¹.

through Christ could have been set forth so clearly that it could be used with advantage side by side with what was said by Christ Himself, and, after the completion of His redeeming work, by His disciples ? Or if it be thought that inspiration does make this possible, would not in consequence an entirely different reception of the Saviour and the form in which He preached the Kingdom of God have been prepared for among the Bible-reading part of His nation ? The effect is in no sort of keeping with the cause to which it is ascribed. Further, the history of Christian theology shows only too clearly on the one hand how gravely this effort to find our Christian faith in the Old Testament has injured our practice of the exegetical art, and how on the other it has submerged the later development of doctrine and the controversies regarding its more exact definition under a flood of useless complications. Thus a thoroughgoing improvement is only to be looked for when we utterly discard Old Testament proofs for specifically Christian doctrines, preferring to put aside what chiefly rests on such support.

3. But if a practice which has so long been prevalent in the Church is to be reformed, it is necessary to show how the practice arose. There are two grounds on which this external equating of both Testaments rests. In the first place, not only did Christ Himself and the Apostles give instruction on portions of the Old Testament that had been read aloud, but the same custom was perpetuated in Christian public gatherings, before the New Testament Canon had been formed and even later. But from this it by no means follows that a similar homiletical use of the Old as well as of the New Testament ought still to be continued, or that we must put it down to the corruption of the Church that the Old Testament is not so much read by Christians of our time as the New. On the contrary, the ecclesiastical status of the Old Testament was due to its historical connexions, so that its gradual retirement into the background lies in the nature of the case ; and these historical connexions are very far from vouching adequately for the normative dignity or the inspiration of the books of the Old Testament. The Pauline passages which testify to the value of the Old Testament [1] relate chiefly to the usage above described ; and the freedom with which the Apostle employs it is in perfect agreement with our contention, so that we might well call him as a witness in support of the position that Old Testament proofs are no longer required.

The second ground is that Christ and the Apostles themselves

[1] Rom. 15⁴, 1 Cor. 10¹¹, 2 Tim. 3¹⁶.

refer to the books of the Old Testament as divine authorities favourable to Christianity.   But from this it does not in the least follow
that for our faith we still need these earlier premonitions, since we
have actual experience ; and the New Testament approves of men
ceasing to believe on the ground of such witness when once they
have gained immediate certainty through their own perception.[1]
Only, for that very reason historical fidelity and completeness of
view demand that what Christ and His first preachers appealed
to should be preserved.   This, however, scarcely covers more than
the prophetic books and the Psalms ; which would justify the
practice of adding these to the New Testament as an appendix.
But in the time of Christ these books did not exist separately, but
only as parts of the sacred collection ; they are often cited exclusively
in that character ; certain quotations, moreover, occur from other
books.   Hence, although for us the Old Testament cannot be an
indivisible whole as it was for the Jews, there can be no objection
to its being added in its entirety to the New Testament.   None the
less, the real meaning of the facts would be clearer if the Old Testament followed the New as an appendix, for the present relative
position of the two makes the demand, not obscurely, that we
must first work our way through the whole of the Old Testament
if we are to approach the New by the right avenue.

SECOND DOCTRINE : THE MINISTRY OF THE WORD OF GOD

§ 133. *Those members of the Christian fellowship who maintain chiefly
the attitude of spontaneity perform by self-communication
the Ministry of God's Word for those who maintain chiefly
the attitude of receptivity ; and this Ministry is partly an
indeterminate and occasional ministry, partly formal and
prescribed.*

1. The assumption, true for every corporate fellowship, that the
common spirit is unequally distributed, we have already [2] made
for the fellowship of the Christian Church.   This distinction between
strength and weakness, between purity and impurity in the presentation and grasp of truth (each of these antitheses viewed in itself and
also in combination with the other) can be seen in the early Church ;
and in each province of the Church it is most clearly marked at the
beginning and gradually diminishes.   Yet in every part of the
Church it will long remain important enough as an inequality of

---

[1] John 4[42].   [2] § 129, 2.

persons. And even if it had wholly ceased to exist as such, none the less in each individual so much of inequality of feeling and mood remains that at one moment he finds himself spontaneously active and at another only stimulated receptively. The suggested antithesis, then, is always present, and the problem thus raised has to be solved. For those who are even momentarily weak and impure only belong to the fellowship in so far as they have a receptive capacity to be purified and strengthened, and the fellowship can retain them only as there are those within it who spontaneously supply to them purification and strengthening. This must here be considered—apart from the distinction of an outer and an inner circle within the Church [1]—as a distinction even among the regenerate themselves.

That the relation of the spontaneously active to the receptive is a communication from the former to the latter, and that every such communication is a service and supply of the Word of God, may be shown as follows. There can be no self-communication except through self-presentation acting by way of stimulus ; the imitatively received movement of the self-presented person becomes in the receptively stimulated person a force that evokes the same movement. If this produces a purifying or strengthening, it can only be an effect such as is found in all similar cases where one common spirit works in each of many—an effect of the Holy Spirit working in each of many Christians. And as the Spirit, taking all from Christ, is ever the same Spirit as inspired the Scriptures, no expression of the individual can evoke a similar effect except in so far as it is analogous to Scripture and hence can justify itself as scriptural. Thus with equal justice it may be said that every self-communication that makes for salvation is certainly also scriptural, and every scriptural one is also edifying. For no true Christian can wish to retain anything in his inner life, and at work there, in which he does not recognize Christ ; so, too, no one can wish, in his self-communication within the Christian fellowship, to commend and disseminate himself and his own things, but rather Christ alone and whatever of Christ lives in him. Similarly, no one can wish to take up anything into his life for self-advancement, save as he takes it from Christ. Hence with every communicative and stimulating activity within the Christian fellowship is bound up self-knowledge (to call it self-denial would be inaccurate), to the effect that the communicated gifts are not to

---

[1] Cf. § 115, 2 and § 116, 1.

be ascribed to the person communicating them, or to any private divine revelation of his own. Everything must be traceable to the view of Christ given in Scripture, so that the individual can only act as the recollecting and developing organ of Scripture ; otherwise unchristian personal claims and separatist influences would break the fellowship in pieces. So, too, a genuinely Christian receptivity will disdain to take the words and acts of any mere individual as example, or to receive them as truth. And this critical attitude, to avoid being deceived, will not hesitate to make distinctions even within what is scriptural ; as in a case where some particular point can be defended by a single Biblical passage, but is out of harmony with the spirit of the whole.

2. If now we consider this influence of the stronger on the weaker, we can see that it embraces the whole Christian life. Even the acts of individuals, in so far as expressive of the same Spirit, are an offering to others of the Word of God ; as follows indeed from what was said above [1] regarding Christ's prophetic office, on which this Ministry depends. Hence the distinction stated at the close of our paragraph is important. All the personal influences just indicated, occurring separately in individual lives, often unintended in part and in part unsought, are the indeterminate and relatively fortuitous ministry of which we cannot speak here, because it belongs to Christian Ethics. But although we have here to do exclusively with the formal and ordered Ministry, the other had to be mentioned ; for the Evangelical conception of the ordered Ministry has its firmest basis in the fact that in all essential respects it is homogeneous with that which is more general and indeterminate. This view, which forbids any sharp distinction between those who discharge the ordered Ministry and other Christians, we find in Scripture itself. When Paul enumerates the different gifts and offices, he mixes both kinds together indistinguishably.[2] So, too, many persons were called by Christ into His discipleship in a more indefinite fashion as contrasted with the definite relationship in which the Twelve stood to Him, or the Seventy-and-two who were sent out on a definite Ministry. In the early Church, too, the Ministry of the Apostles was an ordered one, for they kept to a definite number [3] and acted upon common decisions. The same is true of the office of deacons at first in Jerusalem [4] and on the same model in other churches. But the polemical effort of Stephen in defence of Christianity was no part

---

[1] § 103.   [2] I Cor. 12$^{8-10. 28-30}$.   [3] Acts I^{17}.   [4] Acts 6^2.

of the definite Ministry assigned to him ; he was acting *ad extra* simply as an individual. So, too, the general and indeterminate ministry within the churches was recommended to, and demanded of, all suited for it.[1] Indeed, the distinction lies in the nature of the case ; not that higher and special qualities necessarily belong to the regular Ministry : but if even in civil society the common life cannot be wholly resolved into definite functions assigned to each by the society as a whole, much less is this compatible, in the fellowship of the Church, with religious influence and communication. For, on the one hand, the Holy Spirit can never be inactive, and therefore can never be tied in its activities to definite times ; rather it moves each believer to do whatever comes to hand. On the other hand, even so spiritual a society cannot be regarded as wellordered unless there be a division of labour ; otherwise none of the different gifts could attain to its maximum of activity. Especially as the division can be made with more ease and certainty in proportion as the One Spirit guides in completer harmony the judgments of different minds.

§ 134. *First Theorem.*—*There is in the Christian Church a public Ministry of the Word, as a definite office committed to men under fixed forms ; and from this proceeds all organization of the Church.*

Conf. Aug. v. : 'For the obtaining of this faith, the ministry of teaching the Gospel . . . was instituted by God ; even as by the Word and Sacraments, as by instruments, the Holy Spirit is given ; who worketh faith, where and when He pleaseth.' xiv. 'Concerning Church Government they teach that no man should publicly in the Church teach or preach or administer the Sacraments without a regular call.'—*Conf. Saxon.* (p. 196 Tw.) : Agimus autem gratias Deo . . . quod . . . conservavit publicum ministerium et honestos congressus, qui ipse etiam distinxit quaedam tempora,—*Expos. simpl.* xviii. : Deus ad colligendam vel constituendam sibi ecclesiam eandemque gubernandam et conservandam semper usus est ministris. . . . Nemo autem honorem ministerii ecclesiastici usurpare sibi . . . debet. Vocentur et eligantur electione ecclesiastica et legitima ministri ecclesiae. . . . Eligantur autem . . . homines idonei, etc.—*Conf. Helv.* xv. : Atque hanc ob causam ministros ecclesiae cooperarios esse Dei fatemur, per quos ille cognitionem sui et peccatorum remissionem administret, homines ad se convertat erigat consoletur . . . ita tamen ut efficaciam in his omnem Deo, ministerium ministris adscribamus.—*Conf. Gall.* xxix. : Credimus veram ecclesiam gubernari debere ea disciplina, quam Dominus noster Jesus Christus sancivit, ita videlicet ut in ea sint pastores presbyteri et diaconi, ut doctrinae puritas retineatur, vitia cohibeantur, pauperibus consulatur et sacri coetus habeantur.—*Conf. Angl.* xxiii. : Non licet cuiquam sumere sibi munus publice praedicandi . . . nisi prius fuerit legitime vocatus et missus.

---

[1] Eph. 4²⁹, 5¹⁹.

1. If in our inquiry as to the origin of this public Ministry we go back to the commission given by Christ to the Apostles,[1] we find that this commission was chiefly directed to those without ; for any instance of a Ministry internal to the Church might be taken as coming under the more general and indeterminate ministry.[2] The internal, however, grew out of the external, for the newly converted required steady teaching and admonition ; so that the internal was included in Christ's commission as the natural prolongation of the external. It was the Apostles themselves, however, who proposed a division of this internal Ministry and left it to the whole body to transfer the ministry of serving tables to others ;[3] thus the teaching office became something entrusted to the Apostles by the community, just as the community had formerly transferred both offices combined to the new member of the Twelve. Thus both offices have been perpetuated in the Church as the main branches of the public Ministry, for it is self-evident that the diaconate can be a Church office only if it be a supplying of the Word ; that is, if it be an expression and manifestation of Christian brotherly love in act. But the triple division, however construed, is arbitrary ; in essence it must reduce to that double division between teaching and serving tables which really rests on the fact that the gifts requisite for the one task are as nearly as possible independent of those which constitute qualifications for the other. Indeed, from the first, women have always taken part in the public service of tables,[4] but have always been excluded from the public discharge of the office of teaching.

2. No individual or small group of individuals can represent Christ : all the more must we regard this transference of offices as deriving solely from the whole body, and the formation of the clergy into a self-contained and self-propagating corporation has no Scriptural basis of any kind. When it is a case of propagation, Scripture signalizes only two points—determination of the qualities requisite for the performance of the task, and selection from among those who are known to be so qualified. Here, then, there remains a wide freedom of choice in assigning different tasks to different people, without infringement of the principle that it is the whole body that organizes the discharge of its functions and distributes these amongst its members. Such distribution is impossible without a definite fixing of objects and an exact delimitation of the

---

[1] Matt. 10⁶·ˡ·.
[3] Acts 6².
[2] *E.g.* Matt. 18¹⁵⁻²⁰.
[4] 1 Tim. 5⁹· ¹⁰, Luke 8³.

area within which each is to function. It must be decided what is transferable and what is not ; we therefore indirectly subsume the indeterminate ministry under organization, so as to soften the contrast between the two ; as is also done when temporary associations of more closely related individuals are formed, from time to time, in the interest of what has not been transferred. But even the Ministry of the Word can never be transferred in so exclusive a sense that self-communication of the same kind could not take place between individuals apart from the public Ministry ; this would be to lord it over conscience [1] and quench the Spirit.[2] From the transference there arise two sorts of relationship—that of each needy soul to a variety of communicators as determined by his peculiar needs and their methods, and that of each communicator to various receptive souls with reference to some definite need and within the area assigned to him. It is—if we think of a great continuous mass of Christian life—through these two relationships taken together that churches are delimited and separated ; each as an area in which there are present all the gifts needed for the promotion of Christian life, and in which all the transferable tasks are advantageously distributed. The ramification of Church offices, as well as the forms under which they are transferred, may be very different ; and the theory of such matters belongs to Practical Theology. Here we need only say in general terms that they are good in proportion as, on the one hand, the distribution takes place, and is recognized, as the act of the whole body directly or indirectly ; and as, on the other, the most spiritual Ministry of all—namely, the ordered presentation of the Word of God— keeps its place as the mid-point, from which all radiates out and to which all is in relation.

3. Without this ordered public Ministry and the constitution of the churches that goes along with it, Christian communication would merely be isolated and sporadic in character, and to all appearance fortuitous. In fact, however, it would be impossible to avoid a confusing uncertainty, leading to a fruitless and self-consuming waste of varied forces, were the receptive soul with his needs not referred to definite communicators, and conversely were communicators with their gifts not referred to definite circles of the receptive. But even granting that in the power of the Spirit each gifted person were doing everything possible to employ his gifts for the common good, and similarly that each needy soul had dis-

---

[1] 2 Cor. 1²⁴.   [2] 1 Thess. 5¹⁹.

cernment enough to try the spirits—in other words, that individuals left nothing undone that might be done, a state of matters only imperfectly realized by the very best distribution of forces—still, everything would rest on the stimulation of personal religious feeling and of individual sympathy. No true common conscious-ness, no living conviction of the identity of the one Spirit present in all, could arise thus. But without it there could be for us no recognition of the Holy Spirit in ourselves or any proper conscious-ness of the nature of our vital fellowship with Christ ; to ensure that, we must be conscious of ourselves as members of His Body. Hence nothing but an utterly superficial view of Christianity will find it possible to reduce Christian fellowship to the area of domestic life and to silent, private relationships devoid of publicity. On the contrary, public gatherings for common confession and common edification are the principal thing, and the transference to certain persons of predominance and leadership in these gatherings is merely a side-issue. Indeed, so far as this point is concerned, a Church fellowship can be quite in the evangelical spirit which knows nothing of such transference, and concedes to every Christian the right of leadership.

§ 135. *Second Theorem.—The public worship and service of the Church is in all its parts bound to the Word·of God.*

1. Even the isolated and informal communications of Christian people must, in so far as what they communicate is due to the Holy Spirit, be explanations and active manifestations of the Word of God. If the same is to be true of the public Ministry, not in the same fashion merely, but in a fashion peculiar to itself, it must be owing to the fact that this characteristic of being bound to the Word of God definitely enters into the form of public communication. As regards doctrine, this is secured in part directly by the individual expositions of religious truth being so arranged throughout as evidently to be interpretations of particular passages of Scripture ; partly indirectly through the Creed, which is a brief compendium of doctrine based on Scripture, and which (assuming its scriptural character) ought to be controllingly present to every mind ; by which, too, it ought always to be possible to have the doctrine tested. Both securities, however, must inevitably degenerate into empty forms, easily circumvented, unless the free and informal communication prevailing in the same circle of persons is itself scriptural. If it is not, the Creed will usually assert itself as the

authentic sense of Scripture, so as to prevent any still wider divergence therefrom ; but the result is an unevangelical worship of the letter, and the deeper penetration of Scripture is made impossible.

The same scriptural character is required of Christian poetry if its creations (although originally meant only for the individual) are to pass into public Church use. It comes out in one way in the psalmodic type of Christian verse, which, attaching itself as it does more or less loosely to paraphrastic translations of the Psalms in the style of the earliest Christian hymns, treats of particular passages and situations in Scripture. It comes out differently in the confessional type, which points back to the ecumenical Creeds and clothes the sum of common doctrine in poetic harmonies. The more Christian poetry departs from these two basal forms and represents purely individual aspects of the religious life, the more its influence is confined to small coteries.

Under the conception of public Ministry we have subsumed everything that is the act of the Christian body as such, and the demand for scripturalness must cover such acts too. Hence these active public communications also are seen to be bound to the Word of God ; in part directly, since particular admonitions rest on definite exhortations contained in Scripture and seek to realize them, or are attached to scriptural models ; in part indirectly, through the fixing of Church rules which, derived like the Creed from Scripture, seek to establish an order of Christian life in relation to public worship and service—an order to which all public active communication must be conformed, and from which it can be known which actions of the individual the Church acknowledges as its own, and which it does not.

2. Thus we can see how Confessions or Symbols and Church rules or Canons arise in the Church, not so much as standards by which to test the varied presentations of faith in word and act, as rather the more certainly to secure that the individual shall conform to the original utterances of the Spirit. But it by no means follows that in every age it is possible for them to correspond as perfectly to this ideal as in the period of their formation. That this is not the case is a consequence of the simple fact that they are always the work of the whole Church—using that word as embracing the antithesis used above—not merely of the spontaneous and communicative but also (at least indirectly) of the needy and receptive : and this not merely in the sense that while they originate

with the communicative they yet owe their influence solely to the freely given recognition of the needy, but also because a diffused knowledge of the spiritual state of the needy—in other words, the special circumstances of the moment—was one motive in their production. Hence from the nature of the case every product of the kind falls short of its ideal, the reason being that the progress of the Church is faltering and that at every moment the effects of reactionary tendencies are a part of the situation. They have validity for us only with the reservation that their scriptural character must always be liable to scrutiny. Hence the public worship and service of the Church must always have attached to it a highly developed organization designed to keep up the expert interpretation of Scripture and to bring it to perfection by ceaseless industry. This need not mean that everywhere and in every age those who are charged with the public Ministry must form a special class within the Christian fellowship. On the contrary, our two theorems show that the ecclesiastical distinction, strongly marked as it may be in particular cases, between those who discharge the public Ministry and those to whom they minister is always subordinate on the one hand to the unity and identity of the Spirit in both, on the other to the fact that both are directly dependent on Scripture. This, as also the unfailing affinity between activities which are sporadic and informal and those officially assigned and ordered, means that the antithesis between the two types of member is an ever-decreasing one. If we further consider that on its critical side the normative use of Scripture must one day cease, the antithesis of the two types, in so far as personal, is lost in a direct assurance, common to both, as to the scriptural character both of the accepted doctrines and the canons of practice.

Third Doctrine: Baptism

§ 136. *Baptism as an action of the Church signifies simply the act of will by which the Church receives the individual into its fellowship; but inasmuch as the effectual promise of Christ rests upon it, it is at the same time the channel of the divine justifying activity, through which the individual is received into the living fellowship of Christ.*

1. We have already [1] put the case for what is essential in this paragraph, namely, that the reception of an individual into the

[1] § 114, 2.

Christian fellowship and his justification or regeneration must be one and the same act. Otherwise, if reception into the Church were solely an act of the Church, then, since the act in question cannot be conceived as taking place without the Holy Spirit, the Supreme Being in preparing His union with human nature under the form of the common Spirit, would be in a state of passivity. But the outpouring of the Holy Spirit is conditioned by Christ,[1] and rests on His promise ; the same must therefore hold good of the impartation of the Spirit to the individual, even if (as is essential to the unity of the Church) the Spirit comes to all from Christ in the same manner. Thus the Church is relieved of a great uncertainty by the fact that Christ Himself enjoined baptism as the act of reception into the Church. For now every such reception is an act of Christ Himself, if performed in the manner He enjoined and according to His command. Hence the Church can neither depart from this form of reception through baptism nor, on the other hand, doubt that in every case where the command of Christ is properly carried out, His promise will be fulfilled that with such reception the salvation of the person received begins. The latter would be to doubt the redeeming power of Christ Himself ; the former would be an audacious notion which could not possibly be derived from the Holy Spirit, for the Spirit takes all from Christ.

This fixes it that baptism must be retained by the Church in the form in which it received it. But it is impossible either to obtain or to give any information as to whether, or how, the outward form of the act is connected with its inward content and purpose. On that point we can only say that if Christ had enjoined an utterly different outward rite for the same purpose, we should regard it as equally sacred and expect from it the same results. Only so much is certain, that if Christ had specially instituted something that was altogether new, it would be incumbent on us in that case to seek for a relationship of the closest possible kind between the outward rite and the alleged inward result ; for it is only under the severest compulsion that we could bring ourselves to suppose that any institution of Christ was purely arbitrary. It is otherwise inasmuch as He attached His institution to something already in existence, and since baptism was already historically conditioned by its connexion with the preaching of John. This historical basis is perfectly sufficient, without our being tempted to develop the symbolism universally recognized in that sphere further than is done in Scrip-

[1] § 124, 3.

ture, or to regard the symbolism as so essential as to justify the position that the act itself is only complete and can only secure its purpose when even outwardly it is so performed as perfectly to bring out its importance.

2. In spite of this undeniable connexion between the baptism of Christ and that of John, we can scarcely hold that the two are precisely the same without in some degree lessening the importance of the former.[1] Even if in John's baptism the idea of the Kingdom of God as coming through redemption was fundamental, yet prior to his recognition of Jesus in the act of baptizing Him the person of the Redeemer was undetermined alike for John and for those whom he baptized. Hence we should at least have to distinguish between his baptism before and after this incident, in the sense that the former, to equal Christian baptism, needed supplementing. This distinction, however, could only be important if John later had baptized in Jesus' name, which, all things considered, we have more reason to deny than to assert.[2] Thus it can scarcely be conceded that the baptism of John can have been either reception into the Christian Church or a bath of regeneration ; in other words, it could only be construed as being identical with Christian baptism if we regarded both as equally ineffectual,[3] or if, virtually abrogating the distinction between the old covenant and the new, we held that John, without any definite relation to Christ, was able to give precisely what Christ gave.

On the other hand, not only is it impossible to maintain that for those baptized by John the recognition of Jesus as the Christ was an insufficient additional step, and a new baptism indispensable, but it is not even clear that so long as the Redeemer lived, baptism was invariably essential for entering into fellowship with Him. It rather appears that when by word He imparted forgiveness to someone, and called him to follow Him, this acceptance was itself the act of Christ, and baptism would have been no more than an utterly meaningless supplement. Indeed, it is impossible to hold that even the Apostles had received the baptism of John, not to say all the disciples of Christ, especially those from Galilee ; still less that Christ Himself baptized any single person on whom it would then have been incumbent to baptize others.[4] Hence we must apply

---

[1] See Gerhard, *Loc.* ix. p. 101 f.   [2] Cf. John 3[22ff.] and Acts 19[3-5].
[3] As Zwingli does, *de ver. relig.* p. 208 : Quid vero distent Joannis baptismus et Christi multa tum olim tum nunc est quaestio, sed inutilis plane, nam discrimen omnino nullum est. . . . Nihil efficiebat Joannis tinctio . . . nihil efficit Christi tinctio, etc.   [4] John 4[2].

at this point the distinction between the Church as it still awaited institution and the Church as it already existed, and it is no matter for surprise if many of the Christians who had not been won by the already existing Church were unbaptized. The personal choice of Christ as an act of His will must have been completely sufficient of itself to secure both the blessings which our paragraph ascribes to baptism—namely, the application of the divine decree of redemption to the individual, and the placing of the individual in fellowship with all who already believe. This makes it as clear as possible that baptism as Christ's universal ordinance has taken the place of His particular personal choice.

3. Suppose we hold to this point of view and conceive each act of baptism, if it is to have this effect, as a decision of the whole Church, to which through the action of the Holy Spirit in its fulness there attaches the highest canonical authority ; so that the Church could baptize no one who was not as mature and as ready actually to begin a new spiritual life in fellowship with Christ as everyone chosen by Christ Himself must have been. There would in that case be no occasion to raise questions as to the possibility that baptism and regeneration might be separated from each other ; we could assert without more ado that everyone is regenerated in baptism, and only so. For since the Holy Spirit was bestowed on the whole body of disciples, it might be held that the divine activity in regeneration and justification was so exclusively attached to the administration of baptism that everyone whom in baptism the Church presents to God not only is acknowledged by Him, subsequently as it were, but in and with baptism itself is given a share in the Holy Spirit and divine sonship. In fact, however, this is not the case ; baptism is only granted and administered by a relatively self-contained part of the Church, in a transitional phase of its development, for none of whose particular actions therefore any such canonical perfection can be claimed. Hence no particular act of baptism can do more than approximate more or less to perfect correctness. And if we add that the moment of the individual's regeneration cannot humanly be exactly determined and still less exactly foreseen, it will appear that the supposed incorrectness in the administration of baptism is traceable to the fact that the Church does not approach the baptism of a catechumen in quite the same way as the soul of the catechumen himself (though all is mediated through the activities of the Church) moves on to regeneration. And thus, what on the formal view of the Church's action

would be an absolutely simple process now falls apart into two series of events, with two different terminations. Now if it were demonstrable that the series of the Church's actions which lead up to regeneration were, just because derived less personally and more directly from the power of the Word of God, more closely representative than the other series of the influence of the whole body, and that accordingly what would be most perfect in this imperfect state of things would be that the administration of baptism should always be attached to the rightly discerned moment of regeneration, yet it is undeniably in the nature of the case that the inclination of the Church to baptize will sometimes run ahead of the inward workings of the Spirit for regeneration and sometimes lag behind them, according as those whose office it is to baptize lean to one estimate or the other of the catechumen's inward state. Hence—as if to mitigate our dissatisfaction with this imperfect state of things— already in the Apostolic Age we find both forms of variation : the impartation of the Spirit before baptism and of baptism before the Spirit ; it is obvious, besides, that the distance between the one and the other may be greater now than it was then. In every case, however, where the decisive gracious workings of the Spirit precede, there is a peremptory summons to let baptism follow immediately as reception into the fellowship ; and, conversely, the priority of baptism is only justified by the assured faith, based on the living activity of the Church, that the regeneration of the person received will now result from the influence of the whole body. Thus taken as a whole, the number of the baptized and of the regenerate should always be identical ; yet, owing to the above-mentioned variations, though in an ever-diminishing ratio to the whole as the Church becomes more perfect, there will always be some regenerate persons who are not yet baptized but who might well have claimed to be received earlier into the Church ; similarly there will be baptized persons who are not yet regenerate but in the most active way are being commended to divine grace for regeneration by the prayers of the Church. Hence the relation of the two elements is always at bottom essentially the same, and both must be conceived as absolutely correlative, however they may now and then diverge in time.

4. It is easy to see from this how widely opinions about the worth and effects of baptism may differ without our being justified in stigmatizing as unchristian those that diverge farthest on the one side or the other. If we start with the fact that, in the actual state

of the Church, baptism and regeneration do not always coincide, it is only giving emphatic expression to this fact if we say that even if they did coincide it would be an accident, and that a man is by no means regenerate simply because he has had baptism administered to him. The same position to which, when rightly understood, there is nothing to object, may also be expressed by saying that baptism of itself produces no inward result, but is only an external sign of entrance into the Church.[1] This also is true ; but only if the external particular action, the exact moment of which is for the most part externally conditioned either by general regulations for public worship or by special circumstances, be viewed as quite independent of the activity of the Spirit in the Church. In other words the statement is true, but only as indicating the imperfection of the Church in the matter of baptism ; but if taken as a complete and general description of baptism, it is false. Without the action of the Spirit, baptism with water is certainly no more than an external rite which Christ Himself declares to be insufficient ;[2] but, as was the case with its first administration in the Church proper on the first day of Pentecost, so ever after baptism is meant to be evoked by the action of the Spirit and bound up therewith in the closest possible way. If, however, on the ground that baptism by itself does not produce regeneration, which alone matters, this position be further extended to mean either that baptism is superfluous and were best omitted, or at least that there is no better reason for retaining it than a laudable reverence for ancient institutions, such a view as this last would so entirely reverse the relationship indicated above between the baptism of John and Christian baptism that the latter would seem to be no more than an appendix to the former—an appendix always more meaningless, too, as time went on. But the former view, that baptism is superfluous, by destroying all connexion between the influences of the Christian fellowship (and on these influences baptism sets the crown) and the inward development of the individual up to regeneration, or at least by refusing it any outward expression, really destroys the Church itself, at least as an external institution ; and in all outward respects the Christian fellowship takes on as shadowy and all but fortuitous an aspect as in the case of the Society of Friends. Still, even this

---

[1] Zwingli, *l.c.* p. 220 : Externa vero res est quum tinguntur . . . ac verae rei signum ac ceremonia. . . . Sic sunt ceremoniae exteriora signa, quae accipientem aliis probant, eum se ad novam vitam obligavisse, etc.

[2] And that, as is shown by the connexion in which John 3[2] occurs, even when it is a confession of repentance.

view cannot be called absolutely unchristian ; for it disparages baptism as no more than outward in order to exalt the sole worth of what is inward, namely, regeneration.[1]

On the other hand, if we start from the fact that regeneration and entrance into the fellowship of believers are essentially bound up together and reciprocally conditioned—the more so that it is from this fellowship that all the influences of the Spirit which produce regeneration are derived—the most natural and most original statement of this is to say that one and the same series of Church actions terminates in both things—baptism and regeneration. Now this certainly is also true ; but, as has been shown, it is true only as describing a certain ideal perfection of the Church, which is not at any single point really *given*, and cannot really be manifested in any single action. From this a further inference may be drawn. It may be held that the one termination and goal must be conditioned by the other ; but that baptism cannot be conditioned by regeneration (for as regeneration is only recognizable in the facts of the new life, this would presuppose that the influence of the Church acted on the individual prior to his being received into it, which is absurd), therefore regeneration must be conditioned by baptism. Also since the earlier inward states of the individual preparatory to regeneration are evoked by earlier influences and actions of the Church, regeneration itself can only be evoked by the last action of the Church in the series, namely, baptism. This reasoning also is true and accurate if taken in a purely spiritual sense, and if even in the case of baptism as the final item in the series regard is paid solely to an inward reality which is not bound up with any particular moment of time—I mean the self-expanding movement of the Church, which can only attain its goal through the regeneration of new members. If we consider further that the inner fact of regeneration does not become fully certain in time to a man's own consciousness except through his progressive sanctification,[2] and that for a while it may often be imperilled by whatever interrupts or hinders sanctification, it must be admitted in this reference also that regeneration, as an inner possession, is conditioned by baptism. The personal self-consciousness, if uncertain and vacillating, may be

---

[1] The attitude to the Church which this view represents is revealed in the classical passage in Robert Barclay's *Apolog. Theol.* xii. p. 269 : Ea hac in re sicut in plerisque aliis inter nos et adversarios stat differentia, quod frequenter nedum formam et umbram substantiae et virtuti praeponunt, sed umbram saepe opposite ad substantiam stabiliunt.
[2] Cf. § 108, 3.

strengthened and confirmed by the common consciousness of the
Church expressed in baptism and hallowed by prayer in the name
of Christ.[1] The statement, however, is false if taken in a temporal
sense and related to the outward action, all the more if this action
be conceived in abstraction from the motives on which it is based,
as well as from their antecendent influence. For then what emerges
is the monstrous position that God must necessarily justify the man
to whom the Church grants baptism, however little ground there
may be for that in his inward condition. Such distortions of the
truth we cannot all the same describe as absolutely unchristian,
though they come very near to magic and therefore are censurable
and dangerous and have done most to provoke the above-cited
assertions, which are one-sided in the opposite sense. For the power
thus ascribed to the Church is after all traced back to Christ Himself,
and the fruit of baptism is represented as being not merely the
remission of sin but also living union with Christ.

In the following paragraphs we shall develop what can be put
forward as Church doctrine within these limits, allowing for the
necessary margin of freedom.

§ 137. *First Theorem.*—*Baptism bestowed according to the institution
of Christ confers, along with citizenship in the Christian
Church, salvation also as conditioned by the divine grace in
regeneration.*

Conf. Aug. ix. : De baptismo docent quod sit necessarius ad salutem,
quodque per baptismum offeratur gratia dei.—*Art. Smalc.* v. : Baptismus nihil
est aliud quam verbum dei cum mersione in aquam secundum ipsius institu-
tionem et mandatum. . . . Quare non sentimus cum Thoma qui dicit deum
spiritualem virtutem aquae contulisse . . . quae peccatum per aquam
abluat. Non etiam facimus cum Scoto, qui docet baptismo ablui peccatum
. . . et hanc ablutionem fieri tantum per Dei voluntatem, et minime per
verbum et aquam.—*Conf. Saxon* : Ego baptizo te, id est ego testificor hac
mersione te ablui a peccatis et recipi iam a vero deo . . . quem agnoscis
. . . et certo statuis tibi tribui beneficia, quae in evangelio promisit, te esse
membrum ecclesiae dei.—*Luth. Catech. maj.* : Sola fides personam dignam
facit, ut hanc salutarem et divinam aquam utiliter suscipiat. . . . Eo enim
quod te aqua perfundi sinis baptismum nondum percepisti aut servasti
ut inde aliquod emolumenti ad te redeat. . . . Deinde hoc quoque dicimus
non summam vim in hoc sitam esse, num ille qui baptizetur credat necne ; per
hoc enim baptismo nihil detrahitur.—*Expos. simpl.* xix. : In baptismo enim
signum est elementum aquae, ablutioque illa visibilis quae fit per ministrum.
Res autem significata est regeneratio vel ablutio a peccatis. Baptizari in

---

[1] Ita baptismus intuendus est et nobis fructuosus faciendus, ut in hoc
freti corroboremur et confirmemur, quoties peccatis aut conscientiâ gravamur.
Luther, *Catech. maj.*

nomine Christi est inscribi initiari et *recipi* . . . in haereditatem filiorum Dei . . . et *donari* varia dei gratia ad vitam novam.—*Conf. Gallic.* xxxv. : Baptismus nobis *testificandae* nostrae adoptioni datus, quoniam in eo inserimur Christi corpori, ut eius sanguine abluti, simul etiam ipsius spiritu . . . renovemur . . .—*Conf. Belg.* xxxiv. : Mandavit ut omnes qui sui sunt . . . baptizentur, ut eo significet, quod sicuti aqua in nos infusa . . . sordes abluit, sic et sanguis Christi per Spir. s. idem praestat interne in anima, adspergens eam et a peccatis suis eam mundans, nosque ex filiis irae in filios dei regenerans.—*Colloq. Lips.*, p. 400 : ' Although the grace of God doth not work salvation through baptism *ex opere operato* . . . or through the mere outward washing ; yet is it done in virtue of the word of institution and promise by means of baptism.'

1. In the statements of the two Protestant Churches there is obvious a certain vacillation of opinion, so that if we compare the different passages it is not easy to decide whether in baptism something is given and communicated from the one side and acquired on the other, or whether something is merely indicated and attested or offered. Of this vacillation our paragraph shows no trace ; it places itself on the side of those who ascribe most to baptism ; hence the greater the effect attributed to baptism, the more important it is to determine how much belongs to the institution of Christ to which such an effect is attached. Here we may first of all distinguish between the action itself and the intention with which it is performed : the first by itself alone is only the external side of baptism, the second the internal ; and since the alleged effect is something purely spiritual and inward, this means that the external action simply by itself cannot produce the effect, and the connexion between the two is mediated solely by the intention on which the whole is based. According to the words of Christ Himself [1] and the interpretation of them in act given by His disciples,[2] this effect is reception into the fellowship of disciples ; for only within this fellowship is that ' teaching them to hold ' all that Christ commanded to be found which differs from the evocation of faith or ' making disciples.' Only, the effect of the action does not depend on the intention being pure and unmixed, or on its always being definitely present to the mind of the person by whom baptism is administered.[3] For the action is not the action of any single individual ; the individual only performs it in virtue of the authority therefor which he has received from the Church, and thus as an action of the Church. But the intention of the Church in bestowing this authority can have been none other than the right and true intention indicated

[1] Matt. 28[19, 20].   [2] Acts 2[41, 47].

[3] Here the canon is applicable : Licet uti sacramentis quae per malos administrantur. *Conf. Aug.* vii. and elsewhere.

above.   On this assumption, it is a general principle for all ages
during which the Church may continue to be divided into a number
of relatively antagonistic communions, that baptism which anyone
of them causes to be administered is valid not only for the administering Church itself but for all Churches whatsoever, because
in baptizing they all have the intention to receive into the Christian
Church.   Nay, even supposing some one Church were to add to the
action something having a special relevance to its own party
interest, the other Churches might certainly correct this necessarily
improper addition, and deny its value, but they would not on that
account challenge the validity of the action as a whole, provided the
institution of baptism was not itself challenged.   This principle
is rightly taken to cover heretical parties also ; for they regard
themselves as the true Christians, and their intention always is to
receive those baptized into Christendom.   It is true, in doing so
they likewise intend to propagate their heresy ; but all the orthodox
Church need do is to counteract such heresy strongly in the minds
of the persons baptized, without having on that account to destroy
the original common Christian foundation that has been laid.

As regards the action itself, what ought principally to be noted
in the descriptions given of it in the passages cited is this, that not
only does the water not have any importance in itself apart from
the action, but even the external action, be it complete or partial
immersion—and to the latter type belongs every kind of laving
or sprinkling with water—is connected with the intention solely
through the accession of the Word of God ; without this the action
would be incomplete.   Obvious as this may be, we would not
thereby assert that in His institution Christ gave command that
specific words should be pronounced during the outward action, and
that a baptism therefore is invalid which is lacking in the words
meant to be uttered uniformly, always and everywhere.   What we
do hold is that along with the action there must go a presentation
of the Word of God on which discipleship rests, and this in point of
fact is the Word of Father, Son, and Spirit ; and through appeal to
this Word, as of equally sacred significance for baptizer and baptized,
baptism has its higher significance conserved, for that appeal expresses the intention of the Church and the assenting wish of the
catechumen.   The utterance of the regular formula, however, can
only be described as an ancient Church tradition ; the only general
rule we can state is this, that as no man performs baptism except
by the authority of the Church, he ought to perform it in a manner

consonant with his authority. Hence it cannot be right to make the validity of baptism administered by different religious parties depend on their keeping the formula unchanged, as though in baptism the formula were the substantial thing.[1] Such a demand would certainly bring us into conflict with baptism as performed by Christ's disciples during His lifetime, for they cannot at that time have baptized in the name of the Holy Spirit.[2] Nay, it will probably never be possible to make out whether later, from Pentecost onwards, the Apostles themselves used the formula, or felt that Christ's teaching enjoined them to use it. Occasion has been found in hypothetical cases of extreme urgency, such as could never really occur, to raise the question whether in such a case something else might not be substituted for water ; but it might also be asked whether, if a case arose in which for the sake of the baptized person signs had to be substituted for words, such signs would be valid as reproducing not the words themselves but only their meaning, whereas spoken words differing from the formula but the same in meaning would be invalid. What, however, is much the most essential point in the relation to the Word of God that goes to constitute baptism, is just that the Word must be known to the baptized person and acknowledged by him. For obviously this implies that his being made a disciple, which can only take place through the power of the Word, preceded baptism ; this is the practice which everywhere we find observed by the Apostles, so far as our information goes. Indeed, apart from this the action cannot be regarded as complete. For just as it is only through the accession of the Word to the external rite that the Church expresses her intention, so, too, it is only through his appropriation of the Word that the baptized person's assent to this intention is expressed.

2. From what has now been said regarding the nature of the action, and especially from the fact that the baptized person is asked to give a confession of the Word joined to the action, it follows very clearly that the baptized person's faith is a precondition of the action really being what it is intended to be. So much lies before us in Christ's two sayings about baptism.[3] For even if in the first saying we seek to combine ' making disciples ' and baptizing as closely as possible, what we there have is a later elaboration which only reached its final stage in the second saying, and which from the outset could only represent an approximation to faith ; and even in

[1] Cf. Gerhard, *Loc. Theol.* ix. p. 90.   [2] John 4[2] ; cf. 7[39].
[3] Matt. 28[19, 20] and Mark 16[16].

baptism this approximation could only be fully realized if the baptized person were prepared to make confession of the Word that accompanies baptism. Similarly, the faith which in the other passage Christ makes an antecedent of baptism must be the very faith of which we have been speaking all along. Peter, indeed, seems to demand merely repentance, not faith, before baptism ;[1] still, it was repentance for the part which his hearers, as members of the Jewish nation, had had in the rejection of Christ, a repentance which had only been rendered possible through the acknowledgment of Christ and adoption of His cause which they owed to Peter's address ; and this of itself must involve faith. Peter brings in this demand at the close of his sermon ; he must therefore have started with the same assumption as Paul,[2] and been convinced that his preaching had already produced faith in every case where this was a possibility. Similarly, our thought of the Church, as constantly engaged in preaching, must be that it ought to conclude preaching by baptism, but not interrupt preaching to baptize. Now in the quoted credal passages it is also stated that baptism is proper and complete even without faith, and it tallies with this that other thinkers represent faith as the fruit and consequence of baptism. But against both views we must enter a protest. Baptism is received wrongly if it be received without faith, and it is wrongly given so. True, the ordinance loses none of its significance, whether considered as originally an institution of Christ or in its more definite form as an ordinance of the Church ; but this is so only because the Church can never have laid down that it is a matter of indifference whether those baptized are believers or not. For the same reason, baptism as an act of the mere individual has never been such that the Church could approve of it and regard it quite as its own ; in any case such acts of baptism fall under the head of imperfect Church administration. But if this only means that even in such cases baptism need not be repeated, the point is one which requires to be stated more emphatically, lest we should seem to be ignoring what are manifest imperfections. Baptism, that is to say, is ineffectual only when it is imparted prematurely, before the work of preaching is complete and has awakened faith. It is different with the assertion that faith springs from baptism as its fruit.[3] This is obviously in contradiction to the whole practice of the Apostles

[1] Acts 2[38].   [2] Rom. 10[17].
[3] See Gerhard, *Loc. Theol.* ix. p. 152, where the statement is made that baptism kindles faith in the heart of the person baptized, but not the slightest proof is given of the connexion between the two things.

and the whole experience of the Church as it grew in consequence of mass-baptism ; nay, even in the individual case, where one who is still an unbeliever has been baptized too early, the Church does not rely on baptism alone but carries on the work of preaching in the full sense of the word ; and if in these circumstances faith arises later, no simple Christian mind will ascribe this to the wrongly administered baptism, but to what subsequently to baptism has been done by the Church.

As regards complete baptism, which implies the existing faith of the person baptized, what we say is that it effects salvation, but only along with citizenship in the Christian Church ; that is to say, only in so far as it mediates reception into the fellowship. To this it might be objected that if baptism presupposes faith, then salvation precedes baptism, for we ourselves have explained faith as the appropriation of the perfection and blessedness of Christ ; [1] and a study of this objection is peculiarly fitted to cast light on the whole problem. It goes back to the relation of this Section to the second Division of the previous Section. Faith as an inward state of the individual is the appropriation just described, but the influence of the appropriated perfection of Christ and the enjoyment of His appropriated blessedness become real only within the fellowship of believers ; hence the man in whom faith develops also has the desire to enter the fellowship. In this sense baptism as direct reception into the fellowship of believers is also named the seal of divine grace,[2] because the real enjoyment of grace is thereby guaranteed. Hence all such persons can be regarded as seeking baptism which then the Church grants, just as conversely in other cases the Church offers it and those who have become believers receive it. In the same way we called baptism the channel of God's justifying action, because it is only within the fellowship that an individual can come to have the forgiveness of sins, which is essentially conditioned by the influence of the new communal life, and divine sonship, which is essentially conditioned by fellow-citizenship with the saints. If we want to separate in word what is inseparable in fact, we may on the one hand say that where faith is, conversion must have been ; and where complete regeneration is, there too is justification. Hence if faith was there before baptism, all that is ordinarily represented as the fruit of baptism was there also ; thus baptism would really effect nothing, but only attest and point to what had been effected already ; and thus the one class of credal passages

---

[1] See § 108.　　　　[2] *Heidelb. Catech.*, Quest. 69–72.

can take the form they do without in the least impairing the true force of baptism. On the other hand, it may be said that even if faith is not yet present at the time of baptism, yet it will arise not merely *after* baptism but—baptism being the first item in the whole series of influences which the Church brings to bear on the baptized —*through* baptism. Thus every sort of connexion between personal spiritual life and the perfection and blessedness of Christ would arise out of baptism ; the more so that if (to suppose the case) a regenerate person remained unbaptized and hence was not received into the Christian fellowship, we should have to admit that he could have no real share in the perfection and blessedness of Christ because he had neither come under Christ's fellowship-forming action nor shared in His blessedness as mediated through the communal consciousness. This, it is true, would hold good in a still greater degree if it were the personal desire of the person in question to remain outside the fellowship, and in a less degree if it were only through an ecclesiastical oversight that, although regenerate, he was not yet baptized. Hence the other set of our credal passages is able to ascribe to baptism both faith and all that flows from faith without giving to its mode of operation the least colour of magic. The meaning is not that the outward performance works even in the faintest degree *ex opere operato*, whether by itself or in conjunction with the utterance of certain words (the utterance would itself in that case be no more than an outward performance), but that it works solely in union with the Word which ordains baptism for the Church and along with the Church, and which is uninterruptedly active in the Church throughout its whole extent. And as our paragraph only asserts the efficacy of baptism in connexion with divine grace in regeneration, and thus links up the act of the Church with what is going on in the individual soul, magical conceptions are very definitely barred out. But it distinctly ascribes a saving efficacy to baptism, as the conferring of Christian citizenship, and this is a rejection of the view according to which baptism is a merely external act. Thus our paragraph lends itself to both readings of the credal phrases, which otherwise mutually impute responsibility for one or other of the misconceptions we have been discussing.

4. Hence we may say that everything that is taught about the efficacy of baptism is perfectly clear if we only assume a correct and sound administration of the sacrament ; in that case there is absolutely no reason to ascribe to it magical effects or to depress it into a merely outward usage. It is only the assumption of a wrong

administration that raises difficult questions : that is, if our aim is
to formulate doctrines which shall be equally valid for both cases.
For then one party sets up a principle which obviously isolates the
outward aspect, namely, that the effects of divine grace ought not
to be made dependent on any external act ; [1] the other urges the
principle, plainly favourable to magic, that no state of human consciousness can make inoperative divine promises which have been
attached to an external act ; [2] both without sufficiently remember-
ing that God is not a God of disorder in the assemblies of His people.
Hence everything depends on a sound rule of administration.
Against the Donatists it is rightly taught that the validity of
baptism does not depend on the state of heart in him who performs
it ; but the same cannot be said equally regarding the saving virtue
of baptism.   If the person baptizing is not a pure organ of the
Church in judging of the inward state of the person baptized, the
saving virtue of baptism must be impaired in every case.   Every
such baptism, however, is an act of sin ; and the oftener it occurs,
the more imperfect the Church is.   Hence the first rule is that not
only the decision when baptism should take place, but its administration too, ought to rest in the hands of the ministers of the Word in
the strict sense ; [3] for obviously the person who must have the
most vivid conviction of the faith evoked in the candidate for
baptism is also the best organ of the Church in performing the act
itself.   And for the same reason baptism is not put at the mercy of
some one hour of exalted feeling ; it is only performed as a well-
considered act at a prearranged time, no exception being permissible
except under special circumstances.   The rule to follow will always
be this, that the administration must be conditioned by the sympathy
of the Church (for of those operations of the divine Spirit on the
soul which may be trusted to evoke faith there can scarcely be
knowledge proper), and that when such sympathy is absent, it is
best to wait for the recognizable tokens of faith.

§ 138. *Second Theorem.—Infant Baptism is a complete Baptism
      only when the profession of faith which comes after further
      instruction is regarded as the act which consummates it.*

Conf. Aug. ix. : docent . . . quod pueri sint baptizandi, qui per baptismum oblati deo recipiantur in gratiam Dei.   Damnant Anabaptistas, qui
improbant baptismum puerorum et affirmant pueros sine baptismo salvos

---

[1] Zwingli, *de ver. relig.*, p. 200 : Nam hac ratione libertas divini spiritus
alligata esset, qui dividit singulis ut vult.
[2] *Catech. Rom.* ii. *de bapt.* 58.
[3] *Expos. simpl.* xx. : Baptismus autem pertinet ad officia ecclesiastica.

fieri.—*Art. Smalc.* v. : . . . docemus infantes esse baptizandos. Pertinent enim ad promissam redemtionem per Christum factam ; et ecclesia debet illis baptismum et promissionis illius annunciationem.—*Expos. simpl.* xx. : Cur non per sanctum baptisma initiarentur, qui sunt peculium et in ecclesia Dei.—*Conf. Gallic.* xxxv. : Praeterea quamvis baptismus sit fidei et re-sipiscentiae sacramentum, tamen cum una cum parentibus posteritatem etiam illorum in ecclesia Deus recenseat, affirmamus infantes sanctis paren-tibus natos esse ex Christi auctoritate baptizandos.—*Conf. Belg.* xxxiv. : . . . quos (infantes) baptizandos et foederis signo obsignandos esse credimus. Quin etiam revera Christus non minus sanguinem suum profudit ut fidelium infantes quam ut adultos ablueret, ideoque signum seu sacramentum ejus quod Christus pro eis praestitit, suscipere debent.—*Decl. Thorun.*, p. 429 : . . . Quamvis necessitatem illam adeo absolutam non esse statuamus, ut quicunque sine baptismo ex hac vita excesserit sive infans sive adultus . . . propterea necessario damnandus sit.

1. Thus far we have treated of baptism in general, without even considering the difference between the original institution and the present almost universal practice of the Christian Church, though certainly with the intention that the propositions laid down should not be limited in their application to the baptism of adults but be valid for every baptism that means to be genuinely Chris-tian. Hence we insisted on at least incipient faith and (in line with former paragraphs [1] and therefore necessary) repentance also as preconditions of baptism. With this the practice of the Apostolic Age completely agrees, as far as we know ; for every trace of infant baptism which people have professed to find in the New Testament must first be inserted there. Similarly, in the absence of definite information it is difficult to explain how such a diver-gence from the original institution could arise and could prevail over so wide an area. It might be difficult to specify *one* sufficient reason for the change, but there might well be a multiplicity of reasons which, taken together, were able to win over Christian feeling. First, the desire to be able to include among those who die in the Lord those Christian children who had died before the age of instruction.[2] Next, to make the Christian community more definitely responsible for the children of Christian parents in cases where the parents might not themselves be in a position to imple-ment the obligations of the congregation. And finally, in order to separate off Christian children from Jewish and pagan youth. These may from the first have been the strongest motives. When, how-ever, it became an established custom to regard children who had re-ceived baptism as for that reason members of the Church, it was felt as being in itself a source of comfort that in this act there should be

---

[1] Those referring to regeneration, §§ 107–109.   [2] 1 Thess. 4[16].

expressed a firm confidence that children born of Christian parents would not miss the nurturing care of the Holy Spirit. Our credal passages, however, view infant baptism entirely apart from history and undertake to vindicate it in and for itself, but they do so ineffectively and on grounds that are mutually destructive. If the children are already God's possession, they have no need of baptism in order to be thus offered to God and received by Him to grace ; and conversely, if they need baptism for this, the justification of its being administered to them cannot lie in the fact that already they are God's possession. Similarly it needed to be specially proved (for it does not prove itself) that God reckons offspring along with parents as forming part of the Church ; also a certain qualification—which is not mentioned—needs to be attached to the principle that we ought to baptize children because Christ shed His blood for them also. On these grounds we should have to baptize all men whatsoever, as we could lay hold of them. The missing qualification of this last position rests ultimately on the peculiar situation of the children of Christian parents, as the special justification of the former position does also ; hence it can be seen that our paragraph is an effort to supply these defects and at the same time to solve the contradictions first alluded to. For while, if we take it in close connexion with the previous paragraph, it gives an inadequate explanation of infant baptism, which here is administered in the absence of repentance and faith in those baptized, yet it tacitly admits that infant baptism cannot produce in those baptized the effects of which repentance and faith are the necessary conditions. And just as we cannot suppose that before baptism children are subject to misery due to a consciousness of sin which is ·growing into penitence, we cannot after baptism ascribe to them blessedness due to a dawning sense of divine sonship. Hence there need be no talk of proving that even in such children faith can be produced by baptism. Our paragraph shows, nevertheless, why there is occasion to administer baptism in this form, namely, because in the case of such children we have reason to count upon their future faith and their confession of it. With this is bound up the question how far we may consider them as reckoned by God part of the Church ; the answer being that it is part of Church order to bring them, as the outer circle most intimately entrusted to us, into direct relation to the Word of God, and to maintain them therein until faith awakens. It is from this point of view that the contradictions referred to are most easily resolved. For we only wish to avoid saying that we baptize children because they are already in the Church and in order to commend them to divine grace ; we baptize them rather because already they are marked out for it by their natural connexion with the Christian order in which God has placed them, and with a view to bringing them into the Church. The full truth of both aspects is expressed by saying that for us personal confession of faith is the goal of infant baptism, a goal which it must reach, and by reaching which it has to vindicate itself. On the other hand, it is certain that where this point is not carefully attended to, the ecclesiastical custom of baptizing infants is largely responsible for the fact that some people attribute magical powers to baptism, while others disparage it as a purely external custom.

2. Clearly then this sort of baptism merely by itself, while a bond between the individual and the Kingdom of God, does not straightway imply the possession and enjoyment of salvation but only a normal preparatory operation of the Holy Spirit. Hence any such act taken by itself is in no sense to be equated with baptism according to Christ's original institution, where a personal confession of faith is included in the act itself. Yet this defect does not render the act invalid, as though it were positively wrong ; and the Anabaptist assertion that, in the case of persons baptized so, baptism must be repeated, has rightly been felt to give offence. On such terms no baptism at all would be secure except such as in the early Church—and it was certainly not a laudable custom— was administered shortly before death ; for there can be no surer sign of real regeneration than steady progress in Christian sanctifica- tion. Thus infant baptism is the same as any other baptism which has erroneously been imparted prior to the full faith of the person baptized and yet is valid ; only, its proper efficacy is sus- pended until the person baptized has really become a believer. Our paragraph, however, has still to vindicate itself on the point that we made these imperfect baptisms in detail a reproach to the Church, whereas we now are seeking to find a legitimate place for them as a whole. But this is one of those cases in which conscious divergence must be judged more leniently than unconscious. The latter is at all events overhasty, and on the other hand, it repre- sents as a believing Christian one who as yet is not so ; the former, on the contrary, is a Church rule, and by its forward reference to the personal profession of faith it definitely marks off those baptized in this way from those who already believe. It is there-

fore unjust to infant baptism when confirmation—which for us is simply the depositing and acceptance of a personal profession of faith, and thus supplies a lack in baptism—is regarded as non-essential ; for it is only as combined with confirmation that infant baptism answers to Christ's institution. Hence our paragraph, by making confirmation a part of the administration of baptism, lays it as a duty on the Church to give confirmation very close attention, in order that, so far as the Church can secure it, the later rite may approve itself the true and worthy consummation of infant baptism. It is equally unjust when confirmation is torn away from this context and represented as a sacrament by itself. Whatever we ought to think otherwise of the importance and benefit of confirmation, to isolate it is to render infant baptism incomplete and ineffectual.

Still, we cannot affirm the necessary character of a baptism thus divided into two parts, as is done when the Anabaptists or Baptists are condemned on the ground that they believe that children dying unbaptized may be saved. In this matter we take sides unhesitatingly with the last credal passage quoted above. It is certainly the case that as soon as large numbers of children born of Christian parents had to be nurtured in the Christian Church. a situation emerged which previously had been unknown ; and it seems as if it were in the highest degree natural to mark this by a symbolic act, the more so that nearly everywhere just such acts are performed to indicate that the newly-born do not belong exclusively to their parents, but corporately to the whole fellowship. Besides, nothing was more natural than to select baptism for this purpose. Hence it would have been quite intelligible if, to recover touch with Christ's institution, infant baptism had been abolished at the Reformation ; and this we might do even yet, without thereby losing continuity with a fellowship in whose history there was a period when nothing prevailed except infant baptism—provided only we did not declare infant baptism to be invalid. And we might equally well give up the practice altogether without doing our children any injury. For it is only if we ascribe magical powers to baptism that we can believe that it confers a claim relating to the life after death, quite irrespectively of its influence on this life. Hence no one who does not believe in such magical powers can suppose that there is any difference between children who have been baptized but die before renewing their baptismal covenant, and children who pass out of time without any baptism at all. It would therefore be a natural thing to leave it to each Evangelical household to decide whether it will present its children for baptism in the ordinary way or only when they make a personal profession of faith ; and we ought to make it known that in regard to this point we cancel the sentence of condemnation passed on the Anabaptists, and that on our side we are prepared to enter into Church fellowship with the Baptists of to-day, if only they will not pronounce our infant baptism absolutely invalid, even when supplemented by confirmation. On this point it should easily be possible to reach an understanding.

FOURTH DOCTRINE : THE LORD'S SUPPER

§ 139. *Christians in partaking of the Lord's Supper experience a peculiar strengthening of the spiritual life ; for therein, according to the institution of Christ, His body and blood are administered to them.*

1. Our paragraphs ought in every case to contain simply the expression of our Christian consciousness ; hence at this point we must start with the experience we ourselves have of this sacramental action, and (proving that we do not regard the experience as a purely personal thing) expect all believers to have. Only thereafter can we take up the further question how this experience first originated. The two questions hang together only in this respect, that the experience would not repeat itself perpetually, or at least the interpretation and treatment of the subject would have taken a quite different line, if there had not been some need which thus found satisfaction. To keep touch with the previous Doctrine, the subject of the present one would be utterly devoid of content if the salvation beginning with rightly administered baptism were so conferred that automatically it sustained itself unimpaired and adequately secured its own growth. The analogy of all life, however, argues the contrary ; and it lies in the indissoluble bond between entrance into the living fellowship of Christ and entrance into the fellowship of believers that each of these two must be supported by the other. But just for that reason the mode in which the Church coexists with the world, as well as the hampering influence of the world on the Church, demands that this fellowship should periodically be nourished and strengthened ; and it is the satisfaction of this need that believers seek in the sacrament of the altar. If now we provisionally regard the fellowship of believers with each other and the fellowship of each individual

with Christ as being each of them separate and by itself, the latter fellowship will be fortified against the influences of the world by every moment of devout self-recollection in the believer's life, during which on the one hand he closes his heart to worldly influences and on the other presents Christ to himself, out of Scripture—for it is always out of Scripture, directly or indirectly, that the thing is done.   Over and above this, the fellowship of believers with each other is strengthened by every energetic and affecting manifestation of Christian love in any sphere of the common life.   But each of these kinds of fellowship should influence the other ; therefore between lonely contemplation and common active life there lies that intermediate sphere which we describe by the general term, public worship.   This, viewed on one side, is simply the common life itself, withdrawing from outward activity to communicative representation of what is inward ; viewed on the other side it is simply contemplation itself, moving out of privacy and expanding into the communal.   Here, therefore, the two kinds of fellowship unite—that of believers with each other and that of each soul with Christ ; and hence it is clear that everything that takes place here must have effects on both ; while at the same time every effect one kind of fellowship has on the other seems necessarily to emanate from this intermediate sphere and to pass through it.   It is to this sphere that the Lord's Supper too belongs ; for Christ instituted it as a communal act, which, while it is a presenting of Himself, is certainly a strengthening of both kinds of fellowship.   For this reason, in the Church it is invariably celebrated in gatherings of the congregation : every other sort of celebration is an exceptional case, which ought also to be representative of the congregation assembled together.

But as it is only through trust in what other people profess as their experience that the individual can come to have the same experience as his own, we are led back by an unbroken tradition to the beginnings of the Church, and to the Supper itself as Christ held it with His disciples.   Now from of old the essential thing has been held to, be the bestowal of Christ's body and blood, and elsewhere He makes participation in His flesh and blood essential for having life.   These two, accordingly, are the principal points which have first to be discussed—namely, how the Supper as the bestowal of Christ's body and blood is related to the purely spiritual participation, and how the Supper as an element in public worship is distinguished from other parts thereof.

2. To begin with the second point, it is pretty clear that Christen·dom as a whole in its public teaching and practice has from of old regarded the Supper as the climax of public worship.[1] The rounded whole of our united experience in public worship would seem to us incomplete unless at definite points—and most often at the highest and holiest points—the Supper held its place as the most intimate bond of all. Similarly we should feel it to be a morbid thing—whether in the case of individuals or of entire congregations—if any other element of worship were to have attributed to it a greater power of sustaining and heightening blessedness than the Supper has. But we cannot rest satisfied with this ; we must inquire as to the specific difference between what has come to be practised in the Church (even though it were with an unerring sense for the common good) and what Christ has thus ordained ; and the difference appears to be this. In all other elements of public worship the aforesaid twofold effect on the fellowship of believers with each other and on the fellowship of each with Christ respectively is unequal ; and for that reason they seem one-sided. The more markedly an individual stands out and draws others to himself, or the more powerfully a common mood of feeling finds expression and is heightened by being communicated to others, the intenser is the reaction on the common life. But what the effect on the fellowship of each soul with Christ will be depends on the personal spontaneity with which each brings that which has been publicly represented and expressed to bear on his relation to Christ and inwardly digests it. Each of the two kinds of effect, that is, depends on something else ; hence one may be strong while the other is weak. In the Supper, on the other hand, it is impossible for the two to be separated or distinguished ; the Supper rests on nothing that is individual or peculiar, which might turn the effect to one side or the other ; nor does the distributing minister exert any personal force on the receivers, or the receivers individually exert any special and inward spontaneity. Rather it is simply the whole redeeming love of Christ to which we are pointed there ; and as the distributing minister is nothing more than the organ of Christ's institution, the receivers uniformly find themselves simply in a state of completely open receptivity for Christ's influence. Without the special interposition of any individual, therefore, every effect flows directly and undividedly from the Word of institution in which the redeeming and fellowship-

[1] Cf. *Conf. Saxon.*, pp. 170 f.

forming love of Christ is not only represented but made newly active, and in trustful obedience to which the sacramental action is ever anew performed. It is in this undivided and exclusive immediacy and in the resulting freedom of its effects from dependence on changing personal moods and circumstances, that the Supper differs from all other elements of public worship.

As regards the second point, it is clear that in the discourse,[1] where Christ recommends as essential the eating of His flesh and the drinking of His blood, He had in mind neither the Supper nor any other definite act. He wished rather to indicate in how profound a sense He Himself must become our being and well-being ; and clearly, if we compare His words here with that other saying that we must be related to Him as the branch to the vine,[2] there is no difference between the two except this—that the latter lays stress more on the continuity of the relationship, the former on its periodical renewal. Nor can anyone doubt that the same expression may be used to denote the periodically recurring effect of the Supper ; and not merely the effect which it has on the fellowship of the individual with Christ, as a repeated nourishing of personal spiritual life out of the fulness of Christ's life, but the effect which it is also bound to exert on our fellowship with each other. For, as it is a simultaneous act of many, and has the same effect in all, the consciousness of benefit in each is accompanied by a sympathetic sense that the same thing is happening to others ; and as each knows that the others are being united more closely with Christ, he feels himself more closely united with them. This is not in any sense an exclusive relation to each other of those who are communicating at any one time ; as explained above, each represents to the others the whole congregation. But while indisputably the spiritual participation in the flesh of Christ referred to above can take place more generally in a variety of ways, the Lord's Supper is distinct from all else in this respect that in it the same result is bound up with this definite action, blessed and hallowed by the word of Christ. In itself this is not something unintelligible to believers or requiring special explanation, all the more that it follows the analogy of all important memorial rites ; and deeply as the external side of the action, in its actual form, appeals to us by its varied significance, we yet can easily concede that if it had pleased Christ to give His ordinance a different form we should

[1] John 6[52.56].   [2] John 15[4.6].

nevertheless expect from it the same result, and that that outward form would soon have come to possess a like suggestiveness of meaning. Hence anything that is obscure and, in the degree in which it is explained, more or less unintelligible is to be found solely in the terms used by Christ in relating the outward action to the effect as above described.

3. With a view to more exact discussion of this, assuming (as our paragraph does) that the effect of the action depends on the action being in harmony with Christ's institution, we must first clear up our minds on the point, what precisely such harmony implies. Even if different parties did not protest that the Supper as celebrated by others than themselves was no Supper at all, the variety of eucharistic practice within the Church sufficiently declares that on this point no agreement has so far been reached. It is not difficult, however, to show that such agreement is impossible. As regards both the action and the elements used there are a material and a formal identity which, owing to changed modes of life, cannot be attained together, but only one at the cost of the other ; and in such a situation it is virtually impossible that all should make their choice on the same principle. In general it may be said that insistence on material identity betrays an imperfect inward state, and a truly spiritual Christianity without troubling about the matter would be content if only the rite were so arranged as to represent the original action in its essential features. On the one hand, the historical unity and continuity of the ordinance would be endangered, and there would be no limit to the arbitrary variations introduced, if we were to be wholly indifferent to material identity. On the other, the representation of the original action may be made to depend on quite different points. Hence the problem to be solved can hardly be stated otherwise than by saying that we ought to try for just so much of each sort of identity as can be obtained without sacrifice on the other side. Thus in regard to the elements, we ask that in the Supper there should be eaten what, as used, can rightly be called bread, but not that it should be prepared from the ordinary materials or in the ordinary way ; on the other hand, that in what is drunk there should be wine of the grape, but not the common drink of this place or that, even supposing the common drink to be something different from wine. In regard to the action, we consider it essential that all the communicants should eat and drink in the same way, and that bread and wine should be distributed and received, also that the action

as a common meal should follow upon a devotional address and common prayer. But that it should take place in the evening and be merely the conclusion of another more complete meal, in itself of a worshipping character, so that what is partaken of in the Supper is only what remains over from the former meal—this, it would seem, we cannot insist on, for under present conditions it is unattainable. Indeed, if, still keeping to the last point, it were held that the Supper had such a close relation to the Jewish feast of the Passover that no representation of the impression originally made could be attained unless the Passover too were represented in all its original significance, it would be easy to infer that in that case the Supper can never again be what in Christ's institution it was, and therefore cannot really have been ordained by Him for the Church as an independent and never-ending institution. This objection is so natural that it may yet easily make itself more audible in the Evangelical Church than has hitherto been the case, and it of course raises the question on what in this matter our faith really rests. It can hardly be maintained that the intention to institute a permanent rite is revealed with perfect clearness in the words of Christ, as they have actually been preserved. On the contrary, some of the narratives contain no such injunction ;[1] in others it is only indistinctly expressed ;[2] and as the Apostles deduced no such command from Christ's words at the foot-washing,[3] they could (it is said) have had no more right to make of the Supper a perpetual and universal institution.[4] But as it is obvious that they did the one and did not do the other, we may well keep to the procedure they actually enjoined, without having to decide whether Christ expressly gave them still other injunctions touching the Supper,[5] or whether they deduced such injunctions from His words, or whether it was simply by their direct impressions of the case or by the accompanying circumstances that they were led to take different courses in regard to the Supper and in regard to the foot-washing. In the last of these cases we should not be able to view the Supper as in quite the same sense directly instituted by Christ, but we should still have to hold that the Apostles acted in His sense—unless, indeed, we are going to give up their canonical authority in a matter which touches the very heart and core of their vocation.

---

[1] Matt. 26²⁶⁻²⁸ and Mark 14²²⁻²⁴.
[2] Luke 22¹⁹⁻²⁰ and I Cor. 11²⁴⁻²⁵.
[3] John 13¹⁴⁻¹⁶.
[4] Cf. R. Barclay, *Apol. Th.* xiii.
[5] Cf. I Cor. 11²³.

§ 140. *With regard to the connexion between the bread and wine and the body and blood of Christ in the Lord's Supper, the Evangelical (Protestant) Church takes up an attitude of definite opposition only, on the one hand, to those who regard this connexion as independent of the act of participation, and, on the other hand, to those who, regardless of this connexion, would not admit any conjunction between participation in the bread and wine and spiritual participation in the flesh and blood of Christ.*

Augs. Conf., Art. 10 : ' On the Lord's Supper accordingly it is taught that the true body and blood of Christ is veritably present in the Supper under the form of bread and wine, and is there distributed and received.'—*Apol. Conf.* iv. : Quod in coena domini vere et substantialiter adsint corpus et sanguis Christi, et vere exhibeantur cum illis rebus, quae videntur, pane et vino his qui sacramentum accipiunt. . . . Cum enim Paulus dicat panem esse participationem corporis domini, sequeretur panem non esse participationem corporis sed tantum spiritus Christi, si non adesset vere corpus domini.—*Art. Smalc.* vi. : De sacramento altaris sentimus panem et vinum in coena esse verum corpus et sanguinem Christi, et non tantum dari et sumi a piis sed etiam ab impiis Christianis.—*Expos. simpl.* xix. : In coena domini signum est panis et vinum sumtum ex communi usu cibi et potus, res autem significata est ipsum traditum domini corpus, et sanguis eius effusus pro nobis, vel communio corporis et sanguinis domini.—*Ibid.* xxi. : Foris offertur a ministro panis, et audiuntur voces domini, etc., ergo accipiunt fideles et edunt, etc. : intus interim opera Christi per spiritum sanctum percipiunt etiam carnem et sanguinem domini et pascuntur his in vitam aeternam.—*Conf. Gallic.* xxxviii. : Dicimus itaque . . . panem illum et vinum illud, quod nobis in coena datur, vere nobis fieri spirituale alimentum, quatenus videlicet velut oculis nostris spectandum praebent carnem Christi nostrum cibum esse et eiusdem sanguinem nobis esse potum.—Itaque fanaticos illos omnes reiicimus qui haec signa et symbola repudiant.—*Conf. Anglic.* xxviii. : Panis et vini transsubstantiatio in Eucharistia ex sacris litteris probari non potest, sed apertis scripturae verbis adversatur. . . . Corpus Christi datur accipitur et manducatur in coena tantum coelesti et spirituali ratione. Medium autem, quo corpus Christi accipitur et manducatur in coena, fides est.

1. If the question in view here were a merely exegetical one, Dogmatic might await the close of hermeneutical discussion, and then accept the result just as it does other propositions which are not dogmatic in the full sense because what they contain is not statements about our immediate self-consciousness but facts which we receive on testimony. It is only as a fact in this sense that we could accept the conclusions of exegesis on the meaning of the words, ' This is My body,' etc. But the question is far from being purely exegetical. The language of the different narratives is not uniform ; hence (this belongs to historical criticism) we must first

of all ascertain what kind of expressions Christ can have used, from which these reports may have arisen ; only then will the time have come for inquiring into the sense of Christ's *ipsissima verba* as thus ascertained. Here we may start from very different points of view, and it is improbable that we shall be able to fix Christ's original language in a way to satisfy everyone. Also we are specially bound in dealing with the different views valid within the Evangelical Church to set forth the conviction, fundamental to the Union [of the Lutheran and Reformed Churches], that these differences are not such as to prevent common participation in the Supper. Hence we must endeavour to settle points of controversy as well as may be, and then set forth the principles on which we, so to speak, abolish the differences prevalent within our Church ; whereas we should still retain, on the one hand, the points of difference with the Catholic Church brought out in the credal passages quoted above, and, on the other, with communions and individual thinkers who deny all reality to the sacrament.

Now, to fix the points of controversy, since the differences are all due to the words of Christ just cited, and we can only recur here to what has already been made out in the previous paragraph, the question arises how the meaning of His words bears first on participation in the bread and wine, and next, on the strengthening of spiritual life expected from that ; a second question is, how far insight into the meaning of these words is requisite to the completeness of the action, and hence how far agreement in their interpretation is requisite to its communal character. To the last of these questions we can only reply by saying that the interpretation of Christ's words is essential just in so far as the expected result— namely, the strengthening of spiritual life—depends on it ; and agreement is only beneficial if differences have to be reconciled which might hinder the common performance of the rite. Regarding the first question we can only say—whether the difficult words uttered by the Redeemer be referred more to the bodily action or to the spiritual effect—that any explanation of them which can establish its own exegetical validity may be accepted as sound, provided it does not endanger for the believer the bond between the action and its effect.

2. The first kind of antagonism stated in our paragraph is that to the Catholic Church. It is on the whole wrong to look for this chiefly in the doctrine of transubstantiation. For the real issue it is an unimportant point of difference whether the body and blood

of Christ are partaken of corporeally along with the bread and wine, or the body and blood of Christ are produced in place of bread and wine for corporeal reception. The only distinction between the two is this, that in the one case bread and wine are also partaken of, while in the other we do not partake of them also ; and for the intended result this is quite immaterial. And if there had only been a willingness to give up the further notion that this change in the elements persists even apart from the act of reception, or that even what is not partaken of in the Supper undergoes the same change as the rest of the elements, the Saxon Reformers, as may be seen from the third passage quoted above, would have had little to object. On the other hand, if a disposition had been shown in any quarter to take so physical a view of consubstantiation as that the body and blood of Christ are present in the bread and wine, after the words of Christ have been spoken over them, even when they are not partaken of in the Supper, Luther would have made a serious protest. Even where he is setting forth his own view in the strongest antagonism to the Reformed doctrine, he nowhere affirms any such presence of the body and blood outside the eucharistic action ; on the other hand, ever since the rise of the doctrine of transubstantiation in the Catholic Church, this assumption of a physical and permanent change has been fundamental in all casuistical discussion. Essentially, therefore, what, on this side, provoked persistent opposition was every kind of elevation and adoration of the consecrated elements, as well as every pretension thereby to achieve something apart from actual participation ; and similarly, everywhere within the Evangelical Church it would be distinctly denied that partaking of the consecrated elements outside the celebration of the sacrament conduces either to salvation or to judgment. Hence the chief reason why (apart from its exegetical unsoundness) we reject the theory of the Catholic Church is that, advancing beyond common participation, it seeks by its so conceived union of the elements with the body and blood of Christ to attain quite different ends, and to attach magical spiritual effects to an effect that is bodily.

3. By the second antithesis indicated in our paragraph the Evangelical Church marks itself off from the Sacramentarians— taking that word not, of course, in the sense used by Luther and other theologians in the heat of controversy as applying even to the adherents of the Helvetic and the Gallic Confessions (*their* opinions lie wholly within the limits laid down in our paragraph),

but as denoting those who reject the sacrament. They assert that partaking of the bread and wine indicated by the phrase ' body and blood ' is only a shadowy emblem of that spiritual participation in the body and blood of Christ which is in no sense bound up with any such sacramental action, and that as soon as we have the assurance of this spiritual reality, the merely figurative action is better given up. Now we own that spiritual participation, to which Christ invited men long before the institution of the Supper as to something not merely future, is in no sense bound up by His institution exclusively with the sacrament or confined to it. None the less we confide in Christ's word that in the later institution that invitation is so realized in fact by His power that every believer may count on finding spiritual participation in the sacramental action, and that the action, if it be rightly administered in all respects, gives believers certain and infallible access thereto. Hence, as the most perfect common spiritual participation, the Supper is related to private participation in Christ apart from the Supper as the organized is related to the accidental, just as organized edification in public worship is related to edification which is individual and sporadic. But the opposed view, even when it does not deny that spiritual participation may be found in the sacramental action also, none the less protests that the conjunction of the two things is uncertain and purely fortuitous ; otherwise it would not seek to dissuade men from communicating. And in this it misconceives the value of Christ's institution.

Almost the same thing might be said of those who desire that the Supper should be permanently retained in the Church as Christ commanded, yet abolish its connexion with spiritual participation in the body and blood of Christ, declaring it to be no more than a custom whereby we bear witness, or make a profession of faith.[1] These we oppose, partly because they do not even regard the Supper as the climax of public worship, believing as they do that in the Supper they receive absolutely nothing ;[2] which means that to this gathering of people (which is pre-eminently a gathering in Christ's

---

[1] *Catech. Racov.*, Qu. 334–345. Zwingli is not to be confused with this party. He does call participation in the bread and wine in the Supper merely a thankful remembrance, but at the same time he always assumes a spiritual participation : Cum ad coenam domini cum hac spirituali manducatione venis . . . ac simul cum fratribus panem et vinum, quae jam symbolicum Christi corpus sunt, participas, jam proprie sacramentaliter edis cum scilicet intus idem agis quod foris operaris (*Expos. fid. chr.* Opp. ii. 555).

[2] Apparet coenam domini non eo institutam esse ut aliquid illic sumamus (*Catech. Racov.*, Qu. 338).

name) they would not even apply the general promise given by Christ to all such : partly because on their showing the Supper would not be the same thing in every age. For not only was there no one present at the original institution before whom the disciples could bear witness, but the ancient Church did not admit non-Christians as spectators ; while in their congregational relationships, apart from the sacrament, there is no lack of opportunities for Christians to make themselves known to each other as members of the Church.

4. If we leave open to the Evangelical Church the whole intervening ground between these two views—the one ascribing a magical value to the sacrament, the other depressing it into a bare sign—the historical reason for this is first of all that at the very beginning of Protestantism two views developed, one of which (within these limits) approximated most to the Catholic view, the other to the Socinian ; while on the other hand both clung to a consciousness of common antagonism to the other two. In part there were ever-renewed efforts to reconcile their differences ; in part out of these very efforts there arose a third Protestant view intermediate between both. Hence wherever these two views came in contact, the common conviction came in time to prevail that as they all looked for the same result under the same conditions—namely, the presence of true and living faith—each side must believe that the other had the same right as itself to expect this result, since neither could be certain that it was interpreting the connexion between the action and the result (so far as its production is beyond our power) precisely as the Redeemer intended it, while yet each side was eager to conform to the mind of the Redeemer as closely as possible. This conviction rests simply on a recognition of the exegetical difficulties attaching to the manner in which Christ speaks of His body and blood in offering the bread and wine. One side in interpreting words of such significance will admit nothing but literal explanation, which yet they cannot apply consistently owing to the fact that the reports of Christ's words differ—' this ' in one case having ' blood ' as its predicate, ' cup ' having ' testament ' in the other. So that our Supper and the original Supper cannot be the same if the offered body is literally the same as the body offering it. From this the other side argues that this equating of the bread and the body is only to be taken loosely, the former being a sign of the latter. They have then to explain not merely why in that case a special sign of the blood had to be offered in addition to the sign of the

body, but also whether the disciples (assuming that they were meant to understand Christ's language) were intended to interpret His words analogously to previous words of His own, or rather in the light of the Old Testament rite to which Christ's institution was attached. These problems have not so far all been solved by either side; yet it is possible that new attempts may still be made deserving of a place among the helpful efforts of the Evangelical Church, and that an adequate explanation may at last render all other imperfect ones superfluous. The three views, however, which have stood out from among these imperfect attempts and established their position most firmly may best be exhibited as follows. The first or Lutheran view declares that with the bread and wine Christ conjoined for participation the real presence of His body and blood, but only for the action of bodily partaking in both elements. The second or Zwinglian view declares that Christ conjoined nothing with the bread and wine in themselves ; by His command He merely conjoined spiritual participation in His flesh and blood with the action of partaking in the bread and wine. The third or Calvinistic view declares that while it is true that Christ conjoined something exclusively with the action of eating and drinking, this was not merely spiritual participation, available quite apart from the sacrament ; it was a real presence of His body and blood not to be had anywhere else.[1] The second view recognizes two things only, bodily participation and the spiritual effect, both linked together by the Word. Beyond all question this view is the clearest and the easiest to grasp, for it sets up an exact analogy between the Lord's Supper and baptism, and leaves the real presence of body and blood (which it is scarcely possible to describe) altogether out of account, so that by sacramental participation it can only mean the conjunction of spiritual participation with bodily participation as defined above. But even though we emphasize the words of Zwingli as just quoted, even though many other expressions by which it might be thought he meant to minimize or even abolish the powers of the sacrament be explained in the light of his polemic against Roman doctrine [2]—still this view leaves it unexplained

---

[1] Itaque si per fractionem panis dominus corporis sui participationem vere repraesentat, minime dubium esse debet quin vere praestet atque exhibeat (Calv., *Institt.* IV. xvii. 10). . . . Dico igitur in coenae mysterio per symbola panis et vini Christum vere nobis exhiberi, adeoque corpus et sanguinem eius . . . quo scilicet primum in unum corpus cum ipso coalescamus, deinde participes substantiae eius facti in bonorum omnium communicatione virtutem quoque sentiamus (*ibid.* 11).

[2] Sacramentum vim nullam habere potest ad conscientiam liberandam.

why, if Christ meant no more than this, He made use of these particular expressions. In addition to these two things, both the other views recognize a third thing, namely, a real presence of Christ's body and blood. According to Luther, through a special and secret power of the Word this presence is so conjoined with the elements of bread and wine as to yield what resembles bodily participation ; according to Calvin, it merely is so conjoined with the believer's spiritual participation as to yield a peculiar sacramental intensification thereof, to effect which no other power is required than the power of the divine promise familiar to us all. In both theories this supposed third thing explains why Christ had to use such very peculiar expressions in stating His intention. But, apart from the fact that Luther's view is too near the Roman type not to have encouraged the transference of many superstitious ideas, the mode in which the body of Christ is partaken of along with the bread, as well as the mode in which this sacramental participation differs on the one hand from bodily participation in the symbolic elements, and on the other from spiritual participation in the flesh and blood, is so difficult to make intelligible that while formulæ about it can be composed out of unscripturally devised words, the fact itself can never be made clear. The Calvinistic theory escapes many of these difficulties by holding aloof, alike from the over-intellectual bareness of the Zwinglian view and from the mysterious sensuousness of the Lutheran ; but no more than the latter does it succeed in making it clear that we have an interest in the body and blood of Christ, and no more than the former does it yield any explanation of the kind of relation obtaining between the body and the blood, or the ground of distinction between them. Hence, although this view has had a strong power of attraction, it provides new excuses for vacillating between the charm of symbolism which allures men to seek more in the sacrament than is brought out in the explanation itself, and on the other hand resting satisfied with something more external, on the ground that it is impossible to make out what the peculiar significance of the Supper is. We need not therefore expect that this view will become universally predominant in the Evangelical Church. As a result of the steady unprejudiced work of interpreters we may rather expect yet another view to emerge which will not make ship-

---

. . . Toto igitur coelo errant qui sacramenta vim habere mundandi putant.
. . . Sunt ergo sacramenta signa sive cerimoniae, quibus se homo ecclesiae probat (*De vera et falsa relig.*).

wreck on any of these rocks. Till then it will not be possible to state any common Church doctrine except regarding the effects of the Supper, and all that can be set forth under that head is the contents of the following two paragraphs.

§ 141. *First Theorem.—Participation in the body and blood of Christ in the Lord's Supper conduces in the case of all believers to confirm their fellowship with Christ.*

Luther's *Larger Catech.*, 247 : 'For this reason we go to the sacrament, because we there receive the treasure through and in which we secure forgiveness of sin.'—248 : ' Hence it is well named a food of the soul, which nourishes and strengthens the new man.'—*Expos. simpl.* xxi. : Est ea spiritualis manducatio corporis Christi . . . qua manente in sua essentia corpore et sanguine domini ea nobis communicantur spiritualiter . . . per spiritum s. qui videlicet ea quae per carnem et sanguinem domini pro nobis in mortem tradita parata sunt, ipsam remissionem peccatorum liberationem et vitam aeternam applicat et confert nobis ita ut Christus in nobis vivat.—*Conf. Scot.* xxi. : Sed unio haec et conjunctio quam habemus cum corpore et sanguine Jesu Christi in recto sacramenti usu operatione spiritus sancti efficitur, qui nos vera fide supra omnia quae videntur vehit, et ut vescamur corpore et sanguine Jesu Christi semel pro nobis effusi et fracti efficit.— *Conf. Belg.* xxxv. : Convivium hoc mensa est spiritualis, in qua Christus seipsum nobis cum omnibus bonis suis communicat efficitque ut in illa tam ipsomet quam passionis mortisque ipsius merito fruamur.—Melanchth., *loc. theol.* : Ad hoc igitur prodest manducatio poenitentiam agenti, videlicet ad fidem confirmandam.—Calv., *Institt.* iv. vii. 5 : In hunc modum dominus voluit . . . vera etiam sui communicatione fieri ut vita sua in nos transeat et nostra fiat. . . . *Ibid.* 11 : Per effectum autem redemtionem iustitiam sanctificationem vitamque aeternam . . . intelligo.

1. The one benefit of this participation is stated as being the confirming of our fellowship with Christ ; and this includes the confirming of Christians in their union with each other,[1] for the latter rests so entirely on their union with Christ that the union of an individual with Christ is unthinkable apart from his union with believers. In the credal passages just quoted this is made less prominent than could be wished, owing to the fact that in such discussions the question of the benefit of the sacrament customarily came up only in connexion with the questions we discussed above, where each individual participant is considered only *as* an individual. Hence light on the subject now before us is only to be sought from the enumeration of the benefits won by Christ, or under the all-embracing idea of sanctification. The general expressions for the effects of participation which stand out most clearly are confirmation

---

[1] Cf. 1 Cor. 10¹⁷ 12²⁷.

in faith, and the nourishment of the new man or the passing over of Christ's life into ours. Essentially both are the same, for living faith in Christ is simply the consciousness of our union with Him. It is usual, however, to emphasize two points specially—namely, that in the Supper we have renewed or confirmed to us the forgiveness of sins, and that we experience a heightening of the powers that make for sanctification. The two things really cannot be separated, and both rest on the fact that owing to the incomplete removal of sin even the new spiritual life has its progress interrupted by tendencies of a partially retrograde kind. For just as regeneration only becomes really firm and sure through our being in the status of sanctification, so, too, when union with Christ has been disturbed by sin, the certainty that the sin has been forgiven can only be made really secure through the feeling of restored and strengthened life. And for this the representation of the whole body of believers natural in the action of the Supper is an important factor. For it cannot but give rise in each individual to a strong excitation of the common Spirit, as well as to a heightened consciousness both of his general and his special vocation within this fellowship ; and this cannot but be accompanied by a new impulse to develop his gifts.

As regards the relation of the Supper to the forgiveness of sins, it must first be observed that in this respect no distinction ought to be drawn between original and actual sin, as if baptism referred only to original sin and the Supper only to actual. Apart from the fact that baptism cannot be completed until a time when actual sin has already issued from original, and that it could not be an index of the beginning of the new life unless in consequence of it actual sin ceased to hinder fellowship in the blessedness of Christ—apart from this, baptism as the seal of regeneration has itself a relation to all actual sins, inasmuch as the sins of the regenerate are always *ipso facto* forgiven.[1] But so it is, too, with the Supper ; just as it is original sin which is perpetually being manifested in the actual sin which obstructs vital fellowship with Christ, so it is the forgiveness of original sin that we ever anew require to have confirmed to us. In the second place, the forgiveness of sins ought not to be divided in two, nor ought the sin-pardoning power of the sacrament of the altar to be regarded as of a special character, as though sins were first forgiven in one way through the justifying action of God in regeneration and then in another way through the special presence

[1] Cf. § 111.

and communicative action of Christ in the sacrament.[1] On the contrary, there is but one and the same sin-pardoning power ; and just as regeneration is nothing but the general and ever-active relation of Christ to the totality of the human race, as that relation first comes in touch with the individual life, so the forgiveness of sins in the Supper is simply this living relationship as it reveals itself at a moment when Christ is presented in common to a number of individual believers.

In this connexion it may appear an enigma (for this does not rest on Christ's institution) why, on their confession of sin, the Church should declare forgiveness to those communicating at any given time, before they have taken the sacrament. As an anticipation, however, this declarative act belongs to the Supper in the same way as, conversely, confirmation belongs to baptism as its subsequent consummation. Hence the practice in the Evangelical Church, which at first obtained here and there,[2] of regarding absolution as a sacrament by itself, was soon given up. The confession of sin has no public ecclesiastical character save in relation to the Supper, and the wish to participate in the Supper cannot be otherwise expressed than through confession, for apart from sin there would be no need to renew our union with Christ. But when the Church proclaims the forgiveness of sin in connexion with such confession, what it really does is first to declare that the man who at this very moment feels the need of renewing his fellowship with Christ is put by the Church on an equal footing with those who already have satisfied that need, and next to give the needy soul thereby an assurance that he will find the satisfaction of his need in the sacrament. Hence every evangelical Christian will probably find that the sense of forgiveness which follows absolution imparted by the Church is no more than a shadow of that which he enjoys in partaking of the Supper itself, for it is there combined with the sense of a new influx of living spiritual power out of Christ's fulness, such as really removes the obstructions of the new life and the lingering effects of sinfulness in general.

2. The consequences of all this for the procedure of the Church

---

[1] *Conf. Saxon.*, p. 173 : Monemus etiam ne existiment propter hoc opus . . . remitti peccata, sed ut fiducia intueantur mortem et meritum filii Dei . . . et statuant propter ipsum nobis peccata remitti.

[2] Melanchth., *loc. theol.* : Numerantur haec sacramenta, baptismus, coena domini, absolutio. The same thing is meant by the order of Articles 8–13 in the *Augsburg Confession*. Hence, too, the *Apology* says : Vere igitur sunt sacramenta baptismus, coena domini, absolutio, quae est sacramentum poenitentiae.

in the sacramental action are as follows. First, the Supper refers back to baptism, and therefore, as long as infant baptism is maintained, there can be no participation in the Supper before confirmation in the Protestant sense of that word. The communicating of children, in whom neither the consciousness of sin nor the consciousness of grace can be properly developed, is for that reason a grave abuse infested with superstition. Secondly, on none of the different views can participation in the Supper take place without Christ being presented in the spirit ; hence there can rightly be no eucharistic action designed for those whose mental condition is defective or whose consciousness is obscured or on the very point of disappearing. Thirdly, the Supper was instituted by Christ as a common action ; hence it should always be held so in the Church. Fourthly and lastly, the doctrine of the Greek and Roman Churches that the conjunction of the body of Christ with the bread even apart from its use in the sacrament constitutes a perpetual sacrifice offered to God,[1] finds no support on our side and is for ever excluded ; even when allowance is made for the mitigating explanation that this repetition (as it were) of the sacrifice of Christ upon the cross is merely a memorial thereof.[2] We know nothing of merits or satisfactions as intended here.[3] The evasive suggestion that such sacrifice is not different from but identical with that accomplished on the cross,[4] has for us no value whatever, for in that case we should have to separate altogether the sacrifice in the death of Christ from the obedience in His life,[5] and His original sacrifice would then be just as arbitrary a transaction and just as magical as the sacrifice of the Mass. In any case this latter sacrifice would have to be regarded as supplementary to Christ's original sacrifice ; the consequence of which would be, for one thing, that apart from this supplement God would not behold believers in Christ, and thus justification would be cancelled all over again, in defiance of the fact that the circumstances which alone could bring this about must already have been present to God's foreknowledge in His justifying action. Along with this goes a second consequence, namely, that

---

[1] Ἔκθεσις ὀρθοδ. πίσ. 107. *Catech. Rom.* ii. 77 : Ut ecclesia perpetuum sacrificium haberet, quo peccata nostra expiarentur.
[2] Sacrosanctum missae sacrificium esse non solum nudam commemorationem sacrificii quod in cruce factum est, sed vere etiam propitiatorium sacrificium.
[3] Qui hoc sacrificium offerunt, quo nobiscum communicant, dominicae passionis fructus merentur et satisfaciunt (*ibid.* 79).
[4] Unum itaque et idem sacrificium esse fatemur et haberi debet, quod in missa peragitur et quod in cruce oblatum est (*ibid.* 53).
[5] Heb. 2[10. 17] 3[2] 5[8].

redemption—not merely as concerns its realization in men, viewed, that is, in its temporal aspect (where the matter is self-evident), but even when taken as the ground of the divine good-pleasure, *i.e.* in its eternal aspect—is only made complete through this supplementary action of the Church. And this means that in part men redeem themselves, for the priestly work of Christ would be insufficient apart from the sacrifice of the Mass. Hence, while there is no longer any need to describe the Mass as idolatrous, we persist in rejecting unconditionally the whole idea of a sacrifice subsequent to the end of all sacrifices ; issuing as it does from a demonstrable misunderstanding, it confuses faith and therefore necessarily encourages superstition, and in particular falsifies the idea of the priesthood of all believers. It is thus that we regard it simply in itself, and irrespectively of the doctrine of transubstantiation, with which, of course, it hangs together.[1]

§ 142. *Second Theorem.—Unworthy participation in the Lord's Supper conduces to judgment for the partaker.*

Apol. Conf. iv. : Christus ait (1 Cor. 11[19]) : illos sibi iudicium manducare qui manducant indigne, ideo pastores non cogunt hos qui non sunt idonei, ut sacramentis utantur.—*Conf. Belg.* xxxv.: Nemo itaque ad hanc mensam se sistere debet, qui prius sese recte non probaverit, ne de hoc pane edens et de hoc poculo bibens iudicium sibi edat et bibat.—*Catech. Heidelb.* lxxxi. : Hypocritae autem et qui non vere resipiscunt, damnationem sibi edunt et bibunt.

1. It is not easy to explain to oneself clearly how this paragraph is to be applied. In the first place, it is difficult to form an exact idea from what quarter the unworthiness indicated could arise ; for one who is not a member of the Church has no access to the sacrament, while every true member of the Church is a partaker all the more worthy that the Supper through Christ's institution so possesses a peculiar and independent power which marks it off from all other expressions and media of piety, that everyone must feel stimulated to the most appropriate mood of feeling. What first suggests itself, however, is this. The Supper was instituted as a common action and is publicly administered by the ministers of the Word, hence by Church order definite times and seasons must be appointed for it. Such order has the look of a summons, and it is possible that individuals—whether from custom merely or to meet the views of others—obey this summons without an inward longing for communion being awakened by any sense of their own spiritual

[1] *Heidelb. Catech.*, Qu. 80 ; *Artic. Smalc.* ii., *de Missa* ; *Expos. simpl.* xxi.

deficiencies.   In its origin such participation is unworthy, for it has
no connexion with the purpose of the institution ; without a lively
sense of personal relationship to Christ there can be no active recollection of Him, as He is represented in the Supper.   This will
always be lacking whether we conceive the inward state in question
as one of dull thoughtlessness not banished even by the action
itself, or as the steady presence in consciousness of alien motives,
which can hardly fail to be accompanied by a real, even if temporary,
disbelief in the power and greatness of the sacrament.

2. If, however, the judgment described as a consequence of this
unworthiness be taken as meaning consignment to eternal damnation, then it seems impossible to establish any connexion between
the two things.   Indeed, assuming that unworthy participation is
an actual possibility and is attended by these dangers, and on the
other hand that saving spiritual participation in Christ's flesh and
blood may be had elsewhere than in the sacrament, it looks as if we
might well wish that the sacrament had never been instituted, and
that we had been relegated solely to the extra-sacramental participation just referred to.   But let us put the idea of eternal damnation
provisionally on one side and concentrate on the question of unworthiness.   In that case the thoughtlessness which turns so rich
an opportunity into a meaningless external performance, and the
insincerity which masks unfitting motives by an action so sacred,
are a degradation of it which is eminently calculated to induce a
condition of unreceptivity and hardening, such as we have every
reason to regard as one element in damnation.   This entirely
justifies the wording of our paragraph.   The Supper, that is to say,
is seen to be a means of discrimination ; fit and worthy participation in it promotes living fellowship with Christ, while participation
of an unworthy kind is always rendering more ineffectual what
is the most powerful means by which such fellowship can be
strengthened, and thereby is always enhancing the power of hindrances.   If now we consider how insuperable thoughtlessness must
be, and still more how shameless insincerity must be, if they prove
stronger than what is so sacred, and how little faith can keep hold
of the Redeemer if what He has instituted can thus be torn away
from its purpose, we shall find it quite possible to understand the
fearful awe into which the devotional language of the ancient
Church falls when treating of this subject.   All the more essential
is it that the public teaching of the Church should refrain from
discouraging pronouncements not necessitated by the facts.

3. It is worth while to look back once again from this point at the distinction between the Lutheran and the Calvinistic view of the Supper, and feel how incapable it is of excusing a breach of Church fellowship. Neither of the two is at all successful in clearing up the third element which they accept, and which we have indicated by the phrase ' sacramental participation.' But a reference to our paragraph makes plain how much the distinction between them amounts to. The Lutheran view insists upon it that as sacramental participation in the body and blood is bound up with participation in the bread and wine, it is shared in by worthy and unworthy communicants alike ; only that in the one case it conduces to judgment, but in the other to spiritual participation and, thereby, to salvation. The Calvinistic theory, which attaches sacramental participation to spiritual, can only rejoin that in such sacramental participation the unworthy have no share. If this is the one point of distinction that can be clearly formulated, the difference will become quite negligible, once unworthy participation has disappeared from actual practice. Such difference in doctrine in any case would vanish of itself, as the two Churches approximate to perfection, and is therefore no justification of their separate existence ; for unworthy participation always is an evidence of imperfection in the Church. If the action of those who come to the sacrament is in harmony with the common sentiment of the whole body, and if the Church administering the sacrament develops a perfect sympathy between the whole body and the inward state of each member, no one in that case will seek to come to the sacrament unworthily, and the congregation will offer it to none whose participation would be unworthy. As the Church really advances to a better state, the only cases which tend to recall the difference between the two theories are bound to become fewer in number and gradually to disappear.

APPENDIX TO THE LAST TWO DOCTRINES : THE NAME ' SACRAMENT '

§ 143. *The Evangelical (Protestant) Church uses the name ' Sacrament ' only for these two institutions, Baptism and the Lord's Supper, which were instituted by Christ Himself and which represent His priestly activity.*

1. It is natural enough that a term taken over from a realm wholly foreign to theology should have no exact delimitation. Hence it was only very gradually that the Roman Church reached

its seven sacraments, and it was also by gradual steps that we fixed upon these two. Now the fundamental elements in the meaning of the term ' sacrament ' we must accept very cautiously, for the word, although based on the New Testament representation of a good soldier of Christ, has given prominence to one of its elements which is of most precarious application. Hence we may well wish even more unreservedly than Zwingli did [1] that Church terminology had never adopted the word, and also that it might be found possible to dispense with it. This might be done by way of approximation to the Eastern Church, which has never adopted it, and which instead uses the term ' mysteries '; but anything of the kind will certainly have to wait to a later time. A wish, however, is only rational in so far as it contributes to its own fulfilment ; we have therefore prepared a way here for the change by treating of baptism and the Supper each by itself and without any definite relation to the term ' sacrament,' though as it is familiar we have used it now and then for convenience. The ordinary procedure (to begin with an explanation of this so-called general notion) is always tending to confirm the false idea that it is a strictly dogmatic conception expressive of something that is essential to Christianity, and that it is from the fact that they are exemplifications of this conception that baptism and the Supper derive their special value. That prejudice we may at least claim is not fostered by the treatment adopted here, for even the close relation we have established between baptism and the Supper has been kept quite independent of this traditional term (sacrament), and—like that between the two other pairs of doctrines in this Division—been based solely on a common relation to one of the essential activities of Christ's vocation. So that it has the look of a mere accident that this middle pair of our six doctrines bears a common name, while the other pairs do not.

2. In any case it would be a fruitless proceeding to enter upon an etymological examination of the name, and seek thereby to decide what can and what cannot be subsumed under it. The controversy with the Roman Church, too, is quite an empty one, if it concerns merely the interpretation of the name and does no more than raise the question whether our interpretation is right or theirs, which applies the name to five other ordinances. The controversy has a meaning only if in some vital connexion our opponents are trying to give those five other actions an equal place with these two. In fact, however, there is an obvious dissimilarity among the

---

[1] *De vera et falsa relig.*, p. 194.

actions and situations which for the Roman Church are embraced under the term 'sacrament,' while the closeness of the connexion between the two to which our Church restricts the term has already been shown. Hence, if the name is still to be used, nothing remains but to fix its meaning in a purely arbitrary way without regard to its original sense, as a communal designation of these two institutions. The usage of the Evangelical Church at first was not fixed either ; not only was absolution received as a third sacrament, but Melanchthon also proposed to make ordination a sacrament as well.[1] Absolution, however, failed to keep its place, and the latter suggestion obtained no support. In general we think it more correct (and it is wholly on this model that our eucharistic service has been formed) to regard the absolution as a part of the communion service, as contrasted with which it has lost its sacramental independence ; and it was equally correct to take confirmation as a part of baptism, once confirmation had had restored to it a definite significance. Baptism, however, was also a consecration to the true priesthood common to all Christians, whereas the Ministry of the Word in the narrower official sense is not common to all ; hence dedication to it is not to be put on the same level as baptism. Marriage was only brought in because Scripture uses of it the term ' mystery,' which the term ' sacrament ' displaced ; but not only has it as a permanent state no similarity to our two ordinances, so that by analogy only consecration to marriage could be called a sacrament but not marriage itself, but in addition it has no place here because as a divine moral institution it has existed from the beginning quite irrespective of the mission of Christ. Finally, as regards the virtue sought to be attributed to extreme unction as a usage of the Apostolic Age, this could only be based upon the efficacy of the Church's prayer in the name of Jesus, and the benediction of marriage could only rank as prayer of the same kind. Clearly enough, then, these other usages are distinct from our two sacraments. What is common to both, let the Church name them as it may, will always be this, that they are continued activities of Christ, enshrined in Church actions and bound up therewith in the closest way. By their instrumentality He exerts His priestly activity on individuals, and sustains and propagates that living fellowship between Him and us in virtue of which alone God sees individuals in Christ.

3. We cannot quite ignore here the connexion between our two

[1] *Loc. theol., de num. sacram.*

sacraments and two Old Testament institutions, namely, circumcision and the Passover ; a connexion which has been emphasized more or less at different times, but which has often been quite wrongly conceived.   It is an entirely erroneous idea, for instance, that circumcision and the Passover had any particular relation to each other, as baptism and the Supper have.   Circumcision as an Abrahamitic institution had no other relation to the Passover than to other Mosaic institutions.   Apart from this, it is going much too far to assert that baptism took the place of circumcision and the Supper that of the Passover.   Baptism was instituted quite independently of circumcision ; moreover, circumcision was not put a stop to by baptism but by the preponderance of Gentile Christians over Jewish Christians, as well as by the intermingling of the two. The Supper did indeed attach itself to the Passover, but it was at once separated from it ; while the Passover continued to be celebrated by Jewish Christians without any relation to the Supper. Still, it is not impossible that a closer examination of the original relation between the two might be the very thing to yield a more correct understanding of the difficult expressions used by Christ in instituting the Supper.   And a comparison of the two New Testament institutions with those of the Old Testament has the very definite result of bringing out with great clearness the real difference between the old covenant and the new.

Fifth Doctrine : The Power of the Keys

§ 144. *By reason of its coexistence with the world there exists in the Church a legislative and an administrative power, which is an essential effluence from the kingly office of Christ.*

1. If the Church were completely self-contained, so that in none of those who belonged to it there survived anything of the world, the soul of each Christian in the whole system of its powers rather being a perfect organ of the Holy Spirit, then always and everywhere all events in the Church would happen of themselves as the Spirit prompted.   Owing to the identity of the Spirit in all, everything that happened would show a spontaneous consistency ; there would exist no difference between the general will and that of individuals, and there would nowhere be any occasion for law.   If general conceptions were applied to Church affairs, those so applying them would in reality only be formulating the ways in which men actually behaved.   This ideal, however, has never been realized

except in Christ Himself ; hence the utterances and impulses of the Spirit, when resisted, take the form of law and are accepted as such. This being the case, the analogous activities of Spirit-filled men also take on a relation to law as well as to the resistance which law implies, and assume the form of executive power. Not in any external fashion, as with civil authority (for an external apart from an internal out of which it springs has not the slightest value for the Church), but owing simply to the natural predominance of the common Spirit over persons—a predominance such as every member of a community feels has won his free assent. Should there be someone who does not feel this, or who in his own person is consciously antagonistic to the challenge of the common Spirit, that fact denotes an anti-church element in his life, and the predominance of the common Spirit must be re-established inwardly before the person in whose case it was infringed can again be acknowledged as a true member of the Church. Now this power of producing without any external means a steady voluntary submission, is the very power exerted by Christ ; and in every case where men were united to Him this power was manifested precisely in the fact that impulses coming from Him were recognized as law, and that His judgments regarding men were felt to be final pronouncements on what is in man—the new community thus becoming His Kingdom. In this respect, too, the Spirit actualizes in the Church what is to be received out of Christ's fulness. Or to put it otherwise, when Christ breathed the Spirit on the community of His people, He thereby conveyed this power to it—a power which cannot be conceived apart from this original ruling influence of Christ, and without which the union of the Divine Essence with human nature exemplified in the Church must either be much more or much less than is involved in the conception of a guiding common Spirit.

2. At first this explanation does not at all seem to lead up to what is generally understood by the Power of the Keys, for that spiritual power is ordinarily taken to refer to the expansion and maintenance of the Church, in the sense that it rests with the Church to decide who shall and who shall not be received into the Christian fellowship, and also who shall remain there or be expelled —a matter so far not even mentioned here, but left to be inferred by way of appendix to the foregoing. But the two things can easily be combined, and the path we are now taking is merely that which enables us better to subsume the whole of Church govern-

ment, as is fitting, under one conception. If we start with the kind
of resistance mentioned above, every case of permanent submission
produced subsequently by the Church's legislative authority is a
new conquest for the common Spirit, which thereby wins a place
for itself in an individual life which previously was, at best, a disputed possession hovering on the border between Church and
world. By every such removal of hesitation through legislative
action, the Church's realm is extended. But it is also through
such action that the first entrance of the individual into the Church
is brought about, for regeneration is the effect of the same cause,
for the first time presenting to men the preponderance of the God-
consciousness as the law of spiritual life. The same is true of the
power which applies this law in particular judgments and pronouncements ; these define the place taken in the community by
each individual as a consequence of his inward state, and determine
whether much or little can be entrusted to him.

Another peculiarity seems to be that we formerly [1] described
the Power of the Keys as a prolongation of Christ's kingly activity,
whereas it is here taken more as an effluence thereof, mediated by
the Spirit. But in this respect there is no more than a slight difference between the institutions treated of in this Division. The
mediation of the Spirit comes in in every case, otherwise these
institutions would not be actions of the Church ; and the actions
are all of them effluences of Christ, for it is always from Christ that
the Spirit draws. It is less easy to describe this power as a prolongation of Christ's activity, for the difference between legislative
and administrative activities essentially relates to the organized
community, while Christ's own activity preceded it. If, then, the
difference has no application to His case, the Power of the Keys as
thus defined cannot in the strictest sense be called a prolongation of
His activity, although it does develop the outline of the common
life as Christ drew it, and that without absorbing alien accretions
from without.

§ 145. *Theorem.—The Power of the Keys is the power in virtue of
which the Church decides what belongs to the Christian life,
and disposes of each individual in the measure of his conformity with these decisions.*

Conf. Aug. de abus. vii. : Sentiunt potestatem clavium esse . . . mandatum
Dei praedicandi evangelii, remittendi et retinendi peccata et administrandi
sacramenta.—*Ibid.* : Respondent quod liceat Episcopis seu pastoribus facere

---

[1] § 127.

ordinationes ut res ordine gerantur in ecclesia.—*Expos. simpl.* xiv. : De
clavibus regni Dei . . . simpliciter dicimus omnes ministros legitime vocatos
. . . exercere . . . usum clavium, cum . . . populum . . . increpant inque
disciplina retinent. — *Ibid.* xviii. : Atqui debet interim iusta esse inter
ministros disciplina. Inquirendum enim diligenter in doctrinam et vitam
ministrorum in synodis.—*Conf. Basil.* xvi. : Ipsa pascendi gregis auctoritas,
quae proprie clavium potestas est . . . cunctis aeque inviolabilis esse, et
. . . electis tantum et idoneis administrandum committi debet.—*Conf. Gall.*
xxxii. seq. : Credimus expedire, ut . . . ecclesiae alicuius praefecti inter se
dispiciant qua ratione totum corpus commode regi possit . . . eas tantum
leges admittimus, quae fovendae concordiae et unicuique in obedientia
debita retinendo subserviunt, qua in re sequendum nobis putamus quod
dominus noster . . . de excommunicatione statuit quam quidem approbamus
et una cum suis appendicibus necessariam esse arbitramur. Rom. 16¹⁷.
Cf. *Conf. Belg.* xxxii.—*Conf. Tetrapol.* xiii. : Hi (ministri) claves habent regni
coelorum ligandi et solvendi peccata remittendi et retinendi potestatem, sic
tamen ut nihil nisi ministri Christi sint, cuius hoc ius solius et proprium
est.—*Conf. Saxon.* : Et ad ministerium haec pertinent . . . exercere iudicia
ecclesiae legitimo modo de iis qui manifestorum criminum in moribus aut
doctrina rei sunt, et contra contumaces sententiam excommunicationis ferre,
et conversos rursus absolvere et recipere. Haec ut rite fiant, etiam con-
sistoria in ecclesiis nostris constituta sunt.

1. The term Office or Power of the Keys, in combination with
the terms ' bind ' and ' loose,' occurs in a discourse of Christ [1] which
bears upon the first part of our paragraph ; the terms ' bind ' and
' loose ' occur in another and related discourse,[2] where, at least
judged by the context, they bear upon our second part ; and this
again is very like a third passage,[3] which probably has to do with
the second part exclusively. To say that this or that shall be bound,
means that it shall be fixed by command and prohibition, while
that is loosed which is exempt from such rule and is left to the
self-determination of each individual [4]—the common feeling of the
whole body taking the same attitude to one who adopts one course
and to another who adopts the opposite, provided only that a good
conscience can be assumed in both cases. Now here we have the
legislative activity of the Church described in the previous paragraph, and its limitations as well. The common feeling of the
body has no occasion to express itself in a determinative way
except when, through the imperfect permeation of the Holy Spirit,
there is not being realized in certain members something which
common feeling demands as an essential manifestation of faith, or
when, in certain lives, there is still going on what, if left uncensured,

---

[1] Matt. 16¹⁹.   [2] Matt. 18¹⁸.   [3] John 20²³.
[4] *Conf. Aug. de abus.* vii. : Necesse est enim retineri in ecclesiis doctrinam
de libertate christiana.

would tend to injure the Spirit's action in others.   But it is equally essential, and equally pertinent to the same legislative activity, that things should be ' loosed ' which presumption or spiritual arrogance might seek to bind.   The unity of the Church cannot continue to exist if individuals try to make their personal modes of acting or thinking obligatory, as the only proper expression of the common Spirit.   Now if people insist on taking the scriptural passage referred to (and it is the chief Biblical authority for the doctrine) in the literal sense that Christ conferred this power on Peter alone, we should have to carry through that view strictly ; and then, with the death of Peter, the legislative activity of the Church would have come to an end—in so far, that is to say, as it rests on this injunction of Christ.   Nobody will doubt that in that case it was bound to reappear ; for otherwise, if we suppose everything to have been decided for all time in the first generation, this could only have come about in a supernatural fashion which would destroy the genuinely historical character of events ; and this could never have led up to a free and living development.   It follows that if this were the literal sense of Christ's words, the legislative activity of the Church could not be based on them alone.   But it would not for that reason cease to be a prolongation of Christ's activity.   It would still be an effluence from His will that a community should exist, and without legislative activity its existence is impossible.   Peter himself cannot have understood Christ's words in any such sense, for, when general pronouncements became necessary, he did not arrogate to himself alone the right of making them, but brought the questions at issue before the community. Even in the second passage quoted from Scripture, the ecclesiastical activity which applies the law in judgments and represents law executively is ultimately attributed to the community ; hence it goes without saying that even earlier individuals must have worked in the name of the community, and as its organs ; the more so that the Redeemer certainly did not mean to give any irritated person the right to call his brother to account.   But once we regard the individual as the organ of the community in dealing with a brother, every sin against the whole body is also done against the individual ; and the natural organ of the whole body in each case is the individual who first has certain knowledge of the facts.   If we further bring in the third Scripture passage quoted—and it is always reckoned as bearing on our problem—it may no doubt at first sight be interpreted as meaning that the forgiveness of sins is first

imparted in baptism, and that one whose baptism is postponed
to a later time therefore has his sins longer retained.[1] We have
no desire to exclude this ; clearly the right administration of
baptism (or, as now with us, of confirmation), which is to be expected from the action of the Spirit, also belongs in essence to the
Power of the Keys. But this certainly does not exhaust the
meaning of the passage. The Apostles themselves and the Early
Church after them applied it to persons who had already been
received into the Church ; [2] further, the passage contains the promise
given by Christ with regard to every judgment declaring whether
or not a given person is in that fellowship with Christ in which sin
disappears. Now all regenerate persons are in this fellowship ;
hence their actual sins, which alone could evoke a judgment of the
Church, are already forgiven. If we add the fact that no one
simply as an organ of the Spirit is within the Church, and that
activity within the Church can only take place through powers
which are themselves channels of the Spirit, *i.e.* spiritual gifts (since
there must be sin where there are still vestiges of resistance to the
Spirit's indwelling), it is clear that the Redeemer's promise entails
that the Church will judge rightly on the question what, and how
much or how little, is to be entrusted to the individual member
of the Church, and to what extent his influence on the Church or
his collaboration with it ought to be restricted, if the minimum of
disturbance is to result from his inward state. Thus all that
belongs to the second part of our paragraph we find based on the
words of Christ.

2. If now we survey the credal passages quoted above, we find
that they refer to the same principal points which we have seen to
be constitutive of the Office of the Keys, though not everywhere
expressed quite definitely or distinguished with equal clearness ;
and all that need be added by way of comment is the following.

First, we often find the Ministry of the Word taken as part of
the Office of the Keys. This is obviously the case with regard to
the administration of the sacraments, which is so closely bound up
with the forgiveness of sins ; and what we have already conceded
respecting baptism must hold good also of the Supper, namely, that
its right administration belongs to the Office of the Keys. It is,
however, a mere misunderstanding to say the same of preaching

---

[1] Cf. Matt. 10[14. 15]. For wheresoever the disciples thus withdrew, there
no community arose, and sins were retained in every case.
[2] Acts 8[20-23], 1 Cor. 5[4. 5].

considered by itself ; yet viewed as a special instance of the general principle formulated above, it does belong to the Office of the Keys to determine rightly who is to be admitted to the Ministry of the Word of God—a matter which incontestably must be regarded as one of the most important aspects of the Office. Assuming this, we cannot but judge it natural that with this Ministry nearly everywhere the Church should have combined the administration of both sacraments.

Secondly, many of the credal passages, taken by themselves, appear to suggest that the whole Office of the Keys resides in the whole body of Ministers of the Word. If it were so and if (the testing and the authorization of ministers of the Word being, as it is, an essential part of the whole Office) the entire body of Church teachers were a self-propagating organism and thus in exclusive possession of the Power of the Keys, then the distinction between the clergy (in this narrower sense) and the laity would be sharpened to such a degree that the difference between us and the Roman Church would entirely disappear. This, however, cannot be the intention ; for Christ Himself assigns one part of the function to the congregation, and from the very outset the congregation was given a share in the most important tasks of administration.[1] Indeed, the very passage which gives ministers exclusive power to execute the congregation's judgment takes for granted that it is by the congregation that the judgment is pronounced. As for legislative action, it cannot occur until there has developed in the Church an important distinction or antithesis ; but this distinction is not the same. It is specially incumbent on those entrusted with preaching to train themselves to be ever more perfect interpreters of the Word of God in Scripture, but it is one thing to explain the words of Christ and the Apostles rightly and quite another to apply them profitably in more or less general forms under very different conditions of life ; so, too, it is in one way that Scripture is applied from the pulpit and in quite another that rules for the life of the congregation under definite circumstances are evolved in a spirit of loyalty to Scripture, even though they often cannot be supported by any particular Scripture passage. Hence the distinction between one who grasps the religious meaning of life's conditions and tasks swiftly and surely enough to tell how the law bears on them, and one who accepts the law as law because he hears in it the sound of his own true inner voice, is a quite

---

[1] Acts 1^{15-23} 6^{2-6}.

different distinction from that between minister and hearer. Hence in public teaching it is best to avoid giving even an impression that Church legislation and administration ought to belong chiefly to ministers. We must not then overlook those passages which assign the duty of consulting on the government of the whole body to the leaders of congregations, and among the leaders reckon not only elders but deacons, in spite of the fact that they have no part in the teaching office.[1] Thus both legislative action and administrative action derive ultimately from the congregation.

Thirdly, while so much can be gathered from our credal passages, they do not make clear the scope or manner in which this whole Office resides in the congregation, or how the congregation exercises it. In point of fact, it exercises it not merely indirectly, by ordering and distributing the offices to which legislation and judgment are formally assigned (for how could the holders of these offices come to have such abilities and faculties, unless they have previously had some experience of them ?), but each individual as such also exercises a punitive office, in an independent and informal manner, by the judgments he passes upon what goes on in the congregation, and by praise or blame. Not only so : legislative action is exerted by each through everything he does that goes to form public opinion ; and public opinion must always be the living fount of expressly legislative acts, for these acts are simply a definite way of gaining recognition for public opinion in Church affairs. If in this sphere anything be attempted which is not a pure expression of the way in which, at a particular time and place, human nature in union with the divine Spirit is seeking to give actual form to itself and its concerns, then the attempt fails, and the law, which is thus incapable of securing its own recognition, simply reveals an imperfection in the Church. Inevitably the Church is disturbed, and it is only through controversy that agreement (all the more conscious for what has occurred) can be regained, and along with it a less ambiguous state of the whole body.

Fourthly, the direct consequence of the foregoing is nowhere expressed so clearly that we feel dispensed from stating it, although in a sense it takes us back to what we first said regarding our present enterprise—namely, that all legislative acts within the congregation are always subject to revision. For just as there was a time when none of the now prevailing usages could have been made law, because the law would not have been acknowledged, so, too, a time

[1] See § 134.

may come when the law will be acknowledged no longer ; and if it still struggles to keep up its legal validity, the outcome will be false appearances, of an injurious kind. This is by no means to assert that every enactment publicly made a rule of faith or life is equally mutable, but only that none should rank as immutable ; for we may be sure that certain items will always reassert their validity. If, finally, the right to pronounce excommunication be also reckoned as part of administrative action, this right must be understood in a very limited sense. If this aspect of the Office of the Keys be traced back to the undivided rule of Christ, it is true that in addition to choosing Apostles and calling disciples and entrusting tasks to both, we find Christ pronouncing woes on the Scribes and Pharisees and on places that had not received Him. These, however, were persons who had not yet been received into His fellowship ; He needed only to withdraw from them but not to expel them ; indeed, He Himself did not cast out the prodigal son. Thus we can have no such thing as complete excommunication, breaking off all fellowship. Every condition which might rightly provoke a judgment excluding from all share in the life of the Church ought to be regarded as merely temporary, and no judgment should seek to terminate the influence of the Church on the individual who has once been received into its bosom.

SIXTH DOCTRINE : PRAYER IN THE NAME OF CHRIST

§ 146. *The right prevision which it befits the Church to have of what will be salutary for it in its coexistence with the world naturally becomes Prayer.*

1. The manner in which the Church forms and propagates itself in history necessarily involves that, owing to the influence of worldly factors both within (for something of the world still clings to every member) and without, there will arise within it more or less marked obstructions and fluctuations. The same holds good of its external task of absorbing the world into itself, for here too it fails to attain to a uniform or an easily discernible progress. The common consciousness of this is therefore a consciousness of the imperfection of the Church. As, however, the desire fully to attain the ends of Christ's coming lives on in the Church unbrokenly, the consciousness of the Church's imperfection, closely in touch with this impulse, becomes the consciousness of a defective state ; and this, being as it is simply the correct self-

knowledge of the Church in relation to its love for the Redeemer, must necessarily in the measure of its purity be regarded as an effect of the divine Spirit. Now as the consciousness of the Church thus moves to and fro between the present and the future, it enters in a twofold way into combination with the God-consciousness. In view of the fact that every success attained is due not solely to its own activities but also to the divine government of the world, it becomes thankfulness or resignation for what in the present is the outcome of previous exertions, according as the average result of human effort is surpassed (thankfulness) or un-achieved (resignation). But for that which still remains undecided it becomes prayer—*i.e.* the inner combination with the God-consciousness of a wish for full success.

If we always considered and kept clearly in view the fact that in every case we arrive either at resignation or thankfulness (both of which are inward states in which our share in the perfect blessedness of the Redeemer finds expression, so that in this respect we are perfectly sure of good either way), then the Church, wholly intent on its own activities, would do well to refrain from wishes altogether. And since everything that seems fixed and done with is only a point of transition, so that what at first is accepted with resignation makes itself felt later as a subject for thankfulness and *vice versa*, both resignation and thankfulness ought to disappear—the Church leaving all such transitional stages behind and holding fast exclusively to the irrefragable certainty of ultimate success, and thus through joy in God attaining to perfect peace. But the mind of man (ever anticipating as it does the temporal development of things) is unable to refrain from painting what is possible in a variety of imaginative pictures and comparing their values for its own projects, or from coming to cling by preference to those from which it expects most advantage ; and as long as this mental activity lasts, it is bound to combine with the God-consciousness and become prayer. This is always going on, so that we have no cause to regard the injunction to pray without ceasing [1] as hyperbole. If we did not pray, that could only be due to a disappearance either of our interest in the Kingdom of God, which evokes these ideas of an advantageous but uncertain future, or of our God-consciousness, which keeps present to our mind the absolute powers of the divine world-government.

2. The injunction of the Apostle just mentioned seems rather to

---

[1] I Thess. 5[17].

be addressed to the individual, as indeed it is only in this individual
mind that the play of fancy over the as yet indeterminate events
of the future occurs.   In individuals, however, even correctness of
prevision in no way leads to prevision turning into prayer ; differences here are usually due to the importance of the matters at stake.
So that it is only in a minor degree that our paragraph is elucidated
by what has so far been said.   It will be different if we note carefully the relation of the Church to the individual at this point.   The
individual here has in view first of all his own sanctification, and
next the activity within the whole body made incumbent on him
by the gifts he has already received.   Each of these is a manifold,
the separate parts of which it is impossible to promote equally
by each act, and very soon there comes home to everyone the
experience that while his purposes and hopes may be veering in one
direction, there come to him, from the divine government of the
world, demands and challenges which bend him in another.   Hence
he cannot trust his own presentiment of what is for the moment
best for him personally.   No more can the individual from his
standpoint reach certainty of judgment as to what is advantageous
for the whole body in the actual state of its total task.   True,
individuals will differ in this respect ; and only those would rightly
be judged fitted to exert a definite influence on the whole body who
have developed their capacities on this side into a gift analogous
to that of the prophet.   Besides, this presentiment as found in the
corporate consciousness might be more sure and certain in those
times when the individual still formed a large part of the whole [1]
and was able to apprehend it *as* a whole.   So that from Christ
onwards (and He must be conceived as having possessed this
faculty, humanly considered, in the highest possible perfection)
this gift must be regarded as present approximately, but certainty
of insight diminishes in proportion as a personal element enters
more and more into the individual's premonition of the future.
What is true of the individual will also be true of every group of
people, whether freely associated or constituted by nature, in proportion as they form a smaller or larger part of the whole, and
feel for the others a less or more disinterested love.   Hence, when
matters have reached that point, we must say, on the one hand, of the
whole body that, as personal consciousness and common consciousness are here no longer distinct but completely one, it forms the
most faithful likeness of Christ, and therefore that it is in the whole

[1] Cf. Acts 16[6, 10].

body, revealed as a unity, that the most sure and certain prevision will be found.   On the other hand, the Church is the common home of all those imperfect presentiments which, in their differing imperfections, are so often controversially opposed to each other. It is first of all incumbent on the Church to compare itself with that perfect reflexion of Christ which in its temporal consciousness it is not yet, and to make it its prayer that those of its members may gain an ever larger influence who are the most fully developed organs of the divine Spirit for rightly discovering and introducing whatever may be necessary for the increase and progress of the Kingdom of God.   This is the one presentiment of the Church which it is absolutely right should become prayer, and in which therefore all individuals are at one with the whole body.   In the next place, the Church's duty is first to reconcile the uncertain elements of prevision (so far as they may be discordant) which flow from the imperfect common consciousness of individuals, and then to appease the feeling of uncertainty by turning it into prayer. Both these things are done through the gathering together of individuals for common prayer ; for through the very form of common religious action each individual feels himself drawn away from what is more personal in origin to that which could be the same in all, and is guided by the content and meaning of such common action to that which lays hold on all equally.   Both results are aided by the fact that when a difference emerges between personal presentiments and wishes, each joins in prayer for the others that, through the facts of the divine world-government, they may be led ever more into pure joy in God, whether in the form of resignation or that of thankfulness.   And to this all Church prayers may be reduced.

§ 147. *Theorem.—Every prayer in the name of Jesus—but only such prayer—has the promise of Christ that it is heard.*

Expos. simpl. xxiii. : Oratio fidelium omnis per solum Christi interventum soli deo fundatur ex fide et caritate.—*Conf. Belg.* xxvi. : Proinde secundum mandatum Christi patrem coelestem per unicum mediatorem nostrum invocamus . . . certo persuasi nos ea omnia impetraturos, quae a patre in nomine ipsius petierimus.—*Catech. Heidelb.* cxvii. : . . . huic firmo fundamento innitamur, nos a deo, quamquam indignos propter Christum tamen certo exaudiri.

1. When we use the phrase ' praying in the name of Jesus,' [1] we may have more in mind praying about the concerns of Jesus or

[1] John 16²⁵. ²⁶.

praying in His sense and spirit ; but in fact the two things cannot really be separated. If we could desire to further men's spiritual welfare otherwise than in His sense, we should have to conceive that welfare otherwise than as He did ; in which case it would not be His concerns that were being thus laid before God in prayer. So far, then, it is true that every prayer is prayer in Jesus' name where the petition (whatever it be) is offered with reference to the Kingdom of God. But the more definite the prayer is, the more necessary it becomes that its object should be conceived of as in agreement with the order according to which Christ rules His Church, so that the person who prays may as such be regarded as a true and acceptable representative of Christ. It follows that none can be true prayer in Jesus' name except that which springs from the self-consciousness of the Church as a whole, *i.e.* such prayer as in its content keeps the whole condition of the Church in view. Prayer of this kind certainly belongs to the common prayer of the Church at any given moment, and that such prayer is heard it is impossible to doubt. If the Church's need has been rightly appre-hended, and if the dominating presentiment has arisen out of the Church's whole consciousness of its own inner condition and out-ward circumstances, then the prayer is charged with the full truth : it represents Christ's knowledge of His spiritual body and defines His ruling activity. Hence, in view of the power received by the Son from the Father, its content cannot but be fulfilled. Every other prayer springing from a less perfect Church consciousness, even though it touch equally Christ's concerns and arise from a sincere endeavour to act in His spirit, can look for fulfilment only in the measure in which it harmonizes with the normative prayer as just described ; indeed, it is only thus far that it ought to claim fulfilment. Such prayer, accordingly, can only gain confidence by subordinating itself to prayer that is normative and seeking to be heard only on that condition. An example of such ' condi-tional ' prayer (as it is best named) used by Christ [1] is found in more than one book of Scripture ; but it merely concerns times and seasons, and therefore does not conflict with what we said above as to the utterly right character of His presentiments. From it we can see how such prayer may be without sin, including as it does resignation as a corrective of its own uncertainty, and only desiring to be heard in so far as what is asked for could form part of a nor-mative prayer. So understood, our views are in perfectly natural

[1] Matt. 26¹²ᶠᶠ..

accord with the explanation ordinarily given, for the most part, with respect to conditional prayer, namely, that the man is praying in Jesus' name who only desires to be heard for Christ's sake, or in so far as what is asked for is God's will relatively to the divine purpose in Christ.

2. Still, the objection is constantly put forward that if this explanation really exhausts the matter, then the whole doctrine of the hearing of prayer is a delusion. The objection assumes that we really believe that by prayer we can exert an influence on God, His will and purpose being thereby deflected. Now this conflicts with our primary and basal presupposition that there can be no relation of interaction between creature and Creator ; and a theory of prayer which starts with ideas like those just indicated we can only describe (even though it be held by Christians as devoted as they are believing) as a lapse into magic. True, the promises of Christ [1] are adduced in support ; but either the promises themselves are misunderstood, or the conditions to which the promise is attached are not fully taken account of. For how could one fail to have doubts regarding what—to use the ordinary phrase—can only be called a future accident, unless in another respect he took it to be necessary ? And what can the Christian as such take to be necessary except that without which a regenerate person could not be sustained in the state of sanctification, or the Kingdom of Christ persist and advance ? But this simply means that in this way we are brought back to unconditional prayer. When Christ makes faith the condition of prayer being heard, He does not in the least by faith mean a separate faith that prayer *is* heard, but faith in Himself, in the full sense of the word, therefore faith in the imperishable and supreme value of the Kingdom of God He was founding. In faith so understood all that has here been set forth is embraced. Thus by repelling all magical conceptions of the hearing of prayer, we do the promises of Christ no wrong. For as we do not grant that things, the prayer for which is heard, take place for that reason, even contrary to the original will of God, because prayer has been offered about them, so we do not assert that they would have taken place even had there been no prayer. But between prayer and its fulfilment there exists a connexion due to the fact that both things have one and the same foundation, namely, the nature of the Kingdom of God. In that Kingdom the two are one—prayer as Christian presentiment growing out of the whole action and

[1] Matt. 17[20] and 21[21, 22].

influence of the divine Spirit, and fulfilment as expressive of Christ's
ruling activity in relation to the same object.   Seen thus, fulfilment
would not have come had there been no prayer ; for then the point
would not yet have arrived in the development of the Kingdom of
God on which the fulfilment must follow.   But fulfilment does not
come because prayer was offered (as though prayer could here be
regarded isolatedly as a cause in itself), but because the right
prayer can have no other object than what is in line with the divine
good-pleasure.   Neither would it have come, in virtue of the divine
decree, even had there been no prayer (as though the divine decree
bore upon particulars apart from their natural nexus) ; it comes
because the inward state that gives rise to prayer itself forms
part of the conditions under which it was possible for the result
effectually to emerge.

This view of the case meets another objection to the doctrine
of the hearing of prayer, namely, that it is fitted to depress the
activity of believers, or, to express it more fully, that if we believe
in the hearing of prayer we are certain to separate ' praying ' from
' working ' and substitute prayer for work all through.   Over
against the formula ' pray, and thou needst not work ' is set (if
the hearing of prayer be denied) the other, ' work, and leave no
time for prayer.'   We are bound to reject both views, for, according
to the explanation just given, right prayer only arises when we are
engaged in the activities that go to fulfil our Christian vocation.
Thus every true moment of prayer rests on a moment or element of
action, so that prayer cannot destroy action without being itself
destroyed ;   on the other hand, the presentiment expressed in
such prayer as originates otherwise is bound to be purely arbitrary,
and can carry with it no certainty whatever that it is in harmony
with the ruling activity of Christ.   No more can action destroy
prayer, for action of such a kind could not be directed upon the
Kingdom of God.   The agent is readily satisfied with what he
himself can achieve ; and such action could give no guarantee of
its being under the influence of Christ's rule.

3. In thus interpreting prayer solely by its bearing on the
concerns of the Kingdom of God, we started with the assumption
that prayer in the name of Jesus is the only kind natural to the
Christian.   At the same time, our paragraph does refer to another
kind, familiar to us all from common experience.   Now, to prayer
of this sort we can allow no share in Christ's promise, yet it is so
far suggested by conditional prayer in Jesus' name that it ought

not to be rejected. For human feelings and emotions always exist in combination with the God-consciousness, and in this combination they will always find for themselves a less passionate and more spiritual expression than without it. This sort of prayer (be it the prayer of piety, or of self-love, whether in its nobler or its more inordinate form) is not specifically Christian ; whereas the hearing of prayer is a special promise of the Redeemer to His people. Hence such prayer can only share in the promise in so far as it stands in a close relation to the subject of the promise, *i.e.* in so far as the wishes laid before God can also be regarded as needs of the Church. The prayers of ' piety ' (*pietas*) come nearest to this. For the higher place we give an individual, the more easily we may be seduced to believe that it is a distinct loss for the Kingdom of God that he should be snatched away from his sphere of influence, or hindered in his work. But on closer inspection we shall always be compelled to own that except Christ Himself no individual is indispensable to the Kingdom of God. At a still greater distance stand all wishes relating to our own external welfare or that of others, where too we are less easily deceived. But yet, as long as we have not attained to simple resignation that excludes all wishes, it is natural and wholesome for us even as Christians to combine these wishes with the God-consciousness.[1] It is wholesome for us, however, only as we are led to simple resignation by the feeling that we cannot spread these wishes before God in the name of Jesus. Nay, if this is not the result, the prayer in question would have to be changed, almost in the moment of utterance, into a prayer for resignation ; and this *would* be prayer in Jesus' name. But every such prayer is simply an item in the individual discipline of the soul ; it is therefore best that it should be confined to the circle of personal and domestic life, which is its natural sphere. But public and common Christian prayers ought always to be representative of the pure type of prayer in Jesus' name, without bringing in subjects the connexion of which with the progressive development of the Kingdom of God is doubtful. Otherwise it would be part of the public cure of souls by means of public prayer to turn common wishes, springing from some worldly interest, into prayer for resignation. This is the rule which all public intercessions should follow, and scriptural injunctions on the subject [2] must be interpreted in the light of the promise of Christ here treated as fundamental.

---

[1] 1 Pet. 5[7] ; cf. Matt. 6[31. 32].   [2] 1 Tim. 2[1-4], Phil. 4[6].

§ 148. *The fact that the Church cannot form itself out of the midst of
the world without the world exercising some influence on the
Church, establishes for the Church itself the antithesis between
the* Visible *and the* Invisible *Church.*

1. If every person in the world who has been laid hold of by the
Spirit of Christianity were instantly so to become a possession of
the Spirit that every element in his life was solely determined by his
reception of the Spirit's influence, and he became entirely free from
vestigial traces of his former life, it would certainly mean that the
world might persist alongside of the Church, opposing the Church's
further advance ; and in this way the world might modify the
Church's action and throw it back upon itself. But yet the Church,
as actually existing, would none the less be without any worldly
admixture ; the two would be entirely separate and mutually
exclusive societies. In point of fact, however, regeneration is not
a sudden transformation ; even though delight in God's will has
become the man's proper self,[1] there remains in him everywhere an
activity of the flesh striving against the Spirit ; and thus even in
those who taken together compose the Church, there is always
something that belongs to the world.[2] Hence Church and world
are not spatially or externally separate ; at each point of human life
as we see it, wherever there is Church, because there faith and
fellowship in faith are to be found, there is world as well, because
there exist also sin and fellowship in universal sinfulness. Each
visible part of the Church, accordingly, when more closely examined,
is a mixture of Church and world ; and only if we could isolate
and collect the effects of the divine Spirit in men, should we have
the Church in its purity. Now not merely are these effects certainly
present, inasmuch as the Holy Spirit is only given in this active
union with human nature ; they also form a connected and co-
operative whole. Yet they cannot be exhibited in isolation ; it is
only invisibly that they are contained within the whole complex
as the element in it which opposes the world and separates it from

---

[1] Rom. 7[17. 20], 1 John 1[8-10].   [2] Cf. § 126, 1.

the world. Thus the *invisible* Church is the totality of the effects of the Spirit as a connected whole ; but these effects, as connected with those lingering influences of the collective life of universal sinfulness which are never absent from any life that has been taken possession of by the divine Spirit, constitute the *visible* Church.

2. By the Invisible Church is commonly understood the whole body of those who are regenerate and really have a place within the state of sanctification ; by the Visible Church, all those besides who have heard the gospel and therefore are called, and who confess themselves outwardly members of the Church, or who (as we should prefer to express it) form the outer circle of the Church, inasmuch as they receive preparatory gracious influences through the medium of an externally constituted relationship.[1] But if this externally constituted relationship be taken as consisting in the fact that they have received baptism and call themselves Christians, it must be pointed out that according to Christ's original intention there was not to be any such visible Church, since only those were to be baptized who had repented and were mature enough to receive, in and with baptism, the forgiveness of sins and the bestowal of the Spirit. Thus the called too were to remain outside the Church until both the community and they themselves were at one in the conviction that a living fellowship had been established between Christ and them ; and the outer circle aforesaid was to be composed, not of members of the Church, but of candidates for the Church. It may be urged that this original arrangement cannot now be restored, not merely because of infant baptism, but much more because the nations have been Christianized *en masse* and Christianity has been given civil privileges, and that therefore the arrangement may in a way be regarded as having been altered by Christ Himself. Yet this would not make it any more fitting to describe the fellowship of the regenerate as invisible. Even though the moment of regeneration cannot be fixed, and many Christians may feel uncertainty regarding many other Christians, questioning whether they really are in the state of sanctification ; still, this uncertainty regarding some cannot make the whole invisible. On the contrary, the fellowship or community of those who, just because most firmly settled in the state of sanctification, are most strenuously opposed to the world, cannot but in this sense be the most visible of all.[2] The body, then, which in ordinary usage is known as the invisible Church is for the most part not invisible, and what is

[1] Cf. § 115, 2.   [2] Matt. 5[14].

known as the visible is for the most part not Church. On the other hand, as we have explained it, the antithesis affirms something true and necessary. Even if it were possible to keep all the non-regenerate outside the Church, the whole body of the regenerate would only constitute the visible Church in our sense of the term, and, because visible, would for that very reason not be pure from alien admixture. The pure Church cannot everywhere be made visible ; but it is necessary to treat of it separately as the peculiarly active element in the other. The institutions dealt with in the doctrines of the First Half are the principal organs of the invisible Church, and most of all represent its forces at work within the visible. Here we treat of those general conditions of the visible Church which, as perpetually self-renewing consequences of the persistence of the world within the Church, do most to bring to clear consciousness the antithesis between the visible Church and the invisible.

§ 149. *The antithesis between the Visible and the Invisible Church may be comprehended in these two propositions : the former is a divided church, while the latter is an undivided unity; and the former is always subject to error, while the latter is infallible.*

1. If we merely recur to what was said above regarding the sphere and manner in which the sinless perfection of Christ is communicated,[1] we are in a position to assert that what is innermost in every truly regenerate life is simply the whole truth of redemption ; and it is solely as limited to this domain that we affirm the infallibility of the invisible Church. There is first of all the consciousness of divine sonship in living fellowship with Christ, a consciousness which each has for all and all for each ; and to this is essentially attached the consciousness that in them and for their good there is being vouchsafed a leading into all truth.[2] But when this innermost consciousness comes to be particularized in definite ideas, it no longer has the same full truth ; for the individual's ideas are the outcome of his previous life and are formed out of his previous thought and interests, and for this reason regeneration cannot be a sudden transformation of his whole style of thinking. Hence the outward expression of the inner truth becomes more or less distorted, and of its organized form the Spirit takes possession only gradually. The same holds true of the bent imparted to the will by the life of Christ within us ; it is the pure bent of Christ Himself, against sin and for the dissemination of His life. But when this

---

[1] Cf. § 88, 3.   [2] John 16[13].

takes shape in particular acts, it comes to be mediated not only through the view taken of a specific situation, but also through the purpose in which the action is pre-formed. Both of these, again, are conditioned by ideas formed during the period when the will was still the slave of sense ; hence they can no longer give pure expression to the new inward impulse. Thus, starting from the point to which the new life attaches itself, the pure and the impure very soon separate, and appear as the visible and the invisible ; for that which passes over into the phenomenal consciousness is *eo ipso* no longer pure. Yet both belong to the Christian fellowship ; for to say that redemption is being realized in anyone, and that he is beginning to form a part of the believing fellowship, are the same thing. Someone may say that he acknowledges the distinction between the pure and the impure as a distinction between the visible and the invisible, but that the invisible is not really a fellowship, because what is absolutely inward is absolutely isolated too, and a fellowship (which only becomes possible through means of self-expression) cannot from its very nature be the pure and the true. This objection certainly has to be admitted inasmuch as the invisible Church is not a fellowship by itself alone, entirely separate from the visible. But even in the ordinary usage of these terms, this is not the case ; there as for us the invisible Church as a fellow-ship (and in our reading of these matters the conception of fellow-ship is given greater prominence than ever) is mediated through the visible. But in daily experience everyone will certainly make a distinction between the two. In the one case, reaching over and abstracting from the confused multiplicity of particular acts (our neighbour, too, contemplating us in exactly the same way), we each of us enter into a mutually strengthening and supporting union with the innermost impulses of the other, and thus constitute an element of the invisible Church ; in the other, we enter into a fellowship of these very particular acts and forms of self-expression, so as uniformly to occupy a common area with those who have closest affinity with ourselves and to repel what is alien—and thus constitute an element of the visible Church.

It need not be explained that in the infallibility of the invisible Church we include also its purity, and in the fallibility of the visible also its sin. This is due partly to the fact that particular acts have underlying purposes that determine their range and are themselves subject to the imperfection of the ideas present in the mind, partly to the fact that the development of religious ideas also depends on activities of will, which are affected by the lack of purity in particular resolves.

2. Closely connected with this is the fact that the invisible Church is everywhere essentially one, while the visible is always involved in separation and division. The innermost consciousness and impulses of believers are nothing but the presence and living movements of the Spirit itself ; their fellowship is nothing but the Spirit's knowledge of itself ; and this fellowship must extend wherever the Spirit is the same, *i.e.* over the whole of Christendom. Since it is only an invisible fellowship, it lacks everything that might give it a definite form, and everywhere and always it is simply the direct relationship to one another of all in whom the Spirit dwells and who, meeting and touching as they do in their innermost being, include in their fellowship all like souls. That is to say, it is the common striving of all to recognize everywhere the same Spirit through what is outward, and draw it to themselves. But particular forms of outward expression, ideas no less than acts, which are the channels through which this one fellowship is mediated, are also in themselves the divisive element in the visible fellowship ; not only because, by the laws of physics, attractive force radiating out from the chief controlling points must find its limit somewhere, so that the connexion is broken, but principally because the uniting consciousness of affinity, being bound up with what to our perception are sensible differences between men, takes the form of self-love, thus imposing limit and division.

And here it once more appears, as we have elsewhere shown, that the Christian fellowship as being one cannot possibly impose limits on itself, *i.e.* cannot actively will to have other fellowships alongside of it. That would mean either that the attractive power of Christ stopped at a certain point, His living fellowship thus narrowing itself to a certain circumference, in which case He would not have been inspired and endowed as Saviour of the whole human race ; or the impulse emanating from Him would of necessity be confined in self-love to the fellowship of believers, thus keeping others alongside of them who would not share the same advantages ; and such love could not be identical with the love of Christ.

3. It can, however, be easily shown that in these paragraphs we have stated the whole difference between the visible and the invisible Church. Whether we start from the life of Christ within us or from the action of the Spirit within us, they both issue simply in the twofold fact that everything human in the individual is ap-

propriated by the divine, and then as appropriated enters actively into the communal spiritual life. Now if the still worldly element in the individual has a disturbing influence on this activity, one of these activities must thereby be obstructed and diverted ; indeed, it will be possible everywhere to trace what seems mere negation or omission to what is positively real, namely, an act. But all action within the fellowship is productive of fellowship, which can only continue to exist through actions bearing upon it ; thus whatever disturbs such action must carry with it division. Similarly, if the Spirit present in each is one that leads into all truth, everything in the individual that works disturbingly must be a lapse into untruth. The fact that at this point our paragraph includes in untruth any aberration of the will in sin is justified by the consideration that when we speak of the Church, we have the actions of individuals in view only so far as they take place within the fellowship. And there they can only be disturbing in so far as they are perceived by others and constitute a process ; which again can only be the case when they are adopted as guiding maxims, and maxims that contradict the basal forms of self-expression characteristic of the new life or are asserted as false subsumptions under maxims that are sound—in either case, therefore, in so far as they can be traced to error. On the other hand, isolated sins which spring from no purpose disappear in the life of the fellowship, without leaving a trace. There is no influence arising from the still worldly element within us able to disturb our relationships in the Church, other than those influences which confuse the Spirit— error affecting the Spirit as it leads into truth, and division as it binds and unites. Not only so, these two things are so closely connected that it is only through the presence of either that the other can be detected. Much may appear to be a disturbance of fellowship and yet not be so, unless it.is also a defection from truth ; so, too, nothing that seems to be error or sin really is so unless it at the same time disturbs fellowship.

First Doctrine : The Plurality of the Visible Churches
in Relation to the Unity of the Invisible

§ 150. *Whensoever separations actually occur in the Christian Church,
there can never be lacking an endeavour to unite the separates.*

1. If every worldly element present in individuals is as such disturbing to fellowship, the visible Church always and everywhere

has dispersed within it germs of division.   But each of those germs in itself is infinitely small ; and in the measure in which these elements fall apart or unite to form masses, there will in the latter case appear in the Church more or less division, while in the former nothing more will result than temporary disturbance in restricted circles.   It is obvious that from the outset those elements united most powerfully and became most strongly antagonistic to each other, which sprang from the former religious life of the first Christians as Jews and Gentiles.   Hence even in the age of primitive Christianity, which we can scarcely help regarding as an exception to the general divisive tendencies characteristic of the visible Church, the basis of a separation between Jewish and Gentile Christians existed in so developed a form that only the counter-force of the community-forming principle operating in its primitive strength could delay its actual outbreak.   From this it is clear that the more the uniting Spirit pervades the mass and drives the worldly elements in it apart, the more these elements will lose their divisive force.   Hence this force was never again present, in particular differences that arose in the course of the development of doctrine, with the strength it possessed in the age of heresies and the General Councils.   But, on the other hand, the tendency to division invariably becomes active in proportion as aberrations, which otherwise would fade away of themselves, almost unnoticed, are strengthened by some selfish motive.

2. Yet even in the state of division each part of the visible Church remains a part of the invisible, for in it are found the confession of Christ and therefore also the activity of the Spirit. Hence the impulse from which the division sprang will gradually weaken, and where these different parts of the Church are in contact with each other, the community-forming principle which is the same in all will bring its influence to bear against division, and an impulse towards reunion will arise which of course in the Church as we see it is subject to the same changes and vacillations as its opposite. Indeed, even when this impulse fails entirely to make itself perceptible in history, it is none the less moving sporadically in individuals ; we cannot but assume this if we are right in believing that the Holy Spirit cannot wholly disappear or be banished from any part of the Church, nor can it ever neglect any of its essential functions.

Still, the undeniable experience that apart from this there are frequently also efforts at union which do not originate in the Spirit of the Church, and the success of which cannot therefore be regarded as a gain, reminds us that there may also be divisions which are not due to the worldly elements in the Church, but must ultimately be reckoned among the effects of the Holy Spirit. So that the truth we have established can only be of subordinate importance, and seems to call for further definition. But just as those unions may be only apparent, and the united elements may certainly tend to separate from the whole body in some other fashion, so too that which is in fact only seeking closer union within the great fellowship in a way that will do it no injury, or again that which is really a return to a formerly abandoned fellowship with earlier forms of the Church, may seem to be a division, and yet not be such. Hence it is universally true that the Spirit unites, and that it is the fleshly mind that disunites. But the application of this may be difficult ; and when several communions separated from each other exist side by side in Christendom, it must be left to criticism to decide on which side the disuniting principle is entrenched, and which therefore is responsible for division. This is a question which it will often be as difficult to solve as the question which of two sides in a war has been the aggressor.

§ 151. *First Theorem.—The complete suspension of fellowship between different parts of the Visible Church is unchristian.*

1. What was said in the Introduction [1] about religious fellowship as such, can also be said of Christendom in view of its wide expansion over so great a number of peoples and tongues, namely, that no uniform sort of connexion between its various members is possible, not merely owing to unlike internal affinities and external contacts, but also owing to the unequal distribution of the common Spirit. It is natural that the first of these unlikenesses should be connected with the influence of language and of the whole system of social relationships, and that Christians who speak the same language and belong to the same nation should form a separate communion. But such national and territorial Churches are simply the form in which alone, by the appointed divine order, a larger fellowship is possible ; and they by no means involve a suspension of fellowship with other Christians, for fellowship can exist after as well as before, once the natural conditions for it are present. The same is true of those societies (always strongly marked in external form) of Christian people who, drawn by various affinities, gather

[1] § 6.

specially round those who give a strongly original expression to their individual thought ; for this too can happen without any existing fellowship with other parts of the Church being suspended. It only begins to be suspended when more restricted societies which have originated in the manner just described get into antagonism to each other, and find themselves unable to enjoy their own peculiar life without drawing apart from others and shutting the door upon them. Such a polemical relationship is certainly a suspension of fellowship, and yet only in part. Even though controversy should actually break out over their incompatible peculiarities, it really depends solely on the interest which each side has in the other, and thus is merely the mode in which under the given conditions fellowship can exist between them. Nay, since it is implied in the case that the *lowest common denominator* on which in controversy they fall back is a Christian principle, they cannot fail (if each side is to understand itself and the other) to distinguish the non-controversial region from the controversial, by saying that they maintain a different kind of fellowship in the former region and in the latter. Hence a complete suspension of fellowship only arises when each of the two communions refuses to recognize in the other any element that is identical simply because it is Christian ; that is to say, when all religious communications between the two have ceased, and no sort of Church hospitality obtains between them which would not be shown by either to non-Christians. In that case, all they still have in common is the empty name of Christianity.

2. A complete suspension of fellowship in this sense is unchristian as long as the communion that has been cut off retains its historical connexion with the preaching of the gospel by which it was founded, and does not, itself breaking the connexion, trace the origin of its present form to a different revelation. For as long as in any given communion the acknowledgment of Christ is still found, the action of Christ must be telling there, in however hampered a form ; while, if we cast loose from this, then, since all who have been received into the living fellowship of Christ ought to have fellowship with each other, we are excluding and separating ourselves from the unity of the invisible Church.[1] On this principle, even heretics in the narrower sense (much more, later degenerate forms in which other communions say they find heresy) are still part of

---

[1] Quidam ita perturbant ecclesiae pacem, ut conentur ante tempus separare se a zizania, atque hoc errore excaecati ipsi potius a Christi unitate separentur. August., *de fide et opp.* c. 4.

the Church, and fellowship with them ought not to be completely suspended.   Indeed if, to fix a limiting point, we consider that in the most heretical of all, *e.g.* Manichaeism, elements non-Christian in origin are mingled with Christian, and if, on the other hand, the Indians (say) were ready to acknowledge Jesus as one of their many divine incarnations (which would be merely the introduction of one Christian ingredient in an unchristian whole), we should not own the latter as Christians in any sense,[1] but neither should we describe them as heretics.   Thus for external fellowship we can fix no other limit than this, that we ought not to break completely with any communion which persists in attaching itself to the Christian tradition and on its side cherishes the desire to belong to the Christian Church.

Clearly, too, between all religious bodies of which this holds there is no complete suspension of true Church fellowship ; and so round the whole compass of the field there is exhibited the unity of the Church invisible.   But this all-pervading fellowship consists not merely in the fact that each acknowledges the scriptural baptism of the others, but in this, that all can look back in common to a primitive period of the Church which in the main extends much farther down than Scripture and the Apostolic Age ; that each accords to the others the right to expansion at the cost of the non-Christian world ; and that they accept each other, if not in the fellowship of other forms of Christian work, at all events in the fellowship of this work of extension.

§ 152. *Second Theorem.—All separations in the Church are merely temporary.*

1. If between the separate portions of the Church, fellowship is not completely suspended—if, that is, each separation is relative— we must recognize (if each part is conceived as having a life of its own) that in each there is a twofold movement : at one time the motive of unity is more prominent, at another this weakens and the motive of separation becomes stronger.   This of itself implies the possibility that if a moment of the first kind should coincide with the emergence of a new antithesis within the whole, the previously active motive of separation might merge in the latter, and the particular Church which had hitherto stood by itself thus throw itself wholly on one side of the new antithesis, so becoming an integral part of it, and its previous character passing over with it as a merely subordinate feature.   Or the Church in question may break up

---

[1] It is probably only to *individuals* of this kind that 1 John 4⁵ refers.

altogether, some of its members turning to one side of the new antithesis and some to the other. In this case, however, the old antithesis will gradually lose its intensity, having become subordinate to the new one. And even without this, if any of the other circumstances change, the interest felt in the old antithesis may so decline that it no longer retains power to hold a special communion together. Or, to assume the best that could be said of such a particular Church, namely, that it rests on some spiritual peculiarity which the Spirit appropriates as a special instrument, even such a case, spatially limited as it is, is one of merely transient validity. This is a view, however, which it is only possible to take of such communions as show Christian piety assuming all round an individual form ; there must be greater transience in proportion as the unity that forms the core of the particular communion is small and inadequate. Hence no special communion ought ever to be based on the peculiarities of a specially prominent individual,[1] and no communion has the prospect of long life which seeks to base itself merely on divergent moral practice in the absence of relatively different doctrine, or conversely simply on certain peculiar doctrines in the absence of different ways of life.

To the more fixed divisions belong also those which rest on physical grounds and are delimited by national affinities or by language. And yet for one thing these natural forms are themselves temporary ; for another, Christianity more than anything else has exerted a helpful influence on the inter-communion of languages and peoples. Hence inward forces of division often overflow these limits ; at one time they bind together the Churches of different peoples and tongues in a whole of like spirit and form, at another they sever in opposition elements that naturally belong together.

2. From this it follows of itself that the zeal with which the individual clings to his particular communion can only be genuine, in the sense that no injury is thereby done to full interest in the all-combining unity of the Church invisible, if it is kept within certain limits. The essential thing is that each should love the special form of Christianity to which he adheres only as a transient form of the one abiding Church, though a form that involves a temporary being of its own. A love so qualified is very far from indifference, for it starts with the fact that it is only through his special communion that each stands in union with the whole Church. But equally it is very unlike the partisan assumption, often to be met with when

[1] Cf. 1 Cor. 1¹².

the ardour of ecclesiastical antagonism has risen to a certain point, that antagonism can only be removed by the other side coming over to our side. The extremes here (which need not now be touched upon) we usually describe by the terms ' indifferentism ' and ' proselytizing.'   But to accept in advance the position that a form already acknowledged to be temporary will one day actually disappear is not indifferentism in the least : that can only be charged on one who is unable to regard his relationship to the communion to which he belongs as more than casual, and is unconscious of having any inward reason for decision one way or the other.   Nor is the effort to commend one's own communion in the strongest way to members of other communions what we call proselytizing in the bad sense, otherwise Christianity as such, and Evangelical Christianity in particular, would have been objectionable from the first. No : nature itself prompts to such efforts whenever in another communion we see an enervation or corruption of Christian piety. Indeed, in the partisan assumption just mentioned, this very fact is accepted generally, and therefore the effort, if organized on this basis, is justified as an effort operating on universal lines ; and for that reason it ought not to be charged upon the members of an opposed communion as unchristian.   Proselytizing of the objectionable type is that which regards the extension of one's own communion as an absolute end, and uses individuals for this purpose as mere means.

SECOND DOCTRINE : THE FALLIBILITY OF THE VISIBLE CHURCH
IN RELATION TO THE INFALLIBILITY OF THE INVISIBLE

§ 153. *As in every branch of the Visible Church error is possible, and therefore also in some respects actual, so also there is never lacking in any the corrective power of truth.*

1. Every error, in so far as it is an act of thought completed with knowledge and will yet not in agreement with the object thought of, is sinful in character, and hence must be in general overcome or prevented by the increasing action of the Holy Spirit, not directly, but by the Spirit's counteracting its sinful cause.   Yet here we speak solely of truth and error in the religious sphere. What was said above [1] regarding the absolute purity of impulse must be applied here ; yet error is possible everywhere, alike in the formation of religious ideas and in the religious formation of purposes, and possible on every point.   If a sensuous movement of

[1] § 110, 3.

feeling should pervert a purpose unconsciously, it is possible that the will, as it bears on religious ideas, may be perverted at the same time, and error must then enter into every part of the execution of the purpose. And so long as the view we take of our relations within the Church may be corrupted in this fashion, no purpose can be formed wholly without error, so that no real element of life in its fulness has its being in pure truth ; in every act of the religious consciousness truth is more or less infected with error. The formulæ just used reflect the whole circle and compass of error as it mingles with the action of the Spirit of truth, and at every point each individual will find the source of falsification in himself ; his own consciousness will not suffer him to doubt that error is everywhere real, although in particular cases it may be reduced to scarcely perceptible dimensions.

It is equally certain, however, that even if in this or that quarter of the Church error has accumulated in mass, yet we cannot suppose that any part of the Church, organized as a separate whole, could be wholly devoid of the action of the Spirit of truth. Where acknowledgment of Christ forms the basis of common life, a foundation is thereby laid for all worship of God in spirit and in truth, even if corruption of such worship should be the most conspicuous feature of the body in question. This follows from the simple fact that in no branch of the visible Church (even though the sacraments were absent or had to be regarded as absent in consequence of the abnormal style of their administration) is there lacking the recognition of Scripture or the Ministry of the Word of God. Hence in every communion there are at least some who rise superior to prevailing errors, and in whom the germs are to be found of a more precise development of truth.

2. Our statement, however, assumes the presence of error everywhere, if only in a minute degree, and thus appears to contradict what we formerly asserted about Scripture.[1] For if even Scripture be so exposed to the possibility of error as in some degree to contain it, it cannot be the norm of all religious thinking ; for its normative authority, thus communicated to error, could only spread and confirm it. In that case truth would have to find within the Church some other firm seat, so as to bring its corrective forces to bear on the errors contained in Scripture itself. But at the moment we have to do not with Scripture as it lies before us now, but with its origin ; and in perfect consistency with what has just been said

[1] §§ 129 and 131.

we can easily make the admission that even in the religious thinking of the Apostles the general possibility of error became a reality
here and there without affecting Scripture, for Scripture precisely
as a collection of all that was freest of error was brought together
under the Spirit's guidance.   Nay, Scripture itself testifies [1] to the
fact that human error occurred as a passing phenomenon even in
the thought of the Apostles, and allows us to surmise from this how
perhaps still oftener the first movements of error may have been
suppressed before their influence could make itself felt.   Hence in
the second place (in order not to sever its natural connexion with the
rest of things) we may well admit as regards Scripture that among
the many peripheral ideas which prevailed at the time yet were not
ultimately given a place in the Bible, but none the less belonged to
the thought-processes of the sacred writers, slight traces of human
error might have been found.   This does not in any way detract
from the normative authority of Scripture, or from the influence of
the Holy Spirit in its composition.

§ 154. *First Theorem.—No presentation of the Christian religion*
issuing from the Visible Church contains pure and perfect
truth.

1. If it be the case that Scripture itself is not such a presentation issuing from the visible Church, but rather itself constituted
the visible Church, Scripture does not so far come under the scope
of our paragraph.   But the objection might well be raised that the
very principles which our paragraph affirms suggest that error will
be at its minimum in all acts of ordination, and hence in the appointment of those persons in whose hands the duty is placed of purifying
pre-existing ideas for the dissemination of Christian truth.   If each
of these persons, taken by himself, was exposed to error, then in
the discharge of this duty the controlling power of the common
Spirit must have manifested itself in the fact that wrong individual
tendencies in the community cancelled each other out.   This, however, would imply that every such tendency found its exact counter-
weight in some other.   It is true that in the whole body all possible
tendencies exist ; but if the whole be divided by inner differences,
the onesidedness of each part of the whole cannot find its corrective
opposite within itself ; each particular Church may err even in its
official presentations of truth.   But from this it does not follow
that if there was a time when the Church was as yet undivided, the

[1] Acts 10^{14} 16^{7}, Gal. 2^{11}.

presentations then given were pure and perfect truth. For the tendencies which cancel each other are not all present in the Church at the same time ; ages too can be onesided, in ways that can only be cancelled in a later age. Indeed, if we are bound to hold (and it is a position which alone can justify the existence of the Evangelical Church) that specially inspired individuals may exert on the whole body a reforming influence, and an influence which at first was not official, it at once follows that what has its seat in the official organization of the body is not the reforming power, but the need for reformation. This is a condition of things which may arise anywhere and may recur periodically, wherever and as long as the relation between the whole body and individuals varies between preponderating spontaneity and receptiveness on the one side or the other.

2. No definition of doctrine, then, even when arrived at with the most perfect community of feeling, can be regarded as irreformable and valid for all time. This is pre-eminently true of definitions which arose after controversy as presentations put forth by a larger or smaller majority, for controversy more than anything else rouses all those impulses that lead to error. Hence no one can be bound to acknowledge the contents of such presentations as Christian truth except in so far as they are the expression of his own religious consciousness, or commend themselves to him by their scriptural character. On the other hand, the revision of the Church's public doctrine is a task in which every individual is bound to take a share, testing the established ideas and propositions in the measure of his power and the helps at his command ; he has rights in this matter, in the exercise of which he must be left free. Still, through the whole course of this work there runs a natural agreement with regard to the principles on which, and the aims with which, error is to be counteracted ; but even this agreement is a thing of gradual formation in each Church, and can only arise when the Church has come to self-consciousness. Hence we must always reflect with satisfaction that as regards the doctrines which had come to be matters of controversy, the incipient Evangelical Church declined to submit to the decisions of a General Council ; but we can no longer approve of its having none the less accepted all the ecumenical Creeds ; for these Creeds are but the product of similar Councils, which besides were due to divisions within the Church, and hence were not pre-eminently fitted for the ascertainment of truth. Similarly, it is a matter for satisfaction that the convictions then held were set forth in brief Confessions for the whole of Chris-

tendom, which was the first thing to give reforming influences acting on the whole body their assured place ; but it is a matter of regret that by means of these very documents (as if they had been irreformable) an effort was subsequently made to hinder the performance of the very task to which they owed their birth.

§ 155. *Second Theorem.—All errors that are generated in the Visible Church come to be removed by the truth which never ceases to work in it.*

1. This paragraph is so closely connected with the previous one that, on the whole, no objection can reasonably be made to it.   If, however grave it be, error is only attached to truth in the way just described, its influence within each organic part of the whole body must diminish in proportion as the Holy Spirit takes possession of the organism of thought ; and error is restrained by two forces, prevalent in different degrees at different times : in the individual whose errors are peculiar to himself, it is restrained by the influence of public thought, which makes its pressure felt on him from every side, while in the mass of believers it is restrained by the influence of men of spiritual distinction, spreading clear views ever more widely. If it be thought, however, that in addition to such error *in* the truth, there exists in Christendom also absolute error *from* the truth, and that different methods must therefore be adopted for dealing with *it*, the matter really stands thus.   Not merely may certain ideas issue from an imperfect faith in Christ—they may even be directed against other ideas that reveal a faith more perfect— yet none the less underlying them may be that truth which in the Church remains ever the same.   On the other hand, conceptions and maxims which in no sense issue from the Christian consciousness, and of which accordingly it cannot be said that they constitute merely error *in* the truth, belong to Christendom only in so far as those who cherish them have become subject in other ways to the influence of the Christian Spirit, although as yet they are not definitely aware of the fact. For where no relation to the Spirit exists of any kind, there no part of the visible Church exists ; and in that case the Church has to do with the wrong ideas of individuals only in so far as they offer a point of attachment for its self-expanding action.   In the first case, however, even where there is absolutely no Christian truth on which it seems to rest, error is only a forerunner of such expansion, for it means that already a point exists from which the Christian consciousness may spread.

2. But of course it is impossible for our paragraph to fix times and seasons ; indeed, in the history of Christendom one can actually mark off important periods in which error grows and gains the upper hand, while truth is forced back.   Yet such phenomena are more calculated to suggest a revision of our judgment on previous apparently favourable conditions than to justify the view (incompatible with belief in the Kingdom of Christ) that the truth had disappeared from the Church or been even partially lost.   It all comes to this, that the progress of truth and the consequent removal of error within the Church visible takes either of two forms—one when the truth gradually destroys the opposed error, the other when the error which unconsciously has clung to the expression of real truth is, with all its effects, cut away from the truth ; while the truth, although seeming to lose in power and influence, is purified and thereby exerts a completer influence.

Irrespectively of this, history often exhibits an apparent diminution of the domain of truth due to apostasy, usually under the pressure of external violence.   But if the apostasy is more than apparent, it means that the Christianity rejected was itself merely apparent ; for there is no conceivable point of contact between violence of any kind and living fellowship with Christ.   Hence the Christian consciousness can never really be repressed in this way, much less wholly exterminated.

§ 156. *Appendix to these two Doctrines.—The assertion that the true Church began with the beginning of the human race and remains one and the same on to the end of it, must not be taken as implying that the Christian Church properly so-called is in itself only part of a larger whole.*

Augsburg Conf. vii. : '. . . that a holy Christian Church must ever be and abide . . . in which the Gospel is purely preached and the holy sacraments are administered in harmony with the Gospel.'—*Apol. Conf.* iv. : At sic discernit Paulus ecclesiam a populo legis, quod ecclesia sit populus spiritualis. . . . In populo legis praeter promissionem de Christo habebat et carnale semen promissiones rerum corporalium. . . . Igitur illi tantum sunt populus juxta evangelium qui hanc promissionem spiritus accipiunt.—*Expos. simpl.* xvii. : Quando autem Deus ab initio salvos voluit fieri homines . . . oportet omnino semper fuisse, nunc esse et ad finem usque seculi futuram esse ecclesiam.—Haec aliter fuit instituta ante legem inter patriarchas, aliter sub Mose per legem, aliter a Christo per evangelium.—Agnoscimus hic tamen diversa fuisse tempora, diversa symbola promissi et exhibiti Messiae.—*Conf. Scot.* v. : Credimus Deum . . . omnibus aetatibus ecclesiam suam ab Adamo usque ad adventum Christi in carnem vocasse.—*Conf. Belg.* xxvii. : Credimus —unam ecclesiam catholicam. . . . Haec porro ecclesia et ab initio mundi fuit et usque ad eius finem perdurabit.

1. It is not merely the last-quoted Confessions on the Reformed side which definitely assert the unity of the Old Testament and the New Testament Church; the same is the case on the Lutheran side. Some people might infer the opposite from the language of the Augsburg Confession, but the same view as the Reformed is unmistakably expressed in the authentic explanation of that Confession —the *Apology*. Only in the Saxon Confession does Melanchthon appear in a more cautious mood; in his examples there he goes no further back than the birth of Christ. But he really does this intentionally; his inconsistency is only apparent, for, after all, Christ could not have exerted any redeeming influence on Simeon and Hannah and the others there named.[1] But Melanchthon indubitably regards the faith of Simeon and the Messianic faith of earlier times as being of the same type. If this unity of the Church from the beginning were to be understood (as appears from one passage) in the sense that Christ was the same for the third period as Moses was for the second, our divergence from these credal statements would be even greater. But we appeal to what was said above on this subject.[2] The one point we are concerned about is to define more exactly the difference between our paragraph and these credal passages. Both sides start from the position that the Church only exists where there is faith in Christ; the Confessions, however, assert that this Church has been in existence from the beginning of the world, whereas we hold that it only began with the personal action of Christ. The Confessions therefore must assume that faith in Christ existed before His personal action, but we make such faith conditional on, and derive it from, His personal action: this, then, is the first point we have to decide. But along with this goes the fact that, while we both start from the position that faith saves, the Confessions assert that the personal action of Christ is not necessary to effect human salvation, but we hold that the saving love of God did not become effective till Christ appeared; and the question arises whether, in point of fact, we have to choose between these positions, and on what principle in this instance the choice is to be arrived at. Now these paragraphs are not in themselves utterances of our immediate consciousness; also by its negative form our paragraph shows that it has been constructed simply in contrast to positions which we do not share; hence, in the comparison now to be undertaken, we can recognize no other criterion than agreement with what has already been established as the expression of our immediate consciousness.

---

[1] *Repetit. Conf.* (ed. Twesten), p. 164.   [2] § 12, 2.

2. As regards the first point, we have already shown [1] that the fulfilment of Old Testament prophecies does not constitute them grounds of faith for us, in the sense that we believe in Christ because He was foretold as that which He was later found to be ; this could be no ground of faith in our evangelical sense. But this certainly does not make it impossible that before Christ appeared, promises as such might have become for men a ground of salvation. Given an acute sense of sin and of the need of redemption, this yearning might (if a Redeemer were promised) attach itself to the promise, and a presentiment might arise of the salvation of future ages in fellowship with Him—a presentiment which as sympathetic joy might in a sense overcome the feeling of personal unblessedness. Even granting so much, this was no more than a shadow-life, a dim premonition of the Christian Church, not the Christian Church itself. All we say is that the Church exists wherever there is faith, because faith is the complete appropriation of Christ and is, in addition, of an essentially fellowship-forming character. In the case in question, it is true, we can in a way admit the appropriation of Christ's blessedness, not however the appropriation of His perfection. And this faith in the Messianic promises was never anywhere in the Old Testament a fellowship-forming thing ; that the existing fellowship rested on the Law is obvious historical fact. Hence it is no adequate statement of the difference merely to concede that there was one kind of symbols so long as the Messiah was promised and another after He appeared ; on the contrary, faith itself changed in kind, and in the time of the Law true New Testament faith was merely in the future.[2] Indeed, the position conceded above is incapable of proof, namely, that Messianic promises in the Old Testament really contained the idea of a Redeemer in the sense that we along with the Protestant Confessions, accept, or that in this sense they offered a Redeemer to the consciousness of sin as we understand it. But if it is sought not merely to affirm all this, but actually in respect of the perfection of Christ as it works upon us and of the bond of brotherly love to identify faith before Christ appeared with faith as we know it, it will have to be admitted that the hearers of the promise were able to construct the idea of sinless perfection out of extremely imperfect indications, and not merely construct it but put it in action. And this, of course, leads to the position that the actual appearance of Christ was not necessary for our salvation, and that nothing more

[1] § 14, Postscript.   [2] Cf. Gal. 3[22. 23].

was requisite than that all the time the promise should be kept alive.

3. However little we may agree with this, it looks as if equally inconvenient consequences followed from our own position that men did not attain to salvation before Christ appeared. The inference, however, that the saving love of God only began with the appearance of Christ, we must forthwith qualify (as our principles demand) by saying that it was only the temporal manifestation of that love which then began. Put thus, there can be no objection to its acceptance ; for it simply means that we and the whole human race find ourselves in the same case as even now every individual does who for the first time comes to enjoy redeeming love through becoming regenerate. In the same way, until the appearance of Christ humanity was in a condition of living under preparatory grace—the whole of humanity, and not merely that descending succession of persons through which we are led by the Jewish historical books, from Adam and the patriarchs to the founding of Mosaism. For this preparatory grace was manifested in every place where, and in the measure that, there were to be found the workings of the divine holiness and righteousness ; and from this point of view we obtain that very equality between Jews and Gentiles which Paul took as his starting-point. This harmonizes more closely than may at first sight appear with the mode in which Paul relates Christ's appearance to the promise and the faith of Abraham, when he argues that the preparatory divine grace was not manifested in a special or exclusive fashion in the statutory Law, but pre-eminently in the fact that monotheism should have had a place kept for it ; and action so motived is faith, which can equally well be regarded as obedience. It therefore was reckoned to Abraham for righteousness, because he now became the instrument of preparatory divine grace, and in this relation to future generations could through his faith be an object of the divine favour. In this sense, then, we may also accept a justification for Christ's sake before Christ, analogous to blessedness in sympathy with the future ; and thus scattered rudiments of the Church, although not the Church itself. But if for the position that from the beginning of the human race there has existed a true Church, there be substituted the position merely that from the beginning there has never been any source of salvation for men, or any ground of divine favour towards men, other than Christ—to this there can be no objection.

§ 157. *Since the Church cannot attain to its consummation in the course of human life on earth, the representation of its consummated state is directly useful only as a pattern to which we have to approximate.*

1. The Holy Spirit, as the common vital principle of the Church, is of itself the sufficient reason of this consummation ; but, His action being subject to the laws of temporal life, the consummation can only arrive when all opposition is so completely overcome that in the field of His activity nothing in time remains which is hostile ; when, that is to say, all the influences of the world upon the Church have exhausted themselves. This implies first of all that Christianity has spread over the whole world,[1] in the sense that no other religion survives as an organized fellowship. As long as these antiquated and imperfect forms of religion persist alongside of Christianity, striving to maintain themselves side by side with the Church, their character will be so deeply impressed on their adherents that when these have been captured by Christianity, whether individually or in the mass, they will (even if it be unconsciously) carry over many corrupting elements, which must prove a source of division and error. Now our self-consciousness testifies that in general the origination of faith in the Redeemer is not conditioned by any special circumstance, but depends solely on the common consciousness of sin which can be evoked in all, as well as on the equally universal faculty, due to the sameness of human nature everywhere, of receiving a specific impression from the Redeemer. We therefore cherish the hope that the expansion of Christianity will be accelerated in proportion as the glory of the Redeemer is ever more clearly reflected in the Church itself.[2] It is an undeniable possibility that this might take place in the course of human history ; yet we cannot forget that during all that time the propagation of the species goes on, and that sin develops anew in each generation. Thus even assuming that the power of sin is being ever more widely and thoroughly repressed, and hence more easily broken, the Church is thus ever anew admitting worldly elements. Thus it is always

[1] Rom. 11²⁵. ²⁶.   [2] Eph. 1²². ²³ 2²¹. ²².

involved in the conflict described above, and hence is never perfected.   In this state it is usually designated the *Church militant*,
because it has not only to stand on the defensive against the world
but must seek to conquer the world.   Just for that reason, as
conceived in the state of consummation it is called the *Church
triumphant*, because all that in this sense was worldly has now been
wholly absorbed in it, and no longer exists as its opposite.

2. Strictly speaking, therefore, from our point of view we can
have no doctrine of the consummation of the Church, for our
Christian consciousness has absolutely nothing to say regarding
a condition so entirely outside our ken.   We have recognized
Christ as the end of prophecy;[1] which implies that even the
Church does not acknowledge any gift of the Spirit enabling her to
form a prophetic picture of a future on which (since it lies altogether
beyond human experience) our action can exert no influence whatever ;   indeed, in the absence of all analogy we could hardly understand the picture aright or retain it securely.   None the less, these
prophetic pictures fill a great place in the Church, and it is incumbent on us, before pronouncing for their exclusion from this exposition, to inquire as to their source.   In the first place, reference
must be made to the New Testament predictions of the consummation of the Church, all of which we certainly must trace back to
prophetic utterances of Christ.   Now if these are to be treated by
the rules of art, and yet not to be made doctrines proper, but only
propositions which we receive on testimony, yet which do not stand
in so intimate a relation with our faith as do similar propositions
regarding the Person of the Redeemer, we shall hardly be able to
give them a place in our Dogmatic, or at least only in so far as they
concern the Redeemer and our relation to Him.   While, however,
these propositions are not doctrines of faith, since their content
(as transcending our faculties of apprehension) is not a description
of our actual consciousness, the matter takes on another aspect if,
abstracting from the fact that they transcend our present conditions,
we concentrate on the point that they must contain no reference
to anything in our present state due to the influences of the world.
That these influences may be restrained, in a higher degree than
the mere co-operation of individuals could secure, is the constant
object of our prayers ; and the consummated Church is accordingly the sphere where such prayer is answered in full measure.
Hence this idea of the consummation of the Church is rooted

[1] § 103, 3.

in our Christian consciousness as representing the unbroken fellowship of human nature with Christ under conditions wholly unknown and only faintly imaginable, but the only fellowship
which can be conceived as wholly free from all that springs from
the conflict of flesh and spirit.

§ 158. *As the belief in the immutability of the union of the Divine
Essence with human nature in the Person of Christ contains
in itself also the belief in the persistence of human personality, this produces in the Christian the impulse to form
a conception of the state that succeeds death.*

1. The meaning of this paragraph cannot be that belief in the
continued existence of personality after death or (as we usually
express it) the immortality of the soul arose in the way here indicated ; for traces of that belief exist everywhere, and especially
in the times of Christ and the Apostles it was prevalent among the
Jewish people. The only thing the paragraph can mean is that
apart from this connexion the belief could not have been given a
place in our Christian Dogmatic. Indeed, the whole of the preceding argument has been set forth and proved without reference
to this belief, and only one paragraph, that on the ascension of
Christ (which is not directly a doctrine of faith) points in its direction. So that the reader who so far has found his Christian consciousness reflected in our exposition must own—assuming the facts
of Christianity and our acquaintance with them—that faith in the
Redeemer as it is here described may develop out of a sense of sin
calling for redemption, and that from it we might infer the communication of Christ's blessedness at every moment of life, including the last moment of all, even though we had no conception whatever of a life after death. Thus the question naturally arises
whether, and how, this belief would have come to be bound up
with our religious consciousness, had not the Redeemer accepted
and sanctioned it. Only two possibilities are open. Either the
survival of personality would have been ascertained as a truth
through the activities of knowledge, that is by way of objective
consciousness ; or it might have been given us originally in our
immediate self-consciousness, whether vitally bound up with the
God-consciousness which everywhere is fundamental, or independently thereof and by itself. As regards the first, it would
mean that the doctrine of immortality belonged to the higher
natural science, and in that case the certainty of it could only exist

for those who had mastered scientific method, while others got it from them at second hand. But this evidently is not how matters stand ; it is undeniable that on the scientific plane the belief has always been attacked by some people as vehemently as it has been defended by others. Indeed, anyone who considers the so-called rational proofs of immortality more closely will scarcely find it possible to believe that the idea itself originated with science. It came from some other source, and what science did was to seek to combine it with other scientific results ; and from the nature of the case any such procedure must always be liable to attack. Hence in the event of Dogmatic wishing to make a further use of the idea of immortality, it is not entitled to adopt these proofs ; still less is it obliged to scrutinize them and supply their defects. On the contrary, its duty would be to await scientific demonstration of the idea, leaving the matter on one side till this was forthcoming. Otherwise, Dogmatic would be made dependent on a philosophical theory still under dispute.

As regards the second possibility, if belief in immortality were bound up with the God-consciousness in general, it would be a serious error on our part not to have developed it at the outset when dealing with that subject. This error, however, would have revealed and revenged itself before now, which in point of fact it has not done—a circumstance not calculated to predispose us to believe that the two things are really bound up together. True, there is an impious denial of immortality which is bound up with the denial of God ; both things go along with a materialistic or atomistic type of thought ; but there is also a surrender of the survival of personality which is of a quite different sort, and which, far from regarding spiritual activity as a mere phenomenon of matter, or making matter superior to spirit, strictly regards spirit as the power which produces living matter and conforms it to itself. From this point of view it may similarly be affirmed both that the God-consciousness constitutes the essence of every life which in the higher sense is self-conscious or rational, and that while spirit is essentially immortal in such productivity, yet of such productivity the individual soul is only a transient act, and thus essentially perishable ; in which case every ' act ' over and above the definite point reached by evolution and transcending the definite realm of human existence (to which personality belongs) would forfeit all significance. Between such a surrender of the survival of personality and the predominance of the God-con-

sciousness (even a predominance which insisted on the purest
morality and the loftiest spirituality of life) there would be no incongruity whatever. Added to this is the fact that there certainly
is a belief in personal survival which is in harmony with the general
spirit of piety, a belief which regards the presence of the God-
consciousness in the human soul as explaining why the soul cannot
share the general lot of transience ; but there is also a belief which
is impious. For how could this belief have any affinity with the
God-consciousness, if it merely issued from an interest in the sense-
aspect of life, even were that interest in some degree ennobled
and refined ? And yet this invariably is the case when immortality
is postulated for the sake of retribution, on the assumption that no
such thing exists as a pure and direct impulse to piety and morality,
but both are sought only as means to the attainment of perfect
felicity in a world to come. If then it must be admitted that
there is a way of denying the survival of personality in following
which we may be more deeply pervaded by the God-consciousness
than if we accepted it, we must not continue to assert that this
belief and the God-consciousness are bound up together.

2. None the less, it may well be held that belief in the survival
of personality is bound up with faith in the Redeemer. The
Redeemer ascribes such survival to Himself in everything that He
says about His return or reunion with His people ; and (since He
can only say these things of Himself as a human person, because
only as such could He have fellowship even with His disciples) it
follows that in virtue of the identity of human nature in Him and in
us, the same must hold good of ourselves. Self-evident as this may
seem, we must nevertheless inquire whether objections can be made,
and what these objections are, whether to the correctness of the
underlying assumption or the legitimacy of the inference. Objections of the former kind could only relate to a divergent interpretation of Christ's sayings, and so far they would not be matters for
discussion here, but would belong to exegesis. Here it need only be
said that even if in good faith one were to maintain that, in one way
or another, the relevant sayings of Christ are all figurative, and not
to be interpreted strictly, and that He nowhere claims personal survival, yet faith in Christ as we have here presented it would certainly
still be possible. (For although the surrender of personal survival
as just described would then be common to Christ and to ourselves,
yet this would not necessarily abolish the specific difference between
Him and us.) None the less, a complete transformation of Chris-

tianity would be the result were such a mode of interpretation to prevail within the Church and be made fundamental to the Christian faith. And this of itself implies that we cannot assume that such an interpretation could be put forward in good faith. The case would not be greatly altered were anyone to impugn the legitimacy of the inference referred to above on the ground that even if Christ did ascribe personal survival to Himself, it was an opinion which He merely took over from current belief without definite personal conviction, making no other use of it than He did of similar opinions in similar cases ; so that His utterances on the point do not belong to the type which is so closely bound up with His assurance regarding His own dignity and destiny that neither of these could really be believed in if those utterances were rejected. In fact, it would scarcely be possible for anyone to hold sincerely that it was without personal conviction that Christ rejected the view of the Sadducees, or that His faith in the irresistible progress of His Word did not depend on His faith in the persistence of His personality. But if we cannot deny His firm conviction on the subject, the only further objection that could be suggested is that the survival of His personality (His belief in which we, in that case, should have to share) implies nothing for our own ; on the ground that His survival depends exclusively on what is peculiar to Him, namely, the union of the Divine Essence with human nature which alone constitutes His human person, and that therefore we must say that just because the Redeemer is immortal, all other men are not. Such an explanation would be docetic, and none the less docetic that it is so only in one particular respect. For the difference between an immortal and a mortal soul cannot consist, or reveal itself, solely in the fact that at some time or other one of them really dies ; the activities and states of each must always and in every respect be different from those of the other. Hence, if the soul of the Redeemer were imperishable, but our souls perishable, it could not justly be said that as man He was like us in all points, except sin. For if it were to be maintained that originally it was the nature of the human soul to be immortal, but that each soul becomes mortal by the transmission of sin, this would imply that the whole original work of God had been destroyed by sin, and its place taken by something else. Hence we must put aside a distinction favoured by some, to the effect that all souls become mortal through sin, and at death perish with the body, but that through fellowship with Christ believers obtain a share in immortality and pass through death to life along with Him.   Either this goes back to an assumption which is Manichean in spirit, namely, that those who do not attain to living fellowship with Christ could not in any case have become immortal ; or, if the others are like them in nature, that very nature must have been made totally different by regeneration.   Nothing remains therefore but to say that if we take the utterances of the Redeemer about His eternal personal survival as being imbued with His perfect truth, as His disciples undeniably did, then all who are of human race can look forward to survival too.   Even so the Redeemer continues to be the mediator of immortality, only not exclusively for those who believe on Him here, but for all, without exception ; in this sense, that if personal immortality did not belong to human nature, no union of the Divine Essence with human nature to form such a personality as that of the Redeemer would have been possible ; and conversely, that since God had determined to perfect and redeem human nature through such union, human individuals must all along have possessed the same immortality as the Redeemer was conscious of.   Such is the true Christian assurance concerning this belief ; every other guarantee for it, even were it clearer than efforts at proof would so far lead us to expect, must remain alien to the Christian mind, at least until this belief comes to be one of the ideas constituting the complete and universal body of human conviction.

3. This belief naturally is accompanied by a desire to form and keep clear ideas as to the condition of personality after death.   But it is wholly impossible for us to claim that in this we shall definitely succeed.   The question as to the conditions of existence after death (and a knowledge of them must form the basis of any clear conception) is a purely cosmological question ; and space and spatialities are so closely connected with times and seasons that equally with these they lie outside the range of those communications which the Redeemer had to make to us.   Hence all the indications He gives are either purely figurative,[1] or otherwise so indefinite in tenor that nothing can be gathered from them more than what for every Christian is so much the essential thing in every conception he may form of existence after death, that without it such existence would be mere perdition—namely, the persistent union of believers with the Redeemer.   Similarly, what the Apostles say on the subject is said merely by way of dim presentiment, and with the confession

---

[1] The sayings I refer to are familiar to everyone, and are too numerous to be cited in detail.

that definite knowledge is lacking. True, then, as it may be that each moment of our present life is intrinsically more perfect and wise the more completely and clearly it embraces both past and future, we should not seek to determine our purposes by picturing to ourselves the form of our future life. Such efforts, which spring from the interest of our sensuous self-consciousness in the survival of personality, are always sensuous in character, even when nobler than those of Judaism and Islam ; and we must carefully guard ourselves against allowing them an influence (as though they derived from our Christian faith) which may only too easily injure Christian faith and life, and thereby spoil for us the present. Hence, as regards the idea of the future life, what we shall chiefly have to do is to scrutinize carefully the propositions put forward by others, as well as the opinions which have become dominant.

§ 159. *The solution of these two problems, to represent the Church in its consummation and the state of souls in the future life, is attempted in the ecclesiastical doctrines of the Last Things ; but to these doctrines we cannot ascribe the same value as to the doctrines already handled.*

1. The phrase, ' the Last Things,' which has been somewhat generally accepted, has a look of strangeness which is more concealed by the word ' Eschatology ' ; for the term ' things ' threatens to carry us quite away from the domain of the inner life, with which alone we are concerned. This of itself indicates that something is being attempted here which cannot be secured by doctrines proper in our sense of the word. The terms have this in common, that if the beginning of a wholly new and ever-enduring spiritual form of life be represented as from our point of view ' the last thing,' that endless duration appears merely as the end of a time-life which, as contrasted therewith, is almost a vanishing quantity. This can only be justified by bringing in the idea of retribution, and that idea accordingly becomes dominant. On the other hand, if the same endless duration be regarded as the further development of the new life begun here, the brief time-life appears rather as its preparatory and introductory first stage. The former view, insisting on the idea of retribution, appeals for support chiefly to those passages in which Christ represents Himself as one to whom judgment has been committed ; the latter, based on the idea of development, to passages in which He says that He is come to save. Indisputably this latter view is more closely akin

to the premonition of personal survival as that is demonstrably present in the Christian consciousness ; on the other hand, the former is more in harmony with the idea of the consummation of the Church, an idea which, in order to find a point of attachment in our present life as a whole, insists on the exclusion of all that can be called 'world' even from the Church's environment. Thus doctrines of the Last Things have connexions equally with both these problems ; each doctrine relates to both. If we tried to form a Christian idea of a state subsequent to this life, and it failed to agree with our idea of the consummation of the Church, we could not believe that it really expressed the absolutely final stage ; we should have to suppose that there still remained a further development, in which the Church would be perfected. Conversely, if we viewed the consummation of the Church as arriving within the present course of human affairs, we should have to add something in thought for the state after death, in order to give it a content of its own ; the material for this, however, could not be drawn from our Christian consciousness, for its contents are all of the other kind. Hence it was in the nature of the case that both elements should be thus conjoined—the consummation of the Church (which we cannot regard as possible in this life) being placed in that future life of which we cannot but form a conception, and the idea of that life (based as it must be on fellowship with Christ) being filled out with content from the perfected state of the Church. It must be so, if the new form of life is decisively to transcend the present.

At the same time we are not in a position to exhibit the confluence of the two factors, or to guarantee it. The consummated Church cannot be thought of as analogous to the Church militant ; nor do we know whether into the future life we ought to project the idea of an interdependent common life and work, to which no proper goal can be assigned. On the other hand, if we seek to conceive the future life by analogy with the present, as an ascending development, we cannot but have doubts whether any such development is possible in the consummated Church. Thus the solution of one problem seems never exactly to fit the other. We encounter the same difficulty if we keep to the indications of Scripture. There much is said by way of representing the consummated Church ; but it is not so said that we can affirm with certainty that it ought to be dated subsequently to the end of all earthly things ; [1] and for that reason from of yore many Christians

---

[1] John 6^{53-58}, Acts 1^{6, 7}, Eph. 4.

have actually expected the consummation of the Church here on earth. Other passages are meant rather to describe the life after death,[1] but whether they are also a representation of the consummated Church may be doubted.

2. Hence the following paragraphs, which treat of the Last Things, cannot have ascribed to them at all the same value as the previous doctrines. It is certainly not to be denied that we are conscious of our spiritual life as being the communicated perfection and blessedness of Christ, or that of itself this implies that in every case only the perfect is the originally real, whereas the imperfect owes its being to it ; or that this conviction is likewise faith in the reality of the consummated Church, yet only as an actively motive force within us, which is the really operative element in every aspect or moment of life which promotes the Church. If, however, the distinction (ineradicably bound up with our self-consciousness) between inner principle and outward manifestation be abolished (this active principle being also conceived as somehow attaining to expression in space and time), the position stands on a less firm foundation. Similarly, the equating of all human individuals with Christ implies that the general premonition of the imperishability of spirit, even in individual form, becomes certain for the Christian mind ; but this in no way involves any particular way of conceiving survival. Indeed, we cannot really make a picture of it either in the form of an infinitely progressive development or in that of an unchanging completeness ; to such a task our sensuous imagination is unequal. If, on the other hand, we treat these paragraphs, irrespectively of their source in our self-consciousness, as matters simply to be received on the authority of Scripture, even so they are not comparable to the doctrine of Christ's resurrection ; for what is in question there is statements made by the disciples regarding a fact connected in the closest possible way with their vocation. True, if we had evidence to show how, in ways we could reproduce, Christ formed these two conceptions in His own mind, we should endeavour with perfect confidence to appropriate His thought for ourselves ; for here too we should ascribe to Him nothing less than a perfectly developed human power of premonition, free from all uncertainty due to sin. But the content of these paragraphs cannot be so derived. We nowhere find in His teaching a connected and unambiguous treatment of these subjects, obviously meant to convey definite instruction about them. In

[1] I Cor. 15²³ᶠ·, Phil. 3²¹.

each particular saying either the subject is doubtful, or the outline drawn is indistinct and the .interpretation in a variety of ways uncertain. Hence there is nothing for it but that we should bring up those thought-forms which early became prevalent in the Church and passed over into our Confessions without being submitted to a fresh scrutiny, and should adduce them, under the title of *prophetic doctrines*, merely as the efforts of an insufficiently equipped faculty of premonition, adding reasons for and against. But we give fair warning that in any new forms which these doctrines may assume, the fancy (for to it belongs everything alien to the scope of our present experience which is set forth as object of a possible future experience), if it is to remain Christian, must place itself under the protection of exegesis, and only elaborate the material which exegesis supplies. What it must not do is to let itself become the plaything of caprice or of alleged new revelations.

3. Under the circumstances, an exact construction of these paragraphs in a closely knit context is not to be thought of. We must be content to assume their sense as generally acknowledged, and let the facts prove that in their regard matters really are as I have indicated. This means exhibiting the two points—personal survival and the consummation of the Church—in their relation to each other, in a picture appealing to the sensuous imagination. Hence, in the first place, the survival of personality, above all, as the abolition of death, is represented under the figure of *the resurrection of the flesh*. The consummation of the Church, on the other hand, is represented in a twofold manner—first, as conditioned by the fact that no further influence upon the Church can now be exerted by those who form no part of the Church, it is introduced in its character as the separation of believers from unbelievers, by the *Last Judgment*. But as excluding (in contrast to the Church militant) all the activities of sin and all imperfection in believers, it is represented as *eternal blessedness*. Since the survival of personality, and therefore also the resurrection of the flesh, had to be taken as applying to the whole human race, and some mode of existence had to be found for those separated from believers, over against eternal blessedness stands (also introduced by the Last Judgment) the eternal damnation of the unbelieving. It is clear that, as this last pictorial representation is not an anticipation of any object of our future experience, it cannot be given the form of a special doctrine ; all we can do is to treat it as the shadow of eternal blessedness or the darker side of judgment. These separate pictures

fit together into a single imaginative picture, for this reason that
the new form of existence is conditional on the *Return of Christ*, to
which everything which belongs to the completion of His work
must be related.   Hence it seems entirely natural to begin with the
Return of Christ, which introduces all the rest ; in this way the other
items develop out of it, and in relation to it, in their natural
sequence.

FIRST PROPHETIC DOCTRINE : THE RETURN OF CHRIST

§ 160. *Since the disciples of Christ could not consider the comforting*
promises of His Return [1] *as having been fulfilled by the days*
of His resurrection, they expected this fulfilment at the end
of all earthly things. [2] *Now since with this is bound up*
the separation of the good and the bad, we teach ' a Return
of Christ for Judgment.'

Symb. Roman. : ὅθεν ἔρχεται κρίνειν ζῶντας καὶ νεκρούς.—Symb. Nic. : καὶ
πάλιν ἐρχόμενον μετὰ δόξης κρῖναι ζῶντας καὶ νεκρούς· οὗ τῆς βασιλείας οὐκ ἔσται
τέλος.—It is solely to this point that the *Augsburg Confession* refers, Art. 3.
A much fuller statement in *Expos. simpl.* xi.   Ex coelis autem idem ille
redibit in judicium, etc.—*Conf. Belg.* xxxvii. : Credimus . . . dominum
nostrum Jesum Christum a coelo corporaliter et visibiliter sicut ascendit
magna cum gloria et majestate venturum, ut se vivorum atque mortuorum
declaret iudicem.

1. From the days immediately subsequent to Christ's resurrection we have no record of His having repeated promises of this
kind ; [3] rather He speaks exclusively of His entering into His
glory, and refers His disciples to His spiritual presence. [4]   But this
could not cause doubt in the disciples' minds, leading them to
explain the former promises as having been fulfilled already ; for
His words in their context had pointed too clearly to a Return of
Christ, in which He would manifest Himself to the whole world.
Hence the disciples were so deeply impressed by a definite assurance [5]
(although not given them in Christ's name) which interpreted these
sayings of His literally, that later, when the destruction of Jerusalem occurred (in distinctly prophesying which Christ had spoken
also of His own future), the question was not even raised among
Christians whether all those sayings might not be referred to

---

[1] Omitting all the passages which are obviously parabolic, we have the
following : Matt. 16[27. 28] 24[20ff.] 25[31ff.], Mark 13[26ff.], Luke 21[27. 28], John
14[3. 18] 16[16].
[2] 2 Cor. 5[1-10], 2 Thess. 1[7-10] 2[8], 2 Tim. 4[1], 1 Pet. 4[5-7. 13], 2 Pet. 3[10ff.].
[3] John 21[22. 23] is surely not sufficiently definite in its terms.
[4] Matt. 28[20], Luke 24[26], John 20[17].   [5] Acts 1[11].

Christ's future understood in a non-literal way. Accordingly, after everything Chiliastic had been purged out, the opinion very early became fixed and almost universally accepted that the Return of Christ would coincide with the close of the present state of the earth.

2. If, however, we consider more carefully such passages as are most generally taken to refer to this subject, and also are most explicit, it turns out either that they excite the suspicion (some owing to the dates they fix, the others on account of their predominantly ethical tone) that they are not to be taken literally, or that, even if we interpret the personal Return literally, still there is much else in the context which cannot be taken literally on any terms, because any interpretation of the kind would destroy the whole unity of the discourse. Yet, apart from this literal exegesis we have no Biblical warrant for the position that the reunion of believers with Christ (which is the essential content of our belief in personal survival) is conditional on such a personal Return; indeed, elsewhere He Himself speaks of the first without any mention of the second.[1] Still less have we Biblical warrant for believing that there is bound up with both a prior universal separation of the good and the bad (of which even Paul says not a word[2]), or for thinking that this event, due to a definite reappearance of Christ, will be accompanied by the termination of our present form of existence. Thus all that might go to form a definite picture falls asunder; and, as the essential content of our paragraph, there remains simply this—that (if we substitute the efficacious activity of Christ for His bodily presence) the consummation of the Church, regarded as the cessation of its wavering growth and development, is possible only through a sudden leap to perfection, and on condition that procreation ceases, as also the coexistence of the good and the bad; and that, therefore, this leap to perfection must simply be regarded as an act of Christ's kingly power. This is certainly rooted deeply in Christian faith; even if it does not of itself emerge as a distinct idea in every mind, yet all feel attracted by it when presented to them. For in Christ the Divine Essence is permanently united with human nature; hence human nature cannot be so inseparably restricted to a particular planet as to be involved in that planet's destruction as resulting from cosmic laws. On the contrary, everything pertaining to it must be capable of being conceived in the light of this union and as an effect of it.

So that in this doctrine everything that is figurative and

---

[1] John 17²⁴. [2] I Cor. 15²⁰ff., I Thess. 4¹⁴ff.

necessarily uncertain in quality flows from our interest in personal survival, whereas everything that can be stated with assurance relates to the consummation of the Church.

Second Prophetic Doctrine: The Resurrection of the Flesh

§ 161. *Not only did Christ sanction, by figurative utterances*[1] *and also by His teaching,*[2] *the idea, prevalent among His race, of the resurrection of the dead, but He further in His utterances ascribed this awakening from death to His own agency ; and it is an extension of this His teaching—a perfectly natural extension based on kindred utterances—to say that the general awakening of the dead will in a sudden manner interrupt the usual course of human life on earth.*[3]

1. We are so much aware of the connexion of all our mental activities, even the most inward and profound, with those of the body, that we really cannot form the idea of a finite spiritual life apart from that of a bodily organism. Indeed, the spirit we only conceive as soul when in the body, so that it is impossible to speak of the soul's immortality in the strict sense apart from bodily life. Since the activity of the spirit as a definite soul ceases at death simultaneously with the bodily life, it is only with bodily life that it can recommence. Indisputably, however, the idea of the resurrection of the flesh implies something more than this ; it implies such an identity of life that life after resurrection and life before death constitute one and the same personality ; and this formed part especially of the Jewish conception of the matter.[4] Clearly, too, the soul as an individual entity only persists by itself in the continuity of consciousness, which again appears to us as conditioned by memory ; and memory in its turn is as much bound up with bodily states as any other mental activity. We cannot then conceive how under absolutely different bodily conditions such a unifying memory could get to work ; yet in its absence the soul itself would not be the same. But insistence on this appears to bring us back to the position which we rejected above—namely, that the human mind is rigidly restricted to the surface of this globe. On the one hand, every organism is a product of the planet on which it appears, and dependent on the specific nature of that

---

[1] Matt. 25[31ff.], John 5[28. 29] 6[40. 54].
[2] Matt. 22[30-32].
[3] I Cor. 15[51. 52], I Thess. 4[13-18].
[4] Luke 20[28-33].

planet ; hence the similarity of the future body to the present would imply a similarity of the two worlds ; but even memory, again, in virtue of its organic aspect is dependent on the near affinity of impressions ; thus, for example, in the present life our memory of a definite period of time grows extremely faint once the whole scene has changed.　If we further add that, the greater the excellence of the future life, the less could a definite volition come to the aid of such memory, it must be owned that the more the soul in itself remains the same, the more must the future life be a simple, easily attachable prolongation of the present.　But, in that case, the other point of departure for all these eschatological ideas—namely, the consummation of the Church—gets less than justice ; for in such a life as that just described no consummation is possible.　Hence the latter interest compels us, if we wish to escape the other extreme, once again to limit more strictly the similarity between the future organism and the present ; and it is on this that the description of the resurrection body as immortal [1] and without sex [2] is based.　The first of these qualities, which of itself implies a world of a quite different constitution, completely gets rid of that interest in bodily self-preservation which by experience we know to be so fruitful a seed of strife between flesh and spirit.　The second quality, in addition, guards against the entrance into the consummated Church of new souls called into being through procreation ; for we cannot conceive of such souls not being handicapped by natural forces in the development of spirit, *i.e.* we cannot conceive them without sin.　But obviously both qualities are inimical to the identity of the soul and the continuity of consciousness.　The immortal body will then at every moment and in every function reveal its difference from the mortal ; and the soul in that case will be all the less capable of appropriating the share which the mortal body had in the formation of our present consciousness, and of retaining it in memory.　And as regards the second quality, it is impossible to see how, if the relations of sex cease, the organic system on which they rest can be retained ; or, again, how a male and a female soul can as such fail to be different.　And thus, if owing to changed organization each soul ceased to be either male or female, no soul would be the same as before.　Thus it is clear that in our doctrine both points of departure must be provided for, but that the two really represent different interests ; for the resurrection of the flesh must be conceived in one way if individuals are to remain

[1] I Cor. 15⁴². 　　　　　　　　　[2] Matt. 22³⁰.

absolutely the same, and in another if one and all they are to be merged in the consummated Church.   Hence the different items cannot be combined in an idea capable of clear representation ; any idea we can form suffers from the indeterminateness peculiar to these doctrines, a characteristic harmonizing with the special name we have given them.

2. The general and simultaneous resurrection of all men implies that those who rise have existed since death in a state different from that which they enter by resurrection ; and upon this implication rests the reality of the idea of a Last Judgment.   It is naturally to this intermediate state, as immediately impending, that our sense-bound interest in the survival of the individual is primarily directed ; and the question arises whether at our point of view we possess any rule by which to guide efforts at explanation, or are at all bound to supervise them.   The first would be the case only if we found something laid down about this state in the New Testament ; but all the passages [1] which might be reckoned in here are either of uncertain doctrinal character or of doubtful meaning.   The second would be necessary if such explanations contained anything inconsistent with our Christian consciousness.   Now, the intermediate state can be conceived of in a purely negative way, as meaning simply that the old life activities have ceased and the new have not yet begun—and this is the idea of the sleep of the soul.   To this our Christian consciousness can make no distinct objection ; but while thereby, on the one hand, all Christians are made equal (since, alike for those who first fell asleep and for the last, the interval is nil), yet on the other hand, if the waking of the soul is to be conceived as synchronous with the origin of the new body, it is difficult to imagine how recollection of the former state can simultaneously be implanted and retained.   If the intermediate state be conceived as a conscious state, Christian faith certainly will insist that it cannot be a state devoid of fellowship with Christ ; for in that case it would be a lapse from grace which could not be regarded otherwise than as punishment, and would mean the reintroduction of an idea which the Evangelical Church discarded soon after its formation.[2]   But if

---

[1] Luke 16[22ff.] 23[43], 1 Pet. 3[19, 20].

[2] *Art. Smalc.* ii.: Quapropter purgatorium . . . mera diaboli larva est. Pugnat enim cum primo articulo qui docet Christum solum et non hominum opera animas liberare.   Et constat etiam de mortuis nihil nobis divinitus mandatum esse.—*Expos. simpl.* xxvi. ; Quod autem quidam tradunt de igne purgatorio, fidei christianae, credo remissionem peccatorum et vitam aeternam purgationique plenae per Christum, et Christi domini sententiis (John 5[24] 13[10]) adversatur.

the intermediate period is to be conceived as one of fellowship with Christ, it must be freed from all resemblance to ancient or even Jewish notions of an impoverished sort of life in the underworld. For all the obstacles to blessed fellowship with Christ, which in this life arise from the sense-world, have fallen away ; the intermediate state, therefore, must be a state of enhanced perfection.   But in that case it is difficult not to regard the general resurrection of the dead as superfluous, and reunion with the body as a retrograde step. Indeed, it looks as if in consistency only one way of escape were left open, namely, to suppose that in the intermediate state each individual soul by itself is in fellowship with the Redeemer, but that the fellowship of the blessed with each other, and hence too the activity of individuals, is conditional on the resurrection of the flesh, which therefore is necessary to perfection.   Still, even on this supposition, the existence of the Church remains interrupted till the resurrection, as the existence of the individual does on the former supposition ; and so one of the two elements comes to be more endangered as the other is better secured.   Hence some have taken the simultaneous general resurrection in a merely figurative sense, and have wished to infer from other scriptural passages [1] that for each individual the future life begins immediately after death.[2]   But for one thing this means that the soul is already in possession of the new body when it parts from the old, an idea we find widely accepted ; on the other hand, the simultaneous Last Judgment and also (since its alleged purpose has wholly lapsed) the personal Return of Christ must in that case be taken just as figuratively as the simultaneous general resurrection.   Thus we cannot help wavering between this more Biblical idea, which represents the action of Christ, in conjunction with great cosmic changes, as suddenly giving existence to the future life and the Church triumphant as a great whole (though at the cost of unbroken continuity), and the less Biblical view which (though in a fashion which compels us to ask for scientific proof, since so much emphasis is laid on exact affinity with the conditions of earthly life) maintains the continuity of personality as strictly as possible, the consummated Church only growing little by little out of the earthly life which goes on alongside of it.

[1] Directly, though not with certainty, from Luke 23^{43}; indirectly from Phil. 1$^{21\text{-}24}$.
[2] *Expos. simpl.* xxvi.: Credimus enim fideles recte a morte corporea migrare ad Christum . . . Credimus item infideles recte praecipitari in tartara.

3. If we now turn to the general resurrection, and the predominant modes of conceiving the subjects treated of in the following doctrines, there is one more difficulty to be solved. If saved and unsaved enter upon utterly different states, there is an unanswerable case for holding that the new bodies which they receive cannot be the same in both cases. The organism must be adapted to the conditions of life which are impending ; and this gives rise to a new difficulty if we seek to conjoin the idea of the general resurrection with that of the Last Judgment. If both classes equally become different at the resurrection, sentence has already been pronounced upon them before the judgment comes on, and judgment becomes superfluous ; the more so that such a difference in bodies which originate simultaneously could not be produced by the action of identical cosmic forces combined with differences of a purely ethical kind, but only by a directly creative divine fiat. On the other hand, if those destined to bliss and those destined to perdition are still alike at the resurrection, the resurrection is not an execution of the judgment, and since in one class or the other or in both inward changes must later take place which transform the organism, the reality of the idea of the Last Judgment depends solely on these changes occurring simultaneously, but there is no further need for the simultaneity of the resurrection of the dead and the transformation of the living.

Taking all these considerations together, we find that the various ideas of how the future life is attached to the present are incapable of being made perfectly definite. As the essential content of the doctrine there remains only this, that the ascension of the risen Redeemer was possible only if all other human individuals too can look forward to a renovation of organic life which has links of attachment to our present state ; and further, that the development of the future state must be posited on the one hand as dependent on Christ's divine power and on the other as a cosmic event for which arrangements have been made in the universal divine world-order. The first of these last two ideas is certified as implied in the faith underlying the endeavour to form ideas on this matter ; the second hovers before the mind as indicating a problem we can never completely solve.

THIRD PROPHETIC DOCTRINE : THE LAST JUDGMENT

§ 162. *The idea of the Last Judgment, the elements of which are like-*
wise found in the utterances of Christ, is meant to set forth

the complete separation of the Church from the world, inasmuch as the consummation of the former excludes all influences of the latter upon it.

1. The main element in the idea of the Last Judgment, namely, that Christ will utterly separate the believing and the unbelieving from each other, so that they are consigned to quite different places and can exert no further influence on each other, does not at all involve the consummation of the Church. As has been shown,[1] the imperfections of the Church are due much less to the influence of unbelievers mingling with believers in this world than to the carnal elements still present in the regenerate themselves. Hence if at the resurrection believers were the same in soul as at their departure from this life, they would enter the new life, in spite of the supposed separation, as persons in whom sin, though in process of disappearing, was still at work. Thus the value which in this respect is attributed to separation rests solely on an incorrect reading of the distinction between the visible and the invisible Church.[2] But if this distinction, as we have understood it, is to cease with the beginning of the new life, it follows that at that point the regenerate themselves must discard those elements of sinfulness and carnality which still cling to them. But this is not effected by the outward separation itself, and it was for this reason that in his own exegetical fashion Origen [3] sought to interpret one of the relevant passages as indicating an *inner* separation. Apart from the fact that to have all worldly and carnal motives and ideas so abruptly torn away would so far endanger the continuous identity of personal life, such an inner separation would simply be completed sanctification ; and, as all sanctification must flow from vital fellowship with the Redeemer, the Christian consciousness is unable to recognize itself in any view from which this is absent. Indeed, in any such abrupt cessation of sanctification, not mediated by our own spontaneous action, we cannot help finding something magical, which, had it only been applied to each individual earlier, would have made superfluous the whole redemption which depends on living fellowship with Christ. Thus it always seems as if one of these two things excluded the other. John does appear to offer a mediating idea which might reconcile the discord ; [4] for if the inner separation is effected by the perfect knowledge of Christ consequent on His

[1] Cf. § 126, 1.   [2] Cf. § 148, 2.
[3] *Comment. in Matt.* x. 2 (on Matt. 13$^{36-40}$), ed. R., vol. iii. p. 444.
[4] 1 John 3^2.

Return, it is a work of redemption. But if considered more closely, this suggestion too breaks down. If the Return of Christ effects this change only in proportion to each person's receptivity, it still remains that such receptivity is not equally great in all the regenerate when they leave this world. So that the complete purification of the soul due to the appearance of Christ would not be wrought in each case with equal instantaneousness, but more swiftly in some and more slowly in others. Hence even this separation would not be simultaneous ; it would only come to be gradual after the new life began. If, on the other hand, whether the degree of receptivity for the knowledge of Christ be higher or lower is a matter of no importance, the inner separation certainly would be effected abruptly ; but the same change would necessarily be produced in the unbelieving, for Christ appears to them also at His Return, and in them, too, the receptivity in question is present, even in the worst of cases, in some infinitely small degree. In that case, we should find this growing on our hands into a sudden recovery of all souls for the kingdom of grace, which, while making the separation of persons meaningless, would in itself not be wholly free from an admixture of magic.

2. If now we turn back to the idea of a separation between persons according as they have reached the close of life in a state of belief or unbelief (and it is this idea which has become dominant, because it seems to be approved by Christ's own words), we can hardly deny that it is better fitted to bring about the blessedness of believers in the new life than their perfection. For if the influences emanating from the unbelievers mingled with believers are received by the regenerate solely in their character as organs of the Holy Spirit, and lead solely to action derived from, and determined by, the Spirit, many perfections will be evoked thereby, such as we find likewise in the Christ's pattern life—perfections which apart from such influences could never have developed. But it seems to be otherwise as regards blessedness. The evils due to sin always spread over the entire common and corporate life ; hence even in the next life believers, if involved in the same common life with unbelievers, would have to suffer from the evils these brought with them. But here too people have not recurred as they should have done to the idea of living fellowship with Christ. During His sojourn here Christ also partook in the common life shared by sinners, but we do not suppose that, apart from sympathy and bodily pain, He was a sufferer. Similarly, those united to Him in living fellowship will

experience nothing which tends to hamper their spiritual life and could therefore be felt by them as evil—just as Christ Himself never felt bodily pain and sympathy as evils. Besides, even bodily pain (if a possibility at all in the life after resurrection) would necessarily be capable of being produced in other ways than through sin, so that separation would be no guarantee against it. Sympathy, too, would still be inseparably bound up with identity of nature ; so that the blessed would still have sympathy with the others, though wholly separate from them. Thus the separation contemplated at the Last Judgment remains, even from this point of view, both inadequate and superfluous. All that might be said is that it takes place for the sake not of the blessed but of the others, whether to ensure that they reap no benefit from what the good might do to alleviate the evils pervading the fellowship of the new world, or lest in that very fellowship they might find means of themselves attaining to communion with Christ. But either this would mean attributing jealousy to the Supreme Being, an idea against which even the higher paganism protested ; or it must rest solely on that familiar and widespread idea of the divine righteousness which in its one-sidedness looks so like caprice that before we could feel ourselves entitled, not to say obliged, to regard the idea as in harmony with the mind of Christ, it would have to be much less equivocal in its origins, the expression given to it much more decisive, and the Apostles' use of it much more comprehensive.

3. The idea of the Last Judgment, then, we are unable to state in a final form which perfectly satisfies both demands. None the less, in view of its almost universal prevalence in Christendom, we must try to elicit its essential meaning. By way of preliminary it may be remarked that in so far as it can be traced to an all but vengeful desire to enhance the misery of unbelievers, and to exclude them from all the redemptive influences of the good, or again so far as there has contributed to its prevalence a fear lest, even after attaining perfected fellowship with Christ, we might be pained by the company of the bad, it springs from an unpurified Christian temper and obscures the essential meaning of the whole conception. It follows that this essential meaning can only be what remains over, when we have completely freed our thought from fear and vengefulness. This appears to consist in the following two points. First, once our fellowship with Christ has been perfected, we are so completely freed from evil that even though evil men and evil things be present, both as such are for us non-existent Wrong and evil being

thus wholly shut out from the common consciousness of believers, that consciousness can embrace nothing but the untroubled and unimpeded fulness of divine grace ; the Church is really then a wholly self-enclosed body, so that an outlook (and of this we can never rid ourselves here) that dwells upon opposition and contrast will there give place utterly to one for which evil has ceased to exist, because God cannot originate it. Secondly, if we conceive the Church as consummated, but at the same time suppose that there still exists a part of the human race which has not been captured and pervaded by its spirit, such a supposition is possible only on the assumption that the part in question is completely isolated from all influences issuing from the Church, which means shut off from all contact with it. There is indeed one discourse of Christ,[1] at least very closely related to this theme, which clearly implies that every influence (even the faintest) passing from the seats of the blessed to those who during their earthly life have failed to turn to God, touches them to better issues.

FOURTH PROPHETIC DOCTRINE : ETERNAL BLESSEDNESS

§ 163. *From the resurrection of the dead onwards, those who have died in fellowship with Christ will find themselves, through the vision of God, in a state of unchangeable and unclouded blessedness.*

1. The state of believers after their full reinstatement in life may be conceived under two forms, either as a sudden and unvarying possession of the highest, or as a gradual ascent to the highest— an ascent, however, which like the development of Christ Himself must be thought of as without retrogression and without conflict. Both views have their own special difficulties, when we try to fill in the general outline and to shape the mere formula into a clear imaginative picture. As regards the first, we can hardly explain to ourselves how the consummation can be reached by us, or implanted in us, just at the resurrection, without destroying all connexion with our present life ; which would not be the case if this life were gradually forgotten, like our childhood, as we grew by degrees in perfection. Still more, if we are to conceive a perfection incapable of any further increase—and this in a finite being completely severed from all that admitted of cultivation, or required it—then we find it embarrassingly difficult to imagine how this

---

[1] Luke 16^{19-31}.

being, now deprived of every object for its activity, could express its perfection. We cannot separate communal life from man's nature as such, still less can the Christian conceive himself apart from such a life ; for the fellowship of believers with each other and that of each with Christ are one and the same thing. Not only so ; a common life, devoid of every object of common activity, a life which therefore must limit itself exclusively to the mutual presentation of the contents of the inner life, can scarcely be thought of as an absolutely perfect state. It is true, we have in our present life an element which is akin to such a state, namely, common worship, and all æsthetic representations of the God-consciousness. But we find it deplorable that for such things pious Christians should neglect their practical obligations ; such a life impresses us as meagre ; hence we cannot bring ourselves to think that the highest perfection of existence can be reduced to such an alternation of giving and receiving empty and aimless representations. Instead, our imagination strains to discover some work which in that life might be entrusted to us. On the given assumptions, however, nothing remains but either the cultivation of some external nature or the oversight of some less perfect spiritual world—both such that occupation with them could not disturb our bliss. But we do not find in Scripture any encouragement to such an idea,[1] nor have we the power to fill out such a formula with real meaning.

It is no easier, supposing we try to imagine that at the resurrection there will begin a perfection which rises up and up to infinity. We can hardly conceive such a thing without inequalities and variations, and, even were it not so, at all events not without such a dissatisfaction with what is present as naturally goes along with the expectation of something better yet to come ; and this after all is a sense of imperfection, and therefore in free beings a sense somehow of guilt. Indeed, progress can scarcely be thought of apart from external relations and conditions of development. But if once we open this sluice, there sweep in at once diversities among those who are the same in kind, the antithesis of the pleasant and the unpleasant, and, as a consequence, everything that characterizes human life here below. In fact, nothing remains (and perhaps on these assumptions it is a position we cannot avoid without inconsistency) but that we should accept the change from life to death as itself an element in that future experience. This makes it clear that what we have conceived in this form is not the consum-

[1] Matt. 19[28] and 2 Tim. 2[12] cannot really be taken in that sense.

mation of the Church, but merely a gradually self-amending and self-purifying repetition of the present life. Thus the problem remains unsolved.

2. If now, selecting either form, we inquire as to the real vital content of this future state, and concede at the start that this content, so far as our activity is concerned, is limited to representation; then, in order to gain a clear imaginative picture, we should have to know what there will be for us to represent there ; *i.e.* what influences will affect us and be taken in by us. To this question the usual answer is to say that eternal life will consist in the vision of God.[1] This we can only take to mean the completest fulness of the most living God-consciousness : the next question is how this will be distinguished from our present God-consciousness. The simplest reply would be that while our God-consciousness now is always a mediated one, inasmuch as we have it only in and with some other element, there it will be unmediated. But this can scarcely be harmonized with the retention of personality. For as self-conscious individuals we can only have the God-consciousness, if it is really to be ours, along with our self-consciousness ; and even if the latter has to be distinguished from the former, this will only be conceivable in one of two ways. Either we merely distinguish our self from our God-consciousness, as the subject in which the God-consciousness dwells, without our self-consciousness having any other content ; and this is an idea which hardly anyone will tolerate. Or our self-consciousness, as being changeable and constantly affected, must differ from the other conceived as something which remains ever the same. Hence, if the individual life is to persist in human nature and even in finite nature as such, our God-consciousness must always remain a mediated one ; and it is exclusively within this sphere that we shall have to seek the distinction between its present and its future form. In that case, nothing remains but that (even here we strive after it, though with a sense of inability to attain) we should have an unimpeded knowledge of God in all and along with all ; and also, so far as finite nature allows it, that we should steadily have knowledge of all that wherein and whereby God makes Himself known ; and this without conflict arising between this desire in us and in any other, or between the steady God-consciousness and consciousness in any other of its aspects. This certainly would be pure and assured vision ;

---

[1] A thought first derived from Matt. 5⁸ and 2 Cor. 5⁷, but with what justice is disputed.

it would render us completely at home with God. Only, we can no more understand how we are to find ourselves at this point just at the resurrection without thereby imperilling the continuity and identity of our existence, than we can see how, if we start there at the point we have attained here, we can ever reach the consummation. Thus we can take our departure from either point—from the problem of imagining an unchangeably identical blessedness, or from that of conceiving an endlessly progressive advance. But we really can solve neither problem ; and we therefore always remain uncertain how the state which is the Church's highest consummation can be gained or possessed in this form by individual personalities emerging into immortality.

APPENDIX : ON ETERNAL DAMNATION

The figurative sayings of Christ, which have led to a state of irremediable misery for those who die out of fellowship with Christ [1] being accepted as the counterpart of eternal bliss, will, if more closely scrutinized, be found insufficient to support any such conclusion. Either these passages cannot without extreme arbitrariness be separated from others which must allude to some earlier event,[2] or they are countered by others which forbid us to think of the definitive victory of evil over one part of the human race, and from which we must rather infer that before the general resurrection evil will have been completely overcome.[3] Still less can the idea of eternal damnation itself bear close scrutiny, whether considered in itself or as it is related to eternal bliss. If we once agree that eternal damnation cannot mean condemnation to bodily pains and sufferings, for the simple reason that (if human nature is not to be utterly destroyed) the alleviating influence of custom must be allowed for ; and if the sense of ability to bear what has been inflicted entails some satisfaction, so that what results on the whole is something less than pure and irremediable misery—if all this be so, there is scarcely any firm ground on which we can stand. If the misery is of a spiritual kind, and if accordingly it consists of the pains of conscience, then the lost are better by far in their damnation than they were in this life ; yet although they are better, they are to be more wretched. We cannot imagine this ; for even if such a lot were in keeping with divine justice,

[1] Matt. 25⁴⁶, Mark 9⁴⁴, John 5²⁹.
[2] Cf. Matt. 24³⁰⁻³¹ and John 5²⁴, ²⁵.
[3] I Cor. 15²⁵, ²⁶.

still there would be no way of preventing the self-approval of the awakened and quickened conscience from supplying a counter-weight to misery. Indeed, we cannot imagine how the awakened conscience, as a living movement of.the spirit, could fail to issue in some good. If it be rejoined that what is to be regarded as the source of everlasting torment is not any sharpened feeling for the difference between good and evil, but only the consciousness of self-forfeited bliss, yet such a consciousness could not be living and acute except in so far as bliss could be pictured in the mind ; nor could it be torturing unless a capacity were present to share in the blessed state. But this capacity would itself imply a moral improvement, and the mental picture of bliss would constitute an enjoyment by which the misery was lessened.

If we now consider eternal damnation as it is related to eternal bliss, it is easy to see that once the former exists, the latter can exist no longer. Even if externally the two realms were quite separate, yet so high a degree of bliss is not as such compatible with entire ignorance of others' misery, the more so if the separa-tion itself is the result purely of a general judgment, at which both sides were present, which means conscious each of the other. Now if we attribute to the blessed a knowledge of the state of the damned, it cannot be a knowledge unmixed with sympathy. If the per-fecting of our nature is not to move backwards, sympathy must be such as to embrace the whole human race, and when extended to the damned must of necessity be a disturbing element in bliss, all the more that, unlike similar feelings in this life, it is untouched by hope. For, reflect as we may that if eternal damnation exists at all, it must be just, and that the vision of God embraces also His righteousness, yet even so sympathy persists ; indeed, even in this life we rightly expect a deeper sympathy to be shown to merited than to unmerited suffering. In some form or other personal survival includes memory of our former state, in which it will always happen some of us were associated with some of them in a common life ; and sympathy will be all the stronger because in that earlier time there was a point when we were as little re-generate as they. In the divine government of the world every-thing is inseparably conditioned by everything else ; hence we cannot ignore the fact that the circumstance of our having enjoyed helpful dispensations was due to the very same disposition of things as insured that such help should not reach them. Thus our sym-pathy cannot fail to be attended by the bitter feeling always present when we see a real connexion between our own gain and another's loss.

From whichever side we view it, then, there are great difficulties in thinking that the finite issue of redemption is such that some thereby obtain the highest bliss, while others (on the ordinary view, indeed, the majority of the human race) are lost in irrevocable misery. We ought not to retain such an idea without decisive testimony to the fact that it was to this that Christ Himself looked forward ; and such testimony is wholly lacking. Hence we ought at least to admit the equal rights of the milder view, of which likewise there are traces in Scripture ; [1] the view, namely, that through the power of redemption there will one day be a universal restoration of all souls.

POSTSCRIPT TO THE PROPHETIC DOCTRINES

What seems to emerge from these considerations is this. Both elements—the consummation of the Church and personal survival—can each for itself be taken up with perfect truth in our Christian consciousness ; it is certain, too, that the consummation of the Church can never be manifested in this life, and that the state attained in the next life must bear a different relation to the consummation of the Church from that of our present state. And yet the combination and correlation of these two elements yields no firmly outlined or really lucid idea, nor can any such idea of either the one element or the other be developed out of the intimations of Scripture. If we try to use the idea of the consummation of the Church so as to determine, from its relation to what as yet is unconsummated, the relation of the single life in the next world to the single life here, or the difference between the two, we can reach no fixed conclusion. And if we seek, by means of the idea of the future life, to assign a place to the consummated Church where it will no longer be a productive factor but a product only, again we fail. The one point of view will always tend to merge in what is mythical, *i.e.* in the historical presentation of what is supra-historical ; the other point of view will always approximate to what is visionary, *i.e.* the earthly presentation of what is more than earthly. These were everywhere the forms of prophetic thought, which in its higher import makes no claim to furnish knowledge in the strict sense, but is meant only to give stimulating expression to principles already known.

[1] 1 Cor. 15$^{26.\ 55}$.

THIRD SECTION

The Divine Attributes which relate to Redemption

§ 164. *When we trace to the divine causality our consciousness of fellowship with God, restored through the efficacy of redemption, we posit the planting and extension of the Christian Church as the object of the divine government of the world.*

1. This is the only meaning which can be attached to the conception of the government of the world, as we are able to employ it here. For our Christian consciousness, all other things have existence only as they are related to the efficacy of redemption—either as part of the organization in which the reawakened God-consciousness finds expression, or as so much raw material which this organization is to elaborate. The word ' govern,' however, means to set in motion, and direct, forces whose presence is due to other causes ; hence the term may easily mislead us into thinking even here of a divine direction of earthly forces conceived of as already existing, as also into separating the government of the world from creation in such a way that it comes to look like something that has supervened later or been interjected, and as if from the creation onwards everything could have happened otherwise than in point of fact it did happen. The Christian faith that all things were created for the Redeemer [1] implies on the contrary that by creation all things (whether as prepared for or as overruled) were disposed with a view to the revelation of God in the flesh, and so as to secure the completest possible impartation thereof to the whole of human nature, and thus to form the Kingdom of God. Similarly, the world of nature is not to be considered as going its own way on the strength of the divine preservation, the divine government only exerting influence on it through special isolated acts, so as to bring it into harmony with the kingdom of grace. To us, rather, the two things are absolutely one, and we have the certainty that from the beginning the whole disposition of nature would have been different had it not been that, after sin, redemption through Christ was determined on for the human race.

[1] Col. 1[16].

2. The conception of divine government laid down in our paragraph seems, it is true, to belong to a time when nothing suggested the existence of any other form of spiritual life than that of man, with the exception of angels. The angelic nature, however, glorious as were the descriptions given of it, was placed beneath the human by the first Christians owing to its defective union with the Divine Essence, and put in exclusively subservient relations to men. But even though we assume most willingly that the world forms the richest revelation of God of which it is possible to conceive, though we had become fully persuaded that on every one of the planets organic life is developed up to the level of rationality ; still the subject of angels would be one on which we had nothing to say. Even if our racial consciousness were able to transcend the human and embrace intelligence of every kind, yet such extra-human intelligence does not affect us in such wise as to compel us to expand our ideas of the divine government, so long as we receive no clear impression of how such intelligence operates in time. No such impression is given us, however ; it is therefore only within the compass of our own world that the divine government is known by us—within the sphere, that is, in which redemption makes its power felt. Now the element in our consciousness which becomes the sense of sin does not carry us back directly to the divine causality, so that the conception of the divine preservation of the world derives its full meaning exclusively from the relation obtaining between the divine causality and that element in our consciousness which becomes the sense of grace. Hence we can say, regarding two points formerly made out [1]—both the essence of things in their relations to each other and the order of reciprocal interaction between them—that they exist through God (in so far as they do exist) relatively to the redeeming revelation of God in Christ, by which the human spirit is developed to perfection. Everything in our world, that is to say—human nature in the first place and all other things in direct proportion to the closeness of their connexion with it—would have been disposed otherwise, and the entire course of human and natural events, therefore, would have been different, if the divine purpose had not been set on the union of the Divine Essence with human nature in the Person of Christ, and, as a result thereof, the union of the Divine Essence with the fellowship of believers through the Holy Spirit. And with respect to our conclusion as to the idea of the unity and identity of

[1] Cf. § 46, Postscript, p. 175.

the Church in all ages,[1] we must mark off two periods in the divine
government of the world—one before the union just mentioned was
realized in time and space, when all was merely preparatory and
introductory ; the other subsequent to its being realized, and this
a period of development and fulfilment.

3. In the divine causality there is no division or opposition
anywhere, nor can we regard the government of the world as other
than a unity, directed towards a single goal.   Hence the Church,
or the Kingdom of God in its whole extent as well as in the whole
course of its development, forms the one object of the divine world-
government ; whereas any particular thing is such an object only
in the other and for it.   True, we cannot avoid affirming the independent existence of the particular as an element within this
whole ; but we instantly leave the right track when we assume for
this particular a special divine causality in any way separate from
connexion with the whole, and thus view the particular in question
as the special object or result of divine government, to which other
things therefore are subordinated as means.   As a necessary
correction, rather, we must at once subordinate it to other things ;
each particular thus appearing, simultaneously and equally, as
both conditioning and conditioned, a point at which the threads
of relation cross.   Even the Redeemer, while He does represent
particular disciples at particular junctures of their life as objects of
the divine care, always in doing so has their vocation (*i.e.* their
activity in the Kingdom of God) in view as that on which strictly
the divine care is bent.

Hence for us the usual division of divine Providence into
generalis, *specialis*, and *specialissima* is nearly useless.   The first is
supposed to cover everything, the second the whole human race,
and the third the saints or the Kingdom of God ; but for us it is
only under the third that everything can be subsumed, for to its
object all else is referred.   In any case, the term ' providence ' is
of foreign origin and was first taken over from heathen authors
into later Jewish writings and adopted later by Church teachers,
not without many disadvantages for the clear exposition of the
authentic Christian faith, a circumstance which would have been
avoided by the use of the scriptural terms ' predestination,' ' fore-
ordination.'   These words express far more clearly the relation of
each single part to the connected whole, and represent the divine
rule of the world as an inwardly coherent order.   They do so in a

[1] Cf. § 156.

way by no means equivalent in meaning to the equally unchristian term ' fate,' which always implies that the particular is determined by the co-operation of all other things without the least respect to what would have issued from the independent existence of the object.   Similarly, the term ' providence ' chiefly suggests that the particular is determined without respect to what would naturally have resulted from its coexistence with other things ; and this onesidedness, too, is foreign to the idea of predestination.   Scripture itself does not hesitate to admit that even sin is embraced under divine fore-ordination, in spite of its really being contrary to the notion of the Kingdom of God ; it reckons sin, however, as among the preparatory and introductory elements of the divine govern-ment of the world ; and we can also recognize as perfectly self-consistent the divine decree that all men should share this earlier state previous to the new creation, so partaking in the powers thereof only by way of *contrast*—a form of experience that runs through the whole of human life.   Only, the difficulty which we encountered above of forming the idea of eternal damnation now reappears ; the problem being how to combine this idea with that of a divine government which is a unity in itself and is directed to a single end.

§ 165. *The divine causality presents itself to us in the government of the world as* Love *and as* Wisdom.

1. The one and undivided divine causality cannot without anthropomorphic error be represented in a circle of divine attri-butes ; hence, to bring clearly to consciousness its nature and its aim we must look for differences which, as being human, depend on some antithesis.   Now in all human causality we distinguish between the underlying temper or disposition and the more or less corresponding form in which it is given effect to.   By the former, what is innermost in the spontaneously active being as a unity is represented as will stimulated in a particular way ; the latter is traceable rather to the understanding, and shows us the spontaneous activity in relation to its object as a multiplicity.   The divine attributes named in the paragraph above are conceived on the lines of this human distinction, thus corresponding to the meaning we have attached to the divine government of the world.   Love, that is to say, is the impulse to unite self with neighbour and to will to be in neighbour ; if then the pivot of the divine government is redemption and the foundation of the Kingdom of God, involving

the union of the Divine Essence with human nature, this means that the underlying disposition cannot be conceived otherwise than as love. By wisdom, on the other hand, is understood the right outlining of plans and purposes—these regarded in their manifold characteristics and in the whole round of their reciprocal relations. Hence, since the divine government manifests itself in the self-consistent ordering of the whole sphere of redemption, alongside of the divine love we rightly place wisdom as the art (so to speak) of realizing the divine love perfectly.

2. These two attributes, love and wisdom, are of course separable in human life, and this the more easily that owing to the distinction between understanding and will which is essential to man, it is only in a few persons (and never completely even in them) that disposition and the formation of purposes merge in each other ; either ability of understanding more or less lags behind purity of will, or *vice versa*. No such dualism can be conceived of in the Divine Essence ; hence the two attributes are never separate in any way ; they are so entirely one that each may be regarded as being intrinsically contained in the other. Without ascribing any limitation to God, therefore, we may assert that the divine wisdom is not capable of producing any other disposition of things, or any other ordering of their course, than that in which the divine love is most perfectly realized ; and just as little is the divine love capable of leading to self-impartations other than those in which it itself finds perfect satisfaction, and in which accordingly it presents itself as absolute wisdom. This agreement must be brought out still more clearly in the two doctrines that follow.

First Doctrine : The Divine Love

§ 166. *The divine love, as the attribute in virtue of which the divine nature imparts itself, is seen in the work of redemption.*

Conf. Basil. v. : Status huius scripturae canonicae totius is est, bene Deum hominum generi velle et eam benevolentiam per Christum Dominum declarasse . . . quae fide sola recipiatur.

1. The two points indicated in the paragraph are not infrequently questioned even in the circles to which we belong. That the Supreme Being imparts Himself, and that this constitutes the very essence of divine love, is a position rejected by many as mystical ; and the second point, that, namely, which restricts to the channel of redemption a divine self-impartation alleged to be

going on everywhere, is rejected as unduly exclusive, and as confining the manifestations of the divine perfection to too narrow a range. Moreover, those who diverge from us in this way are chiefly people who, generally speaking, tend to conceal the distinctive features of Christianity rather than give them prominence. As regards the first point, such thinkers recognize the divine love in all those arrangements of Nature and all those dispositions of human affairs which protect life or further it. And yet, apart from redemption, and taken only in this sense, the divine love must always remain a matter of doubt. Supposing we regard the single life as its object, then, if we are not going to lapse into the grossest particularism, it is impossible from such aids to life to infer the divine love ; they involve restraints upon the lives of others ; so that the presence of love would always imply the presence of its opposite.[1] Indeed, this is true not merely of helps and hindrances to sensible well-being ; it applies also to the spiritual development of the single life ; in very many respects favour to one involves the neglect of others. But if we put the single life aside and rather consider humanity—that is to say, our racial consciousness—then (since in this case helps and hindrances ot individuals cancel each other, because each conditions the other) we shall be all the readier to return to the position that divine love does not reveal itself unequivocally except where it shows a generally protective and fostering care of what is highest and most specific in man, namely, his God-consciousness. And this, to Christian eyes, seems everywhere outside the sphere of redemption to be in a depressed condition. Thus we again find ourselves in the sphere of the divine self-impartation. So that, even when we are only seeking to exhibit the divine love as beneficent and protective, we cannot as Christians afford to insist on anything less or lower than that impartation of God in Christ and the Holy Spirit whereby the God-consciousness is renewed and made perfect. For even though every form of the God-consciousness, however imperfect (indeed, even its latent presence as something merely longed for), ranks for us as a divine impartation to human nature, it yet is not such that we can rest in it. On the contrary, such a divine impartation viewed from whatever side appears merely as a transitional stage, to which belong only human states that are provisional and imperfect.

2. On the other hand, it is objected to our paragraph, for one thing, that it was not necessary to wait for redemption in order to

[1] Cf. § 85, 1.

perceive the divine love even in its character as a divine self-impartation, and for another that it is in the highest degree unsym-
pathetic and ungrateful to find that love solely and exclusively in
redemption. Now as regards the first point, people say that an
impartation of God occurs in whatever in man can be taken as belonging to the image of God, therefore in reason with all its endowments—nay, in everything on which the original perfection of man
is based, as well as in all those germs of spiritual development with
which our nature is endowed. To this, it is granted, there certainly
also belongs that God-consciousness which underlies piety ; but if
we were on that account to bind up the knowledge of divine love
with redemption alone, we should be attaching the highest worth
of all to what is really less important. For, it is argued, the difference in God's dealings with creatures incapable of God-consciousness, and with such as develop this consciousness even in the feeblest
and most imperfect way, is greater by far than that existing between
His dealings with the latter and with those whom we call regenerate ;
for obviously the difference between the content of the God-consciousness in the last two classes is far less than that between the
first two. To this we may reply that in virtue of their capacity for
the God-consciousness all men certainly are also objects of the
divine love ; but the divine love dòes not realize itself in them
simply as such ; rather, starting from the fear of God (which was,
of course, the prevailing religious temper under the law) they at
most get through to the negative consciousness that the Supreme
Being is devoid of jealousy—which is still very far from being a
recognition of the divine love. *That* only comes with the efficacious
working of redemption, and it comes from Christ. As for those who
still (this we can say in a true sense of the whole non-Christian
world) hover between idolatry and godlessness, just in so far as
they do not love God, He cannot love them. And thus here, too,
we come back to the position that He loves them only as He sees
them in Christ, just as it is only when they themselves are in Christ
that they come to a knowledge of the divine love.

As regards the second point, it is urged that even if wherever
self-consciousness as such includes God-consciousness, the love of
God first comes out in redemption, yet elsewhere it reveals itself
in much that is exactly the same outside Christianity as within,
and pre-eminently in all the triumphs of human knowledge and
mastery of Nature. But to this we reply that all human life is to
be pervaded by the powers of redemption, and that it is only as so

pervaded that it reaches perfection. So that no human good of any kind is conformed to the relevant divine will, except as it is thus brought into connexion with that predominance of the God-consciousness in our soul which we owe to Christ. On the other hand, nothing which does not represent the divine will can reveal the divine love. Our paragraph, therefore, has only to be taken in the sense made inevitable by what went before [1] to justify itself perfectly.

§ 167. *God is Love.*

1 John 4[16].

1. Already it has been stated repeatedly that in God there can be no distinction between essence and attributes, and that just for that reason the conception ' attribute ' is not particularly well fitted to set forth the Divine Essence. Still, this also implies that, in so far as anything true is predicated of God by means of what we posit as a divine attribute, what is thus truly predicated must also express the Divine Essence itself. On this account it must necessarily be possible to form similar propositions, affirming of Him all other attributes, if these as such have any claim to be posited at all. However, no such propositions occur in Scripture, nor has it ever been laid down in Church doctrine that God is eternity, or omnipotence, or the like. And while certainly we might venture to say that God is loving omnipotence or omnipotent love, yet we must admit that in the first of these forms as much as in the second love alone is made the equivalent of the being or essence of God. Hence it is in this exclusive form that our paragraph has to be established and justified, namely, that love alone and no other attribute can be equated thus with God. Only, it is understood that here also we wish to have nothing to do with any conception of God reached by way of speculation, but that what we have to show is merely why this attribute is thus distinguished from the others which we have come to affirm in the course of our argument.

2. To begin with, as regards the attributes which we arrived at in the first part of this work, they made then no claim to rank as such designations of the Divine Essence that they could be substituted for the name ' God.' [2] Even although we explain omnipotence as the attribute in virtue of which all finite things are through God as they are, while we certainly in that case posit the

---

[1] § 164.   [2] Cf. § 56, Postscript.

divine act in its entirety, it is without a motive, and therefore as an action wholly indeterminate in character ; and it can only be incorrectly, and under the influence of quantitative standards of measurement, that we name God omnipotence. The finite as such is not merely a manifold ; it is also something mutable, and is invariably given to us solely in impermanent states or stages of transition. So that the statement in question really conveys nothing but what the finite is through God, as willed and posited by Him ; and unless we pass out beyond the finite sphere we all the time remain uncertain as to the nature of the will of God which as such is implied in omnipotence. The same thing of course holds true of the other divine attributes treated of in the same context. We arrived at each of them by abstraction from the definite feeling-content of our God-consciousness ; hence, if we are not to project them in thought into the attributes yielded by reflection on this feeling-content (as happens in the formula that God is omnipotent or eternal love), but rather to take them strictly by themselves, we are bound to say that belief in God as almighty and eternal is nothing more than that shadow of faith which even devils may have.[1]

Nor are the two attributes (holiness and justice) discussed in our Second Part, under its second aspect, such as originally could stand as expressions of the Divine Essence. For we cannot say that God in Himself is justice or holiness ; for neither of these attributes can be conceived apart from a relation to evil as well as to the antithesis between evil and good. And neither the antithesis nor its solution has any existence for God, considered solely in Himself. Hence the action of these attributes separately from the others is exclusively limited to a certain sphere, and it is only when we cancel this separation and resolve them into those attributes which we are now discussing as the result of the second half of our exposition, that they are recognizable as divine attributes at all. So that what was formerly considered as the work of divine holiness and justice is now properly (even though it be more by way of preparation than of fulfilment) reckoned in as part of the work of redemption. Thus both of these attributes, like the others, merge for us in the divine love, this last viewed solely in its preparatory manifestations ; and the divine love is holy and just love inasmuch as essentially it begins with these preparatory stages ; in the same way it is almighty and eternal love. Love and wisdom alone, then, can claim to be not mere attributes but also expressions of the very essence of

[1] Jas. 2[19].

God, while yet we do not say God is wisdom precisely as we do God is love ; and the point is one which we can elucidate as follows, even before we deal with the conception of wisdom. If we look at the way in which we become aware of the two attributes respectively, it turns out that we have the sense of divine love directly in the consciousness of redemption, and as this is the basis on which all the rest of our God-consciousness is built up, it of course represents to us the essence of God. But the divine wisdom does not enter consciousness thus directly, but only as we extend our self-consciousness (as personal, but even more as racial consciousness) to cover the relation of all the elements of reality to each other. Indeed, since the two attributes cannot be conceived in separation from each other, and since love is not the perfection of wisdom but wisdom the perfection of love, it follows that love would not be implied in so absolute a degree if we thought God as wisdom, as wisdom would be if we thought Him as love. For where almighty love is, there must also absolute wisdom be.

SECOND DOCTRINE : THE DIVINE WISDOM

§ 168. *The divine wisdom is the principle which orders and determines the world for the divine self-imparting which is evinced in redemption.*

1. The special relationship, previously lacking,[1] which is required to justify our positing the divine wisdom as an attribute distinct from the divine omniscience, is found in this connexion of wisdom with the divine love. Yet it remains true that, no less definitely than was brought out in that earlier context, the divine omniscience indicates in God precisely the same as the divine wisdom does ; only that the timeless relation involved naturally has for us a twofold aspect, wisdom being the word that looks forward, omniscience the word that looks backward. Moreover, the latter is in the same relation to the divine love as the former ; all existence being posited in God simply as that which is mediated by His love. All this forms a supplement to what I have written elsewhere [2] for another discipline as to the relation between love and wisdom—in this respect, that the antecedent word is also directly the creative word. From the fact that we take the divine love as being also wisdom it follows, first of all, that we cannot

---

[1] Cf. § 55, p. 221.
[2] In my article on the scientific treatment of the conception of virtue see *Werke*.

possibly regard all finite being in its relation to our God-consciousness except as (whatever else be the meaning we give to the term
'world') an absolutely harmonious divine work of art.   Even in
human affairs the primary work of wisdom is correctly and completely to outline the idea which the work of art is to embody, so
that actions proper are only traceable to wisdom in proportion as
both in the context of a man's life and in themselves they can be
regarded as works of art or parts thereof ; and he would be the
most perfect man all of whose plans for works or actions formed
a complete whole of self-communicative presentation.   Similarly,
the divine wisdom is nothing but the Supreme Being viewed as
engaged in this absolute (not compositely, but simply and originally, perfect) self-presentation and impartation.[1]   Only we must
think away all division between those two ; there is no distinction
between divine works and acts, nor is it the case that (as with us
men) impartation preponderates in acts, but presentation in works.
It is only for our minds that divine acts are primarily impartation
and then become presentation, and divine works the reverse.   The
sending of Christ, however, is for us primarily divine impartation,
and it is for this reason that the term 'impartation' is put first.
The growth of our consciousness of the wisdom of God consists in
this, that His impartation in its temporal progress becomes for us
ever more and more a perfect presentation of the almighty love of
God.

Next, we must be on our guard lest we again falsify the conception we have reached, by introducing the contrast of end and
means.   The reason for caution lies in what has just been said.
Every human work of art is the more perfect, the more it conforms
to the idea that elements within it should not be distinguishable
as end and means, but are all reciprocally related as parts to the
whole ; whereas means remain external to it.   In a still higher
degree of perfection, this manifestly applies to a complete human
life.   How then could it be that divine wisdom did not exclude
the contrast of end and means even more completely ?   There is
nothing outside the world which could be used as means ; all
things within it, rather, are so ordered that viewed in connexion
with one another they each stand related as parts to the whole ;
while every particular in itself is so entirely both things—means and
end—that each of these categories is constantly abrogating itself
and passing over into the other.   So generally recognized is this

[1] Acts 17$^{24-28}$.

that no one imagines that in God, as distinct from wisdom (taken exclusively as meaning rightness of purpose) there is to be found sagacity as well, in the sense of perfectness in the choice and use of means. Yet it is common enough, and equally confusing, for people to include sagacity as an *additional* element in the idea of divine wisdom, and to interpret wisdom as meaning the divine perfectness alike in the fixing of ends and the determination of means. Means are never employed except where the agent has to have recourse to something not originated by himself. Nor can we easily conceive the determination of means otherwise than in the form of choice, which means reverting to that very mediate knowledge which we discarded. With this is in keeping also the fact that both the wisdom and the omniscience of God are each equivalent to the other and to the divine creativeness, and that we cannot set this equivalence aside without spoiling the conceptions themselves, and *vice versa*.

2. Our recognition of redemption as the real key to the understanding of the divine wisdom is itself the specifically Christian view of this subject. Our Christian consciousness, however expanded, cannot transcend that which stands in relation to us ; and all the divine ordering of the world within this sphere, if we would truly appropriate it, we can only interpret by reference to the revelation of God in Christ and the Holy Spirit. But this ought never to degenerate into an inquisitive search (unfriendly to scientific inquiry) with a view to discovering particular aids to the Kingdom of God in particular events ; for in such a case we should always be dealing merely with transition stages, of whose value for the whole we were utterly ignorant. But we shall do well to be on our guard against ascribing to divine wisdom the divine ordering of external and physical nature, as well as institutions for the all-round development of the human mind, in such a manner as to separate them from the sphere of redemption. Anything wholly out of touch with redemption, and not at the same time totally isolated from human life (a description which would not hold true of any part even of external nature), might just as easily be injurious to the progress of redemption, and in that case would not be pre-formed by the divine wisdom. How could we think we had fathomed the divine wisdom, if we had no better grasp of its manifestations than to suppose that, even if only occasionally, it could conflict with the highest interests of man ? Hence everything in the world, in proportion as it is attributed to divine wisdom, must also be related to the redemptive or

new-creating revelation of God. Thus the proper work of divine
wisdom is precisely the spread of redemption ; or, to put it otherwise, it is on the one hand the mode and the order in which election
is carried out, and the regeneration of individuals as well as of whole
masses of humanity effected, and on the other hand the changing
transformation of the Christian fellowship, as often as living
Christian piety enters, or ought to enter, into combination with this
or that new aspect of human experience. Hence every effort to
penetrate those depths of the divine wisdom still hidden from us,
is in itself to be approved. Nor does it cease to be praiseworthy
though at times it tends to go too much into detail (for what may
be regarded as detail in the sphere of divine grace is not too small
to be considered an object of divine wisdom) ; it is censurable only
when we obscure the absolute unity of divine wisdom by introducing the contrast of end and means.

§ 169. *Theorem.—The divine wisdom is the ground in virtue of which
the world, as the scene of redemption, is also the absolute
revelation of the Supreme Being, and is therefore good.*

1. This proposition, which we indicated at an earlier point [1] but
can only now set forth, and which rather summarizes in sharper
outline what has already been said than contains anything new,
makes in essence the demand that we should not look for a larger
divine impartation than has been effected in the human race by
means of redemption through Christ. And in this sense it has to be
tested first by two propositions, which we find at either end of this
Second Part of our exposition. In the first place, sin invariably
brings with it a diminution of the God-consciousness, and therefore
of the divine impartation. Now if we suppose a real condition of
purity or even of moral and spiritual perfection to have existed
before sin (a condition which might or might not be interrupted
by sin), our paragraph would compel us to suppose that if no fall
had taken place, no redemption would have been necessary, which
means that the impartation of the Divine Essence would have been
less than is now the case, owing to the presence not only of sin but
of redemption. In the second place, as long as the unregenerate
live here in company with the pious, they too experience gleams of
blessedness through the God-consciousness latent in them ; and
these make their presence felt powerfully as preparatory workings
of grace. Now if we suppose that all who had not thus attained

[1] See § 59, Postscript.

to regeneration would have to bear an eternity of unmitigated wretchedness in hell, our paragraph would compel us to assert that even so the sum-total of the divine impartation would be larger than if the regeneration of those also who in this life had not been brought so far, had remained a possibility after death.

2. These implications of our paragraph we must consider from yet another side. If Christ be placed at the summit, as the individual who was entirely pervaded by the God-consciousness and therefore taken up into full unity with the Highest, everywhere else there exists only an imperfect and unequal pervasion, which decreases steadily within the sphere of rational being throughout the various areas in which corporate life is being prepared for redemption, and in irrational and inanimate nature (if this be taken as having independent existence) wholly disappears. And yet, according to our paragraph, this limited and sporadic impartation of the Supreme Being is the whole outcome in which the divine wisdom exhausts itself and the divine love finds complete satisfaction. In that case, we cannot but be extremely doubtful whether the non-rational and non-conscious is to be taken as in itself an object of the divine love merely on the ground that we find it within the domain ordered by the divine wisdom ; or whether it is excluded even from the divine wisdom since it can have no part in the divine love. For the plea that reason needs all these different stages of subordinate being as a substructure for its own life, is always unsatisfying ; it means that here the divine wisdom is assumed to be conditioned. Hence we must add, that whatever in itself is insusceptible of divine impartation shall yet be brought into vital connexion with that in which such impartation can dwell. Thence it follows that so long as this vital connexion is not in operation all round, so long as the Spirit is not yet expressing and presenting itself somehow even in all that is non-rational, the divine wisdom cannot exhibit itself as everywhere present. But when through us the world is become fully ready for us, it will appear clearly that nothing can really *be* save as it is also an object of the divine love.

3. It is only thus, by relation to the divine love, that the divine attributes expounded in the First Part gain their full significance. The divine wisdom, as the unfolding of the divine love, conducts us here to the realm of Christian Ethics ; for we are now confronted with the task of more and more securing recognition for the world as a good world, as also of forming all things into an organ of the divine Spirit in harmony with the divine idea originally underlying

the world-order, thus bringing all into unity with the system of redemption. The purpose of this is that in both respects we may attain to perfect living fellowship with Christ, both in so far as the Father has given Him power over all things and in so far as He ever shows Him greater works than those He already knows. Hence the world can be viewed as a perfect revelation of divine wisdom only in proportion as the Holy Spirit makes itself felt through the Christian Church as the ultimate world-shaping power.

CONCLUSION

THE DIVINE TRINITY

§ 170. *All that is essential in this Second Aspect of the Second Part of our exposition is also posited in what is essential in the doctrine of the Trinity; but this doctrine itself, as ecclesiastically framed, is not an immediate utterance concerning the Christian self-consciousness, but only a combination of several such utterances.*

Symb. Quic. : Fides autem catholica haec est, ut unum Deum in trinitate et trinitatem in unitate veneremur.—*Conf. Aug.* i. : 'Firstly we teach . . . according to the decree of the Nicene Council that there is one single Divine Essence . . . and yet in the same single Divine Essence there are three Persons, equal in power, equal in eternity, etc.'—*Exp. simpl.* iii. : Eundem nihilominus Deum . . . credimus . . . personis inseparabiliter et inconfuse esse distinctum, Patrem, Filium et Spiritum sanctum, etc.—*Conf. Gallic.* vi. : Scriptura nos docet, in illa singulari et simplice essentiâ divinâ subsistere tres personas, Patrem, Filium et Spiritum sanctum.—*Conf. Hung.* : Hunc unum et solum Deum tres in coelo testes Patrem, Filium et Sp. s. esse credimus : qui, licet tres sint subsistentibus suis proprietatibus et officiis dispensatoriis, tamen hi tres unum quoque sunt.

1. An essential element of our exposition in this Part has been the doctrine of the union of the Divine Essence with human nature, both in the personality of Christ and in the common Spirit of the Church ;[1] therewith the whole view of Christianity set forth in our Church teaching stands and falls. For unless the being of God in Christ is assumed, the idea of redemption could not be thus concentrated in His Person. And unless there were such a union also in the common Spirit of the Church, the Church could not thus be the Bearer and Perpetuator of the redemption through Christ. Now these exactly are the essential elements in the doctrine of the Trinity, which, it is clear, only established itself in defence of the position that in Christ there was present nothing less than the Divine Essence, which also indwells the Christian Church as its common Spirit, and that we take these expressions in no reduced or sheerly artificial sense, and know nothing of any special higher essences, subordinate deities (as it were) present in Christ and the

---

[1] Cf. § 94 and § 123.

Holy Spirit. The doctrine of the Trinity has no origin but this ; and at first it had no other aim than to equate as definitely as possible the Divine Essence considered as thus united to human nature with the Divine Essence in itself. This is the less doubtful that those Christian sects which interpret the doctrine of redemption differently are also necessarily without the doctrine of the Trinity— they have no point of belief to which it could be attached—which could not possibly be the case if even in Catholic doctrine there existed at least some other points than this to which the attachment could be made. It is equally clear from this why those divergent sects which are chiefly distinguishable by their denial of the Trinity are not thereby forced into still other divergences in the doctrine of God and the divine attributes, as must have been the case if the doctrine of the Trinity were rooted in a special view of the nature of the Supreme Being as such. But on the other hand, they *are* forced to set up a different theory of the Person of Christ, and hence also of man's need for redemption and of the value of redemption. In virtue of this connexion, we rightly regard the doctrine of the Trinity, in so far as it is a deposit of these elements, as the coping-stone of Christian doctrine, and this equating with each other of the divine in each of these two unions, as also of both with the Divine Essence in itself, as what is essential in the doctrine of the Trinity.

2. But at this point we would call a halt ; we cannot attach the same value to the further elaboration of the dogma, which alone justifies the ordinary term. For the term ' Trinity ' is really based on the fact that each of the two above-mentioned unions is traced back to a separate distinction posited independently of such union, and eternally, in the Supreme Being as such ; further, after the member of this plurality destined to union with Jesus had been designated by the name ' Son,' it was felt necessary to posit the Father in accordance therewith as a special distinction. The result was the familiar dualism—unity of Essence and trinity of Persons. But the assumption of an eternal distinction in the Supreme Being is not an utterance concerning the religious consciousness, for there it never could emerge. Who would venture to say that the impression made by the divine in Christ obliges us to conceive such an eternal distinction as its basis ? Anyone who were to find this task set us in the Johannine conception of the Logos, as if that conception definitely included one element of the doctrine of the Trinity and the completion of the doctrine were called for by

that simple fact, would be in so difficult a position that he could hardly maintain his ground. For one thing, it is in this very passage that Arianism sought a foothold ; and the exegesis of both sides in that controversy is so exposed to equal though opposite objections that we cannot help saying that if either of the two antagonistic views was in John's mind as fundamental to the passage, it must be confessed that he went to work to express it in a highly unsatisfactory and ineffective manner. On the other hand, if the Trinity had been in the Apostle's mind, his exposition would very easily have lent itself to a similar introduction of the Holy Spirit, whose name occurs so often in Christ's discourses as reported by John ; nor would he have lacked opportunity elsewhere to bring in this other member, and to speak of the place of the Spirit as that which was in the beginning with God and was God. Assuming, however, that John here declares of the divine united in Christ with human nature that it existed in God from all eternity in a distinct form, it does not follow by any means that this was meant in the sense of the doctrine of the Trinity, and that that doctrine is therefore the true and the only natural completion of the Johannine statements. For underlying the elaboration of the doctrine is not merely a desire to reproduce very exactly our Christian consciousness that the Divine Essence in both forms of union is the same, and also is equal to the being of God *per se* ; rather, it was only after the distinction had been eternalized and made antecedent to the union that there arose a need to guard against the semblance of polytheism, and to secure that this, in a sense separated, being of God was none the less embraced within the unity of the Divine Essence. But of such a need there is in John no trace whatever, which means that he was not on the way to the doctrine of the Trinity as we have it.

3. Hence the second part of our paragraph must not be understood as meaning that the orthodox doctrine of the Trinity is to be regarded as an immediate or even a necessary combination of utterances concerning the Christian self-consciousness. On the contrary, the intermediate step has been taken of eternalizing, in separation, the being of God in itself, and the being of God which makes union with human nature possible. Now if this arose so definitely out of the utterances of Christ Himself and of the Apostles concerning Him that we had to accept it on their testimony, the doctrine of the Trinity in that case would be a fully elaborated doctrine of this type, and we should accept it as a combination of testimonies regarding a supersensible fact ; but it would no more

be a ' doctrine of faith ' in the really original and proper sense of that phrase than the doctrines of the resurrection and ascension of Christ ; [1] and it would resemble these last also in this respect that our faith in Christ and our living fellowship with Him would be the same although we had no knowledge of any such transcendent fact, or although the fact itself were different. But the exegesis meant to establish the position just mentioned has never been able to entrench itself so strongly as to escape constant attacks upon it. Hence it is important to make the point that the main pivots of the ecclesiastical doctrine—the being of God in Christ and in the Christian Church—are independent of the doctrine of the Trinity.

Let it be supposed that we further elaborate our knowledge of this supersensible fact and—to avoid the idea that the said distinction within the Supreme Being led to nothing up to the beginning of the union—teach besides that both the Second and the Third Person in the Trinity were implicated even in the creation of the world, while the Second Person was also the subject thereafter of all the Old Testament theophanies, and it was from the Third Person that the whole prophetic movement of the Old Testament received its impulse. Then these statements are still further removed from being utterances about our Christian consciousness. And we can wait all the more calmly to see whether the exegetical results on which these expansions of the doctrine rest are any more fully confirmed by the latest work on the subject than has hitherto been the case.

Postscript.—If success ever had attended, or ever could attend, the attempt to exhibit or prove a trinity in God from general conceptions or *a priori* (an effort perhaps stimulated by Church doctrine, apart from which it would hardly occur to anyone, but yet without any relation to the facts of redemption or any appeal to Scripture), still such a doctrine of the Trinity even though worked out with much greater elaboration than the ecclesiastical doctrine (bound up as it is with the basal facts of Christianity) has ever obtained or ever could obtain, could find no place in a Christian Dogmatic. Even although it kept strictly to the use of the same terms in denoting both the trinity and the unity as are employed in the ecclesiastical doctrine, we should firmly maintain that as a doctrine it was different. For deductions of that kind, standing in no connexion with those basal facts, do not merely show it to be quite different from the other in origin ; on that very account they are of no sort of use in Christian doctrine. Therefore we must

[1] Cf. § 99.

simply put them aside as ' philosophemes ' ; nor are we in any way
called upon to submit them to criticism, whether they originate
with ancient [1] or modern [2] Church teachers.

§ 171. *The ecclesiastical doctrine of the Trinity demands that we
think of each of the three Persons as equal to the Divine
Essence, and vice versa, and each of the three Persons as
equal to the others. Yet we cannot do either the one or the
other, but can only represent the Persons in a gradation,
and thus either represent the unity of the Essence as less
real than the three Persons, or vice versa.*

Symb. Quic. : Fides autem catholica haec est ut unum deum in trinitate,
et trinitatem in unitate veneremur.—Patris, filii et spiritus sancti una est
divinitas, aequalis gloria, aequalis maiestas.—Et in hac trinitate nihil prius
aut posterius nihil maior aut minus, sed totae tres personae coaeternae sibi
sunt et coaequales. . . . Neque confundentes personas neque separantes
substantiam.—*Augs. Conf.* I. : ' That there is one Divine Essence, which is
named and truly is God, and yet in this same one Divine Essence there are
three Persons. . . . And by the word Person is understood not a part, not an
attribute inhering in something else, but what subsists in itself (sed quod
proprie subsistit), as the Fathers have used the word in this matter.'—*Conf.
Belg.* viii. : . . . qui est unica essentia, in qua tres sunt personae incom-
municabilibus proprietatibus ab aeterno revera ac reipsa distinctae.

1. There can be no doubt that from this assumption of eternal
distinctions in the Divine Essence, there necessarily follows the
implication of the double equality of the divine in all three Persons,
and of the divine in each Person with the Supreme Being as a
unity. If divinity or power and glory were less in all the three
Persons together than in the Supreme Being conceived as a unity,
the three Persons would not be in but under the Supreme Being.
In that case, the divine in them would only improperly be called
divine, and our living fellowship with Christ as well as our participation in the Holy Spirit would not be fellowship with God. The
result would be the same if the divine in the Persons themselves
were not the same, only the divine in (say) the Father being truly
and properly divine, but the divine in Christ and the Holy Spirit
unreal and subordinate. In that case our indwelling sense of need
for redemption would necessarily take a different form of expression, if indeed as a hindrance to fellowship to God it would in
any way be met by a redemption which did not bring us to fellowship with God. In short, everything most important in Christianity

[1] *E.g.* Anselm, *Monolog.* ep. 29–61.
[2] *E.g.* Daub, *Theolog.*, §§ 126, 127.

would be changed. On those assumptions, no other definition can be reached than that posited by the ecclesiastical doctrine, and the ever-renewed zeal shown in its defence is perfectly intelligible.

2. The cited credal passages undeniably assert, to begin with, that power and divinity is not less in any of the three Persons than in the other two ; and this obviously would be sufficient to bar out all inequalities, if it were not for the inconsistency which emerges as soon as side by side with this equality the attempt is made to perpetuate the method of distinguishing the Persons. For it is then necessary to make this equality a canon to be followed in setting forth the difference between the Persons, in the sense that no element implying an inequality of the kind described can be admitted. If, however, Father and Son are distinguished by the fact that the Father eternally begets, but is Himself unbegotten, while the Son is begotten from all eternity but not Himself begetting, then (although this eternal generation is as different as possible from any generation that is temporal or organic in character), the term itself, if it means anything at all, must at least indicate a relationship of dependence. Hence if power has dwelt in the Father from all eternity to beget the Son as a second divine Person, whereas in the Son no such power dwells, and no relationship of dependence in which the Father stands to Him can be adduced as a counterweight, undeniably the power of the Father is greater than that of the Son, and in addition the glory which the Begetter has with the Begotten must be greater than that which the Begotten has with the Begetter.

The same holds true of the Spirit, whether as in the Greek dogma He proceeds from the Father only, or, as the Latin Church teaches, from the Father and the Son. In the former case, the Son has a twofold incapacity as compared with the Father : He does not beget, nor does a Person proceed from Him. In the latter case the Spirit alone exhibits this twofold dependence—for ' procession ' too is a relation of dependence, though meant to be a different one from being begotten, in spite of the fact that no one has ever succeeded in making clear what the difference between the two is. In this case, however, the Son has one capacity in common with the Father which places Him above the Spirit, whereas in the former case the Spirit is equal to the Son. Whichever way we take it, then, the Father is superior to the other two Persons, and the only subject of controversy is whether these two are equal to each other, or one of them subordinate to the other. But if such distinctions are made, the equality of the Persons is lost.

3. Similarly, the position that the divinity in all the three Persons is the same with that of the one Divine Essence ought to be the rule which controls our ideas of the relationship between the trinity of the Persons and the unity of the Essence. But if we are to take along with this what has just been dealt with, namely, the position that the Persons are distinguished from each other by peculiar properties not predicable of the Divine Essence in itself, while the Divine Essence itself has existence only in these three Persons, but not outside or apart from them (whether as a fourth Person or impersonally), and even in them does not distribute different attributes to different Persons,[1] but resides in each Person whole and undivided, on such terms the desired equality cannot result. For such a relationship as is here asserted we have no closer analogy, on which to form our thought of it, than that of the conception of a species with the individual members it contains ; for the conception of a species is similarly present whole and undivided in its individuals, but nowhere outside them. It is true, this has always been a moot point ; some thinkers admit the analogy,[2] others reject it.[3] But if the relationship is not to be conceived as of this type, then, as even its opponents allow,[4] we really are not in a position to form any definite ideas on the subject, and hence can have no interest in it. If, on the other hand, we do adopt the analogy, no equality is possible between the unity and the trinity ; either more realistically we must make the unity superordinate as the essence common to all three, in which case the distinction of Persons appears subordinate and falls into the background, while the divine *monarchia* stands out ; or more nominalistically we must make the trinity superordinate, in which case the unity as being abstract falls into the background. Then what has immediate existence for our religious consciousness—namely, the

---

[1] Passages like the following : . . . filium eius (*sc.* patris) sapientiam . . . spiritum s. eiusdem virtutem potentiam et efficaciam (*Conf. Gallic.* vi.), even if credal, are too vague to be taken into account.

[2] Τὸ οὐσία φύσιν σημαίνει, τὸ δὲ ὑπόστασις ἰδιότητας (Greg. Naz., *Encom. Athan.*). Ὅν ἔχει λόγον τὸ κοινὸν πρὸς τὸ ἴδιον, τοῦτον ἔχει ἡ οὐσία πρὸς τὴν ὑπόστασιν (Basil, *Ep.* ccxiv.). Κατά γε τὴν τῶν πατέρων διδασκαλίαν, ἣν ἔχει διαφορὰν τὸ κοινὸν ὑπὲρ τὸ ἴδιον, ἢ τὸ γένος ὑπὲρ τὸ εἶδος ἢ τὸ ἄτομον, ταύτην ἡ οὐσία πρὸς τὴν ὑπόστασιν ἔχει (Theodoret, *Dial. I.* ed. Hal. iv. p. 7).

[3] Non itaque secundum genus est species ista dicimus. . . . Nec sic ergo Trinitatem dicimus tres personas unam essentiam tanquam ex una materia tria quaedam subsistant (Augustine, *de Trin.* vii. 11).

[4] . . . propter ineffabilem coniunctionem haec tria simul unus Deus (Augustine, *ibid.* 8).

divinity of the Holy Spirit and the divinity of Christ, as also the relation of Christ as Son to the Father—comes to the front ; but so, too, does the danger of falling into tritheism. Between these two lines of thought (for we must always start either from the unity or from the trinity) no genuinely middle course seems possible which would not really be an approximation to one or the other. But from our assumptions neither the subordination of the unity to the trinity nor the converse follows ; hence as regards the distinctions existing in the Supreme Being from all eternity there is nothing for it but either to accept one of the two courses indicated, which conflicts with what the credal passages insist on, or, if we shrink from what they insist on, to conclude that it is impossible for us definitely to reach either point—the unity or the trinity ; we remain hesitating between the two.[1] In these circumstances the doctrine can do little to secure those two main points (which alone are in question), or to place them in a clearer light.

4. It still remains to show how unity and trinity are related to the divine causality (apprehended in our self-conscious feeling of absolute dependence) alike in redemption and sanctification and generally in creation and preservation. The divine causality must not be divided between the Persons, however natural it might be to say that the Father alone is Creator and Preserver, the Son alone Redeemer, and the Spirit alone Sanctifier. And if it is to be kept undivided, we reach here the same conclusion as before, either that these causalities all belong to the one Divine Essence as such, and to the Persons only in so far as they are in the Essence, but not in so far as they are distinct from each other, or they belong to the three Persons as such, and to the unity of the Essence only in so far as it consists of the Persons. The former view failed to establish itself, obviously because in it the trinity falls more into the background than was permitted by the ruling tendencies of the time ; [2] for it may almost be said that the Persons have reality only in the previously mentioned special acts. The Father is real, in so far as He begets the Son from all eternity, but creation and preservation would appertain solely to the unity of the Divine Essence. The Son, it is true, would not be merely begotten, or the Spirit merely

---

[1] Οὐ φθάνω τὸ ἓν νοῆσαι καὶ τοῖς τρισὶ περιλάμπομαι. οὐ φθάνω τὰ τρία διελεῖν, καὶ εἰς τὸ ἓν ἀναφέρομαι (Greg. Naz., l.c.).

[2] That the tendency of Church teaching tends to emphasize the Persons rather than the unity of the Essence may be seen clearly enough from the following words of the *Symb. Quic.*, 19 : Sicut singillatim unamquamque personam et deum et dominum confiteri christianâ veritate *compellimur*, ita tres deos aut dominos dicere catholica religione *prohibemur*.

breathed into being, for the former also became man and the latter was also poured forth ; but the justifying divine activity would not be that solely of the Son or the sanctifying divine activity that of the Spirit ; both would belong to the unity of the Divine Essence. Hence the second view came to be accepted universally, that the whole divine causality belongs to the three Persons ; but the form it took in ecclesiastical doctrine appears to suffer from a hidden contradiction. For if the divine causality belongs to the Persons as such, it belongs to each of them in so far as distinct from the others ; and hence the same causality is, in the first Person, that of the Unbegotten, in the second that of the Begotten, and thus is in each case triple, because issuing in each case from that which is personally distinctive, though but one in effect ; much as Christ executes the same thing with His two wills, the three Persons execute the same thing each in its own way, and thus each by its own act. This consistent scheme, however, failed to commend itself, obviously because the divine unity is obscured in a wholly nominalistic way, and almost nothing is left for it but to represent the equality of the three in essence and will. On the other hand, the accepted view that those causalities do indeed belong to the three Persons as such, but that each causality is one and the same in all three, and not a peculiar causality in each, means that the causality is really traced back, not to the Persons, but after all to the Divine Essence in its unity. Thus, once the eternal trinity in the unity is assumed, from this angle we arrive simply at the same difficulty as before, of choosing between the preponderance of the one and the subordination of the other, or *vice versa*.

5. If we now consider the manner in which this doctrine is handled almost everywhere in dogmatic expositions, it becomes still clearer to how slight an extent what is insisted on in general formulæ may be given effect to in the developed statement. In the first place, the doctrine of the Essence and attributes of God is treated apart from the trinity, God being considered in His unity. Here, however, the particular attribute under consideration is not shown within the unity, as triply divided or separated in a definite way. Instead, the doctrine of the Persons is later treated of by itself, apart from any such connexion and without being prepared for by the consciousness of the being of God in Christ and in the Christian Church. It is so treated of, however, that when it is shown that this or that attribute also belongs to the three Persons, the proof is specially led only for the Son and the Spirit, while that

it belongs to the Father is usually held to be self-evident. But if the equality of the Persons is asserted not merely as a formula but as an operative rule, such self-evidence must hold either of all three Persons or of none. The pre-eminence given to the Father in this respect proves that He is after all conceived as standing in a different relation to the unity of the Essence ; so that those who feel it to be superfluous to prove that divine attributes and activities belong to the Father, while they insist on proof for the Son and the Spirit, are all of them far from being strict Trinitarians ; for they identify the Father with the unity of the Divine Essence, but not the Son or the Spirit. This can be traced right back to the idea of Origen, that the Father is God absolutely, while Son and Spirit are God only by participation in the Divine Essence [1]—an idea which is positively rejected by orthodox Church teachers, but secretly underlies their whole procedure.

§ 172. *We have the less reason to regard this doctrine as finally settled since it did not receive any fresh treatment when the Evangelical (Protestant) Church was set up ; and so there must still be in store for it a transformation which will go back to its very beginnings.*

1. If we reflect, on the one hand, that the formulæ now accepted in the doctrine of the Trinity originated at a time when Christendom was still being recruited by mass-conversion from heathendom, and consider how easily, when it became necessary to speak of a plurality or distinction in God, unconscious echoes of what is pagan could find their way in, it is not surprising that the descriptions of such plurality should from the start have been vacillating and liable to misconception, and such as were no longer suited to later times, when no further admixture of heathenism was to be feared. Cautions could not but be attached to the use of such descriptions, to guard against aberrations on different sides ; but even so it is seldom that such cautions do not approximate to one extreme in seeking to guard against the other. Also they must lose their value once the danger of misunderstanding to which they relate has disappeared, and in that case the sinister suggestion they contain of the opposite error will come out all the more emphatically. If we take the original tendency of the doctrine, namely, to make clear that it is no hyperbolical expression of our consciousness of Christ and of the

---

[1] αὐτόθεος ὁ θεός ἐστι . . . πᾶν δὲ τὸ παρὰ τὸ αὐτόθεος μετοχῇ τῆς ἐκείνου θεότητος θεοποιούμενον κτλ. *Comm. in Joann.* (ed. R. iv. p. 50), where the connexion puts it beyond doubt that αὐτόθεος is the Father. Cf. *de princ.* i. vol. i. p. 62.

common Spirit of the Church to assert that God is in both, the first task of the doctrine is clearly this—to define this peculiar being of God in that which is other, in its relation both to the being of God in Himself and to the being of God in relation to the world in general.   And obviously there is no prospect of ever so accomplishing this task that a formula adequate for all time could be constructed, and every departure therefrom repudiated as unchristian. We have only to do with the God-consciousness given in our self-consciousness along with our consciousness of the world ; hence we have no formula for the being of God in Himself as distinct from the being of God in the world, and should have to borrow any such formula from speculation, and so prove ourselves disloyal to the character of the discipline at which we are working.   Further, if we feel that our dogmatic expressions for the relation of God to the world inevitably suffer in every case from faults of anthropomorphism, how could we suppose that we should have more success with the more intricate task of distinguishing the peculiar being of God in Christ as an individual, and in the Christian Church as an historical whole, from the omnipotent presence of God in the world in general, of which these are parts ?   Rather we shall have to put up with the fact that the problem can only be solved approximately, and that formulæ which have antagonistic points of departure must always remain opposed in tendency ; for interest in the problem is bound always to spring up afresh.

2. This being so, it might seem very surprising that while so many other problems of later origin have been solved in a tolerably satisfactory way, precisely this one, so comprehensive in character, has remained so long stationary at the very unsatisfactory point to which it was brought at (so to say) the first rush.   But the fact is, those later questions—particularly that of the Person of Christ and of the gracious operations of the Spirit—dealt with the same subject on the side next to the direct interests of faith ; and the Trinitarian definitions proper (all the more that they were made fundamental in the discussions just referred to) had to remain as they had already come to be, in spite of the undeniable fact that impassioned polemical zeal—so prone to error—had had only too large a share in their construction.   But if the doctrine of the Trinity is not even yet free from vacillations as indicated above between equality and subordination on the one hand, and on the other between Tritheism and such a Unitarianism as must obscure all over again what was felt to be of the very first importance, namely, the eternal

distinctness of the Persons, we ought not to feel too much surprise
that anti-trinitarian opinions should ever and again emerge and
should occasionally gain ground ; nor ought we to be precipitate
in condemnation. It is here as with the doctrine of God in general :
many not merely profess to be but actually think they are opposed
to every belief in God, when in fact they are simply repelled by
ordinary presentations of the subject, but have by no means parted
with all those spiritual affections which spring from the God-consciousness. Similarly, it is natural that people who cannot reconcile
themselves to the difficulties and imperfections that cling to the
formulæ current in Trinitarian doctrine should say that they repudiate everything connected with it, whereas in point of fact their
piety is by no means lacking in the specifically Christian stamp.
This is the case often enough at the present moment not only in
the Unitarian societies of England and America, but also among
the scattered opponents of the doctrine of the Trinity in our own
country. That circumstance supplies a further reason why we
should strive to secure freedom for a thoroughgoing criticism of the
doctrine in its older form, so as to prepare the way for, and introduce,
a reconstruction of it corresponding to the present condition of
other related doctrines.

3. The position assigned to the doctrine of the Trinity in the
present work is perhaps at all events a preliminary step towards
this goal. One who is a believer in the ecclesiastical sense of that
word can scarcely arm himself with the equanimity needful alike
for an impartial criticism of the old procedure and for a new construction, until he has become convinced that it is possible for our
faith in the divine present in Christ and in the Christian communion
to find fit theological expression, even before anything has been
heard of those more exact definitions which go to form the doctrine
of the Trinity. But this independence of mind can never attain to
clearness so long as that doctrine is dealt with before the chief points
of faith just mentioned ; for that arrangement of topics only too
easily leads to an impression (utterly contradicted by the history
of the Church) that acceptance of the doctrine of the Trinity is the
necessary precondition of faith in redemption and in the founding
of the Kingdom of God by means of the divine in Christ and in the
Holy Spirit. Not to speak of the fact that the theological character
of the entire presentation is distorted, and that neither the criticism
nor the points of attachment needed for the new construction can
be placed on a right foundation if the doctrine in question (which

is not directly a statement about our Christian consciousness at all) is set up as a fundamental doctrine, and therefore, of course, arrived at in a speculative way. The same speculative tone then comes to be imported into the doctrine of the Redeemer and of the Holy Spirit, as being dependent on the doctrine of the Trinity ; and thus the door is opened wide to the influx of speculative elements.

We ought not, however, to rest satisfied with this preliminary step ; we must at least give some indications of what yet remains to do. And on the present state of the question we may base, I think, the following reflections. The first unsolved difficulty lies in the relation of the unity of the Essence to the trinity of the Persons ; and here everything depends on the original and eternal existence of distinctions within the Divine Essence. Hence it would first be necessary to inquire whether this idea is so clearly and definitely present in passages of the New Testament that we are bound to regard it as a self-descriptive utterance of Christ and of the divine Spirit that guided the thinking of the Apostles. Of this there can scarcely be a better test than to ask whether these passages could not also be explained by the Sabellian view set up in opposition to our ecclesiastical interpretation. If this question must be answered in the negative, nothing is left but to try whether the ecclesiastical doctrine could not, without injury to the essential presuppositions mentioned above, be stated in formulæ which should not contradict the Biblical passages and yet should avoid the rocks on which the ecclesiastical presentation comes to grief. If, on the other hand, the question can be answered affirmatively, so that it is no longer possible to hold that the ecclesiastical doctrine, even if not purely exegetical in origin, can at least be sustained by purely exegetical proof, then the Athanasian hypothesis is simply on a par with the Sabellian ; and the question must be raised whether the latter cannot render us equal service, without involving us in equally insoluble difficulties. In other words, the question is whether formulæ cannot be devised which, without asserting eternal distinctions in the Supreme Being, are yet equally capable of exhibiting in their truth both unions of the Essence with human nature. Only, no mutability must thereby be ascribed to the Supreme Being ; and although the activities of the Supreme Being in effecting the unions are represented as taking place in time, this must be done no otherwise than we do it everywhere else ; for we cannot conceive the divine causality otherwise than as decree in its eternity, while yet we cannot represent its fulfilment otherwise than as in time. The second difficulty suggested by the ecclesiastical doctrine was this, that the designation of the First Person as Father, as well as the relations of the First Person to the other two Persons, seems rather to set forth the relation of the Persons to the unity of the Essence than to be consistent with the equality of the three Persons. Here the question really comes to be, whether it was right at the outset to give the name ' Son of God ' solely to the divine in Christ, and to relate the term ' Father ' to one of the distinctions in the Divine Essence and not rather to the unity of the Divine Essence as such. If it transpires that by ' Son of God ' Scripture always and exclusively means the whole Christ Himself, and recognizes no difference between ' God,' as denoting the Supreme Being, and ' the Father of our Lord Jesus Christ,' but uses the latter name in exactly the same sense as the former, we should then have to try whether a similar question might not be raised with regard to the Holy Spirit, with a similar answer, leading to such forms of statement as would solve our second difficulty. If the results of both problems combined in one, a new construction could easily be arrived at ; if otherwise, we should have to seek new solutions, as we could, of the remaining differences. This is of itself a sufficient explanation why we are here unable to go beyond these indications in such a way as to complete the whole task.

INDEXES

A. SUBJECTS

B. AUTHORS AND SOURCES

C. SCRIPTURE REFERENCES